ISBN 978-1-5283-9827-5
PIBN 10974063

English
Français
Deutsche
Italiano
Español
Português

www.forgottenbooks.com

Mythology Photography **Fiction**
Fishing Christianity **Art** Cooking
Essays Buddhism Freemasonry
Medicine **Biology** Music **Ancient**
Egypt Evolution Carpentry Physics
Dance Geology **Mathematics** Fitness
Shakespeare **Folklore** Yoga Marketing
Confidence Immortality Biographies
Poetry **Psychology** Witchcraft
Electronics Chemistry History **Law**
Accounting **Philosophy** Anthropology
Alchemy Drama Quantum Mechanics
Atheism Sexual Health **Ancient History**
Entrepreneurship Languages Sport
Paleontology Needlework Islam
Metaphysics Investment Archaeology
Parenting Statistics Criminology
Motivational

OFFICIAL EDITION

REPORTS OF CASES

HEARD AND DETERMINED IN THE

APPELLATE DIVISION

OF THE

SUPREME COURT

OF THE

STATE OF NEW YORK.

MARCUS T. HUN, REPORTER.

VOLUME LXX.

1902.

J. B. LYON COMPANY,

J. B. LYON COMPANY,
PRINTERS, ELECTROTYPERS AND BINDERS,
LYON BLOCK, ALBANY, N. Y.

Justices

OF

THE APPELLATE DIVISION OF THE SUPREME COURT.

———————•———————

First Department.

Hon. CHAS. H. VAN BRUNT, P. J.
" EDWARD PATTERSON.
" MORGAN J. O'BRIEN.
" GEORGE L. INGRAHAM.
" CHESTER B. McLAUGHLIN.
" EDWARD W. HATCH.
" FRANK C. LAUGHLIN.

Second Department.

Hon. WILLIAM W. GOODRICH, P. J.
" WILLARD BARTLETT.
" JOHN WOODWARD.
" MICHAEL H. HIRSCHBERG.
" ALMET F. JENKS.

Third Department.

Hon. CHARLES E. PARKER, P. J.
" WALTER LLOYD SMITH.
" S. ALONZO KELLOGG.
" EMORY A. CHASE.
" EDGAR L. FURSMAN.

Fourth Department.

Hon. WILLIAM H. ADAMS, P. J.
" PETER B. McLENNAN.
" ALFRED SPRING.
" PARDON C. WILLIAMS.
" FRANK H. HISCOCK.
" JOHN M. DAVY.*

———————————————————————

* Designated by the Governor on December 30, 1901, to sit temporarily.

CAUSES *in which the decisions contained in Hun's Reports and in the Appellate Division Reports have been passed upon by the Court of Appeals from June 10, 1901, to May 8, 1902 (including 170 N. Y. 622).*

The attention of the profession is called to the fact that the Court of Appeals in many cases decides an appeal upon other grounds than those stated in the opinion of the court below.

The affirmance or reversal of the judgment of the Appellate Division does not necessarily show that the Court of Appeals concurred in, or dissented from, the statements contained in the opinion of the Supreme Court. (*Rogers* v. *Decker*, 131 N. Y. 490.)—REP.

A TABLE

OF THE

NAMES OF THE CASES REPORTED

IN THIS VOLUME.

TABLE OF CASES CITED.

H.

TABLE OF CASES CITED.

UNITED STATES STATUTES AT LARGE CITED.

UNITED STATES REVISED STATUTES CITED.

NEW YORK STATE CONSTITUTION CITED.

NEW YORK REVISED STATUTES CITED.

BIRDSEYE'S EDITION.

GENERAL LAWS CITED.

SESSION LAWS CITED.

SECTIONS OF THE CODE OF CIVIL PROCEDURE CITED.

SECTION OF THE PENAL CODE CITED.

Cases

FIRST DEPARTMENT

IN THE

APPELLATE DIVISION,

March, 1902.*

ARTHUR DANIEL CAVANAGH, Respondent, *v.* METROPOLITAN
STREET RAILWAY COMPANY, Appellant.

Negligence — bill of particulars as to what injuries are permanent.

Where the complaint in an action to recover damages for personal injuries, after
setting forth a number of injuries which the plaintiff claimed to have received,
alleges that "some of the said injuries are permanent," the defendant is entitled to a bill of particulars specifying what injuries the plaintiff claims are
permanent.

APPEAL by the defendant, the Metropolitan Street Railway Company, from an order of the Supreme Court, made at the New York
Special Term and entered in the office of the clerk of the county
of New York on the 30th day of December, 1901, denying the
defendant's motion for a bill of particulars.

Addison C. Ormsbee, for the appellant.

T. B. Chancellor, for the respondent.

PER CURIAM:

This action was brought to recover damages for personal injuries
alleged to have been sustained by reason of the negligence of the
defendant. The complaint, after stating the formal allegations as
to the defendant's incorporation, etc., the happening and manner of
the occurrence of the accident and the negligence of the defend-

---

* The other cases of this term will be found in volume 69 App. Div.—[REP.

APP. DIV.—VOL. LXX.   1

ant, alleges that " the plaintiff received severe and permanent injuries and suffered great pain ; " then follow specific allegations of permanent injuries to the ear and hearing, and then the following, " his right shoulder, head, neck, back and hip were bruised and lacerated and he was in other respects bruised and wounded and became and was sick, sore, lame and disordered and so remained and continued for a long space of time ; and he also received a severe shock to his nervous system, and that some of the said injuries are permanent." The complaint is quite full and complete upon the subject of injuries, and the order denying the motion for the bill would be affirmed were it not for the fact that in the last statement in the 5th paragraph of the complaint it is stated " some of the said injuries are permanent." This statement leaves the whole matter of permanent injuries open and gives to the defendant no notice of the injuries which are claimed to be permanent as distinguished from those that are temporary. We think, therefore, in view of this allegations, that the defendant becomes entitled to a bill of particulars specifying what injuries the plaintiff claims are permanent.

The order should, therefore, be reversed, with ten dollars costs and disbursements, and the motion for a bill of particulars granted to the extent of specifying the injuries which plaintiff declares are permanent, with ten dollars costs.

Present — VAN BRUNT, P. J., O'BRIEN, McLAUGHLIN, HATCH and LAUGHLIN, JJ.

Order reversed, with ten dollars costs and disbursements, and motion granted to extent stated in opinion, with ten dollars costs.

2
157
457
———
2
488

ELI S. SCHREIER, as Trustee of the Estate in Bankruptcy of GEORGE B. CHRISTMAN, JR., Respondent, *v.* WILLIAM F. HOGAN, Appellant, Impleaded with JOSEPH HOGAN and Others.

Security for costs — section 3268 of the Code of Civil Procedure does not apply to an action by a trustee in bankruptcy to set aside transfers by the bankrupt.

Section 3268 of the Code of Civil Procedure, authorizing the defendant to require security for costs, if the plaintiff is " the official assignee or official trustee of a debtor, or an assignee in bankruptcy, where the action is brought upon a cause of action arising before the assignment, the appointment of the trustee or the adjudication in bankruptcy," does not apply to an action brought by a trustee in bankruptcy to set aside transfers made by the bankrupt.

APPEAL by the defendant, William F. Hogan, from an order of the Supreme Court, made at the New York Special Term and entered in the office of the clerk of the county of New York on the 8th day of January, 1902, vacating an order theretofore entered in the action requiring the plaintiff to give security for costs.

Section 3268 of the Code of Civil Procedure, which is referred to in the opinion, provides as follows : " The defendant in an action brought in a court of record, may require security for costs to be given as prescribed in this title, where the plaintiff was when the action was commenced   *   *   *   the official assignee or official trustee of a debtor ; or an assignee in bankruptcy, where the action is brought upon a cause of action arising before the assignment, the appointment of the trustee or the adjudication in bankruptcy."

George F. Hickey, for the appellant.

Herman H. Oppenheimer, for the respondent.

PER CURIAM :

The order requiring security for costs was properly vacated. Section 3268 of the Code of Civil Procedure does not apply to an action by a trustee in bankruptcy to set aside transfers made by the bankrupt. This precise question was determined by this court in *Rielly* v. *Rosenberg* (57 App. Div. 408), and, therefore, upon that authority, the order here appealed from must be affirmed, with ten dollars costs and disbursements.

Present — VAN BRUNT, P. J., INGRAHAM, McLAUGHLIN, HATCH and LAUGHLIN, JJ.

Order affirmed, with ten dollars costs and disbursements.

FANNIE MARKEY, as Administratrix, etc., of JOSEPH P. MARKEY, Deceased, Appellant, *v.* THE SUPREME COUNCIL, CATHOLIC BENEVOLENT LEGION, Respondent.

Mutual benefit association — a benefit certificate, uitra vires because in favor of a brother, is not enforcible by the administratrix of the member.

The objection that a mutual benefit association had no power, under its constitution, to make a benefit certificate issued to a deceased member payable to his brother, is not available to the deceased member's administratrix, and does not entitle her to recover from the association the amount stated in the certificate.

APPEAL by the plaintiff, Fannie Markey, as administratrix, etc., of Joseph P. Markey, deceased, from a judgment of the Supreme Court in favor of the defendant, entered in the office of the clerk of the county of New York on the 19th day of November, 1901, upon the decision of the court, rendered after a trial at the New York Special Term, sustaining the defendant's demurrer to the complaint.

The action was brought to recover the amount of a benefit certificate issued by the defendant to Joseph P. Markey.

Charles Haldane, for the appellant.

Edwin C. Low, for the respondent.

PER CURIAM:

If it be true, as urged by the appellant, that the defendant had no authority, under its constitution, to make the certificate issued upon the life of Joseph P. Markey payable to the brother, Edward J. Markey, it does not follow that the plaintiff can, by reason of that fact, recover the amount stated in the certificate. If the defendant's act in issuing the certificate was *ultra vires* the plaintiff cannot take advantage of it, inasmuch as she has no certificate at all, and comes into court without the basis of any claim whatever. (*Luhrs* v. *Supreme Lodge Knights & Ladies of Honor,* 27 N. Y. St. Repr. 88.) But the precise question here presented was determined adversely to the plaintiff's contention in *Maguire* v. *Maguire* (59 App. Div. 143), and, therefore, upon that authority, this judgment must be affirmed.

Judgment affirmed, with costs.

Present — VAN BRUNT, P. J., INGRAHAM, McLAUGHLIN, HATCH and LAUGHLIN, JJ.

Judgment affirmed, with costs.

In the Matter of the Judicial Settlement of the Account of UNION TRUST COMPANY OF NEW YORK, as Trustee of the Estate of GEORGE P. LAWRENCE, Deceased, Appellant.

70
83

LAWRENCE CRAUFURD and ROBERT B. CRAUFURD, an Infant, Respondents.

Commissions to an executor and trustee — when full commissions should be allowed in each capacity.

A testator by his will, after directing his "executor" to pay all his debts, funeral and testamentary expenses as soon as possible after his decease, gave the residue of his estate to his "executor" in trust, to manage and invest the same and "to collect the interest and income and apply so much thereof as my sister, Minnie H. Craufurd of Norwalk, in the State of Connecticut, may require for the support, education and maintenance of her children during the terms of their minority, and in the event of the death of my said sister so much of said interest or income as my executor for the time being shall deem fit and proper for such support, education and maintenance of my said sister's children during their minority, and as each of such children comes of age I direct my said executor to pay over to such child an equal proportion of the capital and accumulated interest unexpended at that time. In case any child shall die before reaching full age his or her share shall go to increase the shares of the surviving brothers and sisters." He nominated one Marbury to be "the sole *executor* of and *trustee*" under the will and provided that, in the event of Marbury's death or his failure to act, the Union Trust Company of the city of New York should be "the *executor* of and *trustee*" under the will.

Marbury qualified as executor and collected and distributed the income from the residuary estate down to his death in March, 1895. His executrix, on whose accounting as executrix of the deceased executor commissions to the deceased as executor were allowed and as trustee were disallowed, transferred the estate to the Union Trust Company.

In 1900 the Union Trust Company filed its accounts as executor and a decree was entered adjudging that "said executor pay and deliver to Union Trust Company of New York, as trustee, * * * the balance of said estate remaining in its hands."

In 1901 one of the beneficiaries became of age and the trust company instituted a proceeding for a judicial settlement of its account.

Held, that the trust company was entitled to commissions as trustee upon such portion of the *corpus* of the estate as was payable to the beneficiary who had attained his majority, for the reason that the will imposed double duties upon the trust company, namely, those of an executor, and, after the period of administration had passed, those of a trustee, and for the additional reason that the trust company had been discharged as executor and remained liable solely as trustee.

APPEAL by the Union Trust Company of New York, as trustee of the estate of George P. Lawrence, deceased, from that portion of a decree of the Surrogate's Court of the county of New York, entered in said Surrogate's Court on the 6th day of September, 1901, refusing to allow commissions to said company as trustee.

This proceeding was brought to settle the account of the appellant, the Union Trust Company of New York, as trustee of the estate of George P. Lawrence, who died December 15, 1891, leaving a will and codicil thereto which were duly probated in New York county on or about February 26, 1892.

The provisions of the will bearing on the questions involved are as follows:

"*First.* I direct that all my just debts, funeral and testamentary expenses be paid by my executor hereinafter named as soon as may be after my decease.

"*Second.* All the rest, residue and remainder of my property, estate and effects of whatsoever name, nature or kind, and wheresoever situate, I give, devise and bequeath to my executor, hereinafter named, to have and to hold the same upon trust with authority to manage and invest the same, and to keep the same invested in bonds and securities of the United States or of the State of New York, or of the City and County of New York, or upon good first mortgage railroad bonds, or upon bonds secured by mortgages on unincumbered and improved real estate in the Cities of New York or Brooklyn, and to collect the interest and income and apply so much thereof as my sister, Minnie H. Cranfurd of Norwalk, in the State of Connecticut, may require for the support, education and maintenance of her children during the terms of their minority, and in the event of the death of my said sister so much of said interest or income, as my executor for the time being shall deem fit and proper for such support, education and maintenance of my said sister's children during their minority, and as each of such children comes of age I direct my said executor to pay over to such child an equal proportion of the capital and accumulated interest, unexpended at that time. In case any child shall die before reaching full age, his or her share shall go to increase the shares of the surviving brothers and sisters."

"*Fourth.* I hereby nominate, constitute and appoint Francis F.

Marbury, of the city of New York, counsellor at law, to be the sole *executor* of and *trustee* under this my last will and testament, and I hereby declare that in no event shall he be required to give bonds or security in this State, or elsewhere, as such executor. In case of the death of the said Francis F. Marbury, or of his declining or failing to qualify and act as my executor, then I hereby nominate and appoint The Union Trust Company of the City of New York to be the *executor* of and *trustee* under this my last will and testament, in place of the said Francis F. Marbury, with all the powers, rights and duties hereinbefore conferred upon him, and without requiring any bonds or security from said Union Trust Company in this State or elsewhere."

Upon the probate of the will Francis F. Marbury qualified as executor thereunder and collected and distributed the income from the estate down to his death in March, 1895. His wife, who was his executrix, then transferred the estate to the Union Trust Company, since which time it has collected and distributed the income and managed the business of the estate. Mrs. Marbury, in June, 1897, accounted as executrix of the deceased executor, Francis F. Marbury, and her claim for commissions as trustee, in addition to those as executor, was disallowed. From 1896 until September, 1900, the Union Trust Company continued in the management of the estate, and in that month filed an account as executor, and thereafter a decree was entered, September 8, 1900, by which it was adjudged that "said executor pay and deliver to Union Trust Company of New York, as trustee, * * * the balance of said estate remaining in its hands."

Upon one of the beneficiaries arriving at majority the trust company, in 1901, initiated this proceeding by petition, filing a new account and claiming commissions as trustee. This claim was disallowed by the surrogate, and it is from that portion of the decree that the trust company appeals.

Hoffman Miller, for the appellant.

Edwin C. Ward, for the respondent Lawrence Craufurd.

William B. McNiece, special guardian, for the respondent Robert B. Craufurd.

O'BRIEN, J.:

The question here involved is whether the appellant, the Union Trust Company, is entitled to commissions as trustee, having already received full commissions as executor. As formulated in *McAlpine* v. *Potter* (126 N. Y. 289), "The principal question which is presented by this appeal is whether the commissions to be allowed are to be governed by the doctrine of *Johnson* v. *Lawrence* (95 N. Y. 154), or *Laytin* v. *Davidson* (95 id. 263)." This requires that we should examine those authorities and apply them to the case at bar.

In *Johnson* v. *Lawrence* it was said: "Taking the adjudged cases together, they appear to establish that to entitle the same persons to commissions as executors and as trustees the will must provide, either by express terms or by fair intendment, for the separation of the two functions and duties, one duty to precede the other and to be performed before the latter is begun, or substantially so performed; and must not provide for the co-existence continuously and from the beginning, of the two functions and duties; and that where the will does so provide for the separate and successive duties, that of trustee must be actually entered upon and its performance begun, either by a real severance of the trust fund from the general assets, or a judicial decree which wholly discharges the executor and leaves him acting and liable only as trustee." Applying this rule to the will under consideration, it was held that the two functions of executor and trustee co-existed from the death of the testator and the issue of letters testamentary until the final discharge of the plaintiff, and were inseparately blended, so that double commissions were not allowed.

In *Laytin* v. *Davidson* (*supra*) it was held that the will there in question contemplated a time when the duties of the executors as such should cease and they should assume the character exclusively of trustees, and that while the decree of settlement of their accounts did not in terms discharge the executors that was its legal effect, and as trustees they were entitled to the commissions claimed, though they had not made an actual division of the trust fund into shares, as directed. This latter case is also authority for the proposition that it makes no difference upon the question of the right to commissions whether it is the same person or different persons who act in the capacity of executor and trustee.

The solution of the question, therefore, is to be found in the terms
of the will, as to whether, in addition to the ordinary duties of
administering the estate as executor, there is a point of time when
such duties cease and the same or different persons are, by direction
of the will, to manage the estate as trustees. The distinction
between the two cases referred to consists in the fact that in *Johnson* v. *Lawrence* the plaintiffs, as they were required under the will
to carry on the business of the estate and directed not to reduce the
estate for the purpose of division until a certain time, acted throughout as executors, while in *Laytin* v. *Davidson*, after such time had
arrived and the duties of executors had been performed, there
remained the necessity for the persons named continuing in charge
of the estate as trustees.

To determine in what capacity one acts, it is important to keep in
view what ordinarily are the duties of an executor. They are similar to those which in the event of intestacy would devolve upon an
administrator. That is to say, in either capacity, the duties are to
administer upon the estate by collecting and reducing to possession
the assets of the estate and, after paying debts, to have the balance
in hand for distribution. It is only at this point that a distinction
arises, which is that an executor makes distribution under the will
and an administrator under the law.

The duties of an executor and those of a trustee are well defined
in *Drake* v. *Price* (5 N. Y. 430), as follows: "To take possession
of all the goods and chattels, and other assets of the testator, to collect the outstanding debt and sell the goods and chattels so far as is
necessary to the payment of the debts and legacies; to pay the
debts and legacies, and under the order of the surrogate to distribute the surplus to the widow and children, or next of kin of the
deceased. These acts embrace all the duties which appropriately
belong to the executorial office. If any other duty is imposed upon
the executor, or any power conferred, not appertaining to the duties
above enumerated, a trust, or trust power, is created, and the executor becomes a trustee, or the donee of a trust power. And such
powers are conferred and such duties imposed upon him, not as
incidents to his office of executor, but as belonging to an entirely
distinct character — that of trustee. And in all such cases the trust
and executorship are distinguishable and separate."

FIRST DEPARTMENT, MARCH TERM, 1902.   [Vol. 70.

In the case at bar we think the will imposed on the trust company duties other than those appertaining to an executorship,
assuming, what in our view is implied — that upon the completion
of the executorial duties, the duties of trustee were to commence,
for it will be noted in this connection that the trust created is of the
residuary estate which can be ascertained only after the completion
of the work of the executor.   Ordinarily the duties devolving upon
an executor include, as stated, paying debts and legacies, and collecting and reducing to possession the assets of the estate.   These
duties usually are completed within the year or eighteen months
which the law allows for such purpose, unless under the terms of the
will something remains to be done other than to then distribute the
estate.   Such duties are purely executorial.   Where, however, in
addition to the ordinary offices of administering upon the estate, there
is a provision in the will that after a period fixed the property is to
be held in trust, whether by the same or other persons, there then
devolves upon such persons the duties of the trustee.

Another test to apply as to the capacity in which one holds is,
upon whom, if the person acting were to die or resign, would the
power of appointment of a successor devolve ?   In case of a trustee
it would, under the statute, devolve upon the Supreme Court.
Applying that test here, it is evident that should the trust company
resign, the Supreme Court would appoint its successor, for the
duties are such that they should be performed by a trustee.

Referring again to the will before us, it will be noted that the
person named is directed, first, to pay the debts, funeral and testamentary expenses ; and these acts are to be performed, in the language of the testator, " by my executor hereinafter named as soon
as may be after my decease."   Although not expressly stated, the
duty also devolved upon such executor to reduce the estate to possession, to advertise for claims against the estate, and, within the
time prescribed by law, to discharge all purely executorial functions.
It was only when this work was completed that the residue of the
estate, which thereafter was to be managed for certain purposes,
could be determined.   " All the rest, residue and remainder," is,
by the 2d paragraph of the will, given to the same person to
hold " upon trust " for certain of the children of the testator's
sister, he to pay over so much of the income thereof as he may

think proper for their support, education and maintenance during their minority, and their share of the principal and accumulated interest when they arrived at full age. The trust so created is one of the express trusts allowed by law; and no argument is needed to sustain the proposition that a person who is thus required to carry out its clearly defined terms is a trustee. Under this will, therefore, we think double duties were imposed, first, those of executor, and then, after the period of administration as such had passed, those of trustee.

Although it is claimed that the part of the decree of September 8, 1900, which directs the estate to be delivered to the Union Trust Company " as trustee," was inserted through inadvertence, the fact is that such a provision remains therein, and the decree has never been set aside or appealed from, and for that reason was just as binding upon the learned surrogate as it is upon us. In all the cases, including the one on which most reliance has been placed, that of *Johnson* v. *Lawrence* (*supra*), it will be seen that one of the controlling features in the determination of the question of double commissions has been whether, to use the language of the opinion · in that case, there was "a judicial decree which wholly discharges the executor and leaves him acting and liable only as trustee." That surely was the condition here, because the trust company had been discharged as executor and the property had been turned over to it as trustee; and when this proceeding was commenced, it was by the trust company " as trustee." We think, then, that it was beyond the power of the learned surrogate to disregard that decree, so long as it remained a valid and binding adjudication upon the question of the status of the trust company.

Our conclusion is that the decree so far as appealed from must be reversed, and the decree modified by directing the payment to the accounting trustee of commissions on such portion of the *corpus* of the estate as is payable to Lawrence Craufurd, with costs to appellant out of such portion.

Van Brunt, P. J., Ingraham, Hatch and Laughlin, JJ., concurred.

Decree modified as directed in opinion, with costs to appellant out of the portion of the estate payable to Lawrence Craufurd.

ELIZA PRINGLE, Appellant, *v.* FANNIE LOUISE BURROUGHS, *née* TEMPLE, Individually, and as Executrix, etc., of JOSEPH HAMILTON BRYAN, Deceased, Respondent; ELIZA J. BRYAN and Others, Appellants, Impleaded with Others.

Physician's testimony as to information acquired while attending a patient — what constitutes a waiver by the next of kin.

Where one of the heirs at law and next of kin of a decedent brings an action against the other heirs at law and next of kin of the decedent and the chief beneficiary under his alleged will to set aside the probate of such will on the ground that it was not the voluntary act of the decedent, and all of the defendant heirs at law and next of kin join in the prayer of the complaint, the act of the plaintiff in calling a physician who attended the decedent during the month in which he died to testify concerning the decedent's condition at the time he attended him, constitutes an express waiver, under section 836 of the Code of Civil Procedure, of the provisions of section 834 of that Code, preventing a physician from disclosing any information acquired by him in his professional capacity.

APPEAL by the plaintiff, Eliza Pringle, and by the defendants Eliza J. Bryan and others, from a judgment of the Supreme Court in favor of the defendant, Fannie Louise Burroughs, *née* Temple, individually, and as executrix, etc., of Joseph Hamilton Bryan, deceased, entered in the office of the clerk of the county of New York on the 17th day of December, 1900, upon the verdict of a jury rendered by direction of the court, and also from an order entered in said clerk's office on the 5th day of January, 1901, denying the appellants' motion for a new trial made upon the minutes, and also from an order entered in said clerk's office on the 5th day of January, 1901, denying the plaintiff's motion to amend the judgment by inserting after the word " verdict " the words " by direction of the court."

The action was brought to determine the validity of the probate of the will of Joseph H. Bryan who died September 20, 1899. The will was executed September 6, 1899, and was admitted to probate on November 6, 1899. By it the testator, after directing the payment of his debts and giving to his aunt, the plaintiff herein, an annuity of $200 for life, devised all the rest of his estate to Fannie Louise Temple (the defendant Fannie Louise Burroughs), his cousin,

" to have and to hold absolutely," expressing the wish that she attend to the wants of his two sisters. He also made her executrix of his will, and as such authorized her to sell and convey his real estate as she deemed advisable.

The complaint alleges that the deceased left him surviving a widow and two unmarried sisters, both of whom are of unsound mind, no children or issue of deceased child, no father or mother, and no children of deceased brother or sister; that he owned certain real estate at the time of his death, and by a will executed prior to the one in question had given to this plaintiff the sum of $5,000, and such will is the true and valid will of the deceased; that the will admitted to probate was not his will and its execution " was not the free, unconstrained or voluntary act of said deceased," and that at the time it was or purports to have been executed he was not " of sound mind, memory or understanding or capable of making a will." The defendants, other than Burroughs, who were also interested in the will, took sides with the plaintiff in their answers.

It appears from the evidence that the plaintiff, who lived at the home of the deceased at the time of the trial, was seventy-seven years old; that the deceased when he died was fifty-two years of age and had been in ill-health for about two years; that the defendant Fannie Burroughs was a cousin or second cousin of the deceased, but not of the Bryan blood, and that she used to come to the house regularly and take his mother (sister of the plaintiff) to church, and after her death came into the " house and stayed there all the time. * * * She began to nurse " Mr. Bryan, who was then much worse, and looked after the house and gave orders to the maids up to the time of his death some months later; that during this time a new will — the one in dispute — was made, two lawyers coming to the house for that purpose, one being the lawyer who had previously acted for the deceased.

Upon the evidence adduced, the court directed the jury to find a verdict sustaining the probate of the will; and from the judgment so entered, the plaintiff and the defendants other than Fannie L. Burroughs appeal.

Lewis E. Carr, for the appellants.

W. W. Buckley, for the respondent.

O'BRIEN, J.:

Were it not for a ruling upon evidence we should have no hesitation in affirming this judgment; for the inferences most favorable to plaintiff were insufficient to warrant any finding by the jury that the will of Joseph H. Bryan was not valid or that its execution was not his "free, unconstrained and voluntary act." The ruling, however, to which we will briefly refer, requires that the judgment be reversed.

One of the physicians, who had attended the deceased before he died, was called as a witness by plaintiff, and after testifying that he had first visited Mr. Bryan during September, 1899, the month of his death, and had obtained information while so acting professionally for him, was asked to state his condition at that time. Objection was interposed, which the trial judge sustained, and the physician was prevented from giving such testimony.

It is to be noted in passing that all the defendants other than the chief beneficiary, Fannie Louise Burroughs (*née* Temple), had joined with the plaintiff in asking that the will should be declared invalid; and, together, they represented the heirs at law and next of kin of Joseph H. Bryan. The exclusion of the testimony sought to be elicited was because of the prohibition contained in section 834 of the Code of Civil Procedure; and such ruling, if made prior to the amendment of 1893 embodied in section 836 of the Code, would have been right. (*Renihan v. Dennin,* 103 N. Y. 573; *Matter of Coleman,* 111 id. 220.)

By that amendment, however, it is provided: "But a physician or surgeon may, upon a trial or examination, disclose any information as to the mental or physical condition of a patient who is deceased which he acquired in attending such patients professionally, except confidential communications, and such facts as would tend to disgrace the memory of the patient, when the provisions of section eight hundred and thirty-four have been expressly waived on such trial or examination by the personal representatives of the deceased patient, or if the validity of the last will and testament of such deceased patient is in question by the executor or executors named in said will, or the surviving husband, widow, or any heir at law or any of the next of kin, of such deceased, or any other party in interest." (Laws of 1893, chap. 295.)

As held in *Matter of Murphy* (85 Hun, 575), "The purpose of the amendment evidently was to open more widely the door to the introduction of the evidence of medical attendants of a deceased patient when the validity of his will should be in question. The right of waiver was, therefore, extended to others having the relations mentioned to the deceased, and to those having the legal relation of parties in interest, and who are properly in the action or proceeding in which the question arises before the court."

It is insisted by the respondent that here there was no "express waiver" and that the mere calling of the physician as such, was insufficient to constitute a waiver. This precise question, however, has been determined adversely to the respondent in *Holcomb* v. *Harris* (166 N. Y. 257, 263), where the court said : "It is difficult to imagine a clearer act of waiver than for the legal representatives of a deceased patient to call his former physician to the stand and ask him to disclose professional information falling within the provisions of section 834 of the Code. * * * The rejected evidence was material, and, while regretting the necessity for a new trial, we are compelled to hold that this ruling of the trial judge presents reversible error."

We can add nothing to this authority, which is controlling upon us, and requires that the judgment and order appealed from should be reversed, and a new trial ordered, with costs to the appellant to abide the event.

VAN BRUNT, P. J., INGRAHAM, McLAUGHLIN and HATCH, JJ., concurred.

Judgment and order reversed, new trial ordered, costs to appellant to abide event.

16
*557
*558

16
636
593

E. MARTIN BLACK, Appellant, *v.* WILLIAM K. VANDERBILT and EDWARD V. W. ROSSITER, as Trustees for E. MARTIN BLACK, Respondents, Impleaded with FRANCIS D. CARLEY, as Trustee for E. MARTIN BLACK.

A complaint framed in equity — when demurred to, it will not be sustained on the theory that the facts stated will sustain an action at law.

The complaint in an action alleged that the plaintiff was the editor and manager of a newspaper, and that in consideration of services to be rendered by the plaintiff, through the medium of his newspaper, in enhancing the value of the stock of a railroad company, the defendants agreed to set apart for the benefit of the plaintiff 500 shares of the stock of such company and to place such 500 shares, together with other shares owned and controlled by them, in a pool to be formed for the purpose of manipulating the price of said stock; that the agreement provided that if the undertaking should result in a loss, such loss should be borne by the defendants, while if a profit resulted therefrom, " the said defendants were, upon demand of said plaintiff, to account for and pay over to said plaintiff the profit that would be and become due to him on account of the shares so set apart for him up to and at the time such demand was made."

It was further alleged that the pool was formed and that the plaintiff performed his part of the agreement, and that by reason thereof said stock "rose rapidly in value and large profits accrued in favor of the defendants and said plaintiff, and said plaintiff thereafter demanded of the defendants that they account for and pay over to him his share of such profits, as represented by the 500 shares aforesaid; that said trust is still open and the accounts of said trustees have not been settled or adjusted, or the amount due said plaintiff under said trust agreement ascertained."

It was further alleged that the defendants allowed one of their number, who was insolvent, to manage the stock in the pool, including the 500 shares held for the plaintiff, and also "that said defendants during the pendency of this action are doing, and procuring to be done, various acts in violation of the said plaintiff's rights respecting said five hundred shares of stock and the profits already, or to be derived from the sale thereof, which tend to render any judgment which may be recovered herein ineffectual; that said plaintiff has a substantial interest in said shares of stock and the profits already, or to be derived from the sale thereof, now in the possession or under the control of said defendants, as such trustees, and there is danger that such stock or the profits already, or to be derived from the sale thereof, will be removed by said defendants beyond the jurisdiction of said court, or will be lost, materially injured and destroyed."

The complaint demanded as relief that an accounting be had and that the defendants pay over to the plaintiff any and all sums of money or profits found to be due him thereon; that the defendant be restrained, *pendente lite,* from disposing of the 500 shares of stock, if still in their possession or under their control, and any and all sums of money or profits due said plaintiff under the terms of said agreement; that a receiver of such 500 shares of stock or, if said shares have been sold, of the profits derived by the defendants "as such trustees" from the sale be appointed, and that the plaintiff have such other and further relief as might be just and equitable.

The plaintiff's counsel stated in his brief that "the amended complaint states a good cause of action for equitable relief, and upon the allegations contained in the amended complaint the plaintiff is entitled to maintain an action for an accounting."

Held, that the complaint was demurrable;

That it did not state a cause of action for equitable relief and that, as equitable relief alone was demanded and no answer had been interposed, the court would not sustain the complaint on the theory that the facts stated therein entitled the plaintiff to legal redress.

LAUGHLIN, J., dissented.

APPEAL by the plaintiff, E. Martin Black, from an interlocutory judgment of the Supreme Court in favor of the defendants, William K. Vanderbilt and another, as trustees for E. Martin Black, entered in the office of the clerk of the county of New York on the 21st day of May, 1901, upon the decision of the court, rendered after a trial at the New York Special Term, sustaining the said defendants' demurrer to the complaint.

The complaint herein is as follows:

" I. That the plaintiff now is, and at all times since the year 1887 has been, the editor and manager of a newspaper known as *The Wall Street Daily News.*

" II. That in or about the years 1897–1898 the said defendants entered into an agreement with said plaintiff, which agreement was in part in writing and in part oral, wherein and whereby they, the said defendants, for and in consideration of the services of the plaintiff, as hereinafter mentioned, agreed to and did set apart, as the property of and for the benefit of said plaintiff, five hundred shares of the common capital stock of the Pittsburgh, Cincinnati, Chicago and St. Louis Railroad Company, of the par value of $100 per share, which said five hundred shares they, the said defendants, placed with other like shares of the capital stock of the said railroad company, owned by them and others, and controlled by them, for the purpose of forming a pool or combination of said stock and dealing in or manipulating the price of the same on the New York

Stock Exchange and elsewhere, with the view of enhancing the value of all of such shares; that it was in and by said agreement further provided that in case a loss should be incurred in such dealings or manipulation it should, so far as the said plaintiff was concerned, be borne by the defendants, while if a profit resulted therefrom the said defendants were, upon demand of said plaintiff, to account for and pay over to said plaintiff the profit that would be and become due to him on account of the shares so set apart for him up to and at the time such demand was made.

"III. That said agreement further provided that, in consideration of the terms thereof to be performed, as aforesaid, by said defendants as such trustees, said plaintiff was to perform certain work and services on request and on behalf of said defendants, in and about the enhancement of the value of said stock through the medium of the said newspaper; that said plaintiff fully performed all the matters and things by him to be performed under said agreement.

"IV. That after the formation by the defendants, as aforesaid, of the said pool or combination, the market price of the shares of the said Pittsburgh, Cincinnati, Chicago and St. Louis Railroad Company, by reason of the services of the plaintiff, as aforesaid, and the dealings and manipulation, as aforesaid, rose rapidly in value, and large profits accrued in favor of the defendants and said plaintiff, and said plaintiff thereafter demanded of the defendants that they account for and pay over to him his share of such profits, as represented by the 500 shares aforesaid; that said trust is still open and the accounts of said trustees have not been settled or adjusted, or the amount due said plaintiff under said trust agreement ascertained.

"V. On information and belief, that the said defendants William K. Vanderbilt and Edward V. W. Rossiter allowed and still allow said defendant Francis D. Carley to manage, control and manipulate said stock, including said five hundred shares held as aforesaid, for said plaintiff; that said defendant Francis D. Carley is insolvent and unable to pay his debts, and has unpaid, outstanding judgments against him; that said defendants during the pendency of this action are doing, and procuring to be done, various acts in violation of the said plaintiff's rights respecting said five hundred shares of stock and the profits already, or to be derived from the sale thereof, which tend to render any judgment which may be recovered herein ineffectual; that said plaintiff has a substantial interest in said shares of stock and the profits already, or to be derived from the sale thereof, now in the possession or under the control of said defendants, as such trustees, and there is danger that such stock or the profits already, or to be derived from the sale thereof, will be removed by said defendants beyond the jurisdiction of said court, or will be lost, materially injured and destroyed.

" Wherefore, said plaintiff demands judgment against said defendants:

" I. That an accounting be had of and concerning the matters and things aforesaid, and that said defendants pay over to said plaintiff any and all sums of money or profits found to be due him upon such accounting.

" II. That said defendants and each and every of them, and the agents, brokers and employees of each and every of them, be restrained by injunction, during the pendency of this action, from interfering with or disposing of said five hundred shares of stock, held, as aforesaid, for said plaintiff, if still in their possession or under their control, and from interfering with or disposing of any and all sums of money or profits due said plaintiff under the terms of said agreement.

" III. That a receiver be appointed of the said five hundred shares of said stock, held, as aforesaid, for said plaintiff, or if the said shares have been sold, then and in that case, of the profits derived by said defendants, as such trustees, from the sale or transfer thereof.

" IV. That said plaintiff have such other and further relief in the premises as may be just and equitable, together with the costs and disbursements of this action."

The defendants demurred to the complaint on the ground that it does not state facts sufficient to constitute a cause of action, one of the reasons assigned being that the plaintiff's remedy, if any, is legal, and not equitable, as demanded. The court sustained the demurrer, and from the interlocutory judgment thus entered, the plaintiff appeals.

Robert L. Stanton, for the appellant.

Henry B. Anderson, for the respondents.

O'BRIEN, J.:

Reading the allegations of the complaint in the light of the prayer for relief, there can be no doubt that what the plaintiff sought was equitable relief in an equitable action. Were there any such doubt, it would be dispelled by the statement in the brief of the plaintiff on this appeal that "the amended complaint states a good cause of action for equitable relief, and upon the allegations contained in the amended complaint the plaintiff is entitled to maintain an action for an accounting."

It is true that in a subsequent part of the brief is the contention that if, upon the facts stated, the plaintiff was entitled to any redress, legal or equitable, it was error for the court to sustain the demurrer. This latter proposition for which the appellant contends has been applied in cases where an answer has been interposed and thereafter the sufficiency of the complaint was questioned. We can find, however, no authority for the proposition that where a suit is brought in equity for equitable relief, and the defendant demurs, it then becomes the duty of the court, where the facts would not warrant equitable redress, to hold that the demurrer is bad because it might be concluded, upon some construction of the allegations of the complaint, that the plaintiff has stated certain facts which, disregarding all the others, might convert the suit into an action at law. It is true that a party is not to be turned out of court merely because he has failed to demand the precise remedy to which he is entitled, and that he may state in this complaint the facts upon which he relies in such a manner as to entitle him either to legal or equitable relief. But here, no legal redress is demanded, and it conclusively appears that the complaint was framed for equitable relief alone.

In *Swart* v. *Boughton* (35 Hun, 287) it was said: "Where all of the allegations of the complaint are made for the purpose of procuring equitable relief, and where equitable relief alone is asked for, the complaint cannot be sustained for legal redress where no answer has been interposed." That case was followed by this court in *Cody* v. *First Nat. Bank* (63 App. Div. 199); and in view of the very full discussion there of the exact question here presented for consideration, it is unnecessary to add to what was therein said.

Regarding the question as settled, therefore, so far as this court is concerned, we think that the disposition made by the Special Term in sustaining the demurrer was right. The interlocutory judgment appealed from should accordingly be affirmed, with costs, with leave to plaintiff within twenty days to amend the complaint upon pay· ment of costs in this court and in the court below.

VAN BRUNT, P. J., PATTERSON and McLAUGHLIN, JJ., concurred; LAUGHLIN, J., dissented.

LAUGHLIN, J. (dissenting):

The sole ground of the demurrer is that the complaint does not state facts sufficient to constitute a cause of action. The complaint alleges that in 1897, the plaintiff being then the editor and manager of *The Wall Street Daily News,* the defendants entered into an agreement with him, partly in writing and partly in parol, whereby they "agreed to and did set apart, as the property of and for the benefit of said plaintiff," 500 shares of the common capital stock of the Pittsburgh, Cincinnati, Chicago and St. Louis Railroad Company, of the par value of $100 each, and placed said stock with other like shares of the capital stock of said railroad company, owned by them and others, and "controlled by them for the purpose of forming a pool or combination of said stock, and dealing in or manipulating the price of the same on the New York Stock Exchange and elsewhere, with the view of enhancing the value of all of such shares;" that it was further provided by said agreement "that in case a loss should be incurred in such dealings or manipulation it should, so far as the said plaintiff was concerned, be borne by the defendants, while if a profit resulted therefrom the said defendants were, upon demand of said plaintiff, to account for and pay over to said plaintiff the profit that would be and become due to him on account of the shares so set apart for him up to and at the time such demand was made;" that in consideration of the said agreement on the part of the "defendants as such trustees," the "plaintiff was to perform certain work and services on request and on behalf of said defendants in and about the enhancement of the value of said stock through the medium of the said newspaper;" that plaintiff has fully performed said contract on his part, and that by reason of the services so performed by him, and of the dealings and manipulation of said stock by the defendants, as contemplated in the agreement, the market price of the stock rose rapidly and large profits accumulated thereon in favor of the parties hereto; that plaintiff thereafter demanded of defendants "that they account for and pay over to him his share of such profits;" that "said trust is still open and the accounts of said trustees have not been settled or adjusted, or the amount due said plaintiff under said trust agreement ascertained;" that the other defendants allow the defendant Carley, who is insolvent, to "manage, control and manipulate said stock;" that the defendants are doing and procuring to be done "various acts in violation of the said plaintiff's rights, respecting said five hundred shares of stock and the profits already, or to be derived from the sale thereof, which tend to render any judgment which may be recovered herein ineffectual; that said plaintiff has a substantial interest in said shares of stock and the profits already, or to be derived from the sale thereof, now in the possession or under the control of said defendants, as such trustees, and there is danger that such stock, or the profits already, or to be derived from the sale thereof will be removed by said defendants beyond the jurisdiction of said court, or will be lost, materially injured and destroyed."

The prayer for relief is: (1) That "an accounting be had," and that defendants pay over to plaintiff "any and all sums of money or profits found to be due him upon such accounting." (2) That defendants be enjoined *pendente lite* from interfering with or disposing of said 500 shares of stock, if still in their possession or under their control, or any money or profits due to plaintiff under said agreement. (3) That a receiver of said stock or of the profits derived by defendants "as such trustees" from a sale or transfer thereof be appointed. And (4) the usual prayer for "other and further relief."

On demurrer, every allegation of fact and every fact that may be implied therefrom by reasonable and fair intendment must be taken as true. (*Sage* v. *Culver*, 147 N. Y. 241; *Coatsworth* v. *Lehigh Valley R. Co.*, 156 id. 451; *Greeff* v. *Equitable Life Assurance Society*, 160 id. 19.) Under the chancery practice, a demurrer would of course lie to a bill of complaint not showing a cause of action in equity. (*Grandin* v. *Leroy*, 2 Paige, 509; *Wiswall* v. *Hall*, 3 id. 313.) The Code of Civil Procedure (§ 3339) provides that "there is only one form of civil action. The distinction between actions at law and suits in equity, and the forms of those actions and suits, have been abolished."

The demurrer follows strictly the language of the 8th subdivision of section 488 of the Code of Civil Procedure, which authorizes a demurrer where it appears on the face of the complaint " that the complaint does not state facts sufficient to constitute a cause of action." The plaintiff is not obliged to expressly state in his complaint whether he is proceeding at law or in equity. The only requirement is " a plain and concise statement of the facts constituting " the cause of action, " without unnecessary repetition," and " a demand of the judgment to which the plaintiff supposes himself entitled." (Code Civ. Proc. § 481, subds. 2, 3.) The complaint does not denominate the action a suit in equity, and the plaintiff has neither placed it upon the Special Term calendar nor moved for a reference, nor done anything by which he has elected to stand or fall upon his complaint as sufficient for equitable relief. The prayer for relief is a limitation upon the right to recover only where no answer has been interposed. In such case, the judgment may not be more favorable to plaintiff than that demanded in the complaint; but where the defendants have answered, the plaintiff may have any judgment warranted by the proofs and embraced within the issues. (Code Civ. Proc. § 1207; *Chaurant* v. *Maillard*, 56 App. Div. 11.)

The doctrine has been announced in general terms that if a case for either legal or equitable relief is alleged, the complaint is not demurrable, because the plaintiff has not demanded the precise relief to which he is entitled. (*Lester* v. *Seilliere*, 50 App. Div. 239; *Wetmore* v. *Porter*, 92 N. Y. 76; *Parker* v. *Pullman & Co.*, 36 App. Div. 208.) This rule, however, is not to be applied literally to all cases. The judgment must follow the allegations as well as the proof; and where the complaint is clearly framed in equity for equitable relief, it may, in the discretion of the court, be dismissed even at the trial, although the evidence shows a cause of action at law (*Arnold* v. *Angell*, 62 N. Y. 508; *Hawes* v. *Dobbs*, 137 id. 465; *Ketchum* v. *Depew*, 81 Hun, 278); but the better practice in such cases is for the court to retain the action and send it to the trial calendar. (*Thomas* v. *Schumacher*, 17 App. Div. 441, 447, 448; affd. on opinion below, 163 N. Y. 554; *Ashley* v. *Lehmann*, 54 App. Div. 45; *Emery* v. *Pease*, 20 N. Y. 62; *Cuff* v. *Dorland*;

55 Barb. 482.) The preponderance of authority seems to be to the effect that on a demurrer, for the purpose of ascertaining whether a good cause of action is stated, the inquiry is whether the plaintiff would be entitled to a judgment for any relief by default. Accordingly, it is held that where a pleading is framed as an action at law, and there is no prayer for any form of equitable relief, if the complaint fails to state a good cause of action at law, it is demurrable even though the facts would afford ground for equitable relief; and it is likewise held that where all the allegations of a complaint are for equitable relief, and equitable relief only is demanded, if a good cause in equity be not alleged, the complaint is demurrable even though the facts stated show that the plaintiff has a cause of action at law. (*Cody* v. *First Nat. Bank*, 63 App. Div. 199; *Swart* v. *Boughton*, 35 Hun, 281; *Kelly* v. *Downing*, 42 N. Y. 71.)

I am inclined to think the complaint cannot be sustained in equity. The allegations are not sufficient, if proved, to establish a partnership between the parties, and plaintiff is not entitled to an accounting on that theory. Sharing in the profits as compensation for services rendered does not constitute one a partner. (*Smith* v. *Bodine*, 74 N. Y. 30; *Richardson* v. *Hughitt*, 76 id. 55; *Merchants Nat. Bank* v. *Barnes*, 32 App. Div. 92; *McCullough* v. *Pence*, 85 Hun, 271.) If the plaintiff owned the stock and intrusted it to the defendants to manipulate, or if by the agreement it was to become his, a trust would exist between them concerning it, and he would be entitled to an accounting (*Marston* v. *Gould*, 69 N. Y. 225; *Marvin* v. *Brooks*, 94 id. 71; *Parker* v. *Pullman & Co.*, 36 App. Div. 208; *Schantz* v. *Oakman*, 163 N. Y. 148); but as I read the complaint, the plaintiff is only interested in the profits. Nor does he show that the taking of the account of defendants' transactions with the stock will be so complicated or difficult as to warrant a court of equity in taking cognizance of the action within the authority of *Parker* v. *Pullman & Co.* (*supra*).

I think, however, that within the rules stated, the allegations of the complaint and the relief demanded do not necessarily stamp the action as in equity. The complaint sufficiently avers a cause of action for services rendered and for the breach of the contract to account for profits on the stock and pay the same as consideration for such services. In effect, these allegations of the complaint

show that profits have been earned under the agreement; that
plaintiff is entitled to share therein, and that the defendants have
refused upon demand to pay the amount owing to him. The ultimate object of the action is to recover a judgment for the amount
of such profits. It will be necessary to take an account to determine the amount to which the plaintiff is entitled; and, therefore,
the complaint, even if the action be deemed at law, properly
demands that an accounting be had. The demand concerning the
account is not in the form adopted in equity practice, viz., that
defendants be directed to render an account, but in the form authorized by the Code in an action at law, viz., that "an accounting be had
to ascertain the amount owing to plaintiff and for which he is entitled to judgment." The complaint as thus construed is for a cause
of action specified in section 420 of the Code of Civil Procedure; but
inasmuch as the sum of money demanded is not fixed by the terms
of the contract or capable of ascertainment therefrom by computation only, judgment could not be taken by default without an application to the court. (Code Civ. Proc. §§ 419, 420, 1212, 1215.) On
such application the court or a judge thereof must render the judgment to which the plaintiff is entitled, and may, "without a jury or
with a jury, if one is present in court, make a computation or assessment, or take an account or proof of a fact for the purpose of
enabling it or them to render the judgment or to carry it into effect;
or * * * direct a reference or a writ of inquiry for either purpose," except that in an action for personal injuries or an injury to
property, the damages must be ascertained on a writ of inquiry.

If the action be regarded as one to recover money only, it is thus
seen that the taking of an account to determine the amount of the
recovery is expressly authorized by the Code, even if the defendant
should make default. It is also authorized by the Code upon a trial
or upon a reference. (Code Civ. Proc. §§ 1013, 1015; *Smith* v.
Bodine, supra; Wisner v. *Consolidated Fruit Jar Co.*, 25 App.
Div. 362; *McCullough* v. *Pence, supra; Parker* v. *Pullman &
Co., supra.*) An action to recover compensation determinable by
the profits of an individual or firm is an action at law, and under
the authorities above cited, the account may be taken by the court
or upon a reference. (*Thomas* v. *Schumacher, supra; Ashley* v.
Lehmann, supra; Wisner v. *Consolidated Fruit Jar Co., supra.*)

In the case at bar I think the complaint does not attempt to state a cause of action of which a court of equity would have exclusive jurisdiction, nor is the prayer for judgment confined to a demand for equitable relief. A judgment for money only is demanded, and the taking of the account is necessary solely to determine the amount. A temporary injunction, such as may issue in an action at law, is prayed for; but there is no demand for injunctive relief by final judgment. It is true that some of the allegations indicate that the pleader undertook to frame his complaint in equity, but as no equitable relief could in any aspect of the case be awarded, this should not be deemed a controlling election. I see no insuperable obstacle to the plaintiff's sustaining and prosecuting his action to trial and final judgment in a court of law. I find no authority for sustaining a demurrer to a complaint in an action at law upon the ground that, while demanding a money judgment, the amount is not stated, owing to the fact that it depends on an accounting. In this respect the *McCullough* and *Wisner Cases* (*supra*) were like the case at bar.

In my opinion, therefore, the demurrer should have been overruled and the interlocutory judgment should be reversed, with costs, but with leave to the defendants to answer upon payment of the costs of the appeal and of the demurrer.

Judgment affirmed, with costs, with leave to plaintiff to amend on payment of costs in this court and in the court below.

FANNIE CORNELIA HANDY, as Administratrix, etc., of WILLIAM COLE HANDY, Deceased, Appellant, *v.* METROPOLITAN STREET RAILWAY COMPANY, Respondent.

26
•420

26
334

Negligence — a pedestrian injured by a street car in full view, which, without slowing up, strikes him just as he has crossed the tracks — a nonsuit is improper.

In an action brought to recover damages resulting from the death of the plaintiff's intestate, who, while crossing from the east to the west side of Third avenue, in the city of New York, at a point seventy feet south of Seventy-second street, about nine o'clock on a summer evening, was struck by one of the defendant's south-bound electric street cars and killed, the evidence tended to show that when the intestate started from the sidewalk, which was thirty-three feet from the south-bound track, the car was at the south crosswalk of

Seventy-second street; that the intestate proceeded at an ordinary walk and that when he had reached the easterly rail of the south-bound track the car was fifteen or twenty feet away; that when he reached the westerly rail of the south-bound track the car was only five feet away, and that, before he could step off the westerly rail, he was struck by the car.

The evidence also tended to show that the car was traveling about twenty miles an hour and that the motorman made no effort to stop it until after the collision, and did not succeed in doing so until it had traveled about ninety feet.

The plaintiff offered to show that the motorman did not sound his gong, or give any other warning to the intestate; but this evidence was excluded by the court.   Both the car and the avenue were brilliantly lighted, and if either the motorman or the intestate had looked he could have ascertained the position of the other.

Held, that it was error for the court to dismiss the complaint;

That the jury might infer that the motorman's failure to slacken the speed of the car or to give any warning of its approach was due to an error of judgment, in assuming that the intestate would be able to cross in safety, which error of judgment would not necessarily constitute negligence, or else that his failure to slacken the speed of the car or to give any warning of its approach was a failure to observe that degree of care which he should have observed with respect to a person in the position in which the intestate then was;

That, by the same process of reasoning, the jury might have found that the intestate was guilty of a mere error of judgment, and not of contributory negligence, in attempting to cross the street in front of the car without accelerating his steps.

Upon an appeal from a judgment, entered upon a nonsuit, the plaintiff is entitled to the most favorable inference which can be drawn from the evidence admitted or which should have been admitted.

VAN BRUNT, P. J., and McLAUGHLIN, J., dissented.

APPEAL by the plaintiff, Fannie Cornelia Handy, as administratrix, etc., of William Cole Handy, deceased, from a judgment of the Supreme Court in favor of the defendant, entered in the office of the clerk of the county of New York on the 6th day of April, 1901, upon the dismissal of the complaint by direction of the court after a trial at the New York Trial Term, and also from an order entered in said clerk's office on the 11th day of March, 1901, denying the plaintiff's motion for a new trial made upon the minutes.

James Russell Soley, for the appellant.

Charles F. Brown, for the respondent.

O'BRIEN, J.:

The plaintiff's intestate, while crossing to the westerly side of Third avenue, about seventy feet south of Seventy-second street, at a few minutes after nine o'clock on the evening of July 11, 1900, was struck by the defendant's south-bound electric car and thrown from the track and killed.

The deceased was a man about fifty years of age. The evidence is that he was walking, and continued to walk until he was struck, at a natural and ordinary gait, and that he started from the sidewalk, which is thirty-three feet from the track where the accident occurred, when the electric car was at the south crosswalk of Seventy-second street — seventy feet north of the place of the collision. The avenue was well lighted from the electric lights and store windows, and the plaintiff's witnesses clearly saw the deceased at a distance of one hundred feet. There were no other cars or vehicles about, and the electric car was brilliantly illuminated. The car did not stop at Seventy-second street, and there is evidence that it did not lessen its speed until the accident occurred, and that it then ran some eighty or ninety feet further on. When struck the deceased had passed the middle of the track, and was about to step over the westerly rail when he was hurled through the air and landed some fifteen feet away from the car in a southwesterly direction, sustaining a fractured skull, from which injury he soon died.

One of the plaintiff's witnesses, Strauss, apparently a hostile witness, was sitting at the time of the accident in front of a store on the easterly side of the avenue, about one hundred feet away, and testified that as the deceased crossed the track his face appeared to be about west — about half-way position — not looking up the street, but looking towards the northwest slightly. Formerly he had made the statement: "He was turned a little up the street; he seemed to be looking in that direction," and upon being further interrogated, said the deceased was looking "slightly up the street." This witness also testified (and no other witness testified on the subject) that the car was about fifteen or twenty feet away from plaintiff's intestate when he stepped on the easterly rail of the south-bound track — and was five feet away when he stepped on the westerly rail. He also testified: "The motorman reversed his brake immediately after the collision * * * the car was coming very fast." A policeman, who had seen the accident and had testified among other things that the car could have been seen and heard a considerable distance, was asked: "Did you hear any ringing of a bell by the motorman?"

and objection was made to the question, which objection was
sustained and exception taken. Other questions as to whether any
warning was given by the motorman and whether the witness had
called out to the motorman to stop and he did stop after such calling,
were ruled out, exceptions being duly taken. This witness and
others testified that the deceased was facing directly west.

At the close of the plaintiff's evidence the learned trial judge
dismissed the complaint, and the question on this appeal is as to
whether such ruling was right.

The rule has been frequently stated that in reviewing a judgment
upon a nonsuit the plaintiff is entitled to the benefit of the most
favorable inference that can be drawn from the evidence admitted
or which should have been admitted. If there are two inferences,
one favorable and the other unfavorable to the plaintiff's cause of
action, in determining whether a dismissal of the complaint is right,
we must take that inference which is favorable to plaintiff.

Another rule supported by *McDonald* v. *Metropolitan St. Ry.
Co.* (167 N. Y. 66) is thus summarized in the headnote of that
case: "The court cannot in any case where the right of trial by
jury exists and the evidence presents an actual issue of fact,
properly direct a verdict; if in such a case it is dissatisfied with the
verdict because against the weight or preponderance of evidence, it
may be set aside, but a new trial must be granted before another
jury, and the direction of a verdict under such circumstances is
reversible error."

It follows, we think, from these rules, that where the complaint
is dismissed at the close of the plaintiff's case, then if from the evidence two inferences can be drawn, one supporting and the other
destroying the alleged cause of action, it is for the jury to say
which of the two shall be drawn.

Taking the facts most favorable to the plaintiff, it here appears
that the deceased on the night in question was desirous of crossing
between Seventy-second and Seventy-first streets from the east to
the west side of Third avenue, and when he reached the easterly
tracks upon which the north-bound cars were propelled, the car
which subsequently struck him was a considerable distance away on
the other track bound in a southerly direction; and that having
reached the south-bound track, he proceeded at an ordinary walk to

cross, the car at that time, when he reached the easterly rail of the south-bound track, being from fifteen to twenty feet away, but coming at a speed so rapid — as testified by one of the witnesses — that it took only three seconds to run eighty or ninety feet after the collision, which would be at the rate of over twenty miles an hour. The deceased had almost cleared the track, having reached the westerly rail, when he was struck. One witness testified that when he arrived at this point the car was five feet away, but before he could leave the rail, which would have required no more than a second (evidently but a step or two), the car hit him. From this it would appear that the car went a distance of at least five feet before the man could take the step necessary to clear the track.

An effort was made, but under the rulings of the court, unsuccessfully, to show that no gong was sounded nor any signal given by the motorman, by shouting or otherwise, to warn the deceased of his danger, and, such evidence being competent, we must regard the case as though it were admitted. Further, it appears that the deceased was thrown violently a distance of fifteen feet to one side and ahead of the car, and that no effort whatever was made by the motorman to stop the car until after the collision.

We have, therefore, an accident which occurred on an avenue which was sufficiently lighted and in no way obstructed by vehicles so as in any manner to obscure the vision of the motorman or of the deceased. Either of them by looking could have ascertained the position of the other, and it remains to determine whether upon the evidence adduced, drawing the inferences most favorable to the plaintiff, the learned trial judge was justified in holding as matter of law either that the motorman was not guilty of negligence or that the plaintiff's intestate was guilty of contributory negligence.

Upon the former proposition, it appears that while the man was plainly in sight endeavoring to cross the south-bound track, the car, without a signal or warning of any kind, or any attempt to stop or retard it, came at a high rate of speed and struck him. From this evidence two inferences can be drawn. One is that the motorman assumed that deceased would or could cross the tracks in safety without it being necessary to slacken the speed of the car or to give any warning, which assumption, although it might constitute an error of judgment on the part of the motorman, would not necessarily show that he was negligent. The other inference is that the failure to slacken the speed or give any warning was a failure to observe that degree of care which the motorman should have observed with respect to a person in the position of danger that the man then was, while crossing the tracks; and, in this connection, it is evident that if a warning had been given so as to call the attention of the plaintiff's intestate to the necessity of hurrying, or if the speed of the car were slackened in the slightest degree, he could have crossed in safety. Upon the question of the defendant's negligence, therefore, facts were presented from which the jury might have inferred either culpable negligence or a mere error of judgment.

Upon the subject of contributory negligence, the rule is thus stated in *Kettle* v. *Turl* (162 N. Y. 255): " The question of contributory negligence is generally one of fact to be determined by the jury, and it is not within the province of the court. It is only where it clearly appears from the circumstances, or is proved by uncontroverted evidence that the party injured has, by his own acts or neglect contributed to the injury, that the court can determine that question. The cases are exceptional where it can be held that contributory negligence was so conclusively established that nothing was left either of inference or of fact to be determined by a jury."

What has been said with respect to the conduct of the motorman is equally applicable to that of the plaintiff's intestate. He undertook to cross the tracks at a place where, the car being in plain sight, he saw, or should have seen, it; and if, owing to its distance from him, he miscalculated its speed as it came towards him, and thus did not accelerate his steps, this might be regarded by the jury as an error of judgment on his part. We do not think it can, as matter of law, be held to have been negligent.

That he could have passed over unharmed, and that he was not guilty of contributory negligence as matter of law in attempting to cross at all, may be inferred from the fact that, although walking at an ordinary gait, he had almost cleared the westerly rail in safety, and would have done so had it not been for the great speed at which the car approached him. "Assuming that the plaintiff saw the car approaching very fast, still there was nothing to indicate to him that it was not under control of the driver, and he had a right to

FIRST DEPARTMENT, MARCH TERM, 1902.   [Vol. 70.

believe that the latter would exercise proper care. The plaintiff supposed he would clear the car, and although subsequent events proved that he erred in this conclusion a mere error of judgment was not necessarily negligence, when the proof shows that had the car been properly managed, as the plaintiff had a right to assume it would be, he would have been enabled to cross in safety." (*Buhrens* v. *Dry Dock, E. B. & B. R. R. Co.*, 53 Hun, 571; cited as authority in *Johnson* v. *Rochester Railway Co.*, 61 App. Div. 12, 17.)

And this court in *Copeland* v. *Metropolitan St. Ry. Co.* (67 App. Div. 483.) said : " We do not understand the rule to be with respect to the rapid passage of electric cars, that a person seeing a car in the distance is obliged to wait until it has passed and cars are no longer in sight. * * * On the contrary, we have many times held that pedestrians are entitled to a reasonable use of the *streets* and street crossings, and, when exercising such rights, they are justified in assuming that those managing the cars will respect them."

It may properly be urged that if we assume that the deceased, seeing the car, concluded he could under the circumstances get over in safety and thus was guilty merely of an error of judgment and not of negligence, the application of the same rule to the motorman would absolve him from negligence, leaving him responsible only for an error of judgment. As matter of argument this is good, although it may be observed in passing that the motorman should be more familiar with the actual speed of the car than is a pedestrian. The court, however, cannot, as matter of law, determine whether either or both are guilty merely of errors of judgment and not of negligence without usurping the functions of the jury, it being, as already said, where there are two inferences that may be drawn from the facts for the jury to say which of the two should be drawn. (*Weil* v. *Dry Dock, E. B. & B. R. R. Co.*, 119 N. Y. 147.)

We think the dismissal of the complaint was error for which the judgment should be reversed and a new trial ordered, with costs to the appellant to abide the event.

INGRAHAM and HATCH, JJ., concurred; VAN BRUNT, P. J., and McLAUGHLIN, J., dissented.

Judgment and order reversed, new trial ordered, costs to appellant to abide event.

Theresa Storm and Others, Respondents, *v.* Sophie McGrover | 70
and Elizabeth F. Drake, Appellants, Impleaded with Others. | D174 N

Action to have real estate purchased by a committee adjudged to have been purchased with the money of the lunatic — proof required to sustain it — an account by the committee, how far evidence — short form of decision, what it should contain.

In an action, brought by the heirs at law of a lunatic against the heirs at law of the committee of the lunatic, to establish a resulting trust in property purchased by the committee in her individual name, with money alleged to have belonged to the lunatic, the plaintiffs must prove, by a fair preponderance of evidence, that all, and not merely a portion, of the consideration paid for the property belonged to the lunatic.

In such an action an account presented by the committee to the Supreme Court and approved by it, in a proceeding instituted, without notice to the plaintiffs, is not binding upon them, but is competent evidence upon the question as to the identity of the particular money used in the purchase of the property.

A decision, purporting to be in the short form, permitted by section 1022 of the Code of Civil Procedure, should not contain a long and detailed statement of the facts proved upon the trial.

Appeal by the defendants, Sophie McGrover and another, from an interlocutory judgment of the Supreme Court in favor of the plaintiffs, entered in the office of the clerk of the county of New York on the 31st day of May, 1901, upon the decision of the court rendered after a trial at the New York Special Term.

Robert H. Barnett. for the appellants.

Eugene Cohn, for the respondents.

Ingraham, J.:

The plaintiffs in this action seek to enforce a trust which they claim resulted from the purchase of certain property in the city of New York with the money of one Charles Preiss, a lunatic, by his committee ; the committee having taken the title in her own name. The interlocutory judgment determined that such a trust resulted ; that the fee of the property vested in the said Charles Preiss, and the plaintiffs, as his heirs at law, are entitled thereto ; and it directed the defendants, as administrators of the committee, to account for the income received therefrom.

It appeared that Charles Preiss was, on the 28th day of February, 1880, adjudged a lunatic, and his wife, Caroline Preiss, appointed committee of his person and estate. Upon her appointment as such committee, she received the personal estate of the lunatic, and subsequently purchased the property in question; received a conveyance thereof on the 20th day of January, 1883, and paid as the consideration therefor the sum of $3,950 in cash, the said property being subject to a mortgage of $5,000.

The plaintiffs allege that this sum of $3,950 was the money of the lunatic, which the committee invested in the purchase of the said real estate, taking the title to herself individually and without the knowledge and consent of the said lunatic; that the said Charles Preiss died on the 10th day of April, 1899, leaving as his only heirs at law the plaintiffs Theresa Storm and Julia Brockman, his sisters, and the other plaintiffs, who were the children of a brother and sisters of the said Charles Preiss, who died before him; that Caroline Preiss, the widow of the said Charles Preiss, died on the 16th day of January, 1900, leaving her surviving her sisters, the defendants Sophie McGrover and Elizabeth F. Drake, her only heirs at law. The court decided that a trust resulted in favor of the said Charles Preiss and that the property descended to his heirs at law, the plaintiffs in this action.

The court filed its decision, in which the facts found and the conclusions of law are not stated separately. Section 1022 of the Code of Civil Procedure provides that the decision, when it does not state separately the facts found, shall state concisely the grounds upon which the issues have been decided and direct the judgment to be entered thereon. The decision in this case takes up eight pages of the printed record, and apparently sets forth the facts alleged in the complaint as having been found upon the trial. The defendants filed a notice by which they excepted to the rulings of the court upon questions of law, contained in its written decision, which decision fails to separately state its conclusions of law. Then follow four quotations from the decision which are largely statements of facts to which the defendants stated that they intended to except. The exception also states that the defendants give notice that they except to certain findings of fact set forth between folios 10 and 11 of the decision, on the ground that there is no evidence to support such findings. Just what findings of fact there are between folios 10 and 11 of the decision, does not appear by the record. They also excepted to other findings of fact, and then there is another statement that the defendants except to the directions for the entry of judgment; and then follow three separate quotations from the decision directing the judgment to be entered.

Section 1022 of the Code, to which attention has been called, provides that whenever judgment is entered on a decision which does not state separately the facts found, the defeated party may file an exception to such decision, in which case, on an appeal from the judgment entered thereon upon a case containing exceptions, the Appellate Division shall review all questions of fact and of law, and may either modify or affirm the judgment or order appealed from, award a new trial, or grant to either party the judgment which the facts warrant. Neither the decision nor exceptions strictly comply with this provision of the Code. The decision is not one stating the facts found and the conclusions of law separately, nor does it state concisely the grounds upon which the issues have been decided and direct the judgment to be entered thereon. By the decision the learned trial justice first states that "having heard the proofs and allegations of the parties, I decide as follows:" He then decides that the committee of this lunatic paid the consideration for the property in question out of the money belonging to the lunatic in her hands as a committee, and that thereupon the said lunatic, by the operation of the statute, became seized of the said premises in fee simple absolute; and that upon the death of the said lunatic the estate descended to his heirs at law, the plaintiffs in this action. The decision then proceeds to state as the grounds of the decision, concisely stated, four pages of printed matter reciting certain facts as having been proved upon the trial.

All these statements of facts as the grounds of the decision were entirely out of place. They required no notice by the defendants, and all the defendants had to do to raise on appeal the question that had been before the Special Term was simply to except to the decision as filed. This course, plainly prescribed by the statute and being perfectly simple, was not the course adopted by the defendant. He first excepts to what he calls conclusions of law; the first of these "conclusions" is a statement of certain facts which are the grounds of the decision. This was that the committee of the lunatic paid the consideration for the conveyance out of the money belonging to the said Charles Preiss, then in the hands of the said Caroline Preiss as the committee of the person of the lunatic, the said Charles Preiss, and without his knowledge and consent. The three other statements excepted to would probably be conclusions of law.

It is somewhat doubtful whether these exceptions really bring up anything for review. As, however, in form the defendant excepts to all that part of the decision which really states the grounds upon which the case was decided, the long statement of facts contained in the decision being really no part of it and having no business there, we are probably justified in treating these exceptions to what the defendant calls conclusions of law as an exception to the whole decision, so that there is before the court upon this appeal all the questions of fact and law which were before the court below on the trial. The difficulty has arisen by the form of the decision, which gives a long and detailed statement of the facts, not contemplated by the provisions of the Code allowing the court to file a decision stating concisely the grounds upon which the issues have been decided.

The first question presented is whether the evidence justified the finding that all the consideration paid for the purchase of the premises by the committee was out of the moneys of the lunatic, Charles Preiss. The evidence to sustain this finding was mainly that of one Henry Storm, the husband of one of the plaintiffs, who was a sister of Charles Preiss. He testified that he took Charles Preiss to the lunatic asylum about March 31, 1880 ; that Caroline Preiss, prior to her marriage with him, was a dressmaker, and that after her marriage she helped her husband in his business, which was that of a saloon-keeper ; that he had a conversation with the decedent and his wife in which it was stated — by whom it does not appear — that they had saved quite a little money and that the decedent wanted to know how much it took to start a cigar store, but that the witness declined to advise him on the subject. Three savings bank accounts were then introduced in evidence, one in the name of Caroline Preiss in the German Savings Bank, one in the same bank in the name of Charles Preiss, the lunatic, and one in the Dry Dock

Savings Bank in the name of Charles Preiss, the lunatic. The account in the Dry Dock Savings Bank shows a balance on May 2, 1879, of $1,081; and of this $900 was drawn out in May and June, 1879, before the decedent had been declared a lunatic; and a balance of $190.14 was withdrawn on March 13, 1880, which was after the appointment of the committee, she having been appointed on the 28th day of February, 1880. The account in the German Savings Bank in the name of Charles Preiss showed a balance of $459.14, $400 of which was transferred in May, 1880, to the individual account of the committee. It thus appears from these savings bank books that the committee received from the estate of the lunatic after she was appointed committee, $649.28. The witness also testified that the committee sold the saloon in which the business was conducted, for which she received $1,200, and that she also received as committee of her husband, certain pension moneys that were paid to him by the government of the United States; in the year 1881, $450, and in the year 1882, $600. This made an aggregate amount of $2,899.22. There was also evidence that the committee had received about $2,200 for back pensions. The witness further testified as to a conversation he had with Caroline Preiss, the committee, after she had received this money, as to the best way to invest the money she had got from the accumulations of Charles Preiss, and the witness told her she had better deposit the money with the firm of which he was a member; and that in pursuance of that advice she deposited with that firm $4,000, and that subsequently the witness advised her to purchase the house in question, and to complete such purchase the witness' firm gave to the committee two checks, one for $200, which appears to have been paid upon the execution of the contract to purchase the house, and the other check for $3,750, which paid the balance of the consideration for the purchase of the premises in question. Witness further testified that after the decedent had been declared a lunatic, his wife resumed the dressmaking business and conducted the same up to the time of her death; that he knew that the committee after she went into possession of those premises spent a large amount for repairs, and that before the title was finally passed she had about $5,000 invested in the property.

On behalf of the defendant it was proved that Caroline Preiss prior to her marriage had conducted a dressmaking business for from one and a half to two years; that she had a first class establishment and had numerous customers; that after her marriage she continued the dressmaking business down to the time that her husband was taken to the lunatic asylum, and that after that time she still continued the business and had several assistants in her employ, and apparently did a prosperous business. At the time that the decedent was taken to the insane asylum he had a son living, who died before his father.

There was also introduced in evidence an account of this committee of the lunatic, presented to the Supreme Court in a proceeding instituted by the court to compel the committee to account. In that account the committee charges herself with all moneys received as said committee, including the pensions, and credits herself with amounts paid out during the period in question up to the time of the purchase of the house. From that account it would appear that the committee had received from the estate of the lunatic prior to the 1st of January, 1883, the sum of $5,158, and that she had paid out for the support of the lunatic and his family during that period (less the amount of $1,000, which she claims to have paid to herself for money loaned to the lunatic prior to the time he became incompetent) $4,166.47; leaving in her hands on the 1st of June, 1893, the sum of $981.53. This account was passed upon and approved by the referee appointed by the Supreme Court, and the report of the referee approving this account was confirmed by the court. It is not disputed that up to this time the committee supported the lunatic in the asylum, and also herself and her son.

As this accounting was not upon notice to these plaintiffs, it cannot bind them as an adjudication. It was, however, competent evidence to be considered in determining this question in relation to the particular money used in the purchase of this property. The fact that this money so used was money entirely realized from the estate of her husband, depends solely upon the evidence of Mr. Storm, the husband of one of the plaintiffs. The account from the German Savings Bank introduced by the plaintiffs shows that on the 10th day of February, 1882, she drew $4,000 from that bank, and that was undoubtedly the $4,000 that was deposited with Mr. Storm's firm. That amount taken from the savings bank account of the wife was not directly connected with the money of the husband. All of the husband's money that was shown to have gone into that account was the balance transferred from the account of the lunatic of the sum of $400. There is nothing to show that the balance of the money in this bank was the money of the lunatic. It may be surmised that the amount in this savings bank of $2,193.80, deposited on March 23, 1881, was the arrears of the pension drawn by the committee, but there is no evidence of that fact. And in view of the evidence that during this period, from the time that her husband was declared a lunatic down to the 1st of January, 1880, she had out of the moneys received by her supported him in the lunatic asylum and his child and herself, there certainly cannot have been as much money that she had received as committee in her hands at the time that this purchase was made.

To entitle the plaintiffs to maintain this action, which is to have a resulting trust declared of this property so that the property itself belonged to the husband and not to the wife, the plaintiffs must prove by a fair preponderance of evidence that all of the consideration applied to the purchase of this property was the money of the husband. (*Schierloh* v. *Schierloh*, 148 N. Y. 103; *Bryant* v. *Allen*, 54 App. Div. 500.) It will not do that part of this consideration paid for the property was the money of the husband, but there must be a fair presumption from the evidence that all of the money used was his money. In view of the testimony as it stands I do not think that the plaintiffs can be said to have proved that fact. Mr. Storm's recollection of the conversation happening twenty years before he testified, is consistent with the fact that this money was the united savings of the husband and wife, as she at that time made no distinction between them. She and her son, in the absence of a will, were entitled to this property upon the death of her husband. In the conversations between the husband and wife as to the investment of their savings, the money was spoken of as their joint savings and not as the property of the husband only. The evidence would seem to disclose that the wife had supported herself by dressmaking before her marriage; that she assisted her husband in his business before he was declared a lunatic, and up to that time had a bank account of her own in which she made deposits of money, and after that business had been given up, resumed her dressmaking, and there is nothing to justify the presumption that the money in her possession subsequent to the time of her appointment as committee of her husband was his. The husband had certainly nothing to do with the purchase of this property. It was purchased and paid for by the wife and the title taken in her own name, with the knowledge of Mr. Storm and with no protest from him. There was evidently no intent to defraud the husband or his estate, and from the whole case I do not think that the evidence supports the finding that the money used in the purchase of this property or the $4,000 deposited with Mr. Storm's firm, was the money of the lunatic, Charles Preiss.

There are several other questions presented by this record which it is unnecessary to discuss, as we disagree with the court below on this crucial question of fact. The evidence of the declaration of the decedent's husband, as against the defendants, was certainly not competent evidence, and whether or not the declarations of the committee, made long after the transaction, are competent evidence against these defendants is at least a doubtful question, but we think upon the evidence as it stands the finding of the court below was not justified, and that the judgment should, therefore, be reversed and a new trial ordered, with costs to the appellants to abide the event.

VAN BRUNT, P. J., O'BRIEN, McLAUGHLIN and HATCH, JJ., concurred.

Judgment reversed, new trial ordered, costs to appellants to abide event.

JULIAN BENEDICT, Respondent, *v.* ALFRED DUANE PELL, Appellant.

Real estate broker — proof insufficient to establish his right to commissions.

In an action brought by a real estate broker to recover commissions upon the sale of a parcel of real estate owned by the defendant, it appeared that the plaintiff suggested to one Smith the advisability of purchasing the piece of property in question, and upon being informed by Smith that he would be interested in the property if it was in the market, went to the defendant's house and was informed that one Potterton was the defendant's agent; that the plaintiff called upon Potterton, who said that he represented the defendant but that the property could not be sold until the defendant returned from Europe; tnat subsequently the plaintiff and Smith called upon Potterton, who informed the plaintiff that, if he would make a written offer for the property, it would be delivered to the defendant upon his return from Europe; that Smith then made a written offer of $325,000 for the property and delivered it to Potterton; that at a subsequent interview Potterton told the plaintiff that the defendant wanted $375,000 for the property; that the plaintiff made an appointment to see the defendant, and at the hour appointed the plaintiff and Smith called upon the defendant and were introduced to him by Potterton, who then left the room; that the defendant then offered to sell the property for $375,000, which proposition Smith accepted.

The contract between Smith and the defendant contained a provision that "George A. Potterton is the only broker who brought about this transaction, and, so far as the vendee knows, no other broker is concerned herein." It did not appear that Potterton employed or had authority to employ the plaintiff to act on behalf of the defendant, or that the defendant had any knowledge that the plaintiff was a broker or claimed any commissions on the sale or that he had assumed to represent the defendant.

Held, that there was no evidence of any employment of the plaintiff by the defendant;

That the defendant was not chargeable with the knowledge possessed by Potterton of the plaintiff's relation to the transaction, which he did not communicate to the defendant.

APPEAL by the defendant, Alfred Duane Pell, from a judgment of the Supreme Court in favor of the plaintiff, entered in tLe office of the clerk of the county of New York on the 11th day of November, 1901, upon the verdict of a jury, and also from an order entered in said clerk's office on the 11th day of November, 1901, denying the defendant's motion for a new trial made upon the minutes.

George H. Gilman, for the appellant.

Robert L. Stanton, for the respondent.

INGRAHAM, J.:

The action was brought by a real estate broker to recover commissions upon the sale of a piece of real estate by the defendant. At the end of the plaintiff's case the defendant moved to dismiss the complaint upon the ground that the plaintiff was not employed by the defendant, and that the defendant had no knowledge that the plaintiff was a broker or assumed to act for him. This motion was denied to which the defendant excepted.

The plaintiff testified that he called upon a Mr. Smith and

suggested that he (Smith) purchase a piece of property on the northwest corner of Thirty-fourth street and Broadway; that Mr. Smith informed the plaintiff that if the property could be had he (Smith) would be interested in it; that after this interview the plaintiff called upon a Mr. Bollinger and asked whether he knew if the corner had been sold; that Bollinger said so far as he knew the corner was not sold, that it could still be bought, but the owner was not in the city, that he was abroad, somewhere in Spain, and that it could not be bought until he returned; that the plaintiff subsequently called at the house of the defendant and was informed by somebody, in the absence of the defendant, that a Mr. Potterton was the defendant's agent; that the plaintiff subsequently called on Potterton who said that he represented the defendant, but that the property could not be sold until the defendant's return from Europe; that subsequently the witness, with Smith, the proposed purchaser, called upon Potterton, when the plaintiff was told that if he had any proposition to make for the property and would put it in writing it would be delivered to Mr. Pell when he returned from Europe; that Smith then wrote a letter to the defendant in which he offered $325,000 for the property, and this letter was delivered to Potterton who informed the plaintiff and Smith that he thought the property could be purchased for that sum; that at a subsequent interview with the plaintiff Potterton said that the defendant had been offered $350,000 for the property, but that he would take $375,000 cash for it, and the plaintiff made an appointment to see the defendant at three o'clock that afternoon; that at three o'clock the plaintiff and Smith called upon the defendant and were introduced to him by Potterton, who then left the room; that the defendant stated that he would not consider an offer of $325,000, but that he had told his agent, Mr. Potterton, that $375,000 was what he wanted and it would have to be all cash; that after talking a few minutes Smith agreed to take the property for $375,000 and paid $5,000 cash, $70,000 to be paid on signing the contract, and $300,000 on July eighteenth at ten o'clock, when the deed was to be delivered. Subsequent to the signing of this contract the plaintiff sent the defendant a bill for his commissions as a broker, which the defendant refused to pay. In a contract that was signed between Smith and the defendant there was a provision that "George A. Potterton is the only broker who brought about this transaction, and, so far as the vendee knows, no other broker is concerned herein." There is no evidence that at any time the defendant was informed that the plaintiff was a broker, or assumed to represent him in the transaction, and there is no evidence that the defendant either directly or indirectly employed the plaintiff, or accepted Smith's offer with knowledge that the plaintiff purported to be a real estate broker, or to represent him in the transaction.

We have thus a case in which there was no employment of the plaintiff by the defendant, and in which the defendant had no knowledge that the plaintiff assumed to represent the defendant in any way. Upon the evidence it would appear that the plaintiff acted as the agent of Smith in procuring the property, as he first called on Smith and suggested a purchase of the property and subsequently acted at Smith's request or in his behalf in procuring the property. To justify a recovery there must be an employment of the broker either express or implied from the circumstances surrounding the transaction. There was certainly no express employment in this case, and no facts were proved to justify an implied employment which would make the defendant liable for the services rendered by the broker in procuring a purchaser of the property. The mere fact that the plaintiff was a broker raised no such implication.

Potterton was called as a witness for the defendant and testified that he had a power of attorney from the defendant on his bank account, but had no authority over his property; that the rents were sent to him by the real estate agent and he deposited them for the defendant; that he never stated to the defendant that the plaintiff was a broker, or claimed to act in that capacity; that he stated to the defendant that there were no brokers in the transaction, but that Smith and Benedict had come to the witness to buy the property and had waived any right to commissions. The defendant testified that at the interview between the plaintiff and Smith nothing was said about brokers or commissions; that the defendant had no knowledge that Benedict was a broker or claimed any commissions, or that he had assumed to represent the defendant.

At the close of all the testimony the defendant asked the court to direct a verdict for the defendant, upon the grounds that there was no employment and no evidence to show that the defendant knew at the time the contract was made that the plaintiff assumed to act as a broker or had any relation to the transaction, except as an associate or employee of the purchaser. This motion was denied and the defendant excepted. The court then submitted the question of the plaintiff's claim to the jury as follows: "It is claimed that at that time Potterton was acting, in this transaction, as the agent of Mr. Pell. If he was acting as the agent of Mr. Pell in the transaction, his acts would be binding upon his principal." The court then, at the request of the plaintiff, charged the jury that "If the plaintiff was the procuring cause of the sale by the defendant to Smith, or Smith's assign, he is entitled to his commission. 2d. If the plaintiff brought the minds of the purchaser and the defendant together, so that they definitely agreed on the price to be paid, and the terms of the sale, and those terms were executed so that the defendant got his price for the property, the plaintiff is entitled to a verdict." To this the defendant excepted.

These requests of the plaintiff charged by the court entirely eliminated from the consideration of the jury the question of the employment by the defendant, and even if there had been evidence to justify the jury in finding that there was an implied employment, the charge of these requests in the form that they were charged was error and require a reversal of the judgment.

We think, however, that there was no evidence of any employment of the plaintiff by the defendant. There is no evidence that Potterton had authority from the defendant to employ brokers to act for him in the sale of his real estate; no evidence that Potterton did employ the plaintiff to act for the defendant for that purpose; no evidence that the plaintiff ever assumed to act for the defendant. The offer to purchase the property was submitted by the purchaser to Potterton, who transmitted it to the defendant. There is no authority to which our attention has been called that would justify a recovery for commission because a broker called upon the owner of property.

The plaintiff seems to rely in proving this employment upon the fact that Potterton was the defendant's agent, but there is not a particle of evidence to justify a finding that Potterton was authorized by the defendant to employ a broker to act for him or that he ratified an employment of the plaintiff by Potterton, or that Potterton ever employed the plaintiff.   Before there could be a ratification there must be knowledge by the principal of the act of the assumed agent which it is claimed the principal ratified.   It is a general principle of the law of agency that a principal is not bound by the acts of the agent not within the actual or apparent scope of the agency, simply because the agent falsely asserts that they are within it.   (*Edwards* v. *Dooley*, 120 N. Y. 540.)   Here there was neither an actual nor apparent authority conferred upon Potterton to employ brokers for the defendant, and whatever knowledge Potterton had of the plaintiff's relation to the transaction not communicated to the defendant, the defendant is not chargeable with.

It is hardly necessary to cite authorities to prove that there must be an employment to entitle a broker to commission for the sale of the property ; but what was said by Judge WOODRUFF in *Pierce* v. *Thomas* (4 E. D. Smith, 354) so concisely states the legal principle involved that the decision of this case can be rested upon his opinion.   He says : "To entitle a broker to recover commissions for effecting a sale of real estate, it is indispensable that he should show that he was employed by the owner (or on his behalf) to make the sale.   A ratification of his act, where original employment is wanting, may, in some circumstances, be equivalent to an original retainer, but only where there is a plain intent to ratify.   An owner cannot be enticed into a liability for commissions against his will. A mere volunteer without authority is not entitled to commissions, merely because he has inquired the price which an owner asks for his property, and has then sent a person to him who consents to take it.   A broker has no better claim to recover for voluntary service, rendered without employment, and not received and acted upon by the owner as rendered in his behalf, than any other volunteer.   * * *   If, upon this proof, an owner is liable, and against his express refusal to employ the plaintiff, then no man is safe in stating to applicants the terms upon which he will sell.   It is not true that an owner may not declare his price to whom he will without the hazard of paying commissions to those who volunteer, unasked, to send him a purchaser on his own terms." In *Bright* v.

Canadian Int. Stock Yard Company (83 Hun, 482) the presiding justice says: " Take the ordinary case of a broker. In order that he should recover he is bound to show employment, and that he was the procuring cause of a sale, if a sale be the subject which is involved. If the broker introduces one party to the other and a sale results, unless he is able to show employment, that fact does not entitle him to compensation." (See, also, *Fowler* v. *Hoschke*, 53 App. Div. 327.)

The judgment and order appealed from should, therefore, be reversed and a new trial ordered, with costs to the appellant to abide the event.

VAN BRUNT, P. J., McLAUGHLIN, HATCH and LAUGHLIN, JJ., concurred.

Judgment and order reversed, new trial ordered, costs to appellant to abide event.

STANDARD NATIONAL BANK OF THE CITY OF NEW YORK and NATIONAL BROADWAY BANK, Appellants, *v.* GARFIELD NATIONAL BANK, Respondent, Impleaded with NATIONAL SILK LABEL COMPANY and Others.

Conveyance fraudulent as to creditors — the proceeds of the property, sold under an execution against the vendee, cannot be followed by a creditor of the vendor.

Where property transferred by a debtor, in fraud of his creditors, is levied upon and sold, under a judgment obtained against the vendee by a creditor of the latter, and the proceeds are paid over to such creditor before any action is taken to set aside the fraudulent transfer, creditors of the fraudulent vendor are not entitled to follow the proceeds of the property fraudulently transferred into the hands of the execution creditor.

APPEAL by the plaintiffs, the Standard National Bank of the City of New York and another, from that part of a judgment of the Supreme Court in favor of the defendant, the Garfield National Bank, entered in the office of the clerk of the county of New York on the 18th day of July, 1901, upon the decision of the court, rendered after a trial at the New York Special Term, dismissing the complaint as against said defendant, the Garfield National Bank.

The action was brought by creditors of the defendant, the National Silk Label Company, to reach the proceeds of property which that defendant fraudulently transferred to the firm of Macfarlane & Co. and which was sold under an execution issued upon a judgment obtained by the defendant, the Garfield National Bank, against Macfarlane & Co.

H. H. Walker, for the appellant Standard National Bank.

Henry B. Twombly, for the appellant National Broadway Bank.

John J. Adams, for the respondent.

INGRAHAM, J.:

Upon the former appeal in this action, when a judgment in favor of the plaintiffs was reversed, we held that the defendant the Garfield National Bank could not be compelled to account for the money realized upon an execution issued on a judgment against Macfarlane & Co., upon the ground that goods in the possession of Macfarlane & Co. upon which the execution was levied, the legal title to which had been transferred to that firm by the Silk Label Company, had been transferred in fraud of that corporation's creditors, no action having been taken to avoid the transfer at the time of the sale under the execution and the payment of the proceeds thereof to the Garfield National Bank. The reasons for our conclusion are stated in the report of the decision (56 App. Div. 43). We can see no difference between the facts upon which that judgment was based and the facts developed upon this trial. The plaintiffs have attempted to reargue the questions there determined upon this appeal, but after a re-examination we see no reason to change the views before expressed. Upon the trial the plaintiffs conceded that whether or not the assignment of Macfarlane & Co. to Richardson was fraudulent, does not affect the case so far as the plaintiffs are concerned, and this concession is an answer to the position now taken by the plaintiffs as to the effect of the assignment to Richardson. The plaintiffs, however, do not claim through Richardson. Their claim is as creditors of the Silk Label Company, and as such creditors they must establish their right to compel the Garfield Bank to repay the money that it received in payment of its debt from Macfarlane.

A transfer of property by a debtor, fraudulent as to creditors, is not void *ab initio,* but voidable only at the election of the creditors of the vendor. The title to the property passes, and the vendee has a title which he can transfer and which is subject to levy and sale at the suit of his creditors. When the execution of the Garfield National Bank judgment against Macfarlane & Co. was issued, Macfarlane & Co. had, as against the Silk Label Company and its creditors, the legal title to the property transferred. The assignment to Richardson was alleged to be fraudulent as to Macfarlane & Co.'s creditors, and the Garfield National Bank, acting upon that assumption, directed the sheriff to levy upon Macfarlane & Co.'s property. That levy was made, the goods of Macfarlane & Co. that they had transferred to Richardson were sold and the proceeds paid to the Garfield National Bank. Neither the Silk Label Company nor their creditors had up to that time elected to avoid the transfer of the property of the Silk Label Company to Macfarlane & Co. Assuming that the assignment to Richardson was void, Macfarlane & Co. had a leviable interest in the property, and it was that leviable interest of Macfarlane & Co. upon which the sheriff levied under the Garfield Bank judgment. That was what he sold under the levy which produced the money that was paid to the Garfield National Bank. Subsequently, when the creditors of the Silk Label Company sought to set aside the transfer from the Silk Label Company to Macfarlane & Co., the Garfield National Bank had in its possession none of the property of the Silk Label Company ; nor had it ever in its possession any of the property of that company. It is impossible to see upon what principle the Garfield National Bank could be held accountable for the value of any property of the Silk Label Company which had been transferred by a voidable transfer to Macfarlane & Co. It had a right to levy under its judgment against Macfarlane & Co. upon the goods and property of Macfarlane & Co., and that it did. The proceeds of a sale of the property of Macfarlane & Co. under such a levy having been paid to the Garfield National Bank in satisfaction of its judgment against Macfarlane & Co., such proceeds could no more be reached by the creditors of the Silk Label Company than could money which Macfarlane & Co. had realized from a sale of the goods transferred to them by the Silk Label Company and which they had subsequently paid to the bank as a payment of their indebtedness. In either case the money was the proceeds of goods to which Macfarlane & Co. had the legal title and which had been received by the Garfield National Bank from Macfarlane & Co. in payment of its debts.   There could be no difference in principle whether Macfarlane & Co. had actually sold the goods and paid the proceeds to the bank, or whether the bank under an execution had levied upon the goods and the goods had been sold by the sheriff and the proceeds thereof paid by the sheriff to the bank.   In either case the bank had received in payment of its debts money realized from the sale of goods to which Macfarlane & Co. had the legal title.   A different question would have been presented had Macfarlane & Co. turned over to the bank the goods that it had received from the Silk Label Company; and it is not necessary to determine upon this appeal what would have been the rights of the creditors of the Silk Label Company in that situation.   The proceeds realized at the sale of Macfarlane & Co.'s interest in that property did not stand in the place of the goods sold which would entitle the creditors of the Silk Label Company to follow such proceeds into the hands of the bank.   The rule to be applied, as I understand it, is that stated in *Justh* v. *Nat. Bank of the Commonwealth* (56 N. Y. at p. 484): "In the absence of trust or agency I take the rule to be that it is only to the extent of the interest remaining in the party committing the fraud that money can be followed as against an innocent party having a lawful title founded upon consideration; and that, if it has been paid in the ordinary course of business, either upon a new consideration or for an existing debt, the right of the party to follow the money is gone."   The subject is exhaustively examined in *Hatch* v. *Fourth Nat. Bank* (147 N. Y. 184), and upon the principle there established I cannot see that there is any difference in the application of the rule because the money that was received by the creditors was realized upon a sale of property in the hands of the debtor and in which he had a leviable interest and paid to the creditor by the sheriff as the proceeds of the debtor's property, rather than money realized by the debtor himself from the sale of the property.   That the debtor obtained the property from which the money was realized by fraud gave the vendor or his creditor the right to rescind the transfer; but until such rescission the vendee remains the owner of the property ; and, if during that time it is sold and the proceeds paid to a creditor of the vendee, the debt on account of which such money has been paid is satisfied and the money becomes the absolute property of the creditor; and upon the payment of the proceeds of the sale by the sheriff to the Garfield Bank, Macfarlane & Co.'s debt to the bank was paid and the money became the property of the bank.

We think that upon both principle and authority the plaintiffs as judgment creditors of the Silk Label Company had no claim against the Garfield National Bank.

The judgment should, therefore, be affirmed, with costs.

VAN BRUNT, P. J., HATCH and LAUGHLIN, JJ., concurred.

Judgment affirmed, with costs.

INSURANCE PRESS, Respondent, *v.* MONTAUK FIRE DETECTING WIRE COMPANY and CHARLES A. HANSON, Defendants, Impleaded with JOHN D. GOULD, Appellant.

Examination of a defendant before trial — as to the value of patents transferred to a corporation for $3,000,000 of its stock.

A plaintiff who brings an action, based on the fact that $3,000,000 of the stock of a corporation were issued to the defendants in payment for patents owned or controlled by said defendants, the value of which did not exceed $10,000, is entitled to an order permitting him to examine one of the defendants before trial as to the value of the patents.

VAN BRUNT, P. J., and LAUGHLIN, J., dissented.

APPEAL by the defendant, John D. Gould, from an order of the Supreme Court, made at the New York Special Term and entered in the office of the clerk of the county of New York on the 9th day of January, 1902, as amended by an order made at the New York Special Term bearing date the 14th day of January, 1902, and entered in the office of the clerk of the county of New York, denying a motion made by said John D. Gould to vacate an order for his examination as a party before trial.

Irving L. Ernst, for the appellant.

A. Walker Otis, for the respondent.

INGRAHAM, J.:

We think the affidavit upon which the order for the examination of this defendant was granted was sufficient to justify the order and that the court below properly refused to vacate it. The fact upon which the plaintiff's cause of action depends is that $3,000,000 of the stock of a corporation were originally issued to the defendants John D. Gould and Charles A. Hanson as a consideration for the purchase of certain patents then owned or controlled by John D. Gould and Charles A. Hanson, and that said patents did not exceed in value the sum of $10,000. The plaintiff desires to examine the said Gould for the purpose of obtaining testimony to be used upon the trial to prove that fact. The plaintiff must prove, to sustain his cause of action, that this patent was worth much less than the amount of stock which was issued for it. The Code provides for such an examination before trial where it is evident that the testimony of the person sought to be examined will be material upon the trial. The plaintiff is not bound to wait until the trial, when the defendant can keep out of the way and avoid the service of a subpoena, but he is entitled to have the testimony taken before trial so that it can be available for use when the case is tried.

We think the affidavit was sufficient to justify the court in ordering the defendant to be examined as a witness and that the order appealed from should be affirmed, with ten dollars costs and disbursements.

McLAUGHLIN and HATCH, JJ., concurred; VAN BRUNT, P. J., and LAUGHLIN, J., dissented.

LAUGHLIN, J. (dissenting):

I think the affidavits were clearly insufficient to require the granting of the order, and that the motion was properly denied. What is the assigned object of the proposed examination? Not to obtain evidence of a fact, but merely the opinion of the defendant Gould as to the value of the patents, which are a device for the discovery of fire. The patents have been purchased by the company of which plaintiff is a stockholder, and presumably they are in its possession and open to examination by the plaintiff, or any experts whose opinion he may desire concerning their value, at any time. It does

not appear, nor is it alleged, that the defendant Gould possesses
any special knowledge concerning them not readily obtainable by
others.   It is not claimed that he has made any admission as to
their value conflicting with the price charged on the sale to the
company.   It is alleged that this examination is material and necessary for the plaintiff in the prosecution of the action, but it is not
alleged either in substance or effect that the plaintiff intends to use
the evidence upon the trial.   This is not a case where we may dis-
pense with formal allegations of intention to use the testimony
upon the trial, upon the ground that such is the reasonable inference
to be drawn from all the facts and circumstances disclosed.   Here
the inference is plain that the plaintiff does not intend to use this
evidence upon the trial.   His object is to ascertain how the defendant Gould thinks these patents can be utilized to produce a return
which will justify the valuation at which they were turned over
to the company.   That is Gould's defense, if he has any, and is
something the plaintiff is not entitled to know in advance.

VAN BRUNT, P. J., concurred.

Order affirmed, with ten dollars costs and disbursements.

———

JOHN R. TODD, Respondent, *v.* UNION CASUALTY AND SURETY
COMPANY, Appellant.

*Complaint on a policy of insurance against liability for accident — when
demurrable, as not specifying the conditions of the insurance or the hazards
insured against — allegation of performance, except as waived.*

The complaint in an action alleged that the defendant issued to the plaintiff a
policy of insurance by which it "contracted to insure and did insure this plaintiff, upon certain terms and conditions in said contract of insurance specified,
* * * against legal liability for damages" to the extent of $5,000 to any
one person "respecting fatal or non-fatal injuries from accidents occurring to
any person or persons at the place or places mentioned and specified in the
application for the said contract of insurance and in the policy of insurance
issued on said application * * * against the hazards enumerated and set
forth under a certain premium schedule to said contract of insurance annexed;"
that while said contract of insurance was in force, one Brown, a workman in the
employ of the plaintiff, sustained injuries by reason of an accident occurring at
the place specified in the policy, and that Brown and the work in which he was

employed were included in the class of persons and hazards covered by the contract of insurance and against "liability to whom and because of which, due to injuries from accidents, this defendant insured plaintiff;" that subsequently Brown brought an action against the plaintiff to recover for the injuries sustained by him, and recovered $8,856.57 damages, interest and costs, which the defendant refused to pay; "that plaintiff duly complied with and observed all the provisions of the said contract of insurance by him to be complied with and observed as conditions precedent to defendant's liability to him thereunder, except in so far as such compliance and observance were waived or rendered unnecessary by the position and action of this defendant." Judgment was demanded for the sum of $5,000 and interest.

The policy on which the defendant's liability was predicated was not made a part of the complaint.

Held, that the complaint was demurrable, as it alleged simply that the defendant insured the plaintiff upon certain terms and conditions, which were not specified, against certain hazards which were not set forth, and that the plaintiff had performed in so far as performance had not been waived — setting forth no facts from which a waiver could be presumed.

APPEAL by the defendant, the Union Casualty and Surety Company, from an interlocutory judgment of the Supreme Court in favor of the plaintiff, entered in the office of the clerk of the county of New York on the 30th day of November, 1901, upon the decision of the court, rendered after a trial at the New York Special Term, overruling a demurrer to the complaint.

Arthur C. Rounds, for the appellant.

Charles J. Hardy, for the respondent.

McLAUGHLIN, J.:

This action is brought to recover the sum of $5,000 under an employer's liability policy of insurance.

The defendant demurred to the complaint, upon the ground that it did not state facts sufficient to constitute a cause of action. The demurrer was overruled and defendant has appealed.

The complaint, in substance, alleges that at a time specified, a contract of insurance was made between the plaintiff and defendant by which the defendant "contracted to insure and did insure this plaintiff upon certain terms and conditions in said contract of insurance specified, * * * against legal liability for damages" to the extent of $5,000 to any one person "respecting fatal or non-fatal injuries from accidents occurring to any person or persons at the place or places mentioned and specified in the application for the said contract of insurance and in the policy of insurance issued on said application   *   *   *   against the hazards enumerated and set forth under a certain premium schedule to said contract of insurance annexed;" that while said contract of insurance was in force, a workman by the name of Brown, in the employ of the plaintiff, sustained injuries by reason of an accident occurring at the place specified in the policy, and that Brown and the work in which he was employed were included in the class of persons and hazards covered by the contract of insurance and against "liability to whom and because of which, due to injuries from accidents, this defendant insured plaintiff;" that the defendant was duly notified of the accident in accordance with the requirements of the contract of insurance, and that it thereupon disclaimed and repudiated any liability; that subsequently Brown brought an action against the plaintiff to recover for the injuries sustained by him, and in that action the defendant had notice of the commencement of the same, but it refused to take charge of the defense or to relieve plaintiff of all responsibility or care thereof, as provided in the policy, and that in that action Brown recovered $3,856.57 damages, interest and costs, which the defendant refused to pay; "that plaintiff duly complied with and observed all the provisions of the said contract of insurance by him to be complied with and observed as conditions precedent to defendant's liability to him thereunder, except in so far as such compliance and observance were waived or rendered unnecessary by the position and action of this defendant;" and judgment is demanded for the sum of $5,000 and interest.

We are of the opinion that the appeal is well taken. The complaint does not state facts sufficient to constitute a cause of action. The policy upon which defendant's liability is predicated is not made a part of the complaint, nor are its terms sufficiently set forth to enable the court to see that, assuming every allegation alleged in the complaint to be true, the plaintiff has a valid and subsisting claim against the defendant. The plaintiff, it is true, pleads the legal effect of the policy, but he has not alleged the terms and conditions of it, nor the hazards against which he was insured. The allegations in this request are merely to the effect that the defendant insured the plaintiff " upon certain terms and conditions in said contract of insurance specified" against "the hazards enumerated and set forth under a certain premium schedule to said contract of insurance annexed." What "the terms and conditions" of the contract are, what the hazards insured against were, or the nature of the work on which Brown was employed, are not stated, nor is there anything in the complaint from which these facts can be determined. The complaint is also fatally defective in another respect. The plaintiff does not allege performance of the conditions of the policy on his part, nor does he set forth any facts showing a waiver of any of those conditions. The only allegation in the complaint, with reference to the performance of the conditions upon which defendant's liability depended, is:

" X. That plaintiff duly complied with and observed all the provisions of the said contract of insurance by him to be complied with and observed as conditions precedent to defendant's liability to him thereunder, *except in so far as such compliance and observance were waived or rendered unnecessary by the position and action of this defendant.*"

To entitle the plaintiff to recover he must show that he has performed all of the conditions of the policy on his part to be performed or that performance has been waived, and this he does not do by alleging that he has complied with the policy in that respect, except where the same has been waived. If he has performed, then that fact must be alleged without qualification. If he has not performed, for the reason that defendant waived performance, then the conditions waived and the facts and circumstances constituting such waiver must be alleged. (*Smith* v. *Brown*, 17 Barb. 431; *La Chicotte* v. *Richmond R. & El. Co.*, 15 App. Div. 380; *Oakley* v. *Morton*, 11 N. Y. 30; *Crane* v. *Knubel*, 43 How. Pr. 389; *Elting* v. *Dayton*, 43 N. Y. St. Repr. 363; S. C. affd., 144 N. Y. 644.)

We have, therefore, a complaint which alleges that the defendant insured the plaintiff, upon certain terms and conditions which are not specified, against certain hazards which are not set forth, and which only alleges performance on the part of the plaintiff in so far as performance has not been waived, and not a fact has been set out from which the court can infer any waiver whatever. We do not think it can be said that this complaint contains a plain and concise statement of the facts constituting a cause of action upon which a recovery is based (Code Civ. Proc. § 481), and for that reason the demurrer should have been sustained.

The judgment appealed from, therefore, must be reversed, with costs, and the demurrer sustained, with costs, with leave to the plaintiff to amend on payment of the costs in this court and in the court below.

VAN BRUNT, P. J., INGRAHAM, HATCH and LAUGHLIN, JJ., concurred.

Judgment reversed, with costs, and demurrer sustained, with costs, with leave to plaintiff to amend on payment of costs in this court and in the court below.

EDWARD S. FOWLER, Substituted Trustee under the Last Will and Testament of JANE FERGUSON, Deceased, Appellant, *v.* SELIGMAN MANHEIMER, Respondent.

Marketable title — what is — title acquired by a widow of the deceased owner by virtue of an escheat act of the Legislature — when the release by the State is "subject to any right," etc., the Statute of Limitations does not run in her favor.

In 1860, John Furgeson died seized of real property, located in the city of New York, having been naturalized just prior to the time that he acquired title thereto. His widow obtained letters of administration upon his estate and alleged in the petition therefor that the only next of kin of her intestate was his sister: Elizabeth, who resided in Scotland when last heard from, about four-teen years previous to the filing of the petition. By chapter 603 of the Laws of 1867, the interest of the people of the State of New York in the premises was released to Mrs. Furgeson, the act providing that she should hold the land, "subject to any right, claim or interest of any purchaser, heir at law or devisee, or of any creditor by mortgage, judgment or otherwise, in the said real estate."

Mrs. Furgeson remained in possession of the premises until her death, which occurred in April, 1897. Thereafter the trustee under her will entered into a contract to sell the premises, and, upon the refusal of the vendee to accept the title, brought an action to compel the specific performance of the contract of sale. Upon the trial it appeared that the sister of John Furgeson, referred to in the petition for letters of administration upon his estate, had married, but the record did not disclose whom she married or the time when the marriage occurred.

Held, that the plaintiff was not entitled to the relief sought;

That the evidence did not establish that the sister, Elizabeth, at the time John died, was an alien, or that intermediate the time when she was last heard from and John's death, she had not married a citizen of the United States and did not then have living issue of such marriage;

That, in the absence of evidence bearing upon the subject, it could not be assumed that she was dead at the time the petition for letters of administration was filed, simply because she had not been heard of for fourteen years, and that the statement of Mrs. Furgeson in the petition and her subsequent declarations were not sufficient to establish that John Furgeson did not leave other heirs at law capable of inheriting the property;

That the plaintiff had not acquired a good title by adverse possession, because the act of the Legislature expressly provided that Mrs. Furgeson should hold subject to the rights of any heirs at law.

A vendor in a contract for the sale of land is not entitled to a judgment requiring the vendee to specifically perform the contract, unless he has tendered a title which is free from reasonable doubt, and if, after a fair consideration of the title tendered, a reasonable man would hesitate to take it, it cannot be said to be free from reasonable doubt and the vendee is justified in refusing to perform.

APPEAL by the plaintiff, Edward S. Fowler, substituted trustee under the last will and testament of Jane Ferguson, deceased, from a judgment of the Supreme Court in favor of the defendant, entered in the office of the clerk of the county of New York on the 12th day of March, 1901, upon the decision of the court rendered after a trial at the New York Special Term.

Abel E. Blackmar, for the appellant.

Samson Lachman, for the respondent.

McLAUGHLIN, J.:

This action was brought to compel the specific performance of a contract for the sale of certain real estate in the city of New York, the defendant having refused to perform upon the ground that the title tendered was unmarketable, and the question presented upon this appeal is whether or not the defendant was justified in his refusal.

The facts, so far as the same are material to the question presented, are as follows: In 1860 one John Ferguson, it is conceded, acquired good title to the premises by a deed of conveyance, which was recorded on the ninth of March of that year. He died intestate on the 11th of October, 1865, leaving him surviving his widow,

Jane Ferguson, who applied to and obtained from the Surrogate's court of the county of New York letters of administration upon his estate. In .the petition filed for such letters, she stated that the only "next of kin" of her intestate was a sister Elizabeth, who, when last heard from, which was about fourteen years previous, resided in Scotland.

In 1867, by an act of the Legislature of that year (Chap. 603), all the estate, right, title and interest of the People of the State of New York of, in and to the premises in question were released to Jane Ferguson, the widow of John Ferguson, but the act expressly provides that she shall hold the land under such release, "subject to any right, claim or interest of any purchaser, heir at law or devisee, or of any creditor by mortgage, judgment or otherwise, in the said real estate."

John Ferguson, at the time of his death, was in possession of the premises in question, and Mrs. Ferguson, from the death of her husband, continued to occupy the same until her death, which occurred in April, 1897. She left a will which was admitted to probate, and in which certain trusts were created, and the trustee therein named having died, the plaintiff in this action was substituted, and, as such substituted trustee, he entered into the contract with the defendant. At the time fixed for the closing of the contract, the plaintiff was ready and willing to perform, but the defendant refused to perform, upon the ground that the title to the land is in the heirs at law of John Ferguson, and that Jane Ferguson, through whom the plaintiff claims, never had any title at all. Other objections were raised, but it is unnecessary to consider them in view of the conclusion at which we have arrived.

An action for specific performance is an equitable one, and to entitle the plaintiff to the relief asked proof must be presented which clearly and satisfactorily establishes that he is equitably entitled to it. (*Heller* v. *Cohen,* 154 N. Y. 306.) He is not entitled to such relief under a contract for the sale of land, unless he has tendered a title which is free from reasonable doubt (*Vought* v. *Williams,* 120 N. Y. 257), and if, after a fair consideration of the title which he has tendered, a reasonable man would hesitate to take it, then it cannot be said to be free from reasonable doubt, and a party who has agreed to take is justified in refusing to perform,

and as has many times been said for the reason that a purchaser of
real estate ought not to be compelled to take a title which he may
be obliged to defend by litigation (*McPherson* v. *Schade*, 149 N.
Y. 16) ; that he is entitled to a marketable title free from doubtful
questions of fact or law. (*Brokaw* v. *Duffy*, 165 N. Y. 391.)
Under these authorities and many others that might be cited to the
same effect we are of the opinion that the defendant was justified
in his refusal to accept the title tendered him. If the plaintiff has
good title it must be conceded it is solely by virtue of the act of the
Legislature, and whether that act accomplishes that purpose, of
course, depends upon the fact as to whether John Ferguson, when
he died, had heirs at law who were capable of taking the title under
the statutes of the State of New York. It is true, in the petition
made by Jane Ferguson for letters of administration upon her husband's estate, she stated that his only "next of kin" was a sister,
Elizabeth, who had not been heard of for about fourteen years, at
which time she resided in Scotland, and in this connection it also
appeared that John Ferguson was naturalized just prior to the time
he acquired title, and that he came from Scotland, but this proof
fell far short of establishing that the sister Elizabeth, at the time
John died, was an alien, and for which reason she could not
inherit from John, or that intermediate the time when she was last
heard from and John's death she had not married a citizen of the
United States and had living issue by such marriage. It, however,
did appear that the sister was married, but the record fails to disclose whom she married or the time when the marriage occurred.
It cannot be presumed, in the absence of evidence bearing upon the
subject, that because the sister had not been heard of for fourteen
years that she was dead, any more than it can be presumed that she
was, at the time of the death of John, an alien, or did not have
children who could inherit. (*Vought* v. *Williams*, *supra*.) Nor
do we think that the statement of Jane Ferguson, in the petition
referred to, or her subsequent declarations upon the subject, were
sufficient to establish the fact that John did not leave other heirs at
law capable of inheriting under the statute.

The plaintiff is asking for a specific performance of the contract,
and before he can become entitled to that relief he must establish,
beyond a reasonable doubt, that the title which he tendered was

good, and this he can only do by showing that John Ferguson, at the time he died, did not leave any heirs at law, capable of inheriting under the statutes of the State of New York, and for that reason the title is escheated to the State. (*Simis* v. *McElroy*, 160 N. Y. 156.)

In the case last cited the court held that title by adverse possession is not shown where there is a failure to *negative* the possibility of an outstanding claim by the heirs of a former owner as to whom the adverse possession was open to contingencies of remaindership and infancy. So here, we think the plaintiff failed to show the title he tendered was marketable, inasmuch as he failed to negative the possibility that John Ferguson left heirs at law capable of inheriting. The burden was upon the plaintiff, and not upon the defendant, to establish such facts. But it is said that plaintiff has acquired good title by adverse possession. This cannot be, because the only interest which Jane Ferguson acquired was by virtue of the act of the Legislature, and that expressly provided that her interest must be held subject to any right of heirs at law.

It follows, therefore, that the judgment appealed from must be affirmed, with costs.

VAN BRUNT, P. J., O'BRIEN, INGRAHAM and HATCH, JJ., concurred.

Judgment affirmed, with costs.

60
386 KATIE V. HOEY, as Administratrix, etc., of JAMES J. HOEY, Deceased, Appellant, *v.* METROPOLITAN STREET RAILWAY COMPANY and THE DRY DOCK, EAST BROADWAY AND BATTERY RAILROAD COMPANY, Respondents.

Power of the court where specific questions are answered and a general verdict is rendered by the jury — when acute pulmonary tuberculosis will not be presumed to have resulted from the weakness caused by muscular atrophy, induced by an accident.

Where the judge presiding at a jury trial submits to the jury, under section 1187 of the Code of Civil Procedure, certain specific questions of fact with instructions to render a general verdict also, he has no power, after the jury have answered the specific questions of fact and rendered a general verdict, to dismiss the complaint upon the merits nor to set aside the answers, except one, made by the jury to the specific questions of fact submitted to them, or the general verdict. In such a case he may either nonsuit the plaintiff or direct the jury to render a general verdict.

In an action to recover damages resulting from the death of the plaintiff's intestate, in which it appears that the intestate sustained very serious injuries, in consequence of the defendant's negligence, and that a short time thereafter he developed progressive muscular atrophy, but that the immediate cause of his death was acute pulmonary tuberculosis, a germ disease, in no way connected with the accident, nor shown to have resulted from the progressive muscular atrophy, a finding that the acute pulmonary tuberculosis resulted from the accident will not be sustained, upon the theory, unsupported by any evidence, that the intestate was so weakened by his injuries and the progressive muscular atrophy resulting therefrom, that it made him susceptible to tuberculosis, and that by reason thereof he contracted the latter disease.

O'BRIEN and LAUGHLIN, JJ., dissented.

APPEAL by the plaintiff, Katie V. Hoey, as administratrix, etc., of James J. Hoey, deceased, from a judgment of the Supreme Court in favor of the defendants, entered in the office of the clerk of the county of New York on the 23d day of October, 1901, upon the decision of the court, rendered after a trial at the New York Trial Term, dismissing the complaint upon the merits and setting aside the general verdict and the special findings of fact brought in by the jury, except the first finding, with notice of an intention to bring up for review upon said appeal the order dismissing the complaint and directing the entry of the judgment.

William Rumsey, for the appellant.

Charles F. Brown, for the respondents.

McLAUGHLIN, J.:

On the 11th of December, 1899, James J. Hoey, the plaintiff's intestate, while a passenger in one of the defendants' cars, was seriously injured by the car in which he was riding colliding with another car belonging to the defendants. He died on the 30th of September, 1900, and this action was brought to recover damages for his death, on the ground that the negligence of the defendants was the cause of it.

At the trial the defendants' negligence and the intestate's freedom from negligence were conceded, and the sole question litigated was whether the injuries sustained by the intestate at the time of the collision were the proximate cause of his death.

At the close of the case, defendants' counsel moved for the dismissal of the complaint, or for the direction of a verdict, and pending the consideration of such motion, the trial court submitted to the jury, under section 1187 of the Code of Civil Procedure, certain specific questions of fact, with instructions to also render a general verdict. One of the specific questions of fact was: "Did James J. Hoey die September 30, 1900, from hasty consumption?" This was answered in the affirmative and a general verdict rendered, awarding plaintiff, as damages, $12,500. The jury was discharged and the trial court, after consideration, directed that a judgment be entered dismissing the complaint upon the merits, setting aside the general verdict and the answers to all of the questions except the one above given. To this ruling the plaintiff excepted. Judgment was entered accordingly, from which this appeal is taken.

The court had no power to dismiss the complaint upon the merits, nor to set aside the answers of the jury to the specific questions of fact submitted to or the verdict rendered by them. It will be observed that the section of the Code referred to provides that after the jury shall have rendered a special verdict upon such submission, or shall have assessed the damages, the court may then pass upon the motion to *nonsuit,* or direct a general verdict, and on appeal from the judgment entered upon such nonsuit or general verdict, such special verdict or general verdict shall form a part of the record and the Appellate Division may direct such judgment thereon as either party may be entitled to. The trial court, therefore, could, after the rendition of the special verdict by the jury, have adopted either one of two courses; he could nonsuit the plaintiff or direct the jury to render a general verdict. He did not direct a general verdict, nor did he nonsuit the plaintiff, but instead directed judgment dismissing the complaint upon the merits. This was clearly erroneous, but in view of the conclusion at which we have arrived, inasmuch as the special verdict is in fact set out in the record, it is of no importance, since this court has power to direct such judgment as either party may be entitled to. The judgment should have been one nonsuiting the plaintiff, instead of dismissing the complaint on the merits. This brings us to the consideration of the main question presented, and that is, whether the injuries which the plaintiff's intestate sustained in the collision were the proximate cause of his death. If they were not, then the plaintiff was not entitled to recover. The uncontradicted evidence adduced upon the trial was to the effect that a few weeks prior to his death he was stricken with acute pulmonary tuberculosis, which disease the jury found caused his death. Any other finding would have been clearly against evidence. Was the disease then, from which the intestate died, the direct result of the injuries which he sustained in the collision; in other words, was defendant's negligence the proximate cause? A proximate cause, as defined by the Court of Appeals in *Laidlaw* v. *Sage* (158 N. Y. 73, 99), " ' is one in which is involved the idea of necessity. It is one the connection between which and the effect is plain and intelligible; it is one which can be used as a term by which a proposition can be demonstrated, that is, one which can be reasoned from conclusively. A remote cause is one which is inconclusive in reasoning, because from it no certain conclusion can be legitimately drawn; in other words, a remote cause is a cause the connection between which and the effect is uncertain, vague or indeterminate. * * * The proximate cause being given, the effect must follow. But although the existence of the remote cause is necessary for the existence of the effect (for unless there has been a remote cause there can be no effect) still, the existence of the remote cause does not necessarily imply the existence of the effect. The remote cause being given, the effect may or may not follow.' " A proximate cause as thus defined was quoted with approval in a recent case by the same court. (*Seifter* v. *Brooklyn Heights R. R. Co.*, 169 N. Y. 254.)

There is no doubt that the deceased sustained very serious injuries in the collision, and by reason thereof, within a short time thereafter, developed what is termed in the record as "progressive muscular atrophy," but there is nothing in the evidence which would justify a finding that the tuberculosis which resulted in his death was caused by, or necessarily flowed from, that disease. On the contrary, the evidence is uncontradicted that tuberculosis is a germ disease and that in order to contract it in the lungs the germ must be inhaled, and that these germs were not the result of or produced by the accident; that they came from a source independent of, and not connected with, it. What is claimed is that the intestate's condition was so weakened by his injuries, and the disease resulting from them, that is, progressive muscular atrophy, that it made him susceptible to tuberculosis and by reason thereof he contracted it.   There is nothing in the evidence to sustain this claim, and such conclusion is based upon conjecture and speculation alone.   To entitle the plaintiff to recover she was bound to prove that the death of her intestate was the direct result of his injuries; that his injuries were the cause and his death the effect, an unbroken chain extending from the cause to the effect (*Weber* v. *Third Ave. R. R. Co.*, 12 App. Div. 512), and any link in that chain could not be supplied by a mere possibility.   (*Milwaukee & St. Paul R. Co.* v. *Kellogg*, 94 U. S. 469.)   If it could, then it is not difficult to see how easy it would be to take property from one person and give it to another, sanctioned by judicial procedure.   The negligence of the defendants may have been the cause of the intestate's death, but whether it was or was not is a pure guess and nothing more, and a judgment in law cannot stand upon a guess or bare possibility.

Our conclusion, therefore, is that the judgment should be corrected as indicated in this opinion, and as thus corrected affirmed, without costs to either party.

VAN BRUNT, P. J., and PATTERSON, J., concurred; O'BRIEN and LAUGHLIN, JJ., dissented.

Judgment corrected as indicated in opinion, and as thus corrected affirmed, without costs to either party.

64
Y123
REAL ESTATE CORPORATION OF NEW YORK CITY, Plaintiff, *v.* J. HENRY HARPER, as Executor, etc., Defendant.

Assessment on real property in the city of New York for a street opening — when it becomes a lien — breach of a covenant against incumbrances.

February 25, 1898, the Supreme Court, upon the presentation of the report of commissioners of estimate and assessment appointed in a proceeding to open a street in the city of New York, made an order confirming the report in respect to the awards of damages and sent it back to the commissioners with directions to assess two specified lots separately, and also not to exceed one-half the tax valuation of 1896 in determining the assessment for benefits.   The city of New York alone appealed from the order, and its appeal was only from the provision thereof relating to the tax valuation of 1896.

December 8, 1899, the Appellate Division reversed the portion of the order appealed from and ordered that in all other respects the report of the commissioners be confirmed. A property owner took an appeal from this order to the Court of Appeals, which court, May 1, 1900, affirmed the order of the Appellate Division. May 14, 1900, the order of the Court of Appeals was made the order of the Supreme Court. July 18, 1900, the commissioners of estimate and assessment filed an "amended and supplemental report," stating that they had assessed the two specified lots separately. This report was confirmed August 15, 1900, and on October 4, 1900, the lists of assessments were, for the first time, entered with the collector of assessments in arrears, in pursuance of the statute.

December 3, 1900, an assessment levied upon property affected by the proceeding (but not one of the two lots as to which the report had been sent back to the commissioners) was paid by a person to whom such property had been conveyed on January 23, 1900, by a deed containing a covenant against incumbrances.

Held, as under sections 159, 986 and 1017 of the Greater New York charter (Laws of 1897, chap. 378) the report was not *wholly* confirmed until August 15, 1900, that the assessment was not a lien upon the property in question at the time the conveyance was made;

That consequently there had been no breach of the covenant against incumbrances, and that the grantee was not entitled to recover the amount of the assessment from the grantor.

VAN BRUNT, P. J., dissented on the ground that the submission of the controversy was irregular in form.

SUBMISSION of a controversy upon an agreed statement of facts, pursuant to section 1279 of the Code of Civil Procedure.

Francis B. Chedsey, for the plaintiff.

Robert E. Deyo, for the defendant.

McLAUGHLIN, J.:

The question here presented comes before the court upon a submission under section 1279 of the Code of Civil Procedure.

Upon the facts contained in the submission, plaintiff seeks to recover from the defendant $3,868.87, with interest at the rate of four per cent per annum from December 3, 1900, which sum it paid on that date in discharge of an assessment for benefits imposed on certain real estate in the city of New York, conveyed to it by the defendant's testatrix on the 23d of January, 1900, by a deed which contained a covenant to the effect that the premises conveyed were free from incumbrances. The plaintiff predicates its right to recover upon the ground that there has been a breach of that covenant, inasmuch as the assessment was, at the time of the delivery of the deed, a valid and subsisting lien upon the land conveyed.

The defendant claims that there has been no breach of this covenant, since the assessment did not become a lien until several months after the plaintiff acquired title to such land.

The facts upon which the claims of the respective parties depend are as follows : In August, 1895, proceedings were taken by the city of New York for the opening of Whittier street. The defendant's testatrix appeared in the proceeding in December, 1897, and filed objections to the preliminary report of assessments made by the commissioners of estimate and assessment. On the 24th of December, 1897, the commissioners made their report, in which the land subsequently conveyed by the defendant's testatrix to the plaintiff was assessed in her name for benefit in the sum of $3,868.87, and a few days later the report of the commissioners was presented to the Supreme Court, and on the 25th of February, 1898, an order was made confirming such report in respect to the award for damages but referring the same back to the commissioners with directions to apportion between two lots, as indicated upon a certain map — lots 14 and 16 — a sum which had been assessed against them jointly in the name of one owner — it having been made to appear that these lots had different owners ; and also to make all assessments for benefit, in no case more than one-half of the valuation of the property assessed as valued for purposes of taxation for the year 1896.

The city appealed to the Appellate Division from *only* that portion of the order directing the commissioners to follow the tax valuation of 1896 in determining the assessments for benefit, and this was the only appeal taken.

On the 8th of December, 1899, the Appellate Division reversed so much of the order as was appealed from and ordered that in all other respects the report of the commissioners be confirmed. From this order an appeal by a property owner was taken to the Court of Appeals, where the same, on the 1st of May, 1900, was affirmed, and on the fourteenth of the same month the order of the Court of Appeals was made the order of the Supreme Court. On the 18th of July, 1900, the commissioners made an " amended and supplementary " report to the Supreme Court in which, after reciting all the proceedings theretofore taken, including the appeals, it was stated that the commissioners had apportioned, as indicated in their report, the assessment upon lots 14 and 16 between the different owners thereof and had also, at the request of parties interested in other lots, made similar apportionments as indicated, and that " in all other matters our report herein made by us and dated the 24th of December, 1897, is in all respects unchanged." This report, on the fifteenth of August following, was confirmed by an order of the Supreme Court, and on the 4th of October, 1900, the lists of assessments were for the first time entered with the collector of assessments and arrears in pursuance of the statute, which provides that there shall be kept a full and complete record in detail of all the lists of assessments confirmed and that the assessment shall become a lien upon the real estate affected thereby immediately upon its entry in said record. (Greater New York Charter [Laws of 1897, chap. 378], §§ 159, 1017.) The statute further provides that on an application for the confirmation of a report of commissioners, etc., the Supreme Court may confirm the report or refer the matter back to the commissioners, as justice shall require, and this may be done from time to time until a report shall be made in the premises which the said court shall *wholly* confirm, and such report, when so confirmed, shall, unless set aside or reversed on appeal, " be final and conclusive, as well upon The City of New York as upon the owners, lessees, persons and parties interested and entitled unto the lands, * * * mentioned in the said report, and also upon all other persons whomsoever." (Id. § 986.)

Upon the foregoing facts and under the provisions of the statute referred to, was there a valid and subsisting lien upon the land conveyed at the time of the delivery of the deed to the plaintiff? We think there was not. There was no lien upon this land for benefit until the report of the commissioners had been *wholly* confirmed. This is necessarily so, because the statute in relation to the subject so provides. The report had not been *wholly* confirmed at the time the deed was delivered, and manifestly could not be until after the commissioners had made a report concerning that part of the matters which had been sent back to them and from which no appeal had been taken, and that report had been confirmed by the court.

The order of the Appellate Division, reversing the order of the Special Term, and providing that the report of the commissioners was confirmed, did not and could not affect the report which had been sent back to the commissioners, but which had not been questioned or appealed from by anybody; that portion of the order referring the matter back to the commissioners, from which no appeal had been taken, was not before the Appellate Division, and, therefore, it had no power either to reverse, modify or confirm it. It having been made to appear, when the report of the commissioners was first presented, that the assessments made upon lots 14 and 16 (which did not include any part of the land conveyed to the plaintiff) should be apportioned between the different owners of those lots, the court could do nothing, under the statute, except to refer the matter back for correction, and until the commissioners had made the correction and submitted their report, there could be no such thing as the report being *wholly* confirmed, and there could not be a lien until that had been done. The report was not *wholly* confirmed until the 15th of August, 1900. The deed was delivered to the plaintiff on the 23d of January, 1900. The assessment paid by the plaintiff was not a lien upon the land at the time of the conveyance, and, therefore, there has been no breach of the covenant against incumbrances.

The defendant is entitled, under the stipulation, to a judgment to this effect, with costs.

O'BRIEN, INGRAHAM and HATCH, JJ., concurred; VAN BRUNT, P. J., dissented.

VAN BRUNT, P. J. (dissenting):

I dissent. The submission is entirely irregular in form. Questions are submitted to the court, and as the court answers those questions then certain judgment is to be given. There is no authority for a submission of questions to the court. The facts only are to be submitted to the court. It may be proper for the plaintiff to state what judgment he demands upon those facts, and also for the defendant to state what claims he makes upon those facts; but the court is to award any judgment which such facts warrant, and this right cannot be limited.

Judgment ordered for defendant, with costs.

INSURANCE COMPANY OF THE STATE OF NEW YORK, Respondent, *v.* ^70^ a174 N
THE ASSOCIATED MANUFACTURERS' MUTUAL FIRE INSURANCE COR-
PORATION, Appellaut.

*Reinsurance — when the reinsurer is bound by the adjustment of loss made by the
insurer.*

A fire insurance company reinsured a portion of a risk under a contract which
provided that it should be "subject to the same risks, valuations, endorsements
(excepting transfers of location) and conditions as the original insurance, and
loss, if any, to be settled and paid *pro rata* with the reinsured and at the
same time and place, and upon the same conditions."

The property insured was subsequently destroyed by fire.

Held, that the reinsurer, in the absence of fraud or of bad faith on the part of the
insurer, was bound by the adjustment of the loss made by the insurer, especially where it appeared that, under such a policy of reinsurance, it was customary for the reinsurer to pay the reinsured its proportion of the adjustment
expenses.

APPEAL by the defendant, The Associated Manufacturers' Mutual
Fire Insurance Corporation, from a judgment of the Supreme
Court in favor of the plaintiff, entered in the office of the clerk of
the county of New York on the 9th day of March, 1900, upon the
verdict of a jury rendered by direction of the court, and also from
an order entered in said clerk's office on the 16th day of March,
1900, denying the defendant's motion for a new trial made upon
the minutes.

Archibald C. Shenstone, for the appellant.

Frederic R. Coudert, Jr., for the respondent.

McLAUGHLIN, J.:

On the 1st of September, 1897, the plaintiff entered into a contract by which it insured, to the extent of $60,000, the Santa Fe and
Pacific Railroad Company against loss or damage by fire for a specified term upon certain property contained in or on cars awaiting
movement while in transit and until unloaded at destination. Subsequently it applied to and obtained from the defendant a contract
of reinsurance to the extent of $5,000 against a portion of the risk.
The contract of reinsurance provided that it was "subject to the

same risks, valuations, endorsements (excepting transfers of location) and conditions as the original insurance, and loss, if any, to be settled and paid *pro rata* with the reinsured and at the same time and place, and upon the same conditions." During the term of the policy property covered by the original insurance was destroyed by fire. Notice was given of the loss by the insured to the plaintiff, and it, in turn, notified the defendant. The plaintiff, through its adjuster, proceeded to adjust the loss, and after such adjustment a settlement was made with the railroad company by which the plaintiff paid, in satisfaction of its liability under its policy, the sum of $33,633.04, and it thereupon requested the defendant to pay its share of such loss, in accordance with the terms of the policy of reinsurance. The defendant refused, and thereupon this action was brought to recover such sum.

At the close of the trial the court directed a verdict for the plaintiff for the amount claimed, and from the judgment thereafter entered the defendant appealed.

During the course of the trial upwards of one hundred exceptions were taken, and we are asked to hold that "every exception * * * was well taken." We are unable to see any merit whatever in any of the exceptions. Indeed none of them are deserving of consideration, except those relating to the evidence as to the adjustment of the loss and payment of the same by the plaintiff to the railroad company. What is claimed in this respect is that the defendant is not bound by the adjustment made by the plaintiff, but that in order to entitle the plaintiff to recover against this defendant it was required to prove every fact which the railroad would have been required to prove had the plaintiff resisted its claim and an action been brought to recover under the original policy. We think that a proper construction of the contract of reinsurance fails to sustain this claim. The defendant agreed that the reinsurance should be subject to the same risks, valuations and conditions as the original insurance, and that the loss should " be settled and paid *pro rata* with the reinsured and at the same time and place and upon the same conditions." Not only this, but it will be observed that the defendant admitted upon the trial that under a policy of this kind it is customary for the reinsurer to pay the reinsured its proportion of the adjustment expenses. In the absence, therefore, of fraud or bad faith on the part of the plaintiff, the defendant, by the terms of its policy, as well as by the construction placed upon it by the admission, is in no position to object to the mode of adjustment as made by the plaintiff. When, therefore, the plaintiff had ascertained by a proper investigation that it was legally liable to pay a certain amount to the railroad company under its contract, and such payment had been made, the defendant could not question the validity of the plaintiff's act, unless it alleged and proved that the plaintiff had acted fraudulently or collusively to its injury. The amount of the loss to be paid by the defendant was to be evidenced by the plaintiff's adjustment and payment. This sum it had agreed to and was obligated to pay, unless, as already said, it proved that the plaintiff, in making such adjustment and payment, had acted fraudulently and collusively with the railroad company. (*Jackson v. St. Paul Fire & Marine Ins. Co.*, 99 N. Y. 124; *Consolidated Real Estate & Fire Ins. Co. v. Cashow*, 41 Md. 59.) There is nothing to show, either by allegation or proof, that the plaintiff did not act in entire good faith in adjusting the loss and in making the payment which it did, and no reason is suggested why the defendant should not pay to the plaintiff the sum which it agreed to by its contract of reinsurance, and for this reason the trial court properly directed a verdict for the plaintiff.

It follows that the judgment and order appealed from must be affirmed, with costs.

Van Brunt, P. J., Patterson, O'Brien and Laughlin, JJ., concurred.

Judgment and order affirmed, with costs.

Clark W. Dunlop, Respondent, v. Frederic T. James, Appellant.

Landlord and tenant — right of a mortgagee of a leasehold to pay the rent which the tenant's assignee has assumed and to sue the assignee therefor — basis of such right.

Where a lease for a term of twenty-one years contains a covenant obligating the lessee and its assignee to pay a stipulated rent and the taxes assessed upon the premises during the term of the lease, and authorizes the lessor to re-enter in case of a breach of said covenant, a mortgagee of the leasehold interest, in the event of the failure of an assignee of the lease, who took the same subject to the "rents, covenants, conditions and provisions therein," and also subject to the mortgage, to pay the rent and taxes in compliance with the covenant, may pay such rent and taxes and then maintain an action against the assignee to recover the amount so paid.

Such right is not based upon any contract relation between the mortgagee and the assignee of the lease, but rests upon the mortgagee's right to protect his interest in the estate.

APPEAL by the defendant, Frederic T. James, from a judgment of the Supreme Court in favor of the plaintiff, entered in the office of the clerk of the county of New York on the 10th day of May, 1901, upon the verdict of a jury rendered by direction of the court, and also from an order entered in said clerk's office on the 7th day of May, 1901, denying the defendant's motion for a new trial made upon the minutes.

John P. Everett, for the appellant.

O. J. Wells, for the respondent.

McLAUGHLIN, J.:

In April, 1890, the Rector, Church Wardens and Vestrymen of Trinity Church leased for the term of twenty-one years certain real estate in the city of New York to Peck, Stow & Wilcox Company. The lease contained a covenant to the effect that the lessee and its assigns would pay the rent stipulated and also the taxes assessed upon the premises during the life of the lease, and also provided for a re-entry by the lessor in case of a failure to make these payments.

By mesne assignments the lease was acquired by the defendant in this action, who took the same subject to the "rents, covenants conditions and provisions therein also mentioned," and also subject to a mortgage then held by the plaintiff upon the leasehold estate. While the defendant was the owner of the leasehold estate, ground rent became due to the amount of $1,125, and taxes payable to the amount of $1,362.62, which sums the defendant having neglected and refused to pay, notwithstanding he was requested to do so, were paid by this plaintiff to protect his interest in the estate, and thereupon he brought this action to recover from the defendant the amount paid.

At the close of the case the learned justice at Trial Term directed a verdict for the plaintiff for the amount claimed, and the defendant has appealed. The judgment is right. The defendant, as the owner of the leasehold estate, as well as under the covenants contained in the lease, which he expressly agreed to perform when he took his assignment, was obligated to pay the rent and taxes (*People ex rel. White* v. *Loomis,* 27 Hun, 328; *Pardee* v. *Steward,* 37 id. 259; *Sayles* v. *Kerr,* 4 App. Div. 150), and he having failed to perform that obligation, the plaintiff, in order that he might protect his interest in the estate, had the right to make such payments, and when he did he became, by operation of law, subrogated, to this extent, to the rights of the lessor, and he could thereafter enforce his claim against the defendant in the same way and to the same extent that the lessor could had such payments not been made. This right the plaintiff had, not by reason of any contract relation with the defendant, but because of the fact that it was necessary for him to make good the default of the defendant in order that his own property rights might be preserved.

The judgment, therefore, must be affirmed, with costs.

VAN BRUNT, P. J., O'BRIEN, INGRAHAM and HATCH, JJ., concurred.

Judgment affirmed, with costs.

In the Matter of the Judicial Settlement of the Account of Proceedings of ANN HAMILTON, as Administratrix, etc., of WILLIAM HAMILTON, Deceased.

| 70
a172 N

ANN HAMILTON, Individually, Appellant; JAMES HAMILTON and Others, Respondents.

Husband and wife — what recognition by the husband of an obligation to pay for support furnished by his wife will be enforced.

A woman, who, at the time of her marriage, was engaged in the business of keeping a boarding house, continued after her marriage to conduct that business on her separate account, her husband, who lived with her, contributing nothing towards the support of the household and using all money earned by him in his business. After many years of married life, the husband, desiring to protect the wife, executed the following statement :

FIRST DEPARTMENT, MARCH TERM, 1902. [Vol. 70.

"I ouw Mrs. Hamilton for Home Keap for 17 years, at $1,500 Per year

"The amount of time I have Bean in Bussines, which amounts to.. $25,500.00"

and delivered it to his attorney with instructions to give the same to his wife or keep it for her. The attorney delivered the paper to the wife after her husband's death.

Held, that the wife was entitled to recover from her husband's estate the amount specified in the acknowledgment of indebtedness, no objection having been made that such amount did not represent the value of the board and lodging so furnished;

That where a wife assumes the burden of supporting her husband and her family out of her separate estate, any proof tending to show that the husband recognized an obligation upon his part to reimburse the wife for her outlay will be sufficient to create a valid obligation against his estate.

APPEAL by Ann Hamilton, individually, from so much of a decree of the Surrogate's Court of the county of New York, entered in said Surrogate's Court on the 20th day of May, 1901, upon the report of a referee, as disallows her claim against the estate of the decedent and sustains certain exceptions taken by the contestants to the referee's report.

Ann Hamilton was the widow and administratrix of William Hamilton. She filed her account as administratrix, at which time she also presented claims individually against her husband's estate. The matter was duly referred and the referee found in favor of the claimant. When the matter came before the surrogate he disallowed a portion of the said claim, amounting to $25,500.

William Hamilton, a Scotchman, came to this country in the early seventies with his friend Donald Mitchell. They both boarded with Mrs. Gardiner, at her boarding house on East Twenty-fifth street, in New York city. In 1876 Hamilton married Mrs. Gardiner. At that time he was a journeyman carpenter, but after his marriage became a boss carpenter and builder. At the time Mrs. Hamilton first became acquainted with Mr. Hamilton she was keeping a boarding house and had from twenty to twenty-five boarders. When she married Mr. Hamilton she removed from Twenty-fifth street to Thirty-first street, where she still resides. She purchased the house and continued to take boarders, and always had either boarders or lodgers from that time until the present. She received the money from her boarders, purchased her own supplies and ran the house in the same manner that she had conducted the same prior to her marriage. Hamilton contributed nothing toward the support of the household, but used all the money he earned in his business. He told his friend Mitchell that all the property he had he owed to Mrs. Hamilton, because she had supported the household and allowed him to use his money in his business, and had at times loaned him money and had furnished the money for him to start in business. There was a time when he came to Mitchell, who had always been his adviser, and told him he was afraid that he would get into some financial difficulty, and he wished to do something that would insure the protection of Mrs. Hamilton's rights, inasmuch as he was owing her for all the property which he had. He also told the same story to his friend and attorney, Mr. Finck, and told Finck that he wished to do something to protect Mrs. Hamilton's rights. Finck told him to make a statement of his affairs, what property he had and what he was owing, and bring it to him. Hamilton made a written statement of the property he possessed, and in connection therewith appeared the following:

"I ouw Mrs. Hamilton for Home Keap for 17 years, at $1,500 Per year
"The amount of time I have Bean in Bussines, which
    amounts to................... .... $25,500.00
"WM. HAMILTON,
    "210 East 26 St."

The written statement he delivered to Finck, and told him to give the same to Mrs. Hamilton or keep it for her. Finck delivered the paper to Mrs. Hamilton after her husband's death.

Motion was made to confirm the report of the referee; the surrogate denied the same as to the claim for board, and from such determination this appeal is taken.

George Finck, for the appellant.

Arthur C. Rounds, for the respondents.

HATCH, J.:

The referee found upon substantially undisputed testimony that the claimant furnished the board and house for the deceased during the period for which she makes claim. The obligation thus assumed by the claimant was a duty which was imposed upon the husband. The primary obligation rested upon him, not only to support himself, but to support his family. Her assumption of an obligation not resting upon her, but which was imposed upon him, could not create a presumption that the food and lodging so furnished were intended to be gratuitous. It is a general rule that where the relation of the parties is of such a character as repels the presumption of a promise to pay for service rendered, it will be presumed that the service was intended to be gratuitous. The rule is well stated in *Ross* v. *Hardin* (79 N. Y. 84) and *Lind* v. *Sullestadt* (21 Hun, 364). But where the relation is such as casts upon the husband the duty of maintenance and support of his wife and family, no such presumption obtains. Undoubtedly if the wife chooses to assume the burden and does in fact apply her income to the maintenance of the family, intending that the same shall be gratuitous, no recovery can be had for the amount so expended. But where it appears that the husband recognized the obligation to support himself and not be supported by her, there is no presumption that the wife intended the application of her income as a gratuity to him. (*Hendricks* v. *Isaacs*, 117 N. Y. 411.) Under such circumstances, where the husband has been supported by the wife, any competent proof tending to show that the husband recognized an obligation upon his part to reimburse the wife for her outlay will be supported and upheld as sufficient to create a valid indebtedness against his estate.

In the present case it is practically undisputed that the board furnished was continuous and covered the period claimed in the account presented by the claimant. The paper introduced in evidence is a declaration upon the part of the husband not only that he received the board and paid nothing therefor, but that he was also indebted for the same. Consequently, every element of a good cause of action in favor of the claimant was established at the trial, and the wife became entitled to recover therefor. (*Matter of Gallagher*, 153 N. Y. 364.) The admission in that case which was held sufficient upon which to found an obligation against the estate, when connected with proof of the rendition of service, is no stronger in form than is the present declaration made by the husband, while the proof to show the rendition of the service is very much stronger than appeared in that case. Therein the proof of service was slight and nearly inconclusive ; here it is strong and undisputed. It furnishes, therefore, a controlling authority of the right of the plaintiff to recover.

It is suggested that no proof of the value of the board and lodging was given and, therefore, that the admission of an indebtedness in the amount of $25,500 was excessive. It is sufficient to say that no point whatever was raised before the referee in respect to such matter, the whole claim of the respondents being based upon the theory that no recovery could be had of any sum, conceding all that appeared. But it is clear that the proof was sufficient upon which to found a claim, and the admission of the husband was of an existing indebtedness and sufficient upon which to found the promise to pay.

It follows that the decree of the surrogate disallowing this claim should be reversed, and the report of the referee be in all respects confirmed, with costs to the appellant.

VAN BRUNT, P. J., O'BRIEN, INGRAHAM and McLAUGHLIN, JJ., concurred.

Decree reversed and report of referee confirmed, with costs to appellant.

BRADLEY & CURRIER Co., Appellant, *v.* GREGOR GEORGE HOFMANN and Others, Defendants.

DUDLEY S. HARDE and GLOBE REALTY COMPANY, Intervening Petitioners, Respondents.

Mortgage foreclosure — arrangement between a third mortgagee and the holders of the first and second mortgages for a certain disposition of the rents — a receiver appointed thereafter at the instance of the third mortgagee without notice will be compelled to dispose of them in the same way — how far the act of the attorney binds the client.

An action having been brought to foreclose a third mortgage upon certain property, the first and second mortgagees, who were not parties to the action, entered into negotiations with the third mortgagee's attorney respecting the appointment of a receiver of the rents and profits of the property. The negotiations resulted in an agreement that the mortgagor should execute an assign-

ment of the rents to the third mortgagee and that the rents should be applied
in the manner set forth in the assignment. After the assignment of the rents
had been executed by the mortgagor and while the first and second mortgagees
supposed that the rents were being collected under the assignment, the third
mortgagee, without notice to the first and second mortgagees, obtained an
order appointing a receiver of the rents and profits of the mortgaged premises.

Held, that the first and second mortgagees were entitled to intervene in the action
brought by the third mortgagee and to obtain an order directing the receiver of
the rents and profits to apply the money collected by him in the manner stipulated in the assignment of the rents;

That, assuming that the attorney for the third mortgagee had no authority to
make a binding arrangement as to the application of the rents collected, he had
actual knowledge that the first and second mortgagees were taking steps to
secure their rights in connection with the rents, and that such knowledge was
imputable to the third mortgagee;

That, under such circumstances, the third mortgagee could not defeat the superior rights of the first and second mortgagees in the rents, by procuring the
appointment of a receiver, without notice to them.

VAN BRUNT, P. J., dissented.

APPEAL by the plaintiff, Bradley & Currier Co., from the following portions of an order of the Supreme Court, made at the New
York Special Term, bearing date the 7th day of January, 1902, and
entered in the office of the clerk of the county of New York:

" *Ordered* and determined that all and singular the allegations in
the petition are true and that the assignment of rents annexed to
the petition and moving papers was and is valid and in full force and
effect, and that the receivership of said receiver was and is in aid
thereof ; and it is further

" *Ordered* that the motion and petition of the petitioners herein
be and the same hereby is granted; and it is further   *   *   *

" *Ordered* that any moneys which may have come into the possession of the plaintiff, Bradley & Currier Company, under or in
pursuance of the assignment of rents above mentioned, shall be by
it paid to said receiver to be by him applied as in said assignment
provided, and that James R. Cherry, Esq., as such receiver, shall,
and he is hereby directed to pay and apply all moneys now in his
hands as such receiver, and all moneys which shall upon his final
accounting be determined to be in his hands as such receiver for
payment and distribution, in the following manner and in the following order to the extent of said moneys:

" 1st : In payment of the running expenses of said property including necessary repairs.

" 2nd : In payment of taxes now existing against and a lien upon said property.

" 3rd : In payment of the interest and principal now due upon the mortgage held by Dudley S. Harde, one of the petitioners herein upon said property, dated June 28th, 1900, and recorded July 2, 1900, in Section 7, Liber 116 of Mortgages, page 213.

" 4th : In payment of the deficiency resulting from the sale of said premises under foreclosure in the action of Globe Realty Company, plaintiff, against Gregor George Hofmann and others, defendants, for the foreclosure of the mortgage in said action foreclosed."

Austin E. Pressinger, for the appellant.

Nathan Ottinger, for the respondents.

HATCH, J. :

This action was brought to foreclose a mortgage upon certain premises situate on Eighth avenue in the city of New York. The mortgage sought to be foreclosed was subject to the lien of two prior mortgages, one held by the Globe Realty Company, and the other by Dudley S. Harde, the latter being president of such company. Neither the company nor Harde were made parties defendant in the action to foreclose the plaintiff's mortgage. During the pendency of plaintiff's action, some negotiations were had between the attorney for the plaintiff and Harde, respecting the appointment of a receiver for the collection of the rents and profits of the property, and it was agreed between them that Harde should procure from the mortgagor an assignment of the rents to the plaintiff to be by it applied to the payment of running expenses, necessary repairs and taxes upon the property ; the residue to be applied upon the principal and interest and upon the mortgage held by Harde; and it is claimed by the respondents that said assignment was never revoked by Hofmann and is still outstanding and operative. Upon this subject there is serious dispute between the parties, the plaintiff contending that it never made such arrangement with Harde, and that while the assignment of the rents was executed and delivered by Hofmann, yet he immediately nullified the same by refusing to admit the person sent to collect the rents to the premises, and thereby the plaintiff was unable to collect any rents thereunder. Upon this subject, however, it was quite competent for the court to find, as it did, that the respondents' version was correct.

The assignment of the rents by Hofmann was executed February 28, 1901. On March first following, plaintiff applied for and obtained an order appointing a receiver of the rents and profits of the premises. Of this application the respondents had no notice, and they were not aware that it would be made, they relying upon the arrangement under which Hofmann executed the assignment. About April 24, 1901, the Globe Realty Company commenced a foreclosure of its mortgage, making the plaintiff a party defendant therein, but omitting as a defendant Dudley S. Harde, the holder of the other mortgage. This action proceeded to judgment of foreclosure, and upon a sale the property produced the sum of $11,000, leaving a deficiency of about $3,500 due upon the judgment of foreclosure. The effect of this judgment was to cut off the rights of the plaintiff and to leave intact as a lien upon the premises the Harde mortgage. On December 6, 1901, Harde and the Globe Realty Company applied by petition to the Supreme Court for leave to intervene in plaintiff's action, and asked for an order requiring the receiver to apply the money in his hands as was directed in the assignment of the rents made by Hofmann, the mortgagor. The petition set up in substance the above facts, among others, and supported the same by affidavits, and upon the hearing additional affidavits were read in rebuttal of the opposing papers. This application resulted in an order determining that the facts stated in the petition were true; that the motion be granted; that the defendants have leave to intervene as parties, and that the moneys in the hands of the receiver be applied as directed in the assignment by Hofmann.

The appellant appeals from all this order except that part which allowed the petitioner to intervene and have notice of the accounting and disposition of the money under the receivership. It is claimed that this order should be reversed for the reason that the plaintiff has by diligence on its part procured the appointment of a receiver of the rents and profits of the property prior to any action having been taken by the Globe Realty Company or Harde, and that thereby the plaintiff becomes entitled to receive the benefits of its diligent action, and that the money collected by the receiver should be paid to it.

If it be assumed that such claim is sustained by the facts, there would be much force in the contention. The law protects a party when by superior diligence he acquires a specific lien upon the rents, which are superior to any equities of the first mortgagee, and under such circumstances he is entitled to retain them and to apply the same upon his mortgage. (*Ranney* v. *Peyser*, 83 N. Y. 1; *Washington Life Ins. Co.* v. *Fleischauer*, 10 Hun, 117.) The facts, however, as found by the court show that the receivership was obtained without any notice to the petitioners, after they had arranged for securing the rents and profits of the premises and for making particular application thereof in a manner assented to by the plaintiff's attorney. It is undisputed that there was a negotiation between these parties about procuring an assignment of the rents from Hofmann and making disposition of the same without the interposition of a receiver. It may be assumed that the plaintiff's attorney could not make a binding agreement as to a particular disposition of the rents and profits in the absence of an assent thereto by the client whom he represented; and if we assume that the attorney had no authority to make a binding arrangement as to the application of the rents collected, it, nevertheless, follows that the attorney had actual notice of the fact that the petitioners were taking steps to secure their rights in connection with the rents derived from the property. The attorney's knowledge upon this subject was the knowledge of the plaintiff; and, having taken the assignment of Hofmann, he could not, without some notice to the petitioners, acquire rights which would defeat their equities. The liens of the petitioners were superior to the lien of the plaintiff, and all things being equal, they possessed superior equities, and could not lose the same, so far as all of the proceeds of the property were concerned, unless they lay idly by and permitted the plaintiff to acquire rights by diligent effort. (*Ross* v. *Vernam*, 6 App. Div. 246.) After notice to the attorney by Harde that he intended to assert the right of the company and himself in the application of these moneys upon the liens held by the company and himself, the plaintiff could not by diligence, in absence of any notice to him, acquire superior rights. The proofs tend to show that the petitioners supposed that the rents were being collected under the assignment, and as the application of the money when so collected would be for their benefit, the plaintiff could not defeat their right thereto by surreptitiously procuring the appointment of a receiver. The condition was such that the petitioners were lulled into the belief that they were secure, and of that fact the plaintiff's attorney had notice when the receivership was created. As the petitioners had the superior equity, this act could not result to defeat their rights in the premises. The plaintiff has not contested, or at least does not now contest, the right of the court to order the intervention of the petitioners in the action ; and as they acquired right in the rents by action upon their part, such right attaches to their superior equity and entitles them to insist upon the application of the moneys as provided in the assignment.

The present order confirms such right. It should, therefore, be affirmed, with ten dollars costs and disbursements.

INGRAHAM, McLAUGHLIN and LAUGHLIN, JJ., concurred ; VAN BRUNT, P. J., dissented.

Order affirmed, with ten dollars costs and disbursements.

––––––––

WILLIAM COVERLY and Others, Respondents, *v.* TERMINAL WARE-HOUSE COMPANY, Appellant.

Agreement to purchase the vendor's right in a New York city pier, for which both the vendor and vendee had made applications to the dock department — it is without consideration — an agreement not to bid at a city auction sale is against public policy — a pleading must cover the cause of action proved.

A written agreement, under seal, made between two parties who had filed applications with the dock department of the city of New York for a lease of the same pier, by the terms of which one of such parties assumed to sell to the other all his right, title and interest in and to such pier and all his claim upon the dock department of the city of New York in respect thereto and any lease thereof, in consideration of a certain sum of money, to be paid annually thereafter for a period of ten years, is not enforcible against the vendee, as the filing of the application with the department of docks did not vest in either of the parties any property right or interest in the pier which would furnish a consideration for the vendee's promise.

Where it appears that the dock department intended to dispose of the lease at public auction to the highest bidder, an oral agreement made between two applicants, by which one of them agreed that, if the other party would abandon his endeavor to secure the pier, the former party would pay to him any bonus which he might be obliged to pay in order to obtain another pier, is void as against public policy.

Semble, that in an action brought to recover upon the written agreement mentioned in the first paragraph, the plaintiffs would not be entitled to recover upon the oral agreement mentioned in the second paragraph.

APPEAL by the defendant, the Terminal Warehouse Company, from a judgment of the Supreme Court in favor of the plaintiffs, entered in the office of the clerk of the county of New York on the 19th day of June, 1901, upon the verdict of a jury, and also from an order entered in said clerk's office on the 15th day of July, 1901, denying the defendant's motion for a new trial made upon the minutes.

John M. Bowers, for the appellant.

Charles C. Burlingham, for the respondents.

HATCH, J. ·

This action was brought to recover upon an agreement under seal, made and executed between the parties hereto on the 30th day of January, 1891. By the terms of the agreement, the plaintiffs sold to the defendant all their right, title and interest in and to pier 57 (new), North river, and all their claim upon the dock department of the city of New York in respect to said pier and in respect to any lease thereof. The consideration for such sale was the sum of $25,000, payable in installments of $2,500 on the first day of May in each and every year for a period of ten years, until the whole sum should be paid. After the making and execution of the agreement the defendant made payments thereunder in accordance with its terms for a period of four years, when it made default and refused to make further payments thereunder. This action was commenced in October, 1897, to recover for the sums falling due for the years 1895, 1896 and 1897.

The averments of the complaint show that the action is based exclusively upon the written agreement, and no suggestion is made therein of the right to recover upon any other ground. Issue was joined by the service of an answer setting up the defense that there was no consideration for the agreement sued upon and that the plaintiffs had no right, title or interest in pier 57 or any claim thereto; that about the time of the execution of the agreement, the city of New York, under the supervision and direction of the department of docks, was about to lease said pier at public auction, when the plaintiffs, for the purpose of extorting money from the defendant, threatened to attend upon said sale and bid upon the property a sum far in excess of its leasehold value, and that the defendant, believing that the plaintiffs would carry out their threats and force the bidding for said pier very much in excess of the real market value thereof, made and executed the agreement in question, and, based upon the facts stated in the answer, the defendant claims that said contract tended to stifle competition at such auction sale, and is, therefore, void as against public policy.

Upon the trial the plaintiffs proved the making and execution of the agreement in question, the default in payment thereunder and the amount due, together with interest due thereon at the commencement of the action, and rested their case. It is clear, therefore, that both by the complaint and the proof upon the trial the plaintiffs stood squarely upon their right to recover upon the terms of the written agreement.

When the plaintiffs had rested, the defendant called as a witness the plaintiff Coverly, who testified in substance that the plaintiffs were the agents of the Anchor line of steamers and of other lines, and, desiring further wharf accommodations for their business, they made application to the dock department of the city of New York about January, 1889, for a lease of pier 57 mentioned in the agreement; that subsequent thereto, Mr. Rossiter, the president of the defendant, made application to the dock department for a lease of the same pier and was informed that the plaintiffs had already applied for a lease and were entitled to consideration. Thereupon, and about two years after the plaintiffs' application had been filed with the dock department, Rossiter applied to the witness Coverly to release the plaintiffs' right in and to the pier and to seek accommodations elsewhere. After considerable negotiation, the plaintiffs undertook to make an effort to secure other accommodations, the defendant agreeing to pay therefor whatever bonus the plaintiffs were compelled to pay in order to enable them to secure a pier and leave the defendant to obtain pier 57. Pursuant to such arrangement, the plaintiffs did succeed in obtaining pier 54 upon a payment therefor of a $30,000 bonus. While these negotiations were pending, and on the 30th day of December, 1890, the dock department of the city of New York adopted a resolution to lease pier 57 for a term of ten years, with privilege of additional renewal for a further term of ten years, at public auction in the board room on Friday, January 30, 1891, at twelve o'clock noon ; and pursuant to the negotiation, and just prior to the sale, the parties entered into the agreement the subject of this action.

By the provisions of section 716 of the Consolidation Act (Laws of 1882, chap. 410), which was in force at the time these negotiations were had, the dock department was not authorized to make a lease by private contract, except in districts where wharves and piers were appropriated by the department to special commercial interests. All other leases were required to be made at public auction to the highest bidder. The general power in the department to make leases is contained in section 711 of the Consolidation Act. In making disposition of this case, we assume that the department of docks could make a lease of this pier by private contract, but they were also invested with power to make such lease at public auction. There is nothing contained in the provisions of the act which vested any right in or to the pier in question upon making application to the board for a lease. Such application could be made by any person or corporation at any time prior to the making of a lease by the department. No property right could be obtained thereunder until a contract was made binding upon the parties thereto. It is evident, therefore, that the application which the plaintiffs made for a lease of this pier did not vest them with any legal or equitable right therein. Any person had the right, whether he had filed application for a lease of the pier with the dock department or not, to appear and bid at the auction sale, if such sale was determined upon by the department, and was entitled to receive a lease if he bid the highest price therefor offered at the sale, and which the city was willing to accept. The purpose of such a sale is to secure the highest price to the city which interest, under free and open competition, would be willing to give. Every engagement or negotiation which in any manner or form tended to stifle freedom of exercise in this regard was void as against public policy. When, therefore, Rossiter made application for this pier, he stood upon an equal footing with the plaintiffs, and was possessed of the same legal and equitable right in the premises, and neither of the parties could acquire property right or equitable interest therein save as it was fairly acquired by highest bidding at the auction sale. It follows as an inevitable result that there was no consideration for the agreement in question, as the plaintiffs never acquired, by anything which they did, any property right or other interest which could by any possibility furnish consideration for a sale of the pier or interest therein. The plaintiffs, therefore, failed utterly to prove any cause of action, and a verdict should have been directed in favor of the defendant upon the motion made therefor at the close of the trial.

It is said, however, that although the plaintiffs failed to prove the cause of action averred in the complaint, they did prove a good consideration based upon the agreement to pay the bonus which they were required to pay to obtain pier 54. Such agreement, as we view the testimony, was quite independent of the agreement set out in the complaint and proved by the plaintiffs upon the trial as their cause of action, and was so far a departure therefrom as, if effect be given to it, to authorize a recovery upon a cause of action not alleged — which of itself would be fatal to this recovery, if there were no other infirmity. The court, however, seems to have concluded that the plaintiffs were authorized to recover upon the oral agreement which the defendant had developed in the course of its examination of the witness Coverly, as he submitted such question to the jury, charging that there might be a recovery unless the agreement itself tended to stifle competition at the auction sale. Upon such question the jury found in favor of the plaintiffs. The question, therefore, which confronts us, assuming that the plaintiffs may avail themselves of it, is whether upon the evidence the court was justified in submitting such question to the jury.

The court seems to have adopted as the law applicable to the facts the rule as established by the case of *Marie* v. *Garrison* (83 N. Y. 14). That was an action brought to enforce an agreement made upon the foreclosure of a railroad mortgage. The complaint, among other things, averred that the plaintiffs and another person agreed to relinquish their opposition to the mortgage sale, they being stockholders, in consideration of the defendants and others being permitted to bid in the road at the foreclosure sale and issuing to the plaintiffs and others, upon a reorganization of the same, stock in the new company in an amount equivalent to their holdings in the old company. The action sought to enforce a delivery of the stock which the defendant Garrison had refused. The defendants demurred upon the ground of alleged illegality of the contract, as stifling fair competition in bidding at the sale. Upon this subject the court says : "The plaintiffs, who together owned a large number of shares, had a right to enter into any arrangement for the protection of their interests not prohibited by law. This was not the case of a combination between persons having no prior interest in the property to suppress bidding at a judicial sale for speculative purposes. The arrangement made was, so far as appears, a reasonable and honest attempt on the part of the plaintiffs to save their property from being sacrificed on the foreclosure. The other stockholders and bondholders were at liberty to bid on the sale. The mere fact that an arrangement fairly entered into with honest motives for the preservation of existing rights and property may incidentally restrict competition at a public or judicial sale, does not, we think, render the arrangement illegal. The question of intent, at all events, is one for the jury upon the whole facts as they shall appear on the trial." Many other cases, both before and since this decision, have enforced the rule there laid down.

It is evident that, aside from the testimony bearing upon the agreement to prevent bidding, there is a radical distinction between that case and this, and to such distinction was attached great if not controlling weight. There, the parties were all interested in the property and had a specific property right therein. On account of the magnitude of the interests involved no person could bid and protect interests unless possessed of very large means. The agreement itself sought to preserve the property for the benefit of all persons interested therein, and if faithfully carried out would inure to the benefit of every person in interest. In the present case the parties were without the slightest interest in the property ; each desired to obtain it for his respective purposes, and each was desirous of getting it as cheaply as possible ; while the sale was had for the purpose of obtaining the highest price for the benefit of the public

FIRST DEPARTMENT, MARCH TERM, 1902.   [Vol. 70.

Under such circumstances there can be no lawful right, either directly or indirectly, to prevent fair public competition. In the language of Judge FOLGER in respect to such sales: "The rule is, that agreements which in their necessary operation upon the action of the parties to them tend to restrain their natural rivalry and competition and thus to result in the disadvantage of the public or of third parties are against the principles of sound public policy and are void." (*Atcheson* v. *Mallon*, 43 N. Y. 147.) "In all cases where contracts are claimed to be void as against public policy," says Judge EARL, "it matters not that any particular contract is free from any taint of actual fraud, oppression or corruption. The laws look to the general tendency of such contracts. The vice is in the very nature of the contract, and it is condemned as belonging to a class which the law will not tolerate." (*Richardson* v. *Crandall*, 48 N. Y. 348.) "The general rules, condemning as unlawful combinations to prevent bidding at auction sales, have with good reason been applied to offers to the government of services or property in response to a call for proposals with a view to contract with the lowest bidder," says Judge ALLEN, "that is, when the bidding is after what *Gulick* v. *Ward, infra,** called a 'Dutch auction,' a bidding downwards." (*People* v. *Stephens*, 71 N. Y. 527.) And the rule is equally applicable where the auction sale is held to obtain an upset bid. (*Marsh* v. *Russell*, 66 N. Y. 288, 293.)

In respect of this matter, Mr. Coverly states that Rossiter asked him "if we could not retire from our pursuit of this pier," and that he talked with him about the sale upon the thirtieth of January, the day on which it was sold, and further he said, "We had made outlay in connection with pier 57. It was the bonus we paid for pier 54. That had this to do with our obtaining a lease of pier 57, because they wished us to get out of the way so that they could have that pier; they said they must have it." The attention of this witness was called to a conversation respecting his firm being a possible bidder at the auction sale of this pier had with Mr. Rossiter. "Q. Do you mean to say you have no recollection of any such conversation, or do you mean to say that none such occurred? A. Well, it might come up in a way; I do not know;

---

* *Gulick* v. *Bailey* (10 N. J. Law, 87).—[REP.

I cannot recollect exactly. Q. What do you mean by that statement? A. Well, that Mr. Rossiter might say, now we do not want you to come and bid against us at that sale. Q. He might, I know, but did he? A. Well, that was the object of his trying to get us to get accommodation elsewhere. Q. That was it? A. Yes." The witness denied that there was any purpose to extort money from the defendant, and that the claim was without foundation; and it is fair to the witness to say that such was never within the contemplation of either party to the contract, and that the fact that the plaintiffs paid $30,000 as a bonus to enable the defendant to obtain this pier is nowhere disputed, nor is the statement in any wise impugned. There was considerable examination of the witness upon the subject of the conversation with respect to plaintiffs' refraining from bidding at the sale, and many questions and answers were asked and given, but the statement which we have quoted was in no substantial respect denied or qualified, and it is clearly evident that it was the intention of the defendant, acquiesced in at least by the plaintiffs, that the execution of the agreement and the payment of the bonus would result in the plaintiffs' failing to become bidders at the sale. The execution of the agreement itself upon the day before the sale, coupled with the testimony of the plaintiff Coverly, is proof conclusive that its necessary tendency was to restrain the natural rivalry and competition of these parties in bidding at the auction sale, and it resulted in disadvantage to the public. Upon the undisputed proof, therefore, we think that neither the agreement to pay the bonus paid for pier 54, nor the agreement executed between the parties, can be enforced, and that the same are void as being against public policy and, therefore, condemned by the law. If we are right in these views, the court was not authorized to submit any question to the jury. This conclusion renders unnecessary a discussion of the questions raised respecting such submission.

It follows that the judgment and order should be reversed and a new trial granted, with costs to appellant to abide the event.

VAN BRUNT, P. J., INGRAHAM and LAUGHLIN, JJ., concurred; PATTERSON, J., concurred in result.

Judgment and order reversed, new trial ordered, costs to appellant to abide event.

90
2 5
NY 550

REGINA GROSSMAYER, Respondent, *v.* DISTRICT No. 1, INDEPENDENT ORDER OF BENAI BERITH, Appellant.

By-law of a mutual benefit association — when an amendment thereof need not be complied with by a member.

The constitution and by-laws of a mutual benefit association provided that, on the death of a member, the endowment should be paid to his widow, children, father and mother, in the order named, and if he left surviving him none of such relatives, to such beneficiaries as he might direct; that if he left neither wife, child nor parents, and failed to designate other persons as his beneficiaries the endowment should fail. Thereafter, pursuant to a provision thereof authorizing it, the constitution and by-laws were amended so as to provide that the endowment should be paid to the member's widow and children, in the order named, and that a member having neither wife nor child must designate in writing in a book provided for that purpose the person to whom the benefit should be paid, and that, in the event of the member's failure to make such designation, the endowment should not be paid.

Held, that the amendment was not applicable to a member who, prior to its enactment, became insane and after its enactment died without recovering his sanity and without having designated his beneficiaries, leaving surviving him a mother, but neither wife nor children;

That, as the deceased member's disability was created by an act of God, and as the act required to be performed could not be performed for him by any other person, his failure to make the designation which the by-laws required did not work a forfeiture.

Semble, that an amendment to a by-law must furnish the person upon whom it is to operate with an opportunity to comply therewith, and if, by the intervention of the *vis major,* or other equivalent condition, such opportunity is not given, the party will usually be held excused and no forfeiture will result.

VAN BRUNT, P. J., dissented.

APPEAL by the defendant, District No. 1, Independent Order of Benai Berith, from a judgment of the Supreme Court in favor of the plaintiff, entered in the office of the clerk of the county of New York on the 22d day of April, 1901, upon the verdict of a jury rendered by direction of the court, and also from an order entered in said clerk's office on the 8th day of May, 1901, denying the defendant's motion for a new trial made upon the minutes.

Julius J. Frank, for the appellant.

Morris J. Hirsch, for the respondent.

HATCH, J. :

This action was brought to recover the sum of $1,000 from the defendant, a domestic corporation, alleged to be due the plaintiff from and out of an endowment fund established by the defendant under its constitution and by-laws. The defendant is an order organized for benevolent and philanthropic purposes, and among other provisions it established an endowment fund for the benefit of widows, orphans and parents of the members. The son of the plaintiff, Emanuel Grossmayer, became a member of the defendant order in January, 1891, obligating himself thereby to observe the constitution, laws and rules of the order. At the time said Grossmayer became a member, the constitution and by-laws provided that out of this endowment fund the sum of $1,000 should be paid on the member's death, *first*, to his widow ; *second*, to his children, if he leave no widow ; *third*, to his father, if he leave neither widow nor child ; *fourth*, to his mother, if he leave neither widow, child nor father, and *fifth*, such beneficiaries as the member might direct, provided he left surviving none of the relatives designated in the 4th provision. The constitution and by-laws further provided that in case the member left neither wife, child nor parents, and failed or neglected to make any designation as to his beneficiaries, the endowment should fail and go into the endowment fund of the district. Provision was made for amending the constitution and by-laws, and in January, 1896, an amendment was duly made of the laws pertaining thereto and the provisions as to the endowment going to the parents in case of the failure of widow or child to survive the deceased member was stricken out. The amendments to the by-laws provide as follows : " Sec. 5. Upon the decease of a participant in this fund there shall be paid the amount secured by him respectively : *First*, to his widow ; *second*, to his children, if there be no widow ; but the brother may, by a designation in the book provided for that purpose, declare that the Endowment, or a part thereof, shall be paid to such beneficiary or beneficiaries as he may designate, to the exclusion of his children, provided he leaves no widow. In such case a designation to the executors or administrators of the brother is a valid and sufficient designation."

" Sec. 9. A member having neither wife nor child must designate in writing in such book, in the manner hereinbefore provided, to whom the sum secured shall be paid. In the event of a failure of a member to make such designation such sum shall not be paid."

In March, 1892, the plaintiff's son was admitted to Bloomingdale asylum as an insane patient, and from that time until his death in September, 1896, he was incapacitated from performing any act requiring mental operation. His dues to the order, however, were regularly paid, and at the time of his death the deceased was a member in good standing. Deceased did not, however, make the designation in the book as provided by the amended by-laws. He died leaving neither wife nor children, but leaving his mother, the plaintiff in the action, who claims to be entitled to receive the fund. It is the well-settled general rule, applicable to these organizations, that the certificate of membership and its conditions, together with the constitution and by-laws of the order, furnish the contract by which the rights of the members to participate in the benefits are to be determined. (*Bird* v. *Mut. Union Assn.*, 30 App. Div. 346.) Where the constitution makes provision for a change in it and its by-laws by the action of the society, such right to change forms a part of the contract and the members are bound by such changes as are regularly made. The only limitation upon the power seems to be that the by-laws must be reasonable in their terms and operation, and consistent with the provisions of the constitution. (*Parish* v. *N. Y. Produce Ex.*, 169 N. Y. 34.) So far as the amendments to the by-laws in this case are concerned, they are undoubtedly reasonable in character, consistent with the provisions of the constitution, and, therefore, such as the organization had the right to make. Not only must the change be reasonable, however, but the operation of the law must also give fair opportunity for a compliance with its provisions. A by-law, however reasonable in form, would necessarily be unreasonable in its operation, if the members were not given fair opportunity to make compliance with it. The condition always is that the person upon whom the by-law is to operate must be able to and have opportunities for making compliance with its terms, and if by the intervention of the *vis major*, or other equivalent condition such opportunity is not given, the party will usually be held excused and no forfeiture will be worked. (*Wheeler* v. *Conn. Mut. Life Ins. Co.*, 82 N. Y. 543.) In this case it was held that insanity did not excuse the payment of premiums upon a policy of life insurance for the reason that such act could be performed by another for the insane person, with the same force and effect as though performed by him, but it also recognizes that if the contract be of such a character that performance can only be made by the person laboring under the disability, then such condition will excuse non-performance. and no forfeiture will be worked thereby. In *Cohen* v. *N. Y. Mut. Life Ins. Co.* (50 N. Y. 610) it was said : "There is a manifest distinction between mere impediments and difficulties in the way of the performance of a condition and an impossibility created by law or the act of the government. This is clearly recognized in *Wood* v. *Edwards* (19 J. R. 205); *People* v. *Bartlett* (3 Hill, 570). An individual by his covenant may undertake, as against his own acts, and the acts of strangers, but not against the acts of God, or his government or of the obligee. * * * In *Wolfe* v. *Howes* (20 N. Y. 197) the performance of the undertaking became impossible by the act of God in the death of the party, and performance was held excused upon the ground that the parties must be deemed to have made this an exception by implication." In the present case the deceased was and had been for a long time prior to the adoption of the amendments to these by-laws utterly incapacitated from performing any intelligent act. It was, therefore, impossible for him to make compliance with the by-law, and such condition was created by the act of God. The act which the deceased was required to perform could not be so performed by any other person. The by-law required that it should be his act in making designation of the person to whom the endowment fund should be paid. True, a designation might be made of some person by another acting for the deceased, but such designation would not be his act nor could it be said that the designation so made would be of the person selected by the deceased had he the mental capacity to make it. It is, therefore, clear that the disability was of such a character as rendered compliance with the amended by-law by the deceased absolutely impossible, and the act required to be performed could not be performed for him by any other person. So far as the payment of premiums is concerned, that was an act which could be and was performed for the deceased by another, and the defendant had the benefit of all the payments. Under these circumstances, we are of the opinion that the deceased must be held to have been exempted from performance, and such exemption is to be implied from the conditions. To hold otherwise would be to say that the organization could make its by-laws operate unreasonably. If death had intervened before opportunity for compliance therewith had been given, clearly no forfeiture could be worked. We see no difference in principle between an act of God resulting in death, and an act of the same power working a mental death as absolute in bar of performance as though physical death had supervened. We are of opinion, therefore, that the doctrine of the cases we have cited is controlling of this question, and that no forfeiture of the rights of the plaintiff was worked by the failure of the deceased to make the designation which the by-law required. Nothing that is contained in *Hellenberg* v. *District No. 1 of I. O. of B. B.* (94 N. Y. 580) conflicts with this view. The insanity in that case did not supervene until after abundant opportunity had been given to make compliance with the by-law the subject of consideration in that case. Here the disability existed prior to the change, and was continuous during the lifetime of the deceased. Under such circumstances we think that it would be an unreasonable application of this law to hold that its provisions were applicable to the deceased. If these views are sound, it follows that the judgment and order should be affirmed, with costs.

O'BRIEN, INGRAHAM and McLAUGHLIN, JJ., concurred ; VAN BRUNT, P. J., dissented.

VAN BRUNT, P. J. (dissenting):

I dissent. I do not think that a corporation can make its by-laws operative as to some members and not as to others of the same class. The reasonableness of a by-law is not to be judged by the fact that one member is so sitrated that he cannot comply with it.

Judgment and order affirmed, with costs.

Mitchell A. C. Levy, Plaintiff, *v.* George H. B. Hill, Defendant.   70
a174

Marketable title — the projection of a stoop beyond the building line in a street.

The fact that the stoop of a house projects beyond the building line into the street, does not constitute a defect in the title to the premises upon which the house stands, where it appears that the stoop has occupied such position for upwards of thirty years without objection on the part of the municipality or of adjoining property owners or any other person.

In such a case, the contingency that the removal of the stoop will ever be compelled by the municipality or by any person having authority in the premises, is so remote as not to be within reasonable contemplation.

Van Brunt, P. J., dissented.

Motion by the defendant, George H. B. Hill, for a new trial upon a case containing exceptions to the direction of a verdict in favor of the plaintiff, after a trial at the New York Trial Term, ordered to be heard at the Appellate Division in the first instance.

J. Langdon Ward, for the motion.

John Frankenheimer, opposed.

Hatch, J. :

This is the second appearance of the matters in controversy between these parties in this court. The questions in difference arise out of a contract for the sale of real property situate on the northerly side of Thirty-fourth street, between Fifth and Sixth avenues, in the city of New York. After the making and execution of the contract the defendant tendered, pursuant to its terms, a deed of the premises and demanded payment of the purchase price. The plaintiff refused to accept such deed, claiming that the title tendered was defective in that said premises were incumbered by a certain party-wall agreement, and that the stoop of said house extended beyond the street or building line for a distance of fifteen feet and eight inches ; that such projection was unlawful and constituted the same an obstruction in the public street. At the time of the execution and delivery of the contract of sale the plaintiff paid as part of the purchase price the sum of $1,500. This action is brought to recover back such sum, together with the sum of $240, costs and expenses of searching the title.

The first action was brought by the plaintiff for the specific performance of the contract, and judgment was asked that a just deduction be made from the purchase money on account of the defects in the title and on account of the incumbrance and encroachments hereinabove mentioned and, after making such deduction and upon payment of the residue of the purchase money according to the terms of the agreement, that the defendant specifically perform the same. The court held that such action could not be maintained ; that it was not in fact an action for specific performance of the contract in accordance with its terms, but was an equitable action by which it was sought to have the depreciation in the value of the property fixed by reason of the claimed defects in the title, and when such sum was arrived at to deduct it from the purchase price and compel a conveyance upon payment of the residue; that such action could not be maintained, as the court was powerless to grant any such relief; and upon that ground alone a judgment was affirmed which dismissed the complaint. (*Levy* v. *Hill*, 50 App. Div. 294.) The court was unanimous in holding that the claimed defect in the title arising out of the party-wall agreement was frivolous and was not a defect or incumbrance upon the title. A majority of the court further held that the plaintiff obtained by virtue of his contract all of the land, properties and rights which he contracted to purchase, and that the projection of the stoop beyond the building line did not create a defect in the title. It is undoubtedly true that the ground upon which the complaint in that action was dismissed did not involve a determination of the specific questions which the plaintiff claimed constituted defects in the title. The discussion, however, assumed to settle all of the questions involved, and expressed the views of a majority of the judges participating in the decision.

Upon a dismissal of the complaint in that action the plaintiff brought this action. It is clear that if the views of the court in the former decision are to be regarded as controlling, it is conclusive upon the right of the plaintiff to recover in this action. Conceding that the views therein expressed were obiter, and not necessarily controlling, yet the law of the case seems to be settled in accordance with such views by authoritative decision. (*Broadbelt* v. *Loew*, 15 App. Div. 343 ; affd. on opinion below, 162 N. Y. 642.) Therein Mr. Justice PATTERSON, writing for the court, held that the projection of a stoop beyond the line of a city street is not necessarily unlawful, and that the question as to whether it is can only arise between the municipal authorities and the owner of the building, and that such encroachment does not constitute a defect in the title. The stoop in the present case has occupied its present position for thirty years and upwards without objection on the part of the municipality or of adjoining property owners or any other persons. The contingency that its removal will ever be compelled by the municipality or any person having authority in the premises is so remote as not to be within reasonable contemplation. These decisions are authoritative of the questions presented and result in the conclusion that plaintiff is not entitled to recover the sums sought to be recovered in this action.

It follows that the exceptions should be sustained and the motion for a new trial granted, with costs to the defendant to abide the event.

O'BRIEN, MCLAUGHLIN and LAUGHLIN, JJ., concurred; VAN BRUNT, P. J., dissented.

Exceptions sustained and new trial granted, with costs to defendant to abide event.

HERMAN F. KANENBLEY and Others, as Executors, etc., of AUGUST KANENBLEY, Deceased, Plaintiffs, *v.* ALBERT VOLKENBERG and FRANCES VOLKENBERG, Defendants.

Deed to parties " trustees of the separate estate of Margaretta Persse " — the words quoted are descriptive — a deed signed by the grantees as individuals conveys a good title — presumption as to the execution of an express trust.

At the beginning of a conveyance of certain premises following the names of the grantees were the words " *trustees of the separate estate of Margaretta Persse, wife of Dudley Persse.*" Nothing else in the deed indicated the existence of a trust or an intention to limit the estate conveyed to the grantees, and there was no extrinsic evidence of the existence of such a trust. Thereafter the trustees mentioned in said deed and Margaretta Persse conveyed the premises to one O'Gorman for a nominal consideration of one dollar. No other consideration appeared. The trustees signed this deed as individuals and were not described therein as trustees.

Held, that the words "*trustees of the separate estate of Margaretta Persse, wife of Dudley Persse*," contained in the first-mentioned deed, were to be regarded as descriptive merely, and that the persons so described acquired thereunder an estate in fee as individuals;

That, consequently, the deed executed by them for a nominal consideration operated to convey a marketable title which a subsequent purchaser of the premises would be required to accept.

Semble, that if an express trust might be presumed to have been created it would also be presumed that the deed was executed in pursuance of its terms and not in violation thereof.

VAN BRUNT, P. J., dissented on the ground that the submission upon which the question was presented was irregular in form.

SUBMISSION of a controversy upon an agreed statement of facts, pursuant to section 1279 of the Code of Civil Procedure.

George H. Hyde, for the plaintiffs.

Augustus S. Hutchins, for the defendants.

HATCH, J.:

The plaintiffs by this submission seek to procure a judgment compelling the specific performance by the defendants of a contract of sale entered into between the plaintiffs and defendants of certain premises on East Seventeenth street in the city of New York. At the time and place agreed upon in said contract the plaintiffs tendered a deed of the said premises which the defendants refused to accept, claiming that the same did not convey a marketable title. The specific defect is claimed to exist in a certain deed by and through which one Richard O'Gorman became vested with title to the premises.

On June 2, 1856, the fee of the premises in question was vested in Peter Stuyvesant and Benjamin R. Winthrop, as trustees of the separate estate of Julia R. Stuyvesant, wife of Peter Stuyvesant, and upon the above-mentioned day Stuyvesant and Winthrop, as said trustees, together with Stuyvesant and Julia his wife, in their own right, conveyed the premises to Theophilus B. Persse and Robert Gillen, "*trustees of the separate estate of Margaretta Persse, wife of Dudley Persse.*" On February 29, 1860, said trustees and said Margaretta Persse joined in a conveyance of the premises to Richard O'Gorman, the consideration expressed therein being the sum of one dollar; no information of any other or further consideration can be discovered. The signature of the trustees to this deed is as individuals, and they are not described as trustees. On June 19, 1861, for a consideration of ten dollars, O'Gorman and wife conveyed the premises to the said Margaretta Persse, wife of Dudley Persse, which deed was acknowledged in April, 1864. On June 4, 1864, Theophilus B. Persse and wife quitclaimed these premises to Margaretta Persse for a consideration of ten dollars, and on May 1, 1868, Margaretta Persse, *widow* of Dudley Persse, for full and valuable consideration ($26,050), conveyed the said premises to the plaintiff's testator, August Kanenbley, who held the title to the same during his lifetime. The plaintiffs were duly appointed executors under said Kanenbley's will, which contained a good and sufficient power of sale.

It is claimed by the defendants that the deed from Stuyvesant and Winthrop, as trustees, to Persse and Gillen, trustees of the separate estate of Margaretta Persse, wife of Dudley Persse, shows the existence of a trust, undisclosed as to its terms, and as their subsequent deed to Richard O'Gorman was for a nominal consideration only, it must be presumed, in the absence of all other proof, that such conveyance was in violation of the terms of the trust, and, consequently, conveyed no title to the grantee therein. This claim is based upon the supposition that the words in the first deed, trustees of Margaretta Persse, are sufficient to show the existence of a trust, and that said trustees took only the bare, naked, legal title, in consequence of which they could only deal with the property founded upon a sufficient consideration and in accordance with the terms of the trust. It is stated that the most diligent search fails to disclose the existence of any trust estate created for the benefit of Margaretta Persse, and that the only thing which appears, out of which is raised the existence of the trust, is the language contained in the deed to Persse and Gillen, which we have quoted. It is noticeable that the recital is not to them as trustees of anything. The language in form is simply descriptive, and if it be so construed or is susceptible of such construction, then it would create no limitation upon the title in them, and they would take as individuals and an estate in fee. Of course, in order to reach this result all of the terms of the deed and the rules of law applicable thereto are to be considered. In modern construction of deeds it is the office of the premises of the deed rightly to name the grantor and grantee and to comprehend the certainty of the thing granted, and if the *habendum* clause may not be reconciled with the premises of the deed, so that full effect may be given both, the extent of the grant will be determined by the premises, and the *habendum* clause will be made to yield thereto. (*Clapp* v. *Byrnes*, 3 App. Div. 284; affd., 155 N. Y. 535.) It is clear that the language contained in the premises of the deed is, in literal effect, merely descriptive and can easily be construed as such under well-settled authority. (*Towar* v. *Hale*, 46 Barb. 361; *Greenwood Lake & Port Jervis R. R. Co.* v. *N. Y. & G. L. R. R. Co.*, 134 N. Y. 435; *Pfeiffer* v. *Rheinfrank*, 2 App. Div. 574; *King* v. *Townshend*, 141 N. Y. 358.) The granting clause is "do grant, bargain, sell, alien, release, convey and confirm unto the said parties of the third part and to their successors and assigns, * * *." The *habendum* clause reads "to have and to hold the above mentioned and described premises hereby granted and conveyed, or intended so to be with the appurtenances unto the said parties of the third part, their successors and assigns, to their only * proper use and benefit and behoof forever." There is nothing in any of these words which limit their estate. The authority is to hold to their successors and assigns. There is no particular significance attaching to the word successors, in the absence of anything in the other part of the deed showing that a limited estate was granted, and the grant is to the assigns as well as the successors. The grantee in the deed from Persse and Gillen were the assigns of such party in strict legal signification, and under the authorities which we have cited, it is held that no peculiar signification attaches to the word successors in the absence of proof showing that a limited estate was granted. In the present case, taking all the language together, we think it clear that no trust was created and that the words trustees, etc., are to be regarded simply as descriptive, in the absence of all proof tending to show the existence of a trust estate. And giving force and effect to the terms in the deed which authorized a conveyance to their assigns, we have an absolute compliance with the estate as granted. It is significant also that in the deed by Persse and Gillen, they do not

* *Sic.*

assume to execute the same as trustees of anybody. Their act is that of individuals, and is a circumstance to be considered in interpretation of the deed under which they took the estate. As, therefore, there was no declaration of language used in the deed from Winthrop and Stuyvesant to them which created a trust, or which showed that they took as trustees, there was no defect in the chain of title and the plaintiff is entitled to a judgment of specific performance. There is some authority for holding that the court may, in the absence of all proof as to the terms of the trust, presume the existence of an express trust, valid as such in its creation, and thereby reach the conclusion that the trustee is vested with the whole estate, both in law and equity. (*People v. Stockbrokers' Bldg. Co.*, 49 Hun, 351 ; affd. by the Court of Appeals on opinion below, 112 N. Y. 670 ; and cited with approval in *Greenwood Lake & Port Jervis R. R. Co.* v. *N. Y. & G. L. R. R. Co., supra.*) If under such circumstances a valid trust may be presumed, we think there is no violence done in making the further presumption that the trustee, in making a grant of the trust property, complied with the terms of the trust, and if this rule should be adopted in this case, it would result in holding that there was no defect in the title, as the presumption would be that the deed was made pursuant to the terms of the trust and not in violation of it. We prefer, however, to rest our judgment upon the ground that the language of the deed did not create a trust estate in Persse and Gillen, but that they were vested with an absolute title in fee to the estate under the deed to them, and in consequence of which could convey good title. It follows that judgment should be awarded in favor of plaintiffs for the specific performance of the contract, with costs.

O'BRIEN, INGRAHAM and McLAUGHLIN, JJ., concurred; VAN BRUNT, P. J., dissented.

VAN BRUNT, P. J. (dissenting) :

I dissent. I do not think that the submission is in any form which justifies the court in considering the alleged controversy. Questions are submitted to the court and according as it answers them it is to give judgment. There is no warrant for any such form of procedure in the Code. The parties must submit the facts to the court, and the court renders such judgment as the facts warrant ;

and this right cannot be limited by any consent or agreement of the parties to the submission.   This was not done in the case at bar, and the submission is absolutely irregular.

Judgment ordered for plaintiffs for specific performance of the contract, with costs.

HENRY DUCHARDT, Individually and as Executor, etc., of HENRY DUCHARDT, Deceased, and Others, Plaintiffs, *v.* PATRICK M. CASSIDY, Defendant.

Will — when an estate in fee simple absolute is conveyed thereby.

A testator by his will, after devising certain specified real property in fee to each of his children with the exception of his daughter Charlotte, devised certain specified real property to Charlotte "to have the income and rents thereof during her natural life, at her death to be divided amongst all my remaining children, share and share alike."   The residuary clause provided as follows: " All my other real estate and personal property to be divided share and share alike between all my children."   After the residuary clause was the following: "I hereby appoint my son Henry Duchardt to act as trustee for my daughter Charlotte D. Duchardt, her houses to be rented and kept in repair, the money her share to be put in bank or bond and mortgage for her benefit while living." "The real and personal estate of which my daughter Charlotte D. Duchardt is possessed during her lifetime, at her death is to be divided equally between my heirs."

Held, that the testator's children acquired an estate in fee simple absolute in all the property which passed under the residuary clause, and that the clauses following the residuary clause related solely to the property in which Charlotte had a life estate.

VAN BRUNT, P. J., dissented on the ground that the submission upon which the question was presented was irregular in form.

SUBMISSION of a controversy upon an agreed statement of facts pursuant to section 1279 of the Code of Civil Procedure.

Herbert M. Johnston, for the plaintiffs.

George W. McAdam, for the defendant.

HATCH, J.:

The plaintiffs, in June, 1901, made and entered into a contract with the defendant for the sale of certain real estate, situate on the southerly side of One Hundred and Twenty-second street, between

Lexington and Third avenues, in the borough of Manhattan, at the agreed price of $5,850. The plaintiffs trace title to the premises through Henry Duchardt, who died May 14, 1900, leaving a last will and testament, dated December 30, 1897, which was duly admitted to probate. Henry Duchardt, by the terms of the will, was made executor of the same and duly qualified as such. Whether the plaintiffs have good title to said premises is dependent upon the construction of this will, and the point in question is whether that portion of the estate of the deceased, which is the subject of the contract of sale, was vested in the plaintiffs at the time of its execution. The will is short and its scheme seems to be plain. The testator was survived by four children, the plaintiffs in the action. To each one of the children, except Charlotte D. Duchardt, was devised certain specified real property in fee. The clause of the will containing the devise to Charlotte D. is in the following language: "To my daughter Charlotte D. Duchardt, the houses and lots No. 162 East 122d street, also 326 and 328 East 121st street, to have the income and rents thereof during her natural life, at her death to be divided amongst all my remaining children, share and share alike." The residuary clause reads as follows: "All my other real estate and personal property to be divided share and share alike between all my children." It is evident that an estate in fee was devised of all of the real property which passed by the residuary clause. There is no limitation contained in that clause upon the title to the property devised. Thereby all of the children took an immediate vested estate in severalty, in nowise cut down or qualified by any other provision of the will. It consequently follows that there was vested in these plaintiffs, immediately upon the death of the testator, an estate in fee of the property devised in the residuary clause, and they could convey good title thereto. All of the parties in interest have joined in the contract, and when this is followed by the delivery of a deed, properly executed, by the parties thereto, the defendant will have acquired an absolute estate in fee of the premises so conveyed.

It is claimed, however, that two clauses of the will subsequent to the residuary clause cut down and qualify the estate vested thereby in the plaintiffs. These clauses of the will read as follows: "I hereby appoint my son Henry Duchardt to act as trustee for my daughter Charlotte D. Duchardt, her houses to be rented and kept in repair, the money her share to be put in bank or bond and mortgage for her benefit while living." "The real and personal estate of which my daughter Charlotte D. Duchardt is possessed during her lifetime, at her death is to be divided equally between my heirs."

It is clearly evident that there is nothing contained in these clauses of the will which at all interferes with the vesting of an estate in fee of the real property under the residuary clause. A life estate had been given to Charlotte D. in three houses and lots, with devise over to the testator's other children, and it is evident that this is the real property to which reference is made in the last clause of the will, which we have quoted, as it was this property of which Charlotte had possession during her life. By the last quoted clause, the real property in which she was given a life estate, is at her death to be divided equally between the heirs of the testator. It is undoubtedly true that this devise vests an estate in the children living at the death of the testator, subject, however, to open and let in heirs coming into existence after the death of the testator and living at the death of Charlotte. Such construction, however, can have no effect either to qualify, cut down or limit the estate vested in these heirs by the residuary clause of the will, and as the real property therein devised is alone the subject of this controversy, as to it the plaintiffs have title in fee simple absolute, and are authorized to convey the same.

It follows that judgment should be awarded in favor of plaintiff for the specific performance of the contract, with costs.

O'BRIEN, INGRAHAM and LAUGHLIN, JJ., concurred; VAN BRUNT, P. J., dissented.

VAN BRUNT, P. J. (dissenting):

I dissent. I think that the submission is entirely irregular. The parties have attempted to limit the effect of the decision, for which there is not the slightest authority. The judgment to be entered is precisely the same as the judgment in an action and has the same effect, controlling the same parties.

Judgment ordered for plaintiff, with costs.

EDWARD R. LAZARUS, Appellant, *v.* RAY ROSENBERG and Others, Respondents.

Fraudulent conveyance — where an absolute deed is held to be a mortgage, a judgment creditor should be adjudged to have a lien upon the premises subject to the mortgage.

In an action brought by the plaintiff, a judgment creditor of the defendant Mrs. Rosenberg, to set aside as fraudulent and void a conveyance of real estate made by her to the defendant Harris, and subsequently conveyed by Harris to the defendant Mrs. Norton, it appeared that Mrs. Rosenberg, in order to secure Harris against liability as indorser upon a promissory note made by her, delivered to Harris a warranty deed of her interest in the estate left by her deceased father. Upon the maturity of the note Harris was obliged to pay the same, and thereafter Mrs. Rosenberg paid Harris a portion of her indebtedness to him. Subsequently, Harris conveyed the real estate to the defendant Mrs. Norton, upon the latter's agreement to pay the balance of his claim, which amounted to $1,100. The evidence tended to show that Harris transferred his claim against Mrs. Rosenberg to Mrs. Norton when he executed the conveyance. The court found that Harris received the deed in good faith as a security, and also that the defendant Norton succeeded to Harris' interest in the premises, and that the deed to Mrs. Norton was a lien upon the premises to the extent of $1,100. It, however, dismissed the complaint on account of the failure of the plaintiff to tender the amount of the lien before commencing the action.

Held, that this was error;

That the court should have awarded judgment as follows: *First.* Dismissing the complaint upon the merits as against the defendant Harris. *Second.* Adjudging and decreeing that the deed from the defendant Rosenberg to the defendant Harris was intended as security, and is a mortgage, and that the deed from the defendant Harris to the defendant Norton was intended as and is an assignment of the claim of Harris for $1,100 and interest and of said mortgage, and that the same be permitted to stand as security for the payment by the defendant Rosenberg to the defendant Norton of the sum of $1,100 and interest thereon. *Third.* Adjudging and decreeing that the plaintiff's judgment is a lien upon the premises described in the complaint and in said deeds, subject to the lien of the defendant Norton as aforesaid. *Fourth.* That neither party, as against the other, recover costs of the trial.

APPEAL by the plaintiff, Edward R. Lazarus, from a judgment of the Supreme Court in favor of the defendants, entered in the office of the clerk of the county of New York on the 13th day of August, 1901, upon the decision of the court, rendered after a trial at the New York Special Term, dismissing the complaint upon the merits.

Charles G. F. Wahle, for the appellant.

Benno Loewy, for the respondents.

LAUGHLIN, J.:

The plaintiff brings this action as a judgment creditor of the defendant Ray Rosenberg, to set aside as fraudulent and void a conveyance of real estate made by her to the defendant Harris and subsequently conveyed by him to the defendant Norton. On the 12th day of April, 1897, the defendant Rosenberg was and for a long time prior thereto had been engaged in business. Her father, Fink Solomon, and the defendant Harris, who was her uncle, had for many years been accommodation indorsers of her negotiable paper, Harris being the second indorser. On that day a $3,000 note made by her and indorsed by them became due. A note in renewal thereof was signed by her and indorsed by her father, who was then seriously ill, and the defendant Harris was also requested to sign as an indorser. This he declined to do on account of the illness of Solomon, without security. Thereupon, upon the urgent solicitation of Solomon and upon an agreement in writing by the defendant Rosenberg to deed to him, as security for such indorsement, her interest in her father's estate upon her coming into the inheritance, . Harris indorsed the note. On the twenty-eighth day of the same month, Solomon having died in the meantime, the defendant Rosenberg, in compliance with her agreement, executed and delivered to Harris a warranty deed of her interest in the real estate left by her father. The consideration recited in this deed was one dollar, but the true consideration, as already stated, was shown upon the trial.

The action in which the plaintiff obtained judgment against Rosenberg was upon three promissory notes given in renewal of other notes received in payment for goods sold and delivered. That action was commenced on the 11th day of March, 1898, and judgment was recovered on the ninth day of May, the same year. When the note which the defendant Harris last indorsed became due, he was obliged to pay the same. Subsequently the defendant Rosenberg transferred to him certain notes for the purpose of reimbursing him in this regard. He realized upon the sale of these notes the sum of $2,100, leaving the balance of her indebtedness to him on account of this indorsement and payment of the note, the sum of $1,100. The court has found that the deed from Rosenberg to

Harris was for the purpose of securing him on said indorsement, and was received by him in good faith. This finding is fairly sustained by the evidence.

The defendant Rosenberg filed objections to her father's will and was contesting its probate. In these circumstances the defendant Harris did not wish to hold the legal title to the premises, and manifested a desire to transfer the same to any person upon the payment of the balance owing to him. At the suggestion of the defendant Rosenberg or her husband he thereafter and on the 9th day of April, 1898, transferred the premises to the defendant Norton, who was the sister-in-law of Mrs. Rosenberg, by a warranty deed. The consideration recited in the deed is one dollar, but it was shown upon the trial that the real consideration was her agreeing to pay the balance of this indebtedness as security for which she gave two promissory notes, each for $550, one due in six months and the other in twelve months from the date of the transfer. The trial court found in effect that the defendant Norton succeeded to the interests of the defendant Harris in said premises and that the deed to her was a lien upon said premises to the extent of $1,100. The court, however, dismissed the complaint on account of the failure of the plaintiff to tender the amount of such lien before commencing this action.

In this we think the learned trial justice erred. The conveyance to Harris having been valid as security for his liability as indorser, he could transfer his title or interest ; and his grantee, regardless of any notice of knowledge or fraud on her part, could hold the conveyance to the extent of the consideration with which she parted, not exceeding the amount of her grantor's lien. (1 Perry Trusts [5th ed.], § 222; *Popfinger* v. *Yutte,* 102 N. Y. 38; *Cook* v. *Kraft,* 41 How. Pr. 279; *Meltzer* v. *Doll,* 91 N. Y. 365; *Hamilton National Bank* v. *Halsted,* 134 id. 520; *Loos* v. *Wilkinson,* 113 id. 485.) It does not appear that the note which Harris took up as indorser was formally transferred by him to Mrs. Norton, but his cause of action against Mrs. Rosenberg was not on the note but in *assumpsit* (*Griffith* v. *Reed,* 21 Wend. 502; *Wright* v. *Garlinghouse,* 26 N. Y. 539), and the fair inference from his evidence is that he parted with his claim against Mrs. Rosenberg and transferred the indebtedness with the security to Mrs. Norton, and no claim is made to the contrary. The

FIRST DEPARTMENT, MARCH TERM, 1902.   [Vol. 70.

case is, therefore, distinguishable from *Merritt* v. *Bartholick* (36 N. Y. 44), where it was held that the assignment of a lien, without the assignment of the debt for which a personal liability existed, was a nullity. While a mortgage may be given to secure an indebtedness without or in lieu of any personal liability on the part of the debtor (Real Prop. Law [Laws of 1896, chap. 547,], § 214; *Spencer* v. *Spencer,* 95 N. Y. 353; *Mack* v. *Austin,* Id. 513), yet in this case there was a personal liability on the part of Mrs. Rosenberg to Harris which we think he has transferred to Mrs. Norton, and from which Mrs. Rosenberg has not yet been discharged, although she may be discharged from it if she shall ultimately obtain a discharge in the bankruptcy proceedings now pending against her. This, however, is quite immaterial to the plaintiff. It is not claimed that Harris has done anything to discharge his lien upon the premises, except to execute the deed to Mrs. Norton; and if that be ineffectual on account of a failure to transfer the debt, then the lien as well as the debt is left with Harris as before. The fact that Harris in his answer states that he claims no lien upon the premises since his transfer to Mrs. Norton would not estop him from asserting the lien upon which the record remains undischarged, provided the transfer to Mrs. Norton is a nullity so that the notes she gave would not be enforcible for want of consideration.

These conveyances were on their face absolute. Upon proof interposed under the answers the court has found that they were a mortgage and assignment of mortgage and has fixed the amount of the lien for which the assignment is held by Mrs. Norton, but by the dismissal of the complaint the plaintiff is left in no better position than before. He may be obliged to litigate anew this question as to whether the title of Mrs. Norton is absolute or only held as security for $1,100. On these facts the court should have finally determined by the decision and judgment the interest of Mrs. Norton in the premises, and should have declared the legal title thereto in the judgment debtor and that the mortgage be permitted to stand as security so that the plaintiff would be at liberty to sell the property on his execution, subject to the mortgage interest of Mrs. Norton (*Chautauque County Bank* v. *Risley,* 19 N. Y. 369; *Bryer* v. *Foerster,* 14 App. Div. 315; *Harris* v. *Osnowitz,* 35 id. 594; *National Union Bank* v. *Riger,* 38 id. 123; *Clift* v. *Moses,* 75 Hun, 517;

affd., 151 N. Y. 628; *Baldwin* v. *June*, 68 Hun, 284), which is the usual practice where there are no special facts requiring the appointment of a receiver and a sale by him, with directions to apply the proceeds in payment of the mortgage before paying the judgment.

The material facts having been found, we deem this a proper case for the reversal of the judgment and the granting of the appropriate judgment on the facts as found in the decision upon which the judgment was entered. Inasmuch as the security was taken, not in the form of a mortgage, but in the form of a deed, and since the defendant Norton by her answer claimed full title, the defendants should not have been awarded costs. The record does not show the facts essential to enable us to determine whether the plaintiff should have recovered costs of the trial against the defendant Norton, but manifestly he should not have had costs against the defendant Harris.

The judgment is, therefore, reversed, and upon the facts as found in the decision upon which the judgment from which the appeal is taken was based, judgment is awarded as follows: *First.* Dismissing the complaint upon the merits as against the defendant Harris. *Second.* Adjudging and decreeing that the deed from the defendant Rosenberg to the defendant Harris was intended as security, and is a mortgage, and that the deed from the defendant Harris to the defendant Norton was intended as and is an assignment of the claim of Harris for $1,100 and interest and of said mortgage, and that the same be permitted to stand as security for the payment by the defendant Rosenberg to the defendant Norton of the sum of $1,100 and interest thereon from the 9th day of April, 1898. *Third.* Adjudging and decreeing that the plaintiff's judgment is a lien upon the premises described in the complaint and in said deeds, subject to the lien of the defendant Norton as aforesaid. *Fourth.* That neither party as against the other recover costs of the trial.

The appellant, however, after the facts were all disclosed upon the trial, was not awarded the judgment to which he was entitled, and he should, therefore, recover of the respondents the costs of the appeal.

Van Brunt, P. J., O'Brien, Ingraham and Hatch, JJ., concurred.

Judgment reversed and judgment ordered as directed in opinion, with costs to appellant.

PATRICK W. CULLINAN, as State Commissioner of Excise of the State of New York, Respondent, *v.* CHARLES FURTHMANN and THE UNITED STATES FIDELITY AND GUARANTY COMPANY, Appellants.

Request to go to the jury, when in time — sale of liquor on Sundays — proof that the place of the alleged sale was sublet by the licensee — oral proof of the sublease — any conflict of evidence takes a case to the jury — willful false testimony — impeachment of a witness.

Where, upon the denial of a motion by the defendants for a dismissal of the complaint, the plaintiff moves for the direction of a verdict, a request by the defendant to go to the jury upon certain questions, made after the court has announced its intention to direct a verdict in favor of the plaintiff, but before the verdict has been taken or entered, is made in time, and if the request be improperly denied, a new trial must be granted.

In an action to recover the penalty of a bond given upon an application for a liquor tax certificate, in which the defendant's liability is predicated on the fact that liquor was sold on Sundays in a basement under, and connected by a stairway with the licensed premises, it is error for the court to exclude evidence tending to show that the licensee had sublet the basement and that the sublessee was in possession thereof at the time that the sales in question were made.

The sublease being only collaterally involved, secondary evidence of its contents is admissible.

A conflict in the evidence upon a material point requires the submission of the case to the jury.

Where a witness willfully testifies falsely to a material fact, the court or jury may reject his entire evidence.

The credibility of witnesses, whose testimony is substantially impeached or contradicted, is to be determined by the jury and not by the court.

APPEAL by the defendants, Charles Furthmann and another, from a judgment of the Supreme Court in favor of the plaintiff, entered in the office of the clerk of the county of New York on the 29th day of April, 1901, upon the verdict of a jury rendered by direction of the court.

Terence J. McManus, for the appellant Furthmann.

Moses Weinman, for the appellant United States Fidelity and Guaranty Company.

Herbert H. Kellogg, for the respondent.

LAUGHLIN, J.:

This action is brought against the principal and surety to collect the penalty on a bond given on the application of appellant Furthmann for a liquor tax certificate, authorizing him to traffic in liquors on premises No. 2158 Eighth avenue in the city of New York for one year from the 1st day of May, 1898. The application was granted.

The complaint charged and evidence was offered by the plaintiff tending to show violations of the Liquor Tax Law (Laws of 1896, chap. 112, as amended) on Sunday, August 28, and Sunday, September 4, 1898, as follows: (1) In selling liquor in the basement of the premises under the barroom with which there was an open connecting stairway; (2) in having door from street to said basement unlocked; and (3) in permitting persons, not members of the family of the licensee, to enter said basement where liquor was being sold. Other violations of the Liquor Tax Law on Sunday, September 11, 1898, were charged and supported by evidence, as follows: (1) In selling liquor in the barroom; (2) in having the door from the street to the barroom unlocked; (3) in permitting others than members of his family to enter the barroom; and (4) in having a partition across the barroom in such manner as to obstruct the view of persons in the barroom from the street in front.

At the close of the evidence the defendants moved for a dismissal of the complaint, and upon their motion being denied, plaintiff moved for a direction of a verdict. The record shows that the court granted the motion on the ground that the evidence as to selling in the basement on August twenty-eighth and September fourth was uncontroverted. After the intention of the court to direct a verdict was announced, but before the verdict was taken or entered, the defendants' counsel asked to go to the jury upon the questions with reference to the alleged violations of the Liquor Tax Law and specifically upon the credibility of the special agents who gave the only testimony tending to show such violations. These requests were denied, and exceptions taken.

The requests to go to the jury were timely made, and if there was error in their refusal, a new trial must be granted. (*Second National Bank* v. *Weston*, 161 N. Y. 525.)

The verdict cannot be sustained on account of the alleged violations of the law on the first two Sundays, for the court erred, we think, in rejecting competent evidence offered by the defendants bearing upon that question. The plaintiff showed that the licensee had a lease of the basement and that on the Sundays in question liquor was being sold there by a bartender who on week days was in the employ of the licensee in the barroom above. A sign appeared over the basement "Chatauqua Club" and "Gustav Huegel, Billiard, Pool and Shuffle Boards." The licensee testified that he had nothing to do with that business and that he did not at any time in 1898 sell or allow liquor to be sold in the basement. On the objection as incompetent the court precluded the licensee from answering a question as to whether he had in that year a sub-tenant in the basement and sustained a general objection to the question, "Who did business in this basement?" and to the question "Who, to your knowledge, was in possession of the basement underneath the store in the month of August, 1898?"

The licensee also testified that he entered into an agreement in writing with Huegel concerning the basement; that he did not have the writing; that he turned it over to the tenant who succeeded him who was at the time of the trial a resident of Vermont and absent from the State. He was then asked to give the contents of that paper. This was objected to on the ground that it called for secondary evidence and the objection was sustained. The licensee was then asked if he received any money from Huegel in 1898 for rent of the basement. That was objected to generally. The objection was sustained and an exception taken.

We think it was error to exclude the evidence tending to show that the basement had been sublet and was in the possession of Huegel as the licensee's tenant as that would tend to show that Furthmann was not responsible for sales made in the basement. As the lease was only collaterally involved, secondary evidence of its contents was admissible.

The respondent seeks to uphold the verdict principally upon other grounds than those assigned by the court, and the rule is invoked that the judgment may be sustained upon any ground appearing in the record that would have justified the action of the court. (*Scott v. Morgan*, 94 N. Y. 508; *Marvin* v. *Universal Life Insurance Co.*, 85 id. 278.)

We are further of opinion that the testimony of the three special agents relating to the violations of the law was sufficiently contradicted and impeached to require that their credibility be submitted to the jury. One of these witnesses, Sandford, testified to violations on the three days. Waterman claims to have accompanied Sandford and testified to violations on the first two Sundays. Adee claims to have accompanied Sandford on the third Sunday and testifies to the same violations on that day. According to the testimony of these agents the licensee was in the basement on the second Sunday and they talked with him about its being hot there, and he said if they would come around the following Sunday he would have a place open for them upstairs where it would not be so hot. One of them testified that a stairway between the basement and saloon was open and there was no door on it. They testified that on the third Sunday they saw the licensee outside the saloon and he directed them to the side door entering the barroom; that upon entering they ordered drinks and were served by the bartender employed there on week days; that they passed down the inside stairway, which was open, to the basement and back up again; that at this time the licensee had entered and was serving liquor to people in the barroom, and saw them served with some drinks; that there was a partition across the barroom as already described. The licensee testified that he never saw any of these witnesses; that he never sold or allowed liquor to be sold in the basement; that he did no business on Sundays, and did not sell or allow liquor to be sold on the licensed premises during the prohibited hours or on Sunday during that year, and that he never was in the saloon on Sunday; that there was no partition across the barroom as described by plaintiff's witnesses; that there was a door at the foot of the inside stairs cutting off communication with the basement, and that he personally closed and locked this door every Saturday night and it so remained until the following Monday morning. A carpenter was called and he testified that in the fall of 1897, on the employment of the licensee, he built a door at the foot of the inner stairway to cut off communication between the basement and saloon.

It is now well settled that a conflict in the evidence upon a material point requires the submission of a case to a jury.

App. Div.—Vol. LXX.   8

(*McDonald* v. *Metropolitan St. Rway. Co.*, 167 N. Y. 69.) It is equally well settled that where a witness willfully testifies falsely to a material fact the court or jury may reject his entire evidence. (*People* v. *Evans*, 40 N. Y. 1; *Pease* v. *Smith*, 61 id. 477; *Deering* v. *Metcalf*, 74 id. 501.) The credibility of witnesses whose testimony is substantially impeached or contradicted is to be determined by the jury and not by the court. (*McDonald* v. *Metropolitan St. Rway. Co.*, *supra*; *Williams* v. *Del., Lack. & West. R. R. Co.*, 155 N. Y. 158; 11 Am. & Eng. Ency. of Law [2d ed.], 498; 1 Thomp. Trials, § 1038.)

For these reasons the judgment should be reversed and a new trial granted, with costs to appellants to abide the event.

VAN BRUNT, P. J., PATTERSON, O'BRIEN and McLAUGHLIN, JJ., concurred.

Judgment reversed, new trial ordered, costs to appellants to abide event.

SIMON E. BERNHEIMER and JOSEPHINE SCHMID, Respondents, *v.* ALBERT J. ADAMS, Appellant.

Landlord and tenant — right of the latter to remove fixtures — when they will be presumed to remain personal property — when the right of removal may be exercised — estoppel to assert that the right of removal had been lost by a failure to reserve it in a new lease — ordinary trade fixtures distinguished from those distinctively realty — request to go to the jury on certain questions, when in time — it constitutes a consent that the court pass on the other questions.

In an action of replevin, brought against the owner of certain premises to recover possession of a storm house, an iron awning, two urinals, two water closets and twenty feet of oak partition, it appeared that in 1898 the then owner of the premises leased them to the firm of Lee & Block for saloon purposes for a term of five years from May 1, 1898. During the same year the plaintiffs sold and delivered to Lee & Block and installed all the chattels in question except the iron awning, and took back a chattel mortgage covering such property and also the lease. December 19, 1895, the defendant purchased the premises at a foreclosure sale. It did not appear whether the foreclosure terminated the lease to Lee & Block. In or shortly after June, 1896, the defendant executed a lease of the premises to the firm of Mahoney & O'Neill who had become the owners of the saloon business and the fixtures subject to the chattel mortgage. Upon the dissolution of the latter firm, Mahoney succeeded to its rights and obtained another lease from the defendant for a term of five years from May 1, 1896. It did not appear whether the lease contained any reservation of the right to remove the fixtures.

Subsequently Mahoney erected the iron awning with money advanced by the plaintiffs and executed to them a new chattel mortgage covering the property in question and also the lease. The plaintiffs foreclosed this chattel mortgage and on September 10, 1897, Mahoney's wife purchased the property at the foreclosure sale. As security for the purchase price she executed to the plaintiffs a chattel mortgage covering the fixtures and a lease of the premises which the defendant (having previously dispossessed her husband for non-payment of rent) executed to her on the same day. This lease contained no reservation of any right to remove the fixtures. During the term of this lease the plaintiffs foreclosed the last-mentioned chattel mortgage and purchased the property at the sale. They then proceeded to remove the mortgaged property which, in addition to the chattels in question, consisted of a bar and other saloon fixtures.

The defendant admitted the plaintiffs' right to such fixtures, as, in his opinion, could be removed without serious injury to the freehold, and accordingly permitted the plaintiffs to remove the bar which was attached to the wall by screws, and purchased some of the gas fixtures from the plaintiffs, but declined to permit the removal of the chattels in suit.

Upon the trial of the action, the defendant based his title solely upon his deed.

Held, that a judgment in favor of the plaintiffs should be affirmed;

VAN BRUNT, P. J., and McLAUGHLIN, J., dissented.

Semble, that, as it appeared that the sale of the chattels, their annexation to the freehold and the execution of the chattel mortgage constituted one transaction, the law presumed that the parties intended that the chattels should remain personal property, and that when the defendant acquired title he took subject to the plaintiffs' rights therein (per LAUGHLIN and O'BRIEN, JJ.);

Semble, that, even if the lease to Lee & Block was terminated by the foreclosure, the rights of the plaintiffs survived for a reasonable time, to enable them to remove their property (per LAUGHLIN and O'BRIEN, JJ.);

Semble, that, as the defendant did not claim title on account of the failure of the plaintiffs to remove the fixtures within a reasonable time, the plaintiffs were not obliged to prove facts excusing their failure in this respect (per LAUGHLIN and O'BRIEN, JJ.);

Semble, that the defendant was estopped from asserting that the right to remove the fixtures had been lost by the failure to reserve such right in the lease executed to Mrs. Mahoney, inasmuch as he did not assert such claim at the time the plaintiffs attempted to remove the chattels in suit, nor set it up in his answer (per LAUGHLIN and O'BRIEN, JJ.);

Semble, that, even if he were in a position to assert this claim, his contention could not be sustained, as it appeared that the property in question consisted of ordinary trade fixtures as distinguished from fixtures which were distinctively realty, and that they could be removed without injury to themselves and without any material, substantial or serious injury to the freehold (per LAUGHLIN and O'BRIEN, JJ.);

Semble, that, if fixtures are distinctively realty, the acceptance of a new lease
without reserving the right to remove them constitutes an abandonment of
such right, but that this rule does not apply to trade fixtures not distinctively
realty and which are designed to retain their character as personal property,
and are capable of removal without material injury to the freehold (per
LAUGHLIN and O'BRIEN, JJ.);

Semble, that where both parties move for a direction of a verdict, a request made
by one of the parties, after the court had announced its decision, but before
the verdict was taken or entered, to go to the jury upon a certain question, is
timely (per LAUGHLIN and O'BRIEN, JJ.);

Semble, that the party making such request consented that the court should pass
upon the other questions of fact in the case (per LAUGHLIN and O'BRIEN, JJ.).

APPEAL by the defendant, Albert J. Adams, from a judgment of
the Supreme Court in favor of the plaintiffs, entered in the office of
the clerk of the county of New York on the 17th day of January,
1900, upon the verdict of a jury rendered by direction of the court.

William H. Newman, for the appellant.

Gibson Putzel, for the respondents.

LAUGHLIN, J.:

This is a replevin action to recover a storm house, an iron awning,
two urinals, two water closets and twenty feet of oak partition,
which were erected upon or attached to the building known as No.
549 Hudson street in the city of New York, by lessees of the
premises.

The plaintiffs in their complaint base their claim of title on a
chattel mortgage executed to them by Anna Mahoney on the 10th
day of September, 1897, to secure her promissory note. The
defendant in his answer bases his claim of title upon a deed of the
premises executed to him on the 19th day of December, 1895, pursuant to a judgment of foreclosure, prior to which time those chattels had been attached to the freehold. At the same time that the
chattel mortgage was executed, or prior thereto, but on the same
day, the defendant executed a lease of the premises to the plaintiffs'
mortgagor for the term of three years seven months and fifteen
days from the 15th day of September, 1897. This lease makes no
reservation of any existing right on the part of the tenant to remove
these alleged trade fixtures. The chattel mortgage also covered the
lease.

On the 2d day of March, 1893, William H. Ramsey, who then owned the premises, leased the same to Lee & Block for saloon purposes for the term of five years from May 1, 1893. This lease was recorded March 3, 1893. The plaintiffs thereafter and during the same year sold and delivered to said Lee & Block, and installed all the chattels in question, except the iron awning, and pursuant to the contract of sale took back a chattel mortgage thereon and on other property, including the lease, to secure the purchase price of this and the other property. That chattel mortgage was both filed and recorded on the 30th day of March, 1893. There were several transfers of the saloon business and the fixtures, subject to said chattel mortgage, which was assumed by the respective transferees. In June, 1896, after the defendant acquired title to the premises, the firm of Mahoney & O'Neill became the owners of the saloon business and fixtures, subject to said mortgage, which they likewise assumed.

It was not shown whether or not the first lease was cut off by the foreclosure under which the defendant obtained title, but it appears that shortly thereafter the defendant leased the premises to said last-mentioned firm, and upon its dissolution Mahoney succeeded to the rights of the firm and obtained another lease from the defendant for the term of five years from May 1, 1896. Whether he made any reservation of his rights to the property in this lease or otherwise does not appear, but no claim was made upon the trial or is urged here that if the rights of the mortgagees survived the purchase by the defendant they were cut off by this lease.

Mahoney subsequently erected the awning with moneys advanced by the plaintiffs, and thereupon, on the sixteenth day of May, he executed to them a new chattel mortgage covering the property in question and more, and also the lease, to secure the original and this last indebtedness. The plaintiffs foreclosed this chattel mortgage, and said Mahoney's wife, Anna Mahoney, purchased the property on the foreclosure sale on the 10th day of September, 1897, and thereupon, apparently to secure the entire purchase price, executed the chattel mortgage upon which the complaint is based.

It appears that at about the time of said purchase of the property by Anna Mahoney, her husband was dispossessed by defendant for the non-payment of rent. Mahoney's testimony with reference to the lapse of time between his being dispossessed and his wife's obtaining possession is conflicting. He says that she immediately followed him in possession, and also that the place was closed for a time. In December, 1897, the plaintiffs foreclosed the mortgage last referred to and bought in the property themselves. It does not appear definitely, but the presumption is that Anna Mahoney as lessee was then in possession, for her term as lessee had not expired. The plaintiffs then proceeded to remove the mortgaged property, which, in addition to the property in question, consisted of a bar and other saloon fixtures. The defendant was present and did not question their right to remove any of the property which he thought could be removed without material injury to the building. He appears to have asserted no claim of title upon any other ground than by virtue of his deed and because, in his opinion, the articles in question could not be removed without serious injury to the freehold. He accordingly permitted the removal of the bar, which was attached to the wall by screws, and upon its removal the wall was left discolored. Furthermore, he at that time purchased some of the gas fixtures of the plaintiffs, thus clearly recognizing their title.

The case seems to have been tried without much regard to the pleadings, and the plaintiffs were permitted to trace their title without objection on that ground. But the record does not disclose that the defendant made any claim of title other than by virtue of his deed. It appears, however, that at the close of the evidence, in answering the motion made by plaintiffs' counsel for the direction of a verdict, the defendant's counsel asserted that, under the general rule, if the tenant accepted a new lease without removing the fixtures or reserving the right to do so, the right is lost and the fixtures become a part of the realty; but he made his motion for a dismissal of the complaint solely upon the ground that the fixtures were attached at the time of the defendant's purchase.

The articles in question were attached to the premises as trade fixtures. They constituted part of the saloon fixtures, essential to properly equip the leased premises for the accommodation of the patrons of the lessee. It does not appear whether the mortgage was executed before they were attached; but the fair inference is that their sale, annexation to the freehold and the mortgage constituted one transaction. In these circumstances, the law presumes that the parties intended that the chattels should remain personal property. (*Globe Marble Mills Co.* v. *Quinn*, 76 N. Y. 23, 26; *New York Life Ins. Co.* v. *Allison*, 107 Fed. Rep. 179; *Tifft* v. *Horton*, 53 N. Y. 377; *New York Investment Co.* v. *Cosgrove*, 47 App. Div. 35.) The plaintiffs, therefore, as mortgagees, held title at the time of the purchase of the property by the defendant. He has no prior equities over these owners, and he took subject to their rights. (*Sisson* v. *Hibbard*, 75 N. Y. 542; *Globe Marble Mills Co.* v. *Quinn, supra.*)

When the defendant obtained title to the premises, the lease under which the plaintiffs held their mortgage had not expired, unless it was terminated by the decree in foreclosure. Even if it were so terminated, the rights of the mortgagees survived, at least for a reasonable time, to enable them to remove their property. (*London & Westminster Loan & Discount Co.* v. *Drake*, 6 C. B. [N. S.] 798; *Saint* v. *Pilley*, L. R. 10 Exch. Cas. 137; *Updegraff* v. *Lesem*, 62 Pac. Rep. 342; *Royce* v. *Latshaw*, Id. 627; *Alberson* v. *Elk Creek Gold-Mining Co.*, 65 id. 978; 1 McAdam Landl. & Ten. [3d ed.] 716; *Lewis* v. *Ocean Navigation & Pier Co.*, 125 N. Y. 341.) It thus appears that the only claim of title asserted by the defendant in his answer and upon the trial cannot be sustained.

Whether facts existed which excuse the plaintiffs from removing the fixtures within such reasonable time, does not definitely appear; but this might be inferred from the defendant's subsequently allowing the removal of most of the property covered by the mortgage and purchasing part without asserting any other claim of title. Moreover, the defendant having made no claim of title on account of the plaintiffs' failure in this regard, they were not called upon to prove facts constituting a waiver or estoppel on the part of the defendant.

The appellant now contends that by accepting the new lease without removing this property, or reserving the right so to do, Anna Mahoney and these plaintiffs, her mortgagees, forever lost the right to remove the same. We think it may safely be stated that the rule of law invoked is one not well understood by landlords and tenants, and that new leases are generally drawn without reserving such rights. The law does not favor forfeitures. In such cases it lays hold of slight evidence to work a waiver or estoppel. (*Landon*

v. *Supervisors of Schenectady Co.*, 24 Hun, 75 ; *Duffus* v. *Bangs*, 122 N. Y. 423; *Young* v. *Consolidated Implement Co.*, 65 Pac. Rep. 720 ; *Thorn* v. *Sutherland*, 123 N. Y. 236.) We think it may be fairly and justly held that the defendant, by his conduct in not asserting this claim at the time of the attempted removal, but, on the contrary, merely contending that the plaintiffs had no right to remove the articles because their removal would injure the freehold, has led the plaintiffs to employ counsel and bring this action for the purpose of establishing that his contention in this regard was not well founded, and by not invoking the rule in question in his answer, he has permitted them to proceed to final judgment, and should be estopped from now claiming a forfeiture. (*Goodwin* v. *Mass. Mut. Life Ins. Co.*, 73 N. Y. 480 ; *Prentice* v. *Knickerbocker Life Ins. Co.*, 77 id. 483 ; *Brink* v. *Hanover Fire Ins. Co.*, 80 id. 108.)

If, however, notwithstanding these facts and the condition of the record, the defendant still be in a position to assert this claim, we think his contention cannot be sustained. The property in question consisted of ordinary trade fixtures, as distinguished from fixtures which are distinctively realty. The oak partition was only seven feet high, secured to the wall by iron holdfasts three and a half inches long, to which it was screwed, and nailed to the floor. It was placed in a room for the purpose of shutting off and dividing the water closets. The storm house was attached in the same manner. The urinals were attached to the building by the marble slabs forming the back being screwed to a piece of wooden studding three by four, which was nailed to the wall. The water closets were screwed to the waste pipe just above the marble floor, and the seats were screwed to the wall in the same manner as the urinals. The hoppers rested on the marble slabs and were screwed to the wall. The awning was thin corrugated iron, five or six feet in width, extending about seventy-five feet along the side and end of the building outside, and it was fastened to ribs or a frame riveted to heavy holdfasts driven into the wall at intervals of about six feet. It could be removed by taking out the rivets and leaving the holdfasts in the wall, which was customary. These holdfasts, if removed, would leave a hole in the wall at the surface not over one by one and a half inches. The defendant's evidence further showed that tin was nailed to the

wall above the roof of the storm house to prevent water running
down; that the awning was screwed to a wooden bar fastened to the
wall, with tin nailed over that, the same as the storm house. One
witness testified that if the holdfasts were removed from the walls,
new bricks would have to be put in to make the wall the same as it
was before, but he says only a quarter of an inch of the bricks was
broken off. The same witness testified that the floors and wall
would be mutilated by removal of the water closets and urinals, and
that the partition was nailed to the wall, and some of the plaster
would be destroyed in removing it. But by mutilating, he said he
meant a mark would be left in the wall and some of the plaster
would be broken. Another witness testified that part of the flooring had been taken off to put down the floor slabs of the urinals,
and that part of the flooring had been cut away to insert the waste
pipes and drips, and that after the urinals were taken out there
would be a big hole in the floor, and that the wall where the studding was fastened would be injured. It thus appears that the chattels may be removed without injury to themselves and without any
great injury to the inheritance. Manifestly these defects could be
repaired at slight expense. In these circumstances, we are of opinion that the injuries to the building incident to the removal of these
chattels would not constitute a material, substantial or serious injury
to the freehold, within the meaning of those terms as employed in
to the freehold, within the meaning of those terms as employed in
the rule declaratory of the law relating to the right of removal of
trade fixtures by a tenant. (*Tifft* v. *Horton*, *supra* ; *Murdock* v.
Gifford, 18 N. Y. 28 ; *Ford* v. *Cobb*, 20 id. 344 ; *Sisson* v. *Hibbard*,
75 id. 542 ; *Holmes* v. *Tremper*, 20 Johns. 29.)

When Anna Mahoney became a purchaser of these chattels on
the foreclosure of the former chattel mortgage she had the right to
remove them, but it is claimed that she lost this right by not sever-
ing them or reserving it in her lease from the defendant. Why
should she forthwith make her new landlord a present of some
$3,000 worth of trade fixtures ? While it was competent for her
to do so, it is evident that she had no such intention, for concurrently with the defendant's execution of the lease to her she executed the chattel mortgage to the plaintiffs. The taking of a new
lease does not necessarily and conclusively presume the surrender of

a former lease and the transfer of ownership of fixtures to the landlord. The presumption may be rebutted by circumstances showing
that it would be unreasonable to infer that the defendant so
intended. (*Van Rensselaer's Heirs* v. *Penniman*, 6 Wend. 569;
Witmark v. *N. Y. E. R. R. Co.*, 76 Hun, 302; *Second National
Bank of Beloit, Wis.* v. *O. E. Merrill Co.*, 69 Wis. 501, 515;
Abell v. *Williams*, 3 Daly, 17.) In this case Mrs. Mahoney was
not the former tenant. The plaintiffs, as has been seen, had the
right under their former mortgate to remove this property and
that right would survive, for a reasonable time at least, the evic-
tion of the tenant. Mrs. Mahoney succeeded to the same right
and it passed to the plaintiffs by her mortgage. If she purchased concurrently with or after receiving a lease from defendant, the acceptance of the lease would not constitute an abandonment of her right to the chattels. The evidence shows that
she purchased the property, gave the mortgage and received the
lease on the same day. Whether one of these events preceded
the other does not. appear. If we are to indulge in any presumption on that point, it should be one consistent with her
retaining ownership rather than forfeiting her rights. (*Callaghan*
v. *Myers*, 128 U. S. 617.) It was not disputed that these chattels were attached as trade fixtures and that it was intended that
they should retain their character as personal property ; nor were
they of such a character or so affixed as to become necessarily a
part of the freehold and distinctively realty, and, as has been seen,
they can be removed without material injury to the building. We
think no rule of law or public policy requires in these circumstances that the tenants or mortgagees should lose their rights by
a failure to specify in the lease that the right of removal was
reserved, and such a doctrine would be most inequitable.

We deem the true rule on this subject to be, that if fixtures are
distinctively realty, the right to be removed must be reserved in the
lease. The right to remove fixtures which are distinctively realty
is in the nature of a license, and must be exercised while the tenant
is in possession under the lease that grants it. Taking a new lease
without reserving the right is deemed an abandonment thereof.
(*Loughran* v. *Ross*, 45 N. Y. 792; *Talbot* v. *Cruger*, 151 id. 117;
Stephens v. *Ely*, 162 id. 79 ; *Van Vleck* v. *White*, 66 App. Div.

14; *Brooks* v. *Galster*, 51 Barb. 196.) The Court of Appeals has decided that the doctrine of the *Loughran Case (supra)* is not to be extended, and that it will not be applied where a tenant holds over without a new lease after the expiration of a term under a lease in writing. (*Lewis* v. *Ocean Navigation & Pier Co.*, 125 N. Y. 341.) The *Loughran* case involved the right to remove a building which was distinctively real property, and the *Stephens Case (supra)* involved the right to remove general plumbing where a new lease had been taken expressly obligating the lessee to surrender the premises in as good condition as received, and providing that the tenant might make alterations, but must restore the premises to their former condition, and the court held that any parol reservation of the right of removal would be inconsistent with these terms of the lease. In the case at bar the lease is not printed, and it will not be presumed that it contained similar terms. We think the *Loughran* case should further be limited, and that it should be deemed not applicable to trade fixtures, not distinctively realty, designed to retain their character as personal property and capable of removal without material injury to the freehold. (*Smusch* v. *Kohn*, 22 Misc. Rep. 344; *McCarthy* v. *Trumacher*, 108 Iowa, 284; *Wright* v. *Macdonnell*, 88 Tex. 140.)

After counsel for both parties had made a motion for a direction of a verdict and the court announced its decision, but before the verdict was taken or entered, the defendant asked to go to the jury upon the question as to whether these articles could be removed without damage to the building. This request the court refused, and the verdict was then rendered. The request was timely made if that was a question for the jury; but by moving for a direction of a verdict and subsequently asking that only this one question be submitted to the jury, the defendant, in effect, consented that the court should pass upon the other questions of fact in the case. (*Winchell* v. *Hicks*, 18 N. Y. 558; *Ormes* v. *Dauchy*, 82 id. 443; *Thompson* v. *Simpson*, 128 id. 270; *Second Nat. Bank* v. *Weston*, 161 id. 520; *Shultes* v. *Sickles*, 147 id. 704.) We think that as matter of law these chattels could be removed without substantial injury to the freehold, and, therefore, the request was properly denied.

These views require an affirmance of the judgment, with costs.

O'BRIEN, J., concurred; PATTERSON, J., concurred in result; VAN BRUNT, P. J., and McLAUGHLIN, J., dissented.

VAN BRUNT, P. J. (dissenting):

I dissent. While the fixtures might probably be removed during the term of the tenancy, when such term expires the tenant has no right of entry to remove trade fixtures.

Judgment affirmed, with costs.

PASQUALE CAPONIGRI, Respondent, v. HENRY G. COOPER, Appellant.

Undertaking on opening a default in the City Court of New York — the liability thereunder extends to a judgment entered on a remittitur from the Court o Appeals — variance between the undertaking and the provisions of the order.

Judgments having been taken by default against the defendants in two actions brought in the City Court of New York, the court opened the default upon condition that the defendants should give an undertaking in each of said actions, "to secure any judgment that may be recovered in said two actions, which undertakings are to be approved upon notice to plaintiff's attorney and justification of the sureties by one of the justices of this court, and each to be given in the penalty of twice the amount of the claims of the plaintiff in each of the above-entitled actions." Pursuant to this order the defendants gave an undertaking conditioned to pay "the just and full amount of any judgment which may be finally recovered against them * * * in a certain action now pending in the City Court of New York." One of the actions was then brought to trial in the City Court and the defendants recovered a verdict upon which judgment was entered. This judgment was affirmed by the General Term of the City Court of New York and also by the Appellate Term of the Supreme Court, but was reversed by the Appellate Division which ordered a new trial. The plaintiff then appealed to the Court of Appeals, stipulating for judgment absolute. The Court of Appeals affirmed the Appellate Division and directed judgment absolute against the defendants pursuant to the stipulation. Thereafter, on the remittitur from the Court of Appeals, the judgment of the Court of Appeals was made the order and judgment of the City Court.

In an action brought upon the undertaking, after an execution issued upon the judgment entered upon the remittitur had been returned unsatisfied, it was

Held, that the order opening the default and the undertaking contemplated that the liability on the undertaking should not be limited to a judgment recovered in the first instance in the City Court, but should be construed to embrace a judgment entered as the result of a stipulation for judgment absolute in the Court of Appeals;

That, as the undertaking was not a statutory one, the variance between the language thereof and of the order opening the default did not affect the validity of the undertaking;

That, whether the liability on the undertaking was to be determined by the phraseology of the order opening the default or by that of the undertaking, the plaintiff was entitled to recover.

APPEAL by the defendant, Henry G. Cooper, from a judgment of the Supreme Court in favor of the plaintiff, entered in the office of the clerk of the county of New York on the 24th day of June, 1901, upon the decision of the court rendered after a trial before the court without a jury at the New York Trial Term, a jury having been waived.

James C. De La Mare, for the appellant.

Charles W. Dayton, for the respondent.

LAUGHLIN, J.:

This is an action on a common-law undertaking given by Pasquale Altieri and Pietro Altieri, on opening a judgment which had been taken against them by default in the City Court of the city of New York, in an action wherein the respondent was plaintiff and they were defendants. There were two actions pending and two judgments by default, both of which were vacated on the same conditions, but only one of the undertakings is involved here. The order opening the default granted the motion upon condition, among others, that the defendants "give to the plaintiff an undertaking in each of the above-entitled actions executed by two sureties to secure any judgment that may be recovered in said two actions, which undertakings are to be approved upon notice to plaintiff's attorney and justification of the sureties by one of the justices of this court, and each to be given in the penalty of twice the amount of the claims of the plaintiff in each of the above-entitled actions."

The appellant joined in the undertaking as a surety and it was duly approved and bound the parties executing it jointly and severally, in the sum of $2,100. It was conditioned that if the defendants in the action pending in the City Court should pay to the plaintiff therein, the respondent herein, "the just and full amount of any judgment which may be finally recovered against them * * * in a certain action now pending in the City Court of New York * * * then this obligation shall be void, otherwise to remain in full force, effect and virtue."

The action was subsequently brought to trial in the City Court, and the defendants recovered a verdict upon which judgment was entered. On appeal to the General Term of the City Court, taken by the plaintiff, that judgment was affirmed. The plaintiff further appealed to the Appellate Term of the first department where the judgment was again affirmed. An appeal was then taken to the Appellate Division by leave of the Appellate Term, and on such appeal the judgment was reversed and a new trial ordered, with costs of the appeal in the several courts to plaintiff to abide the event. The Appellate Division then granted leave to the defendants to appeal to the Court of Appeals, which they did, stipulating judgment absolute as required by law. The Court of Appeals affirmed the judgment of the Appellate Division and directed judgment absolute against the defendants for the relief demanded in the complaint, with costs. On the 16th day of January, 1901, on the remittitur from the Court of Appeals, an order was duly made and entered in the City Court making the order and judgment of the Court of Appeals its order and judgment, and judgment for the plaintiff and against the defendants in that action for $2,282.75 was thereafter duly entered in the clerk's office of the City Court on the 18th day of January, 1901. The transcript of the judgment was filed and the judgment was duly docketed in the clerk's office of the county of New York, where the defendants resided, and an execution was duly issued on the judgment and returned wholly unsatisfied. It appears that there has been no attempt to take an appeal from the last-mentioned judgment, and that the time for appealing, if an appeal could be taken therefrom, has expired.

The appellant contends that the order of the court and the undertaking contemplated that the liability on the undertaking should be limited to liability for a judgment recovered in the first instance in the City Court, and that it should not be construed to embrace a judgment entered as the result of a stipulation for judgment absolute in the Court of Appeals. We think that both the order and undertaking should be construed in the light of the statutory provisions relating to appeals in such cases. The plaintiff at that time had a judgment. Presumably there was a question with reference to the solvency of the defendants. The court, in requiring the undertaking, doubtless intended to secure the plaintiff on any judgment that he might recover in the action when the same should become final. Stress is laid upon the fact that the language of the order and of the undertaking with reference to the liability differ. This is not a statutory undertaking and the variance is not sufficient to affect its validity. Whether the liability on the undertaking is to be determined by the phraseology of the order or by that of the undertaking is immaterial. In either event the plaintiff would be entitled to recover. The judgment was final, and it was not only recovered in the action, but it was recovered in the court in which the action was commenced, was then pending and in which judgment had been taken by default.

The judgment appealed from should be affirmed, with costs.

VAN BRUNT, P. J., O'BRIEN, INGRAHAM and HATCH, JJ., concurred.

Judgment affirmed, with costs.

STEPHEN F. LEAHY, Respondent, v. HENRY CAMPBELL, as Administrator, etc., of THOMAS S. CLARKE, Deceased, Appellant.

Claim for services rendered and disbursements made for another — when barred by the Statute of Limitations — the statute runs from the date of reference of the claim — when no presumption arises that the services were gratuitous — in the case of an agreement to make the claimant the heir of the decedent the statute does not begin to run before the latter's death.

Ordinarily, no recovery can be had against a decedent's estate for services rendered by the claimant to the decedent, and disbursements made by the claimant at the request of the decedent, more than six years prior to the decedent's death, in the absence of evidence of any payment or of the existence of a mutual, open and current account.

Upon the reference of a disputed claim against a decedent's estate, the entry of the order of reference is deemed the date of the commencement of the action, for the purpose of the application of the Statute of Limitations, and the objection that the statute has run against the claim may be raised upon the trial when the ground therefor first appears from evidence offered or received.

Where it is found that the claimant was the business representative, confidential agent and companion of the decedent and that his duties were to take care of the decedent's real property, secure tenants, collect rents, make and attend to the making of repairs, select and purchase materials, pay and collect bills and to wait upon and attend to the interests of the decedent, and it does not appear that the claimant was related to the decedent, and no facts and circumstances are shown from which it can be presumed that the services were rendered or the disbursements made gratuitously, the law will imply a promise on the part of the decedent, not only to reimburse the claimant for the moneys expended, but to pay the reasonable value of his services.

Where it appears that the decedent agreed to compensate the claimant for his services and disbursements by making him his sole heir, and that he never repudiated such agreement, but failed to perform it owing to the fact that his death was both sudden and unexpected, the claimant is entitled to recover on *quantum meruit* compensation from the estate for his services and disbursements, and as there was no breach of the agreement until the decedent died without having performed it, the Statute of Limitations is not a bar to his right to recover for services rendered and disbursements made more than six years prior to the decedent's death.

VAN BRUNT, P. J., dissented.

APPEAL by the defendant, Henry Campbell, as administrator, etc., of Thomas S. Clarke, deceased, from a judgment of the Supreme Court in favor of the plaintiff, entered in the office of the clerk of the county of New York on the 26th day of January, 1901, upon the report of a referee appointed pursuant to the provisions of the Code of Civil Procedure to determine respondent's claim against the estate for services and disbursements, the justice of which was doubted by the administrator.

L. J. Morrison, for the appellant.

Thomas Cooper Byrnes, for the respondent.

LAUGHLIN, J.:

The respondent presented a claim for $15,000 for "work, labor and services caring for property, looking after the repairs, collecting the rents, keeping the accounts and performing such duties as required of an agent, collector, manager, supervisor and bookkeeper in the various transactions, business and personal requirements of Thomas S. Clarke and for disbursements made for and on account of Thomas S. Clarke and at his request * * * from January 1st, 1889, to July, 1900."

The referee found that the services were rendered from the 3d day of January, 1889, when the respondent was thirty-four and the decedent fifty-seven years of age, until decedent died on the 21st day of July, 1900, covering a period of eleven years one month and eighteen days; that the respondent "became at said Clarke's request his business representative, confidential agent and companion; said Leahy's general duties were to look after and care for the real property of said Clarke, secure tenants, collect rents, make and attend to the making of repairs, select and purchase materials, pay bills, collect bills, and to wait upon and attend to the interests and wants of said Clarke, and to accompany said Clarke from place to place during the day or night, on Sundays and holidays as well as week days, on business and pleasure. That the relationship between said Clarke and said Leahy became from the start, and continued, and was at all times intimate, and one of mutual trust and confidence, viewed and described by said Clarke to his associates and acquaintances as faithful, devoted and honest, and considered as that of 'father and son,' and the duties of said service and employment were exacting and were well performed, and called for and required of said Leahy nearly all of his time and thought." These findings are fairly sustained by the evidence. The referee allowed the claim in full, including services and disbursements for the entire period.

The first question to be considered arises on the objection that the Statute of Limitations is a bar to the recovery for any services rendered or disbursements made more than six years prior to decedent's death. There was no evidence of any payment made by decedent to the respondent, nor was there proof that an account was kept by respondent or rendered to decedent. There was, therefore, no "mutual, open and current account where there have been reciprocal demands between the parties," within the contemplation of section 386 of the Code of Civil Procedure, which provides in effect that the Statute of Limitations only runs in such case from the date of the last item proved on either side of the account. (*Adams* v. *Olin*, 140 N. Y. 150; *Green* v. *Disbrow*, 79 id. 1; *Ross* v. *Ross*, 6 Hun, 80.)

In claims of this character which are litigated without formal pleadings, the entry of the order of reference is deemed the date of the commencement of the action for the purpose of the application of the Statute of Limitations (*Hultslander* v. *Thompson*, 5 Hun, 348), and the objection that the statute has run against the claim

FIRST DEPARTMENT, MARCH TERM, 1902.   [Vol. 70.

may be presented on the trial when the ground therefor first appears from evidence offered or received. (*Covey* v. *Covey,* 64 Hun, 540.) The appellant upon the trial timely interposed the defense of the Statute of Limitations.

It does not satisfactorily appear that the respondent was related to the decedent, and there is no presumption from the facts and circumstances shown that the services were rendered or disbursements made gratuitously. The law would, therefore, imply a promise on the part of the decedent not only to reimburse respondent for the moneys expended, but to pay the reasonable value of his services. (*Wiley* v. *Goodsell,* 3 App. Div. 452; *Woodward* v. *Bugsbee,* 2 Hun, 129; *Markey* v. *Brewster,* 10 id. 16; *Davis* v. *Gallagher,* 55 id. 593; *Bradley* v. *Bradley,* 48 N. Y. St. Repr. 490; *Smith* v. *Long Island R. R. Co.,* 102 N. Y. 190.) This, however, would only justify the recovery for services rendered and disbursements made within the six years immediately preceding decedent's death.

The referee also found that the decedent agreed to compensate the respondent for such services and disbursements by leaving to respondent all his property, both real and personal, but that the death of said Clarke was sudden and unexpected, and on that account he failed to perform this agreement. If the respondent rendered services and disbursed moneys upon the faith of such an agreement, he is entitled to recover of the estate on a *quantum meruit,* the provision for compensation not having been made as agreed. (*Gall* v. *Gall,* 27 App. Div. 173; *Collier* v. *Rutledge,* 136 N. Y. 621; *Porter* v. *Dunn,* 131 id. 314; *Robinson* v. *Raynor,* 28 id. 494.) According to the agreement, as found by the referee, there was no obligation to pay until after the death of the employer. Inasmuch as he never repudiated the agreement, there was no breach of contract until he died without having performed it, and the cause of action for services did not accrue until that time. In such case, the Statute of Limitations is not a bar, and the employee may recover for all services rendered and disbursements made on the faith of the agreement prior to a breach thereof. (*Taylor* v. *Welsh,* 92 Hun, 272; *Quackenbush* v. *Ehle,* 5 Barb. 469; *Robinson* v. *Raynor, supra; Bonesteel* v. *Van Etten,* 20 Hun, 468.)

The point is also made that the evidence is insufficient to sustain this finding of the referee to the effect that the decedent agreed to compensate respondent by will. We are unable to agree with the appellant's contention in this regard. The decedent died intestate, leaving real estate of the value of $22,000, and personal property of the value of $16,000. He was sixty-eight years of age, unmarried, and left no father, mother, brother or sister. The only relative he had in this country was a young man named Gallagher, and their relationship is not shown. There is no evidence of any intimacy between him and Gallagher, and on one occasion when a friend suggested that he supposed decedent would leave all his property to Gallagher, the decedent replied, " No, I will have to take care of Steve," meaning the respondent; that respondent was faithful and honest, had worked for him long, had attended to his business affairs since 1889 ; that " he was the only boy he had and he intended to give him all the property he had." It appears by the uncontradicted testimony of the respondent, which was received without objection and is substantially corroborated by the testimony of other witnesses, that from 1889 he devoted his entire time to looking after the property and business and personal affairs of decedent and to affording him companionship; that decedent owned four parcels of improved real estate in the city of New York, and respondent collected and paid over to the decedent, without deduction for services, commissions or disbursements, rents aggregating for the entire period $27,135 ; that he supervised the care and repair of the buildings on these premises and personally made repairs thereon, and in so doing expended from time to time thereon during this entire period his own money to the extent of $4,140.71.

Evidence was given by disinterested witnesses to the effect that the decedent and respondent were very intimate, constantly together both day and night, and Sundays and holidays; that the former looked upon the latter as his son; that on one occasion, in speaking of respondent, the decedent said, " The only one I am working for is Steve." He spoke to another personal friend of the respondent's having been his faithful servant for a number of years, taking care of him and his property, and that while he had not prepared himself for departing from this world, he said that he intended not to forget " his son." He frequently said to respondent in the presence of a personal friend, when talking about the expenditures made by respondent on his property, " You are only paying it for yourself, Steve ; of course that will be yours some day ; " and within two weeks of his death, while suffering from rheumatism, he said to the same friend that if he could get out the next day " he would see that Leahy was righted before anything happened." He told another friend on more than one occasion, speaking of respondent doing work upon his premises, " I do not know how much, but he pays for it, and it will all be his some day." Another witness, to whom decedent spoke of some trouble the respondent had with one parcel of property, testified that decedent said " that he was glad that he did not have anything to do with it. He said that Steve would be paid for it when he was gone — that that was the way that he was going to pay him." Within a month of his death decedent said to another personal friend that respondent was spending too much money on one of the buildings, but that he was spending it for himself ; that " he is my boy, he can do as he likes ; he can have everything I have got." The respondent's brother testified that the decedent many times remarked to him that no one was to get any part of his property except respondent Another witness testified that when the respondent was only nineteen years of age the decedent told her that he intended " to fix him if he was a good boy."

The decedent was guilty of no affirmative act repudiating his obligations to the respondent, and, as has been seen, he constantly recognized them, and when admonished of his failure to perform by illness shortly before his death, he then declared his intention to keep his agreement.

It is true there is no express evidence of an agreement between the decedent and the respondent by which the latter was to render these services and make these disbursements in consideration of receiving the decedent's entire estate at his death. It is not, however, essential that the agreement be established by direct testimony. It is sufficient if the conduct of the parties and the facts and circumstances clearly indicate that such an agreement was made. Such, we think, is the inference to be drawn from the testimony given in this case. It is not reasonable to suppose that the respondent would disburse his own money in large amounts in making improvements on the decedent's property, and devote his entire time to the decedent's business, while at the same time collecting rents and paying the same over to decedent without deduction on account either of disbursements or services, unless there was some agreement or understanding that reimbursement and adequate compensation were to be made in some manner in the future. The reasonable inference is that the respondent expected that the property would be his upon the death of the decedent. Of course, the conduct of the respondent could not establish his claim, but his conduct, taken in connection with the attitude of the decedent toward him, and the conversation between them in which decedent said in substance that respondent was improving the property for himself and that some day it would be his, and the other declarations of the decedent concerning his intentions, we think fairly justify the inference that the services were rendered and the disbursements made upon an agreement and understanding between the respondent and the decedent to the effect that the former was to receive all the property — at least all of the real property — of the latter at the time of his death.

If these views are sound, we do not understand that it is seriously contended that the amount of the judgment was not justified. The services rendered were given in detail, but there was no direct express evidence as to their value. The difficulty of proving the value of such services was commented on by the court in *Gall* v. *Gall* (*supra*), where a hypothetical question to witnesses not familiar with the value of all the items of the services was sustained. In this case, no expert testimony was given, but it was proved without objection or exception that the respondent was obliged to hire a clerk at an expenditure of two dollars and fifty cents a day to look after his butcher business during this entire time, to enable him to devote his time and attention to the decedent and his business. While this evidence would have been incompetent if objected to, yet it having been received without objection, the appellant cannot now be heard to claim that it is no proof of the value of respondent's services. It could have been received in evidence for no other purpose than to show the value of such services; and, having been received for that purpose without objection, the respondent may have been misled into omitting to make other proof.

It was further shown that the usual commission on the collection of rents was five per cent. If the respondent were allowed commissions on the collections and for the disbursements in employing a clerk, his claim would have considerably exceeded the amount allowed by the referee. In *Gall* v. *Gall* (*supra*) the court held that in estimating the value of services in this class of cases the position and standing of the parties, the circumstances under which the services were rendered, the amount of property owned by the decedent, and the estimate placed by the decedent upon the value of the services, were all important and should be considered. We are impressed with the justice of this claim and with the fairness of the conduct of the respondent, and are satisfied that the recovery is not excessive.

Our conclusion is, therefore, that the decision of the referee was correct, and the judgment should be affirmed, with costs.

O'BRIEN, McLAUGHLIN and HATCH, JJ., concurred ; VAN BRUNT, P. J., dissented.

VAN BRUNT, P. J. (dissenting) :

I dissent. I do not think that there was any proof of any agreement to make a will. Much stress is laid upon the fact that there was no proof of a repudiation of such an agreement. But as there is no proof that the deceased ever heard of any claim that there was such an agreement, there does not seem to have been a very pressing necessity for repudiation.

Judgment affirmed, with costs.

WOLDEMAR KITTEL, Appellant and Respondent, *v.* CHARLOTTE DOMEYER, Respondent and Appellant.

THE PROVIDENT SAVINGS LIFE ASSURANCE SOCIETY OF NEW YORK and WILLIAM M. HOES, Public Administrator, as Administrator, etc., of FREDERICK DOMEYER, Deceased, Respondents, Impleaded with Others.

Insurance for the benefit of the wife of the assured — how affected by chapter 272 of the Laws of 1896 — an action for the insurance money in excess of the statutory amount lies by the legal representative, not by a creditor, of the deceased husband — policies pledged to creditors, how far considered.

Section 22 of chapter 272 of the Laws of 1896, relating to policies of insurance procured by married women upon the lives of their husbands, and which provides that a married woman shall be "entitled to receive the insurance money payable by the terms of the policy as her separate property, and free from any claim of a creditor or representative of her husband, except that where the premium actually paid annually out of the husband's property exceeds five hundred dollars, that portion of the insurance money which is purchased by excess of premium above five hundred dollars is primarily liable for the husband's debts," applies to policies of insurance obtained by a wife upon the life of her husband previous to its enactment, and while chapter 277 of the Laws of 1870, which provided, "when the premium paid in any year out of the property or funds of the husband shall exceed five hundred dollars, such exemption from such claims shall not apply to so much of said premium so paid as shall be in excess of five hundred dollars, but such excess, with the interest thereon, shall inure to the benefit of his creditors," was in force.

Under the act of 1896 a creditor of the deceased husband cannot maintain, in his individual right, an action to reach "that portion of the insurance money which is purchased by excess of premium above five hundred dollars," as the fund thus created is for the benefit of all the creditors of the husband.

Semble, that such an action can only be maintained by an administrator or executor of the deceased husband; or, in the event of his refusal to act, by a creditor of the deceased husband, suing on behalf of himself and all other creditors.

Semble, that in determining what portion of the insurance money was purchased by premiums in excess of $500, there should be excluded from the calculation premiums paid on policies issued to the wife upon the husband's life, and which, prior to the husband's decease, had been assigned by the husband and the wife as collateral security for a debt owing by the husband.

Cʀoss-ᴀᴘᴘᴇᴀʟs by the plaintiff, Woldemar Kittel, and by the defendant, Charlotte Domeyer, from a judgment of the Supreme Court in favor of the plaintiff, entered in the office of the clerk of the county of New York on the 27th day of April, 1901, upon the decision of the court rendered after a trial at the New York Special Term.

George H. Fletcher, for the plaintiff,

Charles C. Sanders, for the defendant Charlotte Domeyer.

William T. Gilbert, for the respondent Provident Savings Life Assurance Society of New York.

McLᴀᴜɢʜʟɪɴ, J. :

Frederick Domeyer died January 31, 1900, and at the time of his death his wife, the defendant Charlotte Domeyer, held three insurance policies for $10,000 each upon his life, by the terms of which the amounts assured thereby were payable to her; one issued by the Provident Savings Life Assurance Society of New York, June 1, 1892; one issued by the United States Life Insurance Company, August 30, 1893, and one issued by the Penn Mutual Life Insurance Company, August 26, 1895. The plaintiff also held three policies aggregating $10,000, issued on the 4th of June, 1891, by the Provident Savings Life Assurance Society of New York upon the life of Frederick Domeyer, payable to the defendant Charlotte Domeyer, and which were, on the 25th of September, 1894, assigned by Mrs. Domeyer and her husband to the plaintiff as collateral security for the payment of a debt then due him from the husband.

The United States Company and the Penn Company paid to Mrs. Domeyer the amounts covered by their respective policies, after deducting the premiums due. The Provident Company paid into court the amount secured by the policy issued June 1, 1892, but refused to pay the policies assigned to the plaintiff, for the reason that the proceeds of such policies were claimed by both the plaintiff and the defendant Charlotte Domeyer.

Thereupon this action was brought to procure a judgment establishing an alleged claim of the plaintiff against the estate of Frederick Domeyer, deceased, and adjudging that the proceeds of the three policies theretofore assigned belonged to him to be applied towards the satisfaction of his claim, and also adjudging that he had a lien, sufficient to satisfy his claim, upon the proceeds of the other policies for any sum that might remain after such application. The plaintiff had a judgment establishing his claim against such estate at $18,939.28, and directing the Provident Company to pay to him the proceeds of three policies theretofore assigned, such proceeds to be applied towards the satisfaction of his claim, and also adjudging that he had a lien upon the proceeds of the other policies, except the one issued by the United States Company, and as to that he had a lien for so much of the proceeds as was purchased by the annual premiums in excess of $74, and directing the wife to pay to the administrator of Frederick Domeyer, deceased, so much of the proceeds of the policy issued by the United States Company as was purchased by the annual premiums in excess of $74, and the entire proceeds of the policy issued by the Penn Company; also directing that the money theretofore paid into court on the $10,000 policy issued by the Provident Company be also paid to the administrator.

From this judgment both parties have appealed. The plaintiff apparently succeeded at the trial and he seeks to sustain the judgment in this court, substantially upon the theory that, inasmuch as Frederick Domeyer for several years prior to his death was insolvent, and during that time the premiums on all of the policies referred to exceeded $500 a year, and such premiums were paid by the deceased out of his own property, the plaintiff, as a creditor, is entitled to recover, after applying the proceeds of the policies assigned to him, the balance of his claim out of the proceeds of the other policies; in other words, that he has a lien given to him by statute on such proceeds.

The question presented, therefore, is whether the plaintiff, as a creditor of the estate of Frederick Domeyer, deceased, is entitled, after applying the proceeds of the policies theretofore assigned to him, to so much of the proceeds of the other policies as will be sufficient to satisfy his claim in full. The determination of this question necessarily involves a consideration of the statutes in relation to insurance obtained by a wife on the life of her husband, when the premiums upon the policies have been paid out of the property of the husband. The first statute giving to the wife the right to insure the life of the husband is chapter 80 of the Laws of 1840, but it did not, in terms, permit the use of the husband's property to pay the premiums upon such policies, and the first statute which did was chapter 187 of the Laws of 1858, which was amended by chapter 277 of the Laws of 1870, and further amended by chapter 272, section 22, of the Laws of 1896. The statute as amended by the Laws of 1896 provides that " A married woman may, in her own name, or in the name of a third person, with his consent, as her trustee, cause the life of her husband to be insured for a definite period, or for the term of his natural life. Where a married woman survives such period or term she is entitled to receive the insurance money payable by the terms of the policy as her separate property, and free from any claim of a creditor or representative of her husband, except that where the premium actually paid annually out of the husband's property exceeds five hundred dollars, that portion of the insurance money which is purchased by excess of premium above five hundred dollars is primarily liable for the husband's debts." The amount of premiums annually paid on the policies, the proceeds of which are here in dispute, largely exceeded the $500 provided by this statute, inasmuch as they amounted to $1,262. In order, therefore, to determine the rights of the plaintiff, it is necessary, as already indicated, to construe this statute and ascertain, if possible, just what the Legislature intended by its enactment.

The manifest purpose of the statute of 1858, as it seems to us, was to exempt from the rights of creditors a certain share of the income of the husband which he might apply towards the establishment of a fund for the benefit of his widow. By the act of 1858 the wife was permitted to cause to be insured for her sole benefit the life of her husband, for any definite period or for the term of his natural life, and in case of her surviving her husband the insurance becoming due by the terms of the policies payable to her was to be her own property, free from all claims of creditors of her husband. The act, it will be observed, further provided that such exemption should not apply where the amount of the premium annually paid out of the property of the husband exceeded $300. Thus, by the express language of the act, it would seem that the Legislature intended to exempt for the benefit of the wife certain property of the husband, and to put it beyond the reach of his representatives or creditors. That this was the intent is apparent from the fact that the statute expressly provides that the exemption shall not apply; that is, there shall be no exemption where the amount of premiums paid by the husband on policies for the benefit of his wife shall annually exceed the sum of $300. This was the condition of the statute until the act of 1870 was passed (Chap. 277) by which it was amended, so far as the benefits to be derived by the wife were concerned, so as to provide that " when the premium paid in any year out of the property or funds of the husband shall exceed five hundred dollars, such exemption from such claims shall not apply to so much of said premium so paid as shall be in excess of five hundred dollars, but such excess, with the interest thereon, shall inure to the benefit of his creditors." The exemption provided in the act of 1858 was thus increased from $300 to $500, but the whole exemption was not forfeited if there was an excess of premiums paid; only so much of the premium paid as was in excess of

$500 should inure to the benefit of creditors; that is, not one but all of the creditors of the deceased husband, and such excess was evidently intended to be administered as part of his estate and in that way distributed *pro rata* among all the creditors according to their respective claims. The principal and substantially the only change which seems to have been made by the act of 1896 was that the excess of premium was not the fund which was to inure to the benefit of creditors, but that the insurance purchased by premiums in excess of $500 should be " primarily " liable for the husband's debts, and should be no longer free from the claims of creditors and representatives of the husband. It is, however, claimed on the part of the defendant Charlotte Domeyer that the act of 1896 cannot apply to the proceeds of the policies here in question, inasmuch as they were obtained by her on the life of her husband prior to the passage of that act. We cannot agree to this contention. When the history of the legislation on the subject is taken into consideration with the object and purpose of it, it seems to us that the legislative intent is a mere exemption from the claim of creditors and nothing else. It is, in other words, a gratuity given by the Legislature to his wife. The rights involved are not of contract but of legislative intent. The statutes which were in force at the time the policies were issued did not give to the husband, by the mere issue of such policies, the right, for the term of his life, to appropriate money, which in equity, except for this legislation, belonged to his creditors, to keep alive policies for the purpose of creating a fund for the benefit of his wife when he died. Any change in respect to the right of the husband to use money for the purpose of creating this fund is a mere matter of State regulation, determining what property shall be exempt from execution and nothing more. Of course, it could not be said that if a man purchased a farm, and at the time it was exempt from execution by levy from creditors, the Legislature would have no right thereafter to remove or alter that exemption. So here, all the Legislature has done is to alter the exemption so that the creditors can reach the fund created in excess of $500 per year. This is in harmony with the rule which would have existed had there been no statute whatever on the subject, viz., that the executor or administrator of the estate of the deceased insolvent could, for the benefit of creditors, recover the insurance which had been bought by him with money which should have been applied to the payment of his just debts.

But then the question presented is as to how this claim of the creditors can be enforced. The statute provides that that portion of the insurance money which was purchased by excess of premiums above $500 is "primarily" liable for the husband's debts. The word "primarily" is used as a synonym for the word "first" — that is, that the excess of the insurance shall be first liable for the husband's debts, and secondly that after the husband's debts have been satisfied, the remainder of the excess shall belong to the wife. If we are right in thus construing the statute, it necessarily follows that this excess of insurance is a fund for not one but all the creditors of the deceased. It is an equitable asset of the estate of the husband who died insolvent, without sufficient property to pay all his just debts. Therefore, the executor or administrator of the husband's estate, in the administration of the same, is obligated to reduce this equitable asset to possession, under the powers conferred by chapter 314 of the Laws of 1858, and distribute the same among all the creditors of the deceased. Of course, the wife cannot be deprived of any part of this insurance which is not necessary for the payment of the debts of the deceased. That this was the legislative intent is indicated by the phrase that this excess of insurance shall be "primarily" liable for the payment of the husband's debts; in other words, if the husband does not leave sufficient property to pay his debts, then the claims of all the creditors are to become a lien upon the insurance purchased by annual premiums in excess of $500, and until such claims have been paid, the wife has no interest in such proceeds; that is, the proceeds of the excess of insurance is property which has been produced by the misapplication of assets of the insolvent husband and which, under the statute, forms a part of his estate to be distributed, after his other property has been exhausted, among all his creditors.

It may be suggested that the executor or administrator might be unwilling to take the necessary legal proceedings to reduce this insurance to possession. That may be. But if an administrator or an executor refuses to perform his duty, he can be removed and some one appointed in his place who will properly execute the duties of his trust; or, in case of his refusal, it is possible a creditor, on behalf of himself and all other creditors, might bring an action, making the executor or administrator a party defendant, and alleging that he had refused to bring such action.

It seems to us clear, however, that a creditor situated as the plaintiff is, has no standing whatever to maintain an action of this character.   In this connection it may not be out of place to call attention to the fact that in no event can the premium paid upon the three policies assigned to the plaintiff be charged to the defendant Charlotte Domeyer; in other words, such premiums cannot be considered as a part of the $500 in determining what insurance she is entitled to under the statute.   These policies were assigned as collateral security for the payment of the husband's debts long before his decease.   By virtue of the assignment, in which she joined, she thereby, until the husband's debts had been paid, parted with all her interest in such policies.   The premiums thereafter used in keeping such policies alive were not for her benefit, but for the benefit of the husband and this plaintiff.   The husband had the right, and it was a laudable act on his part, to use so much of his own property as he saw fit to keep those policies alive in order that he might secure to his creditor the payment of his claim.   It needs no argument to demonstrate that if the plaintiff's claim against the husband's estate exceeds the proceeds of the policies, and for that reason he is entitled to take the entire proceeds, that the premium paid cannot be included in the $500 which the husband had a right to use for the purpose of creating a fund for the benefit of his wife after he had died.

It follows, therefore, that the judgment appealed from must be reversed, with costs, and, inasmuch as the plaintiff cannot under any circumstances recover in this action, the complaint must be dismissed, with costs to the defendant Charlotte Domeyer.

VAN BRUNT, P. J., INGRAHAM, HATCH and LAUGHLIN, JJ. concurred.

Judgment reversed, with costs, and complaint dismissed, with costs to the defendant Charlotte Domeyer.

MAX STERN, Respondent, v. JOSEPH J. McKEE and ERNEST G. HOFFMANN, Appellants.

A plea of performance of a contract, not sustained by proof of an excuse for non-performance — the facts constituting the excuse must be pleaded — proof of readiness to perform — subscription to the stock of a corporation to be organized — what departure in its organization from the prospectus discharges the subscribers.

Where the plaintiff in an action to recover damages for the breach of a contract alleges full performance on his part, he cannot recover without establishing that fact. If he relies upon proof that he was excused from full performance he is bound to allege the facts constituting such excuse, and, in addition thereto, that he was at that time ready and able to perform, and would have done so except for the acts of the other parties to the contract. The refusal of the other parties to proceed under the contract will not relieve the plaintiff from the necessity of proving his ability and readiness to perform the contract on his part.

Where subscriptions to the stock of a corporation about to be formed are obtained in connection with a prospectus stating that the object of the corporation is "to acquire all patents and rights for all countries, except the United States and Canada, to metal turning machines, known as the 'Hoffmann machines,' and of which E. G. Hoffmann is the inventor and patentee, as well as all improvements, additions, etc.," the organization of a corporation, "to make, contract for the manufacture, or purchase of, buy, use, sell, lease, rent or mortgage all mechanical or other apparatus, machinery and implements for metal turning machines, or any other article or articles connected therewith or incident thereto, or any or all of them, and *in general to do a manufacturing business*," constitutes such a material departure from the agreement entered into by the subscribers as will render the subscriptions unenforcible as to non-assenting subscribers.

APPEAL by the defendants, Joseph J. McKee and another, from a judgment of the Supreme Court in favor of the plaintiff, entered in the office of the clerk of the county of New York on the 1st day of May, 1901, upon the verdict of a jury; also an appeal by the defendant Joseph J. McKee from an order entered in said clerk's office on the 1st day of May, 1901, and by the defendant Ernest G. Hoffmann from an order entered in said clerk's office on the 30th day of April, 1901, denying the respective defendants' motions for a new trial made upon the minutes.

This action was brought to recover damages for the alleged breach of a contract between the defendants and the plaintiff's assignor, one

Shainwald. The contract first made was in writing and was as follows :

"NEW YORK, *May* 15, 1896.

"Agreement made and entered into on this date between E. G. Hoffmann, Joseph J. McKee and Ralph L. Shainwald ; in consideration of one dollar to each in hand paid, the receipt whereof each of the parties hereto duly acknowledges, Mr. Hoffmann agrees to give to Mr. Shainwald the sole option until August 31st, 1896, to sell all his rights to all countries outside of the United States, except as hereafter mentioned, to metal turning machines of his invention, and any and all improvements, for a term of years as is customary in the various countries where such patents or rights are in existence or are procurable, and to keep alive all his rights in foreign countries at his expense during term of this option.

"Mr. McKee agrees to give to Mr. Shainwald the sole option to August 31st, 1896, to sell all his rights to the Hoffmann Metal Turning Machine Patents for Great Britain, France, Germany & Belgium, which patents are not included in those referred to in the first paragraph, same having been sold to Mr. McKee by Mr. Hoffmann. Mr. McKee is also to secure to Mr. Shainwald all improvements for same term of years as Mr. Hoffmann agrees upon in the first paragraph.

"The purpose of said option & the Rights to Mr. Shainwald are to enable him to form a company in New York city which is to acquire all the rights to the Hoffmann Metal Turning Machines and all improvements.

"It is agreed between the three parties hereto as follows: that the proposed company is to be formed on the below-named basis: A share capital of $300,000, of which one-half ($150,000) is to be paid for Patents & the remainder ($150,000) sold at 50c. on the dollar to realize $75,000 in cash. The cash to be used to pay $55,000 for patents, & $20,000 to be left in company's treasury as a capital for expenses of introducing & exploiting the machines in Europe.

"The $55,000 cash is to be distributed among the three parties hereto as follows: To Mr. Hoffmann, $34,000, to Mr. Shainwald, $16,000, to Mr. McKee, $5,000. The shares as follows: To Mr. Hoffmann, $62,000, to Mr. Shainwald, $68,000, to Mr. McKee, $20,000. Out of shares received by Mr. Shainwald he is to settle with Continental Commerce Co. for cancellation of their option from Mr. Hoffmann, dated Sep. —, 1895, and also with Mr. H. Liebes, of London, for surrender of his rights acquired under option of Continental Commerce Co.

"It is further agreed that the patent for Canada now existing is understood will be reserved for sale to the Hoffmann Machine Co. of New York, and Mr. Hoffmann agrees that said Company shall have the balance of this year to decide whether to purchase same at not more than one thousand dollars."

Shortly after the execution of the contract the same was modified by a parol agreement to the effect that the proposed corporation should be organized under the statutes of West Virginia, with a capital of 3,000 shares of the par value of $100, of which 2,250 shares were to be delivered to the defendants in payment of the patents, and 750 shares were to be sold for cash, and of the proceeds $20,000 was to be held by the corporation as working capital and the balance to be divided among the parties to the contract in certain proportions, the defendants to transfer and deliver to the persons purchasing said 750 shares an equal number of shares of stock issued to them as an inducement to purchasers to make such purchases. An extension of the option was obtained from August 28, 1896, to September 22, 1896. During the life of the option, Shainwald drew up a prospectus of the contemplated company. He also procured persons to subscribe for a certain amount of the stock of such corporation, when formed. On the 17th of September, 1896, Shainwald procured to be incorporated under the laws of West Virginia, the Hoffmann Foreign Machine Company with a capital stock of $500 — the articles of incorporation stating that the incorporators "desire the privilege of increasing the said capital by the sale of additional shares from time to time to three hundred thousand ($300,000) dollars in all." On the 21st of September, 1896, the parties to the contract met for the purpose of carrying out the same, but were unable to do so for the reason that they could not agree upon certain details. The cause of the disagreement is not entirely clear, the plaintiff contending that the defendants required Shainwald to guarantee the payment of the subscriptions which he had obtained, and he refusing to do so the other parties refused to proceed, and the defendants contending that they refused to proceed because Shainwald would not permit them to inspect the subscription list, or the charter or minute book of the corporation which he had organized. The defendants, in any event, refused to carry out the terms of the contract, and subsequently Shainwald assigned his interest in the contract to this plaintiff, who thereupon brought this action to recover damages alleged to have been sustained by reason of the defendants' failure to perform on their part, he alleging that, prior to the expiration of the option, "Shainwald performed all the conditions and requirements of said agreement as so modified on his part."

The defendants interposed separate answers to the complaint, and among other things denied that the plaintiff was entitled to recover for the reason that his assignor had not performed the contract on his part. At the close of the case the defendants moved to dismiss the complaint upon the ground, among others, that if the defendants, at the time alleged, refused to perform, the plaintiff was not entitled to recover because his assignor had not performed, nor had he the ability to perform at that time. The motion was denied and an exception taken.

The plaintiff had a verdict for $16,000, and from the judgment entered thereon, and an order denying a motion for a new trial, defendants have separately appealed.

William H. Stayton, for the appellant McKee.

Charles A. Wendell, for the appellant Hoffmann.

William B. Hornblower, for the respondent.

McLAUGHLIN, J.:

Plaintiff having pleaded full performance of the contract could not recover without establishing that fact. This he did not do, and, therefore, the motion of the defendants at the close of the trial to dismiss the complaint on that ground should have been granted. The allegation of the complaint in this respect is "that prior to the said 22d day of September, 1896, said Shainwald performed all the conditions and requirements of said agreement as so modified on his part; that said Shainwald caused a corporation to be formed under the laws of the State of West Virginia; that said Shainwald secured purchasers of Seventy-five thousand ($75,000) dollars of the stock of such corporation, and thereupon called upon and required the said defendants to comply with their part of the said agreement and to transfer the patents and improvements set forth therein to said corporation, and receive the consideration and the stock called for by the said contract and modification thereof as hereinbefore set forth." This allegation was put in issue by the answers of the defendants and no proof whatever was offered at the trial tending to establish the truth of the same. On the contrary, the evidence is uncontradicted to the effect that Shainwald did not form a corporation with a capital stock of $300,000; nor did he procure purchasers of stock in any corporation which was formed to the amount of $75,000. The contract in express terms obligated Shainwald to form a corporation with a capital stock of $300,000, and impliedly obligated him to procure purchasers of such stock to the amount of $75,000. This latter obligation is implied from the fact that the plaintiff's assignor was to receive $16,000 in cash and $68,000 in stock; and the plaintiff alleges it in the complaint and his assignor testified upon the trial that the agreement obligated him to do this. The plaintiff, therefore, having alleged performance, was bound to establish that fact, and failing to do so, no recovery could be had. (*La Chicotte* v. *Richmond R. & El. Co.*, 15 App. Div. 380; *Schnaier* v. *Nathan*, 31 id. 225; *McEntyre* v. *Tucker*, 36 id. 53; *Cox* v. *Halloran*, 64 id. 550.) But in this connection it is suggested that the recovery can be upheld upon the theory that Shainwald was excused from full performance by reason of the defendants' refusal to proceed. This cannot be done for the reason that there are no appropriate allegations in the complaint which would permit a recovery upon that ground. The plaintiff having predicated his right to recover on the breach of the agreement, was bound to allege and prove performance on the part of his assignor, or an excuse for non-performance, and if an excuse were relied upon, then he was bound to allege facts constituting such excuse, and, in addition thereto, that he was at that time ready and had the ability to perform, and would have done so except for the acts of the other parties to the contract. But had the plaintiff alleged facts showing an excuse for the non-performance based upon the refusal of the defendants to proceed, it would have been unavailing, inasmuch as it appears, and this fact is uncontradicted, that at the time the defendants refused to perform — September 22, 1896 — the plaintiff's assignor not only had not performed, but he did not then have the ability to do so. The refusal of the defendants at that time to proceed under the contract did not relieve the plaintiff's assignor from the obligations which he had assumed, nor from proving that at that time he was able, ready and willing to proceed to carry out the contract on his part. (*Bigler* v. *Morgan*, 77 N. Y. 312; *Lawrence* v. *Miller*, 86 id. 137; *Eddy* v. *Davis*, 116 id. 247.) The plaintiff's assignor could not then have performed. He had not formed the corporation as agreed, nor had he procured a purchaser to a single dollar of the stock. The most favorable claim that can be made for him in this respect is that he had formed a corporation with a capital stock of $500 and had obtained subscriptions to the extent of $75,000 to the stock of a corporation when formed. The corporation which he had formed, as already said, only had a capital stock of $500, and it is difficult to see, until something further had been done, how the stock which he claims had been subscribed for could have been delivered, or how the defendants could receive the stock which the agreement provided should be delivered to them as a consideration for the assignment of their patents. But it is suggested that had the defendants acted with Shainwald the capital stock of the corporation formed could have been increased to $300,000. It is true that the terms of the certificate of incorporation provided for such increase, but before that could be done it would have been necessary for the stockholders to have taken some action showing that they had voted upon the subject of such increase; and had Shainwald and the defendant McKee favored such increase, it does not necessarily follow that the increase would have been voted, inasmuch as it appears that they were minority stockholders.

Nor do we think that the subscriptions to the stock could have been enforced if the capital stock of the corporation formed had been increased to $300,000. These subscriptions were obtained in connection with a prospectus which stated that the purpose of the corporation to be formed was "to acquire all patents and rights for all countries except the United States and Canada, to metal turning machines, known as the 'Hoffmann machines,' and of which E. G. Hoffmann is the inventor and patentee, as well as all improvements, additions, etc." The subscribers agreed to take stock in a corporation formed for this purpose. The corporation as organized by Shainwald, as appears from the certificate of incorporation, was "to make, contract for the manufacture, or purchase of, buy, use, sell, lease, rent or mortgage all mechanical or other apparatus, machinery and implements for metal turning machines, or any other article or articles connected therewith or incident thereto, or any or all of them, and *in general to do a manufacturing business.*" This was a material departure from the agreement entered into by the subscribers, and to which, so far as appears, none of them ever assented. The corporation having been formed without their knowledge, or at least some of them, and they never having ratified the additions to the contemplated business of the corporation, certainly could not be called upon to pay their subscriptions, or take stock in such corporation. (*Dorris* v. *Sweeney*, 60 N. Y. 463.) Nor do we think it satisfactorily appeared in other respects that valid subscriptions to the amount of $75,000 had been secured. Some $17,500 of such stock appears to have been subscribed for, not by parties purporting to have subscribed for it, but by Shainwald, under an alleged authorization to so subscribe. These authorizations, according to the testimony of Shainwald, were by parol, with the exception of one, which is claimed to be by a cablegram and which cablegram was not introduced in evidence, and as to one of them the alleged subscriber testified that he never signed the list and never authorized Shainwald to sign for him. In addition to this, all of the subscriptions are conditioned upon the payment of the bonus by the defendants, and how the corporation could enforce the payment of such bonus it is difficult to see. If it could not do so, then it could not enforce the payment of the subscriptions contingent upon the bonus.

Other questions are raised by the appellants, but we deem it unnecessary to consider them.

The judgment and order appealed from must be reversed and a new trial ordered, with costs to the appellants to abide the event.

VAN BRUNT, P. J., O'BRIEN, HATCH and LAUGHLIN, JJ., concurred.

Judgment and order reversed, new trial ordered, costs to appellants to abide event.

DAVID McCLURE, as Receiver of THE LIFE UNION, Respondent, *v.* JOHN W. WILSON, Appellant.

Fraud — when the inference thereof will be sustained — proof that money of a corporation was paid upon its void notes to a director thereof — knowledge imputable to a director.

Where fraud is charged, knowledge is generally a matter of inference, and where a state of facts is developed, from which different inferences may be drawn, a jury may draw such inferences and may characterize the act by considering it in the light of all that occurred, and if the inference drawn by the jury is not unreasonable it will be sanctioned by the court.

What evidence given in an action brought by the receiver of a co-operative insurance corporation against a former director thereof, to recover moneys of the association paid to the director in extinguishment of void notes executed by the association to the director, is sufficient to warrant a jury in finding that the defendant took such money with knowledge that it belonged to the corporation, considered.

In such a case the defendant is chargeable with such knowledge as he gained in the capacity of director, or which he might have acquired by the exercise of reasonable care.

APPEAL by the defendant, John W. Wilson, from a judgment of the Supreme Court in favor of the plaintiff, entered in the office of the clerk of the county of New York on the 17th day of May, 1901, upon the verdict of a jury, and also from an order entered in said clerk's office on the 27th day of May, 1901, denying the defendant's motion for a new trial made upon the minutes.

Henry D. Hotchkiss, for the appellant.

David McClure, for the respondent.

HATCH, J.:

The action was brought by the plaintiff as receiver of the Life Union, a co-operative or assessment insurance corporation, to recover a sum of money received by the defendant which the receiver claims equitably belongs to it.

The defendant was for a time acting as a director of said insurance corporation, and during that period three agreements were entered into, which had for their purpose the unlawful transfer of the control of the Life Union over to one Louis P. Levy. This contemplated transfer was a private affair in which certain directors were interested and the money consideration paid for its consummation accrued to their individual benefit. The first of these agreements was made on December 28, 1891, the second and third were made on February 5, 1892; the second agreement merely modified the first in some particulars.

By the terms of the first and second agreements, one Horace Moody, the party of the first part, undertook to deliver to Louis P. Levy and Lucius O. Robertson, parties of the second part, the absolute control of the Life Union, together with its franchise, book accounts and moneys, property and records.

Moody agreed that he would by March 21, 1892, secure the election of a majority of the board of directors, including the vice-president and two members of the executive committee, and that the persons composing the majority should be designated by Levy and Robertson, Moody agreeing at the same time to deliver to them the resignations of the retiring officers and directors. The consideration to Moody for doing this work was a sum of money aggregating $15,000, to be paid through a trustee in installments under the terms of the contract. By the second agreement, $2,000 of the consideration was to be paid to one D. Frank Lloyd on part fulfillment of the agreement, the time for the performance of the original agreement being extended to April 21, 1892. The parties to the third agreement were Moody, Levy, Robertson and D. Frank Lloyd. This agreement shifted the burden of the execution of the scheme from Moody to D. Frank Lloyd, who was a business associate of and had an office in the same suite with William H. Law, the president of the Life Union. Under this agreement Lloyd, instead of Moody, was to receive all the money. Lloyd acted in the matter for Law; it was through Law that Lloyd first knew of the scheme to transfer the control of the Life Union to Levy; the two had talked the matter over together and Law had asked Lloyd to enter into the negotiations and agreements. The third agreement provided, among other things, that eleven notes of the value of $1,000 each, which had been issued by the Life Union on account of the sum of $11,000 which had been advanced to it by certain parties, should be returned *pro rata* to Moody, Robertson and Levy, as the cash was paid to Lloyd.

In April, 1891, what was known as the Flour City deal was in process of negotiation. This was an effort by the Life Union to secure for the consideration of $40,000 the membership of another association having a large amount of insurance. At a meeting of the Life Union directors, held April 10, 1891, being prior to the time defendant became a director, the issuing of thirty-five one thousand dollar notes by the Life Union was authorized in the following form :

" $1,000.   NEW YORK, *April* 13*th*, 1891.

" On or before twenty-four months after date The Life Union of the City of New York promises to pay to the order of ——— one thousand dollars at its office in the city of New York from such portion of the income of said The Life Union as may be properly applicable thereto, with interest. Value received.

" THE LIFE UNION,
" By J. T. BALDWIN, *Pres't.*   [SEAL.]
" RALPH MARDEN, *Secy.*"

Eleven thousand dollars were raised by subscription and notes issued to the subscribers, all being directors of the Life Union, the defendant Wilson, who had then become a director, being one of them ; he subscribed $2,000 and took two notes. The consideration to the Flour City for the transfer consisted of $5,000 in cash, $24,000 of the Life Union notes authorized as above, and the $11,000 raised by subscription held by Mr. Baldwin, and according to the testimony of William H. Law, finally paid over to C. F. Underhill, the president of the Flour City. The transfer failed of completion, for the Flour City went into the hands of a receiver. The notes thus became worthless. None of the $11,000 went into the treasury of the Life Union.

X The defendant Wilson was elected a director June 16, 1891, and resigned May 20, 1892 ; he had been vice-president and resigned such office December 15, 1891. He was made a member of the executive committee on September 30, 1891, and continued as such down to April 1, 1892. His friend Baldwin and Mr. Law, whom he saw frequently, were also members of the executive committee. Up to the time of his own resignation the defendant sat at the meeting of the directors and voted upon the resignation of old directors and the election of Levy and his friends to fill the vacancies. He was present at the meeting at which Louis P. Levy was

FIRST DEPARTMENT, MARCH TERM, 1902.   [Vol. 70.

elected president of the Life Union, after which and at the same
meeting defendant's resignation was presented and accepted and a
friend of Levy was elected in his place.

At a meeting of the directors of the Life Union held September
30, 1891, at which Wilson was present, a resolution was adopted
that such legal steps be taken as might be necessary to recover the
notes and cash paid to the representatives of the Flour City Company, the expenses to be borne by the Life Union and six trustees,
of whom Wilson was one.

On March 28, 1892, a circular entitled "The Life Union Vindi-
cated," dated February 27, 1892, was issued and published in the
New York *Tribune.* This circular was signed by members of the
executive committee, one of whom was Wilson, and the portion of
it in which we are here interested reads as follows: "The $35,000
notes given by The Life Union were specially printed contract
notes, payable out of expense funds derived from the transferred
membership of the Flour City. No such transfer took place.
Therefore, the consideration having failed, the notes are worthless.
The directors have lost $11,000. The company lost nothing."

The scheme of transferring the control of the Life Union to Louis
P. Levy was fully carried out, and, on the part of Levy, his agreements were fulfilled by the payment of the moneys in several
installments to Lloyd from time to time, for which Levy received
notes *pro tanto.* Lloyd gave the money to Law as fast as he
received it from Levy. The payments were made in Lloyd and
Law's office in their presence. Law and Lloyd gave Levy the notes
representing the amount paid. The total amount paid was $12,000,
representing the $11,000 principal of the notes and $1,000 interest.
The payments extended from February to the latter part of May,
1892. All payments were made to Lloyd in bills, and were so
handed over to him by Law. Contemporaneously, Wilson gave up
his notes and got money in bills by installments, $2,000 and interest
from Baldwin, to whom the money had been paid by Law. The
last installment was paid to Wilson a day or two after his resignation
on May 20, 1892.

So far as the law of this case is concerned, it has been settled by
decisive authority that the proposed scheme of the Life Union to
purchase the Flour City Association was illegal, *ultra vires,* and

that the notes given to carry out the arrangement were executed without authority and were void (*McClure* v. *Levy*, 147 N. Y. 215); and that, so far as the persons participating in the transaction were concerned and who received money in payment of such notes with knowledge of the source of the payment, such moneys were unlawfully paid, remained the property of the association and could be recovered by its representatives in an action for that purpose (*McClure* v. *Law*, 161 N. Y. 78); that as to a director of the corporation, who was a holder of one of the notes, but had resigned his directorship prior to the time when the scheme was formulated for the purpose of unlawfully transferring the control of the association, had no knowledge thereof and did not participate therein, was not chargeable with moneys paid to him in payment of one of the notes, it appearing that he acted in good faith, it could not be said that he parted with no value by the surrender of the note, for while the same was not a binding obligation upon the Life Union, it might be that a right of action existed to enforce the same against the Flour City Association or against the persons who received the money represented by the note. (*McClure* v. *Trask*, 161 N. Y. 82.) This case, therefore, comes to rest upon the fact as to whether the defendant herein had knowledge of the unlawful scheme, and the source of the moneys which he received in payment of the two notes held by him.

It is undisputed that from June 16, 1891, down to May 20, 1892, the defendant acted as a director, was elected a member of the executive committee of the board, and was for a time vice-president of the company. On the day when Law resigned as president and Levy was elected in his place, the defendant participated in the action, and when it was consummated immediately resigned, so that during the whole period from the time of the execution of the first agreement which marked the inception of the scheme down to the time of its consummation, the defendant was an active participant in all of the transactions by which it was carried out. As a director he was chargeable with such knowledge as he gained in that capacity or might have learned by the exercise of reasonable care. He could not blindly shut his eyes to what was transpiring about him and shelter himself behind the claim that he was merely acting in the interest of a friend and knew nothing of what he was doing.

The whole subject of the issuing of the notes, the attempted purchase of the Flour City Association, and the fact that the notes were invalid, must have been known to him, because he signed the circular which was promulgated over his signature, and which recited all of the facts, and some things that were not facts.

The acts of the defendant are to be measured and his knowledge inferred from what transpired while he was a director, applying thereto by reasonable interpretation of his acts the knowledge that was fairly necessary in their performance. Knowledge, where fraud is charged, is, in most cases, a matter of inference, and where a state of facts is developed from which different inferences may be drawn a jury is authorized to draw the same, and may characterize the act from all that appears, and if the inference which the jury draw is not unreasonable, it will be sanctioned. (*Bagley* v. *Bowe*, 105 N. Y. 171 ; *Gray* v. *Richmond Bicycle Co.*, 167 id. 348.)

The jury were authorized to find that the payment of the money by Baldwin to the defendant was quite exceptional in character. Both of these men were business men ; Baldwin was the cashier of a bank, and the defendant was entirely familiar with business methods. Baldwin received the money from Law which was paid upon the unlawful agreement, and from time to time he gave to the defendant sums of money in bills, and although he was the cashier of a bank that usually deals largely in evidences of money, yet nothing was made to appear to show by check, entry or otherwise what this transaction was. It was a payment upon what the defendant knew had been characterized as a void obligation. Baldwin had in no measure guaranteed the payment of these notes to the defendant, nor was he under any legal liability therefor, and it may fairly be inferred that business men do not usually pay obligations out of their own pockets upon which there exists no legal liability which may be enforced. There was nothing in the transaction between Baldwin and the defendant, so far as developed by this record, which created against the former even a moral obligation to return the money. A mere representation that a given security is a good investment, where the security is not owned by the person making the representation and he receives no benefit therefrom, and the person purchases of his own volition, creates no liability against the person making the representation, either moral or otherwise, and is not so unusual in character as that such person feels called upon to pay the amount of the investment if it happen to turn out to be bad. The particular circumstances, therefore, that the defendant bought these notes, acted as a director during the period specified, participated in the furtherance of the scheme that transferred the control of the association to Levy pursuant to the agreement, and severed his connection the moment it was consummated, received payment in bills from Baldwin of the notes and Baldwin received money from Law, the proceeds of the illegal action, in bills, together with all the other circumstances which the case presents were sufficient for the jury to find that the defendant received payment of the notes, that it was of money belonging to the association and that he had knowledge of its source. The charge of the court to the jury was clear, full and complete of all these matters. In fact, it was a model charge in the presentation to the jury of the questions which they were called upon to decide.

We think their verdict was justified and should receive support by this court.

The judgment and order should, therefore, be affirmed, with costs.

VAN BRUNT, P. J., O'BRIEN, INGRAHAM and LAUGHLIN, JJ., concurred.

Judgment and order affirmed, with costs.

WILLIAM H. GRAY, Respondent, *v.* CHAPTER GENERAL OF AMERICA, KNIGHTS OF ST. JOHN AND MALTA, and FRANCIS HOUGHTALING, as Grand Chancellor of the CHAPTER GENERAL OF AMERICA, KNIGHTS OF ST. JOHN AND MALTA, Appellants. 70 174 N

Co-operative insurance — forfeiture, when waived — equitable relief for protection of rights — what allegations establish a cause of action — when resort need not be first had to the remedy within the corporation.

Where the constitution of a co-operative insurance company, the subordinate bodies of which are called encampments, provides that assessments shall be paid by the financial chancellor of each encampment to the grand chancellor, and that in the event of the failure to pay the assessment within a specified period the warrant of the encampment shall be canceled, the acceptance by the grand chancellor of an overdue assessment from the financial chancellor of an encampment constitutes a waiver of the right to insist upon the forfeiture.

Where the grand chancellor, acting in violation of the provisions of the constitution, assumes to cancel the warrant of an encampment for an alleged failure to pay an assessment within the prescribed period, and also to suspend from the benefits of the endowment department all the members of the encampment, who were not in default themselves, a court of equity will interpose to protect the rights of a member of such encampment.

An allegation contained in the complaint in an action brought by the aggrieved member, to the effect that the plaintiff had been elected by his encampment a representative to the supreme body of the organization; that at the annual meeting of said supreme body its managing board was elected, the salaries of its officers determined, financial reports made for its approval or disapproval, and amendments to the constitution or other internal legislation passed; that the officers of the association had been guilty of mismanagement, and that the alleged cancellation of the warrant of his encampment was made for the purpose of preventing the plaintiff and others of his encampment who objected to the mismanagement from attending the annual meeting of the supreme body, and protesting against the same, states a cause of action.

The rule that a member of such an association must seek redress in the first instance under the provisions of the laws of the association does not apply to such a case, especially where it is shown that the officers of the association have violated the constitution.

APPEAL by the defendants, Chapter General of America, Knights of St. John and Malta, and another, from an interlocutory judgment of the Supreme Court in favor of the plaintiff, entered in the office of the clerk of the county of New York on the 5th day of December, 1901, upon the decision of the court, rendered after a trial at the New York Special Term, overruling the defendants' demurrers to the amended complaint.

Leopold Leo, for the appellants.

Justus W. Smith, for the respondent.

HATCH, J.:

The amended complaint demands judgment that the plaintiff be adjudged a member in good standing of the defendant insurance corporation and of the endowment department thereof; that the plaintiff's endowment certificate be adjudged to be in full force and effect so long as plaintiff continues to pay his dues and assessments to the financial chancellor of his encampment, and that the defendant corporation, its officers, subordinates and agents, be enjoined and restrained from declaring plaintiff under suspension in the endowment department as well as a member of the defendant corporation, and also be restrained from declaring New York Encampment No. 43 suspended, and from taking possession thereof and from canceling its warrants, and that the plaintiff have such other and further relief as may be just, with costs.

The complaint shows that the "Chapter General of America, Knights of St. John and Malta," is a New York corporation, and a monthly assessment, co-operative insurance company; that the plaintiff is, and has been since March 31, 1888, a member in good standing in the defendant corporation and of New York Encampment No. 43, a subordinate body thereof, and is the holder of a certificate of insurance of defendant corporation in the sum of $2,000, payable to his wife within three months after due proof of his death; that section 38 of the constitution of the defendant corporation provides for the payment to the plaintiff on his arriving at the age of seventy years of said sum of $2,000, in five annual installments, and in case of his death before full payment, any unpaid balance to be paid to his beneficiary; that he has duly paid all assessments and dues, and that no charges have been preferred against him; that assessments are levied by the "Grand Chancellor," upon notification to the financial chancellor of subordinate bodies called "encampments," who thereupon notifies the members to pay to him their assessments and all dues then due within thirty days from the date of the notice, and that failure to pay the same suspends the member from all rights of membership; that such suspension is not absolute, but the member may reinstate himself within thirty days thereafter by making such payment and passing a new medical examination; that non-payment by and the suspension of an encampment does not suspend a member; that the defendant Houghtaling, on March 25, 1901, issued a notice declaring the plaintiff and all the members of the plaintiff's encampment suspended, for the alleged reason that the encampment had failed to pay to the grand body assessments Nos. 221 to 228, inclusive, although the plaintiff had paid the same to the financial chancellor of his encampment, to which financial chancellor, under the constitution of the defendant corporation, the

FIRST DEPARTMENT, MARCH TERM, 1902.   [Vol. 70.

members of the encampment are required to pay their assessments, and who is required to give a receipt therefor to the member so paying, and that the moneys so collected do not go into the encampment treasury, but are to be paid by the financial chancellor direct to the grand chancellor, and that all assessments so paid by the plaintiff have been paid or tendered to the grand chancellor; that the notice declaring the encampment suspended was followed on April 6, 1901, by a notice declaring the warrant of the encampment canceled, because the encampment had failed to pay assessments 221 and 222, and that it had been suspended therefor for three months and had not reinstated itself. The complaint shows that these assessments had been paid, although not in due time, and that provisions of the constitution requiring that in such a case there must be prompt notice of any default on the part of the financial chancellor, an investigation of the matter, and thereupon the encampment declared dormant, and that the state of dormancy exist three months before an encampment warrant can be declared canceled had not been complied with, and that the defendants had waived any default by continuing to direct the collection of assessments from the members; that the supreme body of the defendant corporation, called the chapter general, meets annually in September; that said supreme body consists of its own officers and past grand commanders of good standing, and of elected representatives from the subordinate bodies called "encampments," of which representatives plaintiff was one; that at a meeting of said supreme body its managing board is elected, salaries of officers determined, financial reports made for its approval or disapproval, and amendments to the constitution or other internal legislation passed. Plaintiff charges mismanagement on the part of the officials, and that the alleged cancellation of the warrant of his encampment was not in good faith, but for the purpose of preventing plaintiff and others from his encampment who objected to the mismanagement from attending the annual meeting of the supreme body and exposing their misdeeds.

The notice of the suspension of the members of the encampment, which was given by the grand chancellor, recited as a reason therefor failure to remit assessments from 221 to 228. The averment of the complaint is that numbers 221 and 222 were paid by the financial chancellor of the encampment to the grand chancellor and that the latter gave his receipt therefor. The payment was not made in the time required by the constitution, but it was competent for the grand chancellor to accept the same, and such acceptance constituted a waiver of the right to insist upon the forfeiture, assuming it to have been incurred by such failure. (*Titus* v. *Glens Falls Ins. Co.*, 81 N. Y. 410; *Martin* v. *Equitable Accident Assn.*, 61 Hun, 467.) It is clear, therefore, that this notice, so far as it was based upon failure to pay assessments 221 and 222, was ineffectual, as they had been paid. The notice was also ineffectual because it assumed to suspend the members from the benefit of the endowment department. This was in violation of the terms of the constitution, for by section 79 they, not being in any default themselves in payment of assessments, were authorized to pay thereafter to the grand chancellor and affiliate with another body.

The grand chancellor not only waived default in the payment of assessments Nos. 221 and 222, but he also issued notices to the encampment for the collection of 223 and 224, which were collected by the financial chancellor and not paid over. Instead of then suspending the encampment for this act, or taking steps as provided by the constitution, he issued to the suspended encampment, which had elected a new financial chancellor in place of the defaulting officer, assessment notices Nos. 227 to 232, all of which were paid by the plaintiff to the financial chancellor, to whom they were issued by the grand chancellor. There was, therefore, a recognition upon the part of the grand chancellor that the encampment was authorized to collect these assessments, and his command, as well as that of the constitution, was to pay such assessments to the officer who had been authorized to collect the same. It is, therefore, apparent that the grand chancellor had no authority under the constitution to issue assessments which the members were required to pay, and then, upon payment as commanded, suspend them for failure to do something else which by his own act had been waived. As the notice of the suspension of the encampment was based upon the first notice suspending the members, it is evident that it was ineffectual for the purpose which it sought to accomplish, as it was not authorized by law and the acts of forfeiture had been waived. In addition to this, it was provided by the constitution that, upon default of an encampment to make payment as prescribed, authority was vested in the district deputy to make an inquiry into the matter, take testimony upon notice to the defaulting encampment, render a judgment and report the same to the grand commander and until such steps are taken an encampment may not be declared dormant.

When an encampment is declared dormant after these proceedings have been had by the district deputy, then a member, not otherwise in default, is given opportunity to pay his assessment to the grand chancellor, or to an officer appointed for that purpose by the district deputy, and has three months thereafter to affiliate with another encampment.

It is the averment of the complaint that compliance was not had with any of these provisions of the constitution, in consequence of which it is clear that the grand chancellor could not deprive this plaintiff of his rights in the endowment fund. Equity has jurisdiction of such matter and may interpose to protect the party's rights. (*Meyer* v. *Knickerbocker Life Ins. Co.*, 73 N. Y. 516)

The rule that members must seek redress in the first instance, under the provisions of the laws of the association for the redress of grievances, has no application to such a state of facts. It does not appear that there are any such provisions, and, so far as the constitution is concerned, the complaint shows that it has been violated by the defendants, in consequence of which he could have no redress except by resort to legal remedies.

We are also of opinion that the complaint states a good cause of action respecting the right of the plaintiff to representation in the convocation of the supreme body. It appears that such a body is the general governing body of the order, and that the officers constituting the same threaten to deprive the plaintiff of a seat and voice therein, he being entitled thereto; that the management of the affairs of the corporation has been wasteful, extravagant and in violation of the constitution; and that such acts seriously affect the integrity of the endowment fund, and that if such management is continued the value of plaintiff's certificate will be materially reduced if not wholly destroyed. The encampment of which the plaintiff is a member is entitled to representation, unless it forfeits its right thereto and is, in the manner provided by the constitution, duly and legally suspended and declared dormant for such acts of forfeiture. Undoubtedly a cause of action would exist in its favor for the protection of its rights as an encampment, but such fact does not deprive the plaintiff of his right. The matters averred in the complaint show that he has a property interest, which is not only jeopardized by the attempted suspension of his right to benefit therein, but is also jeopardized by the wasteful and extravagant management of the officers of the corporation. By reason of his election to representation in the grand convocation he has a means to protect his property interest in the endowment fund by taking steps therein to prevent mismanagement and waste. If he be deprived of such right, his opportunity to protect his property interest in this respect is lost, and, as the laws of the order confer upon him the right to be heard in the convocation, a deprivation of such right clearly affects his individual property right and interest. The same equitable principle which protects him from suspension of all right in the endowment fund also protects him in his right to assert and vote for the maintenance of the integrity of the fund and to prevent wasteful and extravagant raids thereon. It is evident, therefore, that this complaint states a cause of action.

The interlocutory judgment should, therefore, be affirmed, with costs, and leave given to the defendant to withdraw the demurrer and answer within twenty days, on the payment of costs in this court and in the court below.

VAN BRUNT, P. J., INGRAHAM, McLAUGHLIN and LAUGHLIN, JJ., concurred.

Judgment affirmed, with costs, with leave to the defendants to withdraw the demurrer and answer within twenty days, on payment of costs in this court and in the court below.

DEMIE W. HILDRETH and HENRY SEGELKEN, Respondents, *v.*
JOSEPH M. McCAUL, Appellant.

162
ª459

*Firm name — what facts establish bad faith in the use of a name and justify the
granting of a temporary injunction.*

An individual who becomes a member of a copartnership has a right to use the
name of his copartner in connection with his business and in advertising the
same, provided he acts in good faith and does not deceive the public or mislead those with whom he seeks to do business, as to the identity of his business or his firm, to the injury or prejudice of others competing in the same
line of business.

What affidavits, submitted on a motion made in an action brought by Demie W.
Hildreth and Henry Segelken, partners, doing business under the firm name
of Hildreth & Segelken, against one Joseph M. McCaul, who claimed to have
entered into a copartnership with one Henry Phelps Hildreth, and who had
leased premises formerly occupied by the firm of Hildreth & Segelken, and
erected a sign bearing the words "Hildreth, McCaul Co.," in large letters
and the words "Jos. M. McCaul, Prop.," in small letters underneath, establish
that McCaul was not using the name "Hildreth" in good faith and justify the
granting of a temporary injunction restraining the defendant from using, in
his business, the name "Hildreth" separately or conjunctively with any other
name, designation or description until the further order of the court,
considered.

APPEAL by the defendant, Joseph M. McCaul, from an order of
the Supreme Court, made at the New York Special Term and
entered in the office of the clerk of the county of New York on the
10th day of July, 1901, restraining and enjoining the defendant, his
agents and servants, "from showing, displaying or otherwise using
during the pendency of this action in or upon any papers, devices,
sign or signs, or otherwise, in the business conducted by the defendant at Nos. 120–122 West Broadway, in the borough of Manhattan,
city of New York, or elsewhere, the name of 'Hildreth' separately
or conjunctively with any other name, designation or description."

William Hughes, for the appellant.

William Victor Goldberg, for the respondents.

LAUGHLIN, J. :

In the year 1883, appellant and Henry Phelps Hildreth formed a
copartnership as manufacturers and commission merchants dealing
in honey, beeswax, maple sugar and maple syrup and carried on

business at No. 90 Hudson street in the city of New York. In 1884 Luther S. Hildreth became a member of the firm and the firm name was changed to McCaul & Hildreth Bros. The firm remained the same until 1888, when appellant retired and Henry Segelken entered the firm as a partner. The business was then continued under the firm name of Hildreth Bros. & Segelken. In 1895 Henry Phelps Hildreth withdrew as a partner and the firm name became Hildreth & Segelken. In 1898 Luther S. Hildreth died, and his wife, Demie W. Hildreth, who succeeded to his interests, became a member of the firm and the business was and still is continued under the name of Hildreth & Segelken.

Each successive firm succeeded to the good will of the former firm. For about thirteen years prior to the 1st day of May, 1901, the firm business was conducted at Nos. 120 and 122 West Broadway. On that day the firm changed its place of business to Nos. 265 and 267 Greenwich street. The appellant, prior to his connection with the firm, had experience in this line of business as an employee of the firm of H. K. & F. B. Thurber & Co., and after withdrawing from the firm to which plaintiffs are successors in 1888, he engaged in the same line of business as a broker on his own account at 198 Duane street and so continued until 1892. After being out of the business for about four years he resumed business in 1896 in Brooklyn, continuing it until 1899. In May, 1899, he entered the employ of plaintiffs and continued in such employ until May 1, 1901.

He claims to have entered into a copartnership with Henry Phelps Hildreth on the 11th day of May, 1901. The articles of copartnership were not produced, but by their terms, as stated by appellant, he was to furnish the entire capital, which was to be $6,000, and was to have charge of the business and Hildreth was to share in the profits as if he had contributed the sum of $500 to the capital.

Hildreth was old, in poor health, had no means, and judgments in large amounts had been entered against him, which remained unsatisfied. He had worked as a clerk for a time after leaving the firm in 1895, but for many years had been out of business. He was defendant's brother-in-law.

The defendant rented the premises 120 and 122 West Broadway for a period of thirteen years shortly after the same were vacated by the plaintiffs. In place of the sign which respondents had on the building, appellant caused the sign "Hildreth, McCaul Co." to be erected in large letters and the words "Jos. M. McCaul, Prop." in small letters underneath. He prepared letter-heads quite like those used by the plaintiffs, excepting that in place of the firm name "Hildreth & Segelken," the firm name of "Hildreth, McCaul Co." in large letters with the words "Jos. M. McCaul, Prop." appeared, and with that heading he caused a circular to be issued to the trade, signed "Hildreth, McCaul Co., Jos. M. McCaul, Prop.," stating, among other things, "We have organized this new honey, beeswax, maple sugar and maple syrup firm, and have located ourselves at the old stand which we established fifteen years ago. We will continue to carry a full line of the different kinds of honey. * * * Our experience for the past twenty-five years in this line of goods enables us to make selections and give you entire satisfaction."

It was shown by affidavit that the Bradstreet Mercantile Agency published a report of appellant's firm and business, stating that appellant represented that Henry P. Hildreth was not his partner, but that he paid a consideration for the use of his name, and that the Wilbur Mercantile Agency published a report to the effect that appellant was successor to the plaintiffs. It also appeared that confusion in business has resulted, and that orders intended for respondents were received by appellant, and that customers of plaintiffs were misled by the circular and supposed that appellant had succeeded respondents in business.

Shortly after the commencement of this action and before the hearing on which the injunction order was granted, Henry Phelps Hildreth died. Other facts were stated in the moving affidavits tending to show that appellant was not acting in good faith in the use of the name "Hildreth," which he caused to be placed before his own as has been seen. These facts were controverted by appellant's affidavit.

We think the moving papers were sufficient to justify the inference of such bad faith in this regard, and to warrant an injunction. The order granted, however, is too broad, in that it absolutely enjoins the use of the name "Hildreth" by the appellant in his business. Doubtless this was owing to the death of Hildreth, it not appearing that appellant had any right to continue the use of his name.

An individual has a right to use his own name in connection with his business and in advertising the same, provided he acts in good faith and does not deceive the public or mislead those with whom he seeks to do business as to the identity of his business or his firm to the injury or prejudice of others competing in the same line of business. (*Devlin* v. *Devlin*, 69 N. Y. 212; *Meneely* v. *Meneely*, 62 id. 427.) The rule was well stated by RAPALLO, J., in *Meneely* v. *Meneely* (*supra*), as follows: " The manner of using the name is all that would be enjoined, not the simple use of it; for every man has the absolute right to use his own name in his own business, even though he may thereby interfere with or injure the business of another person bearing the same name, provided he does not resort to any artifice or contrivance for the purpose of producing the impression that the establishments are identical or do anything calculated to mislead. Where the only confusion created is that which results from the similarity of the names the courts will not interfere. A person cannot make a trade mark of his own name, and thus obtain a monopoly of it which will debar all other persons of the same name from using their own names in their own business." We think he has the same right to form a copartnership with an individual of any name and to use the name of his copartner in connection with the business or in advertising it, and he should not be enjoined from so doing.

If upon the trial the plaintiffs establish a case for permanent injunction the court will protect the defendant's rights by confining the injunction to the manner of using the name as indicated by these authorities. So far as this appeal is concerned, we will merely modify the injunction order by adding at the end of the enjoining clause the words " without the further order of the court," and as thus modified it is affirmed, with ten dollars costs and disbursements.

VAN BRUNT, P. J., O'BRIEN, McLAUGHLIN and HATCH, JJ., concurred.

Order modified as directed in opinion, and as modified affirmed, with ten dollars costs and disbursements.

166
is⁹129|

LOUIS J. FREY, Respondent, *v.* DAVID M. TORREY, Appellant.

Bankruptcy — a discharge does not cover an indebtedness created by fraud — effect of the proof of the claim in bankruptcy on the right to subsequently sue thereon — election.

The words, " while acting as an officer or in any fiduciary capacity," used in subdivision 4 of section 17 of the United States Bankruptcy Law, excepting from the operation of the discharge in bankruptcy an indebtedness " created by his fraud, embezzlement, misappropriation or defalcation while acting as an officer or in any fiduciary capacity," do not qualify the w J ;ds " fraud," " embezzlement," and " misappropriation," but only the word " defalcation." *

Proof in the bankruptcy proceeding of an indebtedness created by the fraud of the bankrupt does not constitute an election which will estop the creditor from subsequently bringing an action against the bankrupt to recover the indebtedness created.

Semble, that if it be conceded that the creditor waived the tort by proving his claim in bankruptcy, he might subsequently bring an action against the bankrupt on contract, and if the discharge in bankruptcy were pleaded he might, in rebuttal, show that the debt was created by fraud, not to change his cause of action from contract to fraud, but to prevent it from being barred by the discharge in bankruptcy.

VAN BRUNT, P. J., dissented.

APPEAL by the defendant, David M. Torrey, by permission, from a determination of the Appellate Term of the Supreme Court, affirming a judgment of the Municipal Court of the city of New York, borough of Manhattan, ninth district, in favor of the plaintiff, entered on the 28th day of June, 1901; and also (as stated in the notice of appeal) from a judgment of the said Appellate Term in favor of the plaintiff, entered in the office of the clerk of the county of New York on the 1st day of November, 1901.

Robert A. B. Dayton, for the appellant.

Walter J. Rosenstein, for the respondent.

LAUGHLIN, J.:

The pleadings in the Municipal Court were oral. The record shows that the complaint was " for money obtained by fraud."

---

* See *Matter of Bullis* (68 App. Div. 5(8).

The answer was a general denial and a plea of discharge in bankruptcy. The defendant was a private banker, and between the 5th and 11th days of October, 1898, the plaintiff deposited with him the sum of $150. The balance of this deposit standing to the credit of the plaintiff on the last-mentioned date was $123.19, no part of which has been paid. The action was brought to recover that sum.

On the 13th day of October, 1898, the defendant made a general assignment for the benefit of his creditors which was filed the next day ; and on the seventeenth day of December thereafter, on the petition of his creditors, he was duly adjudged a bankrupt by the United States District Court. In the bankruptcy proceedings the plaintiff filed proof of a claim in the same amount for "money deposited" with the defendant "while acting in the capacity of banker." On the 29th day of March, 1899, the defendant was duly discharged by said court from all debts provable in bankruptcy which existed on the day he was adjudged a bankrupt "excepting such debts as are by law excepted from the operation of a discharge in bankruptcy."

The appellant, without conceding fraud on his part in contracting this indebtedness, rests his appeal solely upon the grounds : (1) That respondent having proved his debt upon contract waived his right to recover upon the ground of fraud ; and (2) that even if there was actual fraud on his part, still the debt has been discharged by the discharge in bankruptcy. The trial court and the Appellate Term have determined that there was fraud on the part of appellant in receiving these deposits when he was hopelessly insolvent. We do not deem it necessary, inasmuch as the appellant has not seen fit to present the point, to scrutinize the evidence, in the light of the decisions applicable, for the purpose of determining whether a finding that positive fraud, involving moral turpitude or intentional wrong, might be inferred therefrom.

The effect of the discharge in bankruptcy must be determined by a consideration of the Bankruptcy Act of July 1, 1898, and the decisions thereunder, and those construing the corresponding provisions of the former Bankruptcy Laws. . Section 17 of the present Bankruptcy Law, so far as material to our inquiry, provides as follows : "A discharge in bankruptcy shall release a bankrupt from all of his provable debts, except such as * * * (2) are judgments in

actions for frauds, or obtaining property by false pretenses or false
representations, or for willful and malicious injuries to the person
or property of another; * * * or (4) were created by his
fraud, embezzlement, misappropriation, or defalcation while acting
as an officer or in any fiduciary capacity." (30 U. S. Stat. at Large,
550.)

The provisions of the Bankruptcy Act of 1867, corresponding
with the two subdivisions quoted, so far as that act contained provisions on the subject, were embraced in section 33 of the act of
1867 (14 U. S. Stat. at Large, 533), which is the same as section 5117
of the United States Revised Statutes, which provided as follows:
" No debt created by the fraud or embezzlement of the bankrupt, or
by his defalcation as a public officer or while acting in any fiduciary
character, shall be discharged by proceedings in bankruptcy."

The appellant contends that the words " while acting as an officer
or in any fiduciary capacity," in subdivision 4 of section 17 of the
act of 1898, related not only to " defalcation " but also to the words
" fraud," " embezzlement " and " misappropriation." In other
words, he contends that debts created by fraud are not necessarily
dischargeable in bankruptcy, but in order not to be that the fraud
must have occurred while the defendant was acting as an officer
or in some fiduciary capacity. This was neither the grammatical
nor judicial construction of section 5117 of the United States
Revised Statutes. (*Sheldon* v. *Clews*, 13 Abb. N. C. 41; *Bradner*
v. *Strang*, 89 N. Y. 299; affd., 114 U. S. 555; *Schroeder* v. *Frey*,
60 Hun, 58; affd., 131 N. Y. 562; *Stokes* v. *Mason*, 10 R. I. 261;
Bradenberg Bank. [2d ed.] 273.)

The construction of subdivision 4 herein quoted has been frequently discussed judicially, but we find no controlling precedent.
The view presented by appellant seems to have been adopted by the
Appellate Division in the fourth department in *Matter of Bullis* (68
App. Div. 508; 73 N. Y. Supp. 1047), but the construction of subdivision 4 was not essential to the decision in that case. The question
there was whether a *judgment* had been discharged by a discharge in
bankruptcy of the judgment debtor, and the point decided was that the
judgment had been recovered in an action for fraud, and, therefore,
was excepted from the operation of such discharge by subdivision 2
of said section 17. It is true that the provisions with reference to

a discharge in bankruptcy under the present law are somewhat different from those of the former act of Congress, but we think the change has restricted rather than extended the effect of a discharge. Subdivision 2 of section 17 excepts from the discharge judgments for willful and malicious injuries to the property of another. There was no similar exception in the former statute. Under the construction of the former Bankruptcy Law causes of action against factors, agents, commission merchants, bailees and auctioneers for conversion or misappropriation of funds or property were discharged, it being held that the debts for fraud not dischargeable were those where there was actual positive fraud as distinguished from implied or constructive fraud, and that the debts created by defalcation while acting in a fiduciary character embraced only those debts incurred by a breach of a technical as distinguished from an implied trust. (*Lawrence* v. *Harrington*, 122 N. Y. 408; *Mulock* v. *Byrnes*, 129 id. 23; *Hennequin* v. *Clews*, 77 id. 427; affd., 111 U. S. 676; *Neal* v. *Clark*, 95 id. 704; *Upshur* v. *Briscoe*, 138 id. 365; Loveland Bank. § 295.) In view of these decisions we regard the addition of the word "misappropriation" inserted in subdivision 4 of section 17 of the act of 1898, which was not in the former act, as quite significant and as designed to except from the discharge the classes of debts last referred to which were discharged under the former Bankruptcy Law. It will also be observed that the word "public," qualifying "officer," in the former statute has been omitted from the act of 1898.

It seems to be the view of the text writers and of the Federal judges, so far as this question has been considered, that Congress in this change of phraseology intended no change whatever with reference to the character of the debts created by fraud which are not dischargeable. (Collier Bank. [3d ed.] 198, 991; Loveland Bank. §§ 293, 295; *Matter of Thomas*, 1 Am. Bank. Rep. 515; *Matter of Moreau Lieber*, 3 id. 217.) If the words "fraud," "embezzlement" and "misappropriation" are all qualified by the clause "while acting as an officer or in any fiduciary capacity," it is difficult to see the purpose of the use of the word "fraud" at all.

The respondent's claim not having been merged in a judgment, subdivision 2 of section 17, hereinbefore quoted, has no application and we do not think that said subdivision tends to sustain the appellant's contention. It will be observed that there was no corresponding provision under the former law expressly exempting from the discharge causes of action for fraud that have merged in judgments. There appears to have been some doubt whether such judgments would remain enforcible, and, in view of the fact that Congress provided in subdivisions 1 and 5 of section 63 (30 U. S. Stat. at Large, 562) for proving judgments as debts, this subdivision was doubtless enacted to obviate such question as well as to provide for cases, as has been seen, that were neither covered by the former law nor included in subdivision 4 of the present act. (*Matter of Lewensohn,* 3 Am. Bank. Rep. 594, 596; Collier Bank. [3d ed.] 194.)

The application of subdivision 4, relating to debts not in judgments, depends on how the debts were created; while the application of subdivision 2, which is confined to debts merged in judgments, depends not on how the debts were originally created, but on the form of action on which the recovery was had as shown by the judgment, pleadings and record. (*Matter of Rhutassel,* 96 Fed. Rep. 597; *Matter of Thomas,* 1 Am. Bank. Rep. 515; *Burnham* v. *Pidcock,* 58 App. Div. 273; *Matter of Bullis, supra;* Collier Bank. [3d ed.] 194.)

We are of the opinion, therefore, that this indebtedness having been created by the fraud of the appellant was not discharged by the decree in bankruptcy.

The appellant's contention that the respondent is estopped from prosecuting this action by his election to prove his claim in bankruptcy remains to be considered. A binding election can only be made where a party, with full knowledge of all the material facts, adopts a remedy which is inconsistent with another remedy then open to him. (*Crossman* v. *U. R. Co.,* 127 N. Y. 34.) We fail to discover any inconsistency between the remedy pursued by the respondent in the bankruptcy court and that adopted by bringing this action. It does not necessarily appear that the respondent waived the tort by filing proof of his claim in bankruptcy. If not, merely proving the indebtedness which concededly existed and which was induced by fraud, would not be inconsistent with subsequently bringing an action to recover the money obtained by the fraud. (*Stokes* v. *Mason,* 10 R. I. 261; *Sheldon* v. *Clews, supra; Bickford* v. *Barnard,* 8 Allen, 314.) But if the necessary inference from the record be that he waived the cause of action for the tort, still this case may be treated as an action on contract to recover the money on an implied promise to repay the same. The mere fact that it appears to have been alleged that the money was obtained by fraud is not decisive that the action is not upon contract. Subdivision 4 of section 549 of the Code of Civil Procedure classifies an action to recover a debt induced by fraud as an action on contract. The allegation of fraud is essential only for the purpose of obtaining an order of arrest or body execution. (*Ewart* v. *Schwartz*, 48 N. Y. Super. Ct. 390.) The allegations of fraud may be treated as surplusage and perhaps they would have been stricken out if the appellant had pleaded an election of remedies. The law seems to be well settled that proof of a cause of action in bankruptcy does not bar an action thereon subsequently where the claim has not been fully paid. There is no inconsistency where the same claim is asserted in each forum and there can be no bar without complete payment except the debt be dischargable. The claimant may sue on contract, and if the discharge in bankruptcy be pleaded he may in rebuttal show that the debt was created by fraud, not to change his cause of action from contract to fraud, but to prevent its being barred by the discharge in bankruptcy. (*Argall* v. *Jacobs*, 87 N. Y. 110; *Schroeder* v. *Frey*, 60 Hun, 58; affd., 131 N. Y. 562; *Stewart* v. *Emerson*, 52 N. H. 301; Brandenberg Bank. 273.) As to these creditors whose claims would be discharged it is well settled that proof of their claims does not deprive them of pursuing any other remedy if the bankrupt be not discharged. (Collier Bank. [3d ed.] 188; *Whitney* v. *Crafts*, 10 Mass. 23; *Dingee* v. *Becker*, Fed. Cas. No. 3,919.)

There would seem to be no reason in holding that the proof of a claim in bankruptcy is an election which debars the creditor from afterwards pursuing the debtor for the same claim unless it be one dischargeable in bankruptcy. The claim being provable in bankruptcy, there is no inconsistency in permitting the creditor to prove it and share in the distribution and subsequently adopt other remedies for collecting the balance of the claim.

These views lead to an affirmance of the determination of the Appellate Term, with costs.

O'BRIEN, McLAUGHLIN and HATCH, JJ., concurred ; VAN BRUNT, P. J., dissented.

VAN BRUNT, P. J. (dissenting):

I dissent. I am of the opinion that the proving of the claim in bankruptcy was an election.

Determination of Appellate Term affirmed, with costs.

THE TRIBUNE ASSOCIATION, Appellant and Respondent, *v.* EISNER & MENDELSON COMPANY, Respondent and Appellant.

Excuse or waiver of performance of a contract — it cannot be shown under a plea of performance — action for breach of a contract only partially performed by the plaintiff — the expense of the full performance of the contract may be shown by the defendant.

Where the complaint in an action to recover damages for the breach of a contract alleges full performance by the plaintiff, proof of matters excusing or waiving such performance is not admissible and a recovery cannot be had upon that theory — at least, where the defendant did not repudiate the contract.

Semble, that, where the contract has been only partially performed by the plaintiff, owing to the alleged breach of the contract, the amount of the expense to which the plaintiff would be put in performing the contract may be shown in reduction of the recovery.

APPEAL by the plaintiff, The Tribune Association, from that portion of a judgment of the Supreme Court, entered in the office of the clerk of the county of New York on the 11th day of May, 1901, upon the decision of the court rendered after a trial before the court without a jury, as amended *nunc pro tunc* by an order entered in said clerk's office on the 31st day of May, 1901, which dismisses the plaintiff's first cause of action upon the merits.

Also, an appeal by the defendant, Eisner & Mendelson Company, from so much of said judgment as dismisses the defendant's counter-claim upon the merits, and awards judgment in favor of the plaintiff upon the second cause of action.

Selden Bacon, for the plaintiff.

Julius J. Frank, for the defendant.

LAUGHLIN, J. :

The complaint contains two causes of action and the answer interposes a counterclaim. The case was tried before the court, a jury trial having been waived. The decision directed the dismissal of the complaint upon the merits as to the first cause of action and also a dismissal of the counterclaim upon the merits and granted judgment for the plaintiff upon its second cause of action. The plaintiff appeals from the judgment in so far as its first cause of action is dismissed, and defendant appeals from that part of the judgment dismissing its counterclaim and awarding a recovery in favor of the plaintiff upon the second cause of action.

The plaintiff's first cause of action is for a balance due on an agreement in writing for advertising, and it alleges full performance of the contract on its part. The material allegations relating to the first cause of action are put in issue by the answer. The contract on which the first cause of action was founded was in writing and was made on the 10th day of November, 1893. The plaintiff therein agreed to insert for the defendant " 30,000 lines daily & Sunday advertising * * * at the same price as paid heretofore." It was further therein provided that the advertising should be done within the succeeding sixteen months and be paid for in fully paid unassessable capital stock, $100 per share, of the " Johann Hoff " corporation, organized under the laws of West Virginia with a capital of $750,000, which shares were to be issued quarterly as the advertising was done, and were to be purchased of the plaintiff at par by the defendant within two years after such issue.

The plaintiff has only published about two-thirds of the advertising agreed to be published under the contract, and for that it has been fully paid. The price paid by the defendant theretofore for similar advertising was forty cents per line less fifteen per cent, or net, thirty-four cents. The plaintiff seeks to recover at this contract price for the remainder of the advertising which it has not published. The defendant duly raised the objection that as the complaint was for performance, the plaintiff could not recover on the theory of waiver of full performance, and the complaint was not amended in this regard. The contention of the plaintiff is that it was ready and willing to perform, but that the defendant failed to furnish the advertising matter with which it could perform, and its counsel cites the case of *Smith* v. *Wetmore* (167 N. Y. 234) to sustain this proposition. In that case the evidence showing performance on the part of the plaintiff was received without objection, and the complaint was for that reason amended on appeal to conform to the proof, and we think the rule stated by the court, that "when performance of a contract is alleged by the plaintiff and denied by the defendant, it is competent for the plaintiff to prove that the defendant would not allow him to perform, or repudiated the contract, or had committed a breach of it himself, by hindering performance or refusing to abide by its obligations," does not apply in this case. Here the defendant did not repudiate the contract. It merely failed to call upon the plaintiff to perform, and the plaintiff made no request for performance on the part of the defendant. We think this case is governed rather by the doctrine now firmly established that under a complaint for full performance of a contract, proof of matters excusing or waiving performance is not admissible, and a recovery may not be had upon that theory. (*Gatling* v. *Central Spar Verein*, 67 App. Div. 50; *Fox* v. *Davidson*, 36 id. 159; *La Chicotte* v. *Richmond R. & El. Co.*, 15 id. 380; *Weeks* v. *O'Brien*, 141 N. Y. 199.) The defendant had a right to assume that the plaintiff intended to show as it alleged that it advertised 30,000 lines, the full quota specified in the contract. The defendant was justified in resting upon its defense that the contract had not been fully performed and that the plaintiff had been fully paid for the work done. Had the plaintiff alleged a breach of the contract on the part of the defendant in failing to furnish it the advertising matter and sought to recover the profits it would have made on performance, the defendant might have interposed a different defense and would then be in the position of reducing plaintiff's recovery by the amount of the expense to which plaintiff would be put in performing the contract. (*Howard* v. *Daly*, 61 N. Y. 362.) It follows that the complaint as to the first cause of action was properly dismissed.

The second cause of action alleged is both upon an express contract and upon a *quantum meruit* for advertising between the 3d day of October and the 15th day of December, 1895. The plaintiff proved that during this time it published 2,553 lines of advertising matter for the defendant, the reasonable value of which was $1,794 and it has recovered the full amount. This recovery is on the basis of forty cents per line and double charge for display, which was the usual rate charged by the plaintiff in the absence of a special written contract.

If the defendant's liability for this advertising was on a *quantum meruit* we do not agree with the contention of the defendant that the evidence is insufficient to sustain the recovery. It is further claimed, however, that this advertising was done under written contract which fixes the price to be charged at thirty-three and one-third cents per line less fifteen per cent, or twenty-eight and one-third cents net, with no extra charge for display. Mr. Eisner, the secretary of the defendant, testified that in the early part of the summer of 1895 the manager of the plaintiff's advertising department, Mr. Masters, since deceased, called upon him with reference to making a new contract for advertising; that he told Mr. Masters that he understood the plaintiff was giving lower rates to other advertisers than to defendant, whereas he, Masters, had constantly assured the witness that the defendant was getting the lowest price, and that was the reason it made the 30,000-line contract in 1893; that Mr. Masters said that some advertisers got a page rate covering ten pages at thirty-three and one-third cents less fifteen per cent, and that they were allowed to split it up in certain spaces as long as it covered ten pages; that the witness replied that that only made 20,000, and asked how Mr. Masters expected him to obtain a new contract from the defendant when it had been overcharged, and further said that unless Mr. Masters could give the rebate to the defendant on the space already used " we will not start on a new contract in the Fall;" that Mr. Masters replied, " I will try to get you a new contract for the Fall, allowing us the rebate on the space already used ; " that after extended negotiations Mr. Masters finally agreed to this proposition on the 30th day of September, 1895, and the witness, in the presence of Mr. Masters, dictated a letter to his stenographer addressed to " G. H. Haulenbeek Advertising Agency," through which the business between plaintiff and defendant had been theretofore carried on, as follows :

" GENTLEMEN.—We beg to inform you that we have made an arrangement with the New York *Tribune* through Mr. Masters, and we hereby authorize you to give them the contract for 50,000 lines, full preferred position at 28¼ cents per line, to be used during three years; no extra charge for display, cuts or position.

" From the first bills rendered under this contract you will please deduct the amount of $646.83 on the Hoff account and $487.20 on the Carlsbad account, due us from this paper on the old contract.

" Yours very truly,

" EISNER & MENDELSON CO.,

" Per EISNER."

This letter was written out, signed and delivered to Mr. Masters and by him delivered to the advertising agency on October 2, 1895, and he thereupon received copy for advertising matter and commenced performance of the contract. A few days later Mr. Masters received a letter from the advertising agency under date of October 4, 1895, containing an order for this advertising which he accepted in writing for the plaintiff. This letter was as follows :

" Please enter our order for fifty thousand (50,000) agate lines, to be used for the advertising of the Eisner & Mendelson Co. and Johann Hoff, as per copy and instructions furnished by us from time to time. This amount of space to be used within two years if possible. If not, an extension will be given for the balance. Position of this advertising is to be at top of column and alongside reading or first following reading and alongside reading. No extra charge for display, cuts or position. For this please charge us 28¼ cents net per line for space used each month."

Subsequently a misunderstanding arose between the parties as to the terms of the contract for this advertising. It appears from the correspondence that Mr. Masters, representing the plaintiff, contended that the understanding was that the plaintiff, in consideration of the rebate allowed defendant on the old contract, was to receive cash for all stock which it had received from the defendant under the former contract without awaiting the two years therein specified, and the defendant's secretary contended that there was no such understanding. Accordingly on the 13th day of December, 1895, Mr. Masters wrote the defendant reciting his understanding of the contract and the controversy that had arisen between them and said that since the defendant's understanding of the contract seemed to be so entirely different from his, and as defendant did not seem inclined to talk the matter over and adjust it "it seems best to stop all business now running until such adjustment is made, or new contract can be made. Trust that this will be satisfactory, and hope to have a favorable reply." On the following day the defendant's secretary replied asserting his recollection of the parol contract and saying, "If you have changed your mind or your office does not seem to be satisfied we will stop just there where we left off before I went abroad and will consider the matter as if no agreement or contract had been made between us." On the thirtieth day of the same month Mr. Masters replied to this letter, reiterating at length his recollection of what took place between him and the defendant's secretary, and closing as follows: "As you know the advertising has been stopped for the present until an adjustment can be made of this business." On the 2d of January, 1896, the defendant, by its secretary, wrote Mr. Masters again, saying that his recollection seemed to be correct in all respects except where he says the new contract was made on the understanding that the defendant was to pay for the stock held by plaintiff in cash, and asserting that Mr. Eisner had a distinct recollection to the contrary, and this letter closed by saying that Mr. Eisner had informed Mr. Masters at the time of the negotiations that the old contract would have to take care of itself, and that was the only way he could secure a new contract from the defendant and that he was of the same opinion still, and, therefore, could not see how they could come to any settlement and that the defendant would "simply have to do without the *Tribune*."

Down to December fourteenth the plaintiff had charged this advertising to the defendant on its books at the rates specified in the letter from the defendants to the advertising agency and from the advertising agency to plaintiff's representative. The fair inference is that the minds of the parties never met on the new contract. They mutually so agreed by their correspondence and by suspending the advertising. No subsequent agreement was reached. If either of the parties wished to stand upon its claim it should have asserted its intention so to do; but this neither of the parties did. If the defendant wished to insist as a condition of abandoning the contract that the advertising done up to that time should be charged

FIRST DEPARTMENT, MARCH TERM, 1902.   [Vol. 70.

only at the rates intended by the contract, it should have made a reservation to that effect. On the contrary, its proposition was, " We * * * will consider the matter as if no agreement or contract had been made between us."

We are of opinion that neither party insisted that a contract had been made that was to be binding upon the parties either in the past or in the future. In these circumstances the plaintiff was entitled to recover for the advertising thus done as if no contract had been made.

These views also dispose of the defendant's counterclaim. The counterclaim was for the rebate under the contract of 1893, which, as has been seen, for the purpose of obtaining the new contract for 50,000 lines of advertising in 1895, the plaintiff agreed to allow on such new contract. The defendant has proceeded on the theory that the letter from him to the advertising agency, directing the deduction of the two items of $646.83 and $487.20 rebate on the old contract from the first bills rendered by the plaintiff on the new contract, constitutes an account stated. It neither alleged nor proved the facts which would warrant the allowance of this counterclaim on any other theory than that it was an account stated. It is evident that the defendant yielded to the plaintiff's claim concerning this rebate in consideration of the defendant giving it the new contract. The new contract never having been made effectual and having been abandoned by mutual consent, the right to the rebate so far as it rests upon that contract, falls with it. It will be observed that the rebate was to be allowed on the first bills rendered under that contract. As no bills have been rendered, paid or accrued under that contract, it is evident that the defendant cannot be allowed the rebate in the manner contemplated by the parties.

The judgment should be affirmed, but both parties having appealed, the affirmance is without costs.

VAN BRUNT, P. J., O'BRIEN, INGRAHAM and HATCH, JJ., concurred.

Judgment affirmed, without costs.

MICHAEL McNALLY, Respondent, *v.* MARY E. FITZSIMONS, as Administratrix, etc., of ANN CASSIDY, Deceased, and Others, Defendants, Impleaded with MARY E. FITZSIMONS, Individually, and Others, Appellants.

Partition of real property, between the committee of a lunatic and his cotenants, induced by the fraud of the latter — set aside at the suit of his heirs — sufficiency of the complaint in such an action as to an offer and ability to restore.

Where a lunatic and his uncle and aunt are cotenants of a number of parcels of real estate, and the committee of the lunatic, who has no knowledge in respect to the condition of the real estate, at the suggestion of the uncle and aunt, obtains leave of the court to join in a voluntary partition of such real estate, the uncle and aunt, in their dealings with the committee of the lunatic, are bound to exercise the utmost good faith.

Where the uncle and aunt, by means of false representations and fraudulent concealment in respect to the condition of the real estate, induce the committee of the lunatic to accept as the lunatic's share of the real estate, property, the title to which is in dispute and the value of which is much less than the value of the property set apart for the uncle and aunt, the lunatic's heirs may, after his death, maintain an action to set aside the partition.

Where the complaint in such an action alleges in one portion thereof that deeds of the property set apart to the lunatic were executed, and in another portion thereof alleges that such deeds were never delivered, but does not contain an offer or an allegation of ability to restore whatever the lunatic had received under the agreement, the court will, for the purpose of sustaining the complaint against a demurrer, assume that the execution of the deeds to the lunatic was not completed by delivery.

Semble, that if it should appear upon the trial that the deeds had been delivered, the complaint would have to be dismissed because of its failure to contain an offer and an allegation of ability to restore.

APPEAL by the defendants, Mary E. Fitzsimons, individually, and others, from so much of an interlocutory judgment of the Supreme Court in favor of the plaintiff, entered in the office of the clerk of the county of New York on the 25th day of November, 1901, upon the decision of the court, rendered after a trial at the New York Special Term, as overrules said defendants' demurrer to the complaint.

Charles E. Miller, for the appellants.

I. Newton Williams, for the respondent.

VAN BRUNT, P. J. :

I concur in the conclusion arrived at by the court below, but I do not concur in that portion of the opinion in which the learned judge states that in effect the complaint contains an offer to restore what John P. McNally received.

This action is undoubtedly brought for the purpose of rescinding an executed, or partly completed, partition between certain tenants in common of real estate. In consequence of the fact that the drawer of the complaint did not seem to comprehend what was necessary to the execution of a deed, we are left in doubt from the allegations of the complaint as to whether or not any deeds were executed to the deceased John P. McNally. The pleader seems to be ignorant of the fact that for the due execution of a deed, delivery, as well as the other requisites, is necessary. If the deeds of the property alleged to have been assigned to the deceased John P. McNally were executed, then it is clear that the complaint in this action is defective in not containing an offer to restore, and alleging an ability to restore. (*Brewster* v. *Wooster*, 131 N. Y. 473, 477, and cases cited; *Cox* v. *Stokes*, 156 id. 491, 506.) The complaint contains allegations that the deeds to McNally were executed, and it also contains allegations that they were not executed. It says in paragraph 9 of the complaint that the other tenants in common released to said John P. McNally the premises which were assigned to him; in paragraph 11 it speaks of the deed of a part of the premises which were assigned to John P. McNally in the partition as being made and executed, and in paragraph 12, speaking of the defendant Mary E. Fitzsimons, it alleges that she executed and caused or procured others to execute said deed to John P. McNally, and then in paragraph 14 it alleges upon information and belief that the deeds executed to said McNally in release, or pretended release, were never delivered to said McNally or to said Harrigan as his committee, or to any other person on his behalf. But in view of the rule that a pleading is to be most favorably construed in the case of a demurrer where there are inconsistent allegations, I suppose that we are to take the allegation which will support the cause of action, rather than the one which is fatal to it. Assuming, therefore, that the deeds in question were never executed because of non-delivery to the lunatic, or his committee, or to any other person on his behalf, there was no necessity of an allegation of an offer to restore. But if it should turn out upon the trial that these deeds had been executed by delivery, then, clearly, the bill would have to be dismissed because it did not contain any offer to restore, which, under well-settled principles of law, is absolutely necessary in the case of rescission, except under circumstances which are not applicable to the case at bar.

Upon the main question, it seems to us that in view of the fact that the cotenants were dealing with the committee of a lunatic who had no knowledge in respect to the condition of the real estate, they were bound to the utmost good faith. The relations of the parties would have been entirely different had they not been dealing with a lunatic whose committee could not be supposed to be familiar with the condition of the property to be partitioned, and who, as is alleged, relied upon the representations made by the cotenants of the lunatic that the partition was fair and equitable. The ordinary rule of *caveat emptor* cannot be held to apply to parties situated as were those who took part in this partition.

We think, therefore, upon the whole, that the judgment should be affirmed, with costs, with leave to the defendants to withdraw their demurrer and answer upon payment of costs in the court below and of this appeal.

INGRAHAM, MCLAUGHLIN and HATCH, JJ., concurred; LAUGHLIN, J., concurred in result.

LAUGHLIN, J. (concurring):

This action is brought to set aside a voluntary partition of real estate made by heirs of Ann Cassidy, deceased, on the ground of fraud. These heirs were John P. McNally, Mary E. Fitzsimons and Peter A. Cassidy.

It is alleged in the complaint that the plaintiff is the father and sole heir of John P. McNally, who died on the 18th day of July, 1900, at Newark, N. J.; that for ten years prior to his death he was of unsound mind and confined in an insane asylum in the State of New Jersey; that on the 25th day of March, 1898, one William Harrigan was duly appointed guardian of his person and property by the Orphans' Court of Essex county, N. J.; that

FIRST DEPARTMENT, MARCH TERM, 1902.   [Vol. 70.

said Harrigan was thereafter and on the 22d day of April, 1898, also duly appointed the committee of the person and property of said McNally by the Supreme Court of this State; that said Harrigan qualified as such committee and continued to act as such until on or about the 1st day of January, 1899; that said Harrigan, neither as guardian or as such committee, has ever received or held any money or property of said McNally; that, soon after the appointment of said Harrigan as such committee, the said Peter A. Cassidy and Mary E. Fitzsimons represented to him that the only real estate left by said Ann Cassidy consisted of a house and lot known as No. 208 East Fifty-first street, a house and lot known as No. 113 Avenue D, four houses erected on two lots known as Nos. 593 and 595 Second avenue, a moiety of two houses and lots known as Nos. 324 and 326 Cherry street, and proposed and suggested that he petition the Supreme Court for leave to make a partition of said real estate, and as a fair and equitable partition they proposed that they release to McNally the premises No. 208 East Fifty-first street and No. 113 Avenue D, and that he release to them as tenants in common the remaining premises; that they represented to him that this would be a fair and equitable partition of said property; that, acting upon such representations, said Harrigan, as such committee, petitioned the Supreme Court and such proceedings were had in said court that a partition of said property was made, as so proposed by said Cassidy and Fitzsimons, pursuant to an order or judgment of said court made in said proceedings, and the premises Nos. 208 East Fifty-first street and 113 Avenue D were by said Fitzsimons and by the heirs of said Cassidy, who in the meantime had died, released to said McNally and the other property was by said Harrigan, as such committee, released to said Cassidy before his death and to said Fitzsimons; that, in making such partition, said Harrigan relied solely on the representations of said Cassidy and Fitzsimons, or their duly authorized agents or attorneys, to him as such committee and to the plaintiff, that said partition was fair, honest and equitable to said McNally, which statements and representations said Harrigan, as such committee, and the plaintiff relied on and believed to be true, especially as said Fitzsimons and Cassidy were the aunt and uncle respectively of said McNally and professed at that time to be deeply interested in his welfare; that said representations were false and untrue and were well known by said Cassidy and Fitzsimons to be false and untrue at the time they were made; that their falsity and untruthfulness were not discovered by said Harrigan, or by the plaintiff, until about the month of August, 1900; that neither said McNally nor said Harrigan, as his committee, would have been a party to said partition as made and consummated by the judgment of said court had they not believed said representations; that said partition was not fair or equitable and just in that the property set apart to Fitzsimons was worth a sum largely in excess of $8,000 more than that set apart to said McNally; that the building on premises No. 113 Avenue D had been reported or surveyed as an unsafe and dangerous building by the building department of the city of New York to the knowledge of said Cassidy and Fitzsimons and they knew that the entire southerly gable wall of said building was unsafe and dangerous, and by the order of said building department had to be torn down and rebuilt or otherwise made safe, but that they fraudulently concealed these facts from the said Harrigan, as committee, and the court in said partition proceedings; that on or about the 1st day of August, 1900, the plaintiff first learned that at the time of the rendition of the judgment of the Supreme Court and of the making of the deed of premises 208 East Fifty-first street, so made and executed to said McNally, the title to said property was in dispute and that one Theresa G. Graham claimed to be the lawful owner thereof by virtue of a deed from said Ann Cassidy; that an action was subsequently commenced by said Graham against the plaintiff and others to recover said property, which action is now pending in the United States District Court for the southern district of New York; that said Cassidy and Fitzsimons were fully aware, while said proceedings were pending, of the claim of said Graham to be the owner of said property, but they wrongfully and fraudulently concealed said fact from said committee, the plaintiff and the court; that the deed to said McNally of the property set aside to him in said partition proceedings did not convey all the right, title and interest of said Peter A. Cassidy therein; that the deeds and releases to said McNally " in release or pretended release of the said real estate to him " were not delivered to him or to his committee or to any other person in his behalf and for that reason were void; that the said Cassidy and Fitzsimons, without the knowledge, consent or approval of said committee, agreed to pay the attorneys who represented him a large amount of money if said partition proceedings went through, and did pay to said attorneys at least the sum of $2,500 for putting through said partition proceedings, which sum was grossly in excess of the reasonable value of the services of said attorneys, "so that said attorneys did not truly represent said committee but represented the said Cassidy and the defendant Mary E. Fitzsimons;" "that all the consents both verbal and in writing and all acquiescence made by (the plaintiff) or the said William Harrigan individually or as such committee of John P. McNally, to the settlement of the said estate" were all induced and brought about by the false and fraudulent representations and wrongful acts and misconduct of the said Peter A. Cassidy and the defendant Mary E. Fitzsimons; and that by reason of the said fraud and deceit practiced by said Fitzsimons and Cassidy the said McNally was wrongfully and unlawfully deprived of property of the value of at least $8,000, and if the said Graham's claim is valid, of the value of at least $20,000, for which plaintiff has no adequate remedy at law. The complaint demands judgment that the said partition of the real estate be declared null and void; that any and all proceedings, orders or judgments made therein be vacated and set aside, and that all deeds made in accordance with said order or judgment may be declared null and void and ordered to be canceled of record; that the plaintiff be adjudged to be the owner in fee of an undivided one-third part of the real estate of which said Ann Cassidy died seized, and that the parties to this action account for all rents received by them respectively from said property and for such other or further relief as to the court may seem just and equitable together with costs and disbursements to be paid by the defendants.

The plaintiff, as the sole heir of said McNally, may maintain this action. (*Prentice* v. *Achorn*, 2 Paige, 30; Code Civ. Proc. § 1909.) On demurrer a pleading is not to be construed strictly against the pleader. It is deemed that the demurrer admits not only every fact specifically alleged, but also every fact that may be inferred or implied therefrom by reasonable and fair intendment. (*Coatsworth* v. *Lehigh Valley R. Co.*, 156 N. Y. 451; *Rochester R. Co.* v.

Robinson, 133 id. 242 ; *Hewlett* v. *Brooklyn Heights R. R. Co.*, 63 App. Div. 423 ; *Waite* v. *Aborn*, 60 id. 521, 524.)

It was said by the court in *Foote* v. *Ffoulke* (55 App. Div. 617, 618) that "where different inferences can be drawn, the one which will support rather than one which will destroy the action or remedy sought should be adopted." If the allegations of a complaint are indefinite the remedy is by motion to make them more certain and definite. Where the allegations are inconsistent the remedy is before answer to compel an election. (*Sarasohn* v. *Miles*, 52 App. Div. 628 ; affd., 169 N. Y. 573 ; *Tuthill* v. *Skidmore*, 124 id. 148 ; *Einson* v. *North River Electric Light Co.*, 34 Misc. Rep. 191.) Tested by these rules, or even by the somewhat inconsistent rules that with reference to matters of substance an ambiguous pleading or one of doubtful meaning must be construed most strongly against the pleader (*Clark* v. *Dillon*, 97 N. Y. 370 ; *Bogardus* v. *N. Y. Life Ins. Co.*, 101 id. 328, 337 ; *National City Bank* v. *Westcott*, 118 id. 468, 474 ; *Browne* v. *Empire Type Setting Machine Co.*, 44 App. Div. 598 ; *Hammel* v. *Washburn*, 49 id. 119), I think the complaint sufficiently states a cause of action for the relief demanded.

It is urged that the plaintiff should have offered to restore what he has received. According to one of the allegations of the complaint he has received nothing, for the releases or deeds have not been delivered. It does not appear whether the releases or deeds have been recorded. But, assuming that they have been delivered and recorded, plaintiff asks to have the proceedings of the court and the deeds all canceled and each party account for the rents and profits received. This will restore all parties to their position prior to the partition and is, I think, a sufficient offer to restore and may be consummated at the trial or properly disposed of by the decree. (*Allerton* v. *Allerton*, 50 N. Y. 670 ; *Powell* v. *Linde Co.*, 49 App. Div. 286.) This being a suit in equity the plaintiff's failure to tender restoration before suit brought and demand restoration by defendants, is no bar to the action, but may affect the allowance of costs. Inasmuch, however, as some of the parties are infants a suit was unavoidable. It is not very definitely alleged in the complaint just what proceedings were had in court, but the fair inference is that they were proceedings under sections 1590 to 1593 of the Code of Civil Procedure, which authorize a voluntary partition of real estate in cases of lunacy and provide that the releases shall have the same effect as deeds would were the lunatic competent.

I doubt whether the action could be maintained merely upon the claim of Theresa G. Graham. Although an heir is not a purchaser from his ancestor within the protection of the recording acts, I think that when heirs who have come into the inheritance, as manifestly these heirs did, voluntarily partition the real estate upon the faith of the record title, that each becomes a purchaser from the other and is protected against an outstanding unrecorded deed of which he had no knowledge where the grantee was not in possession. (Real Prop. Law [Laws of 1896, chap. 547], §§ 240, 241 ; *Oliphant* v. *Burns*, 146 N. Y. 218, 233 ; *Tefft* v. *Munson*, 57 id. 97 ; *Strough* v. *Wilder*, 119 id. 530 ; *Westbrook* v. *Gleason*, 89 id. 641.) But the allegations of fraud and deception by which an inequitable partition of the real estate was procured to the great damage of the plaintiff's incompetent ancestor are sufficient, if established, to warrant the relief for which the action is brought.

It follows that the judgment should be affirmed, with costs.

McLAUGHLIN and HATCH, JJ., concurred in result.

Judgment affirmed, with costs, with leave to defendants to withdraw demurrer and answer on payment of costs in this court and in the court below.

BENNO JAFFE and LUDWIG DARMSTAEDTER, Appellants, *v.* EVANS & SONS (LIMITED), Respondent.

Trade mark — a name generic and descriptive of a patented preparation — use of such name by the public, after the expiration of the patent.

Where a patent is issued for the manufacture of a hydrous wool fat preparation called "lanoline," and during the term of the patent such word becomes the generic and descriptive name of the preparation, a corporation which, after the expiration of the patent, engages in manufacturing a wool fat preparation, essentially similar to the preparation manufactured under the patent, may use the word "lanoline" to designate its product, providing that it accompanies such name with indications showing that it is the manufacturer thereof.

APPEAL by the plaintiffs, Benno Jaffe and another, from a judgment of the Supreme Court in favor of the defendant, entered in the office of the clerk of the county of New York on the 28th day of August, 1901, upon the decision of the court, rendered after a trial at the New York Special Term, dismissing the complaint upon the merits.

The suit was brought to restrain the defendant, a British corporation, from using the word "Lanolin" or "Lanoline," which is claimed to be a trade mark of the plaintiffs', and from selling its product in packages similar to plaintiffs' and for an accounting.

The plaintiffs are citizens of Prussia and are engaged in the manufacture and sale of a hydrous wool fat preparation called "lanoline," and until the year 1896 were protected in such manufacture and sale under the term "lanoline" by United States patent. Although such patent has now expired and they admit that every one is at liberty to manufacture and sell their article, they claim to have a trade mark in the word "lanoline," or words similar to it, and, therefore, seek to restrain the defendant, who sells its product, both of hydrous and anhydrous wool fat in this country, as hydrous and anhydrous "lanolin."

The plaintiffs' and also the defendant's preparation is sold in circular tin cans of very nearly the same size, but a comparison of the labels shows a distinct difference excepting that the defendant's label contains in red letters the words "British Lanolin," printed horizontally and underscored; and on the plaintiffs', in red letters, printed diagonally, are the words "Dr. Oscar Liebreich's Lanoline," the word lanoline being in large type and on a line by itself. The plaintiffs' label further states that the product is made in Germany; and names and addresses there and names and addresses of New York agents are given. It has also on one side two designs denoted "trade mark." The defendant's label states that the product is made by special plant and patent process, "produced by British enterprise and labour only," and is "sweeter and cheaper than most makes." English, Canadian and New York addresses are given and a special trade mark entirely dissimilar from plaintiffs' is placed at the top.

From the testimony it appears that during the continuance of the plaintiffs' patent various manufacturers of wool fat prepared by different processes sold their products under names other than lanoline. The plaintiffs' patent related to the process of manufacture and the product was hydrous wool fat containing a fixed proportion of water which, if driven off, would again be absorbed or taken up. The use of the product was as a base for ointments, salves, etc.

It was testified that the defendant's preparation of hydrous wool fat or "hydrous lanolin" was essentially the same in character as the plaintiffs' "lanoline" and could be used as well. One druggist said "they appeared to be identical," but that when he bought the British product he knew it was not the plaintiffs', and there was no confusion. He would in his work use from either can. Another pharmacist testified that the British manufacture was so labeled he would not be deceived at all as to what he was getting; that he tried it, and as it is cheaper, he now uses no other. The plaintiffs' hydrous lanolin, according to the testimony, contained about forty per cent of water, which brought it within the requirements of the trade.

Leading text books and manuals were used in evidence in which the word "lanoline" is defined as a "mixture of 75% of pure wool fat and 25% of water," and, in the Standard Dictionary, lanoline is defined as "An unctuous fatty mixture * * * with fatty acids, obtained from various keratin tissues, as the wool of sheep * * * (<L. *lana,* wool, + *oleum,* oil)."

Upon the evidence the Special Term dismissed the complaint, and from the judgment so entered the plaintiffs appeal.

Louis C. Raegener, for the appellants.

Charles W. Lefler, for the respondent.

O'BRIEN, J.:

We might well rest our affirmance of this judgment upon the statement of the law as contained in the opinion* of the learned

---

*The following is the opinion of O'GORMAN, J., delivered at Special Term:

O'GORMAN, J.:

The plaintiffs and their assignors for twenty years prior to 1896 had through certain patents a monopoly in the manufacture of a purified wool fat used in ointments, salves and soap, which product they designated "Lanoline." Since 1896 they have used the same name as a trade mark, and this action is brought to restrain the defendants from applying the name to their product, which is

judge at Special Term.   The insistence of the appellants, however, that the case presents questions of fact and not of law, requires that we again examine the record.

In the leading case of *Singer Mfg. Co. v. June Mfg. Co.* (163 U. S. 169) it is said : " The result, then, of the American, the English and the French doctrine universally upheld is this, that where, during the life of a monopoly created by a patent, a name, whether it be arbitrary or be that of the inventor, has become, by his consent, either express or tacit, the identifying and generic name of the thing patented, this name passes to the public with the cessation of the monopoly which the patent created." That case is also authority for the further statement that one who avails himself of this public dedication may use the generic designation in all forms with the fullest liberty, by affixing such name to the machine or product and by referring to it in advertisements, subject, however, to the condition that the name must be so used as not to deprive others of their rights or to deceive the public and that the name must be accompanied with such indications as will show by whom it is made so that the public may be informed of that fact.

In the present case, if the word " Lanoline " or " Lanolin " is generic or descriptive of the article, which we think upon the evi-

---

substantially similar to the one covered by the plaintiffs' patents, and is sold as " British Lanolin Hydrous " and " British Lanolin Anhydrous." The action cannot be maintained.   Upon the cessation of the monopoly created by the patents the plaintiffs reserved no exclusive right to the manufacture of their product or to the use of its identifying and generic name.   Upon the expiration of the patents the name, as well as the right to manufacture and sell the product, became public property, and no trade mark right exists or could be acquired by subsequent use. (*Singer Mfg. Co. v. June Mfg. Co.*, 163 U. S. 169.) The name was the property of the patentee only during the life of the patents, and to permit its exclusive retention thereafter would practically extend the monopoly indefinitely. That somewhat similar articles produced by other processes were known by other names during the period covered by the patents is entirely immaterial. "Lanoline" was then exclusive property, and competitors were driven to the employment of other names for their goods to escape the imputation of infringement of rights under the patents; but now, the patents having expired, the commodity and process and the scientific or descriptive term by which it was designated by the plaintiffs, and by which it has become universally known, have passed to the public, and the plaintiffs are not entitled to the relief which they seek in this case.   The allegations as to deception and unfair competition are without evidence to support them, and the complaint must be dismissed, with costs.

dence adduced it is, it follows that the defendant may use the word provided its preparation is substantially the same product as plaintiffs' and the word is accompanied with *indicia* which show clearly that the defendant is the manufacturer. This necessarily includes the other proposition that the defendant has no right to manufacture something entirely different and call it " Lanolin," nor would it have the right to use that name in advertisements or labels in such a way as to deceive the public into thinking its product was the one manufactured by the plaintiffs.

As said in the case from which we have already quoted (*Singer Mfg. Co. v. June Mfg. Co., supra*): " The public having the right on the expiration of the patent to make the patented article and to use its generic name, to restrict this use, either by preventing its being placed upon the articles when manufactured, or by using it in advertisements or circulars, would be to admit the right and at the same time destroy it. It follows then, that the right to use the name in every form passes to the public with the dedication resulting from the expiration of the patent."

The law being settled, therefore, what the plaintiffs claim is, that the words " British Lanolin Hydrous " and " British Lanolin Anhydrous " do not honestly describe the defendant's product; and, although the word may be descriptive, it was unnecessary for the defendant to use it on its labels and thus injure the plaintiffs. Taking up this last proposition first, if defendant had the right to use the name, even though such use might have injured the business of the plaintiffs, which was likely, since the latter according to the evidence charged sixty cents a can, while the defendant's price was twenty cents — nevertheless, the court would have no right to interfere unless by imitating the plaintiffs' label or by simulating the appearance of the packages, the defendant was guilty of fraud upon the public in endeavoring to palm off its own product as the one manufactured by the plaintiffs.

There was upon the trial no proof offered that would justify the court in finding, nor did it find, there was any fraud or misrepresentation on the part of the defendant ; nor did the defendant introduce any confusion in the trade ; nor did it appear that any one was misled by the expression " British Lanolin," as employed by it, into believing that he was purchasing the plaintiffs' lanoline, which is made in Germany. Nor does it appear that there was any marked likeness in the label or dress of the goods of the parties; and, therefore, the whole dispute turns upon defendant's right to use the word " Lanolin," which, as we have said, being descriptive of the article, it might do, provided the word honestly described the defendant's product and that product did not essentially differ from the plaintiffs'. Both use wool fat as the basic ingredient; and though it was not shown (nor was it important) precisely how either product was manufactured, the goods sold had common characteristics.

The plaintiffs' product consisted of wool fat prepared by a certain process, containing, besides wool fat, about twenty-five per cent of water. The defendant's preparation, referred to as British hydrous lanolin, in addition to wool fat, contains, as testified, about thirty per cent of water. Further, it was shown the two preparations were substantially the same in nature; and there was other proof tending to show that lanoline was accepted as standard if it contained no more than thirty per cent of water. And it appears that the ability of the prepared wool fat to take up a large amount of water, which, if driven off, is again absorbed, is characteristic of the product termed lanoline, which characteristic the defendant's preparations indisputably had.

" Hydrous " is the scientific term indicating the presence of water; while " anhydrous " signifies the absence of water and the quality of taking it up. The term " anhydrous," therefore, might properly be applied to the plaintiffs' product after the water it contained was driven off; and thus it becomes evident that the use of the words " hydrous " and " anhydrous," in connection with lanoline, would have a definite meaning and be entirely understood by every one familiar with its nature and characteristics. Hence, no one would be misled by the addition of these words, although, strictly speaking, the phrase " hydrous lanolin " may be tautological and " anhydrous lanolin " a contradiction of terms. What the defendant sold was the product in its two forms.

In view of the fact that the defendant had two preparations of wool fat, designated as hydrous and anhydrous lanolin, the one containing water in the first instance and the other without water, but capable of absorbing it, as was clearly indicated by the terms used, any question of fraud or deception was eliminated so far as the public was concerned and particularly as the name by whom and the place where manufactured was expressly stated, was there no probability of any one being deceived into thinking that the defendant's was the plaintiffs' product. So far as the manufacture of British hydrous lanolin was concerned, it was substantially the same article or product as was manufactured by the plaintiffs and no deception was practiced. Nor was there any deception in the sale of "Anhydrous Lanolin," which the plaintiffs make no claim of preparing for sale.

We think, therefore, that there was nothing to prevent the defendants from applying to their product as prepared the terms which truthfully represented the inherent elements and characteristics of lanoline.

Upon the facts, therefore, as well as upon the law, we think that the Special Term was right in the conclusion reached, and the judgment, accordingly, should be affirmed, with costs.

Van Brunt, P. J., Ingraham, Hatch and Laughlin, JJ., concurred.

Judgment affirmed, with costs.

Johanna Kalish and Others, as Executors, etc., of Joseph Kalish, Deceased, Respondents, *v.* Luke Higgins and Elizabeth Higgins, Appellants. (Action No. 1.)

192|
613|

Fraudulent conveyance — under what circumstances a conveyance from a husband to his wife for a nominal consideration is not fraudulent as to creditors — burden of proof — declarations by the grantor made after the conveyance.

A conveyance of real estate, made by a man to his wife for a nominal consideration, at a time when his only liability was a contingent one as surety upon a lease under which no rent was then due, will not be set aside as fraudulent, because some two years after the execution of the conveyance the tenant makes default in the payment of rent due under the lease and the surety (the grantor) is then insolvent and is unable to pay the judgment rendered against him therefor, where it does not appear that at the time of the execution of the conveyance, either the grantor or the grantee intended to defraud any one or contemplated any liability under the guaranty, and it is shown that up to a short time before the judgment was entered against him the grantor retained sufficient property with which to satisfy any liability under the lease.

In an action by a judgment creditor to set aside the conveyance, declarations made by the grantor after the execution of the conveyance are not competent as against the grantee for the purpose of showing fraud.

In such a case the burden of showing a fraudulent intent is upon the plaintiff, and the fact that one of the defendants was called as a witness and testified to facts inconsistent with a fraudulent intent, and that the court refused to believe his testimony, is not evidence from which the court can properly find the existence of a fraudulent intent.

APPEAL by the defendants, Luke Higgins and another, from a judgment of the Supreme Court in favor of the plaintiffs, entered in the office of the clerk of the county of New York on the 10th day of May, 1901, upon the decision of the court rendered after a trial at the New York Special Term.

M. J. Horan, for the appellants.

Edward W. S. Johnston, for the respondents.

INGRAHAM, J. :

The plaintiffs, as judgment creditors of the defendant Luke Higgins, seek to set aside a deed made by Higgins conveying certain real estate to his wife, Elizabeth Higgins, for a nominal consideration. The complaint alleges the conveyance of the property sought to be reached in this action on the 5th day of August, 1896, and the recovery of judgment against the defendants on the 18th day of October, 1898; that on the 19th day of February, 1892, and the 14th day of June, 1894, when the instruments upon which the judgment against the defendant Luke Higgins were obtained were executed, Higgins represented to the plaintiffs' testator that he was the owner and seized in fee of the premises described, and that the said plaintiffs' testator accepted the obligation of the defendant as surety, relying upon the said representations and statements; that the conveyance by the defendant Luke Higgins to his wife was made for the purpose of preventing judgments against Higgins from becoming a lien on said premises and was made solely for the purpose of hindering, delaying and defrauding the plaintiffs' testators and other creditors of the defendant Luke Higgins; that the defendant Luke Higgins is wholly insolvent and has no other property or assets out of which said judgment or any part thereof can be collected, and that unless the court grants the relief sought in this

action the plaintiffs will be remediless.   There is no allegation in
the complaint that at the time of this conveyance of the property
the judgment debtor was not solvent, or that he did not retain property sufficient to pay all his debts.

The court in its decision, which was a short decision, under section 1022 of the Code, found that "at that time (time of conveyance) he (defendant Luke Higgins) did not have left enough property to meet his said obligations under his contract of guaranty."
There was no allegation in the complaint of this fact, and not only
is there no evidence to sustain this finding, but it is disproved by
the undisputed testimony.

The decision further contains a statement that " the court decides
that   * * *   the aforesaid conveyances were made by defendant
Luke Higgins with the intent to hinder, delay and defraud the plaintiffs' testator and plaintiffs, within the meaning of said statute."   We
think that the testimony did not justify this finding, and that there
was no evidence to show that this defendant was at the time of making
this conveyance insolvent.   In the opinion of the court below the
decision was based upon the case of *Citizens' National Bank* v.
Fonda (18 Misc. Rep. 114), but in that case it appeared that the
conveyance sought to be impeached was voluntary and included all
of the debtor's property, so that there was not enough left to pay
his debts, the court in that case saying: " The conveyance in question being voluntary, without consideration, and covering substantially all of the property of the judgment debtor, so that there is
nothing left out of which the plaintiff can collect its judgment, is
presumptively fraudulent if the plaintiff at the time the conveyance
was made was a creditor."   This certainly was not an authority for
a case in which not only was that crucial fact unproved, but where
the uncontradicted evidence showed that, at the time of the conveyance sought to be impeached, the judgment debtor retained property much in excess of his actual indebtedness and much in excess
of the claim which subsequently he became bound to pay.

The facts surrounding this transaction show that at the time this
conveyance was made neither the judgment debtor nor the grantee
had an intention to defraud any one.   The plaintiffs' testator, being
the owner of a piece of real estate, leased it on February 19, 1892,
to one Manning for a term of five years, from May 1, 1892, to May

1, 1897, at an annual rental of $1,560, payable monthly in advance, and the defendant Luke Higgins guaranteed the payment of that rent. This lease contained a covenant against the assignment of the lease. On the 21st day of June, 1894, the tenant, wishing to transfer the lease, applied to the plaintiffs' testator for permission to make such transfer; whereupon the landlord consented to an assignment of the lease from Manning to one Reilly, and at the same time covenanted to give a further term of two years, to commence on the 1st of May, 1897, upon the same terms and conditions as the existing lease, either to Manning or to Reilly, and at that time the defendant Higgins executed an agreement whereby he agreed to remain liable on said lease, regardless of such assignment, for any default made by either Manning or Reilly during the remainder of the term, and further agreed that, if default should be made by Manning or Reilly in the payment of the rent and the performance of the covenants contained within the lease or the renewal thereof which the plaintiffs' testator had that day covenanted to and with said Manning and said Reilly to grant at the expiration of the time of the within lease, he would pay the rent mentioned in said lease or renewal, or any arrears thereof that might remain due to the plaintiffs' testator. This instrument was executed on the 14th day of June, 1894. At that time Higgins was again asked whether he was the owner of the property the conveyance of which is sought to be set aside in this action, and he stated that he was. But there was no agreement or covenant, or undertaking that he would remain the owner of the premises, or that the premises should be subject to any lien for the performance of this agreement. It appears that all of the rent under the original lease was paid, and that neither the lessors nor Higgins made any default in the payment of such rent. Higgins, being engaged as a saloon keeper in the city of New York, became ill, and in August, 1896, desired to convey the premises in question to his wife. He went to the office of Messrs. Johnston & Johnston, who were the attorneys for the plaintiffs' testator, and had prepared the lease from Manning, the consent for the assignment of the lease from Manning to Reilly, and the instrument by which the defendant guaranteed the payment of the rent, and requested them to draw up the papers for a transfer of this property from himself to his wife. The deeds making these transfers

FIRST DEPARTMENT, MARCH TERM, 1902.   [Vol. 70.

were drawn up in the office of Johnston & Johnston and recorded
by them. This conveyance was, therefore, made under the direction of the attorneys for the lessor, in whose presence Higgins had
stated that he was the owner of the property, and at the time these
conveyances were made there was no rent due under this lease to
the plaintiffs' testator, and none became due which was not paid by
the tenant for several years thereafter.

There is no evidence that at the time this conveyance was
made Higgins was indebted to any person in any sum of money.
Higgins was called as a witness and testified that at the time he did
not owe anybody one cent. There was a contingent liability to the
plaintiffs' testator under this guaranty for the rent, but no rent was
then due and unpaid, and there is no evidence that either of the
parties to this action contemplated that there ever would be any
rent due or unpaid, or that this conveyance had any relation to any
liability under that guaranty. Both the defendant and his wife
positively swear that they had no suspicion that any liability would
subsequently arise because of this guaranty, and there is no evidence to contradict that statement. It is corroborated by the fact
that the defendant went to the attorneys for the lessor to have
drawn up the conveyance to effect the transfer. Nor at this time
had either Reilly or Manning accepted the renewal of the lease or
agreed to accept such a renewal. After these transfers were made
and duly recorded Higgins continued in business, being apparently
prosperous. He had an account in the Greenwich Bank, and that
account continued until after May 3, 1898, the balance upon the
date of this conveyance being more than $100, afterwards increas-
ing, so that at one time he had over $3,500 on deposit in the bank;
and from January 12, 1897, to March 24, 1898, he apparently had
in this bank at all times a sum of money in excess of that required
to pay the amount unpaid for the rent upon this lease, the payment
of which he had guaranteed. In addition to this Higgins continued
to conduct his business, giving orders for supplies, and promptly paid
his bills. In November, 1897, he sold out this business and received
the consideration therefor.

On the 15th day of April, 1897, Reilly, the person to whom the
lease made to the plaintiffs' testator had been assigned, served a
notice upon the plaintiffs' testator that he elected to take a renewal

of the lease for two years to commence May 1, 1897, and subsequent to that a renewal lease was executed between Reilly and the plaintiffs' testator, but there is no evidence that the defendants had notice of those facts. Reilly continued in these premises under this renewal lease, and during the time he occupied the premises he paid all the rent that accrued. Before the expiration of the two years, however, he left the premises, leaving unpaid the sum of $86, as rent of the premises for the month of June, 1898, and the sum of $130, the rent of the said premises due on the 1st day of July, 1898, making a total of $216, and for that sum the plaintiffs' testator obtained a judgment against Higgins, which judgment was entered on October 18, 1898, and it is to enforce payment of this indebtedness, accrued nearly two years after the transfer of the property upon a lease executed nearly a year after the transfer of the property — it being the only unpaid obligation of the defendant either actual or contingent at the time he made the transfer — that such transfer is sought to be set aside. These facts are all undisputed, with nothing secret about the conveyance, which was made under conditions which showed that it was not intended to conceal it when made, and when there was no rent due the plaintiff and no lease then in existence upon which the defendant could at any time be liable.

To say that the execution of an instrument under those circumstances was fraudulent, would make fraudulent every conveyance made after a man had signed a guaranty which was to continue for several years. If any legal proposition is settled, it is that a person has a right to give away his property as he pleases, and that such a gift is not invalid because he subsequently becomes insolvent and unable to pay his debts. As was said by Judge EARL in *Kain* v. *Larkin* (131 N. Y. 307): " By the express terms of the statute, it is not sufficient to condemn a conveyance of land as a fraud upon creditors that it was not founded on a valuable consideration. A person assailing such a conveyance must go further and show by other evidence that it was made with the fraudulent intent condemned in the statute. An owner of real estate can make a voluntary settlement thereof upon his wife and children without any consideration, provided he has ample property left to satisfy all the just claims of his creditors. If the grantor remains solvent after the conveyance and has sufficient property left to satisfy all his just debts, then the conveyance, whatever his intention was, cannot be a fraud upon his existing creditors; and when a judgment creditor assails a conveyance made by the judgment debtor, he cannot cast upon the grantee the *onus* of showing good faith and of establishing that the grantor was solvent after the conveyance, by simply showing that the deed was not founded upon a valuable consideration. But the person assailing the deed assumes the burden of showing that it was executed in bad faith, and that it left the grantor insolvent and without ample property to pay his existing debts and liabilities, and so it has been repeatedly held." This opinion but reiterates a rule that has always been the law as shown by the authorities cited. If this is the law, then upon the facts stated there is no justification for a finding that this conveyance defrauded the plaintiffs, or any one, or was made with such an intent, and the burden of proof being upon the plaintiffs to show the fraudulent intent, and there being no evidence to show such intent, the finding of the trial judge of such an intent is unsupported by the evidence.

There are several rulings upon questions of evidence which it is not necessary for us to consider upon this appeal, as a new trial must be ordered. It is proper, however, to call attention to the fact that the declarations of Luke Higgins, the grantor, made after the conveyance, are not evidence as against Elizabeth Higgins, the grantee, to show fraud in the transaction; nor would the fact that one of the defendants was called as a witness and testified to facts which are inconsistent with a fraudulent intent, and that the court refused to believe his testimony, be evidence from which the court could find a fraudulent intent.

We think the evidence in this case was entirely insufficient to justify a finding of any fraudulent intent as to either of the parties to the conveyances, and for that reason the judgment should be reversed and a new trial ordered, with costs to the appellant to abide the event.

VAN BRUNT, P. J., McLAUGHLIN, HATCH and LAUGHLIN, JJ., concurred.

Judgment reversed, new trial ordered, costs to appellant to abide event.

THE PEOPLE OF THE STATE OF NEW YORK, Respondent, *v.* MARK
SCHLESINGER, Appellant.

*Assault — charge to the jury where an inspector of the bureau of incumbrances in
New York city is indicted for an assault, committed while he is engaged in removing goods from a sidewalk.*

Upon a trial under a charge of assault, it appeared that the defendant was an
inspector in the bureau of incumbrances of the city of New York, and that he
and another inspector had been sent to a store in which one Scott was employed
for the purpose of removing and taking away whatever merchandise might be
found upon the sidewalk in front of the store. The evidence for the prosecution was that as the defendant and his companion reached the store Scott was
coming out with a leather traveling bag which he was taking to a factory;
that the defendant and the other inspector undertook to take the bag from him,
and that in the altercation which followed the assault was committed.

The defendant's evidence tended to show that as Scott came out of the store he
attempted to seize one of the leather bags which the defendant was removing
from the sidewalk, and was about to take it away; that the defendant and the
other inspector attempted to take the bag from him, but that no unnecessary
force was used.

After the jury had retired they sent the following inquiry to the court: "Will
your Honor please inform the jury that, if Mr. Schlesinger pushed Scott aside
and, in doing so, he fell and received the injury, whether this can be considered
an accident and not an assault?" to which the court responded, "I said to find
him guilty you must find that it was willful and wrongful." Thereupon one
of the jurors inquired, "If it was done by accident?" to which the court
replied, "Oh, the law does not punish people criminally for accidents." The
juror then asked, "Supposing Scott interfered with him in his duties, and he
pushed him aside and he fell?" to which the court replied, "Any unlawful
touching of a person, if done willfully and wrongfully, is an assault. If I put
the tip of my finger upon you, willfully and wrongfully, that is an assault."

Held, that the last instruction, while correct in the abstract, was misleading, and
required the reversal of a judgment of conviction;

That it did not answer the inquiry or give the jury a correct idea of the principle
to be applied, in case they found that Scott interfered with the defendant in
the discharge of his duties:

That the proper rule was that if any one interfered with the defendant in the
discharge of his duties, either in removing or in keeping possession of the
things removed, he was justified in using sufficient force to prevent such interference, and that the court, in answering the inquiry, should have so instructed
the jury.

APPEAL by the defendant, Mark Schlesinger, from a judgment
of the Court of General Sessions of the Peace in and for the city

and county of New York in favor of the plaintiff, entered in the office of the clerk of said court on the 27th day of October, 1899, upon the verdict of a jury convicting the defendant of the crime of assault in the second degree.

William F. Howe, for the appellant.

Howard S. Gans, for the respondent.

McLAUGHLIN, J.:

The defendant appeals from a judgment of conviction of the crime of assault in the second degree and for which he has been sentenced to serve a term of one year in the penitentiary.

The facts charged in the indictment as constituting the crime for which he has been convicted are, in substance, that on the 20th of October, 1896, he willfully and wrongfully inflicted grievous bodily harm upon one William Scott, by striking him, throwing him down, and beating him.

At the trial there was a sharp conflict of testimony between the witnesses offered on the part of the People and those offered on the part of the defendant. The testimony of the witnesses on the part of the former tended to establish that at the time stated in the indictment, the defendant, then an inspector in the bureau of incumbrances of the city of New York, went, by the direction of his superior officer, to a trunk and leather store kept by one David A. Doyle, at Nos. 1 and 2 Vesey street, in that city, for the purpose of removing and taking away whatever merchandise might be found in front of the store, upon the sidewalk, in violation of certain ordinances of the city; that the defendant was accompanied by one Clark, also an inspector in the bureau of incumbrances; that as the defendant and Clark approached the store, one Scott, an employee therein, came out of the store with a leather traveling bag, which he, by the direction of his employer, was taking to a factory for the purpose of having it repaired; that as he met the defendant and Clark, they took hold of him and undertook to forcibly take the bag from him, and that in the altercation which followed, the defendant knocked Scott down, and in doing so, or thereafter beating him, inflicted very serious injuries upon him.

While the testimony on the part of the defendant tended to

establish that the latter was not the cause of, or responsible for the injuries to Scott, so far as such testimony related to Scott's injuries, it was substantially to the effect that, as Scott came out of the store, he attempted to seize one of the leather bags which the defendant was removing from the sidewalk and was about to take away, and that in doing so he slipped and fell to the sidewalk, and in this way sustained his injuries; that he did seize one of such bags, and that the defendant and Clark attempted to forcibly take it from him, but that no unnecessary force was used. There was no dispute but what Scott, at the time, was very seriously injured.

This was the situation at the close of all the testimony, and the case was submitted to the jury with instructions, in substance, that if they found that the testimony of the witnesses of the People was the correct version of the transaction, then it could find the defendant guilty of the crime charged in the indictment, while, on the other hand, if the testimony of the defendant and his witnesses was true, then the defendant was entitled to an acquittal. The charge was eminently fair to both sides, as is evidenced by the fact that no exceptions were taken to it, and we should affirm this judgment were it not for the instructions given to the jury after they had entered upon their deliberations. Some time after the jury had retired, the following inquiry was sent to the court: "Will your Honor please inform the jury that, if Mr. Schlesinger pushed Scott aside and, in doing so, he fell and received the injury, whether this can be considered an accident and not an assault?" To which the court — the jury having returned to the court room — responded: "I said to find him guilty you must find that it was willful and wrongful." Thereupon the ninth juror inquired: "If it was done by accident?" And the court answered, "Oh, the law does not punish people criminally for accidents." And again the ninth juror inquired: "Supposing Scott interfered with him in his duties, and he pushed him aside and he fell?" To which the court replied: "Any unlawful touching of a person, if done willfully and wrongfully, is an assault. If I put the tip of my finger upon you, willfully and wrongfully, that is an assault." While this instruction, in the abstract, was not erroneous, it was misleading and by reason thereof may have resulted to the great prejudice of the defendant. It did not answer the inquiry, or give the jury a correct idea of the legal principle to be applied in case they found that Scott interfered with the defendant in the discharge of his duties. The defendant, of course, not only had the right, as it was his duty, to remove the obstructions from the sidewalk, but also to keep possession of the things removed until the same had been deposited in the place provided by the city (*Scott* v. *Mayor*, 27 App. Div. 240), and if any one interfered with him in the discharge of that duty, either in removing or in keeping possession of the things removed, he was justified in using sufficient force to prevent such interference, and the court in answering the inquiry, should have so instructed the jury.

We are of the opinion, therefore, that justice requires that a new trial should be had. The judgment of conviction is, therefore, reversed, and a new trial ordered.

VAN BRUNT, P. J., O'BRIEN, INGRAHAM and HATCH, JJ. concurred.

Judgment reversed and new trial ordered.

202
NY 539

JEANNETTE CROW, Respondent, v. METROPOLITAN STREET RAILWAY COMPANY, Appellant.

Negligence — injury from a passenger being thrown from a car by its sudden starting after it had slowed up — permanent injuries must be alleged — when an erroneous admission of evidence is cured by the charge.

In an action to recover damages for personal injuries, sustained by the plaintiff while a passenger on one of the defendant's street cars, evidence that the plaintiff indicated to the conductor her desire to alight at a certain point; that the conductor rang the bell, and that, in obedience to the signal, the speed of the car was slackened; that the plaintiff then went to the rear platform and took hold of the rail of the car, and that while she was in this position and before the car had come to a full stop, its speed was, without warning to her, suddenly increased and she was thrown to the street, is sufficient to warrant a finding that the defendant was guilty of negligence.

VAN BRUNT, P. J., and INGRAHAM, J., dissented.

Evidence that the plaintiff sustained permanent injuries as a result of the accident is not admissible, in the absence of an allegation to that effect in the complaint.

The admission of evidence of permanent injuries, over the objection of the defendant that they had not been pleaded, does not, however, constitute error requiring the reversal of a judgment in favor of the plaintiff, where it appears that the court in its charge instructed the jury for what injuries they could award damages, and did not include therein permanent injuries.

VAN BRUNT, P. J., and INGRAHAM, J., dissented.

APPEAL by the defendant, the Metropolitan Street Railway Company, from a judgment of the Supreme Court in favor of the plaintiff, entered in the office of the clerk of the county of New York on the 21st day of September, 1901, upon the verdict of a jury for $1,500, and also from an order entered in said clerk's office on the 20th day of September, 1901, denying the defendant's motion for a new trial made upon the minutes.

Theodore H. Lord, for the appellant.

Lyman A. Spalding, for the respondent.

McLAUGHLIN, J.:

This action was brought to recover damages for personal injuries alleged to have been sustained by the plaintiff through the negligence of the defendant. She had a verdict for $1,500, and from the judgment entered thereon, as well as from an order denying a motion for a new trial, defendant has appealed.

On the 3d of March, 1899, the plaintiff, then upwards of seventy-five years of age, entered one of the defendant's cars at One Hundred and Fifteenth street for the purpose of going to Forty-third street in the city of New York, and when she reached Forty-third street, according to her testimony, she indicated to the conductor her desire to get off at that street, but for some reason the car was not stopped, and after it had passed Forty-third street she called the conductor's attention to that fact and again requested him to have the car stopped in order that she might get off. He thereupon rang the bell of the car once and it immediately commenced to slow up, and she prepared to get off by going to the rear platform and taking hold of the rail of the car; that while she was in this position, and before the car had come to a full stop, its speed was, without warning to her, suddenly increased, or, to use her own language, " the car gave a violent jerk," and she was thrown to the street and injured. She was corroborated as to the fact that the bell was rung for the car to stop by the defendant's witness Aiken, who testified that when the car was on the north side of Forty-second street he heard the conductor ring the bell for it to stop. On the part of the defendant, the conductor testified that he did not remember that the plaintiff asked him to stop the car; in fact, he did not remember seeing her at all until she fell from the car; that it was the custom to slacken the speed of the car in approaching Forty-second street in order to avoid collisions with cars running east and west on that street; he denied that there was any sudden starting of the car after it commenced to slow up, and in that respect as well as to the custom of the defendant to slacken the speed of the car at that point, he was corroborated by the motorman and other witnesses. The conductor, however, did not deny that he rang the bell for the car to stop at Forty-second street, nor did the motorman deny that the bell was rung for him to stop at that place.

We have, therefore, evidence from which the jury might have found that, after the plaintiff had indicated her desire to get off the car, and after the signal had been given by the conductor to the motorman to stop the car for that purpose, that in obedience to that signal the motorman had slackened the speed of the car preparatory to stopping it, and while the plaintiff was preparing to get off, the speed of the car, without notice to the plaintiff, was greatly increased and by reason thereof she was thrown to the street and injured; and if such facts had been found by them, then they might well have found that the defendant had not performed its full duty to the plaintiff. After the car had commenced to slow up at her request she had a right to prepare to leave the car, and she also had a right to assume that the conditions existing at that time would be continued until the car had been stopped and she had been afforded an opportunity to get off. There certainly was sufficient evidence, as it seems to me, to go to the jury upon these questions of fact.

This case is clearly distinguishable from *Armstrong* v. *Met. St. Rway. Co.* (36 App. Div. 525), and *Sims* v. *Met. St. Rway. Co.* (65 id. 270). In each of those cases the defendant was held not liable for the reason that it did not appear that any signal to stop the car had been given to the person in control of the car, or that the plaintiff had a right to assume that the slackening of the speed of the car in each instance was for the purpose of permitting him to get off.

It also urged that the judgment should be reversed, because the learned trial justice erred in allowing the plaintiff to prove special damages in the nature of permanent injuries which were not alleged in the complaint. It is true the complaint did not allege permanent injuries, and upon the trial the plaintiff's physician was asked the following question : " Q. Doctor, how long, in your judgment, will the effects of these injuries remain ? " He answered, against defendant's objection and exception : "A. I think they will be permanent." A motion was made to strike out the answer on the ground of the objection, and this was denied. The objection should have been sustained, and the motion to strike out should have been granted. In the absence of proper allegations in the complaint to the effect that the plaintiff had sustained permanent injuries, she could not prove such facts upon the trial. (*Clark* v. *Met. St. Rway. Co.*, 68 App. Div. 49.) But we do not think the defendant could have been injured by this answer. At the close of the trial the jury were specifically told for what injuries damages could be awarded, and those enumerated did not include permanent injuries. At the conclusion of the charge, plaintiff's counsel requested the court to charge that the jury could award damages for future pain and suffering. This request was denied, the court saying : " I think the evidence upon that subject is so doubtful that it would not be right to say there are any consequences in the future, considering her present age, for which the railroad company is liable." This was equivalent to telling the jury to disregard the evidence as to permanent injuries, inasmuch as they could not award damages therefor. The defendant apparently was satisfied with the instructions given on this subject, inasmuch as no exceptions were taken to the charge and no requests made, so far as appears, which were not granted. Under such circumstances, we do not think the admission of this evidence was injurious to the defendant.

The judgment and order must be affirmed, with costs.

Hatch and Laughlin, JJ., concurred; Van Brunt, P. J., and Ingraham, J., dissented.

Van Brunt, P. J. (dissenting):

It seems to me that the judgment of the court in this case is founded upon the fact that the car slowed up after the plaintiff had

notified the conductor of her desire to alight at the next street, and
that, although not at a regular stopping place, she had a right to
treat this as an invitation to alight. It appears that the car was
approaching a railroad crossing, and that it slowed up for that reason,
and that its proper stopping place was upon the other side of the
street. Under these circumstances, the mere fact that the car slowed
up preparatory to crossing a street upon which ran another railway,
was not an invitation to the plaintiff to alight.

I, therefore, dissent.

INGRAHAM, J., concurred.

Judgment and order affirmed, with costs.

₂₀₆
₅₄₆
THOMAS NELSON, Respondent, v. EDWARD S. HATCH, Appellant,
          Impleaded with LYMAN E. WARREN.

*Attorney and client — contingent fee — agreement by a third person with the attor-
ney to pay the disbursements of the action and share in the recovery — failure of
the attorney to perform the latter agreement — measure of damages where the complaint in the action to which the contract related was dismissed.*

Hatch & Warren, a firm of attorneys who were engaged in prosecuting an action
    under an agreement with their client, which provided that the firm should fur-
    nish the personal services of Warren, pay the expenses of the litigation and
    receive thirty per cent of the proceeds, entered into a contract with one Nelson,
    by which the latter, in consideration of one-half of Hatch & Warren's share of
    the proceeds, agreed to advance $10,000 to the attorneys for the purposes of
    the litigation, the first $5,000 to be advanced by a specified time and the second
    $5,000 to be advanced in such sums as might be desired by Hatch & Warren.
After Nelson had advanced $7,000 under his contract, Hatch & Warren refused
    to advance moneys necessary to the diligent prosecution of the action, although
    they had in their hands funds applicable to that purpose. They also demanded
    of Nelson an additional payment of $1,000 under the contract when the expenses
    of the litigation did not necessitate such a demand, and upon his refusal to comply
    therewith notified him that the contract was terminated. Thereafter Warren
    withdrew from the firm and refused to take any further part in the conduct
    of the litigation. Hatch subsequently procured the action to be tried (but
    not by Warren), and it resulted in a judgment that the client had no cause of
    action.
In an action brought by Nelson against Hatch & Warren to recover damages for
    a breach of the contract,

Held, that Nelson's failure to pay the $1,000 demanded by Hatch & Warren did not justify them in electing to terminate the contract, as he was not obliged to pay the second $5,000 upon the arbitrary demand of Hatch & Warren, but only when the proper conduct of the litigation required it;

That the refusal of Hatch to apply the money advanced by Nelson to the diligent prosecution of the action, and the attempted cancellation of the contract because of Nelson's failure to pay the $1,000, and the refusal of Warren to perform his contract with the client, constituted a breach of the contract with Nelson, and absolved the latter from the necessity of continuing to perform it;

That it could not be successfully contended that the measure of the plaintiff's damages was the benefit to him of having the contract performed, and that as the action to which the contract related had resulted in a judgment of no cause of action the plaintiff's damages were purely nominal;

That, as the contract had been rendered impossible of performance by the action of the defendants, this rule of damages did not apply, and that, under the circumstances, the plaintiff should be permitted to recover the moneys which he had advanced under the contract and the expense which he incurred in connection therewith.

INGRAHAM, J., dissented.

APPEAL by the defendant, Edward S. Hatch, from a judgment of the Supreme Court in favor of the plaintiff, entered in the office of the clerk of the county of New York on the 24th day of July, 1901, upon the report of a referee.

In 1891 Lilyon B. Daniels, who claimed to be the widow of William B. Daniels, entered into an agreement with the firm of Hatch & Warren, attorneys, by which that firm, in consideration of a contingent fee of thirty per cent of the proceeds, agreed to prosecute an action on her behalf to establish her rights as widow in her alleged husband's estate. Hatch & Warren agreed, among other things, to furnish the personal services of Lyman E. Warren and to advance all moneys necessary for the prosecution of the claim.

After the execution of this agreement Hatch & Warren entered into a contract with one Nelson, by which the latter, in consideration of one-half of Hatch & Warren's interest in the recovery, agreed to advance $10,000 for use in prosecuting the action.

The action is brought to recover damages for the breach of the latter contract.

William Rumsey, for the appellant.

Thomas Darlington, for the respondent.

HATCH, J.:

When this case was before this court upon the former appeal, it was held that the action was one to recover damages for a breach of the contract, the subject of the action, and it having been determined by the referee before whom it was tried that it was an action to rescind the contract, we reversed the judgment and ordered a new trial. (56 App. Div. 149.) Upon the new trial the plaintiff has recovered judgment for the damages demanded in his complaint. The facts which appear upon the present trial are not essentially different from those which appeared upon the first trial, and as they have been fully stated in the case as reported upon that appeal, it is not essential that we again restate them in detail.

The obligation which the plaintiff assumed by the terms of his contract was to advance for the purposes specified therein the sum of $10,000, $5,000 of which was to be paid to Hatch & Warren between March 1, 1891, and May fifteenth of the same year, and of the remaining $5,000 it was to be advanced in such " sums as may be desired by the parties of the first part," but no sum greater in amount than $1,000 of the last $5,000 at a time should be required to be paid by the plaintiff, and he was entitled to a notice of thirty days of an intention to draw such sum. Taking into consideration the object sought to be accomplished by the contract and the purpose of the parties thereunder, it is evident that it was contemplated that the first $5,000 would create a fund, by virtue of which the defendants would be enabled to make necessary advances for the diligent prosecution of the action, which had then been begun and was pending in Colorado. We think the fair construction of this contract, relating to the payment to be made by the plaintiff thereunder, required the payment of the $5,000 within the time expressly stipulated, but that the second $5,000 was not required to be paid upon the mere arbitrary desire of Hatch & Warren, but that it intended to provide that as the necessity of the litigation required, Hatch & Warren had the right to demand of the plaintiff payment of the additional $5,000 in sums of $1,000 each as should be required for the diligent prosecution of the action, and unless such sums were required for that purpose, there was no right upon the part of Hatch & Warren to demand the same and no obligation on the part of the plaintiff to pay the same, although demand was made therefor, unless it was required to discharge proper obligations in connection with the prosecution of the action.

Concluding that this is the proper construction of this contract, the testimony is to be examined for the purpose of seeing if Hatch & Warren, or either of them, was guilty of any acts which constituted a breach of the same prior to the plaintiff's refusal to make further payments thereunder, and whether he was excused from so doing. The testimony is undisputed that prior to November 23, 1891, the plaintiff had paid to Hatch & Warren the first $5,000 within the stipulated time, and had also advanced, upon the demand of the defendant Hatch, $2,000 of the second $5,000. At this time it appeared without dispute that the action brought by Mrs. Daniels was pending in the Colorado court and that the same, by reason of default in taking the proper proceeding and necessary steps, was in a condition where it could be dismissed, and was only saved from such result by the consideration and stipulation of the attorneys for the defendant therein ; that the reason for this condition rested in the fact that the attorneys representing Mrs. Daniels in Colorado had not been furnished with sufficient funds to enable them to take the proper and necessary steps in protection of Mrs. Daniels' rights therein. Of these facts the defendants were informed by the attorneys in Colorado, and one of them, Mr. Donnolly, had a personal interview with the defendant Hatch and requested that he make payment in the sum of $500 in order that such attorney might proceed with the action. Hatch refused at that time to make payment of such sum, or any other, and only paid in immediate connection with the lawsuit, a small sum for clerk's fees, and declined to pay more. As appears by the books of Hatch & Warren, there had been paid out up to and including the 30th day of September, 1892, the sum of $2,148.95. This sum was made up in part of $200 in cash for some undisclosed purpose, $423.04 to Warren and $1,075 to Mrs. Daniels. There was at this time in the hands of Hatch, of the payments made by the plaintiffs herein, $4,851.05, and there was no immediate pressing necessity for the advance of this sum at that time. On the contrary, a small proportion only was necessary to relieve the default of Mrs. Daniels in her action and for the orderly prosecution of the same. Under such circumstances, it is perfectly clear that it was the duty of Hatch & Warren to make the necessary advances, and that the plaintiff could not be called upon to pay further sums until there was a necessity therefor. This being the relative condition of the parties at this time, Mr. Hatch, under date of the 27th of February, 1891, made a demand upon the plaintiff for a further payment of $1,000. The plaintiff was excused from making this payment and could not be placed in default by refusal to comply with the demand for two reasons, *first*, there was no right in the defendants to demand the payment under the terms of the contract, and, *second*, the plaintiff after the demand saw the defendant Warren and was informed by him that the money was not then wanted, and that he need not make the payment at that time. In the face of this condition, however, the defendants, under date of November 23, 1891, wrote that the plaintiff was in default by failing to pay the last sum demanded, and that by reason thereof the contract with him " is canceled — has become void and of no further effect." It is clear, therefore, that Hatch & Warren on that date were guilty of a clear breach of the contract. *First*, for the reason that the defendant Hatch, who had the custody of the money, had refused to advance the same for the purposes for which it had been paid, and such refusal was in violation of the terms of the contract; *second*, for the reason that in violation of its terms and when the plaintiff was not in default, they notified him that they canceled the same and elected to treat it as void and of no effect. These acts constituted clear breaches of the contract by the defendants, and the plaintiff, by reason thereof, was absolved from a further fulfillment of the same.

The latter act constituting the breach is averred in the complaint as one of the grounds for the maintenance of this action. The complaint does not in terms aver a breach of the contract in the refusal by Hatch to pay the money as necessity required for the proper prosecution of Mrs. Daniels' action. The evidence, however, of such breach was given and stands undisputed in the record, and no objection was taken that it was not admissible under the complaint; consequently, it may be considered by this court, and the complaint be deemed to be amended in order to give effect to the proof as nobody is prejudiced or misled thereby. (*Drexel* v. *Pease*, 37 N. Y. St. Repr. 166; *Bate* v. *Graham*, 11 N. Y. 237.)

It seems clear, therefore, that a breach of this contract was established by undisputed proof prior to the time when Warren withdrew from the prosecution of the action. But we are also of the opinion that this action in withdrawing and refusing to perform his contract with Mrs. Daniels constituted a breach of the contract with the plaintiff, and that by reason of it the latter was absolved from further fulfillment of its terms. The contract between the parties to this action is to be construed in connection with the contract between Hatch & Warren and Mrs. Daniels. By the terms of the latter, it was stipulated that Mrs. Daniels should have the personal service of Warren in the conduct of the litigation. It is clear that it could not be fulfilled in conformity with its terms unless Warren gave his personal service. The consideration for the plaintiff's contract was the assignment of one-half of the interest possessed by Hatch & Warren therein; consequently, the plaintiff had the right to demand that that contract be fulfilled according to its terms. It may well have been the personal service of Warren in the conduct of that litigation, which was the inducing cause of plaintiff's executing the contract and entering into the engagement which he made. He was entitled to insist that it be performed in accordance with its terms, and Hatch & Warren had contracted with him that it would be so performed. The only way in which Hatch & Warren could avoid this result would be by the plaintiff's consenting that it be otherwise performed. It was competent for him to waive performance by Warren; it was within his right to insist upon it. It is clear that he never waived any of his rights and at all times stood upon the fulfillment of the contract which he made. The defendant Hatch had no right to insist that the plaintiff accept performance by any other person. It may be his misfortune that without his fault Warren withdrew from the fulfillment of the contract and thereby made it impossible for him to perform the same, but the plaintiff is not to be prejudiced in any of his rights by such fact, nor can Hatch complain of such result because the plaintiff stands insisting upon his legal rights in the premises. It is entirely immaterial to any question which concerns the legal rights of the parties to this action that Hatch subsequently procured Mrs. Daniels' lawsuit to be tried and conducted with vigor and skill. That was no concern of the plaintiffs as such act was not in fulfillment of the terms of his contract and he was not bound to accept the same as performance. Under date of October 1, 1892, the plaintiff notified the defendants of their breach of the contract and demanded a return of the money which he had paid thereunder. At this time Hatch was in default under the contract in failing to advance the moneys as required thereby and his letter to the plaintiff canceling the same remained of record, unrevoked, and it was after that time that Hatch attempted to make fulfillment of the contract with Mrs. Daniels. In no view, therefore, upon the undisputed proof, can we escape the conclusion that Hatch and Warren were both guilty of a breach of the contract with the plaintiff at the time when he made his demand for the return of the money paid thereunder, and elected to treat the contract as terminated on account of the defendants' breaches of the same. This was clearly within his legal rights, and by reason of the then condition he became entitled to have and recover such damages as he had sustained which might be properly recoverable.

It is earnestly insisted, however, that if there was a breach of the contract, nevertheless, the proof shows that no damages beyond such as are nominal have been sustained by the plaintiff. It is the claim of the learned counsel for the defendant Hatch that the measure of plaintiff's damages is the "benefit to him of having the contract performed," and that this constitutes the measure of damage. On this hypothesis the claim is advanced that the actual result showed that Mrs. Daniels in fact had no cause of action or right in her husband's estate, and that, therefore, the plaintiff could by no possibility take anything of advantage under his contract. It may be conceded that such rule of damage is the true rule if the means exist by which the measurement can be applied. The rule, however, fails as applied to this action, for the reason that by the defendants' acts the contract never could be performed, in consequence of which all basis for the measurement of damages upon any consideration of result which might have flowed therefrom is futile, and under such circumstances application of the rule is rendered impossible. In *Friedland* v. *Myers* (139 N. Y. 433) an action was brought for a breach of contract in the lease of a building for a special purpose. The court held that ordinarily in case of lease the measure of damage would be the difference between the rent reserved and the actual value of the lease, but that the damages were not limited to that sum, and the lease being for a special purpose, proof of damage under the rule would be practically impossible of ascertainment, and that a recovery could be had for other damages that were the proximate effect of the breach of the covenant so far as they were not speculative or uncertain in character, and might be deemed to be within the fair contemplation of the parties when the lease was made and might have been foreseen as a consequence of a breach of the covenant. The plaintiff therein was permitted to recover for his actual and necessary expenses incurred in preparing for the occupation of the premises, and that such item properly embraced architect's fees in making drawings for cases, counters and other necessary features required in the business, it appearing that this work was done with the knowledge and assent of the defendant, and that his conduct throughout was such as to invite the expenditure. To the same effect is *Bernstein* v. *Meech* (130 N. Y. 354). That was an action to recover damages for the breach of a theatrical contract, where the compensation of the plaintiff was to be fifty per cent of the gross receipts realized from the performances to be given. It was impossible to determine what those receipts would have been, and plaintiff was permitted to prove his expenses in preparing for the fulfillment of the contract. Mr. Justice BRADLEY, writing for the court, said : " His loss also consisted of the expenses by him incurred to prepare and provide for such performance. While the plaintiff was unable to prove the value in profits of his contract, he was properly permitted to recover the amount of such loss as it appeared he had suffered by the defendants' breach." This rule has been uniformly recognized. (*Dickinson* v. *Hart*, 142 N. Y. 183.) The present case falls within the same principle. Here it was impossible to establish what the plaintiff's damages were or would have been had the contract been fulfilled as it was rendered absolutely impossible of performance. But the plaintiff was permitted to prove the moneys which he advanced, and the expense which he incurred in connection with it. These defendants had knowledge of such expense and extent of the same because they received the money. Consequently the case falls squarely within the rule of the cases we have cited.

There is no other question which requires consideration. It follows, therefore, that the judgment should be affirmed, with costs.

VAN BRUNT, P. J., O'BRIEN and LAUGHLIN, JJ., concurred; INGRAHAM, J., dissented.

INGRAHAM, J. (dissenting):

I am unable to concur in the affirmance of this judgment. The contract between the plaintiff and the defendants was made on the 27th day of February, 1891. By it the plaintiff agreed to pay under certain conditions $10,000, and in consideration thereof the defendants sold, assigned, transferred and set over to the plaintiff an undivided half interest in and to a contract theretofore executed between one Lilyon B. Daniels and the defendants, and of any and all moneys and property that the defendants may derive or receive under said contract, except disbursements. The contract between the defendants and Daniels was annexed to the contract between the the plaintiff and the defendants, and by that contract Daniels assigned and transferred to the defendants thirty per cent of her undivided share of, and of her claim, right, title and interest in and to, certain property which had belonged to one W. B. Daniels, deceased, and in or to any claim or chose in action against the said W. B. Daniels, or his estate; the defendants agreed to prosecute the claim of the said Lilyon B. Daniels against the estate of W. B. Daniels and to furnish "the personal services of the said Lyman E. Warren, at any and all times when it shall be necessary, or when reasonably requested by the party of the first part so to do." This agreement also provided that the defendants, who were attorneys and counselors at law, "must assume to and do make provision for obtaining the money for the payment of any and all disbursements, that may be required by them and for carrying out this contract so long as they undertake and continue in the prosecution of the matters contemplated by the terms of this agreement. And the parties of the second part (defendants) shall have the right at any time to withdraw from the provisions of this agreement, and in such event shall be entitled to a lien upon the interests of the party of the first part in and to any of the real or personal estate in which she shall have an interest as the widow of the said W. B. Daniels to the extent of the disbursements or cash that shall have been obtained, advanced or loaned or paid out by the parties of the second part for the purpose of carrying out this contract." This contract between Daniels and the defendants being annexed to the contract between the plaintiff and the defendants, the plaintiff is chargeable with knowledge of its terms.

It seems that in the year 1892 the defendants dissolved partnership as the result of a dispute. Whereupon Warren wrote to Mrs. Daniels a letter dated September 29, 1892, as follows:

"The firm of Hatch & Warren has been dissolved. Under the provisions of the contract made with Hatch & Warren the said Hatch & Warren shall have a right at any time to withdraw from the provisions of that agreement. I hereby withdraw from the provisions of that agreement and declare the same terminated and ended.   Very truly,

"LYMAN E. WARREN."

On the thirtieth of September Mrs. Daniels wrote a letter to the defendants stating that she had received the letter from Warren, and that "in consequence of this letter and the refusal of Mr. Hatch and of Mr. Warren to carry out their contract I hereby notify you that such contract is annulled and terminated. I further notify you that from this date you cease to meddle with my affairs in any way, and to do any further act or thing either for or against me in this matter, as I have made other arrangements for transacting my business.   Very truly,

"MRS. L. DANIELS."

In answer to this letter the defendant Hatch wrote to Mrs. Daniels acknowledging its receipt, claiming that Warren did not have the right to declare her contract terminated; and that Hatch & Warren had advanced a considerable sum of money under the terms and conditions of the contract and were ready to do and perform all the terms and conditions of the contract. Nothing further seems to have been done by Hatch & Warren under the contract to the 10th day of February, 1893, when this action was commenced. Assuming, as we must, that this action was to recover the damages sustained by a breach of the contract between the plaintiff and the defendant, and assuming that there was evidence to justify a finding that

there had been a breach of their contract with Mrs. Daniels prior
to the commencement of the action, the substantial question is as to
the measure of damages to which the plaintiff was entitled. It was
proved without objection that subsequent to the commencement of
the action the defendant Hatch, with the consent of Mrs. Daniels,
did prosecute the action brought by Mrs. Daniels to recover her
interest in the property of W. B. Daniels, deceased; that that action
was tried in the year 1893 and resulted in the defeat of Mrs. Daniels,
and a judgment was entered which was subsequently affirmed on
appeal. It was thus established that Mrs. Daniels had no claim
against the estate of W. B. Daniels which was the subject-matter of
the assignment by Mrs. Daniels to the defendants, which could be
enforced. There was no express obligation in the contract between
the plaintiff and the defendants that the defendants would carry
out the contract with Mrs. Daniels and continue to act for her in
the prosecution of these claims. The plaintiff seems to have been
willing to pay his money upon a transfer to him of one-half of the
amount that the defendants would receive under their contract with
Mrs. Daniels. So far as I can see, the only agreement that the
defendants made with the plaintiff was that they would act in good
faith in carrying out the contract beween themselves and Mrs. Daniels
and realize as much as possible in their conduct of the prosecution of
her claim against the estate of W. B. Daniels. Assuming that this
contract was broken and that Hatch & Warren failed to carry out that
implied agreement, the damages that the plaintiff sustained in consequence of the breach of that undertaking was the amount that he could
show that he would have received in case the agreement had been
carried out; but it seems to me that the plaintiff has failed to establish that any amount could have been recovered upon the claim of
Mrs. Daniels against the estate of W. B. Daniels, or that the plaintiff was entitled to more than nominal damages. It is true that
Warren refused to take part in the prosecution of the claims against
Mrs. Daniels, and that the contract with Mrs. Daniels provided
that the defendants would furnish the personal services of Warren
at any and at all times when it should be necessary or when reasonably requested by Mrs. Daniels, but so far as appears Mrs.
Daniels never requested the defendants to furnish the services
of Warren after his withdrawal from the firm; and she subse-

quently consented to Hatch's proceeding to conduct the litigation with his partner, Mr. Wickes, and such services were subsequently actually rendered and the claims prosecuted. Upon what basis it can be said that the plaintiff sustained any damage by reason of any of the breaches of the contract relied upon I am unable to see. Nothing has ever been realized upon these claims, and upon this record it must be assumed that the claims were without foundation and of no value, and what the plaintiff obtained by his assignment was one-half interest of the defendants in certain claims which were not enforcible and from which nothing has been realized. Basing this action as it must be based upon a claim for the damage sustained in consequence of a breach of the contract by the defendants, it seems to me that the evidence conclusively established that the plaintiff sustained no injury by such a breach, as his interest in the contract between Mrs. Daniels and the defendants was valueless; that nothing has ever been received by them and no recovery has ever been had upon the claims of Mrs. Daniels of which the defendants were entitled to receive thirty per cent, one-half of which was assigned to the plaintiff. This contract between the defendants and Mrs. Daniels was one which upon its face was void for champerty, and the plaintiff, who is a lawyer, must be chargeable with knowledge of that fact. He paid his money upon the chance of obtaining an interest in a recovery, if one was had, upon Mrs. Daniels' claims. As a consideration for the payment of that money he obtained an interest in a contract which could not be enforced, and which the subsequent events have shown to be of no value, and having made such a contract with his eyes open and taking the chances of a recovery of a large sum of money if the speculation had succeeded, I can see no reason why the court should interfere to allow him to recover back what he had paid, the speculation that he entered into having been unsuccessful.

I think the judgment should be reversed.

Judgment affirmed, with costs.

218 MAGGIE A. COLEMAN and Others, Respondents, *v.* THE CITY OF
NY 612,   NEW YORK, Appellant.

*New York city street — right of the city while it remains unopened to maintain a
dumping board thereon — when a property owner is entitled to a mandamus to
compel the opening of the street — right to maintain the dumping board after the
street is opened.*

Chapter 697 of the Laws of 1887, as amended by chapter 272 of the Laws of
1888 and chapter 257 of the Laws of 1889, which vested in the board of the
department of docks in the city of New York authority to establish the boundary lines of Exterior street along a portion of the East river and authorized
the board of street opening and improvement to institute proceedings to
acquire the necessary lands, provided that the street should be laid out as provided by the plan adopted by the dock department, " and the same shall be
the sole plan according to which any wharf, pier, bulk-head, basin, dock or
slip or any wharf, structure or superstructure shall thereafter be laid out or
constructed in that part of the water front included in and specified upon said
plan, and from the time of the adoption thereof, no wharf, pier, bulk-head,
basin, dock or slip, nor any wharf structure or superstructure shall be laid
out, built or rebuilt in that part of the water front aforesaid, unless in accordance with such plan. Excepting, nevertheless, that the board of the department of docks may build or rebuild, or license the building or rebuilding of temporary wharf structures or superstructures to continue and remain for a time not
longer than until the construction of said Exterior street shall be begun, all such
licenses to be then determined without any right to damages or compensation
in favor of the licenses."* A plan of the street was adopted by the dock
department and the lands necessary for the street were acquired by eminent
domain. Nothing has been done by the city to open or grade the street and it
has never been opened for public use and exists only upon paper, except so
far as the city has made use of a part of the land so acquired for its own purposes. Prior to the condemnation of the land the board of dock commissioners
passed a resolution authorizing the street cleaning department to erect and
maintain a dumping board on the land taken for the purposes of the street and
this dumping board has since been maintained.

Held, that as long as the street remained unopened, the department of docks had
the right, under the exception contained in the act of 1887, to permit the
maintenance of a dumping board upon the land taken for the purposes of the
street.

Semble, that the remedy of a property owner, who had been assessed for the
opening of the street, was by mandamus proceedings to compel the city
authorities to lay out the street.

Quære, whether the city would have a right to maintain the dumping board on
the dock after the street had been actually opened.

---

* *Sic.*

APPEAL by the defendant, The City of New York, from a judgment of the Supreme Court in favor of the plaintiffs, entered in the office of the clerk of the county of New York on the 1st day of October, 1901, upon the decision of the court rendered after a trial at the New York Special Term.

The judgment in this action restrained the defendant from using Exterior street with its structures and also perpetually enjoining it from maintaining a dumping board along the bulkhead line of the dock, wharf, cribwork, etc., or on the crib-work on Exterior street, and directed a removal of the same.

Terence Farley, for the appellant.

Louis O. Van Doren, for the respondents.

HATCH, J.:

By chapter 697 of the Laws of 1887 authority was vested in the board of the department of docks to establish the easterly line of Exterior street along a portion of the East river. This act was amended by chapter 272 of the Laws of 1888 and by chapter 257 of the Laws of 1889. By these acts authority was devolved upon the department of docks to determine upon a plan for said street and there was vested in the board of street opening and improvement of the city of New York, after the adoption of the plan and upon the written petition or consent of certain property owners, authority to institute proceedings *in invitum* to acquire land for the purposes of the street, as determined upon by the dock department. The boundaries of the street were laid out and a map and plan of the same was adopted by the dock department. The board of street opening and improvement instituted proceedings thereunder and the city acquired title to the lands necessary for the street. These proceedings were begun April 23, 1891, and were terminated by an order of confirmation of the report of the commissioners appointed in the proceedings, and the same was filed in the office of the clerk of the court on the 14th day of July, 1897. A part of the land so taken was the property of these plaintiffs, and they have been assessed upon their remaining lands a proportionate cost of the proceeding. Nothing further has been done by the city to open or grade the said street, the same has never been opened for public use, and now exists only upon paper, except so far as the city itself has made use of a part of the land so acquired for its purposes.

By the terms of the act of 1887 it was provided (§ 2) that the street should be laid out as provided by the plan adopted by the dock department, " and the same shall be the sole plan according to which any wharf, pier, bulk-head, basin, dock or slip or any wharf, structure or superstructure shall thereafter be laid out or constructed in that part of the water front included in and specified upon said plan, and from the time of the adoption thereof, no wharf, pier, bulk-head, basin, dock or slip, nor any wharf structure or superstructure shall be laid out, built or rebuilt in that part of the water front aforesaid, unless in accordance with such plan. Excepting, nevertheless, that the board of the department of docks may build or rebuild, or license the building or rebuilding of temporary wharf structures or super-structures to continue and remain for a time not longer than until the construction of said Exterior street shall be begun, all such licenses to be then determined without any right to damages or compensation in favor of the licenses *."

It is evident that the exception created by the terms of the act was intended to be applicable to the actual construction of the street, and during the period prior to such time the dock department was authorized to make use of this land and water front for any temporary purpose, provided that a nuisance was not created thereby. On April 27, 1900, over a year prior to the time when the report of the commissioners in the condemnation proceeding had been confirmed and filed by order of the court, the board of dock commissioners, upon the application of the department of street cleaning of the city of New York, passed a resolution granting to such department permission to erect and maintain a dumping board on the crib bulkhead at the foot of East Eightieth street, and under such authority the street cleaning department erected such dumping board and other buildings in connection with the same, and has since used the board and other structures as a dumping place for waste paper, ashes, etc., and for the separation of such material therefrom as was suitable for sale. No garbage has ever been dumped at this place, as the same is separately collected and is disposed of in other places in the city.

By the provisions of the Greater New York charter (Laws of 1897, chap. 378, § 836), the board of the department of docks is

---

* *Sic.*

required to set apart for the use of the department of street cleaning, the board of health and other city departments, suitable and
sufficient wharves, piers, bulkheads, slips, and berths in slips for the
use of said departments, and, by section 542 of the charter, such
dock department is required to make compliance with the request
of the street cleaning department, and to set apart such places,
wharves, piers, etc., as may be necessary. By section 534 of the
charter the commissioner of street cleaning is required to remove
from the streets of the city and make disposition of ashes, street
sweepings, garbage and other light refuse and rubbish, as often as
the public health requires or as may be found practicable. It was
pursuant to this authority and the request of the street cleaning
department that the dock department authorized the construction
of the structure of which the plaintiff makes complaint.

In September, 1900, the plaintiffs brought this action to enjoin
and restrain the city from making use of the property in the manner above specified under a claim that such structures are maintained and used without authority and that the same are a public
nuisance. The complaint proceeds upon two theories, *first*, that the
land and water front is used in violation of law, and especially in
violation of the act under which Exterior street was constituted and
authorized to be laid out and opened; and, *second*, upon the theory
that the business as conducted is a nuisance, as matter of fact. The
first theory, therefore, is that the structures are a nuisance *per se*,
as matter of law; and, second, a nuisance, as matter of fact, assuming them to be lawful structures.

It is evident that the court in its decision has adopted both theories, although it is quite probable that the learned court would not
have found as matter of fact that the business as conducted constituted the same a nuisance if the other element which the case presented had been eliminated. It is undoubtedly true that the defendant, acting through its constituted authority, was commanded to lay
out Exterior street in the manner directed by the statute, and it was
required in the performance of the mandate of the statute to exercise
reasonable diligence in laying out and grading the street for the benefit of the general public, and particularly for the benefit of the persons whose lands have been appropriated for the purpose. Undoubtedly the city has been guilty of *laches* in not proceeding with more

diligence to lay out, regulate and grade this street for purposes of its proper use. Its failure in this regard, however, can in no view be made to furnish ground for this action, as the plaintiffs are not entitled to a remedy to correct the evil by way of injunction. So long as the street in fact remains unopened for public use, the right granted to the city to authorize the land taken and the water front to be temporarily used remains; and if such use is of such a character that it can be terminated at any time when the street is opened and graded for the use of the public, it continues to exist so long as such conditions exist. The failure to perform the duty and open the street as commanded by the statute may be conceded to have been neglectful and a violation of duty on the part of the city; but so long as the street remains unopened, the use authorized by the dock department is a use authorized by the statute and continues to be and is temporary, no matter how long the same lasts, as it cannot be construed into a permanent occupation unless permitted to exist after the street is opened to public use.

The remedy for this neglect upon the part of the city is not by way of injunction, for, no matter how it result, it would not operate as a compulsory process upon the city to open the street, and until it perform that act, the occupation is lawful. The plaintiffs, as parties in interest, have abundant authority to compel the city to make compliance with the statute. Their remedy in that respect, however, is mandatory to compel affirmative action in obedience to the commands of the statute to lay out the street. The dock department is invested with as much authority to authorize the temporary use of a portion of this street and water front by another department of the city as to authorize its use by any other person or corporation. Of course, it could not authorize the maintenance of a nuisance thereon, but it can authorize a legal structure in which to conduct a legal business, and such period of use will continue to be lawful until the public authorities perform their duty and open the street either voluntarily or under compulsion. It seems clear, therefore, that this structure may be authorized for the period prior to the opening of the street, whether the same can be thereafter maintained as matter of right, or not. So far as the present surroundings are concerned, the dock is not occupied by the defendant's dumping board and the use thereof is not, therefore, exclusive as was the case in *Hill* v. *Mayor* (139 N. Y. 495).

We do not find it necessary in disposition of the present case to determine whether the city is authorized to construct and maintain this dumping board at this particular place after the street is opened or not. It is evident, however, that such determination must rest upon the authority vested in the dock department and the character of use which may be made by the street cleaning department. The question is to be solved by a construction of the statutes under which the power is exercised, and for the present it is not necessary for us to express an opinion thereon. It is sufficient now to say that the present use is authorized by the statute; consequently, it is not a nuisance *per se* and cannot become such until the street be opened for public use.

So far as claim is made that the business as conducted constitutes the same a nuisance, we think the evidence is insufficient for such purpose. There is no pretense but that the business is properly conducted with as little annoyance to surrounding persons and property as is compatible with carrying on the business at all. Indeed, upon this subject the city sought to show how the business was carried on and that it was done with care and circumspection. The court ruled that it was not necessary for the defendant to give proof upon that subject until the method and manner of doing the business was attacked. No proof was offered upon such subject as a distinct issue; consequently, it must be regarded that the business was in all respects properly conducted.

The evidence offered to establish the nuisance as a fact tended to show that dust and ashes were blown from the dump across property in the vicinity, but there was no proof, so far as we are able to find, showing that dust and ashes were blown from the dump upon the property of the plaintiffs, while it did appear that considerable dust and other materials came from lime and cement stored and handled in that vicinity, and from brick yards and coal barges which were unladen near by. Indeed, the proof was stronger as to floating dust, ashes and other material from these sources than from the dump. There was proof that some smell arose from the dump, but how pungent and offensive it was, or how far it extended, was not made to appear, nor did it appear that the plaintiffs were affected by it.

Substantially, the whole basis of injury to the plaintiffs' property was claimed to arise from the structure itself, and we think there was no sufficient proof that the business as conducted constituted the same a nuisance.

It is to be borne in mind that the work of the street cleaning department is a work of necessity. Upon it is dependent in large degree the comfort, health and happiness of a large city, and it is common knowledge that some individuals must always suffer more inconvenience and discomfort from the performance of this public necessity than others. If the manner and method adopted in the conduct of the business does not create a nuisance, the right to conduct it must be supported. (*Kobbe* v. *Village of New Brighton*, 23 App. Div. 243; *Pettit* v. *N. Y. C. & H. R. R. R. Co.*, 80 Hun, 86; *Health Dept. of N. Y.* v. *Purdon*, 99 N. Y. 237.)

As before observed, we think the trial court would have failed to find that this business as conducted constituted it a nuisance, had it not been for the fact that it regarded the existence of the structure a nuisance *per se*. As we regard the structure as lawful, and the evidence as insufficient upon which to find that the conduct of the business created a nuisance, it necessarily follows that the judgment should be reversed and a new trial granted, with costs to the appellant to abide the event.

VAN BRUNT, P. J., O'BRIEN, INGRAHAM and McLAUGHLIN, JJ., concurred.

Judgment reversed, new trial ordered, costs to appellant to abide event.

TOBIA PRATA, Respondent, v. SAMUEL GREEN, Appellant.

Agreement to pay to a materialman a specified sum out of an installment to fall due to the contractor at a certain stage of the work — the payment before it becomes due, of the balance of such installment to the contractor, who then abandons the work, entitles the materialman to his money.

Under an arrangement between the owner of certain premises and a mortgagee thereof, the owner was to erect a number of buildings thereon and the mortgagee was to advance to him certain sums at various stages in the erection of the buildings. During the progress of the work the mortgagee, in order to induce a firm which had furnished a portion of the stone used in the construction of the buildings, and for which it had not been paid, to furnish the rest

of the stone, made an agreement with the firm by which he undertook to withhold, from the payment to which the owner would be entitled when the buildings were inclosed, $800 and pay the same to the firm.   After the firm had fur-
nished the stone, but before the building had been entirely inclosed and before
it was due under the terms of the contract, the mortgagee paid to the owner
$4,950, which represented the amount of the inclosure payment less the $800
which he had contracted to withhold.   After receiving such payment, the
owner abandoned his contract and never entirely inclosed the buildings.

In an action brought by an assignee of the firm against the mortgagee to recover
the $800 which the latter agreed to withhold from the inclosure payment,

Held, that the plaintiff was entitled to recover;

That when the mortgagee chose to recognize the owner's right to receive the
inclosure payment before it became due, the right of the plaintiff's assignors
to the $800 immediately attached.

VAN BRUNT, P. J., dissented.

APPEAL by the defendant, Samuel Green, from a judgment of
the Supreme Court in favor of the plaintiff, entered in the office of
clerk of the county of New York on the 25th day of June, 1901,
upon the verdict of a jury, and also from an order entered in said
clerk's office on the 26th day of June, 1901, denying the defendant's motion for a new trial made upon the minutes.

Alexander Rosenthal, for the appellant.

Milton Mayer, for the respondent.

HATCH, J. :

The defendant, being the owner of certain premises, conveyed
the same to one Cohen and entered into an agreement with the latter for the erection of six houses thereon, defendant agreeing to
procure a building loan to be advanced in certain sums as progress
was made with the buildings.   Green took back a mortgage from
Cohen upon the premises, subject to the mortgage securing the
building loan.   By the terms of the contract under which the
houses were erected, Green was to advance to Cohen the sum of
$5,750 when the buildings should be inclosed ; this was called the
inclosure payment.   Cohen made and entered into a contract with
the plaintiff's assignors to furnish stone to be used in the construction of the buildings.   The evidence on the part of the plaintiff
tended to show that Cohen made default in payment for the stone

delivered pursuant to such contract, and that by reason of such default plaintiff's assignors refused to deliver further stone thereunder until payment was made for that already delivered. This being the situation and the defendant being anxious that Cohen should fulfill the contract and complete the houses, he applied to the plaintiff's assignors to furnish the stone, and in order to induce them so to do he entered into the following contract:

"NEW YORK, *November* 2, 1899.

"Received from Samuel Green his check for ($400) Four hundred dollars, for which we promise to deliver the stones needed for the 6 houses which David Cohen is building on 113th Street, between 1st and 2nd Avenues. It being understood that David Cohen has given to Samuel Green an order for the total sum of the enclosure payment he is to receive upon five of said houses, and that Samuel Green promises to hold an additional sum of Eight hundred dollars for us, until the six buildings are enclosed.

"NEW YORK, *November* 2, 1899.

"I agree to withhold $800 from the amount of the enclosure payment & pay the same to S. Pizzutiello & Sons.

"(Signed)   SAMUEL GREEN."

Pursuant to this engagement, Pizzutiello & Sons furnished the stone and in all substantial respects made compliance with the contract. After its execution, but before the buildings were entirely inclosed, Green obtained from the building loan fund, pursuant to the order which had been delivered to him by Cohen, $4,950, leaving a balance due upon the inclosure payment, if the contract had been fulfilled, of the sum of $800. The defendant paid to Cohen the amount that he received of the inclosure payment prior to the time when it was due according to the terms of Cohen's contract. After such payment Cohen abandoned his contract, leaving the same uncompleted and never in fact entirely inclosed the buildings. Green assigned his mortgage to a party who foreclosed the same and upon the sale he bought in the premises and subsequently resold the same. Plaintiff's assignors applied to the defendant after (they) had delivered the stone and asked for payment. Defendant requested them to wait, as he would be obliged to foreclose his mortgage, and when the matter was straightened out he would pay the money.   It never having been paid, Pizzutiello & Sons assigned their contract to the plaintiff, who brings this action.

The rights of the parties are to be determined from a construction of defendant's contract under which he assumed the payment of the $800.   It is undisputed that Green had a substantial interest in procuring the contract made by Cohen to be fulfilled.   His mortgage security very largely depended for its value upon such fulfillment.   It was clearly for his benefit that the stone was furnished, and by virtue of his undertaking he procured its delivery and had the benefit of plaintiff's material in the construction of the buildings, and he had it within his power at all times to protect Pizzutiello & Sons from any loss in connection with the transaction.   The equitable features, therefore, which the case presents are clearly with the plaintiff.   By the terms of the defendant's agreement, no particular sum was reserved from the inclosure payment to which it could be made applicable.   Such payment was all due at one time, and when due, $800 thereof belonged primarily to plaintiff's assignors, and defendant was bound at his peril to see that they received it.

While the defendant had the right to stand upon the terms of his contract with Cohen and make no payment until the houses were inclosed, it was nevertheless competent for him to waive strict performance of the contract and make such payment, but he could not so pay if thereby the plaintiff's assignors were prejudiced.   Eight hundred dollars of the inclosure payment belonged equitably to the plaintiff's assignors, and if the defendant chose to recognize Cohen's right to receive the inclosure payment, the right of plaintiff's assignors to be paid immediately attached thereto.   This money became due to them the moment that the defendant recognized Cohen's right to receive the same, and he did so recognize it when he made the payment.   The act of payment upon the part of the defendant was distinctly prejudicial to the right of plaintiff's assignors, and as defendant was obligated to pay this debt from the inclosure payment, he had no right under the terms of the contract to deplete the fund, without protecting the interest of plaintiff's assignors therein.   (*Beardsley* v. *Cook*, 143 N. Y. 143.)

It being conceded that Green paid upon the inclosure payment $4,950, in utter disregard of his contract to pay for the stone which had been furnished for the building, we think he may not shelter himself from liability by now setting up the claim that he had retained a sum sufficient from the inclosure payment to meet this claim, and would have paid it had Cohen fulfilled his contract. We think that such is not the fair construction of his engagement. On the contrary, we are of opinion that when he recognized the right of Cohen to receive payment for his part of the work, he was immediately charged with an obligation created by his contract to pay the plaintiff's assignors. We, therefore, conclude that the construction placed upon the contract by the court below was correct, and that the defendant, having received and paid to Cohen more than was sufficient to discharge this claim, he became liable therefor.

Under this view of the case there are no other questions which require consideration. It follows that the judgment and order should be affirmed, with costs.

O'BRIEN, INGRAHAM and McLAUGHLIN, JJ., concurred; VAN BRUNT, P. J., dissented.

Judgment and order affirmed, with costs.

WILLIAM B. AXFORD, as Administrator, etc., of WILLIAM H. AXFORD, Deceased, Appellant, *v.* EZRA K. SEGUINE, Defendant.

ELI T. ELY and CLARENCE M. ELY, Subsequent Lienors, Respondents.

Attachment — what is a sufficient averment of an indebtedness — an averment "that deponent will allege in his complaint herein " is insufficient.

The affidavits used on a motion for an attachment alleged that the plaintiff's intestate and the defendant were jointly seized of certain real estate, and that, prior to the intestate's death, portions of such property were sold and purchase-money mortgages taken in the joint names of the deceased and the defendant. The affidavits further alleged "that after the delivery of said mortgages said deceased had an agreement and understanding with the defendant whereby it was agreed that, in dividing the proceeds of the sale of the property covered by the above mortgages, that the said mortgages should be included in the share of the deceased;" that the agreement was made in the presence of the deponent; that since the making of the mortgages the defendant has collected the same and given satisfaction pieces therefor, and has fraudulently taken and converted the money so collected to his own use, and upon demand has refused to pay the same to the plaintiff; that the amount of the moneys so collected is $4,780, which sum is due and owing to the plaintiff by the defendant, with interest from April 21, 1896, over and above all counterclaims known to the deponent; that the defendant is a resident of the State of New Jersey.

Held, that the affidavits sufficiently averred the existence of an indebtedness on the part of the defendant to the plaintiff.

VAN BRUNT, P. J., dissented.

That averments contained in the moving affidavits prefaced by the statement "deponent will allege in his complaint herein," would not support an attachment, as the deponent might change his mind and conclude not to allege such facts.

APPEAL by the plaintiff, William B. Axford, as administrator, etc., of William H. Axford, deceased, from an order of the Supreme Court, made at the New York Special Term and entered in the office of the clerk of the county of New York on the 16th day of January, 1902, granting a motion made by Eli T. Ely and Clarence M. Ely, subsequent lienors by attachment and by judgment, to vacate the plaintiff's attachment against the property of the defendant, Ezra K. Seguine.

Henry G. K. Heath, for the appellant.

William S. Maddox, for the respondents.

HATCH, J.:

The motion to vacate was made by subsequent lienors and was based upon the papers upon which the attachment was granted, the claim being that they were insufficient to support the same. There was no complaint, either drawn or served, and the proof showing right to the attachment was contained in affidavits. The point involved in the application is, whether the affidavits contain an averment sufficient to show the existence of an indebtedness against the defendant in the favor of the attaching creditor. It appears therefrom that the plaintiff's intestate and the defendant were during the lifetime of the deceased jointly seized of certain real property in the city of Buffalo in the State of New York; that prior to the intestate's death certain portions of such property were sold and purchase money mortgages given in the joint name of the deceased and the defendant. The mortgages are particularly specified and the respective amounts due thereon are stated. It is further alleged "that after the delivery of said mortgages said deceased had an agreement and understanding with the defendant whereby it was agreed that in dividing the proceeds of the sale of the property covered by the above mortgages, that the said mortgages should be included in the share of the deceased." The affidavit then proceeds to state that such agreement was made in the presence of deponent; that he heard the same and knows its terms; that since the making of the mortgages the defendant has collected the same and given satisfaction pieces therefor, and has fraudulently taken and converted the money so collected to his own use, and upon demand has refused to pay the same to the plaintiff; that the amount of the moneys so collected is $4,730, which sum is due and owing to the plaintiff by the defendant, with interest from April 21, 1896, over and above all counterclaims known to the deponent; that the defendant is a resident of the State of New Jersey.

The decision of the learned court below proceeded upon the ground that the allegation of ownership of the mortgages and proceeds therefrom was insufficient and did not show that either the mortgages or the proceeds were the property of the deceased at the time of his death; that if such ownership was sufficiently pleaded no breach of the agreement was shown; that conceding that the mortgages and proceeds were to be set apart to the deceased, yet that it did not appear but that there were offsets held by the defendant which might wipe out the specific items, the subject of the action.

We are of the opinion that the allegations contained in the affidavits were sufficient to show that the deceased became entitled to have and receive the sums of money collected from the mortgages. Such fact being established, the learned judge in concluding that such sum might be wiped out upon an accounting between the parties, overlooks the averment of the affidavit that the same is due and owing, over and above all counterclaims known to deponent. This was a jurisdictional fact necessary to be stated, and is sufficient in answer to the suggestion that the item might be wiped out by offsets and counterclaims. As the averment stood, the debt was established as a debt due and owing and not subject to any deduction. All of the jurisdictional facts, therefore, appeared and the plaintiff made a *prima facie* case to warrant the issuing of an attachment. It would be necessary for the defendant to establish that the amount was subject to deduction in order to answer the facts stated in the affidavit, for according to its averments, no such claims existed to·defeat or reduce the amount of the claim.

This motion having been made by subsequent lienors, the parties stand upon their strict legal rights, and if the affidavits contain a statement of the cause of action and the jurisdictional facts, as required by the Code, no authority exists to vacate the same. (*Haebler* v. *Bernharth*, 115 N. Y. 459.) It follows, therefore, that as to the first cause of action sufficient appears to sustain the attachment for the amount of the debt shown therein to exist.

The allegation as to the second cause of action is clearly bad. The statement that "deponent will allege in his complaint herein," states nothing. He might change his mind and conclude not to allege it, or to aver something else. It is not the statement of any fact.

It follows that the order vacating the attachment should be reversed and the attachment sustained as to the first cause of action, without costs to either party.

INGRAHAM, McLAUGHLIN and LAUGHLIN, JJ., concurred; VAN BRUNT, P. J., dissented so far as attachment is sustained for any sum.

VAN BRUNT, P. J. (dissenting):

I dissent. I do not think that the affidavit shows any cause of action, and the attachment should be entirely vacated.

Order vacating attachment reversed and attachment sustained as to the first cause of action, without costs to either party.

232| GUSTAVUS ISAACS, Respondent, *v.* JOHN DAWSON and WILLIAM
537| ARCHER, Appellants.

Contract to erect a city building — obligation of a sub-contractor as to work covered
by the plans but not by the specifications of the principal contract — provision that
anything mentioned in one should be deemed to be included in the other — provi-
sion for a reference of disputes to the architects — a provision of the principal con-
tract as to extra work, not applicable to the sub-contract — a provision as to following
the direction of the commissioner of public works as to changes — rejection of proof
that the sub-contractor had the city plans and specifications — when a reformation
of the contract should be asked for.

The firm of Dawson & Archer obtained a contract for the erection of the new
criminal court building in the city of New York. The plans and specifications,
which were made a part of the contract, provided for a cellar, a basement and
four stories above the basement. The basement rested on the solid earth on
one side of the building, but on the other sides of the building it was supported
by pillars and beams. The plans indicated that terra cotta arch blocks were to
be set between the iron beams of the basement, but the specifications, as well
as the principal contract for the erection of the building, expressly excepted
the " ground floors " from that work. The specifications clearly indicated that
the term " ground floors " meant the basement.

Dawson & Archer sublet the fire proof work to one Isaacs by a contract by which
the sub-contractor agreed, among other things, to "Furnish and set between
the iron beams on all floors (except ground floors), also in top story ceilings
and roof, best approved terra cotta arch blocks 8 inches deep." The sub-contract contained an agreement to do the work in conformity with the specifications and drawings made by the architects, but it did not definitely appear
whether the reference to the specifications referred to the city specifications or
to those contained in the sub-contract. Isaacs refused to set terra cotta arch
blocks between the iron beams of the basement floor, but subsequently did the
work under the express direction of Dawson & Archer.

In an action brought by Isaacs against Dawson & Archer to recover the value of
such work, it was

Held, that, assuming that the reference to the specifications contained in the
plaintiff's contract referred to the city specifications, such contract did not
require him to furnish or set terra cotta arch blocks between the iron beams of
the basement floor;

That a clause in the sub-contract providing, "Should any dispute arise respecting the true construction or meaning of the said drawings or specifications,
the same shall be decided by said architects and their decision shall be final
and conclusive," had no application to the case, as the dispute related to the
construction of the contract and not to the construction of the drawings or
specifications;

That a provision in the city specifications to the effect that the specifications, plans and drawings were intended to mutually explain each other, and that anything mentioned or referred to in one and not shown on the other, and *vice versa*, were to be deemed included in both, was inapplicable, as the plaintiff only contracted to execute that portion of the plans and specifications which was expressly embraced in the sub-contract:

That the provisions of the city specifications with reference to the formalities to be observed with respect to claims for extra work, were designed to protect the city against the principal contractors, and were not binding upon the sub contractor;

That a provision of the sub-contract requiring the plaintiff to deviate therefrom by omitting work or doing extra work when directed by the commissioner of public works or the architects, and in such a case providing for a deduction from the contract price or extra pay as the case might be, did not preclude the defendants from doing the extra work;

That the refusal of the court to allow the defendants to show that the plaintiff had the city plans and specifications when he contracted with them did not constitute a reversible error.

Semble, that if it was the intention of the parties to include the basement floor, the defendants should have pleaded the facts and asked for a reformation of the contract.

Vᴀɴ Bʀᴜɴᴛ, P. J., and Iɴɢʀᴀʜᴀᴍ, J., dissented.

Aᴘᴘᴇᴀʟ by the defendants, John Dawson and another, from a judgment of the Supreme Court in favor of the plaintiff, entered in the office of the clerk of the county of New York on the 17th day of October, 1901, upon the verdict of a jury, and also from an order entered in said clerk's office on the 15th day of October, 1901, denying the defendants' motion for a new trial made upon the minutes.

David Thornton, for the appellants.

Frank M. Avery, for the respondent.

Lᴀᴜɢʜʟɪɴ, J. :

This appeal presents but a single question, and that relates to the construction of a building sub-contract. The defendants were partners engaged in business as builders. On the 28th day of February, 1890, they contracted in the firm name of Dawson & Archer with the city of New York to erect the new Criminal Court building on premises bounded by Centre, Elm, Franklin and White streets. The defendants, by contract in writing, on the 26th day of March, 1890, sublet part of this work to the plaintiff. The plaintiff's agree-

ment, so far as material to the question presented, was to " do all
the work hereinafter mentioned in and on the building to be erected
on Elm, Centre, Franklin and White Streets, in the City of New
York, for the Mayor, Aldermen and Commonalty of the City of
New York, viz. :

" FIRE-PROOF WORK.

" Furnish and set between the iron beams on all floors (except
ground floors), also in top story ceilings and roof, best approved
terra cotta arch blocks 8 inches deep. The skewback blocks against
the beams are to be made to accurately fit the beams, all to be made
thoroughly wet, and each voussoir laid in a full bed of Portland
cement on both beds and ends at one operation. All to be laid true
to a line, the crowns to be keyed with tiles made to fit the different
spans.

" Furnish and set all necessary centres for the proper construction
of these arches, and in no case are the centres to be struck until the
work is thoroughly set and dried.

" The roof blocks are to be of porous terra cotta for the proper
fastening of the tile, all to be set in Portland cement."

The terra cotta partitions throughout the building were also to be
constructed by the plaintiff, but he was not to set the frames for
door or window openings in the partition or do any concreting.
The description of the work so far as it was embraced within the
plaintiff's contract followed the description thereof in the defendants' contract with the city and in the city's specifications. The
plaintiff was to perform the work included in his contract and furnish all the materials for the gross sum of $37,500, payable in
monthly installments of ninety per cent of the value of the work
done, immediately upon the receipt by defendants of their monthly
payments from the city but in no case later than sixty days after
the end of the month for which the monthly installment was to be
paid. The remaining ten per cent was to be paid within six months
after the completion of plaintiff's contract work. The plaintiff
before receiving his pay was required to obtain a certificate from
the architect to the effect that the work has been done and material furnished "in conformity with said plans and specifications "
and are such as is required thereby.

There was no express reference in the plaintiff's contract to the specifications that were made a part of the defendants' contract with the city; but after describing the work as indicated, it provided that the same should be done "agreeably and in conformity to the above specifications and to the drawings made by Thom and Wilson and Schaarschmidt, architects, in a good, workmanlike and substantial manner, to the satisfaction and under the direction of the said architects, to be testified by a writing or certificate under the hand of the said architects."

Although the contract in its reference to specifications is not very definite, the trial justice instructed the jury that it related to the city's specifications and that may be assumed.

The plaintiff testified that he refused to set terra cotta arch blocks between the iron beams of the basement floor on the ground that that work was not included in his contract, but that he subsequently did the work by the express direction of the defendants. The question is whether this was extra work. The plaintiff has recovered on that theory. The appellant maintains that the cellar floor and other floors under the basement are the "ground floors" excepted from the plaintiff's contract. The plans and specifications for the new criminal building provided for a cellar, a basement above and four stories above the basement. The cellar floor was to be concreted four inches thick. Neither the plans, specifications nor any contract provided for, required or contemplated that there were to be any iron beams or terra cotta arch blocks under it. The basement floor was the first floor to be supported by iron beams, and the plans indicated that terra cotta arch blocks were to be set between those iron beams; but the specification expressly excepted the "ground floors" from that work as did also defendants' contract with the city as well as plaintiff's contract with defendants. The specifications clearly indicate that by the "ground floor" is meant the basement floor. The basement floor opened on Elm street where it rested on the solid earth, but at Centre street it was supported by pillars, and between the two streets beams extended supporting it. At Centre street the basement floor was reached by stairs. The clause relating to concreting provides that the cellar and all other rooms "below the basement or ground floor" shall be concreted. The basement floor is the lowest floor below which there are any rooms, and is, therefore, here used as synonymous with

" ground floor." Again, the clause relating to cut stone requires the use of Long Meadow stone above the " basement or ground floor " and cut granite for the basement story " from the grade of the sidewalk up to and including the first story sill course." The plans and specifications call for a staircase in the Elm street vestibule from the basement to the first story above, which staircase was not to extend below the basement. The specifications speak of this staircase as extending from the " basement or ground floor."

We think the plaintiff's contract did not require him to furnish or set terra cotta arch blocks between the iron beams of the basement floor. That floor was expressly excepted from his work. No other construction will give force or effect to the express intention of the parties to except some floor where there were iron beams and where such work would otherwise have been required. The other portions of the specifications clearly identify the basement floor as the " ground floor " referred to in the contract. It was clearly a ground floor since at Elm street it was virtually on a level with the street. The conflict on this point between the specifications and defendants' contract on the one hand and the plans on the other, indicate a mistake. Whether it was originally contemplated to set terra cotta arch blocks between the iron beams on the basement floor, and there was a subsequent change in such intention which resulted in that work being excepted from the specifications and form of contract required of bidders, but not from the plans, or whether the mistake arose on a misapprehension as to the floor to which the exception relates, is wholly immaterial to the present inquiry. Nor were the defendants aided by that clause of plaintiff's contract which provides : " Should any dispute arise respecting the true construction or meaning of the said drawings or specifications, the same shall be decided by said architects and their decision shall be final and conclusive."

The dispute here arose over the construction of the contract, and that was not intended to be left to the architect. The provision in the city's specifications to the effect that the specifications, plans and drawings are intended to mutually explain each other, and that anything mentioned or referred to in one and not shown on the other and *vice versa*, are to be deemed to be included in both, has no application to the plaintiff's contract. If the controversy arose between the defendants who contracted for the entire work and the city, a different question would be presented, as to which it is unnecessary to express opinion. The plaintiff's contract was for the performance of only that part of the work covered by the defendants' contract which is expressly embraced therein. The plans and specifications were undoubtedly to govern as to the manner in which the plaintiff should do this work, but they could not extend his liability to other work not included in his contract. The provisions of the city's specifications with reference to the formalities to be observed to authorize a claim for extra work are not binding on the plaintiff. They were designed to protect the city against the general contractor.

The defendants controverted the plaintiff's testimony to the effect that he refused to do the work on the basement floor and that he was subsequently directed to perform it by them on an understanding which reserved his right to be paid therefor. This question of fact was submitted to the jury, and by their verdict it has been resolved in favor of the plaintiff. The provision of the contract requiring plaintiff to deviate from the contract by omitting work or doing extra work when directed by the commissioner of public works or the architects, and in such case providing for deduction from the contract price or extra pay, as the case might be, did not preclude the defendants themselves from authorizing this extra work.

We think that the refusal of the court to allow the defendants to show that plaintiff had the city's plans and specifications when he contracted with them is not reversible error. As has been seen, he was only bound by those plans and specifications in so far as he contracted to execute them. If, as claimed by the defendants, it was the intention of the parties to include the basement floor, then the defendants should have pleaded the facts and asked for the reformation of their contract. No other question requires special consideration.

The judgment and order should be affirmed, with costs.

O'Brien and Hatch, JJ., concurred; Van Brunt, P. J., and Ingraham, J., dissented.

Judgment and order affirmed, with costs.

Cases

DETERMINED IN THE

THIRD DEPARTMENT

IN THE

APPELLATE DIVISION,

March, 1902.

Herbert P. Bissell, as Receiver of Linus Jones Peok & Co., Appellant, *v.* The State of New York, Respondent.*

Statute of Limitations — what does not suspend its operation — claim against the Buffalo Asylum for work and materials — it might have been presented to the State Board of Audit — what statute conferring jurisdiction on the Board of Claims gives a reasonable time for the presentation of a claim.

The operation of the Statute of Limitations upon a claim against the State of New York, for work performed and material furnished under written contracts with the managers of the Buffalo Asylum, between 1871 and 1877, was not suspended by the commencement, in 1878, of a proceeding by mandamus against the managers of the Buffalo Asylum to compel them to measure stone furnished under the contracts, as that proceeding was not a proceeding or suit against the State of New York or a necessary step preliminary to bringing the matter before the State Board of Audit of the State of New York, the body which then had jurisdiction of such claims.

The fact that the claim was payable out of the appropriations for the construction of the asylum and that this fund was placed practically in charge of the managers, did not operate to deprive the claimant of the right to have his claim adjudicated by the State Board of Audit. The running of the statute against the claim was not suspended by an action brought by the State against the original claimants or by an action brought by the original claimants against the State, which actions apparently related to the contracts upon which the claim was based, but in neither of which the claim was litigated or directly involved.

Chapter 60 of the Laws of 1884, which took effect March 25, 1884, and remedied the omission of chapter 205 of the Laws of 1883 (abolishing the Board of Audit and creating the Board of Claims) to give the Board of Claims jurisdic-

---

* Decided January 14, 1902.

tion to determine certain claims which had accrued prior to the passage of that act, by authorizing the court to adjudicate such claims, provided they should be filed on or before July 1, 1884, allows a reasonable time for the presentation of a claim which had accrued five years, nine months and twenty-five days prior to the passage of the act of 1883.

Semble, that if there had been no provision in the act of 1884 limiting the time in which the claim should be filed, the Statute of Limitations would run against the claim in two months and five days after the act of 1884 went into effect.

Chapter 254 of the Laws of 1895, authorizing the Board of Claims to adjudicate the claim in question, does not prevent the operation of the six years' Statute of Limitations.

Semble, that a statute attempting to effect such a result would be unconstitutional.

APPEAL by the claimant, Herbert P. Bissell, as receiver of Linus Jones Peck & Co., from a judgment of the Court of Claims of the State of New York in favor of the defendant, entered in the office of the clerk of said court on the 21st day of December, 1900, upon the decision of the court dismissing the claim on the ground that it was barred before presentation by the six years' Statute of Limitations.

Fletcher C. Peck, for the appellant.

John C. Davies, Attorney-General, and *George H. Stevens*, for the respondent.

KELLOGG, J. :

The claim of plaintiff is one of considerable magnitude for work performed and material furnished under written contracts with the managers of the Buffalo Asylum between 1871 and August, 1877. The defendant admits all the facts as alleged by plaintiff, and this is an admission of merits in the claim, and plaintiff should have had judgment for a large sum if the defense of the Statute of Limitations is not a complete defense. As to the Statute of Limitations the plaintiff urges that by reason of his efforts to collect the claim the claim has not become stale and the six-year statute has not run. It is admitted that the last item of the claim accrued as early as August 6, 1877, and the proof shows that the larger part of the claim accrued many months prior to that date. The claim upon which the adjudication is here for review was presented to the Board of Claims in August, 1895. We have here at least eighteen years to account for. What is it that suspended the running of the statute during that time? The record shows that the first step taken in the line of collection of the claim was a writ of mandamus to the managers of the asylum, taken out in December, 1878, to compel the managers to measure the stone furnished as by the contract provided. This mandamus proceeding was allowed to slumber until March, 1888. But this proceeding was not a proceeding between plaintiff and the State of New York, and the claim is against the State of New York. The State was not a party and the Court of Appeals, by EARL, J., says in *Peck* v. *State* (137 N. Y. 375): "While they (the managers) represented the State in making the contracts with Linus Jones Peck & Co., they did not stand in the place of the State in any suit brought against them either for misfeasance or nonfeasance in the discharge of the duties devolved upon them by law. No provision is found in any statute giving them authority to represent the State in any litigation, or giving the consent of the State to be bound by any adjudication to be made against them." We must, I think, conclude that this mandamus proceeding against the managers did not have the effect of staying the running of the Statute of Limitations. It was not a proceeding or suit against the State. It was not a necessary step to be taken preliminary to the bringing of the matter before the State Board of Audit where such claims could properly have been adjusted. In the case above cited (*Peck* v. *State*) it was by the court said : "If upon their demand (upon the managers) payment was refused, they could have instituted proceedings before the State Board of Audit and could thus have had their claim adjudicated and could have obtained payment of any award made to them."

I do not think there is any force in the plaintiff's contention that because the appropriations for the construction of the asylum constituted a special fund out of which plaintiff's claim was to be paid, and by the law this fund was placed practically in charge of the managers, that for such reason plaintiff was denied access to the State Board of Audit to have the claim adjudicated. The case of *Peck* v. *State* (*supra*) is authority against that proposition, and the claim there referred to is the claim now before us.

It is also difficult to see how the action brought by the State against plaintiff's assignor, Linus Jones Peck & Co., charging over-estimates and over-payments, or the action by Linus Jones Peck & Co. against the State for damages in stopping the delivery of stone, can have any remote effect in delaying the running of the Statute of Limitations upon this claim. In neither of those actions was this claim litigated, or directly involved. Until October, 1890, this claim was allowed to sleep. At that date it was first presented to the State Board of Claims. The Board of Audit was created in 1876 (Laws of 1876, chap. 444), with power to adjudicate and adjust all claims against the State of this character. This board continued in existence until May 31, 1883, when the Board of Claims succeeded to its functions and duties (Laws of 1883, chap. 205). All that portion of plaintiff's claim which accrued prior to May 31, 1877, was barred by the six years' statute on May 31, 1883. This, as the record shows, included the entire claim except a single item of $1,125 which plaintiff alleges accrued on or about August 6, 1877. The act of 1883 (Chap. 205) abolishing the Board of Audit and creating the Board of Claims failed to give jurisdiction to the new board to adjudicate this claim and claims similarly circumstanced, and while no tribunal existed, competent to adjudicate the claim, the running of the statute was suspended, but, as we have seen, all of the claim was already barred except the item of $1,125, and there remained of the six years only two months and five days as to this last item. In 1884 a law was passed (Chap. 60, amdg. Laws of 1883, chap. 205) which gave to the Board of Claims jurisdiction of this claim and others similarly situated, provided they should be filed on or before July 1, 1884. This act took effect March twenty-fifth and gave, therefore, three months and five days in which to file plaintiff's claim, and this term added to the five years nine months and twenty-five days already run, makes six years and one month the Statute of Limitations had run against this last item on July 1, 1884. It seems to me clear that the moment the door was opened to any tribunal competent to hear and determine this claim the statute would begin immediately to run, and even had there been no provision in this act of 1884 (Chap. 60) limiting the time in which such claims might be presented, the six-year conclusive bar against this claim would have been perfect on June 1, 1884. Hence there can be no force in the contention of plaintiff that this requirement of the act that such claims must be presented before July 1, 1884, is unreasonably short when applied to his case. This requirement did not curtail the time available to plaintiff in which to save his claim. Six years was all the Constitution permitted him in any case to have, and the Board of Claims could not have given him more, nor could the Legislature. The Enabling Act of 1895 (Chap. 254), which authorizes the Board of Claims to adjudicate this claim, does not and cannot interfere with the operation of the six years' statute; and while this question does not appear to have been before the Court of Appeals in *Peck* v. *State* (137 N. Y. 372) for the reason that the Board of Claims was in that case bound by the two years' limitation, the case having been tried in that tribunal before the Enabling Act was passed; and while it is conceded that the claim is a meritorious one the court has no power to give to plaintiff any relief.

The judgment of the Court of Claims should be affirmed.

All concurred, except EDWARDS, J., not voting.

Judgment of the Court of Claims affirmed, with costs.

MAY A. THOMPSON, Respondent, *v.* JOHN R. THOMPSON, Appellant.

Party — an administrator, withholding on a settlement of the estate a sum to pay a tax — he cannot, after he has been released as administrator by the next of kin and a decree entered settling the estate, be sued therefor in his individual capacity.

The administrator of an intestate's estate, with the consent of all the next of kin, set apart $600 of the assets of the estate in order to meet a possible demand for an inheritance tax and agreed to return it to the next of kin if it should not be needed for that purpose. The balance of the estate was then distributed among the next of kin, each of whom executed to the administrator a written release, under seal, acknowledging the receipt of his or her full distributive share and releasing and discharging the administrator and the estate from any further liability. Pursuant to a provision contained in the releases such releases were filed in the Surrogate's Court and a decree was entered thereon judicially settling the administrator's account and discharging him from all liability. No inheritance tax was ever assessed against the estate.

Held, that one of the next of kin of the intestate, who was entitled to a one-tenth share of the estate, could not maintain an action against the administrator to recover $60, being her share of the $600 retained by him;

That the administrator still retained such $600 as administrator and that his liability, therefore, was as administrator only.

FURSMAN and KELLOGG, JJ., dissented.

APPEAL by the defendant, John R. Thompson, from a judgment of the Supreme Court in favor of the plaintiff, entered in the office of the clerk of the county of Delaware on the 16th day of September, 1901, upon the verdict of a jury, and also from an order entered in said clerk's office on the 16th day of September, 1901, denying the defendant's motion for a new trial made upon the minutes.

The defendant was the administrator of the estate of John Thompson, deceased. The plaintiff, as one of his next of kin, was entitled upon distribution to a one-tenth share thereof. In May, 1893, the parties interested got together and mutually agreed upon the total sum which was in the defendant's hands as administrator to be distributed. Each of such parties thereupon executed to the defendant a written release, under seal, acknowledging the receipt of the full distributive share due to each, respectively, and of all moneys due, or to become due, from said estate, and in full payment and satisfaction of all claims held against such estate or the administrator thereof, and releasing and discharging him and the estate from any further liability. Such release also contained an agreement that the same might be filed in the Surrogate's Court, and that upon it a decree might be entered, without citation and without filing any further account, judicially settling the defendant's accounts as such administrator and discharging him from all further liability as such. It also contained a covenant to save the said defendant harmless and to indemnify him from all cost, trouble and expense on account of the payment therein acknowledged. Such releases were duly acknowledged and filed with the surrogate, and a decree was thereupon entered declaring his accounts settled and discharging him from further liability as such administrator.

The plaintiff was present at such settlement and executed one of such releases. Subsequently in November, 1899, she brought this action to recover from the defendant the further sum of sixty dollars, which she claims the defendant on the occasion of the settlement promised to pay to her in the event that no collateral inheritance tax was thereafter assessed against it; that the defendant's promise then made was a personal one, and that the release then executed by her runs to him as administrator only; and, therefore, does not at all affect this claim. The trial court so held, and the jury rendered a verdict in her favor for such amount and interest.

From the judgment entered thereon, and from the order denying a new trial upon the minutes, this appeal is taken.

Charles L. Andrus, for the appellant.

Andrew J. McNaught, Jr., and *John P. Grant*, for the respondent.

PARKER, P. J.:

If the balance which at the time of the settlement was found to be due from the defendant as administrator included the $600 which the complaint claims was then "entrusted" by the next of kin to the defendant to meet a possible demand for an inheritance tax against the estate, then it might perhaps be argued that a retention of the same by the defendant, and a release therefor, was equivalent to a receipt by him of their money, advanced by them to protect him *personally* against such a claim; and his promise to repay the plaintiff sixty dollars thereof as the amount so deposited by her, in the event that he did not have to use the same, might be considered a promise made by the defendant, in his individual character, under an arrangement made subsequent to the transaction to which the release referred. It might then be considered that she had received the sixty dollars and receipted for it, and had thereafter returned it to the defendant for the purpose aforesaid. Such a subsequent arrangement would not be affected by the release.

But the fact, as it appears from the evidence introduced in her behalf, is, that the defendant deducted the sum of $600 from the assets before the balance for distribution was agreed upon. The share then agreed to be due her, and upon the payment of which to her she executed the release, was ascertained upon the theory that it did not include any part of the $600. He deducted that as a possible necessary expenditure, before he struck the balance for distribution, and so such $600 was no more nor less than assets of the estate left in his hands for subsequent distribution. He retained it solely as administrator, and I am at a loss to understand why he does not still hold it as such. He received it from the estate as part of its assets. According to her claim, as it appears upon the trial, he has never yet distributed it, and, therefore, his liability to account for and pay it over is that of an administrator only.

From this view of the transaction — and which is the one stated by the respondent in her points — it is manifest that the plaintiff is not entitled to maintain this action.

Her claim is squarely in conflict with the release which she then executed. Such release and the surrogate's decree subsequently entered is a flat bar to her recovery here, and on the evidence before it the jury was not warranted in rendering the verdict which it did render. All objections and exceptions necessary to raise this question were taken by the defendant upon the trial. The judgment and order, therefore, must be reversed and a new trial granted.

All concurred, except FURSMAN, J., dissenting in an opinion in which KELLOGG, J., concurred.

FURSMAN, J. (dissenting):

One John Thompson having died intestate the defendant was duly appointed sole administrator of his goods, chattels and credits, qualified and entered upon his duties as such. He was one of the heirs at law and next of kin of the deceased. Something more than a year after such appointment he and the other heirs and next of kin met together for the purpose of settling up and distributing the estate. At that time the defendant kept back from the distribution the sum of $600 upon the claim that it might be required to pay an inheritance tax. This was consented to by the plaintiff and other next of kin upon the express promise of the defendant that in case the money was not needed for the purpose mentioned he would pay to each his or her share thereof, being $60, the sum sued for in this action, and thereupon distributed the remainder of the estate. Under this arrangement and in consideration of this promise the plaintiff executed and delivered to the defendant a full release and discharge of "all moneys due or to become due" from the estate "or the administrator thereof."

This paper contained also an express consent that a decree, without an accounting of the administrator being had and without citation or notice, might be entered in the Surrogate's Court settling the estate and discharging the administrator. Like papers were executed and delivered to the defendant by the other next of kin. Thereupon the defendant petitioned the surrogate to be released and discharged as administrator, and without notice or citation a decree was entered finally settling the accounts of the administrator and releasing and discharging him "from all further liability as such administrator." These facts were found by the jury (the verdict having been for the plaintiff) upon sufficient evidence and under proper instructions. There was no inheritance tax to be paid and none is possible.

What was it the parties intended to accomplish by this settlement? Certainly not any continued liability of the administrator as such, for it was at the same time and as part of the same transaction agreed that the defendant should be discharged from all liability as administrator for this money, and a paper was executed fully releasing and discharging him therefrom. Yet he has in his hands sixty dollars of the plaintiff's money which he promised to pay over to her in case it was not used for a certain specified purpose. It is true that this was a part of the testator's estate, but at the time of the settlement it belonged to the plaintiff, and her consent that the defendant retain it and be discharged as administrator notwithstanding was given only upon his promise to pay it over unless required for the specified purpose. This promise was not made by him as administrator, because it was understood that his accounts as administrator were then and there fully settled, that he was to be at once discharged, upon the consent of all parties, by a final decree of the surrogate from all further duties and obligations of his office, the estate deemed fully distributed and his official relation thereto ended. This money was, therefore, no longer a part of the estate nor in the hands of the defendant as administrator. In what capacity, upon what agreement or understanding then, does he hold it? Not as administrator, because he is not administrator, nor as part of the estate, because he could rightfully hold that only as administrator. Moreover, it was clearly contemplated and understood by the parties that his accounts as administrator were then and there settled, a final distribution of the estate then made, and all liability as administrator ended. It seems to me clear that his agreement to pay was made and accepted as his personal agreement. Upon no other theory can it be reconciled with the terms of the paper, executed by the plaintiff at the same time and as a part of the same transaction by which she acknowledged the receipt of her full distributive share of the estate and consented to the discharge of the defendant from his office. If he should be sued as administrator it would be a sufficient answer that he had been duly discharged from that office and from all liability as administrator upon the consent of the plaintiff. The final decree cannot be opened, because there was neither mistake nor fraud in procuring it. He has sixty dollars of the plaintiff's money which in equity and good conscience he ought to pay to her. The promise to pay the money in case it was not needed for an inheritance tax was an independent agreement and proof of it did not tend to contradict the writing executed by the plaintiff (*Chapin* v. *Dobson*, 78 N. Y. 74; *Dodge* v. *Zimmer*, 110 id. 43); and his release from all liability as administrator was a sufficient consideration therefor. (*Andrews* v. *Brewster*, 124 N. Y. 433.) The defendant repudiates all liability, both personally and as administrator, and unless he is held personally liable upon his promise, the plaintiff is remediless. For these reasons I think the judgment should be affirmed.

KELLOGG, J., concurred.

Judgment and order reversed, and new trial granted, with costs to appellant to abide event.

***

EDWARD D. VOSBURY and BENJAMIN T. ASH, Respondents, *v.* CHARLES A. MALLORY, Appellant, Impleaded with WILLIAM E. MALLORY.

Breach of a contract to give the plaintiffs the exclusive sale of a hat manufactured by the defendants — measure of damages — the plaintiffs are not entitled to recover for unsold hats at the price at which they contracted to sell them.

In an action for the breach of a contract made between the plaintiffs, who were the proprietors of a retail hat store in Binghamton, N. Y., and the defendants, who were the manufacturers of the "Hawes Guarantee Hat," it appeared that the plaintiffs agreed to handle, advertise and push the sale of such hat in the city of Binghamton and the county of Broome and to make it their "leader" in preference to all other makes of hats, in consideration of which the defendants agreed to sell such hats to the plaintiffs at the price of twenty-four dollars per dozen, the plaintiffs agreeing to sell the hats for three dollars each and the defendants agreeing not to sell such hats to any other person in that locality — the contract to continue in force as long as the plaintiffs performed on their part. The breach consisted of the action of the defendants in refusing to sell the hats to the plaintiffs and in selling the hats to another dealer in the city of Binghamton. It appeared that at the time such breach occurred, the plaintiffs had on hand 197 hats. Nothing in the contract prevented the plaintiffs from thereafter selling the hats and it was not shown that the breach had in any way depreciated their value.

Held, that the measure of the plaintiffs' damages was the value of the contract; That they were not, however, entitled to recover the value of the 197 hats still on hand and unsold at the time of the breach, at the rate of three dollars for each hat.

APPEAL by the defendant, Charles A. Mallory, from a judgment of the Supreme Court in favor of the plaintiffs, entered in the office of the clerk of the county of Broome on the 16th day of October, 1901, upon the verdict of a jury.

T. B. Merchant and *L. M. Merchant,* for the appellant.

Harry C. Walker and *Rollin W. Meeker,* for the respondents.

PARKER, P. J.:

This action is to recover damages for the breach of a contract which is stated in the complaint, as I analyze and construe the averments therein, to have been as follows:

The plaintiffs, being retail dealers in hats in Binghamton, N. Y., agreed with the defendants, who were manufacturers of the "Hawes Guarantee Hat," that they would handle, advertise and push the sale of such hat in such city and the county of Broome, and make it their "leader" in preference to all other "makes of hats;" and, in consideration thereof, the defendants agreed to sell to the plaintiffs such hats as they should, from time to time, order at the price of twenty-four dollars per dozen, the plaintiffs, however, agreeing to sell the same at retail for three dollars each, and the defendants further agreeing that they would sell such hat to no one in that city or locality other than the plaintiffs. Such arrangement was to continue so long as the plaintiffs "performed the conditions of said agreement on their part."

The phraseology of the complaint in some parts would seem to charge that the plaintiffs were appointed the exclusive *agents* of the defendants to sell such hats for them in such county, but the explicit statement is made therein that the hats were to be *purchased* by the plaintiffs at the price of twenty-four dollars per dozen, and I am clearly of the opinion that under the arrangement as therein intended to be stated the hats were delivered to the plaintiffs, pursuant to their orders as purchasers thereof, and became their property.

The evidence given by the plaintiffs on the trial establishes a contract such as I have above stated, and that evidence is not contradicted. Such arrangement was made in March, 1897, and was acted upon by both parties until in January, 1899. During such period the plaintiffs advertised the hat largely and made it their "leading" hat and substantially performed the arrangement on their part. It appears that during such period they had ordered in the aggregate about 500 hats, and at the time of the refusal of the defendants to further fill their orders they had on hand 197 of such hats unsold.

In January, 1899, the agent of the defendants with whom this arrangement had been made visited the plaintiffs and was informed by them that they were not then prepared to say whether they could further continue the arrangement; that a dissolution of their firm was in contemplation. It was thereupon agreed between them that the plaintiffs would then give an order for hats to be used in the coming spring trade, to be considered a conditional one, and that, if the plaintiffs should within one month notify him that they wished to continue the arrangement, the order should be filled and the arrangement be continued. If they did not so notify him, the order was not to be filled, and the agreement was to end. They thereupon gave to such agent an order for eight or ten dozen hats conditioned as above stated. Within the month these plaintiffs notified the defendants that they wished to continue the arrangement, and to have their last order given to their agent Brainard filled. The defendants replied refusing to fill any further orders by them, and notified them that they had made arrangements to thereafter sell the hats to another party in such city. Thereafter no hats have been furnished to these plaintiffs, and the other party has been the only one in the city to whom they have been furnished. In March following this action was commenced. It was brought to trial in September last; when the plaintiffs rested, the defendants moved for a nonsuit which the trial court denied. No evidence being offered by the defendants, the case was sent to the jury upon the question of damages only. The jury returned a verdict of $708 against the defendants, and from the judgment entered thereon this appeal is taken.

The defendants claim that the agent, Brainard, had no authority to bind them by the contract which he made. But it is not contradicted but that they adopted and acted under it for about two years; and also they give as an excuse for not further selling to the plaintiffs that his agreement with the other party was controlling upon them.

They further claim that there was no time specified in the agreement during which it was to continue, and that, therefore, the defendants were at liberty to withdraw from it at any time. But the plaintiffs testify that it was to continue so long as they were willing to advertise and make it their leading hat. The parties might make such an agreement if they desired, and inasmuch as the plaintiffs' evidence to that effect is not disputed, it was properly considered by the trial court to have been so agreed.

It seems, therefore, that a contract was proven upon the trial, such as is above stated; that it was still in force; and that a breach of it was fully established. The nonsuit was, therefore, properly refused.

The only remaining question is, whether the trial court properly instructed the jury as to the measure of damages which they were to apply to the case.

It may be stated generally that, upon the repudiation of such a contract as is here shown, the value of such contract is the measure of damages to which the plaintiff is entitled. He has been deprived of such contract and he should have its value in lieu thereof. That value must be ascertained by the jury from the nature of the contract, and the consequences naturally and plainly traceable to its breach. There is always more or less difficulty in such cases in determining what elements may be considered without violating the rule that gains or benefits which are uncertain and speculative should not be estimated. Each case depends upon its own peculiar features. The general rules concerning such cases are found in *Wakeman* v. *Wheeler & Wilson Mfg. Co.* (101 N. Y. 205, 210); *Bernstein* v. *Meech* (130 id. 354); *United States Trust Co.* v.

O'Brien (143 id. 285), and an application of such rules to this case is not necessary here, nor could it intelligibly and accurately be made until the facts of this case are more fully presented.

It is clear, however, that the trial court erred in its instruction to the jury that they might allow to the plaintiffs the value of the 197 hats still on hand and unsold at the time of the breach at the rate of three dollars for each hat. Those hats had been purchased and paid for by the plaintiffs, and were their property. It was not part of the defendants' contract to guarantee their sale, nor, in any event, to receive them back at the rate of three dollars apiece, nor at any price whatever. There was nothing in the contract which prevented the plaintiffs selling these hats after its breach at three dollars apiece, or at such price as they chose to sell them. And I am unable to understand why they could not as readily sell them during the year 1899, with another party in the city selling the new style of that year, as if they themselves were selling such new style. But be that as it may, there is no evidence in the case that the breach of the contract in any way depreciated the value of such hats. On the contrary, the evidence shows that the plaintiffs, at once upon the refusal of the defendants to continue the arrangement, packed them up and made no effort whatever to dispose of them. Nothing whatever appears to show what they lost, if anything, because of such depreciation. They are still the plaintiffs' hats. The plaintiffs still hold them as such, and yet they have recovered from the defendants the full value at the rate of three dollars for each of them. Certainly, such an item was not properly considered in ascertaining the value of this contract to the plaintiffs at the time it was broken, nor was it admissible under any of the rules recognized in the cases above cited. Such item makes up nearly six-sevenths of the verdict rendered. It was clearly error to instruct the jury that it was a proper item for them to consider in arriving at the damages, and for that reason this judgment must be reversed.

All concurred.

Judgment reversed and new trial granted, with costs to appellant to abide event.

WILLIAM H. VEDDER and Others, Respondents, *v.* HARVEY LEAMON, Appellant.

Complaint for goods sold at "prices mutually agreed upon" — proof of market value is not sufficient — how far such proof is competent — an allegation that the goods were worth "the prices so agreed upon" is surplusage.

Where the complaint in an action alleged that the plaintiffs sold and delivered to the defendant merchandise "at and for prices mutually agreed upon, which were worth and amounted at the prices so agreed upon as aforesaid, to the sum of $16,702.30, which said price and value the defendant promised to pay to the plaintiffs for said goods, wares and merchandise," and the answer admits that the goods were sold and delivered at prices mutually agreed upon, but denies that the total prices amounted to the sum stated in the complaint, the plaintiffs are not entitled to recover under proof of the market value of the goods.

The allegation of the complaint that the goods were worth "the prices so agreed upon" should be regarded as surplusage.

Semble, that, under such an issue, evidence of the value of the goods would be competent for the limited purpose of determining what were the actual prices agreed upon.

KELLOGG, J., dissented.

APPEAL by the defendant, Harvey Leamon, from a judgment of the Supreme Court in favor of the plaintiffs, entered in the office of the clerk of the county of Schenectady on the 25th day of March, 1901, upon the report of a referee, with notice of an intention to bring up for review upon such appeal an order of the Supreme Court made at the Montgomery Special Term and entered in the office of the clerk of the county of Schenectady on the 25th day of March, 1901, granting to the plaintiffs an extra allowance of costs.

R. J. Cooper, for the appellant.

Edwin C. Angle, for the respondents.

PARKER, P. J.:

The complaint in this action avers that the plaintiffs, at divers times between certain specified dates, sold and delivered to the defendant "lumber and building materials of various kinds, at and for prices mutually agreed upon, which were worth and amounted at the prices so agreed upon as aforesaid, to the sum of $16,702.30, which said price and value the defendant promised to pay to the plaintiffs for said goods, wares and merchandise." It then proceeds to aver that $16,228.14 of such sum has been paid; also that the defendant is entitled to a further credit of $12.17 and $76.11, and prays judgment for the balance, viz., $385.88.

The answer admits, substantially, that all the materials charged to have been delivered were purchased by the defendant and delivered at prices mutually agreed upon. But it denies that, at the prices so fixed and agreed upon, such materials amounted to the sum of $16,702.30, and denies that the balance of $385.88, claimed by the plaintiffs, is due and owing to them. The defendant's claim is, and was upon the trial, that at the prices agreed upon the aggregate price of materials so delivered did not amount to more than the payments conceded to have been made.

On the trial the plaintiffs, under the persistent objection and exceptions of the defendant, proved the market value of the lumber and materials so delivered, and the referee found as a fact "that the *value* of the lumber and building materials furnished by the plaintiffs to the defendant amounted to the sum of $16,702.30." He then deducted therefrom the credits above stated, as being allowed to the defendant in the complaint, and ordered judgment for the balance. He makes no finding whatever as to what the prices agreed upon between the parties were, or what sum they amounted to, although he does find that for some of the articles delivered the prices were agreed upon, and for the others the plaintiffs were to have the market prices at the time of delivery. He makes no finding as to what portion of the whole amount delivered was sold at agreed prices and what portion was sold at market prices; and an exception is filed to this finding upon this particular ground.

Judgment was entered in accordance with this report, and from such judgment this appeal is taken.

Clearly this trial has proceeded in entire disregard of the well-settled rule that the recovery must be had in accordance with the claim made in the complaint. (*Romeyn* v. *Sickles*, 108 N. Y. 650.)

The complaint sets up a claim for lumber sold at agreed prices. The answer concedes that such a contract was made, and differs only as to what such prices were. Here was a distinct and narrow issue tendered by the plaintiffs and accepted by the defendant, and the defendant had the right to expect that upon the trial such issue, and that only, would be tried. He was under no obligations to prepare to meet the other and distinct issue as to what was the market value of the goods so sold. Evidently, the trial of that issue would require a preparation very different from the one tendered; and it violates the first principles of pleading to permit the defendant to be lured into court upon the issue framed by these pleadings and compelled to meet the one upon which judgment has been rendered against him.

It has been held that where, as in this case, neither party denies the making of the express contract, but the difference is only as to the price, evidence of the market value may be given as bearing upon the question : What was the actual price agreed upon ? But in those cases the evidence must be received for that limited purpose only, and the contract price, whatever it is found to be, must determine the amount to be recovered. (See *Cornish* v. *Graff*, 36 Hun, 160, 164; *Knallakan* v. *Beck*, 47 id. 117; *Barney* v. *Fuller*, 133 N. Y. 607.) And such cases are authority for the position above taken, that it is not proper evidence upon which to base a recovery. (See, also, *Dennison* v. *Musgrave*, 29 Misc. Rep. 627.)

It is suggested that the complaint in this action does not limit the issue tendered to a cause of action upon an express contract. To sustain such a claim it must be held either that the language above given may be as well construed as stating a cause of action upon a *quantum valebat*, as one upon an express contract to pay a stipulated price; or else it must be treated as stating both causes of action in one count.

But, very clearly, a claim to recover based upon an implied promise to pay what the materials were reasonably worth, cannot be ascribed to the language there used. No such cause of action could be sustained upon the averments there found. It is elementary law that there cannot be an express and an implied contract, embracing the same subject-matter, at the same time. (15 Am. & Eng. Ency. of Law [2d ed.], 1078.) If, as the averments in this complaint charge, the parties mutually agreed upon a price, then no implication of law can arise as to what should be paid. It is only when there is no agreement as to price that the law implies an agreement to pay what the goods received were reasonably worth; and a party cannot recover on an implied agreement to pay their *value* when he could have recovered upon a special contract fixing their price. (Id. 1111.)

Now, this complaint distinctly avers that the goods in question were sold and delivered "at and for prices mutually agreed upon." This is an averment that there was an express contract or agreement fixing the prices ; and, that being so, it excludes all possibility of their having been sold under such circumstances that the law would imply a contract to pay what they were reasonably worth. Instead of there being statements enough in the complaint to constitute a cause of action to recover upon a *quantum valebat*, the very facts stated exclude the possibility of such a recovery.

I do not deny but that two counts, the one upon an express and the other upon the implied contract, may be now joined in the same complaint; but that two such counts have *not* been merged in the language above quoted is clear. The facts averred show clearly the existence of the express contract and necessarily exclude the existence of an implied one. It is true that in addition to the averments that show that the lumber was purchased at prices mutually agreed upon, there is also a statement that it was worth as much as such prices. Concede that it was, such fact, in connection with all others averred, does not show a right to recover on a *quantum valebat*. On the contrary, it still appears that such a right of recovery does not exist, because there was an express contract as to price, which is controlling. If it had been intended to state a cause of action upon an implied contract to pay the market prices, no averment was proper, nor would one have been made, that prices for the same had been agreed upon. Hence, we must assume that the averments of value are mere surplusage. But the following cases have construed just such a pleading, and are authority for the conclusion which I reach : *Evans* v. *Kalbfleisch* (16 Abb. Pr. [N. S.] 13) ; *Meissner* v. *Brennen* (39 N. Y. St. Repr. 443 ; 15 N. Y. Supp. 671).

It was error, therefore, for the referee to receive evidence upon the value of the lumber sold, and to make up his decision upon that as a basis, instead of from the prices agreed upon. Under the complaint as it now stands, such a recovery ought not to be had. The judgment must, therefore, be reversed and a new trial granted.

All concurred, except KELLOGG, J., dissenting.

SMITH, J. (concurring):

While agreeing with the conclusion reached by the presiding justice, the grounds of my conclusion are not entirely the same. It is unnecessary to cite authorities for the proposition that a plaintiff may unite in the same complaint a cause of action upon express contract and another cause of action, involving the same subject-matter, upon *quantum valebat*. This right, I apprehend, is to enable the plaintiff, if the contract be denied, to recover upon his *quantum valebat*. And such pleading would seem to be sanctioned by the case of *Howarth* v. *Howarth*, decided by this court and reported in 67 Appellate Division, 354. Where, however, the defendant admits that a contract was made as to the price, that fact becomes established for the purposes of that action, and the plaintiff should not be allowed to recover, upon the theory that no price was agreed upon, as against the admission of both parties. I am not prepared to agree that this complaint would not be deemed to include a cause of action upon a *quantum valebat* as well as a cause of action upon contract, if the defendant had not foreclosed the issue by admitting the contract. If the contract had been here denied, and the plaintiff had failed to establish the same, I think he should have been allowed to recover under this complaint upon a *quantum valebat*.

Judgment reversed on the law and facts, referee discharged, and new trial granted, with costs to appellant to abide event.

MARY PRIESTER, Respondent, *v.* FRIEDERICKA HOHLOCH, as Administratrix, etc., of JACOB PRIESTER, JR., Deceased, Appellant.

Lease reserving the rent accruing after the lessor's death to his widow — it gives her no right of action therefor — the rent passes to the heirs of the lessor dying intestate.

A provision in a lease that, in the event of the death of the lessor before the expiration of said lease, the rent for the unexpired term shall be paid to the lessor's wife, who was not a party to the lease, and who, so far as appeared, gave no consideration for the promise, is invalid and will not support an action by the widow for rent accruing after the testator's death.

Where the lessor dies intestate the right to such rents vests in his heirs at law, and his administrator, as such, has no interest therein.

APPEAL by the defendant, Friedericka Hohloch, as administratrix etc., of Jacob Priester, Jr., deceased, from an interlocutory judgment of the Supreme Court in favor of the plaintiff, entered in the office of the clerk of the county of Saratoga on the 24th day of October, 1901, upon the decision of the court rendered after a trial at the Saratoga Special Term overruling a demurrer to the complaint.

This action is brought by the widow of a deceased lessor to recover rent reserved in a lease executed by him prior to his death. The complaint, in substance, avers that the plaintiff's husband leased to Jacob Priester, Jr., his farm for the term of five years from January 25, 1897, for the annual rent of $500, payable October first in each year; that, by the terms of such lease, it was further provided " that in case of the death of said lessor before the expiration of said lease, that the rent for the unexpired term should be paid to the wife of said lessor; that in and by said lease the rent for the unexpired term after the death of said lessor was duly assigned to plaintiff, who was the wife and is now the widow of said lessor, and by the terms of said lease and the death of said lessor, plaintiff became and now is the owner of the rent which became due under said lease on October 1st, 1900." It further avers that such lessee entered under such lease on January 25, 1897, and that he died January 2, 1898, intestate, and that this defendant is his duly qualified administratrix; that the lessor died intestate December 22, 1898; that on October 1, 1900, there became due "under the terms of said lease," from the defendant as such administratrix of said lessee, to the administrators, successors or assigns of said lessor, the sum of $500; that the administrators of said deceased lessor, on December 4, 1900, for value received, sold and assigned to plaintiff the said lease and all moneys due and to grow due thereunder, and all their rights and claims therein and thereunder. It also further avers that the lessor was the owner in fee of the said premises, and that the plaintiff, as the widow of said deceased lessor, has a dower interest in the premises so leased. It further avers a proper demand upon the defendant, as administratrix of said deceased lessee, for the $500 of rent so becoming due on October 1, 1900, and that she has rejected the claim and refused to pay it; the complaint then prays judgment for a recovery of the same.

THIRD DEPARTMENT, MARCH TERM, 1902.   [Vol. 70.

The defendant demurred to such complaint on the ground that it does not set forth a cause of action. The court at Special Term overruled such demurrer, and from the interlocutory judgment entered upon such decision this appeal is taken.

Hiram C. Todd and *Edgar T. Brackett,* for the appellant.

John Foley, for the respondent.

PARKER, P. J. :

The theory that the plaintiff acquired the right to maintain this action as the assignee of the administrators of her deceased husband cannot be sustained, for the reason that such administrators never themselves acquired any right to the rent in question. It is rent accruing for the year beginning January 25, 1900, and the lessor had been dead more than a year prior to that date. Unless the plaintiff's claim, that she took this rent under the terms of the lease, can be sustained it passed with the title of the farm to the heirs of such lessor, and they alone could collect it. The administrators, as such, under the statute took no interest in it (*Fay* v. *Holloran,* 35 Barb. 295), and I understand that the plaintiff's counsel does not now urge any such claim upon us.

The averments in the complaint that, by the lease, this rent for the unexpired term was *assigned* to the plaintiff, and that, by its *terms,* upon the lessor's death, she became the owner of this rent, can be considered as conclusions of law only. No provisions of the lease are given except those above cited, and the plaintifl's rights, if any, are given by that provision.

Does such a provision give to the wife a right of action for the rent in question ?

It cannot be construed as a gift to her of such rent, for the one sufficient reason, if for no other, that there is no delivery to her of the thing given, either actual or constructive. No effort at a symbolical delivery is attempted. Her whole interest rests upon a mere promise, which becomes operative only after her husband's death.

It cannot be deemed a trust created for her benefit, for the reason that it does not assume to put the *title* to such rent in any person as trustee for her. The relation of the lessee is but that of a debtor for the rent as it accrues. The fund, upon which it is claimed a trust is impressed, was not in existence when the lease was executed. It could not come into existence until after the lessor's death, and it might never come into existence. No words importing a trust, or indicating that the lessee had any purpose of assuming such a position, appear in the lease. As to so much of the rent as might accrue after the lessor's death, the lessee agrees, as a debtor, to pay it to the wife; but surely we cannot reasonably construe such language as an undertaking on his part to be liable to account to her as a trustee for the same, nor as indicating an intent, on the part of either, that he should do so. It is to be noticed that there is no claim of any indebtedness from the husband to the wife, and, in cases of "voluntary settlements or gifts, the court will not impute a trust where a trust was not, in fact, the thing contemplated." (*Young* v. *Young*, 80 N. Y. 438.) And no exception to this rule is made in favor of a wife or children. (Id. 437.) (See, also, *Sullivan* v. *Sullivan*, 161 N. Y. 554, 558.)

Moreover, it is plain that this provision in the lease amounts to nothing more than an attempt to make a voluntary disposition of a portion of the lessor's property, for the benefit of his widow, after his death. Had the lease contained no provision as to the payment of rent, save that it be paid on the first of October annually, it would be payable to the lessor for the whole term. In the event of his death, all rent that accrued afterwards would be payable, under the statute, to his heirs. The provision in question seeks to change the statutory succession; to divert such rent from the heirs to the widow. It operates in no other way. The promise to pay the widow is not operative until after the death of the lessor, and she neither acquires any interest nor is there any that she can acquire until after such death. The lessor, during life, parts with nothing; on the contrary, he is to have the entire rent during that period. The promise, therefore, is clearly in the nature of a will, or a testamentary disposition (*Matter of Diez*, 50 N. Y. 88, 93; *Gilman* v. *McArdle*, 99 id. 452, 461), and hence is inoperative because not properly executed.

Being inoperative on that account, of course no action can be maintained upon such promise. Hence the demurrer to her complaint should have been sustained. The interlocutory judgment must be reversed, with costs, with leave to the plaintiff to amend upon the usual terms.

All concurred.

KELLOGG, J. (concurring) :

The plaintiff cannot maintain an action on the lease for the reason that she is not a party to the lease and there is no consideration for the promise to pay rental to her. If she acquired any property right through the terms of the lease, she did so at the time the lease was executed and such property right could not be subsequently destroyed without her consent. The contingency of payment of rental to her only in case she should survive the lessor does not affect the legality of the promise; it is only a measure of the property interest intended to be vested in her. The bare fact that plaintiff was the wife of the lessor is not a sufficient consideration to support the promise for her benefit contained in the lease.

This seems to be the conclusion reached in the following cases : *Lawrence* v. *Fox* (20 N. Y. 268); *Durnherr* v. *Rau* (135 id. 219); *Buchanan* v. *Tilden* (158 id. 109). And for the reasons here stated, I concur in the reversal of the order.

SMITH, J., concurred.

Interlocutory judgment reversed, with costs, and demurrer sustained, with costs, with usual leave to plaintiff to amend on payment of costs.

ALBANY BREWING COMPANY, Respondent, *v.* EDWARD L. BARCKLEY, as Treasurer of Albany County, Defendant, Impleaded with A. PAGE SMITH, as Receiver, etc., of JOSEPH SEENEY, Appellant.

County Court — a judgment establishing an equitable claim upon a liquor tax certificate cannot be rendered by it.

After the holder of a liquor tax certificate had assigned the same as security for an indebtedness, a receiver of his property was appointed in proceedings supplementary to execution. The receiver, finding the liquor tax certificate in the possession of the licensee, surrendered it to the county treasurer and received a statement of the amount of the rebate due thereon. The assignee of the certificate thereupon brought an action against the county treasurer in the County

Court for the conversion of the certificate, and, upon motion of the assignee, the receiver was made a party defendant.

Upon the trial the court dismissed the complaint as against the county treasurer and rendered a judgment in favor of the plaintiff against the receiver, adjudging "that the plaintiff has an equitable claim upon the certificate in question and any rebate thereon, and that such receiver took such certificate subject to such claim."

Held, that the County Court had no jurisdiction to grant such a judgment and that such jurisdiction could not be conferred by consent of the receiver.

APPEAL by the defendant, A. Page Smith, as receiver, etc., of Joseph Seeney, from a judgment of the County Court of Albany county in favor of the plaintiff, entered in the office of the clerk of the county of Albany on the 18th day of June, 1901, upon the verdict of a jury rendered by direction of the court, and also from an order entered in said clerk's office on the 21st day of June, 1901, denying the defendant's motion for a new trial made upon the minutes.

In April, 1897, a liquor tax certificate was issued to one Joseph Seeney, who thereupon assigned the same to this plaintiff as security for an indebtedness. Upon October 27, 1897, the defendant Smith was appointed receiver of the property of Seeney in proceedings supplementary to execution. This liquor tax certificate, having been found in the possession of Seeney, was, upon the first day of November following, surrendered to defendant Barckley, as treasurer of Albany county, together with a petition in due form for its cancellation and the payment to him of the proper rebate. The treasurer thereupon gave to the receiver a receipt for the certificate and a statement of the amount of rebate and by whom payable, and sent to the State Commissioner of Excise, as he was by law required to do, a duplicate of the receipt, together with the certificate and petition for cancellation. Thereupon this action was brought against the said Barckley, as treasurer of Albany county, for a conversion of this certificate. Upon motion of the plaintiff the defendant Smith was thereafter made a party defendant, upon the allegation that he claimed to have some interest in the certificate, which interest, if any, arose subsequent to the plaintiff's interest. The action was brought to trial and the plaintiff recovered a judgment for conversion against the said Barckley, which judgment was by this court reversed and a new trial ordered. (See 42 App. Div. 335.) Upon the new trial, upon motion of plaintiff, the complaint was dismissed against the defendant Barckley, and, against the defendant Smith's objection, the jury were directed to render a verdict that, under the facts in this case and as between the plaintiff and defendant, the receiver, "the plaintiff has an equitable claim upon the certificate in question and any rebate thereon, and that the receiver took such certificate subject to such claim." Thereupon a judgment was entered adjudging that the plaintiff have judgment, without costs, against the defendant Smith, as receiver, etc. "That the plaintiff has an equitable claim upon the certificate in question and any rebate thereon, and that such receiver took such certificate subject to such claim." From this judgment the defendant Smith, as receiver, has appealed to this court.

George H. Mallory, for the appellant.

Robert W. Hardie, for the respondent.

SMITH, J.:

This judgment must be reversed as beyond the power of the County Court to grant. The jurisdiction of that court is prescribed by statute. There is no statutory authority for a trial by the County Court of the issue which was here tried between the plaintiff and the defendant Smith, nor for the granting of any judgment upon such an issue. This want of jurisdiction is not cured by any proceeding on the part of the defendant Smith, as a defendant is powerless, even by consent, to confer jurisdiction of the subject-matter in litigation upon a court of limited jurisdiction. It becomes unnecessary, therefore, to examine the other objections discussed upon the briefs of counsel. The judgment must be reversed and a new trial granted, with costs to appellant to abide the event of the action.

All concurred.

Judgment reversed on the law and facts and new trial granted, with costs to appellant to abide event.

In the Matter of the Estate of David Walker, Deceased,
Polly Walker, as Executrix, etc., of David Walker, Deceased,
Appellant; James Walker, Respondent.

An agreement by a devisee, having a life estate and a right to use the proceeds of
property, with a third person to sell it and pay over the proceeds — it creates an
agency or a loan with collateral, not a trust — the devisee becomes a creditor of the
deceased third person's estate — a surrogate cannot decree payment of such an
unliquidated claim — what surrogate may direct payment thereof after an account-
ing elsewhere.

Harriet A. Walker, a resident of Delaware county, died, leaving a will, which
was admitted to probate in that county, by which she gave to her husband,
James Walker, the use of all her real and personal property for life, with the
added right to sell and dispose of any of the property "so far and so much as
he shall deem necessary for his comfortable support and maintenance during
his life." The will further provided that the portion of the property left at
the death of her husband should pass to her two sons equally. Thereafter
James Walker conveyed to David Walker a vendor's interest in a land contract, which apparently constituted part of his wife's estate, under an agreement that David Walker should collect the moneys unpaid under the land contract, and would, during the term of the natural life of James Walker, advance
to the latter such sums of money as the said James Walker should need for his
support and maintenance, not exceeding in the aggregate the sum collected.

David Walker further agreed to pay the expenses attending the last sickness and
funeral of James Walker, and that, upon the latter's death, he would convey
the land and the land contract to Silas Walker, a son of the said James Walker,
upon being reimbursed for the moneys which he had advanced pursuant to the
contract, less the amount which he had received thereunder.

David Walker, after collecting certain of the moneys due upon the land contract
and paying over said sums to James Walker, died, leaving a last will and testament which was admitted to probate in Broome county, of which county he
was a resident.

In a proceeding instituted in the Surrogate's Court of Broome county by James
Walker to compel the executrix of David Walker to account for the money
and securities received by her testator under the agreement, it was

Held, that the agreement between James Walker and David Walker did not create an express trust in David Walker, as James Walker, under the terms of
his wife's will, had no power to create such a trust;

That, under the circumstances, the contract with David Walker created either
an agency, revocable at the pleasure of the principal or merely the relation of
lender and borrower with security given for moneys to be loaned;

That James Walker was a creditor of the estate of David Walker to the extent of the balance of the proceeds of the agency in the hands of David Walker at the time of his death;

That, as the claim was not liquidated, the surrogate of Broome county had no power, under section 2722 of the Code of Civil Procedure, to direct its payment;

That the claim could be liquidated only upon an accounting and that, as such accounting was an accounting of the acts of David Walker and not of the acts of his executrix, the surrogate would not have jurisdiction to entertain it, except as provided by section 1822 of the Code of Civil Procedure, upon the consent of all the parties;

That if the claim had been liquidated or established, the surrogate of Broome county was the only surrogate having authority to direct its payment.

APPEAL by Polly Walker, as executrix, etc., of David Walker, deceased, from a decree of the Surrogate's Court of the county of Broome, entered in said Surrogate's Court on the 3d day of April, 1901, directing the executrix of David Walker, deceased, to pay a claim against said decedent's estate alleged to be due James Walker.

In 1889 Harriet A. Walker, a resident of Delaware county, died, leaving her surviving her husband, James Walker, and two sons, Walton H. Walker and Silas Walker. She left a will which was duly admitted to probate in Delaware county, by which she gave to her husband, James Walker, the use of all her real and personal property for life, with the added right to sell and dispose of any of the property, " so far and so much as he shall deem necessary for his comfortable support and maintenance during his life." By the second provision of the will what was left of the property, at the death of the husband, was given to the two sons equally. The husband, James Walker, was named as executor of the will. James Walker took possession of the entire estate, and thereafter, and in 1892, entered into an agreement with his brother David Walker, which recited that James Walker had conveyed to David Walker certain real estate, occupied by Richard J. Bundy, and has assigned to David Walker a contract for the sale and purchase of said premises, made by Samuel C. Gilbert of the first part, and the said Richard J. Bundy of the second part. In consideration of this transfer and this assignment the said David Walker by that contract agreed that he would advance him such sums of money for his support and maintenance as the said James Walker should request and need thereof during the term of his natural life, the aggregate of such moneys not to exceed the sum due and unpaid on the said contract. The said David Walker further agreed that he would pay the necessary funeral expenses, and for medical attendance during the last sickness, and that at the death of James Walker he would convey to Silas Walker, his son, the said land and the said land contract, upon being reimbursed for the moneys that he had theretofore advanced pursuant to the contract, less the amount he had received upon the contract.

Thereafter David Walker, who was a resident of Broome county, collected certain of the moneys due upon the contract and paid over certain sums to James Walker, and, in the month of January, 1899, died, leaving a last will and testament, which was admitted to probate in that county, by which Polly Walker, his wife, was made his executrix.

Thereupon James Walker demanded possession of the securities, which were in the hands of David Walker at his death, and an accounting under the agreement made between him and David Walker. The surrogate ordered Polly Walker to account to James Walker for the moneys and securities held by David under the aforesaid agreement. From this order or decree this appeal is taken.

C. T. Alverson and *Taylor L. Arms,* for the appellant.

A. M. Sperry and *James L. Greene,* for the respondent.

SMITH, J. :

By the will of Harriet Walker, James Walker took only a life estate in her property, with the right to use so much of the principal as was necessary for his support. What remained of that estate, at the death of James Walker, was given to their two sons, Walton and Silas. This remainder was not the subject of disposition by James Walker, and his attempt, in his contract with David Walker, to pass the same to Silas Walker was clearly void, as in contravention of the instrument by which he held his title. No evidence was taken upon this proceeding and the decision must rest upon the petition and the answer. While the facts are not clearly stated it is fairly inferable that the interest conveyed under the contract to David Walker was simply a vendor's interest in a land contract. The moneys upon this contract were to be collected by David

Walker and paid to James Walker as his needs should require, and for the balance David was to account. The contention of the appellant is that by the contract David Walker was made the trustee of an express trust, which trust, upon the death of David, vested in the Supreme Court. The answer of the respondent is that by the will of Harriet Walker, James Walker was himself made a trustee of this property, which trust he was powerless to delegate to David Walker, and that the contract with David Walker was, therefore, void. It seems clear that under the will of Harriet Walker, James Walker, as executor and life tenant, held such a trust position as could not be abrogated by the granting of an irrevocable trust or the giving of an irrevocable power of attorney in respect of the property so held. He had the right, however, to constitute David Walker his agent to collect the rents and profits and account to him therefor. As a necessary incident of the agency he probably had the right to give to David his title to the land and land contract such as it was. James then is alone interested in the performance of David's contract. No provision is made for any compensation to David. Under the circumstances of this case the contract with David must be held to create either an agency revocable at the pleasure of the principal, or merely the relation of lender and borrower with security given for moneys to be loaned. (See *Heermans* v. *Ellsworth*, 3 Hun, 473; *Walker* v. *Denison*, 86 Ill. 142; *Blackstone* v. *Buttermore*, 53 Penn. St. 266.) With either construction of the agreement with David Walker, no trust imposed upon James Walker by the will of Harriet Walker has been violated, and at the death of David Walker his executor is required to account for any balance she may have in her hands, which was held by David Walker at his death, as the proceeds of this agency, or as the balance of security after payment of moneys loaned. To the amount of this balance James Walker is, I think, a creditor of the estate.

This decree is not justified, however, by the mere fact that the petitioner is a creditor. The claim which can be directed paid by the surrogate under section 2722 of the Code of Civil Procedure is a liquidated claim undisputed. This claim is not liquidated and can only be liquidated upon an accounting. That accounting is not an accounting of the acts of Polly Walker, as executrix, but the accounting of the acts of David Walker. Such an accounting the surrogate is wholly without jurisdiction to entertain, except upon the stipulation of all parties. Without the consent to try the same before the surrogate, the claim must be liquidated and established against the estate as any other claim, before the surrogate can order its payment. After the liquidation of the claim or its establishment the surrogate of Broome county is the only surrogate with the authority to direct its payment. The appellant's claim that the surrogate of Delaware county is the only surrogate with jurisdiction in this matter is, we think, ill founded. For the reason then that no consent has been given for the adjudication of this claim before this surrogate, as seems to be permitted by section 1822 of the Code of Civil Procedure, we think the order of the surrogate was erroneously made and should be reversed.

All concurred.

Decree reversed, without costs, and petition dismissed.

AMERICAN CASUALTY INSURANCE COMPANY OF ONEONTA, NEW YORK, Appellant, *v.* GEORGE E. GREEN, Respondent.

Surety on the bond of an insurance agent — what modification of the contract between the company and its agent discharges the surety.

A contract between an insurance company and one of its agents provided that the agent should pay all the expenses and claims of his district and, in addition thereto, pay to the company ten per cent of the gross premiums collected in the district. Pursuant to the terms of the contract, the agent furnished a bond conditioned that he should well and truly perform the terms of the contract, which bond was executed by a surety who had knowledge of the terms of such contract. After the delivery of the bond to the insurance company, the insurance company and the agent, without the knowledge or consent of the surety, made an agreement whereby the agent was to deduct ten dollars weekly from the receipts as a living fund and the insurance company was to pay from the home office sick claims, doctors' bills and rent and the agent was to remit to the insurance company all collections, less commissions due to sub-agents and the ten dollars weekly for living purposes.

Held, that the alteration of the arrangement between the insurance company and the agent operated to release the surety from any liability upon the bond.

APPEAL by the plaintiff, American Casualty Insurance Company of Oneonta, New York, from a judgment of the Supreme Court in

favor of the defendant, entered in the office of the clerk of the
county of Broome on the 20th day of February, 1901, upon the
report of a referee dismissing the complaint upon the merits.

T. B. Merchant and *L. M. Merchant*, for the appellant.

James T. Rogers, for the respondent.

SMITH, J. :

We entirely agree with the conclusions of the learned referee,
and with the reasons assigned therefor in his opinion.* We would
add thereto only a single word.   Appellant strenuously contends that

---

* The following is the opinion of the referee:

W. M. HAND, Referee:

This action is brought to recover of the defendant the sum of $200, upon a cer-
tain bond executed by defendant as surety for one Charles E. Frazier, and hereafter fully referred to.

The plaintiff is a domestic corporation having its principal office at Oneonta,
N. Y., and for some years has been engaged in issuing policies of insurance of
the character of sick benefits on payment of small weekly or monthly premiums.

Prior to June, 1898, one Charles E. Frazier had been the agent at Binghamton,
N. Y., for the American Sick Benefit and Accident Association of New York in a
similar character of insurance to that transacted by the plaintiff.   The former
company having been prohibited by the Insurance Department from transacting
business in this State, Frazier, who had a large list of policyholders in that company, made arrangements with plaintiff by which he was to transfer that business
to plaintiff, take charge of plaintiff's business in Binghamton and vicinity, solicit
insurance, collect premiums and transmit the same (less commissions of sub-
agents) to plaintiff, in consideration of which Frazier was to receive a salary of
fifteen dollars per week and plaintiff was to pay all expenses of the business.

Frazier entered upon his work under this arrangement about June 20, 1898, and
continued to act under the same until early in September of the same year, during which period the net loss to plaintiff through Frazier's agency was sixty-nine
dollars and sixty-two cents.

On or about August 16, 1898, plaintiff and Frazier entered into a new agreement, in writing, by which Frazier was to act as plaintiff's agent and agreed to
pay all expenses and claims of the Binghamton district and in addition pay to
plaintiff ten per cent of the gross premiums collected in said district on account
of policies issued by plaintiff.   The said contract further provided that it should
not go into effect or force, nor be binding upon either party, until Frazier furnished plaintiff a bond for $200, with an acceptable surety.

For the purpose of fulfilling the requirements of the contract with reference to
a bond, Charles E. Frazier, as principal, and the defendant, as surety, on or about
September 2, 1898, executed a bond to plaintiff in the sum of $200, conditioned
that if said Charles E. Frazier should well and truly perform and carry out the

the agreement of September seventh in no way altered the liability
of the parties to the contract of August sixteenth; that the agreement of the plaintiff to pay all expenses to be repaid by Frazier in
no way extended the liability of Frazier, who was using plaintiff
only as a medium of payment, and that the agreement that Frazier
might in all events retain from the moneys collected ten dollars a
week for his living may be regarded as an agreement for a loan for
which plaintiff does not claim to hold this defendant. Granting
for the argument the construction contended for, the agreement of
August sixteenth was by the contract of September seventh altered

agreement referred to (that of August 16, 1898), then the obligation to be void
and of no effect, otherwise to remain in full force and virtue.

Before executing the bond defendant had knowledge of the terms of the written
agreement thereby guaranteed.

After execution the bond was delivered to Frazier, who, on or about September
7, 1898, took the same to Oneonta and delivered the same to plaintiff.

On the same day, and while at Oneonta, it was agreed between Frazier and M.
G. Keenan, secretary of plaintiff, the same person who executed the agreement
on behalf of plaintiff and with whom Frazier had had the preliminary negotiations, whereby Frazier was to deduct ten dollars weekly from the receipts as a
living fund and the plaintiff was to pay from the home office sick claims,
doctors' bills and rent, and Frazier was to remit to plaintiff all collections, less
commissions due to sub-agents and the ten dollars weekly agreed to be retained
by Frazier for living purposes.

Under this latter arrangement the business of plaintiff was conducted by Frazier
from that date up to January 9, 1899, and all remittances made by Frazier to
plaintiff were applied by plaintiff upon the advances made by plaintiff for sick
claims, doctors' bills, rent and the ten dollars allowed to be retained weekly for
living purposes.

It will be observed that under this arrangement the business between plaintiff
and Frazier was conducted in a manner very materially different from that contemplated by the original contract; in fact, the written agreement was not observed
in any particular.

It was the performance of the written contract of August 16, 1898, and not the
new agreement of September seventh, which this defendant guaranteed to the
amount specified in his bond, and to recover upon which this action is brought.

Neither Frazier nor plaintiff had the power to change the contract without
defendant's consent (and it is conceded that the above-stated changes were made
without the knowledge or consent of defendant) and still preserve the liability of
defendant on his bond.

It will be further observed that the giving of this bond was, by the terms of
the agreement between Frazier and plaintiff, a condition precedent to the contract becoming of force; and, on the very occasion of the delivery of the bond,
the new agreement was made so that the agreement guaranteed by defendant did

to include plaintiff's covenant to advance to Frazier moneys necessary to pay expenses and to loan to him ten dollars a week whether earned or not. Such an alteration is, in my judgment, material, and prejudicial to the interest of the surety, and when made without the knowledge of the surety must effect his release. Defendant might well have argued when assuming his obligation that unless Frazier's profits were sufficient to pay his expenses, the ten per cent due to plaintiff and reserve to him a substantial income he must soon surrender before an extended liability was incurred, and might further have considered that his need of a net profit to secure his living would be such an incentive to him to work up his business as to make more probable his success. The mere fact that credit was given and a loan made to Frazier not contemplated by the August agreement would probably be immaterial. The insertion, however, into the contract guaranteed of a covenant on plaintiff's part to give

not, in fact, become operative, which, in my opinion, entirely absolved defendant from liability on his bond.

By the original agreement Frazier was bound to pay sick claims, doctors' bills, rent, and find his living expenses from the surplus remaining after remitting to plaintiff ten per cent of the gross weekly collections; by the new agreement all of these payments were voluntarily assumed and agreed to be paid by plaintiff, and Frazier thus became the debtor from week to week in a manner not in the contemplation of the parties at the time the original contract was made and the bond in suit was executed by defendant and in an amount many times in excess of the ten per cent, which only was to be remitted to plaintiff under the original contract.

In my opinion this was such a change in the agreement of August 16, 1898, between plaintiff and Frazier, as to absolutely release defendant from liability as surety on the bond given in pursuance of that agreement. It is not for the court to inquire as to the effect of the changed agreement on the surety, or whether or not it operated to his injury; the guaranty is of a certain specified agreement and not of one in any particular different, and, if changed by the parties without the assent of the surety, the surety is thereby absolutely released from liability. (*Ludlow* v. *Simond*, 2 Caines Cas. 1; *Walsh* v. *Bailie*, 10 Johns. 180; *Grant* v. *Smith*, 46 N. Y. 93; *Paine* v. *Jones*, 76 id. 274; *National Mechanics' Banking Assn.* v. *Conkling*, 90 id. 116; *John Hancock Mutual Life Ins. Co.* v. *Lowenberg*, 120 id. 44; *Page* v. *Krekey*, 137 id. 307; *Livingston* v. *Moore*, 15 App. Div. 15.)

From January 9, 1899, to about March 1, 1899, the business between plaintiff and Frazier was conducted practically in accordance with the terms of the contract of August 16, 1898, but Frazier in the meantime, *i. e.*, from September 7, 1898, to January 9, 1899, had incurred indebtedness to the company under the manner of doing business during that period of more than $160 above all remit-

that credit and make that loan, makes a contract materially differing from that which defendant guaranteed.

The judgment should be affirmed.

All concurred.

Judgment unanimously affirmed, with costs.

HUGH J. BALDWIN, Appellant, v. GEORGE D. GENUNG and CLAYTON A. SMITH, Respondents.

70
89

Libel — a justification of one of several alleged libelous charges is good as against a demurrer — it must be as broad as the libel.

Where the complaint in an action of libel sets forth several independent alleged libelous charges, the justification of a single one of such libelous charges is sufficient to sustain the answer as against a demurrer.

The justification of a charge must be as broad as the charge itself.

APPEAL by the plaintiff, Hugh J. Baldwin, from an interlocutory judgment of the Supreme Court in favor of the defendants, entered

tances, so that the financial situation, as between Frazier and plaintiff, when they assumed to begin doing business according to the original contract, was quite different from that existing at the time defendant executed the bond, a difference directly resulting from the new agreement under which the business had been transacted, because the amount he had fallen behind during that period was less than the $10 per week the plaintiff allowed him to retain for living expenses.

Again, and about March 1, 1899, a further bond was exacted of Frazier by plaintiff, to which B. W. Terry became surety, and it was then agreed that Frazier should be released from paying 10 per cent to plaintiff on such business as sub-agents received 100 per cent commission for.

Under such circumstances, I am of the opinion that the defendant, having been released from liability by the new arrangement of September 7, 1898, his liability was not renewed on January 9, 1899, when the agreement of September seventh was abandoned.

The indebtedness of Frazier to plaintiff at the time of the commencement of this action, arising between September 7, 1898, and September, 1899 (when his agency terminated), exceeded $200.

For the foregoing reasons, based upon the facts above stated, which are established by the evidence, I believe that the plaintiff has, by its own acts, as a matter of law, released defendant from liability on the bond in suit, and that the plaintiff has no cause of action against defendant, and its complaint herein should be dismissed on the merits, with costs.

in the office of the clerk of the county of Tioga on the 22d day of July, 1901, upon the decision of the court, rendered after a trial at the Broome Special Term, overruling a demurrer to the second defense in the defendants' answer, described as a defense in justification.

Frederick E. Hawkes, for the appellant.

H. Austin Clark and *Frank A. Bell,* for the respondents.

SMITH, J. :

The plaintiff asks damages for the publication in defendants' newspaper of certain articles claimed to be libelous. The answer, in the 2d paragraph, seeks to justify the charges made. A demurrer thereto has been overruled, and from the judgment entered upon the order overruling the same this appeal is taken.

The plaintiff was a candidate for the office of president of the village of Waverly. He had been theretofore for two terms the president of the village. The defendants in their paper were opposing his election, and the articles complained of contained matter in which were direct and implied charges against the character and the official conduct of the plaintiff while theretofore in office. Without setting forth at length the numerous articles of the publication of which complaint is made or the extended answer, claimed to be in justification, our conclusion generally is that in no instance is the justification sought to be pleaded as broad as the charge made. We agree with the respondents' contention that the justification of a single charge is sufficient to sustain the answer against this demurrer. But we are unable to find a single independent libelous charge complained of in the complaint which is fully justified in the answer. The respondents seek the protection of the rule that a demurrer searches the record for the first defective pleading, and claims the complaint to be defective. We are satisfied, however, that the complaint sufficiently states a cause of action. Proper matter is stated in inducement and the charges are such as to need no innuendo, and the statement of the intent of the defendants in making the publication, if available for no other purpose, is competent upon the question of exemplary damages. We think, therefore, the judgment should be reversed and the demurrer sustained, with costs, with leave, however, to the defendants to amend upon payment of costs in this court and the court below.

All concurred.

Judgment reversed and demurrer sustained, with costs, with leave to defendants to amend on payment of costs in this court and in the court below.

DANIEL D. DUNKLE, Respondent, v. CHARLES A. McALLISTER, Appellant.

Physician — what testimony of a plaintiff suing for an assault does not entitle the defendant to examine the plaintiff's physician.

In an action to recover damages for an assault and battery, in which an issue arises as to whether the injuries received by the plaintiff were caused by a rifle bullet or by a blow from the rifle, the fact that the plaintiff tells the character of the injury does not operate as a waiver of the provisions of section 834 of the Code of Civil Procedure and entitle the defendant to call the physician who attended the plaintiff to testify, against his objection, that the injuries were the result, not of a gunshot wound, but of a blow.

APPEAL by the defendant, Charles A. McAllister, from a judgment of the Supreme Court in favor of the plaintiff, entered in the office of the clerk of the county of Montgomery on the 23d day of May, 1901, upon the verdict of a jury for $1,800, and also from an order entered in said clerk's office denying the defendant's motion for a new trial made upon the minutes.

The action is in the nature of assault and battery. The plaintiff claimed that defendant shot him with a rifle. The plaintiff received a serious injury, but defendant claimed it was the result of a blow with the rifle and not from shooting.

Charles A. Stone and *A. M. Mills*, for the appellant.

Henry M. Eldredge, for the respondent.

KELLOGG, J.:

The case, so far as determining the amount of damages suffered and whether or not the injury was inflicted by the defendant in self-defense, is peculiarly one for a jury. There is not in the record anything upon which the court on this appeal can predicate passion or prejudice on the part of the jury. It may be true that the verdict is unusually large for a case of this character, but the circumstances as narrated by the plaintiff's witnesses are unusual and the injury considerable. The case cannot, therefore, be properly reversed on the ground that the verdict is excessive or on the ground that it is against the weight of evidence.

The appellant raises a single question of law on the exclusion of the evidence of the plaintiff's physicians, who were produced by defendant to prove that in their opinion, formed from an examination of the wound, while attending plaintiff as a patient, the wound was not a gun-shot wound, but the result of a blow. I think this was material testimony and bore directly upon the question of punitive damages within the discretion of a jury. This evidence being objected to by plaintiff was excluded under section 834 of the Code of Civil Procedure. In this I do not think the court erred. No court, I believe, has yet gone so far as to hold that it is a waiver of this right to enjoin secrecy in an attending physician, when all that can be said is that the patient himself became a witness and told the character of the injury he was suffering from. That appears to be all the plaintiff did in this case. The nearest reported case to this in its facts is *Treanor* v. *Manhattan Ry. Co.* (28 Abb. N. C. 47), but the case was condemned by the Court of Appeals in *Morris* v. *Railway Co.* (148 N. Y. 93). All the plaintiff says on his direct examination in this case, having reference to any physician, is, "Dr. Vedder came and put plasters on," and it was not sought by defendant to deny this statement by the testimony of the physicians.

This judgment should be affirmed, with costs.

All concurred, except SMITH, J., not sitting.

Judgment and order unanimously affirmed, with costs.

WILLIAM EHLE, Appellant, *v.* THE TOWN OF MINDEN, Respondent.

Town — liability of, for an injury from the fall of a bridge, built on private property to temporarily replace the highway bridge destroyed by a freshet.

A highway bridge having been washed out by a freshet, the highway commissioner barricaded the highway to prevent travel in the direction of the washout; built a temporary bridge across the stream on private lands, and obtained a license to drive through such private lands to the temporary bridge.

Held, that, in procuring the license and in constructing the temporary bridge, the highway commissioner acted as a volunteer and not in his official capacity, and that the town was not liable, under section 16 of the Highway Law, for any damages to person or property sustained by a person driving across the temporary bridge by reason of a defect therein, especially where it appeared that the person sustaining the injuries was aware of the situation.

APPEAL by the plaintiff, William Ehle, from a judgment of the Supreme Court in favor of the defendant, entered in the office of the clerk of the county of Montgomery on the 4th day of February, 1901, upon the dismissal of the complaint by direction of the court after a trial at the Montgomery Trial Term.

F. G. Kelsey and *Andrew J. Nellis*, for the appellant.

Henry M. Eldredge, for the respondent.

KELLOGG, J.:

This action is for damages for injuries to plaintiff's horse and person sustained through the fall of a bridge while plaintiff was attempting to cross it with a load of hay weighing 4,299 pounds, horses weighing 2,800 pounds, and wagon weighing 1,400 pounds.

It appears that some days prior to the accident the highway bridge had been washed out by a freshet and the highway itself had been barricaded to prevent travel in the direction of the washout. This was done by the highway commissioner. A passageway by license of the owner of the land had been opened through the private lands of this owner so that teams might drive to a place on the creek and cross the creek by means of a temporary structure in lieu of a bridge This passageway was not intended to be permanent. No other work was done upon it than the work of erecting the temporary structure which was intended to answer for a bridge until the highway bridge could be reconstructed. This entire passageway, including the substitute for a bridge, was wholly outside the limits of the highway. The highway itself was a cross road but little traveled. When plaintiff rested his case I think there was sufficient evidence to warrant a finding by the jury that Emory Walrath, the commissioner of highways of the town of Minden, procured the license from the landowner for this passageway and erected the structure over the creek.

I do not, however, think that the town was liable for the reason that this was not a public highway nor was it a bridge in or over a public highway, nor was it one which it was the duty of the highway commissioner to provide, nor one upon which he had the right to expend the funds of the municipality. It was wholly outside the limits of the commissioner's jurisdiction, entirely on private grounds, and in the procurement of the license and in the construction of this substitute for a public highway and a public bridge, he acted as a volunteer and not as a highway commissioner. That this was not a public highway, and not a bridge in the public highway, was well known to the plaintiff. It was obvious to any one there passing in the daytime, and especially obvious to plaintiff who was familiar with this highway from frequent driving over it before the washout. It is only for the misfeasance or nonfeasance of the highway commissioner when acting within the scope of his official duties that the town is liable. The language of the statute is as follows (Highway Law [General Laws, chap. 19 (Laws of 1890, chap. 568)], § 16):

" Liability of towns for defective highways.— Every town shall be liable for all damages to person or property sustained by reason of any defect in its highways or bridges, existing because of the neglect of any commissioner of highways of such town."

It is under this statute that plaintiff must recover against the town if he recovers at all. It will be noted that the neglect here for which recovery against the town is authorized, is neglect touching defects existing in the *town's* highways and bridges, not defects in private bridges, or bridges on private property, over which the town has and can have no control or jurisdiction. It is only the public highway which can be barricaded for the traveler's protection ; it is only within the limits of the town's highways that the commissioner can exercise his official functions.   The commissioner's duties are plainly and specifically imposed and pointed out in the Highway Law, and his duties here imposed are the exact measure of his powers.   Nowhere in words or by implication is the duty imposed or the authority conferred of erecting temporary passage-ways over private lands, or erecting structures along those passageways in lieu of bridges in the town's highways.   Nor is there any power in any town officer, or board of town officers, to authorize the highway commissioner to do this.   This passageway and temporary structure, it will be observed, was in no way a means to the construction of a highway bridge.   It was not a necessary act in the reconstruction of the washed-out bridge.   No duty is imposed upon the commissioner to facilitate the public travel beyond the construction, in a reasonable time, of a bridge in the town's highway to replace the one destroyed.   The question cannot arise in this case as to the commissioner's duty to warn the public that this passage was not a public highway, because the plaintiff knew it.   He knew it before he attempted it.   It is an ancient rule, and the courts declare it a sound rule, that to charge a person or a municipality with negligence respecting a public work, the law must have imposed the duty so as to make failure in performance culpable.   The duty here imposed relates solely to defects in the town's roads and bridges, and none others.   As this was not a town road or bridge, the town cannot be held for any neglect in its construction, and that is the sole neglect charged in the complaint.   There is no charge of failure to barricade against a danger, or failure to warn plaintiff that this was not a town highway.   Where the duty of erecting and maintaining bridges is imposed upon a county, as is the case in some States, it has been declared that the county is liable only for the class of bridges which the statute requires or authorizes it to build and maintain.   (*Taylor* v. *Davis County*, 40 Iowa, 295 ; *Moreland* v. *Mitchell County*, Id. 394 ; *Long* v. *Boone County*, 32 id. 181.)

In *Mayor* v. *Cunliff* (2 N. Y. 165), CADY, J., after stating the rule of liability of a person or municipality to be confined in public works to the class of acts within the field of statutory duty imposed, says : " Suppose a traveller upon a public road comes to a narrow and deep stream which he cannot cross without a bridge and he immediately goes to work and makes a bridge over which he with his horse and wagon passes, and shortly after another traveller attempts to pass over with a span of horses and wagon, but unfortunately the bridge breaks down and both his horses are drowned. Has he a remedy against the man who built the bridge? Why not? Because the law had imposed on him no duty to build it. And so I apprehend the law to be in relation to the defendants. If the law had imposed upon them no obligation to construct the bridge or to widen and enlarge the draw therein, they must be regarded as mere volunteers and in no way responsible to the plaintiff for what they did or for what they neglected to do." This was a case of a bridge built over the Hudson river by the city of Albany under an unconstitutional act, which fell from faulty construction after the public had begun to travel over it. The judgment of the Court of Appeals is placed squarely on the ground that the city had no authority to build the bridge and the act of the officials could not make the city liable because *ultra vires.* STRONG, J., says: " It was said, however, that the assent of the common council estopped the corporation from raising this objection " (lack of authority). Admitting the principle to be true as applied to individuals, he further says, "But it is, I conceive, different with a corporation. There the officers act for their constituents, who have to pay, when they are responsible at all, and such officers are limited in their legitimate action to the powers conferred by their charters. So long as they confine their agency to such powers, their constituents are responsible for their misfeasance or carelessness. * * * The rule, although it may sometimes operate harshly, is a safe and sound one and should be applied uniformly to all cases of misconduct in persons acting in a representative character where they travel beyond their legitimate powers." Commenting upon this case, MILLER, J., in *Sewell* v. *City of Cohoes* (75 N. Y. 51) says: " It will thus be seen that no duty was imposed upon the defendant to build the bridge in question, and as the law conferred no authority there could be no liability."

The court, in *Smith* v. *City of Rochester* (76 N. Y. 506), declares the rule as stated in the head note of the case, " To establish the liability of a municipal corporation for damages resulting from the alleged negligence or want of skill of its agent or servant in the course of his employment, it is essential to show that the act complained of was within the scope of the corporate powers ; if outside of the powers of the corporation as conferred by statute, the corporation is not liable, whether its officers directed the performance of the act, or it was done without any express direction.''

It is misleading to give to the acts of every person having a little brief authority an official character, though professed to be done by color of office.   The fact that it is so done does not make a *prima facie* case; it must be shown by every complainant that the act was in fact authorized respecting a public work, and always this burden is upon the plaintiff.

Without giving any expression on the question of contributory negligence, I am of opinion that plaintiff's complaint was, for the reasons stated, properly dismissed, and the judgment should be affirmed, with costs.

All concurred.

Judgment unanimously affirmed, with costs.

The United National Bank of Troy, Plaintiff, *v.* Catharine Ida Weatherby, as Administratrix, etc., of Nelson L. Weatherby, Deceased, Appellant and Respondent; The Travelers' Insurance Company of Hartford, Conn., Appellant; James C. Wilbur, Individually and as Surviving Partner of the Firm of Weatherby & Wilbur, Defendant, and International Navigation Company, Respondent.

Deposit, in a bank account in the name of a firm of brokers, of moneys of an insurance company and of a navigation company — under what circumstances they are respectively impressed with a trust — effect of the moneys being from time to time wrongfully withdrawn and thereafter being replaced.

The firm of Weatherby & Wilbur, who were engaged in the insurance and brokerage business, kept a bank account in the name of "Weatherby & Wilbur." In August and September, 1898, Weatherby, who was the agent for the Travelers' Insurance Company, deposited in the account premiums collected by him for that company amounting to $313.64. In September, 1898, he deposited in the account $360.08, which represented the avails of drafts sold by the firm for the International Navigation Company. Weatherby died October 5, 1898, at which time the account contained $724.87. Several times during the month of September Weatherby, by means of withdrawals, made without the knowledge of the insurance company or the navigation company, reduced the account below the sums needed to discharge the two claims, but, as many times, made good such deficiency from some undisclosed source. It did not appear that Weatherby deposited in the account any money except trust money, or that he had deposited therein moneys held in trust for any one but the insurance and navigation companies.

Held, that the several withdrawals and restorations made by Weatherby in his lifetime did not operate to extinguish the identity of the moneys originally deposited belonging to the insurance and navigation companies;

That, in the absence of any other claimants of the $724.87 than the creditors of Weatherby or his administratrix, such moneys constituted a trust fund, applicable to the discharge of the claims of the insurance and navigation companies.

APPEAL by the defendant Catharine Ida Weatherby, as administratrix, etc., of Nelson L. Weatherby, deceased, from that portion of a judgment of the Supreme Court in favor of the defendant International Navigation Company, entered in the office of the clerk of the county of Rensselaer on the 13th day of August, 1901, upon the decision of the court rendered after a trial at the Rensselaer Trial Term before the court without a jury, which awarded the International Navigation Company $360.08, with interest and costs, out of a fund deposited in court by the plaintiff.

Also an appeal by the defendant the Travelers' Insurance Company of Hartford, Conn., from that portion of the said judgment denying said defendant any part of said fund and awarding costs personally against said company in favor of the defendant Catharine Ida Weatherby, as administratrix, etc., of Nelson L. Weatherby, deceased.

This is an appeal from a judgment of a Trial Term of the Supreme Court declaring the interest of the several defendants in a fund of $1,240.89, deposited in plaintiff's bank in the name of "Weatherby & Wilbur." The plaintiff makes no claim to the fund, and the contention is between the defendants. A judgment of interpleader having been entered by consent, the said $1,240.89 has been paid into court. The defendant Catharine Ida Weatherby claims the money as administratrix of Nelson L. Weatherby, who died October 5, 1898. The Travelers' Insurance Company claims a portion of the fund, viz., $418.64 and interest, $313.64 having been collected as premiums on policies of insurance and as agent of the company by Nelson L. Weatherby in his lifetime, and $105 having been collected by the administratrix since his decease. James C. Wilbur appeared, but made no answer. He is the Wilbur named in the firm name of Weatherby & Wilbur. The International Navigation Company claims $360.08 as avails of drafts sold which were by the company remitted to " Weatherby & Wilbur " for sale as brokers, the money realized on sale to be returned to the company.

The Special Term, on stipulation of parties as to the facts, decided that the International Navigation Company was entitled to have the full amount of its claim and interest from October 5, 1898, paid out of the fund.

The court further decided that the Travelers' Insurance Company bore the relation of " creditor to Weatherby," and neither the insurance company nor James C. Wilbur was entitled to any share of the fund.

The court further found that Catharine Ida Weatherby, as administratrix, was entitled to the balance of the fund, and judgment was accordingly directed, with costs, in favor of the administratrix against the Travelers' Insurance Company. From this judgment the Travelers' Insurance Company and the administratrix appeal.

Shaw, Bailey & Murphy, for the plaintiff.

Learned Hand, for the respondent International Navigation Company.

Henry W. Smith and *William W. Morrill*, for the appellant Travelers' Insurance Company.

James B. Egan and *H. D. Bailey*, for the administratrix.

King & King, for the defendant Wilbur.

KELLOGG, J.:

Beyond doubt the claims of the International Navigation Company and of the Travelers' Insurance Company are for moneys held in a trust capacity. Weatherby held them as agent. Hence the decision of the trial court that the relation between Weatherby and the Travelers' Insurance Company was only that of debtor and creditor requires a reversal of the judgment, or a modification of it, if it appears that the Travelers' Insurance Company is entitled as *cestui qu'e trust* to any portion of the fund.

It does not seem to admit of doubt but that the Travelers' Insurance Company is entitled to the $105 (less commissions) collected after the death of Weatherby by the administratrix and forming a part of this fund. As to the $313.64 collected in the lifetime of Weatherby, its recovery in this action depends upon whether the proof is sufficient to warrant a finding that it now forms a part of this fund. It is an admitted fact that in small sums, on different days in the months of August and September, 1898, this was deposited and was made a part of a fund in the plaintiff's bank kept under the name of " Weatherby & Wilbur."

It is also admitted that the $360.08, claimed by the navigation company, was in like manner deposited by Weatherby in this fund during the month of September, 1898.

The fact is admitted also that Weatherby died October 5, 1898, and at that time the fund kept in bank and designated " Weatherby & Wilbur " amounted to $724.87, a little more than enough to satisfy these two claims, not allowing interest.

It is admitted that at all times prior to and on the 1st day of September, 1898, this fund had been kept and was then more than sufficient to satisfy the then deposits on account of these two companies ; that on September 2, 1898, by reason of withdrawals by Weatherby on that day, without the knowledge of either of the companies, the fund was reduced below a sum needed to discharge these claims ; that on September 6, 1898, he made the fund good by restoration and continued the same good until September 17, 1898 ; that between September sixth and September seventeenth Weatherby received and deposited in this fund $290.26 of Navigation Company's money and $199.63 of Travelers' Company's money, and the fund on that date was more than sufficient to satisfy their claims ; that on September seventeenth, without the knowledge of either company, Weatherby by withdrawals again reduced the fund below the sum needed to discharge these claims ; that during the succeeding five days he restored the money, so that on September twenty-second the fund was again in excess of the united claims of these companies ; that on the twenty-third of September Weatherby by withdrawals, without the knowledge or consent of either company, again reduced the fund below what was needed to satisfy these two claims, and subsequently made restoration, so that at the time of his death on October 5, 1898, the fund amounted to $724.87. This seems to be the admitted history of this fund. I think it may be accepted as an uncontroverted fact in the case that deposits by Weatherby in the name of "Weatherby & Wilbur" constituted a trust account. The business was in the nature of a trust business. The agreement of March 9, 1898, between Weatherby & Wilbur, which is set forth in the complaint, is claimed by the administratrix to have been a dissolution of that firm. However that may be, it is there stated that the business was "doing an insurance and brokerage business in the city of Troy." The other undisputed facts show that the "insurance" was only the collection of premiums on insurance policies as agents, and brokerage was the handling of other people's property as brokers for a commission. The agreement was to continue this business. Moreover, the agreement fairly contemplated a separate account and no mixture of funds. "No personal accounts or debts to be made by either party to be charged against the business, or in such manner that the same can be presented as an offset against insurance premiums of the creditor." Then the provision that, "at the end of each year the said Weatherby shall render a full account of the business," required a separate account. Again, the law against the mixing of trust moneys with other moneys requires a separate deposit account; and the fact that this account was so kept in bank by Weatherby after the so-called dissolution seems conclusive that it was intended to represent and did represent a trust account — the depositary of trust money received by Weatherby. The fact that Weatherby on occasion, either inadvertently or intentionally, drew out money from this account for improper use, does not destroy the trust character of the account itself. Once the depositary of trust money it must be regarded as continuing so, and the money found in it must be taken as impressed with a trust until the trust is discharged. If we are right in assuming that this was a trust account, the act of Weatherby in every instance in making deposits in this account was a declaration on his part that such deposits were impressed with a trust. And there is no evidence in this case of any deposit therein by Weatherby of any money other than trust money, and the express admission by all the parties that this account was the depositary of the money held in trust for these two companies it seems to me leaves no room to question that this was exclusively a trust account. It could not have been more so if the account had been designated "Weatherby, agent." The only confusion that can be claimed then is that which arises from the mingling of trust funds with other trust funds, and this claim is one which the various *cestuis que trust* can determine among themselves in the first instance, for the creditors of Weatherby or the administratrix representing them can have no interest in the fund until the various trusts are discharged.

The claim is made by the administratrix that the several withdrawals and restorations made by Weatherby in his lifetime operated to extinguish the identity of the money originally deposited belonging to these companies. The complete answer to that, it seems to me, is that such withdrawals were wrongful whether intentional or inadvertent, and presumably the wrongdoer by making subsequent deposits intended to make restoration and right the wrong. Under such circumstances, the *cestuis que trust* have a right to adopt these acts done for their benefit, and as against all the world besides the act of restoration is conclusive until at least it is shown that the money used to make restoration belonged to some one besides the wrongdoer. The act of restoration impressed the restored funds with the same trust which attached to the money originally deposited. This, if we correctly interpret the opinion of the court, was so held in *Baker* v. *N. Y. Nat. Ex. Bank* (100 N. Y. 31). That was a case of deposits of proceeds of sales on commission made by Wilson & Bro. in the name of "C. A. Wilson & Bro., agents." The court held that this fund could not be reached by a creditor of Wilson & Bro., though that creditor was the bank itself, and the court, by ANDREWS, J., says the bank "could not appropriate it to the debt of Wilson & Bro. even with their consent to the prejudice of the *cestui que trusts*." The court further says as to these deposits not being in fact the proceeds of sales of goods of their principals, "conceding that Wilson & Bro. used the specific proceeds for their own purposes and their identity was lost, yet when they made up the amounts so used and deposited them in the trust account, the amounts so deposited were impressed with the trust in favor of the principals and became substituted for the original proceeds and subject to the same equities." This was in effect held by the Court of Appeals at an earlier date (*Van Alen* v. *American Nat. Bank,* 52 N. Y. 1) and was followed in *Gerard* v. *McCormick* (29 N. Y. St. Repr. 709, 712).

We are lead to the conclusion, therefore, that in the absence of other claimants than the creditors of Weatherby or the administratrix, the $724.87 constitutes a trust fund which is applicable by the direction of the court in this action to the discharge of the claims of these two companies. Nor do I think that we are embarrassed by any suggestion that there may be other *cestuis que trust* entitled to share in this fund and not here represented. A similar suggestion was made in *Baker* v. *N. Y. Nat. Ex. Bank* (*supra*), and it was there disposed of by the court saying: "The objection for defect of parties was not taken in the answer and moreover it does not appear that there are any unsettled accounts of Wilson & Bro. with any other person or persons for whom they were agents." This case, so far as the complaint and several answers and stipulation of facts go, precludes the suggestion that there are other persons interested who have not been made parties to this action.

So far as the claim of the International Navigation Company goes, it might be supported on the grounds that Wilbur was, as to that company, a copartner of Weatherby and the money collected and deposited in name of Weatherby & Wilbur was copartnership money and first applicable to the discharge of this company's claim. The contention that the stipulation by fair construction is an admission that this company had knowledge of any dissolution — if there was one in fact — and that the company dealt with Weatherby as an individual, is refuted by the receipts for the drafts and the letters with which the drafts were forwarded. As to the Travelers' Company there is no question but it dealt with Weatherby alone as its agent. Wilbur under the written agreement of March 8, 1898, has a right to insist that these moneys arising from the business shall be used to discharge the obligations of the business first; if there were any surplus it would be in the nature of profits, one-half of which would have to be applied for his benefit. This right of Wilbur any creditor of the firm may claim to be subrogated to and so work out the application of the copartnership effects to the discharge of the creditor's claim. I do not, however, deem it necessary that the navigation company should exercise its right to these moneys on that theory, I think it is plain that both of these companies are entitled to this fund because it is impressed with a trust for their benefit.

While the money paid into court amounts to $1,240.89, that portion of this which was turned over to the bank after the decease of Weatherby is not impressed with any trust by reason of any declaration or act of restoration on the part of Weatherby; hence only that portion other than the $724.87 actually identified as trust money can be taken by either of these companies. That portion is $9.80 of navigation company's money and $78.75 (being $105 less agent's commissions) Travelers' Insurance Company's money.

The judgment must, therefore, be modified by directing that of the $1,240.89 deposited in court there be first paid the sum of $360.08 to the International Navigation Company and $392.39 be paid to the Travelers' Insurance Company; that the International Navigation Company and the Travelers' Insurance Company are each entitled to costs of the action and costs of this appeal; that the balance of said $1,240.89, less the said taxable costs allowed to each of the companies and lawful commissions, be paid over to the administratrix Catharine Ida Weatherby.

All concurred.

Judgment modified in accordance with opinion, and as so modified affirmed, with costs as indicated in opinion.

HENRY J. SMITH, Appellant, *v.* LOUISE SMITH and Others, Respondents.

Non-resident alien devisee — he takes a good title to land under chapter 38 of the Laws of 1875 until escheat is declared.

In July, 1892, when chapter 38 of the Laws of 1875 was in force, a non-resident alien, related by blood to a naturalized citizen of the United States, could take, by devise, from such citizen, land situated in the State of New York.

The provision of the act of 1875 that in order to "hold" the land as against the State the alien must declare his intention to become a citizen, is available only to the State; as against the rest of the world the title vests in the alien without precedent or subsequent condition, and as against the State the alien may hold until the escheat is declared.

APPEAL by the plaintiff, Henry J. Smith, from a judgment of the Supreme Court in favor of the defendants, entered in the office of the clerk of the county of St. Lawrence on the 18th day of November, 1901, upon the decision of the court, rendered after a trial at the St. Lawrence Special Term, dismissing the complaint upon the merits, on the ground that plaintiff had no interest in the real estate of the testator, Owen Smith.

The plaintiff is a son of Owen Smith, who died July 27, 1892. At the time of his death Owen Smith was a resident naturalized citizen of this State and the owner of some real estate in St. Lawrence county. His son, the plaintiff here, was also a resident citizen. The deceased at the time of his death had a brother, Thomas Smith, in Ireland. He was a non-resident alien. Thomas Smith died intestate October 7, 1892, two months and ten days after the death of Owen, and before he had any knowledge of the provisions of Owen Smith's will. The last will of Owen Smith gave to Thomas Smith, his alien brother in Ireland, a third of his real estate or the proceeds thereof, in case the executors should sell the real estate, which under the will they had power to do.

The plaintiff contends that under the Statute of Wills the devise to Thomas Smith was void and that the third interest so devised, immediately upon the death of Owen, descended to him as sole heir at law; and this action is brought to establish this contention.

Joseph F. Brown, for the appellant.

Ledyard P. Hale, for the respondents.

KELLOGG, J.:

The question presented by this record is, could a non-resident alien in July, 1892, take an interest in lands situated in this State through a devise by a citizen? The answer to the question depends upon the proper construction to be given to the law of 1875 (Chap. 38). For political reasons the common law created a barrier against the ownership by aliens of lands situated here. Aliens, resident or non-resident, could not take by inheritance, but they could take by purchase or devise and hold the fee until "office found" or the State asserted its rights to ownership by escheat. As against all others the title by grant or devise was good. The history of the various statutory enactments by which the common law was modified and materially changed in this State shows a continuous progression along the line of removal of the disabilities attached to alienage, until the act of 1893 (Chap. 207) practically placed aliens and citizens upon the same footing. The act of 1845 (Chap. 115) was a partial relief to *resident* aliens, enabling them to take and hold lands by purchase (which the courts have interpreted to mean by devise also), and by section 4 of that act the alien heirs of such resident aliens, whether such alien heirs were resident or non-resident, may take by inheritance. At the time of the passage of the act of 1845 there existed what is known as the Statute of Wills which provided, "every devise of any interest in real property to a person who, at the time of the death of the testator, shall be an alien *not authorised by statute* to hold real estate, shall be void. The interest so devised shall descend to the heirs of the testator." (2 R. S. 57, § 4.) Such is the statutory law at the present time, but it will be observed that it runs only against "an alien *not authorised by statute* to hold real estate." So fast as the various statutes enabled any class of aliens to take and hold real estate, that class was removed from the operation of this provision of the Statute of Wills. This Statute of Wills, however, from its passage, changed the rule of the common law, which was that an alien could not take by inheritance, but might take by devise or grant until "office found."

The statute of 1845 removed a class of aliens from the effect of this Statute of Wills, and that class were all "resident aliens," as to property acquired by purchase (including property acquired by devise); as to property of resident aliens acquired by descent this statute of 1845 gave no relief. (*Callahan* v. *O'Brien*, 72 Hun, 216.) One relief given by this statute was the right to inherit which the common law denied to aliens. The statute of 1874 (Chap. 261) further enlarged this class, but did not give to any alien the right to take by devise, which the common law did give and which the Statute of Wills cut off. The statute of 1875 (Chap. 38) seems to have been passed expressly to give the same right to alien devisees of the same blood as alien heirs enjoyed under the previous statutes. In effect, no other change was made. It does not seem to admit of any doubt but under this law of 1875 aliens may take by devise. The statute reads as follows: "If any alien resident of this State, or any naturalized or native citizen of the United States, who has purchased and taken or hereafter shall purchase and take a conveyance of real estate within this State, has died, or shall hereafter die, leaving persons who according to the statutes of this State would answer the description of heirs of such deceased person, *or of devisees under his last will, and being of his blood,* such persons so answering the description of heirs *or of such devisees* of such deceased person, whether they are citizens or aliens, are hereby declared and made capable of taking and holding, and may take and hold, as heirs, *or such devisees* of such deceased person, as if they were citizens of the United States, the lands and real estate owned and held by such deceased alien or citizen at the time of his decease;" then follows a provision that in order to "*hold*" as against the State the alien must declare his intention to become a citizen. We find here no impediment to the immediate transmission of the title to realty to the heir in case of intestacy, or to the devisee of the same blood in case there is a will. The condition of holding as *against the State* is a question solely between the State and the heir or devisee; as against all the world other than the State the title vests without precedent or subsequent condition, and as to the State, the heir or devisee may hold, as the courts have decided in analogous cases, until "office found" and escheat is declared.

In this case the important feature of the statute of 1875 (Chap. 38) is the clear intention of the Legislature to place the alien heir and the alien devisee upon the same footing as to the right to take and hold realty in this State. This is a clear modification of the Statute of Wills, or, rather, it takes the alien devisee of the blood of the testator out of the class referred to in the Statute of Wills, "an alien *not authorised* by statute to hold real estate."

So far as I have been able to discover, no court in this State has held that under the statute of 1845, and the amendments of 1874 and 1875, a non-resident alien could not take and hold lands in this State by descent from resident aliens or resident citizens. The decisions seem to be all to the contrary. And if a non-resident alien may take as heir, it would seem to be incontestable that devisees of *the same blood* of testator, dying after the passage of the law of 1875, can take whether resident or non-resident.

The case of *Marx* v. *McGlynn* (88 N. Y. 375, 876), cited by the learned counsel for appellant, is not an authority against this proposition. In that case the devisee was not of the blood of the testatrix and for that reason alone his disability to take is not removed by the act of 1875. The court, at the pages cited, in its opinion said, " In the first clause the devise of the house to Bradley, who is shown to be an alien, is void, as an alien cannot take real estate by devise," is not to be questioned as the law so far as Bradley or that case is concerned. But the broad statement that " an alien cannot take real estate by devise " nullifies the provisions of the statute of 1875 as we have seen. It is quite likely that this statute was not presented to the court's attention, for by it Bradley, being not of the blood of the testatrix, could obtain no relief under it.

The case of *Parker* v. *Linden* (113 N. Y. 28) shows a will of real estate in New York to certain relatives of the *half* blood, non-resident aliens, and the decease of the testator after the passage of the act of 1875. In the General Term, VAN BRUNT, P. J., writing in this case, said, " But it is to be remembered that the testator knew that these half-brothers and half-sister, being aliens, British subjects, could not take real estate by devise," and to save the testator's intention the court construed the will by reason of the power of conversion contained in it as a will of personalty. (44 Hun, 518.) When this case was considered in the Court of Appeals, DANFORTH, J., writing for the court said, as to this forced construction to save the interest of the half brothers and sister, " It was, in fact, unnecessary to accomplish that object ; as to all others, except the State, they could take and hold as *heirs or devisees* (Chap. 38, Laws of 1875)." Whether the General Term or the Court of Appeals regarded a half brother or half sister as coming within the requirement of the act " and being of his blood " is not disclosed. The Court of Appeals, by reference to the law of 1875, declares that being non-resident aliens, these half brothers and half sister could take either as heirs or devisees. If they could take only as heirs, as plaintiff contends, the statement that they could take as devisees is erroneous.

It is unnecessary to consider the question as to whether the testator made by his will a conversion so that the provisions of the will might be effectuated, treating it as wholly personal.

It ·is also unnecessary to consider what may be the exact nature of the title or interest of defendant Mary Rose Reilly in the estate of her father, Thomas Smith. It is enough for all the purposes of this action to determine, as we do, that Thomas Smith took as devisee a title to the realty defeasible only by the State, and that plaintiff as heir at law of Owen Smith acquired no title.

The judgment should be affirmed, with costs.

All concurred.

Judgment unanimously affirmed, with costs.

JONAS M. KILMER, Appellant, *v.* EVENING HERALD COMPANY, Respondent.

Discontinuance of an action for libel — a stipulation by the plaintiff not to bring another action, not required as a condition thereof — when an additional allowance is properly imposed.

Where, on a motion to discontinue an action of libel on the calendar at a Trial Term, it appears that no rights of the defendant will be injuriously affected by such discontinuance, the court has no power to require the plaintiff, as a condition of the discontinuance, to file a stipulation not to bring another action for the same cause.

The court may, however, require the plaintiff to pay to the defendant an extra allowance of $225, where it appears that the complaint demanded judgment for $25,000 and that the questions presented were difficult and called for more than ordinary investigation in preparation for trial.

APPEAL by the plaintiff, Jonas M. Kilmer, from that portion of an order of the Supreme Court, made at the Broome Special Term and entered in the office of the clerk of the county of Broome on the 25th day of January, 1902, requiring and directing as a condition for the discontinuance of the action the payment to the defendant of an additional allowance of $225 and a stipulation not to begin another action for the same alleged cause.

The complaint charges the publication by defendant of libelous matter and seeks to recover $25,000 as damages. The answer denies that the publication was wrongful, false or malicious, alleges matter was privileged, alleges matter in mitigation of damages, and matter which defendant claims to prove in justification of the publication. The action was not tried. No witness on either side had been examined. The cause being on the calendar at a Trial Term, plaintiff made application to discontinue. The defendant asked that as a condition of discontinuance the plaintiff should be required to pay an additional allowance and costs, and file a stipulation not to bring another action for the same cause, and against the protest of plaintiff such conditions were incorporated in the order.

Israel T. Deyo, for the appellant.

Theodore R. Tuthill, for the respondent.

KELLOGG, J.:

In *Matter of Petition of Butler* (101 N. Y. 307) it was held: "Ordinarily a suitor has a right to discontinue any action or proceeding commenced by him and his reasons for so doing are of no concern to the court. A party should no more be compelled to continue a litigation than to commence one except where substantial rights of other parties have accrued and injustice will be done to them by permitting the discontinuance. In such a case, through the control which the court exercises over the entry of its order, there is discretion to refuse; but where there are no such facts and nothing appears to show a violation of the right or interest of the adverse party, the plaintiff may discontinue, and a refusal of leave becomes merely arbitrary and without any basis upon which discretion can exist."

In *Winans* v. *Winans* (124 N. Y. 145) the court said: "But an application for leave to discontinue is addressed to the legal not the arbitrary discretion of the court and it cannot capriciously deny it."

It would, therefore, seem that ordinarily discontinuance is a right, and leave to discontinue is not a favor asked. Without doubt in the action before us the plaintiff had a right to discontinue his action, and a refusal of leave to discontinue would have been a capricious denial. There were no rights of defendant which could have been injuriously affected by such discontinuance. There were no interests of defendant to be protected or which could be protected by a continuance of the action. *Matter, etc., Waverly Water Works Co.* (85 N. Y. 479), cited by respondent, presents quite a different case. There the matter was by law placed in the discretion of the court and it was a favor plaintiff was asking, not the recognition of a right, and the court says: " The right to impose such conditions grows out of and is included in the right to refuse the discontinuance altogether." So we have in all these cases in effect a declaration that if the right to refuse an application for discontinuance altogether does not in a given case exist the court has no right to impose arbitrary conditions, and also that ordinarily the right to discontinue an action on payment of costs and allowances is as broad and as clear as the right to commence an action, and the suitor's reasons in either case are of no concern to the court. This must lead to the conclusion in the case before us that the Special Term had no power to impose, as a condition of discontinuance, the filing of a stipulation not to sue again for the same cause. It is no answer to say that plaintiff is asking a favor of the court in asking leave to discontinue, and he must take the order with any condition the court imposes or leave it untaken. By asking leave to discontinue the plaintiff asks the court to adjudicate upon the case and facts before it that defendant by discontinuance will not be injuriously affected. That is a legal proposition and is not addressed to the judicial discretion.

The appellant urges that the extra allowance of $225 was improper. At the time the application was made to discontinue the application for an allowance was made. The Code of Civil Procedure (§ 3253) provides for an additional allowance " in a difficult and extraordinary case (where a defense has been interposed in an action)." It is not necessary that there should have been a trial to warrant the allowance. The apparent object of this provision is to supply a method of at least partial compensation to the prevailing party for the expense necessary in the litigation not covered by the taxable costs. The questions presented in this case, as the record before us shows, were difficult and called for more investigation than ordinary in preparation for trial. Expert counsel, as a matter of reasonable prudence, were engaged both by plaintiff and by defendant to assist the attorneys of record. The court, we think,

294   PEOPLE ex rel. ARGUS CO. *v.* BRESLER.

THIRD DEPARTMENT, MARCH TERM, 1902.   [Vol. 70.

was justified in making an additional allowance, and the sum he fixes appears to us reasonable.

The order, however, must be modified by striking out the provision requiring the plaintiff to stipulate not to bring another action against defendant for the same cause, and as so modified the order is affirmed, with ten dollars costs and disbursements to appellant.

All concurred.

Order modified by striking out provision requiring plaintiff to stipulate not to bring another action against the defendant for the same cause, and as so modified affirmed, with ten dollars costs and disbursements to appellant.

––––––––––––––––––

THE PEOPLE OF THE STATE OF NEW YORK ex rel. THE ARGUS COMPANY, Appellant, *v.* FREDERICK U. BRESLER, as Clerk of the Common Council of the City of Albany, N. Y., and THE PRESS COMPANY, Respondents.

294|
Y 302|

Designation of official city newspapers — the president of the common council in a city of the second class can vote only in case of a tie vote.

Under section 14 of the charter of cities of the second class (Laws of 1898, chap. 182), which provides that "the president may vote like other members of the common council, upon all resolutions and ordinances submitted to the body for its action in case of a tie vote," the president of the common council has not the same right as aldermen to vote upon all propositions, but can vote only in case of a tie vote upon resolutions and ordinances.

Section 29 of the charter, relating to the designation of the official newspapers, which provides, "each member shall be entitled to vote for one of the papers," does not give the president of the common council express authority to vote upon this question without regard to the existence of a tie vote thereon.

Semble, that it was the intention of the Legislature not to make the president of the common council a member of that body except so far as specific functions are conferred upon him.

APPEAL by the relator, The Argus Company, from an order of the Supreme Court, made at the Albany Special Term and entered in the office of the clerk of the county of Albany on the 13th day of February, 1902, denying the relator's motion for a mandamus directed to Frederick U. Bresler, as clerk of the common council of the city of Albany, N. Y., requiring him to deliver to the relator for publication all matter required by law to be published in the city's official papers.

Amasa J. Parker, Jr., for the appellant.

Arthur L. Andrews, for the respondent Bresler.

John F. Montignani and *William P. Rudd*, for the respondent The Press Company.

KELLOGG, J.:

The question presented by this appeal relates to the right of the president of the common council of a city of the second class to vote in the designation of an official newspaper. The Special Term interpreted the statute as giving to the president such right. I think in this the learned court was in error.

The common council mentioned in the act (Laws of 1898, chap. 182) is a legislative body; "its authority except as otherwise provided in this act, or by other laws of the State is legislative only." (§ 12.) The common council is composed of one alderman from each ward and a president elected from the city at large. The wards have equal representation in the legislative body if we do not give to the president aldermanic powers, and if we do the ward in which the president happens to reside has a representation in the legislative body for all purposes twice that of any other ward. Such a scheme might be the subject of just criticism. That it was not the intention of the Legislature to give to the president all the powers possessed by an alderman is manifest by the provisions of section 14 as follows: "The president may vote like other members of the common council upon all resolutions and ordinances submitted to the body for its action in case of a tie vote." If the president had by the general provisions of the act the right to vote as alderman there would have been no need of giving him the right to vote in case of a tie vote. This must be interpreted as a denial of the right to vote in all other cases. Counsel for the Press Company ask us to interpret the legislative intention as meaning "must vote" instead of "may vote" when there is a tie vote on resolutions and ordinances, but this could hardly be counted a cure for deadlocks. If the president had the same right as aldermen to vote on all propositions, his vote might as often make a tie as dissolve one. But the reasoning of the learned counsel illustrates the difficulty of maintaining any middle ground. It was either the intention of the Legislature to give to the president the right to vote the same as aldermen on all propositions, or it was its intention to give him the right to vote only in case of a tie vote upon resolutions and ordinances. It appears to me that there is no escape from this conclusion. That it was not the intention of the Legislature to invest the president with all the powers of an alderman in the legislative body seems to me very clear. The status and functions of the president are different from those of aldermen. He is elected as a city officer by the city at large, and is to receive a salary fixed by the act. His duties are defined by the act and are not the duties imposed upon the aldermen. He is to preside at the meetings of the common council; he has power to convene the common council; he is made a member of the board of estimate and apportionment; he is required to "discharge such other duties as president as may be defined by ordinances of the common council and other provisions of this act" (§ 14), and he has the right to vote on ordinances and resolutions in case of a tie. "The president and aldermen thus elected shall constitute the common council." (§ 13.) Without doubt he may be regarded as a member of that body, but a member with different powers than those possessed by the aldermen, and not clothed with aldermanic powers. Great stress is laid upon the wording in section 29, "Each member shall be entitled to vote for one of the papers," and it is urged that this gives the president express authority to vote on this question. There appears to be no special reason why he should be permitted to vote on this question unless he is a voting member of the council and entitled to vote on every question. I see no particular significance in the use of the term "each member;" it was a provision restricting a member from voting for more than one paper and was naturally expressed in this way. If the Legislature had intended to give to the president a right to vote on this question it would have included it in the provision (§ 14) conferring a power to vote in case of a tie. The term "member" is used very often in this act, and it does not appear to me that in its use the Legislature intended to refer to any one other than the aldermen, or that it intended to include the president or to give him the right to vote in matters referred to. Section 15 provides for the choosing of a clerk who may be removed " by a vote of three-fourths of all the members." Section 16, " The president of the common council or a *majority of its members* may call a special meeting." Section 17, " *A majority of all its members* shall be a quorum." Section 19, " No appropriation of money shall be made * * * except by an ordinance passed by *three-fourths of all the members* * * * ; and no ordinance shall be passed * * * authorizing a sale or lease * * * except by a vote of *three-fourths of all the members* of the common council." Section 21, after the mayor's veto the ordinance cannot be passed " unless *three-fourths of all the members* of the common council " vote for it. Section 25, " The common council may by ordinances passed by two-thirds of all its members " regulate the powers and duties of any city officer or department. Section 27, no expulsion shall take place or vacancy be declared " except by the vote of three-fourths of all the members of the common council." Then follows section 29, before quoted, as the sole reliance for authority in the president to vote : " Each member shall be entitled to vote for one of the papers." Following this in the same section it is provided : " In case any of the official papers shall refuse or fail to act or perform as such the *common council* may designate another paper in its place." The inquiry is pertinent here : Can the president vote on this proposition ? The " common council " must designate ; that is, the members of the common council ; each member may vote. The act authorizes the " common council " to do many things. That is, it authorizes each member of the common council to vote on the subject, and the act would have no greater significance if it had said " Each member shall be entitled to one vote " on the question before the common council. To give, therefore, to this form of expression occurring in section 29 the meaning claimed for it, that it confers upon the president the power to vote and thereby changes the voting force in the common council, it seems to me does violence to the otherwise apparent intention of the Legislature. It punctures and distorts a reasonable governmental scheme and creates unnecessary confusion and doubt as to when and on what occasions the president may exercise the functions of the aldermen and when not ; when he must be counted in determining a majority vote or a two-thirds or three-fourths vote or a quorum. If, as I believe, it was the intention of the Legislature not to make the president, elected by the city, a member of the legislative body except so far as specific functions are conferred, viz., the right to call the council together, to preside at their meetings, with a vote upon the passage of ordinances and resolutions when there is a tie in the legislative body, then we have a scheme workable and comprehensible, a legislative body constructed on a plan analogous to that of other legislative bodies, composed of members from each separate ward of the city, giving to each section equal representation and with no confusion as to the meaning of the plan or as to powers of its component parts. This is a general act and affects all cities of the second class, and no confusing interpretation should be read into it unless it is impossible to read it otherwise.

The order should be reversed, with ten dollars costs and disbursements against the Press Company, and writ of mandamus prayed for be directed to issue, without costs.

All concurred.

Order reversed, with ten dollars costs and disbursements to relator against the Press Company, and the writ of mandamus prayed for directed to issue, without costs.

298
90

FANNY F. WALLACE and LULU J. WALLACE, as Executrices and Widow and Sole Heir at Law and Devisees under the Will of EDWIN R. WALLACE, Deceased, Respondents, *v.* THE INTERNATIONAL PAPER COMPANY and WILLIAM McECHRON, Appellants, Impleaded with WARREN CURTIS and Others.

Tax — effect on a tax sale of a statement by the Comptroller that there was no tax — chapter 908 of 1896 is a short Statute of Limitations.

A statement made by the Comptroller of the State of New York to the owner of certain lands upon which an unpaid tax was then a lien, to the effect that there was no unpaid tax thereon for the year in question, does not render a subsequent sale of the land for such unpaid tax void, but at most merely voidable; and where the owners fail to assert their right to have the sale set aside within the time fixed by section 132 of the Tax Law (Laws of 1896, chap. 908) they cannot thereafter assert it. (Per KELLOGG and FURSMAN, JJ.)

The provision of the Tax Law relative to the effect of a deed executed by the Comptroller, pursuant to a tax sale, is a Statute of Limitations and applies to such a case. (Per PARKER, P. J., SMITH and CHASE, JJ.)

APPEAL by the defendants, The International Paper Company and another, from a judgment of the Supreme Court in favor of the plaintiffs, entered in the office of the clerk of the county of Hamilton on the 28th day of September, 1901, upon the decision of the court rendered after a trial at the Fulton Trial Term before the court without a jury, holding that certain taxes had been paid and that plaintiffs were owners of two-thirds of 1,128 acres of land in the northwesterly corner of township 4, Totten and Crossfield's purchase, in Hamilton county, and William McEchron, one of the defendants, had no interest therein.

Griffin & Ostrander, for the appellants.

Homer Weston and *Waldo Weston,* for the respondents.

KELLOGG, J. :

This case has been twice tried. The testimony on the second trial does not in any material respect differ from the testimony presented to this court on review of the first trial. We then held that the books in evidence from the office of the State Comptroller (and the same books were in evidence on the second trial) showed conclusively a tax assessed for the year 1862 upon the land in question included in a larger unallotted tract; that such tax was called the "H. H. & L. Road" tax, and was a proper lien upon the premises claimed by plaintiff in this action. No one testifies to having paid this tax or to having seen it paid. No receipt for this tax was offered in evidence from the Comptroller's office. We must, therefore, conclude that the tax was not paid before the sale of 1871, and, therefore, the Comptroller had jurisdiction with power to enforce payment. Whatever there may be in the testimony from which any inference can be drawn that the Comptroller at any time before the sale declared to plaintiffs or their predecessors in title that there was no unpaid tax for the year 1862 on these lands could at most only make the sale voidable. The fact remains that there was an unpaid tax and the sale was not void. If for the inferences suggested the sale was voidable, this infirmity could be only available to the plaintiffs by the assertion of their rights to set the sale aside within the time fixed by the Laws of 1896 (Chap. 908, § 132). They failed to do this, and it is too late to make the defense available in this action.

The judgment is reversed, a new trial granted, with costs to the appellant to abide the event.

FURSMAN, J., concurred; PARKER, P. J., SMITH and CHASE, JJ., concurred in result.

CHASE, J. (concurring):

Whether or not the Hamilton, Herkimer and Lewis road tax for 1862 on that part of township 4 lying in the town of Morehouse has been actually paid to the State, the evidence on the last trial, in my opinion, discloses a state of facts which brings this case within the rule laid down in *People ex rel. Cooper* v. *Registrar of Arrears* (114 N. Y. 19). Were it not for the provisions of section 132 of chapter 908 of the Laws of 1896 relating to the effect of the Comptroller's deed, I would, for the reason stated, be in favor of affirming the judgment to the extent of the lands in the town of Morehouse in the plaintiff's deed described. It is very doubtful whether the land described in the tax deed of December 22, 1845, is identical with the land described in the tax deed of December 29, 1886. With these suggestions, I concur in the result on the ground that the Court of Appeals in *Meigs* v. *Roberts* (162 N. Y. 371) has practically held that the said act of 1896 is a Statute of Limitations and that as such it applies to a case like the one now under consideration, not alone for the reason stated by Justice KELLOGG, but generally against the plaintiff.

PARKER, P. J., and SMITH, J., concurred.

Judgment reversed on law and facts and new trial granted, with costs to appellant to abide event.

ISRAEL P. GRANT, Respondent, *v.* ALICE P. SMITH, as Sole Executrix, etc., of LEWIS M. SMITH, Deceased, Appellant, Impleaded with ALICE P. SMITH, Individually, and Others.

Partnership accounting — when the partners are, and when they are not, entitled to interest on money advanced to the firm.

Where the shares of the several members of a copartnership in the partnership profits depend upon the amount of capital furnished by them, respectively, interest should not, upon an accounting between the partners, be allowed on money furnished by the several partners as part of the original capital or as an addition thereto, but when the amount to be furnished by each partner is fixed and certain and the share of each of the respective partners in the partnership profits is a fixed proportion thereof, advances by one of the partners, in excess of his prescribed proportion, although credited to the special account of such partner and called capital of the firm, are, as between the partners, loans and advancements for the benefit of the partnership and interest should be allowed thereon.

APPEAL by the defendant, Alice P. Smith, as sole executrix, etc., of Lewis M. Smith, deceased, from portions of a judgment of the Supreme Court in favor of the plaintiff, entered in the office of the clerk of the county of Chemung on the 27th day of May, 1901, upon the report of a referee in an action for an accounting.

A. C. Eustace and *J. P. Eustace,* for the appellant.

H. H. Rockwell, for the respondent.

CHASE, J. :

This is an action for an accounting. The plaintiff and the defendant's intestate were partners. Their respective interests in the partnership and the amount that each was to contribute to the capital of the firm was fixed and certain. The only question arising on this appeal relates to the allowance to the plaintiff of interest on the amounts advanced, paid out and expended by him for the benefit of the partnership in excess of the amount required by the partnership agreement.

The rule in regard to the allowance of interest on an accounting between partners has been recently stated by the Court of Appeals in the case of *Rodgers* v. *Clement* (162 N. Y. 422). In that case the court say : " If the moneys advanced by the plaintiff to the firm were contributions of capital or additions to plaintiff's capital, then he was not entitled to interest on the same since he must rely upon the profits of the business to compensate him for the investment unless there was a special agreement between the partners that interest should be allowed. * * *

" But, on the other hand, if the moneys so paid or advanced by the plaintiff for the use of the firm were in fact loans, and the plaintiff as to such advances was a creditor of the firm, he stands upon the same footing as any other creditor with respect to the right to be allowed interest upon the accounting. A partner may loan money to the firm of which he is a member, and when he does his right to interest is to be determined in the same way as that of any other creditor. In such cases the general rule is to allow interest upon the advances, although there was no express agreement by the firm to pay it, in the absence of some agreement to the contrary, express or implied. The right to interest, or an agreement to pay or allow it, is to be implied in such cases without any express promise as in like transactions between parties holding no partnership relations to each other."

Where the share of the several partners in a partnership venture depends upon the capital furnished by them, respectively, it is very clear that interest should not be allowed on moneys furnished to the partnership as capital, either under the original agreement or as additions thereto, but when the amount to be furnished by each partner is fixed and certain, and the share of each of the respective partners in the profits of the partnership venture is a fixed proportion thereof, advances by one of the partners in excess of his prescribed proportion, although credited to the special account of such partner and called capital of the firm, are in fact, as between the partners, loans and advancements for the benefit of the partnership, and equity requires that interest should be allowed thereon. We see no reason for interfering with the findings of the referee herein, and such findings are sufficient to sustain the judgment. Judgment should be affirmed, with costs.

All concurred.

Judgment unanimously affirmed, with costs.

WILLIAM J. FAITH, as Administrator, etc., of WILLIAM J. FAITH, JR., Deceased, Respondent, *v.* THE ULSTER AND DELAWARE RAILROAD COMPANY, Appellant.

WILLIAM J. FAITH, Respondent, *v.* THE ULSTER AND DELAWARE RAILROAD COMPANY, Appellant.

WILLIAM J. FAITH, as Administrator, etc., of MARGARET WATSON FAITH, Deceased, Respondent, *v.* THE ULSTER AND DELAWARE RAILROAD COMPANY, Appellant.

Deposition not certified to have been read to the witness nor filed within ten days — suppressed unless so certified and unless an order to file it nunc pro tunc *be obtained.*

Where on an appeal from an order denying a motion to suppress the deposition of a witness, it appeared that the referee who took the deposition failed to certify that it was read over to the witness and subscribed by her, and that the report of the referee and the original minutes of the examination were not filed in the office of the clerk of the county in which the action was brought within ten days after the deposition was taken, both of which are required by the statute, the Appellate Division considered that the deposition should be suppressed unless the respondents obtained a certificate from the referee, before whom the deposition was taken, showing that after it was completed it was carefully read to, and subscribed by, the witness, and also obtained an order from the Special Term allowing the certificate and the deposition to be filed with the clerk of the county in which the action was brought *nunc pro tunc* as of a date within ten days of the day on which the deposition was taken, and should actually so file such certificate and deposition.

APPEAL by the defendant, The Ulster and Delaware Railroad Company, in each of the above-entitled actions, from an order of the Supreme Court, made at the Rensselaer Special Term and entered in the office of the clerk of the county of Ulster on the 7th day of January, 1902, denying a motion made by the defendant to suppress and set aside the deposition and examination of Margaret Watson Faith.

Lewis E. Carr and *Amos Van Etten,* for the appellant.

Sumner B. Stiles, Francis L. Wellman and *C. Sheldon Carothers,* for the respondent.

CHASE, J.:

On the 6th day of October, 1900, a collision occurred between the engine of a passenger train on the defendant's road and a wagon drawn by one horse, by which the driver of the horse and one William J. Faith, Jr., were killed, and one Margaret Watson Faith was injured. Thereafter William J. Faith, as administrator of William J. Faith, Jr., his son, brought an action against the defendant to recover damages for the death of said William J. Faith, Jr., and alleged that said death was wholly caused by the negligence of the defendant. William J. Faith individually brought an action against the defendant to recover for loss of services of Margaret Watson Faith, his wife, and for medical attendance and services in the care of his said wife. Margaret Watson Faith also brought an action against the defendant to recover damages for her injuries. Issue was joined in each of these actions, the place of trial being Ulster county. On the 26th day of March, 1901, an order was obtained entitled in the three actions for the examination of said Margaret Watson Faith. Such examination was had in New York city before a referee on the 27th day of March, 1901, as provided by said order. On the 29th day of March, 1901, said Margaret Watson Faith died. The action brought by Margaret Watson Faith has abated. Since the death of Margaret Watson .Faith said William J. Faith, as her administrator, has brought another action against the defendant to recover damages for her death. On the 29th day of March, 1901, another order was made in regard to using the deposition of Margaret Watson Faith in an action thereafter brought by the husband. It will be sufficient to determine in regard to the effect of that order when an action contemplated by such order is commenced. The report of the referee and the original minutes of. the examination of Margaret Watson Faith were filed in the clerk's office of the county of New York on the 2d day of April, 1901. On the 15th day of April, 1901, plaintiffs, by an order of the court, removed said report and minutes from the files in New York county, but they were not filed with the clerk of Ulster county until May 25, 1901. On the 7th day of December, 1901, the defendant moved at Special Term to suppress and set aside said deposition. Such motion was made on affidavits and also on all the papers and proceedings in the actions. The defendant urged various grounds for suppressing and setting aside the deposition, but the motion was denied, and from the order denying the motion this appeal is taken. It does not appear that the deposition was read to the person examined before it was subscribed by her, and it was not filed in the office of the clerk of Ulster county until about two months after it was taken and subscribed. The statutory provision (Code Civ. Proc. § 880) in regard to reading a deposition to the person examined after the same is completed, and also in regard to filing the same within ten days, cannot be disregarded. Depositions are taken apart from the court and jury before whom the same are to be used, and by whom the evidence contained therein is to be weighed. Great care should be exercised in taking the evidence, and every reasonable precaution should be taken to see that the person examined fully understands and appreciates the deposition before the same is subscribed. The serious illness and extreme weakness of the person examined in this case emphasizes the necessity of holding that the language of the statute in regard to the manner of taking and certifying a deposition is mandatory. When a deposition has been taken it may be used by either party. Each party, therefore, has an interest in having it filed in the proper clerk's office. Delay in filing a deposition subjects it to additional danger of being altered, mutilated or destroyed. If a deposition can be retained by one party for nearly two months after it has been taken, it might result in seriously interfering with the conduct of the case, or perhaps wholly prevent its use as evidence on the trial. The plaintiffs assert that the deposition was read to the person examined before it was subscribed by her, and that a certificate can be obtained showing compliance with the statute, and that they can satisfactorily explain the failure to have the referee make the required certificate, and also the failure to file the deposition as also required by the statute.

Whether the plaintiffs can explain the failure to comply with the statute sufficiently to obtain an order to file a new certificate and the deposition as signed *nunc pro tunc*, must be left to be determined by the court at Special Term.

All concurred, except FURSMAN, J., not sitting.

Order reversed, with ten dollars costs and disbursements. The motion to suppress and set aside the deposition granted, with ten dollars costs, unless the plaintiffs, within thirty days from the entry and service of this order, obtain a certificate from the referee before whom the deposition was taken showing that the same when completed was carefully read to and subscribed by the person examined, and also obtain and enter an order from the Special Term upon notice allowing such certificate, and the deposition as filed to be filed with the clerk of Ulster county *nunc pro tunc*, and as of a day within ten days after March 27, 1901, and actually so file such certificate and deposition. This order shall not be construed as in any way interfering with the discretion of the Special Term in any question presented on the application for relief herein.

CHARLES H. TURNER, Respondent, *v.* THOMAS S. WALKER, Appellant.

Venue — of an action by a vendor to compel a vendee to specifically perform a contract to buy land.

An action brought to compel the vendee in a land contract to accept the title tendered by the vendor and to pay the contract price therefor, is an action brought " to procure a judgment establishing, determining, defining, forfeiting, annulling, or otherwise affecting an estate, right, title, lien or other interest in real property," within the meaning of section 982 of the Code of Civil Procedure, which provides that such an action shall be brought in the county where the land is situated.

APPEAL by the defendant, Thomas S. Walker, from an order of the Supreme Court, made at the Montgomery Special Term and entered in the office of the clerk of the county of Franklin on the 8th day of July, 1901, denying the defendant's motion to change the place of trial of the action from the county of Franklin to the county of Hamilton.

The complaint avers that a written contract for the sale and purchase of land in Hamilton county, describing it, was entered into between the parties at the agreed price of ten dollars ($10) per acre, the total amount of the purchase to be ascertained by a survey of the land and a determination thereby of the number of acres covered by the contract; that such survey was made, the number of acres found to be 2,481 and 72-100, and the whole amount of the purchase price thereby fixed at twenty-four thousand eight hundred and seventeen dollars and twenty cents ($24,817.20); that the plaintiff executed a good and sufficient deed of this land and tendered the same to the defendant; that defendant refused to accept it and refused to pay the purchase price. The complaint, thereupon, prays for a judgment requiring the defendant to perform the agreement, and pay the purchase price to the plaintiff.

The answer denies, among other things, the making of the contract, and sets up various other matters by way of defense. With the answer the defendant served a demand that the place of trial be changed from Franklin to Hamilton county. This demand being disregarded, the defendant moved upon the pleadings and upon an affidavit showing service of the demand for an order changing the place of trial to Hamilton county upon the ground that the action related to lands situate in that county and is, therefore, local in character. The motion was denied at Special Term, and from the order denying it this appeal is taken.

A. Walker Otis, for the appellant.

Frederick G. Paddock, for the respondent.

FURSMAN, J.:

Section 982 of the Code of Civil Procedure provides that certain actions "must be tried in the county in which the subject of the action, or some part thereof, is situated." Enumerated among these are actions "to procure a judgment establishing, determining, defining, forfeiting, annulling, or otherwise affecting an estate, right, title, lien, or other interest in real property." The scope and object of this action is to compel the defendant to accept a deed of land and to pay the alleged agreed price therefor. It is not an action for damages for a breach of contract, but to enforce performance of a contract relating to lands, to compel the acceptance of a title to lands. It is in no sense an action for damages. It is simply an action to compel a specific performance of a contract relating to the sale and transfer of title to real property. If the action had been brought by the defendant against the plaintiff to compel the execution and delivery of a deed there can, of course, be no doubt that the action would be local, because section 982 expressly declares that such an action must be brought in the county where the subject-matter of the action is situated. In what way does such an action differ from one to compel the acceptance of a deed? We think the subsequent clause of the section above quoted was intended to embrace actions of this character, and, indeed, all actions affecting the transfer of title to real property not therein before enumerated.

The action, as above indicated, is not alone to recover the purchase price, certainly not to recover damages for a breach of contract, but to compel the defendant to take title to the land described in the complaint, as well as to pay the purchase price therefor.

We think, therefore, that the action is governed by section 982 and must be tried in Hamilton county, or according to the provisions of the Code in Fulton county, Fulton and Hamilton counties being regarded as one. (Code, § 232.)

The order must be reversed, with ten dollars costs and disbursements, and the motion granted.

All concurred.

Order reversed, with ten dollars costs and disbursements, and motion granted, with ten dollars costs to appellant to abide event.

THE PEOPLE OF THE STATE OF NEW YORK, Respondent, *v.* MARY JOHNSON, Appellant.

Circumstantial evidence of the crime of arson — to justify a conviction it must be inconsistent with innocence.

To justify a conviction upon circumstantial evidence the circumstances must not only point to guilt, but must also be absolutely inconsistent with innocence, that is, the inference of guilt must be the only one that can reasonably be drawn from the facts.

What circumstances, adduced on the trial of an indictment charging the defendant with burning her dwelling house for the purpose of obtaining the insurance thereon, are insufficient to sustain a conviction, considered.

SMITH, J., dissented.

APPEAL by the defendant, Mary Johnson, from a judgment of the County Court of Tioga county in favor of the plaintiff, entered in the office of the clerk of the county of Tioga on the 10th day of December, 1901, upon the verdict of a jury convicting her of the crime of arson in the second degree, and also from an order entered in said clerk's office on the 10th day of December, 1901, denying the defendant's motion for a new trial made upon the minutes.

Martin S. Lynch, for the appellant.

Oscar B. Glezen, for the respondent.

FURSMAN, J.:

The indictment charges that on July 4, 1900, at Newark Valley in the county of Tioga the defendant willfully and feloniously set fire to and burned in the night time a dwelling house then owned and occupied by her, in which at the time there was no human being except herself, and that Radford aided and abetted the commission thereof by procuring certain policies of insurance to be issued upon the dwelling house, and by directly and indirectly counseling, etc., the defendant to commit the same.   Stated in full, the proof made by the prosecution at the trial is this: The defendant had lived with Radford at a boarding house in Buffalo as his wife; in December, 1898, one Curry transferred to the defendant, then known as Ellen Grey, some real estate and furniture in Buffalo, and afterwards Curry sold it to Radford.   The defendant purchased the house in Newark Valley in February, 1900, for which she paid in money and property about four thousand dollars ($4,000); she bought it through Radford from Meyers; the conveyance to her was expressly subject to two mortgages, one for two thousand dollars ($2,000) and the other for four thousand dollars ($4,000), thus making the entire purchase price about ten thousand dollars ($10,000).   On the 11th day of June, 1900, she procured a policy of insurance on the house for three thousand dollars ($3,000), payable to the German Bank of Buffalo, the then holder of one of the mortgages, and July 19, 1899, a policy of insurance for "not exceeding three thousand dollars" ($3,000), loss payable to Radford as second mortgagee (this policy was for one year, and was on the 5th of May, 1900, assigned by Radford).   The house burned was the best in Newark Valley, and although it cost about sixteen thousand dollars ($16,000) to build and was in excellent repair, owing to the fact that there was no market for such property in Newark Valley it was, in the opinion of some witnesses, worth no more than four thousand dollars ($4,000). After the purchase the defendant received and placed in it three consignments of second-hand furniture, including an organ and a number of pictures, and also a quantity of drugs in boxes.

Among the furniture was that bought from Curry, and the whole was sufficient to properly furnish a house of this character. One witness for the prosecution (Pierson) testified that he helped carry about one-half a carload of furniture into the house and that it was new. After the arrival of the furniture, and on the 11th day of June, 1900, the defendant procured a policy of insurance for one thousand dollars ($1,000) covering household furniture, jewelry, wearing apparel, pictures and many other things, and on the sixteenth day of June another policy covering the same property for one thousand five hundred dollars ($1,500). All the property specified in the proofs of loss was in the house when it burned. Made a compulsory witness before a sheriff's jury, the defendant testified that she had never lived under any other name than Mary Johnson. She testified that she first discovered the fire in the kitchen, and the prosecution gave evidence that the fire was not in the kitchen but in the elevator, or a room off the kitchen. She testified that on discovering the fire she ran to the "fire hall," a few rods distant, screaming, and concerning this the prosecution gave evidence that the first alarm was given by a man named Halliday. The prosecution also gave evidence that after the fire had been burning a considerable time something dropped down the elevator shaft which water did not extinguish, though the chemical engine did. This constituted the evidence of the prosecution. It is a settled principle of criminal law that to justify a conviction upon circumstantial evidence, the circumstances must not only point to guilt, but must also be absolutely inconsistent with innocence. The inference of guilt must be the only one that can reasonably be drawn from the facts. (*Poole* v. *People*, 80 N. Y. 645; *People* v. *Harris*, 136 id. 423.) Analyzed, and applied to the inquiry whether there was sufficient proof to justify this conviction the evidence is this: The defendant's true name is Mary Johnson; she falsely stated before the sheriff's jury that she had never been known by any other name. This was wholly immaterial upon the question of her guilt, and is easily accounted for upon grounds quite consistent with innocence. She bought the property in Newark Valley and paid a fair price for it. She had it insured as collateral to two mortgages already existing upon it, one of which was held by Radford with whom she had lived as his wife, but Radford had parted with his policy before the fire, and had, therefore, no interest in the destruction of the property. She moved into it a quantity of furniture sufficient to furnish it throughout, and insured this for two thousand five hundred dollars ($2,500), but this furniture was, concededly, all in the house at the time of the fire, and there is no proof worthy of the name that it was not fully worth the amount for which it was insured. She asserted that she discovered the fire in the kitchen, when in fact it was in a small room or shaft adjoining the kitchen, a mistake easily made in the hurry and excitement of the moment. She stated that she gave an immediate and first alarm, whereas others thought it was given by a man named Halliday. After the fire was well under way something on fire dropped down the elevator shaft which was not easily extinguished, but there were two packages of drugs in the house, the nature of which is unknown which may have caused this. On this proof was the defendant justly convicted? We think not. There was barely enough to excite suspicion, but by no means enough to establish beyond a reasonable doubt that the fire was of incendiary origin, or to overcome the presumption of innocence with which the law clothes the accused. Every material circumstance proved is as consistent with innocence as with guilt, and taken as a whole falls far short of proving that this was an incendiary fire. There was nothing to be gained by it to either Radford or the defendant. It seems to us that she was accused, tried and convicted upon a mere suspicion that because she had led to some extent an immoral life, and had sustained at one time improper relations with Radford she must be guilty of the crime charged. But the law requires that the evidence of guilt in a criminal case shall be clear and decisive, leaving no reasonable doubt in the mind, *first*, that a crime had been committed, and, *second*, that the accused committed it. It will not do to convict upon a mere possibility. The proof must be convincing, and unexplainable upon any theory consistent with innocence. We do not think that such was the case here, and, therefore, conclude that the judgment of conviction must be reversed and the defendant discharged.

All concurred, except SMITH, J., dissenting; PARKER, P. J., not voting.

Judgment of conviction reversed and defendant discharged.

JOHN DE WITT PELTZ, as Trustee under the Last Will and Testament of BILLINGS P. LEARNED, Deceased, Plaintiff, *v.* HARRIET W. LEARNED and Others, Defendants.

Trust estate — assessments for sewers and pavements made during a life estate, charged against the principal of the trust fund.

A testator devised certain city real estate to a trustee in trust to receive the income thereof and pay the same over to his daughter during her life, the will providing that at the death of the daughter, the trustee should convey the property to such persons as the daughter might appoint by her last will and testament, and that in the event of her failure to exercise the power of appointment the property should pass to her issue then living. During the continuance of the trust the city constructed sewers and vitrified brick pavements along the streets upon which the various parcels of real estate were situated and levied assessments to defray the expense thereof upon such real estate. The testator's daughter was then forty-four years old and unmarried,

Held, that the sewers and pavements were permanent improvements and that, in view of the peculiar provisions of the will and of the fact that there was no remainderman in existence, the entire amount of the assessments should be charged against the principal of the trust estate.

SUBMISSION of a controversy upon an agreed statement of facts pursuant to section 1279 of the Code of Civil Procedure.

Martin T. Nachtmann, for the plaintiff.

Learned Hand, for the defendant Harriet W. Learned.

William L. Learned, for the defendants Lydia L. Hand and others.

FURSMAN, J.:

In and by his last will Billings P. Learned gave, devised and bequeathed to Leonard G. Hun in trust certain real estate situate in the city of Albany to receive the income, rents, issues and profits thereof and pay the same over to his daughter Harriet during her life. By the terms of the will the trust is to cease at her death, and thereupon the trustee is to convey and assign the property to such person or persons as she may by her last will appoint, and in case she fails to exercise this power of appointment the same is to go to her issue then living. It appears from the statement submitted that under the 3d subdivision of the residuary clause of the will there has come into the hands of the trustee certain personal property which is held by him upon the same trust as the real estate above mentioned. John De Witt Peltz has been substituted as trustee in the place of Hun. Harriet is forty-four years old and unmarried. The city of Albany has constructed certain sewers and put down certain vitrified brick pavements along the streets upon which the various parcels of real estate are situated, and, as authorized and empowered by law to do, has levied assessments for the expense thereof upon such real estate. Under the charter some of these assessments may be paid in installments, interest being chargeable on the deferred payments, and that course has been pursued by the trustee. On these facts we are asked to determine whether these assessments should be paid out of the principal of the trust estate or out of the income derived therefrom, and whether an apportionment should be had between the principal and income.

We think the sewers and pavements must be considered to be permanent improvements. The law which authorizes the cost of their construction to be assessed upon the property " intended to be benefited " (see § 29, tit. 9, chap. 298 of 1883) proceeds upon the assumption that it is thereby made of greater permanent value. While it is true that sewers and pavements will wear out with time and use the same is equally true of almost all material structures, and it seems to be the rule now that new structures added to the land which are of a beneficial character are to be regarded as permanent improvements. As between the owner and the city the land is primarily liable for the assessments, since such assessments are made liens thereon, and the land may be sold to pay them, but as between the life tenant, who has the present beneficial estate, and the remainderman, to whom the land is to ultimately come, equity will sometimes apportion the cost of such improvements as are here involved. (*Thomas* v. *Evans*, 105 N. Y. 611.) In *Peck* v. *Sherwood* .(56 id. 615) there was a municipal assessment for flagging a sidewalk, and the court held that the cost should be apportioned between the life tenant and remainderman, and in *Stilwell* v. *Doughty* (2 Bradf. 311) a like apportionment of the cost of a sewer was upheld. There is, however, no fixed rule. Each case must depend on its own circumstances. (*Chamberlin* v. *Gleason*, 163 N. Y. 218, 219.) In the present case, however, there is no remainderman in existence. Harriet has the whole income during her life, and may dispose of the body of the estate by will, for this is the effect of the direction to the trustee contained in the will of Billings Learned to convey the property at her death to such person as she may by her will appoint. Failing this, it is to go to her children. Failing both, it is undisposed of by the will. It was apparently given to the trustee for her use and benefit. It may be assumed, also, that he fully understood that in the city of Albany sewers and street improvements were likely to be constructed, and that the law charged the expense of this construction against the real estate benefited. I think, therefore, that it may be justly concluded that his intention was that the body of the estate should bear these expenses, so that her income should not be lessened, except as it must necessarily be lessened by diminishing the source from which it is derived. The suggestion that this must reduce in value the property that is ultimately to go to whoever may be entitled is met by the legal presumption that the real estate is bettered to the extent of the cost of the improvement assessed against it. It seems to me that the question is of little practical importance in this case. Whether the whole cost of these improvements is cast upon the principal, or apportioned between the principal and income, the life tenant must suffer a loss, because in the one case the source of her income is diminished to the full extent of the cost, and in the other both the source of the income and the income itself is lessened. It is altogether uncertain to whom the principal will go in the end, and, under the peculiar circumstances of this case, I am inclined to the opinion that the intent of the testator will be effectuated and substantial justice accomplished by charging the whole sum against the principal.

All concurred.

Judgment ordered in conformity with the opinion handed down.

JOHN ERDMAN, Respondent, *v.* GEORGE UPHAM, Appellant.

Action for the maintenance of a third person, with whom the defendant had made a contract for his support — the contract cannot be enforced by one not a party to it — exclusion of a deed whose contents are not shown — appeal from a justice's judgment — the return, not the preliminary statement in the "case," prevails.

The complaint in an action brought in a Justice's Court alleged that in 1898 the defendant "made a written contract with Philip Erdman," by which the defendant agreed to maintain and support Philip during his life "for the consideration of some property of the value of about $1,200, which the defendant became the owner of by deed of Philip Erdman then and there;" that between August 1, 1899, and May 1, 1900, the plaintiff maintained and supported Philip with the knowledge and consent of the defendant, and that such support and maintenance was worth the sum of $180. The answer admitted the execution of the deed referred to in the complaint and denied each and every other allegation thereof.

Upon the trial the plaintiff offered in evidence a "deed of property from Philip Erdman to George Upham" (the defendant), but made no statement as to the character of its contents. The court excluded the deed upon the objection of the defendant, and no other evidence being offered by the plaintiff the justice entered a nonsuit against him.

Held, that, in the absence of any information as to the contents of the deed offered in evidence, it could not be said that the justice erred in excluding it;

That, if the contract set forth in the complaint had actually been made, the plaintiff being neither a party nor a privy thereto could not maintain an action upon it; .

That, in the absence of any proof or offer to prove that the plaintiff had furnished support to Philip Erdman upon the consent of the defendant, the justice properly granted the nonsuit.

On an appeal from a judgment rendered by a justice of the peace, the date of the rendition and entry of the judgment will be determined by the return of the justice and not by the statement placed at the beginning of the printed case.

PARKER, P. J., and CHASE, J., dissented.

APPEAL by the defendant, George Upham, from a judgment of the County Court of Sullivan county in favor of the plaintiff, entered in the office of the clerk of the county of Sullivan on the 25th day of March, 1901, upon the decision of the court reversing, upon appeal, a judgment in favor of the defendant rendered by a justice of the peace.

J. M. Maybee, for the appellant.

Charles H. Stage, for the respondent.

FURSMAN, J. :

The complaint avers that in 1898 the defendant " made a written contract with Philip Erdman " by which the defendant agreed to maintain and support Philip during his life " for the consideration of some property of the value of about $1,200, which the defendant became the owner of by deed of Philip Erdman then and there ; " that between August 1, 1899, and May 1, 1900, the plaintiff maintained and supported Philip with the knowledge and consent of the defendant, and that such support and maintenance was worth the sum of $130.

The answer admits the execution of the deed· referred to in the complaint, and denies each and every other allegation thereof.

On the trial the plaintiff offered in evidence a " deed of property from Philip Erdman to George Upham " (defendant) which was objected to on the " ground that plaintiff is not a party to the transaction and cannot maintain an action on any promise or any agreement contained therein." This objection was sustained. No other evidence was offered by the plaintiff, and the justice thereupon entered a nonsuit against him. Assuming that the complaint states a cause of action, none was proved or attempted to be proved. The complaint sets forth two papers, a contract and a deed. A deed was offered in evidence, which may or may not have contained a contract. The record is silent as to its character and contents. No statement was made in connection with the proposed evidence as to its tendency or effect, or tending to show that it would be made material by subsequent proof. If there was such a contract as set forth in the complaint the plaintiff was not a party, nor privy to it, and the rule of law is that one who is neither a party to a contract, nor a privy to it, cannot maintain an action upon it. (*Simson* v. *Brown,* 68 N. Y. 355.) " A mere stranger cannot intervene and claim by action the benefit of a contract between other parties. There must be either a new consideration or some prior right or claim against one of the contracting parties by which he has a legal interest in the performance of the agreement." (*Vrooman* v. *Turner,* 69 N. Y. 280.) The admission that " there is such deed and contract as offered in evidence" is no more than an admission of the execution of the paper. Without any information as to the contents of the paper offered we cannot say that the ruling of the justice was not correct. In the absence of any proof or offer to prove that the plaintiff had furnished support to Philip upon the consent of the defendant, it certainly was correct under the authorities above cited. No other evidence being offered, the justice was right in granting the nonsuit.

It is suggested that the trial was had and the nonsuit granted on the seventh of December and the judgment entered on the ninth, and that this was not in compliance with section 3015 of the Code of Civil Procedure. It is true that in the formal statement at folio 1 of the printed case it is said that the judgment of the justice was rendered December ninth, and the return states that the trial was had December seventh, but the return also states that it contains "all the proceedings" had in the action, "including the evidence and the judgment entered therein," and there is nothing whatever to indicate that the judgment was not rendered and entered immediately upon the granting of the nonsuit. Indeed, on the face of the return it appears that it was rendered and entered immediately. Are we to take the formal statement (which may be a misprint as to the date of the judgment) or the justice's return as our guide? I think the latter, for that is the only official record of the actual fact. I suggest that the date in the formal statement may be a misprint of ninth for seventh, not only because the return indicates that judgment was rendered immediately upon the nonsuit being granted, but because the notice of appeal to the County Court is from a judgment rendered on the nineteenth of December, undoubtedly a misprint. It is sufficient, however, that the return of the justice, which is an official statement required by law upon an appeal being taken to the County Court, furnishes the only proper evidence to the appellate court of the date of the rendition and entry of the judgment. It has been held, moreover, by the Appellate Division of the fourth department that where a judgment of a justice is entered within a reasonable time after the event upon which it depends occurs, although not on the same day, the statute is complied with. (*Sweet* v. *Marvin*, 2 App. Div. 1.) It may be noted that the printed case does not show that any formal judgment for costs was ever entered by the justice from which an appeal could be taken, nor any judgment except the mere statement in the return "Motion for request granted. Judgment rendered for defendant and against plaintiff as above, with the costs of the action."

The judgment of the County Court must be reversed, with costs, and that of the justice affirmed.

All concurred, except PARKER, P. J., and CHASE, J., dissenting.

Judgment of the County Court reversed, with costs, and judgment of the Justice's Court affirmed.

RICHARD SMITH, Respondent, *v.* CHARLES N. MORSE, Appellant.

Contract sale of a wood lot accompanied with authority to cut the wood — surrender of the contract to the vendor while a licensee of the vendee is cutting the wood — liability of such licensee for wood cut before and after notice to stop cutting.

The vendor in a contract for the sale of a wood lot authorized the vendees to cut and sell the timber growing upon the lot. Thereafter the vendees sold to one Smith the timber growing upon a portion of the lot to be thereafter cut by him. Subsequently the vendees surrendered their contract to the vendor, and the latter, who knew that Smith was cutting timber upon the lot and had made no previous objection thereto, notified him to stop cutting. Smith continued cutting for a few days thereafter, and the vendor thereupon brought an action of trespass against him for the cutting done by him both before and after the vendor had notified him to stop.

The jury awarded a verdict of $200 to the plaintiff, and judgment was entered thereon for treble that amount.

Held, that, assuming that the license given by the vendor to the vendees was personal to the latter, the vendees might while it remained unrevoked employ the defendant to do the acts which they were authorized to do, and that consequently the defendant was not a trespasser up to the time when he received notice to quit;

That it was error for the court to allow the plaintiff to prove the value of the timber cut by the defendant before being notified to stop, and at the same time to refuse to allow the defendant to show that he acted in good faith under a claim of right and with the knowledge and consent of the plaintiff;

That, as it was impossible to tell whether the verdict was based upon the cutting done before or that done after the defendant received notice to stop, the judgment entered upon the verdict for three times its amount should be reversed.

APPEAL by the defendant, Charles N. Morse, from a judgment of the County Court of Ulster county in favor of the plaintiff, entered in the office of the clerk of the county of Ulster on the 15th day of May, 1900, upon the verdict of a jury, and also from an order entered in said clerk's office on the 5th day of May, 1900, denying the defendant's motion for a new trial made upon the minutes, and also from that portion of an order bearing date the 4th day of June, 1900, and entered in said clerk's office, allowing to plaintiff treble damages, *nunc pro tunc.*

In December, 1895, the plaintiff entered into a contract in writing with McKnight and Rosecrans by which he agreed to sell and convey to them a wood lot of about 200 acres, for which they were to pay $1,200, $600 to one Cantine who held a mortgage to that amount upon the premises, and the remainder in various prescribed installments. McKnight and Rosecrans were without means, and it was understood between them and the plaintiff that they were to cut off and sell the timber growing on the lot and with the money obtained therefrom make the payments required by the contract. McKnight and Rosecrans entered into possession and began cutting the timber. Of this the plaintiff had full knowledge and even assisted them in the work. On the 11th day of April, 1896, McKnight and Rosecrans sold to the defendant the timber growing on a portion of the lot, to be thereafter cut by him, and also a quantity of timber already cut by them and lying on the lot. Under this arrangement the defendant began cutting timber. The plaintiff knew that the defendant was cutting timber and made no objection.

In January, 1897, McKnight and Rosecrans, although they had kept the terms of their agreement with the plaintiff, surrendered their contract with him, and thereupon the plaintiff forbade the defendant to continue cutting. The defendant did, however, continue for a few days, and for this cutting and for all the cutting by defendant under his agreement with McKnight and Rosecrans this action is brought. The complaint alleges trespasses committed by defendant on various days from April 15, 1896, and particularly on certain named days from the eighth to the sixteenth of February, inclusive, and asks treble damages. The jury awarded two hundred dollars ($200) damages to plaintiff, and judgment was thereupon directed for six hundred dollars ($600) and entered accordingly.

Howard Chipp and *John R. De Vany,* for the appellant.

John E. Van Etten, for the respondent.

FURSMAN, J. :

Although the contract between the plaintiff and McKnight and Rosecrans did not in terms authorize them to cut and sell the timber growing on the lot therein described, the evidence clearly established that the very intent and object of the agreement was that they should cut and sell the timber and out of the proceeds pay the plaintiff the contract price. In furtherance of this object they immediately began to cut and sell the timber with the full knowledge and consent of the plaintiff. In doing this they were not in any sense trespassers, but were cutting under a license from plaintiff. Assuming that this license was personal to them, they might, while it remained unrevoked, employ defendant to do the acts which they were thus authorized to do, so that, until the surrender by them of the original contract on the 31st of January, 1897, and the subsequent notice to defendant, he was clearly acting within his right and was not in any sense a trespasser.

On the trial the plaintiff was permitted to prove the value of timber cut by defendant, not only after the surrender and notice, but also that cut by him while acting under the original contract between plaintiff and McKnight and Rosecrans, and under the proof thus made it is impossible to determine what injury the plaintiff suffered by reason of the acts of defendant committed after his relation to the parties had been thus changed. Moreover, the learned trial court excluded all evidence offered by defendant tending to show that he acted in good faith, under a claim of right, and with the knowledge and consent of the plaintiff. This, we think, was error, for had he been allowed to prove that the plaintiff at the time of the surrender agreed that he might continue cutting under his agreement with them, he would thereby have become a licensee of the plaintiff to that end, and no action could have been maintained against him for any thing done by him while such license remained unrevoked. The jury were charged by the trial court that they were to determine whether the defendant acted in the belief that he owned the property, and were assured that if he believed he had a right to do this he could not be held for treble damages. No finding was made touching this question, but a general verdict of two hundred dollars ($200) was returned. As above suggested, it is impossible to determine from the evidence whether this verdict was based upon the acts of defendant after the license to cut had been revoked, or included also the cutting during the time the defendant was a licensee for that purpose, but the court nevertheless trebled the damages found by the jury and directed a judgment for six hundred dollars ($600).

This also, we think, was error. For these reasons the judgment must be reversed and a new trial ordered, with costs to the appellant to abide the event.

All concurred; PARKER, P. J., in result.

Judgment and order reversed and new trial granted, with costs to appellant to abide event.

In the Matter of the Real Estate of CHARLES J. WOOD, Deceased.

HARRY C. WOOD, Respondent; MARY Q. POLHAMUS and JAMES F. POLHAMUS, Appellants.

Surrogate's decree directing a sale of a decedent's estate for the payment of debts — it is proper, notwithstanding a devise charging the property with the decedent's debts or a power of sale therefor — an infant is bound by a decree the same as an adult.

A decree directing the sale of a decedent's real property for the payment of his debts may be made, notwithstanding that the property was effectually devised expressly charged with the payment of the decedent's debts and funeral expenses, or is subject to a valid power of sale for the payment of debts, if it is not practicable to enforce the charge or to execute the power, and the creditor has effectually relinquished the same.

An infant party to the proceeding, of whose person the court had jurisdiction and for the protection of whose interest a special guardian was duly appointed, is bound by the decree as much as if he had been an adult.

APPEAL by Mary Q. Polhamus and another from a decree of the Surrogate's Court of the county of Montgomery, entered in said Surrogate's Court on the 19th day of June, 1901, setting aside a sale of real estate of the decedent, Charles J. Wood, together with the orders and decrees directing and confirming such sale.

Henry V. Borst and *S. W. Putman*, for the appellants.

George M. Albot, for the respondent.

CHASE, J.:

On the 15th day of February, 1896, Charles J. Wood died, leaving a last will and testament, dated the 5th day of February, 1896, by which he gave all his real estate and personal property to Harry C. Wood and therein provided: "Said Harry C. Wood is to pay out of said real estate all my just debts, and also to pay Katy Adams and Amey Wood one hundred dollars ($100) apiece." The last clause of the will is as follows: "I appoint James F. Polhamus and John V. Putman executors hereof and empower them to sell all or any real estate of which I may die seized." The testator did not leave a widow, but left three children, Katy Adams, Amey Wood and Harry C. Wood, his only next of kin and heirs at law. Amey Wood and Harry C. Wood were minors, the said Harry C. Wood being at the time of his father's death in the seventeenth year of his age. The testator died the owner of an unincumbered piece of real estate, but without personal property, other than such as was thereafter set apart by appraisers, to the minor children in accordance with the provisions of the Code of Civil Procedure.

The testator owed debts amounting to about the sum of $700, and his funeral expenses amounted to about $50. Said will was admitted to probate on the 2d day of March, 1896. Said John V. Putman did not qualify as an executor. Said James F. Polhamus refused for some time to qualify as executor, but did not file a renunciation, and in November, after the probate of said will, an order was served upon him requiring him to qualify as an executor or be deemed to have renounced, and thereafter, at the request of the persons interested, he duly qualified and letters testamentary were issued to him. Said Harry C. Wood refused to accept the property and pay the debts and legacies as in and by said will provided. There was a great difference of opinion among the persons inter- ested in the real estate of said testator as to the value thereof. The creditors threatened to institute proceedings for the sale of the real estate. The executor was wholly unable to find a purchaser for the property at a sum sufficient to pay the debts or at any sum whatever. A petition was duly presented to the Surrogate's Court substantially complying with section 2752 of the Code of Civil Procedure, praying for a decree directing the disposition of the decedent's real property, and a citation was duly issued and served upon all persons interested in said real estate as legatees and devisees, and upon all creditors of the decedent. On the return day of said citation an attorney at law was duly appointed special guardian for said infants for the purpose of protecting their interests in said proceeding. Such proceedings were thereupon had that on the 31st day of January, 1898, a decree was made reciting the appointment of said special guardian, and that "he having duly appeared as such special guardian," and "no one appearing in opposition, such proceedings were thereupon had * * * that the surrogate after hearing all the proofs and allegations of the parties, and after due examination so as aforesaid had, it being established to the satisfaction of the surrogate:

"1. That the petitioner has fully complied with the requisite provisions of the statutes concerning the disposition of a decedent's real property for the payment of his debts and funeral expenses; and that the proceedings herein have been in conformity to title 5 of chapter 18 of the Code of Civil Procedure. * * *

"4. That the property hereinafter described was not effectually devised or expressly charged with the payment of debts and funeral expenses," and directing a sale of said real property as provided by statute.

"Now, on motion of S. W. Putman, attorney for the petitioner, it is ordered, adjudged and decreed: * * *

"2. That for the purpose of paying the claims hereinbefore established a sale of the following described real property of which said decedent died seized be made by James F. Polhamus, said executor."

Thereafter the property was duly advertised for sale, and on the day so advertised the highest bid obtained for the property was $300. The executor refused to sell the property at that price and the sale was adjourned for two weeks, at which time the highest bid obtained for the property was $325. The executor refused to sell the property at that price and the sale was again adjourned for one week, at which time, April 23, 1898, the highest bid obtained for the property was $375, at which price it was sold to one Vernon Newkirk, who had married the minor, Amey Wood.

The sale so made was duly confirmed and the deed was delivered and consideration paid. Subsequently from the net proceeds of the property the funeral expenses were paid and the balance divided *pro rata* among the creditors of said testator in accordance with a final decree for distribution made by the Surrogate's Court and dated July 25, 1898.

Harry C. Wood became twenty-one years of age on the 2d day of November, 1900, and in January thereafter he made a motion in said Surrogate's Court to have said proceedings, orders and decrees, and the sale thereunder set aside, on the ground that the decree was irregular, without authority and unwarranted by law, and that no proper proceedings were taken to protect the interest of said Harry C. Wood, and also on the ground that the sale and order confirming the same were void, for the reason that the executor became interested in said sale before the order of confirmation.

The Surrogate's Court on the 19th day of January, 1901, made an order setting aside said proceedings, orders and decrees, and the sale thereunder, from which order this appeal is taken. The creditors of the intestate accepted their respective *pro rata* shares in the net proceeds of sale. They were apparently satisfied with the action of the executor, and are in no way parties to the proceedings to set aside said sale.

Harry C. Wood, the present petitioner, although the devisee under the will of his father, has no apparent beneficial interest in the property. The Surrogate's Court had unquestioned jurisdiction of all persons interested in the property, and the petition by which the proceeding was commenced substantially complied with the section of the Code relating thereto. It is apparent from section 2759 of the Code of Civil Procedure that a decree can be made notwithstanding the property was effectually devised expressly charged with the payment of debts and funeral expenses, or is subject to a valid power of sale for the payment thereof, if it is not practicable to enforce the charge or to execute the power, and the creditor has effectually relinquished the same.

An infant is bound by a decree where the court has jurisdiction of his person and a special guardian has been duly appointed for the protection of his interest as much as if he were an adult. (*Matter of Hawley*, 100 N. Y. 206.)

Section 2481 of the Code of Civil Procedure is not applicable to this case. It is said in *Matter of Hawley* (*supra*): "The due enjoyment of property rights, and the repose of titles which that enjoyment requires, renders it necessary that the adjudications of legal tribunals upon which rights to a large extent rest, should not be lightly disturbed or arbitrarily set aside and vacated after long lapse of time for errors which should have been discovered and remedied at the time of their perpetration. Some excuse must be shown by a party why he has not availed himself of the right of review provided by the statute, and the character of such excuse is described in section 2481. That section very clearly defines the nature and characteristics of the proof necessary to authorize a proceeding thereunder, and by its expression of the circumstances under which such an application can be made very clearly implies that it cannot be successfully maintained upon other grounds." Certainly a decree affecting the title to real estate should not be disturbed on grounds other than those stated in section 2481, unless it be entire lack of jurisdiction in the court.

There is nothing in the record before us showing what evidence was before the Surrogate's Court on which it based the recitals in the decree as hereinbefore quoted. It is unnecessary to suggest what course this court would pursue in case of an appeal from a decree like the one made herein after a contest in Surrogate's Court, or even what course would have been pursued by this court had an application been made herein before other important equities had intervened.

We are convinced that the sale herein was made in good faith after a determined effort to obtain a purchaser at as large a price as possible, and the grantee from the person to whom the deed was executed in accordance with the order of confirmation has since expended in improvements on the property more than the original purchase price thereof. No good purpose can be subserved by setting aside the proceedings and sale thereunder, and much apparent harm would come therefrom. In view of the peculiar circumstances of this case, including the fact that the petitioner has no apparent interest in the result of a resale, if made by the executor without the aid of the proceeding, and the further fact that the unpaid creditors are apparently satisfied with the sale as made, we think that the surrogate erred in setting aside the proceedings and the sale thereunder, and the order appealed from should be reversed.

All concurred.

Order reversed, with ten dollars costs and disbursements.

———

THE CITY OF GLOVERSVILLE, Respondent, *v.* ELIHU F. ENOS, Appellant.

License to sell milk — penalty for holding oneself out as having a license without having it or after it has expired — when not incurred.

The board of health of the city of Gloversville adopted, pursuant to law, the following regulation: "All venders of milk shall register their names with the clerk of the board, who shall issue to them a certificate of authority to sell milk, under his hand and seal. Every person so authorized to sell shall place in a conspicuous place on both sides of his milk wagon or sleigh the number of the license. Milk tickets shall be used but once. The certificates issued as above shall continue in force one year from the date of issue. Every person who holds himself out as possessing such certificate without having taken out the same, or after the same has been revoked, or has expired, shall be liable to a penalty of ten dollars." A person engaged in vending milk in the city obtained a certificate of authority from the city board of health and placed the number of the certificate in metal figures on the front end of the dashboard of his milk wagon. When the certificate of authority expired the milk vendor refused to register his name with the clerk of the board of health and procure a new certificate of authority, contending that such a certificate was not necessary. He also had his wagon repainted, the metal figures being painted over with the rest of the wagon.

Held, that the milk vendor was not liable for the penalty imposed by the regulation, as such penalty was directed only against a person who held himself out as possessing a certificate, without having taken out the same or after the same had been revoked or had expired.

APPEAL by the defendant, Elihu F. Enos, from a judgment of the County Court of Fulton county in favor of the plaintiff, entered in the office of the clerk of the county of Fulton on the 3d day of September, 1901, upon the decision of the court affirming upon appeal a judgment of the recorder of the city of Gloversville in favor of the plaintiff for a penalty of ten dollars, with interest thereon and costs.

William Green, for the appellant.

Frank Talbot, for the respondent.

CHASE, J.:

The city of Gloversville is a municipal corporation. The board of health of said city, prior to the times hereinafter mentioned, adopted and published, as required by law, certain regulations, among which is the following:

"REGULATION 15 — Milk License. — No milk which has been watered, adulterated, reduced or changed in any respect by the addition of water, or any other substance, thing or material, shall be brought into said city, or held, sold, kept or offered for sale at any place therein. All venders of milk shall register their names with the clerk of the board, who shall issue to them a certificate of authority to sell milk, under his hand and seal. Every person so authorized to sell shall place in a conspicuous place on both sides of his milk wagon or sleigh the number of the license. Milk tickets shall be used but once. The certificates issued as above shall continue in force one year from the date of issue. Every person who holds himself out as possessing such certificate without having taken out the same, or after the same has been revoked, or has expired shall be liable to a penalty of ten dollars." And such regulation has ever since remained in full force and effect. The defendant is a resident of this State, and an honorably discharged soldier of the military service of the United States. On the 19th day of August, 1897, there was issued to the defendant a license by the clerk of the county of Fulton, as provided by chapter 371 of the Laws of 1896. Thereafter the defendant exhibited to said board of health the license so issued to him by the county clerk of the county of Fulton, and said board gave to him a certificate of authority to sell milk as provided by said regulation, to continue in force for one year from August 16, 1897. The number of the certificate of authority so issued by the board of health was "11," and the defendant thereafter placed the number "11" in metal figures on the front of the dashboard of his milk wagon. When the certificate of authority so issued to him by the board of health expired, the defendant had his wagon repainted a reddish color and the said metal figures were painted over with the rest of the wagon. Prior to the commencement of this action the president of said board of health told the defendant's son, who was then in charge of defendant's wagon selling milk upon the streets of the city of Gloversville, that it would be necessary for the defendant to register his name with the clerk of said board of health and procure a new permit or license therefrom, for all of which no fee would be charged. The defendant's son replied to the president of the board of health, " They did not have to register or take out any license and would not do so." The defendant at all times since the expiration of said license so issued to him by said board of health, has claimed and maintained that it was not necessary for him to register again or obtain any other license than that issued to him by the county clerk.

This action was commenced in the Recorder's Court of the city of Gloversville, and the complaint alleges, " That the defendant is indebted to the plaintiff in the sum of ten dollars, being a penalty of that amount duly imposed by the board of health of plaintiff upon the defendant for his willful violation of regulation 15 of said board ; * * * said violation consisting in the refusal of defendant, after repeated requests by said board so to do, to register his name with the clerk of said board. * * *"

A penal statute will not be extended by implication or construction to cases within the mischief if they are not at the same time within the terms of the act fairly and reasonably interpreted. (*Verona Central Cheese Co.* v. *Murtaugh*, 50 N. Y. 314 ; *Commissioners of Pilots* v. *Vanderbilt*, 31 id. 265 ; *Health Department* v. *Knoll*, 70 id. 530.)

The only penalty provided by the regulation is against a person who holds himself out as possessing a certificate without having taken out the same, or after the same has been revoked or has expired. If it was the intention of the board of health to provide a penalty for selling milk without a certificate of authority from them, it was a very simple matter to have said so in plain and unmistakable terms.

The only way prescribed by the regulation for a person to hold himself out as having a certificate of authority from the board of health is by placing the number in a conspicuous place on both sides of the milk wagon or sleigh. This, concededly, was never done by the defendant even when the certificate of the board of health was in full force.

After the certificate expired the defendant not only did not maintain the number in a conspicuous place on both sides of his milk wagon or sleigh, but covered up and concealed such outward evidence as he had theretofore maintained of having such certificate.

From the time the certificate expired the *defendant has at all times claimed and maintained* that it was not necessary for him to register again or to obtain any other license, and refused to do so, thus consistently and expressly negativing any willful or other holding himself out as having the certificate of the board of health.

We are of the opinion that the defendant is not liable under the complaint nor upon the conceded statement of facts herein for the penalty imposed upon him. Judgment should be reversed, with costs in this court and in the courts below.

All concurred.

Judgment of the County Court and of the Justice's Court reversed, with costs, and costs in the courts below.

In the Matter of the Application for an Examination of EDWARD M. SAYRE, Individually and as an Officer of the SAYRE MANUFACTURING COMPANY and the SAYRE BROTHERS MANUFACTURING COMPANY, Appellant, at the Instance of the PORTER SCREEN MANUFACTURING COMPANY, Respondent.

Parties to an action to dissolve a corporation and sequestrate property fraudulently transferred by it — examination, before suit brought, of an officer of such corporation — that it will tend to incriminate him is not a defense to the application — he may be required to produce the books and records of the corporation.

In an action brought by a judgment creditor of a corporation to procure a dissolution thereof and a sequestration of property fraudulently transferred by it, the persons or corporations who hold such property in their possession may be joined as parties defendant.

On an application, under section 870 of the Code of Civil Procedure, to take the testimony of a person whom the applicant intends to make a party to an action to be thereafter commenced by him, the question whether the information sought to be elicited by the several questions to be asked will have a tendency to incriminate the witness should be reserved until the examination occurs.

The order for the examination of the witness may properly require him to pro-

THIRD DEPARTMENT, MARCH TERM, 1902.   [Vol. 70.

duce the books and records of corporations of which the witness is an officer and director, and which the applicant expects to make parties to the action, where it appears that the production of the books and records is required simply as an incident to the examination of the witness, and not for the purpose of allowing the applicant to inspect them.

APPEAL by Edward M. Sayre from an order of a justice of the Supreme Court of the State of New York, made at chambers and entered in the office of the clerk of the county of Chemung on the 11th day of November, 1901, denying his motion to vacate an order made by the county judge of Chemung county on the 16th day of October, 1901, for his examination, individually, as an officer of the Sayre Manufacturing Company and the Sayre Brothers Manufacturing Company and for an examination and inspection of the books and papers of said corporations, in an action about to be brought by the Porter Screen Manufacturing Company against the said Sayre Manufacturing Company, Sayre Brothers Manufacturing Company and others.

The Porter Screen Manufacturing Company is a foreign corporation. The Sayre Manufacturing Company, a domestic corporation, was incorporated on or about the 18th day of November, 1891, and has its principal place of business at Horseheads, N. Y.

Between the 20th day of January, 1899, and the 5th day of July, 1899, the Porter Screen Manufacturing Company sold and delivered to the Sayre Manufacturing Company goods and merchandise to an amount exceeding $2,000 in value. The Sayre Manufacturing Company did not pay for said goods and merchandise, and on the 18th day of January, 1900, an action was commenced in the Supreme Court of this State by the Porter Screen Manufacturing Company against it for the value of such goods and merchandise. An answer was interposed, and the issues so joined were referred to a referee for trial and he subsequently reported in favor of the plaintiff, and judgment was entered in favor of the plaintiff and against the defendant for the sum of $2,764.70 damages and costs on the 6th day of August, 1901.

Thereafter execution was issued against said Sayre Manufacturing Company, and on or before the 1st day of September, 1901, the same was returned wholly unsatisfied and the said judgment still remains unpaid. In January, 1898, and again in January, 1899, the Sayre Manufacturing Company filed its annual report as provided by law, but failed to make a report in January, 1900.

The Sayre-Hatfield Company, a domestic corporation, was duly incorporated on or about the 12th day of January, 1900, and has its principal place of business at Horseheads. On the 7th day of August, 1900, an order was duly granted by the Supreme Court authorizing the Sayre-Hatfield Company to assume the name of Sayre Brothers Manufacturing Company. At the time of the commencement of said action by the Porter Screen Manufacturing Company against the said Sayre Manufacturing Company, said Sayre Manufacturing Company was the owner in fee of two parcels of land at Horseheads, N. Y., on one of which parcels of land was situated the mill and machinery of said Sayre Manufacturing Company, and such real estate, mill and machinery constituted nearly the entire property and assets of said Sayre Manufacturing Company, and was of the value of at least $5,000. On the 13th day of February, 1900, there was recorded in the office of the clerk of Chemung county a deed dated the 1st day of January, 1900, conveying the said mill premises to the Sayre-Hatfield Company for the stated consideration of one dollar, and the Sayre-Hatfield Company and said Sayre Brothers Manufacturing Company, its successor, have ever since continued in the possession and enjoyment of the said real estate and personal property formerly belonging to said Sayre Manufacturing Company.

On or about the 16th day of October, 1901, the Porter Screen Manufacturing Company presented to the county judge of Chemung county an affidavit upon which it asked for and obtained an order that Edward M. Sayre, individually, and as an officer of the Sayre Manufacturing Company and of the Sayre Brothers Manufacturing Company, appear before a referee named in said order at a time and place therein named to be examined in an action about to be brought in the Supreme Court by the Porter Screen Manufacturing Company against the Sayre Manufacturing Company, the Sayre Brothers Manufacturing Company, Edward M. Sayre and others named, and also directing that said Edward M. Sayre produce upon such examination the books and records of said defendant corporations. Said affidavit also states:

"That the nature of the controversy which is expected to be the subject of said action, will be the dissolution of the said corporation, Sayre Manufacturing Company, and the sequestration of its property and the enforcement of the liability of said individual defendants, as officers and directors of said corporation to the creditors of the said corporation and especially to the Porter Screen Co., for their failure to make and file an annual report as of the first day of January, 1900, and compelling them to pay to the creditors of said Sayre Mfg. Co., the value of the property which they have acquired, transferred to others, lost or wasted, by violation of their duties."

The said Edward M. Sayre is, and has been during the times mentioned, secretary of the Sayre Manufacturing Company, and has possession of the books and records of said corporation and is fully informed as to the transfers by said corporation and disposition made of its assets.

The affidavit further states that the examination of Edward M. Sayre individually, and as an officer of the Sayre Manufacturing Company and the Sayre Brothers Manufacturing Company, is necessary to enable the Porter Screen Manufacturing Company to frame its complaint in the action so to be brought.

A motion was made in the Supreme Court by Edward M. Sayre, Sayre Manufacturing Company and Sayre Brothers Manufacturing Company to set aside the order of said county judge, and in the affidavits read by them on said motion it appears that at a meeting of the stockholders of the Sayre Manufacturing Company, held on the 1st day of February, 1900, a resolution was adopted as follows:

" *Resolved*, That the President and Secretary of the Sayre Manufacturing Company be authorized to enter into negotiations for the sale and transfer of land, buildings, and machinery of said corporation unto the Sayre-Hatfield Company for the sum of at least $13,000, and that the said President and Secretary be, and they are hereby authorized and empowered to make, execute and deliver to the said purchaser a good and sufficient deed of said land, buildings and machinery on receiving the consideration therefor."

By the affidavit of Edward M. Sayre, it appears that he had the charge and control of the Sayre Manufacturing Company and that, although but five shares of the stock of such company stood in his name, nevertheless at the time it ceased to do business, he owned and for a long time had owned all of the capital stock of said corporation. He also states in his affidavit that the deed of the property of the Sayre Manufacturing Company was executed to the Sayre-Hatfield Company pursuant to the resolution of the stockholders, and $13,000 of the stock of the Sayre-Hatfield Company was thereupon issued to him, Edward M. Sayre, individually. It also appears by said affidavit that the said Edward M. Sayre is now advised that he should have taken said stock in the name of the Sayre Manufacturing Company and that he, in law, now holds the same in trust for the Sayre Manufacturing Company and its creditors.

The motion to set aside said order of the county judge was denied, from which order this appeal is taken.

Richard H. Thurston, for the appellant.

Hosea H. Rockwell, for the respondent.

CHASE, J.:

A few facts stand out prominently in the record. The Porter Screen Manufacturing Company sold and delivered to the Sayre Manufacturing Company goods and merchandise which were not paid for as agreed. In an action brought on such account, judgment has been entered in favor of the Porter Screen Manufacturing Company against the Sayre Manufacturing Company for $2,764.70. When said goods and merchandise were sold, and when said action was commenced, the Sayre Manufacturing Company was in active business, and owned its plant, consisting of real and personal property. Before the judgment was obtained in said action a new corporation was organized for the purpose of carrying on the same kind of business and in the same town as the old corporation. The persons in control of the new corporation, Sayre Brothers Manufacturing Company, are substantially the same as those who were in control of the Sayre Manufacturing Company.

The Sayre Brothers Manufacturing Company is now in the possession and enjoyment of the plant of the Sayre Manufacturing Company, and the Sayre Manufacturing Company has ceased to do business and has no assets that can be reached by execution.

In an action to procure the dissolution of a corporation where the action is brought by a creditor, and the stockholders, directors, trustees or other officers or any of them are made liable by law in any event or contingency for the payment of the debt, the persons so made liable may be made parties defendant and their liability may be declared and enforced by the judgment in the action. (Code Civ. Proc. § 1790.)

In such an action if a fraudulent transfer of the corporate property is alleged, the creditor may join as parties defendants the persons or corporations who hold such property in their possession. (*Proctor* v. *Sidney Sash & Furniture Co.*, 8 App. Div. 42.)

The Porter Screen Manufacturing Company expects to bring an action against the Sayre Manufacturing Company, its directors and stockholders and the Sayre Brothers Manufacturing Company, for the purpose of obtaining payment of its judgment.

An examination of a person or corporation against whom an action is about to be brought in a court of record is authorized by section 870 of the Code of Civil Procedure. (*Merchants' National Bank* v. *Sheehan*, 101 N. Y. 176.)

Edward M. Sayre, the person to be examined, is not a mere witness, but one of the persons against whom the action is to be brought. He is also the manager of the corporations included among the proposed defendants. The information material and necessary to enable the plaintiff to frame its complaint is peculiarly within his personal knowledge. Many of the facts necessary to enable the plaintiff in such action to frame its complaint are matters of public record and of common knowledge, but it does not appear who were present at the stockholders' meeting of February 1, 1900, nor by what vote the resolution was passed by them, neither does it appear whether the directors of the Sayre Manufacturing Company ever authorized and directed the conveyance to the Sayre-Hatfield Company. The facts relating to the transfer of the property of the Sayre Manufacturing Company, except so far as they appear as matters of record, must necessarily be obtained from some of the persons that are to be made parties defendant in the action to be brought.

Substantially all of the statements in the moving affidavit are made upon knowledge. The statements made on information and belief are so connected with the positive allegations and based upon them that they were properly considered by the judge who granted the order for the examination.

The facts and circumstances detailed in the moving affidavit justify the statement that the examination of Edward M. Sayre is material and necessary to enable the plaintiff in the proposed action to frame its complaint.

The requisite facts having been presented by the affidavit, there is nothing requiring this court to interfere with the discretion exercised by the judge to whom the application was made in granting the order, or by the justice in refusing to set aside the order on motion of the party to be examined. (*Jenkins* v. *Putnam*, 106 N. Y. 272 ; *Pots* v. *Herman*, 7 Misc. Rep. 4.)

The appellant suggests that the evidence sought to be obtained on the examination will have a tendency to criminate the witness. It is not apparent that all the questions to be asked on the examination will call for answers that would tend to criminate the witness. On the examination the personal privilege may or may not be insisted upon. We are of the opinion that the question whether the information sought to be elicited by the several questions to be asked will have a tendency to criminate the witness should be reserved until the examination occurs, and if the personal privilege is then insisted upon, rulings can then be made from time to time as the question is presented. (*Ryan* v. *Reagan*, 46 App. Div. 590; *Matter of Davies*, 168 N. Y. 89.)

The appellant also suggests that the applicant is not entitled to an inspection of the books of the corporation as provided for by the order. We do not understand that the order provides for the discovery and inspection of the books as provided in sections 803 to 809 of the Code of Civil Procedure. The books and records are to be produced under the order herein simply as an incident to the examination of the party. (*Duffy* v. *Consolidated Gas Co.*, 59 App. Div. 580 ; *Bloodgood* v. *Slayback*, 62 id. 315.)

The order should be affirmed, with ten dollars costs and disbursements.

All concurred; SMITH, J., not sitting.

Order affirmed, with ten dollars costs and disbursements.

Cases

DETERMINED IN THE

FOURTH DEPARTMENT

IN THE

APPELLATE DIVISION,

March, 1902.

336|
¹466|
Y 385|
Herbert J. Rice, Respondent, *v.* Eureka Paper Company, Appellant.

Master and servant — injury to an employee from his hand being drawn into a machine of which he has complained to his master — effect of the master's having promised to add a proper device for stopping the machine.

A factory employee engaged in operating a rag cutter, which is not fitted with a belt shifter or other device by which it can be stopped quickly in case of emergency, and who is aware of the danger to be apprehended from the absence of such appliances, assumes the risk incident thereto and cannot recover damages from his employer for personal injuries sustained by him in consequence of the fact that his hand becoming caught in the material which he is feeding into the machine and that he is unable to stop it in time to escape injury.

Evidence that the accident occurred early on a Wednesday morning and that on the previous Saturday the employee narrowly escaped meeting with a similar injury and at once called the attention of his superior to it, and stated to him that he would stop work upon the machine that Saturday night, when his contract of hiring expired, unless a belt shifter was placed on the machine, and that his superior, who represented the employer, assured him that a belt shifter would be put upon the machine the first part of the following week, and that the employee continued to work upon the machine solely in reliance upon that promise, does not render the employer liable — it appearing that the accident happened before the expiration of the time within which the master promised that a belt shifter would be placed upon the machine.

Semble, that the employer would not be liable though it should be assumed that the time within which he agreed to remedy the defect had expired at the time the accident occurred.

Spring and Davy, JJ., dissented.

APPEAL by the defendant, the Eureka Paper Company, from a judgment of the Supreme Court in favor of the plaintiff, entered in the office of the clerk of the county of Oswego on the 24th day of January, 1901, upon the verdict of a jury for $5,120, and also from an order entered in said clerk's office on the 25th day of January, 1901, denying the defendant's motion for a new trial made upon the minutes.

The action was commenced on the 11th day of October, 1900, to recover damages for injuries sustained by the plaintiff on the morning of the 4th day of April, 1900, while in the employ of the defendant, alleged to have been caused solely through its negligence.

James Devine, for the appellant.

Frank C. Sargent, for the respondent.

McLENNAN, J.:

On the morning in question, and for several years prior, the defendant was engaged in manufacturing paper from rags, manila rope, string, etc., at its factory located at Oswego Falls, N. Y. One of the machines used by the defendant was a rag cutter, so called, which cut the material into small pieces preparatory to converting it into pulp. It consisted of a feed table about three feet long upon which the rough material was placed, and at one end there was a large, slowly revolving cylinder having upon its surface spikes or teeth, which caught the material, drew it between the cylinder and a stationary plate below, subjecting it to pressure and bringing it in contact with rapidly revolving knives immediately behind the cylinder, where it was cut and dropped upon a carrier which conveyed it to another part of the machine.

The machine was located in the second story of the factory, and was driven by power taken from a main revolving shaft extending through the first story close to the ceiling, by means of a belt which passed over a pulley on the shaft up through the floor to a pulley on the axle of the cutter. A tight and loose pulley, covered by a box, were close together upon the end of the axle, so arranged that when the belt was upon the tight pulley the machine would run, and when shifted to the loose pulley it would stop. The operator could only move the belt from the tight to the loose pulley, and thus stop the machine, by leaving his place in front of the feed table, going to the end of the axle, removing or opening the box, and pushing the belt with a stick. This was the means usually employed when it was desired to stop the machine temporarily, although the belt and loose pulley would still continue to revolve. When it was desired to stop the machine for a day or for any considerable time, a workman would go to the floor below and with a long stick push the belt from a tight to a loose pulley on the main shaft, and thus not only stop the machine, but the belt and the loose pulley upon the axle as well. There was no other way provided by which the cutter could be stopped, so long as the main shaft in the factory continued to revolve, no matter what the exigencies or necessity for stopping the same. As a rule, rag cutters and machines of similar construction are stopped by pushing the belt from the tight to the loose pulley by means of a belt shifter — a very simple device in common use — and the evidence quite conclusively shows that with such an appliance the machine in question could be stopped almost instantly by the operator without leaving his place, simply by moving a lever close to his hand. When the cutter was constructed it is apparent it was intended it should be stopped in that manner, because it was provided with a loose pulley, the only purpose of which is to facilitate the stopping of the machine, and, ordinarily, a belt is not moved onto such a pulley except by means of a shifter; at least, the machine could be stopped safely and almost instantly by that method. It further appears that by another simple device, also in common use, called a belt tightener, the machine could be stopped with almost equal facility, and for nearly a year prior to the day in question the defendant had in its factory, substantially ready for use, a tightener for this machine, but for some reason it had never been attached. With that attachment the operator would only have to pull a cord, close to his hand, and a weight would be removed from the belt and thus loosen it upon the pulley, when it would immediately cease to revolve. By means of either device in case of necessity the machine could be stopped almost instantly and, substantially, as effectively with one as with the other. Without either of such devices, and with the machine in the condition it was, it would be impossible for the operator to stop it, if for any reason he became unable to leave the place where he was required to stand in order to perform his work, and the danger and risk incident to the operation of the machine were thereby greatly increased. Under such conditions, it is obvious that if the person or clothing of the operator should become caught in the machine serious injury would result which he would be utterly powerless to prevent.

About two o'clock on the morning of the 4th of April, 1900, the plaintiff, who had been in the defendant's employ for more than a year previous, tending the machine in question, was standing in his accustomed place in front of the feed table, placing thereon rags, rope, string, etc., to be drawn under the cylinder and to the revolving knives beyond. While so engaged his right hand was caught in a loop of a strong string, and was being slowly drawn to the cylinder. He attempted to extricate this hand with the other, but in so doing it also became caught, and both were drawn to the cylinder and to the revolving knives, where little by little the entire right hand and all the fingers of the left but one were cut off. A fellow-workman then came to plaintiff's assistance, shifted the belt from the tight to the loose pulley on the axle; the machine stopped and the plaintiff was extricated. This action is brought to recover damages for the injuries thus sustained.

The plaintiff, at the time of the accident, was forty years of age; was ordinarily bright and intelligent; had tended the machine in question for more than a year; was entirely familiar with its construction and operation; knew that it was not provided with a belt shifter or belt tightener; fully understood that proper provision had not been made for stopping the machine, and knew and apprehended the dangers incident thereto. The machine was suitable for the work it was intended to do; all the parts were perfect and all appliances necessary or convenient for its use were supplied, except a belt shifter or belt tightener, which would have enabled the plaintiff to stop the machine at will and almost instantly, but that such appliances had not been furnished and were not in use was apparent and was known to the plaintiff. He also knew the danger to be apprehended from a failure to use such devices. If no other facts existed, clearly the plaintiff assumed the risk of his employment, and would not be entitled to recover.

The correct rule applicable to such a state of facts is stated in *Hickey* v. *Taaffe* (105 N. Y. 26) in the following language : "There is no doubt that an employe in accepting service with a knowledge of the character and position of the machinery, the dangers of which are apparent, and from which he might be liable to receive injury, assumes the risks incident to the employment, and he cannot call upon the defendant to make alterations to secure greater safety."

The rule was in effect reiterated in *Crown* v. *Orr* (140 N. Y. 452). The court said : "If he (the employee) voluntarily enters into or continues in the service without objection or complaint, having knowledge or the means of knowing the dangers involved, he is deemed to assume the risk and to waive any claim for damages against the master in case of personal injury to him."

The proposition of law was in effect stated by the learned trial justice in his charge to the jury, when he said : "Where a servant in the employ of a master knows the danger, understands the machine perfectly, realizes the risk which he undertakes, the law regards him as having assumed all the risk or danger."

The counsel for the respondent does not seek in any manner to controvert the rule of law stated, or to question its applicability to the facts of the case at bar, so far as they have now been recited, but it is insisted that the additional facts to which attention will now be called, take the case out of the rule adverted to. The accident happened on Wednesday morning. The plaintiff testified in substance, and the evidence is sufficient to support a finding to that effect, that on Saturday previous, while feeding the machine, his fingers became caught in the string in such manner that they narrowly escaped being drawn under the cylinder; that he at once called the attention of his superior, a Mr. Webb, to the fact, who, upon the evidence, the jury was justified in finding, represented the defendant, and stated to him that he would stop work upon the machine that Saturday night, when his contract of hiring expired, unless a shifter was connected with it so that it could be stopped ; that Mr. Webb assured him the defendant would put a shifter upon the cutter the first part of the following week ; that he, relying upon such promise and assurance, remained in defendant's employment, believing it would be done, and that he would not have continued to work upon the machine if such promise had not been made.

The jury was also justified in finding, upon the evidence, that the plaintiff's injuries resulted because of defendant's failure to furnish and attach to the rag cutter a belt shifter or tightener, or make proper provision for stopping the machine; that it was negligent in that regard; that such negligence caused the accident, and that the plaintiff was not guilty of negligence because of anything done by him in feeding the machine at the time of the accident.

It is urged by respondent's counsel that the promise and assurance made and given on behalf of the defendant that it would supply a proper appliance for stopping the machine, which was relied upon by the plaintiff, furnishes an exception to the rule applicable to the assumption of risk by an employee, and so that the plaintiff is entitled to recover damages for the injuries sustained by him. It is not contended that the judgment can be sustained upon any other ground, and that presents the only question which requires consideration.

The doctrine of assumption of risk is based upon contract. Independent of any question of public policy or statutory prohibition, a master has a right to hire a servant to operate machinery which as originally constructed is defective and unsafe, or which has become so because permitted to get out of repair, no matter how great the danger incident to its operation, provided the servant knows its condition and fully appreciates the risk. In case a contract of hiring is entered into under such circumstances, the presumption is conclusive that the parties contracted with reference to existing conditions; that the wages of the servant were fixed accordingly, presumably increased because of the assumption by him of the risk incident to operating defective and dangerous machinery, and in case he thereby sustains injury the master is not liable. The servant's right in the premises is to refuse to contract, or, if he has entered upon the employment and does not longer wish to expose himself to its dangers, to stop work. The rights of the parties to such a contract, although simply a verbal agreement to employ by the master and to work by the servant, are no different than if it had been in writing, and had expressly provided that for a certain sum per day or per week, to be paid by the master, the servant would operate a defective and dangerous machine, which was fully described, and would assume the risk incident thereto. If to such a contract is added a clause by which the master, for the purpose of inducing the servant to accept or remain in the employment, agrees to remedy the defective machinery, and thereby make its operation reasonably safe, are the rights of the servant changed or enlarged, in case he is injured, simply because the master failed to remedy or repair the defects as he had agreed to do? We can conceive of no principle of law upon which to rest the proposition that by such a contract of hiring the servant becomes relieved of the assumption of the risk incident to the operation of such machinery, simply because the master promised to remedy or repair the same.

If a manufacturer hires a machinist for two days to run an engine which is dangerous because the flywheel is broken, which defect is known to and the danger is fully appreciated by the machinist, in case he sustains injury because of such defect, the master is not liable, because the servant himself assumed the risk incident to the operation of the engine in that condition. If, when the master employed the servant, and even for the purpose of inducing him to enter the service, he promised to supply the engine with a new flywheel upon the morning of the second day, and during the first day the servant was injured, how can it be said that he did not assume the risk incident to the first day's service? By the contract the servant in effect agreed to run, for one day at least, the defective engine. Presumably his wages were increased because of the dangers attending such work. Knowing all the facts, he contracted to operate an engine for at least one day with a broken flywheel, which made its operation hazardous. But suppose accident does not result during the first day's service, and upon the morning of the second day the servant discovers that the master has failed to keep his promise to supply the engine with a perfect wheel, but the servant, without protest, remains in the employment and continues to operate the engine, and on the second day the flywheel goes to pieces and he is injured. Do not all the elements exist which impose upon the servant the assumption of the risk? He knew the defect; appreciated the danger, which was apparent, yet with full knowledge of the conditions continued in the employment. In the case supposed there could be no suggestion that the servant believed the defect had been remedied, and for that reason continued in the service. He knew that the flywheel upon the engine continued to be in a defective and dangerous condition ; knew that the promise of the master had not been fulfilled, and yet with such knowledge he assumed to commence operating the engine on the morning of the second day. We fail to see how the promise of the master to repair and his failure to do so, even under such circumstances, in any manner changed the relations or rights of the parties. When the servant discovered that the wheel had not been repaired on the morning of the second day, he was under no obligation to continue his work, because the master had broken the contract. He was then entitled to stop work and recover any damages resulting from the breach. It is suggested that he had a right, under the contract, to continue to operate the dangerous machine, knowing it had not been repaired by the master as he had promised, and then insist upon recovering from the master the damages for personal injuries sustained by him on account of the failure to repair; but that is only another way of saying that the risk of operating the machine ceased to be assumed by the servant from the moment the master promised to repair.

An experienced locomotive engineer is upon an engine ready to start upon his trip ; he has the lever in his hand with which to start or stop the engine ; the lever is cracked and is liable to break at any time ; the engineer knows it and knows and fully appreciates the danger attending its use in that condition. He calls the attention of the master to the unsafe condition of the lever, and declares he will quit the service unless it is remedied. The master then and there promises to have it repaired before the engine is started upon another trip. - That promise being made, the engineer, without protest, fully knowing and realizing the danger, starts upon his journey and is injured through the breaking of the lever. On what principle is the master liable? He has procured a defective engine to be run, as he had a right to do, provided only the servant knew of the defects and also knew the danger. He has not broken any agreement. He did not agree to repair until the return of the engine from the trip then commenced. Upon principle we fail to see why the case does not fall within the rule laid down in many cases decided by the Court of Appeals, and which is stated in *Hickey* v. *Taaffe* and *Crown* v. *Orr* (*supra*).

In the case at bar it is not claimed that the defendant would have been liable for plaintiff's injuries if received while operating the rag cutter previous to the Saturday night preceding the accident; but upon that night, the contract period then ending, he being only hired from week to week, the plaintiff declared his intention of leaving defendant's employ unless the machine was supplied with a belt shifter, which would render its operation less hazardous. Thereupon the defendant assured the plaintiff that if he would continue to operate the machine in the condition in which it then was, it would be supplied with a shifter during the fore part of the following week. The plaintiff assented and continued to operate the machine precisely as before. It would seem that the only effect of the new arrangement was that the plaintiff expressly stipulated to operate the dangerous machine for at least two or three days, precisely as he had impliedly stipulated to do and had done for a year previous, but with the assurance that at the end of the two or three days it would be made reasonably safe. How he ceased to assume the risk of such employment during those days which for a year he had assumed, solely because of defendant's promise, it is difficult to understand. The dangers incident to operating the cutter were in no manner increased; the conditions were unchanged; plaintiff's knowledge of the situation and appreciation of the risk were the same; the defendant had not broken his agreement, and, so far as appears, had no intention of so doing. The time in which it promised to remedy the defect had not expired. How then did the plaintiff acquire important rights in addition to those which he had prior to the Saturday night in question, to wit, rights which relieved him from the assumption of the risk of the employment and placed that burden upon the defendant?

On Saturday night, the plaintiff having declared his intention of leaving defendant's employ because no belt shifter was attached to the machine, the defendant said to the plaintiff, in substance, I want my dangerous rag-cutting machine run for a few days longer and until I have an opportunity to repair it, which will be in two or three days at most; you know all about it and I would like to have you do it, but if you do not wish to I will get some one else. The answer of the plaintiff was, in effect, that he would continue the employment upon the conditions specified. He did so; continued to operate the machine, with full knowledge of all its defects and fully appreciating the dangers incident thereto. It cannot be said that the time in which the defendant promised to remedy the defect had expired, the accident having occurred in the early morning of the Wednesday following the Saturday night when the promise was made. There is no pretense that the plaintiff supposed the repairs had been made and thus was induced to remain, or had been assured the cutter could run safely, or comparatively so, and relied upon the superior knowledge of the defendant's superintendent in that regard. But even if, upon the evidence, it might be found that "the fore part of the next week" had expired, and thus that the defendant had violated his agreement to repair, we cannot perceive how that fact would change or enlarge the plaintiff's rights in the premises, because he knew perfectly well the defect had not been remedied, and continued without protest or complaint to operate the cutter. So that we have the precise question presented : Does the bare promise of a master to repair, in the future, defective machinery, which is being operated by a servant who has knowledge of the defects and fully appreciates the danger incident thereto, relieve the servant from the assumption of the risks of the employment, and in effect make the master an insurer of the servant's safety ?

So far as we have been able to discover the question has not been directly passed upon by the Court of Appeals of this State, in any case where the views of the court have been expressed in an opinion, and where the determination of the question was necessary to the decision of the case. As there seems to be some conflict between the decisions of the lower courts and the decisions of the courts of sister States we have deemed it proper to point out why, in our opinion, the rule which was made the basis of the judgment appealed from is unsound in principle, and why it should not be incorporated into the law of this State applicable to actions for negligence brought by employees against employers. Having done so, we will review the adjudicated cases bearing upon the question and endeavor to ascertain whether or not such a rule has been approved by the weight of authority. The question is an important one. If the respondent's contention shall prevail, it will only be necessary in the future, in any action brought by a servant against the master to recover damages for injuries sustained on account of defective machinery, tools or appliances, or because an unsafe place in which to work is provided, to testify that the master promised to remedy or repair, and his liability will be established, or at least an issue will be raised for the determination of a jury.

Laning v. *N. Y. C. R. R. Co.* (49 N. Y. 521) was an action to recover for injuries sustained by the plaintiff, who was in defendant's employ, in falling from a scaffold erected under the supervision of another employee, which collapsed because improperly constructed. It appeared that the employee who had charge of erecting the scaffold was, to the knowledge of the defendant, addicted to the use of liquor to such an extent that he was frequently drunk while engaged in the performance of his duties and at the time when the scaffold was erected, and that the defective construction of the scaffold was the result of such intoxication. It also appeared that the plaintiff knew of the habits of such employee; that the scaffold was erected under his direction, and of the condition he was in at the time. It further appeared that the defendant, through its foreman, prior to the accident, had assured the plaintiff that if the employee who had charge of erecting the scaffold did not do better or mend his habits he would have him discharged. It did not appear that the plaintiff knew the scaffold was dangerous. It was urged that the defendant was not liable because the scaffold fell on account of the negligence of a co-employee, occasioned by his intemperate habits, of which the plaintiff had knowledge. Upon all the facts, including the promise of defendant's foreman, it was held that under the circumstances of that case the question of plaintiff's contributory negligence was one of fact for the jury, and the jury having found a verdict in favor of the plaintiff, the judgment entered thereon was sustained. The decision cannot be regarded as authority for the proposition contended for in the case at bar. It would be somewhat analogous if it had been shown that the plaintiff in that case knew the scaffold was defective; had gone upon it fully appreciating the danger; had thus sustained injury and had then sought to recover damages, claiming that he was relieved from the risk of going upon the scaffold which he knew was dangerous, simply because the defendant had assured him that the person under whose direction it was erected would not become drunk while engaged in the duties of his employment. No such proposition was held. It was only decided that it was proper for the jury to take into consideration all the circumstances adverted to in determining whether or not the plaintiff was free from or chargeable with contributory negligence. It is true the learned judge who wrote the opinion quotes substantially from the opinion in the case of *Holmes* v. *Clark* (10 Week. Repr. 405) and says : " It has been held that there is a formal distinction between the case of a servant who knowingly enters into a contract to work on defective machinery and that of one who, on a temporary defect arising, is induced by the master, after the defect has been brought to the knowledge of the latter, to continue to perform his service under promise that the defect shall be remedied."

But this language was apparently only used for the purpose of showing that it was proper, after it had been proven that the plaintiff in that case knew of the intemperate habits of the other employee, to show that the foreman of the defendant had promised to see that such employee did better, or in case he did not to have him discharged, and that those facts with the others were properly for the consideration of the jury. The proposition stated in the second head note to the case quoted in the brief of respondent's counsel is not, so far as we can ascertain, borne out by the facts, by the decision or by any language contained in the opinion of the learned judge.

In the case of *Sweeney* v. *Berlin & Jones Envelope Co.* (101 N. Y. 520) it was held that a threat by the master to discharge a servant if he does not continue to use a machine which he was engaged to operate, and which is in the same condition it was when he undertook the work, is not coercion which will render the master liable in case the servant is injured by its use. In that case, which was an action by an employee who was injured in operating a defective machine, the plaintiff testified that he told the superintendent it was dangerous; that he was referred to the machinist, who promised to remedy the defect. Judge DANFORTH, in writing the opinion of the court (p. 525), said : " If the defect had been in the pedal and a promise made to repair that, and yet directions given for its use, it might be otherwise ; but here the promise, if there was any, concerned a new appliance, not attached to that particular machine, nor to any machines of that make. The ' Adams machines,' as the plaintiff's witnesses proved, were uniformly furnished with the pedal.   A clutch had never been seen on one. They were for different purposes."

While a portion of the language quoted would seem to indicate that if the promise in that case had been to add something which properly belonged to the machine, the lack of which caused the injury, the plaintiff might have recovered because of such promise. That question was not decided and was not necessary to the decision of the case.

Expressions of similar import may be found in the opinions in other cases decided by the Court of Appeals.

Marsh v. *Chickering* (101 N. Y. 396) was an action brought to recover damages for injuries sustained by the plaintiff in falling from a ladder used by him in lighting lamps in front of defendant's building.   The ladder slipped and the plaintiff was injured because it was not " hooked and spiked."   The plaintiff knew its condition ; that in consequence it was likely to fall, made complaint to the defendant, and was by him directed to go to the superintendent, who promised the plaintiff that he would have the ladder " hooked and spiked."   The superintendent failed to do so.   The plaintiff continued to use the ladder as before and was injured.   It was held that the plaintiff could not recover.   In that case the court apparently regarded the fact important that the plaintiff was a common laborer, employed in doing common work, and was using a common tool or appliance, in regard to the use of which he had perfect knowledge.   The court said : " The fact that he (the plaintiff) notified the master of the defect and asked for another instrument and the master promised to furnish the same, in such a case does not render the master responsible if an accident occurs."

We think the language quoted could not have been intended to be only applicable to common laborers using simple tools and appliances, and not to skilled laborers using complicated machinery, provided the latter, because of their skill, were perfectly familiar with such machinery and with the dangers incident to its operation.

As was said by Mr. Justice CULLEN in *Spencer* v. *Worthington* (44 App. Div. 496) : " There is a great difference between the use of a steam boiler and that of a step ladder.   A servant exercising due care would probably always know when a step ladder was likely to break down, while he might not know when a boiler was likely to blow up. Therefore, there is a marked distinction between a boiler and a step ladder, so far as knowledge of danger and consequent assumption of risk should be imputed to the servant. But when, because the servant is an expert, or for other reasons, his knowledge of the danger arising from the use of the boiler is just as great as that which an ordinary servant would possess in the use of a step ladder, we do not see on what ground any distinction can be drawn between the two cases."

In the case at bar the evidence clearly shows that the plaintiff was quite as familiar with the machine in question, and with the consequences and dangers attending its operation without a belt shifter, as was the plaintiff in the *Marsh* case with the ladder and its operation, and with the danger of using it without hooks and spikes.

The case of *Healy* v. *Ryan* (25 Wkly. Dig. 23; affd., 116 N. Y. 657, without an opinion), cited by respondent's counsel, is by no means decisive of the question involved. Certain of the language in the opinion of the court at General Term is susceptible of the construction contended for by counsel, but an examination of the printed case on appeal discloses that there was abundant ground upon which to sustain the judgment, independent of whether or not the defendant in that case promised to repair the defective brake. Apparently proof of the promise was not made for the purpose of establishing non-assumption of risk on the part of the plaintiff, but for the purpose of proving knowledge on the part of the defendant that the brake was defective, which was the chief issue litigated. The plaintiff gave evidence tending to show that while he knew the brake was somewhat defective, and had complained of it, he believed it would answer the purpose for which it was intended; that at the time of the accident he was in good faith trying to operate it, but that owing to its worn condition it would not take hold of the wheel with sufficient firmness to hold the heavy train on the descending grade where it was necessary to stop in order to avoid the collision. Upon all the facts in that case, including the promise of the defendant to repair the brake, the question of defendant's negligence and of plaintiff's freedom from contributory negligence was submitted to the jury, and those questions having been determined by its verdict in favor of the plaintiff, the judgment entered thereon was affirmed by the General Term, fourth department, and by the Court of Appeals.

A large number of cases might be cited which amply support the proposition that where a servant has been assured by the master that the machinery or appliance with which he is working, or the place in which he is performing his duties, is safe, or that no injury will result from the defects, if any, he has a right to rely upon the superior knowledge of the master and continue the employment, and if injured in consequence of such defects he may recover the damages sustained, notwithstanding he knew of the defects. Belonging to that class of cases are *Hawley* v. *Northern Central Railway Co.* (82 N. Y. 370); *Daley* v. *Schaaf* (28 Hun, 314); *Siedentop* v. *Buse* (21 App. Div. 592). Those and similar authorities have no application to the case at bar, for no assurances were given by the defendant that the machine was safe or that its operation was not dangerous. The plaintiff did not rely upon the superior knowledge of defendant's foreman. The jury was expressly charged that the plaintiff had full and complete knowledge as to the condition of the cutter, and as to the danger attending its operation in the condition in which it was at the time of the accident.

In the case of *Hannigan* v. *Smith* (28 App. Div. 176) the precise question under discussion was raised and decided. In that case the plaintiff was engaged in carrying brick from the street to an elevator in a building being erected by the defendant, by which they were carried to the top of the building where they were being laid into a wall by other workmen. There were no floors in the different stories, only occasional loose plank, and brick from time to time fell from the top of the building to the floor below, to the knowledge of the plaintiff, where he was passing in and out in the performance of his work. The plaintiff complained to the foreman of the defendant of this condition of things; insisted that it was dangerous, and the foreman promised to remedy the difficulty by laying a floor in an upper story which would prevent the brick from falling to the floor below. Upon such premise being made, the plaintiff continued his work, but knew the floor had not been laid or any provision made to render plaintiff's work less dangerous. A brick fell and injured him, and it was held that he could not recover.

Mr. Justice O'BRIEN, writing the opinion of the court, said: "It will be found, upon an examination of the cases relied upon by the appellant (the plaintiff), that none of them sustain the proposition that, with respect to a danger which the servant knows as well as the master, he is absolved from the charge of contributory negligence if he proceeds to ignore the danger, even though he does so on the assurances of the master that at some future time the defect will be repaired. If he proceeds with his work in the face of the obvious danger, and as a result is injured before it is remedied, he cannot be said to have been himself free from negligence."

In the case of *McCarthy* v. *Washburn* (42 App. Div. 252), which was an action to recover damages for injuries sustained by the plaintiff by the caving in of a sand bank while he was engaged in removing sand therefrom, it appeared, as stated in the opinion of the court, that "he (the plaintiff) had worked in and about brickyards and upon railroads for upwards of thirty years, and was thoroughly familiar with the kind of labor upon sand banks in which he was engaged at the time of the accident. Two or three days before he was hurt he had a conversation with the defendant about the condition of the bank, saying that he was afraid of it and was not going to work there any longer. To this the defendant responded, in substance, that he would secure the bank in a day or two, and keep the gravel back, so that there would be no danger. According to the plaintiff's testimony the defendant said: 'I will secure the bank in a day or two, and I will warrant you that nothing will happen you.'"

Nothing, however, was done by the defendant in fulfillment of his promise, and knowing that fact the plaintiff went on with his work and was injured. The plaintiff, at the close of the evidence, was nonsuited. The judgment of nonsuit was affirmed by the Appellate Division. The court said: "We think that this disposition of the case was fully justified by the testimony of the plaintiff himself. He knew everything that the defendant knew about the danger. He also knew that the defendant had taken no measures to lessen or avert it. No sort of constraint was exercised upon him. * * * Under the circumstances, the plaintiff was subject to the rule which was applied in the case of *Hannigan* v. *Smith* (28 App. Div. 176)."

The learned justice then quotes with approval the language of
Mr. Justice O'BRIEN in the *Hannigan* case, to which attention has
already been called.

So in the case of *Spencer* v. *Worthington* (*supra*), which was a
case where the plaintiff was injured because he used an oil can with
a short spout to oil machinery while in motion.   It appeared that
he complained to the superintendent that the can was unfit for the
purpose, and that he was promised that a can with a long spout
would be furnished to him.   He believed such promise would be
fulfilled, but it was not and he continued to oil the machinery with
the can having a short spout, and was injured.   It was held that no
recovery could be had, notwithstanding the promise, its breach by
defendant and plaintiff's reliance upon it.   Mr. Justice CULLEN,
in writing the opinion of the court in that case, reviews the case of
Hannigan v. *Smith* (*supra*), and cites it with approval and, as we
have already seen, held there can be no logical distinction between
the assumption of risk by a servant using a simple or common tool
or appliance, and one using complicated machinery, provided the
knowledge of the latter is as full and comprehensive as to the
machine or appliance used as that of the former.

We believe we have now called attention to all the decisions of
the courts of this State bearing upon the question involved.   In
none of them has it been decided that a servant may recover from
the master for injuries sustained and resulting from the operation of
defective or dangerous machinery, where the servant was fully
aware of the defects and fully understood the danger, simply because
the master promised, at some time in the future, which time expired
after the injury, to remedy such defects, and failed to do so.

Judge Cooley, in his work on Torts (pp. 559, 560) and Mr. Bailey,
in his work on Master's Liability for Injuries to Servant (p. 207)
state the rule quite as broadly as is contended for by respondent's
counsel, and so as amply to cover the case at bar and justify an
affirmance of the judgment.   Judge Cooley says: " If the servant
having a right to abandon the service because it is dangerous,
refrains from doing so in consequence of assurances that the danger
shall be removed, the duty to remove the danger is manifest and
imperative, and the master is not in the exercise of ordinary care
unless or until he makes his assurances good.   Moreover, the assur-

ances remove all ground for the argument that the servant, by continuing the employment, engages to assume its risks. So far as the particular peril is concerned the implication of law is rebutted by the giving and accepting of the assurance; for nothing is plainer or more reasonable than that parties may and should, where practicable, come to an understanding between themselves regarding matters of this nature."

Mr. Bailey, in stating the rule, uses substantially the same language. Neither of the learned authors, however, as it seems to us, at all satisfactorily explain how or why it is that the other rule, which they lay down without qualification, becomes abrogated and annulled simply by the fact that the master has promised to repair and has failed to do so, to the knowledge of the servant. The other rule adverted to, and which is universally recognized, is stated by Mr. Bailey (p. 145) as follows: " Therefore, it has come to be well settled that the master may conduct his business in his own way, although another method might be less hazardous, and the servant takes the risk of the more hazardous method as well, if he knows the danger attending the business in the manner in which it is carried on. Hence, if the servant, knowing the hazards of his employment as the business is conducted, is injured while employed in such business, he cannot maintain an action against the employer, because he may be able to show there was a safer mode in which the business might have been carried on, and that, had it been conducted in that manner, he would not have been injured."

If the suggestion was that the servant ceases to assume the risk after the expiration of the time within which the master promised to repair, and that from then on, for a reasonable time, the master was liable because of the violation of his contract, there would be some reason upon which to base such a rule, but as laid down by the learned authors it is not restricted to such a case, but is such as to make the master liable *instanter* upon making the promise, and without reference to whether or not the time he was to have in which to redeem his promise has expired. As in the case at bar, the servant agreed to run the defective cutter during the fore part of the week upon condition that the master would repair it at the end of that time. Before the time expired, before the master had violated his agreement, and, so far as appears, he had no intention of violating it, the accident occurred and the plaintiff was injured. As before said, we think there is no principle of the law of contracts or of negligence upon which the master in such case should be held liable.

The doctrine asserted by Judge Cooley is approved by a large number of adjudicated cases, one (*Hough* v. *Railway Co.*, 100 U. S. 213) decided by the Supreme Court of the United States, and many decided by the highest courts of several of the western and southern States. (*Ferriss* v. *Berlin Machine Works*, 90 Wis. 541; *Stoutenburgh* v. *Dow, Gilman, Hancock Co.*, 82 Iowa, 184; *Lyttle* v. *Chicago & West Michigan Railway Co.*, 84 Mich. 289; *Snowberg* v. *Nelson-Spencer Paper Co.*, 43 Minn. 532; *Gulf, C. & S. F. R. Co.* v. *Donnelly*, 70 Tex. 371.)

Those cases and several others cited by Judge Cooley approve without qualification the rule as stated by him, and if followed clearly entitle the plaintiff to an affirmance of the judgment appealed from. While the authorities cited are entitled to great weight, in view of the decisions of the courts of this State to which attention has been called, and which we deem to be in conflict with those authorities, we are impelled to adopt what we believe to be the logical result of the decision of the Court of Appeals in *Marsh* v. *Chickering* (*supra*), and the rule laid down by the Appellate Division of the first and second departments in *Hannigan* v. *Smith, McCarthy* v. *Washburn* and *Spencer* v. *Worthington* (*supra*), and to hold: That where, as in this case, a servant was engaged in operating machinery which he knew to be defective, and fully appreciated the danger incident thereto, the master is not liable for injuries sustained by the servant because of such defects, although, for the purpose of inducing the servant to continue in the employment, the master promised to remedy the defects within a specified time, which promise was relied upon by the servant and induced him to remain, when such injury was sustained by the servant before the expiration of the time within which the master promised to repair.

It follows that the judgment appealed from should be reversed and a new trial granted, with costs to the appellant to abide event.

Judgment and order reversed, upon questions of law only, the facts having been examined and no error found therein, and new trial ordered, with costs to the appellant to abide event.

WILLIAMS and HISCOCK, JJ., concurred; SPRING and DAVY, JJ., dissented.

SPRING, J. (dissenting):

I cannot concur with the majority of my brethren in the conclu-clusions reached in this case.

We may regard it as settled by the verdict of the jury that had there been a shifter on this machinery accessible to the plaintiff he might have quickly stopped it, and prevented the frightful injuries which were inflicted upon him. Also that the defendant's manager or superintendent realized the necessity of procuring this shifter, and had, in fact, obtained one which was in the building for the very purpose of enabling the machine to be stopped readily. Further, that on the Saturday night preceding the accident, the dangerous condition of the machine was sharply called to the atten-tion of this superintendent, followed up by the statement of the plaintiff that he would quit unless a shifter was put on. That thereupon the superintendent who represented the defendant stated that he intended to shut down the next week for other repairs, and that the shifter would then be adjusted. The plaintiff, relying upon this promise, continued his work, and during Wednesday morning following received his injuries, by reason of the absence of this shifter. The cases cited in the prevailing opinion from the first and second departments did not involve complicated machin-ery, but perfectly obvious risks, which any man, however simple minded, would understand, and while there are remarks in the opinions which justify the conclusion that the plaintiff cannot recover, yet I think so far as the case itself in each instance is con-cerned, it is not necessarily an authority against the plaintiff. In the case of *Healy* v. *Ryan* (25 Wkly. Dig. 23; affd., 116 N. Y. 657) the plaintiff was injured by a collision attributable to a defective brake. The proof showed that he had complained of the defect and had been assured that it would be remedied. In the charge of the trial court, there being conflicting evidence as to this promise, it was left to the jury to pass upon as a question of fact, and its significance, therefore, was pointedly in the case. The General Term of this department affirmed a recovery, commenting specifically on the effect of the promise to remedy these defects. That case, it seems to me, is quite analogous to the present one, and the Court of Appeals in affirming the judgment did so with the charge squarely presenting the question involved here, and must have assented to the doctrine which thus stood out prominently in the case. In the two or three cases in the Court of Appeals commented upon in the prevailing opinion, while not exactly in point, the court seems to recognize the doctrine that where a promise is made by a master to his servant that he will repair a defect in a machine this is equivalent to saying that he will assume the risk of the defective machinery instead of the employee. The text writers and courts of other States and of the United States Supreme Court, so far as I can find, are substantially a unit on this proposition against the position contended for in the opinion of the court.

The doctrine of assumption of risks is contractual in its nature, and, of course, the parties by agreement can fix their relation. When the machinery is defective the master may not desire to shut down his plant, but prefer to take the hazard of an accident to one of his employees. He, therefore, says to him : " Go on and perform the work as you have done before and in a few days when there is a lull in the business I will remedy the defect." The servant assents to this and is injured because of the defect, and within the time stipulated for making the repairs. It is no more than fair that upon a state of facts like this that the servant should be relieved from assuming the risks by implication imposed upon him when the danger is obvious. The only reasonable interpretation that can be put upon the promise of the defendant's manager is that it was expected to shift the liability to the defendant. Unless this is true the promise of the defendant is meaningless and does not inure at all to the benefit of the plaintiff. The master gets his work done, keeps his machinery moving upon the strength of his promise, and still if injury occurs the plaintiff cannot recover, if the doctrine of the prevailing opinion is true, because he knew of the existence of the defect. The duty is imposed upon the defendant to provide reasonably safe machinery. That is the basic principle of these cases. He becomes aware that he has failed to do this.

Notwithstanding this increased peril, he urges his servant to continue work on this dangerous machinery, promising to repair it within a definite time, and it is just he should stand the consequences. In an arrangement of this kind the defendant, by reason of greater ability, greater contact with men and more experience, has, in the vernacular of the farm, the long end of the evener, and should be held to the legitimate consequences which flow from the promise he has made.

Nor can I see that this is fraught with the peril to a manufacturer contended for in the prevailing opinion. If the person injured is bent on committing perjury to make out a case, he can simply add to the promise as given by the plaintiff the additional fact that the master told him if he would stay and work he, the master, would be responsible for any injuries sustained by reason of the defect called to the master's attention, and the doctrine of assumption of risks confessedly is not applicable to that servant.

Both upon principle and authority I am in favor of affirmance.

DAVY, J., concurred.

Judgment and order reversed upon questions of law only, the facts having been examined and no error found therein, and new trial ordered, with costs to the appellant to abide the event.

WILLIAM A. LATHROP, Appellant, v. WILBUR H. SELLECK, Respondent.

Conditional sale — evidence that the vendor was insolvent is incompetent to establish its character — facts indicating insolvency, not known to the vendee, are incompetent on the question of his good faith — prohibition of transfers by an insolvent corporation.

A corporation which had purchased certain furniture from the firm of Norton & Co. sold it to one Lathrop. Thereafter Norton & Co. brought an action against the corporation to recover the property, and the sheriff took possession thereof under the writ of replevin. Subsequently Lathrop brought an action against the sheriff to recover possession of the property, the issues raised being whether Norton & Co. sold the property to the corporation upon condition that the title thereto should remain in Norton & Co. until the purchase price had been paid, and whether or not the plaintiff was a *bona fide* purchaser of the same.

Upon an appeal from a judgment rendered upon a verdict in favor of the defendant, it was

Held, that evidence that the corporation was insolvent at the time it purchased the goods from Norton & Co., and also when it sold them to the plaintiff, was immaterial and incompetent for the purpose of establishing the character of the sale;

That evidence of facts tending to establish the insolvency of the corporation, which facts were not shown to have come to the knowledge of the plaintiff at the time he purchased the goods, was not competent for the purpose of showing that he was not a *bona fide* purchaser;

That evidence of the insolvency of the corporation was not competent for the purpose of showing that the sale of the goods to Lathrop was within the statute prohibiting transfers by insolvent corporations, as no such issue had been submitted to the jury.

APPEAL by the plaintiff, William A. Lathrop, from a judgment of the Supreme Court in favor of the defendant, entered in the office of the clerk of the county of Oswego on the 23d day of November, 1897, upon the verdict of a jury, and also from an order entered in said clerk's office on the 23d day of December, 1897, denying the plaintiff's motion for a new trial made upon the minutes.

The action is in replevin, and was commenced on the 20th day of October, 1896, to recover possession of certain personal property alleged to be of the value of about $2,000, which the plaintiff claims belonged to him, and which he claims the defendant wrongfully and unlawfully took possession of on the 29th day of September, 1896, and converted to his own use. The property which is the subject of dispute consisted of hotel furniture and furnishings, and on and prior to September 2, 1896, was in the possession of the Lake Ontario and Riverside Railway Company in a hotel which was being run by it. From time to time prior to that date the property had been purchased by the railway company from S. P. Pierce's Sons of Syracuse, N. Y., to the amount of $675 ; from A. S. Norton & Co. of Oswego, N. Y., to the amount of $1,835.20, and from other merchants to the amount of about $1,200. On the day last mentioned the railway company assumed to sell to the plaintiff all of said property for the consideration of $1,282, $600 of which was paid in cash by the plaintiff and the balance by assuming the payment of the account of S. P. Pierce's Sons, and the railway company executed a bill of sale of the property to the plaintiff and delivered possession thereof to him. Thereafter, and on the 29th day of September, 1896, the furniture obtained from Norton & Co. not having been paid for, they commenced an action in replevin against the railway company to recover the same from it, claiming that the property was sold upon condition that the title to it should not pass, but should remain in Norton & Co. until fully paid for by the railway company. In that action the defendant, as sheriff of Oswego county, took possession of the property sold to the railway company by Norton & Co., which constituted a part of the property sold by the railway company to the plaintiff, and refused to deliver it to the plaintiff after demand made. Thereupon the plaintiff brought this action of replevin against the defendant to recover the property so taken by him at the instance of Norton & Co.

W. P. Goodelle, for the appellant.

D. P. Morehouse, for the respondent.

McLENNAN, J.:

The only questions of fact submitted to the jury were whether or not the sale of the furniture by Norton & Co. to the railway company was a conditional sale, the condition being that the title to the property should not pass until paid for, or was such that the railway company became the absolute owner of the property, and was such at the time it assumed to sell and deliver the same to the plaintiff in this action, and whether or not the plaintiff was a *bona fide* purchaser of the same.

The defendant was permitted, over plaintiff's objections and exceptions, to introduce a large amount of evidence tending to show that the railway company, from which the plaintiff purchased the goods in question, was insolvent when it purchased the same from Norton & Co., and also when it sold them to the plaintiff. We are of the opinion that the admission of such evidence constituted reversible error. The evidence was not material and had no bearing upon any issue submitted to the jury. If the sale by Norton & Co. to the railway company was a legal conditional sale, and of such a character that the title did not to pass until the goods were paid for, the solvency or insolvency of the railway company was of no consequence, because its interest and right to the possession of the goods having terminated on account of its failure to pay according to the terms of the sale, Norton & Co. were entitled to retake them, and upon so doing became the absolute owners of the same. Under such a sale Norton & Co. would have had the right to retake the goods even if the railway company had been entirely solvent. Their rights in the premises could in no manner be affected because of the fact that the railway company was solvent or insolvent, and so proof of that fact was immaterial and incompetent for the purpose of establishing the character of the sale.

Many of the facts proven which tended to establish the insolvency of the railway company, and which were objected to, were in no manner shown to have been known to the plaintiff when he purchased the goods from the railway company, and, therefore, were not competent for the purpose of showing that he was not a *bona fide* purchaser of the goods in question.

If we assume that the alleged conditional sale was valid as between Norton & Co. and the railway company, it could have no binding force or effect as against the plaintiff under the proof in this case, if he was a *bona fide* purchaser, and any fact which existed as to the financial condition of the railway company was not competent to impeach his *bona fides*, unless such fact was known or ought to have been known by him. It is urged by the learned counsel for the respondent that it was proper to show the insolvency of the railway company, for the purpose of bringing the transfer by it to the plaintiff within the statute prohibiting transfers by insolvent corporations, or by those whose insolvency is imminent. (Laws of 1890, chap. 564, § 48, as amd. by Laws of 1892, chap. 688.) A sufficient answer to that suggestion is that no such issue was submitted to the jury. It is true defendant's counsel asked the court to charge, and it did charge, the statute, but the court nowhere pointed out its applicability, if any, to the facts of the case at bar, and the jury was not in any manner instructed what effect should be given to the provision of the statute in determining the rights of the respective parties.

Without going over the evidence in detail bearing upon the question of the railway company's insolvency, which was objected to, we think it clear that at least such of the facts proven as were not shown to have come to the knowledge of the plaintiff at the time he purchased the goods in question were incompetent, and had no bearing upon any issue which was submitted to the jury for its determination. It cannot be said that the evidence was not prejudicial to the plaintiff. It is apparent that the financial condition of the railway company, as disclosed by the evidence, would materially influence the determination of the jury. The jury would naturally give weight to the fact that an insolvent corporation had obtained Norton & Co.'s goods, and that while insolvent it had sold them to the plaintiff for much less than the purchase price, perchance for less than their value, and such considerations would be quite likely to influence the determination of the questions submitted to the jury by the court, especially so when the questions submitted were presented in such a manner as to leave the important issues somewhat obscured.

Numerous other objections were made by the plaintiff to the rulings of the court in receiving and excluding evidence, to which exceptions were duly taken, but in view of the fact that a new trial must be had because of the error committed in receiving evidence of the railway company's insolvency, we deem it unnecessary to discuss the other exceptions presented by the record.

It follows that the judgment and order appealed from should be reversed and a new trial granted, with costs to the appellant to abide event.

Judgment and order reversed upon questions of law only and a new trial ordered, with costs to the appellant to abide event.

ADAMS, P. J., SPRING, WILLIAMS and HISCOCK, JJ., concurred.

Judgment and order reversed upon questions of law only, and new trial ordered, with costs to the appellant to abide event.

ANNIE WELCH, Respondent, *v.* SYRACUSE RAPID TRANSIT RAILWAY COMPANY, Appellant.

Negligence — injury to a passenger stepping from a street railroad car into a hole in an asphalt pavement within two feet of the tracks, which a paving company had agreed to keep in repair.

In an action to recover damages for personal injuries, it appeared that the plaintiff was a passenger on the defendant's street railroad in the city of Syracuse, and that while alighting from the car she stepped into a hole in the asphalt with which the street was paved and broke her ankle. The hole had existed for several months, and was four feet six inches long, one foot five inches wide and three inches deep. The inner edge was one foot five inches from the outer rail of the defendant's track.

It further appeared that the pavement had been laid by a paving company, pursuant to a resolution of the common council of the city, authorizing the paving company, at its own expense, to take up the existing pavement and to repave the street with asphaltina and to keep the same in repair for five years, the work to be done in accordance with plans and specifications of the city engineer and subject to the approval of the commissioner of public works.

Held, that the resolution was competent upon the question of the defendant's negligence, as the defendant had a right, in determining whether or not the hole was dangerous, to take into consideration the fact that the duty of repairing the street had been imposed upon the paving company, and that neither the city nor the paving company had taken any steps to repair the defect.

Semble, that the adoption of the resolution operated, during the five years that the paving company agreed to keep the pavement in repair, to relieve the defendant from the obligation imposed upon it by section 98 of the Railroad Law (Laws of 1890, chap. 565, as amd. by Laws of 1892, chap. 676) of keeping in repair the pavement for a distance of two feet in width outside of its tracks.

SPRING and HISCOCK, JJ., dissented.

APPEAL by the defendant, the Syracuse Rapid Transit Railway Company, from a judgment of the Supreme Court in favor of the plaintiff, entered in the office of the clerk of the county of Onondaga on the 4th day of April, 1901, upon the verdict of a jury for $800, and also from an order entered in said clerk's office on the 16th day of April, 1901, denying the defendant's motion for a new trial made upon the minutes.

The action was commenced on the 6th day of September, 1900, to recover damages for injuries sustained by the plaintiff, alleged to have been caused through the negligence of the defendant.

Charles E. Spencer, for the appellant.

M. E. Driscoll, for the respondent.

McLENNAN, J. :

On the 30th day of April, 1899, and for several years prior, the defendant was engaged in operating a street surface railroad in the city of Syracuse, N. Y. On Warren street, which extends north and south, there were two tracks, and the defendant was accustomed to cause its cars going in either direction upon that street to stop just south of its intersection with Genesee street to permit passengers to enter or alight from the same. At that point, on the westerly side of the street, about twelve feet south of the south crosswalk on Genesee street, there was a hole or depression in the asphalt with which the street was paved, which had existed for several months. It was four feet six inches long; its greatest width one foot five inches, and its greatest depth three inches. The edges were beveled and somewhat ragged. The inner edge was one foot five inches from the outer or westerly rail of defendant's track.

About one o'clock in the afternoon of the day in question the plaintiff, who had taken passage in another part of the city upon one of defendant's open cars, along the side of which there was a running board to enable passengers to get on or off, attempted to leave the car at the place described, and in doing so stepped from the running board into the depression without observing it, in such manner that her ankle was broken and she was thrown to the ground. To recover damages for the injuries thus sustained this action was brought.

Two theories were presented to the jury by the learned trial justice, either of which they were instructed might be made the basis of a recovery against the defendant according as they found the facts : *First,* that by statute, section 98 of the Railroad Law (Laws 1890 chap. 565, as amd. by Laws of 1892, chap. 676), the duty was imposed upon the defendant of maintaining the street "two feet in width outside of its tracks" in a reasonably safe condition, and if the place where the plaintiff stepped in alighting from the car, and which caused her to fall, was within that space and was dangerous, the defendant was chargeable with negligence for having neglected to repair the defect in the pavement; *second,* that if the jury should find, as they might upon the evidence, that the plaintiff stepped into the hole at a point outside of the two-foot strip, if it was dangerous, the defendant was chargeable with negligence for having stopped its car opposite such place for the purpose of letting plaintiff off, without adopting some means to prevent her from stepping into the hole in question.

To meet the first proposition the defendant offered in evidence a resolution adopted by the common council of the city of Syracuse on the 22d day of April, 1895, duly approved by the mayor, by which permission was given to the Asphaltina Company of America to take up the pavement then laid on Warren street, on the westerly side of defendant's railroad, between Genesee and Washington streets, and at its own expense to repave the same with asphaltina, and to keep the same in repair for five years, to be done in accordance with plans and specifications of the city engineer and subject to the approval of the commissioner of public works of the city. Prior to the adoption of the resolution, the space between defendant's tracks and a strip two feet wide outside of the westerly rail, which included the place in question, was paved with sandstone blocks. Pursuant to the resolution and under the direction and supervision of the commissioner of public works, the two-foot strip of sandstone pavement was removed by the asphaltina company, and it, with the rest of the street west of defendant's tracks, was paved with asphaltina. This was done without cost to the defendant and, so far as appears, without notice to it by the city, although it had knowledge that a change in the pavement had been made and the manner in which it was done. From the time the change was made, so far as appears, the defendant did nothing to keep the strip of pavement next to the outside or westerly rail of its track in Warren street in repair, and in no manner interfered with it. The resolution was excluded and the defendant duly excepted.

It is urged on the part of the appellant that by the resolution which was offered in evidence, and in view of what was done pursuant to it under the direction of the city, the defendant was relieved from all obligation imposed by section 98 of the Railroad Law to keep the two-foot strip west of its westerly rail properly paved or in repair for the period of five years, or at least until the city had notified the defendant to again assume the responsibility of keeping the same in repair; that the city, as it had a right to do, had assumed exclusive control over such pavement, and that, under the circumstances, the defendant had no right to in any manner interfere with it for the period of five years, during which, the asphaltina company, in consideration of being permitted to lay the pavement, agreed to keep it in repair. It is evident the purpose of the resolution was to enable the asphaltina pavement to be tested to ascertain its durability and wearing qualities, and it is apparent, if the defendant or any other corporation could make repairs at will, such test would be useless and of no practical benefit either to the asphaltina company or to the city.

By the charter of the city of Syracuse (Laws of 1885, chap. 26, § 30) the mayor and common council are given authority to lay out, make, open, regulate, repair and improve highways and streets, and by section 138 (as amd. by Laws of 1888, chap. 449) the common council is given authority to order the construction and repair of pavements, and defray the expenses thereof by assessment upon the abutting property owners. Section 98 of the Railroad Law does not in any manner deprive the city authorities of any of the powers conferred upon them by the charter, but on the contrary, by its terms, provides that a railroad corporation occupying the streets of a city shall keep in permanent repair the portion of the streets between its tracks, the rails of its tracks, and two feet in width outside of its tracks, "*under the supervision of the proper local authorities and whenever required by them to do so, and in such manner as they may prescribe.*" The statute expressly reserves to the local authorities the right of control over any and all portions of the street, that between and adjacent to the tracks, as well as to any other part. The city of Syracuse had the right, acting through its officers or through any other agency, to do with the pavement in question precisely as it saw fit, provided it did not unnecessarily and improperly interfere with the rights of the defendant. It had the right to withdraw from the defendant the power to in any manner interfere with the pavement upon Warren street, or to relieve it from the duty imposed by statute, provided other means were adopted which would better or equally well protect the interests and rights of the public.

So far as appears, at the time the resolution in question was adopted, the pavement upon Warren street adjacent to defendant's tracks was in perfect repair. The defendant had fully performed the obligation imposed upon it by statute. The city, we must assume, for a legitimate and useful purpose, ordered such pavement to be removed; directed that another kind be laid in its place by a party in no manner connected with the defendant, and directed that such party have control of and be responsible for its condition for a period of five years. By such action on the part of the city, the defendant was relieved from the obligation during that time of keeping in repair the portion of the street in question.

In *Snell* v. *Rochester Railway Company* (64 Hun, 476) it was held that the defendant was not liable for the dangerous condition of the street between its tracks, arising from the defective condition of a sewer which had been constructed under the authority of the city.

The resolution was competent as bearing upon the question of defendant's negligence, even if it was not relieved of its obligation to keep the street in repair by reason of the city's action in the premises. It is apparent that the comparatively slight depression in question would not impress the defendant as being dangerous so forcibly when it knew or had reason to believe that the municipality, through the asphaltina company, had assumed responsibility for its repair, and did not so consider it. The defendant had a right, in determining whether or not the defect was dangerous, to take into consideration the fact that the city authorities had taken control of the street, and to assume that they did not regard it as being in a dangerous condition, because of the fact that they had taken no steps to repair or cause the same to be repaired. The jury was entitled to have before it any and all facts which would influence the conduct of a person of ordinary care and prudence in the premises. It had a right to say, not only whether the defendant was negligent in permitting the defect described to exist in the street, as an independent proposition, but also to say whether it was negligent in so doing, in view of the fact that, by the resolution which was offered in evidence, the city had contracted with the asphaltina company that said company, and not the defendant, should keep such street in repair, under the direction and supervision of the municipal officers.

We think the exclusion of the resolution was error, and that it was of such substance as to require the reversal of the judgment. It is impossible to say from the record upon which of the theories presented by the learned trial court the jury found the defendant guilty of negligence. The evidence was conflicting as to whether or not the plaintiff stepped into the hole outside or inside of the two-foot strip. If the jury found that she stepped inside it was instructed, as we have seen, that it might find the defendant guilty of negligence because it failed to discharge the duty imposed upon it by the section of the Railroad Law referred to, and for aught that appears, that was the basis of the verdict rendered. The resolution should have been received in evidence, at least for the purpose of enabling the jury to say whether or not, in view of it and under all the circumstances, the defendant, through its agents, was negligent in not determining that the defect in the street was dangerous, and in not repairing it.

Having reached the conclusion that the exclusion of the resolution offered by the defendant constitutes reversible error, we deem it unnecessary to determine whether the defect in the pavement — assuming that the city of Syracuse was responsible for it — was of such a character as to charge the defendant with negligence because it stopped its car at that place to permit the plaintiff to alight therefrom.

It follows that the judgment and order appealed from should be reversed and a new trial granted, with costs to the appellant to abide event.

Judgment and order reversed upon questions of law only, the facts having been examined and no error found therein, and new trial ordered, with costs to the appellant to abide event.

WILLIAMS and DAVY, JJ., concurred; SPRING and HISCOCK, JJ., dissented.

SPRING, J. (dissenting):

By section 98 of the Railroad Law the duty of keeping "in permanent repair" that part of the street between its tracks, the rails of its tracks "and two feet in width outside of its tracks" is imposed upon the defendant. This is a mandatory obligation resting upon the defendant in consideration of its privilege to use the street, and

is for the benefit of the public.   In the language of the court in
Conway v. *City of Rochester* (157 N. Y. 33, 38): "The duty of
keeping such portion of the streets in permanent repair is not suggested or advised, but is commanded.   So much of the statute certainly is mandatory.   *   *   *   The municipal authorities are
given no authority to relieve the railroad corporation of the whole
or any portion of the needed repairs, or to impose the whole or any
portion of the cost upon the abutting owners or the city at large."

To be sure this reparation must be done under the supervision of
the municipal authorities.   The dominion of the city arises from
the exigency of the situation.   The land occupied by the defendant
is part of the street of the city, and unless the city retain supervision over it the defendant might use different material or construct
in a different manner its part of the street from the residue thereof,
and it is essential, therefore, that the determination of what material
is to enter into any repairs made and the manner of doing the work
shall be vested in the city authorities, but the expense is chargeable to the defendant.   The owner of a city lot is obliged to construct and keep in repair the sidewalk in front of his premises, but
the material to be used and the method of performing the labor are
within the control of the municipal authorities.   I take it that
the owner is liable to a person injured by falling upon a defective
sidewalk in front of such owner's premises, providing the defect
has been of long standing, even though the city has not interfered
or required the defective condition to be remedied.

In 1895 the asphaltina company put in the pavement on this
street pursuant to an agreement authorized by the common council
of the city.   By the agreement the asphaltina company was to
keep this pavement in repair for five years.   The defendant, of
course, knew of the condition of the pavement and acquiesced in
the change made in it in 1895.   The asphaltina company is liable
for failure to comply with its contract, we may assume, but that
does not absolve either the city or the defendant from complying
with the duty of keeping the street in repair, which is a matter of
vital concern to those using the street.   The burden was imposed
upon the defendant to remedy the defect, and it cannot shield itself
from liability to its passenger because the asphaltina company or
the city is responsible for this defect as well as it.   It may be it has

redress against the city as the city may have against the owner of a lot who neglects to keep his sidewalk in repair, whereby injury has resulted, but the person injured, one of the public, is not obliged to investigate the relations between any of these parties. He can base his claim upon the recovery arising because of the violation of the statute.

Nor is it necessary for the city first to notify the defendant to repair before the obligation becomes fixed. (*City of Brooklyn* v. *Brooklyn City Railroad Co.*, 47 N. Y. 475; *Doyle* v. *City of New York*, 58 App. Div. 588; *Simon* v. *Met. Street Railway Co.*, 29 Misc. Rep. 126.) The duty is imperative as the primary one imposed upon the defendant, and if a defect exists which would render the city liable to respond in damages because of it, the street railroad company which has appropriated the street for its purposes is likewise liable, perforce the statute, even though by its contractual relations with the city the latter may be compelled to indemnify it. The duty is imposed originally upon the city to maintain and keep in repair its streets. The statute, without relieving the city, attached the burden as to a definite part of the street on the railroad company using it. If the latter is relieved from liability to a traveler injured by reason of a defect in its part because the city let a contract to a paving company to construct and maintain the pavement, then the city may also be relieved. Upon proper notice to the defendant such an agreement might be made at any time, as the control of the street is vested in the municipality. If it is done with the knowledge and acquiescence of the defendant, the resulting liability of the latter is the same. This pavement had existed for four years prior to this accident, and so far as appears there was no outcry against it by the defendant. The argument is made that the pavement for which the present was substituted was adequate. It is too late now to raise that question when it did not seek to prevent the repairs made and for four years has acquiesced without a murmur. The time to resist was when its pavement was being removed, for the municipal authorities could not remove it arbitrarily.

The plaintiff was a passenger on the defendant's car, which was an open one with a running board to enable the passengers to get on and off. At the place where the car was in the habit of stopping there was a hole in the pavement about four feet and six inches long, one foot five inches in width, and three inches in depth in its deepest part. No warning was given to the plaintiff or to any of the passengers as to the existence of this hole, and the plaintiff stepped from the car into it, unaware of its existence, and was injured. I think the verdict of the jury, that the defendant was negligent in permitting its car to stop at this place for passengers to alight without apprising them of the situation, is supported by the facts, and upon that verdict, as matter of law, the defendant is liable. (*Wolf* v. *Third Ave. R. R. Co.*, 67 App. Div. 605.)

The judgment and order should be affirmed, with costs.

HISCOCK, J., concurred.

Judgment and order reversed upon questions of law only, the facts having been examined and no error found therein, and new trial ordered, with costs to the appellant to abide the event.

In the Matter of the Petition of GEORGE DOHENY and JOHN G. LYNCH, as Trustees under the Will of PATRICK LYNCH, Deceased, for Leave to Resign.

MARY L. PENDERGAST and Others, Appellants; GEORGE DOHENY and JOHN G. LYNCH, as Trustees, etc., of PATRICK LYNCH, Deceased, Respondents.

Trust — taxes on real property, assessed during a testator's life, should be paid from his general estate and not from a trust fund of which the real property is part; — accounting, when it does not create an estoppel.

Taxes levied prior to the death of a testator, upon real property in which a trust is created by the testator's will, are not a charge against the trust estate, but are payable out of the testator's general estate.

Where it appears that the trustees were also the executors under the will, and that pending the probate thereof they were appointed temporary administrators of the estate, and while acting as such paid taxes assessed upon the trust property prior to the testator's death, a decree rendered upon their final accounting as temporary administrators, which simply determined that the temporary administrators had received from all sources a certain sum and had expended for all purposes a certain other sum, leaving a balance of $558 in their hands which, less their commissions and costs, they were directed to pay

(margin) 370| 691|

over to themselves as executors, and which did not attempt to make any distinction between the receipts and expenditures received and made on account of the trust estate from those received and made on account of the general estate, will not estop the *cestuis que trustent*, when, upon the accounting of the trustees, the latter seek to charge the payment of such taxes upon the trust estate, from insisting that such taxes should be paid out of the general estate.

APPEAL by Mary L. Pendergast and others from so much of an order of the Supreme Court, made at the Onondaga Special Term and entered in the office of the clerk of the county of Onondaga on the 9th day of November, 1901, as overrules and disallows the objections filed on their behalf to so much of the account of the trustees as credits themselves with the sums of $359.68 and $85.02.

The proceeding was instituted on the 29th day of May, 1901, by the respondents, trustees, by service of their petition duly verified on that day, in which they asked for a settlement of their account, for allowance of their commissions and for permission to resign as such trustees.

William S. Jenney, for the appellants.

Leroy B. Williams, for the respondents.

McLENNAN, J.:

Patrick Lynch, of the city of Syracuse, N. Y., died on the 15th day of September, 1898, leaving a last will and testament, in which the respondents George Doheny and John G. Lynch were named executors, and which, among others, contained the following provision:

" 2nd. I give, devise and bequeath to my executors hereinafter named, the store and premises known as No. 128 E. Genesee St., in Syracuse, being about twenty feet on said street, and now leased in part to Bartel's Brewing Co., in trust nevertheless for the following uses and purposes, to wit: to rent or let to the best advantage, and from the income thereof to pay all taxes, assessments and repairs, and pay the remainder of the net income and rents thereof to my daughter Mary L. Pendergast quarterly during the term of her natural life, and upon her death they shall convey and deliver said real estate to the children of my said daughter then living."

Upon the will being offered for probate, objections were made, and on the 5th day of October, 1898, the respondents were appointed temporary administrators of the estate, to act pending the hearing of such objections, and were authorized to take possession "of the real and personal property of which said Patrick Lynch died seized and possessed, and receive the income, rents and profits thereof as the same become due and payable, until the further order of the court; and they are also hereby authorized to lease the real estate of which said deceased died seized for not more than one year, and to pay from the income thereof all taxes and assessments thereon, and to keep the same in repair and to pay therefor from the income thereof. Also to pay the debts and expenses tending the last sickness and funeral of said deceased."

The respondents, as such temporary administrators, immediately entered upon the discharge of their duties, took possession of all the real and personal property of which the deceased died seized, collected the rents and income thereof, received from all sources the sum of $13,405.59. From the moneys in their hands they paid the debts and expenses attending the last sickness and the funeral of the deceased and other debts of the estate, amounting in the aggregate to the sum of $12,847.59, leaving a balance in their hands of $558.

The will of Patrick Lynch was duly probated on the 2d day of February, 1899, and thereby the respondents became executors and trustees under such will. Thereupon and on the 8th day of February, 1899, they presented their petition as temporary administrators to the surrogate of Onondaga county, asking for a settlement of their accounts and their discharge, and made a detailed statement of their receipts and expenditures a part of such petition. By such statement of account it appeared that on the 3d day of January, 1899, the temporary administrators paid to "E. F. Allen, Treas., State & County Taxes 1898, Estate of P. Lynch, $1,504.25." Also under date of February 4, 1899, was the following item: "E. F. Allen, Treas., City Taxes 1898, 130 E. Genesee St. (the trust property), $359.68." It appears by the affidavits used upon this proceeding, although not indicated by the account, that of the first item of $1,504.25, $85.02 was for taxes on the trust property, and the account itself indicates that was true of the whole of the second item.

Notice of the presentation of such petition, of which the statement of account constituted a part, was given to all parties interested, and there being no objection a decree was duly made by the Surrogate's Court adjudging, in substance, that the account presented was correct; that there was a balance in the hands of the temporary administrators of $558. Their commissions were fixed at $324.06, and their costs at $70, leaving a balance of $163.94 which they were directed to pay to themselves as "executors" of the will of Patrick Lynch, deceased. Upon such payment being made it was adjudged that the temporary administrators should be discharged and their accounts as such finally settled. Thereupon the respondents entered upon the discharge of their duties as executors and trustees under the will of Patrick Lynch, deceased, and continued to act as such until the order appealed from was made which permitted them to resign as trustees, and settled their accounts. The controversy arises over the order so far as it settles such account, in that the *cestui que trust* was not credited with the two items above referred to paid by the temporary administrators for taxes upon the trust property.

The facts are not in controversy. The temporary administrators, in making up their account as such, did not make any distinction between moneys received from the estate generally and those received from the trust property, and the same was true with reference to their expenditures. Such bookkeeping was entirely proper, or at least it was immaterial so far as the appellants were concerned, because at that time, a contest existing as to the validity of the will, no one could know whether or not there would be a trust estate. If the contest had been successful the deceased would have died intestate, and there would have been no trust estate or *cestuis que trust*. Even under such circumstances it undoubtedly was the duty of the temporary administrators to have kept the income from and disbursements made in connection with the real property separate and distinct from the receipts and expenditures affecting the estate generally, to the end that the real estate, with the net accumulations, might be turned over to the heirs in case there was sufficient personal property to pay the indebtedness against the estate; but the appellants had no interest or concern in what the temporary administrators did in that regard, because, so far as then appeared, they had no interest in the estate and would not have unless the will should be declared valid. The appellants, even had they known that the temporary administrators were paying the debts of the general estate with the net income received from the East Genesee street property, could not have been heard to complain, because at that time, so far as was known, it was not trust property, and the appellants had no interest to protect in that regard. Their interest commenced when it was established that the deceased had made a valid will which created a trust for their benefit. The will, however, having been admitted to probate, and a trust estate having been thereby created, it became necessary to determine the rights of the parties as of the time of the testator's death, and then and only then it became important to determine the rights of the *cestuis que trust* in the real estate in question, and the simple question is presented whether the method of bookkeeping adopted by the temporary administrators, which we may assume was approved by the decree of the Surrogate's Court discharging the respondents as such, can in any manner affect the rights of the *cestuis que trust*.

It appears that the two items paid for taxes above referred to, were paid by the temporary administrators out of funds received from the rents and income of the trust estate. The taxes for the year 1898 upon the real property constituting the trust estate, having been assessed prior to the death of Patrick Lynch, were not a charge against such trust estate, but were payable out of the general estate the same as any other indebtedness of the testator. (*Matter of Babcock*, 115 N. Y. 450.)

It is, therefore, only necessary to inquire whether the decree made by the Surrogate's Court discharging the temporary administrators, and which directed them to turn over all the property of the estate to the executors under the will which then had been admitted to probate, was of such a character as to estop the appellants from claiming credit for the amount which the temporary administrators had paid for the benefit of the general estate, out of the funds belonging to the *cestuis que trust*.

The decree of the Surrogate's Court discharging the temporary administrators in no manner purports to settle the estate as between the several interested parties. It is not a decree of distribution. It in no manner assumes to determine what part or portion was included in the trust or remained a part of the general estate. It in no manner purported to strike a balance between the receipts and expenditures affecting the trust property. It did not assume to direct that any sum should be paid over to the trustees by the temporary administrators. The decree simply determined that the temporary administrators had received from all sources out of the estate a certain sum; had expended for all purposes in connection therewith a certain other sum, leaving a balance of $558 in their hands which, less their commissions and costs, they were directed to pay over, not to themselves as trustees, but to themselves as executors under the will of Patrick Lynch, deceased. Undoubtedly, the decree having been made upon notice to all the parties interested, if it had determined that the balance of $558, less the commissions and costs, belonged to the trustees, and had directed that that amount be paid to them as such, the trustees and those claiming under them would have been bound by such determination, and if mistake had occurred it could only be corrected by a review of such decree. But no such determination was made, and such balance was not directed to be paid to the respondents as trustees, but to them as executors, and such balance and the entire estate was turned over to them as such executors. It, therefore, became their duty to adjust the accounts of the estate between themselves as executors and themselves as trustees. Certainly the *cestuis que trust* were in no position to compel such adjustment until the respondents as trustees presented their account as such, because then, so far as appears, for the first time the *cestuis que trust* knew that it was proposed to use money which belonged to them with which to pay the general indebtedness of the estate. There was nothing in the decree of the surrogate which authorized the respondents to credit the balance which remained in their hands as temporary administrators to themselves as trustees, rather than to themselves as executors. Under the decree as *executors* they became possessed not only of the balance remaining in their hands as temporary administrators, but of the entire estate, and it then became their duty to make proper distribution as between the appellants and the others interested in the estate. There was nothing in the decree which discharged them as temporary administrators to prevent them from so doing, and we think there is nothing in such decree to prevent the appellants from compelling such action. The decree made by the Surrogate's Court on the final settlement of the temporary administrators' account determined nothing beyond the amounts received and paid out by them. (*Johnson* v. *Richards*, 3 Hun, 454.)

The relief sought by the appellants is equitable. By granting it no injustice can result to any interested party. The respondents presumably have the funds in their possession as executors with which to credit the estate, which was in their hands as trustees, with the amount which had been improperly taken from the trust funds and used for the purposes of the general estate.

The conclusion is reached that the order appealed from should be modified, so as to provide that the account of the respondents as trustees be corrected by disallowing the items of three hundred and fifty-nine dollars and sixty-eight cents and eighty-five dollars and two cents, and directing that such sums be paid to the appellants, and as so modified the order is affirmed, with ten dollars costs and disbursements to the appellants, payable out of the money of the estate other than trust property.

SPRING, WILLIAMS and DAVY, JJ., concurred; HISCOCK, J., not voting.

Order modified so as to provide that the account of the respondents, as trustees, be corrected by disallowing the items of three hundred and fifty-nine dollars and sixty-eight cents and eighty-five dollars and two cents, and directing that such sums be paid to the appellants, and as so modified affirmed, with ten dollars costs and disbursements, payable out of the moneys of the estate other than trust property.

ADDISON W. SMITH, Respondent, v. THE FIRST NATIONAL BANK OF CUBA, Appellant.

Usury — recovery of, where paper is discounted by a national bank — when the Statute of Limitations begins to run.

Where a national bank discounts a note for a customer, retaining as the discount an excessive rate of interest, and on the maturity of the note the customer pays the excessive discount in cash and executes a renewal note for the same amount, and this process is repeated several times, each actual payment constitutes a usurious transaction within the meaning of section 5198 of the

United States Revised Statutes, which provides that a person who pays an excessive rate of interest to a national bank may maintain an action to recover, "twice the amount of the interest thus paid, from the association taking or receiving the same, provided such action is commenced within two years from the time the usurious transaction occurred."

The two years' Statute of Limitations commences to run from the date of each cash payment of an excessive discount.

APPEAL by the defendant, The First National Bank of Cuba, from a judgment of the Supreme Court in favor of the plaintiff, entered in the office of the clerk of the county of Allegany on the 3d day of October, 1900, upon the report of a referee.

This action was commenced January 9, 1899, to recover penalties from the defendant, a national bank, for receiving or reserving more than six per cent interest in violation of sections 5197 and 5198 of the United States Revised Statutes. The fact appears without contradiction that as to a series of notes negotiated by the plaintiff with the defendant the latter did receive money in excess of the legal rate of interest, but several defenses are interposed, an appreciation of which renders necessary a review of the various transactions.

On November 18, 1897, the plaintiff presented to the bank a promissory note of $5,000 due in three months, signed by Julia A. Smith, the mother of the plaintiff, to the order of A. W. and C. S. Smith. A. W. Smith is the plaintiff and C. S. Smith his brother. The note was duly indorsed and negotiated with the defendant, which retained for the discount $87.50 which is $12.50 in excess of the legal rate of interest. This note was renewed at its maturity by a note February 18, 1898, signed and indorsed as the original note, but the avails of the said note, $4,911.55, less the discount, were placed to the credit of the maker, and the note of $5,000 was charged to her account. A precisely similar transaction occurred three months later and also upon a further renewal July 18, 1898. At the maturity of this last note of the series the referee has found that the plaintiff paid the note, but disallowed the discount on the preceding notes on the ground that it was paid each time by Mrs. Smith, the maker. No question arises as to the Statute of Limitations over this transaction, and the finding of the referee does no violence to the facts.

On the 10th day of August, 1896, the plaintiff negotiated with the defendant a promissory note for $4,761.48, executed by him as maker to the order of the said Julia A. Smith and indorsed by her and payable at the defendant bank three months from its date. The proceeds of this note, less the discount ($83.35), were credited to the account of the plaintiff. This note was renewed in about three months by a like note, but the avails were credited to the Smith estate and the prior note charged up to that account. A like renewal was had in February, 1897, and the same disposition was made of the proceeds, and that note was also charged to the account of the Smith estate. Again, this note was renewed by another similar in form in May, 1897, and on that day there was charged to the account of Julia A. Smith in the bank $100, and to the Smith estate $37.55, covering the discount on this note and another one, and this note was paid in full by the plaintiff about November 20, 1897. On these notes the excess of interest reserved each time was about one per cent, and the referee finding this was paid by the plaintiff, allowed him to recover therefor less the sum of $100 charged to the account of Julia A. Smith.

On the 2d day of January, 1896, the plaintiff negotiated with the defendant a promissory note of $3,000 made by Julia A. Smith to the order of A. W. and C. S. Smith and duly indorsed and due in three months, and the avails thereof, less the discount of $61.25, or an excess beyond the lawful rate of $16.25, were credited to the Smith estate. This note was renewed from time to time, the avails each time being credited to the account of the Smith estate and the note charged to the same account until the last note of this series, which was given May 10, 1897, the discount whereof was charged to Julia A. Smith, and the $37.55 to the Smith estate as above mentioned. The discount on these several notes was paid by the plaintiff, who finally paid the note in full November 20, 1897.

It is apparent, therefore, that these notes were all made and negotiated for the benefit of the plaintiff, but the evidence is not as clear as it should be as to the person paying some of the payments of interest or discount. There were three distinct accounts in the bank, one of the plaintiff, one of his mother and one denominated that of the Smith estate. Just who composed the latter does not appear, except that the indorsers were brothers, and the defendant seemed to exercise the privilege of charging the discount to any of these accounts which were sufficiently large to meet it in case the plaintiff's account was inadequate for that purpose. The evidence shows unmistakably that the plaintiff paid these notes, and he testified also that he paid the discount each time it arose. The final payments were made by a loan upon his mother's property, but he secured her so that he in fact paid the debts. Pass books were written up at regular intervals of these three accounts and delivered to the persons entitled to them, so that we may assume each party interested was advised of the course adopted by the defendant. There are also other notes involved in this litigation, but as the referee did not allow any recovery for the illegal interest reserved on them, it is unnecessary to go into their history.

Stanley C. Swift, for the appellant.

F. M. Todd, for the respondent.

SPRING, J.:

Section 5197 of the Revised Statutes of the United States restricts the rate of interest which may be charged or reserved as discount by a national bank to the rate allowed in the State where the bank is located. Section 5198 provides, *first,* for the forfeiture of the entire interest as a penalty for taking usurious interest, and, *secondly,* that an action may be maintained by the person who has paid the excessive interest to recover "twice the amount of the interest thus paid from the association taking or receiving the same, provided such action is commenced within two years from the time the usurious transaction occurred."

The sole question for our determination is when did " the usurious transaction " occur ? When the first of each series of notes was given nothing was paid by the plaintiff. He received the face of the note less the discount, but he paid no interest. This was in the note which he transferred to the defendant. A different situation was presented when the note matured. The plaintiff then gave a new note of like amount with the original and paid the discount including the excessive rate. This was, therefore, a genuine payment, a parting with the interest by the plaintiff, and constituted a " usurious transaction " within the letter of the statute quoted. Each actual payment on each renewal was a separate, independent transaction and the Statute of Limitations actually commenced to run from the date of each payment. The plaintiff had withdrawn all the avails of the various loans so that it cannot be claimed that he paid the discounts from time to time out of the identical moneys which he received from the defendant for these notes. The confusion which has arisen over the question as to when the Statute of Limitations commences to run upon payments of excessive interest in contravention of the section referred to is attributable in a large measure in failing to distinguish between an actual payment and one that is carried along with the principal indebtedness. In *McBroom* v. *Scottish Investment Co.* (153 U. S. 318), relied upon by the referee and the respondent's counsel, there is nothing in conflict with this plain rendering of the statute. In that case the defendant loaned to the plaintiff $65,000 payable in six years with interest at the rate of twelve per cent per annum. He gave a note for the principal sum and several notes for the interest at the stipulated rate and also paid out of the avails to the agent of the defendant $6,500 in cash. The plaintiff paid no part of the principal debt and only the first of the notes for interest and sued to recover as a penalty twice the bonus and the interest originally paid, although the claim for the latter was abandoned. The action was brought pursuant to a statute of New Mexico, where the transaction occurred, and which statute is akin to the one under consideration. In the New Mexico statute the action was maintainable to recover "double the amount so collected or received upon any action brought for the recovery of the same within three years *after such cause of action accrued.*" The agent to whom the $6,500 were paid was acting for the company by an agreement which provided that any bonus paid should inure to the benefit of the defendant, so that this bonus was equivalent to a usurious transaction with the defendant. It is, therefore, precisely the same as if the defendant had retained out of the avails of the loan the bonus of $6,500 which made up the usury. It was not money paid by the plaintiff independently of the loan, but it was part of the note, and until he paid that obligation there was no payment of usury exacted. The pointed distinction between that case and the present one is that here as each note matured and was renewed the plaintiff actually paid the discount in cash, and of course the discount or interest was not carried along in the note. When he paid the note in full he did not pay the discount over again, as it was not in the note. When the payment of interest or discount was made that transaction was completed and the defendant had no election after that to apply this in reduction of the note. That principle only applies where the discount is added to the note. Had there been no renewal note given or if given had it in each instance included the interest, the *McBroom* case would be applicable. In *Brown* v. *Marion National Bank* (169 U. S. 416) the court recognizes the distinction here made, citing the *McBroom* case as its authority, and say : " Sometimes interest is said to have been paid when it is evident that it was only included in a renewal note. But that, as we have said, was not *payment* within the meaning of the statute. (*Driesbach* v. *National Bank,* 104 U. S. 52.) If the note when sued on includes usurious interest, or interest upon usurious interest, agreed to be paid, the holder may, in due time, elect to remit such interest, and it cannot then be said that usurious interest was paid to him." And again : " If at any time the obligee actually pays usurious interest as such, the usurious transaction must be held to have then, and not before, occurred, and he must sue within two years thereafter."

In *Nash* v. *White's Bank of Buffalo* (68 N. Y. 396) the notes transferred to the bank by the plaintiff were those of third persons, and the court held this was an actual payment as the plaintiff had parted with all his title, and it was equivalent to the payment of usurious interest in cash. That case is helpful in that it indicates that if the payment is a genuine one, instead of existing as a liability against the person seeking to recover for the overcharge of interest, it is regarded as a transaction separate from the note itself. Had the plaintiff in this action turned over the promissory note of a third person to meet the discount, when one of the notes was renewed under the *Nash* case, that would be regarded as a payment of the discount the same as if made in money, and in either event the transaction would be ended and the statute commence to run although the Statute of Limitations was not considered in that case. In *National Bank of Auburn* v. *Lewis* (75 N. Y. 516 ; 81 id. 15) the action was by the bank on its note, and the defendant answered setting up the illegal interest exacted and claiming that there was a forfeiture of the interest paid and asked for its allowance in abatement of the sum unpaid on the note. It involved the construction of the first part of section 5198 and not that part which controls in this action. There are several cases in other States which recognize the doctrine that where the interest has been paid instead of embodied in the note such payment constitutes a usurious transaction within the import of this section. (*Lynch* v. *Merchants National Bank*, 22 W. Va. 554; *Henderson Nat. Bank* v. *Alves*, 91 Ky. 142; *First Nat. Bank of Dorchester* v. *Smith*, 36 Neb. 199.)

It is a reasonable interpretation of the statute to hold that upon the actual payment of the interest or discount the cause of action accrues, and the two years' Statute of Limitations commences to run from the date of that payment. Several of the payments made by the plaintiff and allowed by the referee were improperly allowed, as they were barred by this statute.

While two of the series of notes were made by Julia A. Smith as maker, yet they were really for the benefit of the plaintiff and he eventually paid them, and testified that he also paid the discount or interest, and we apprehend that these loans may not be said to be those of third parties within the *Nash* case cited above. The payments which were charged to the account of Julia A. Smith were disallowed, while those charged to the Smith estate were treated as if made by the plaintiff. It does not appear definitely who composed the estate, and the plaintiff testified that he paid all the discounts or. interest. In view of the uncertainty of the proofs as to the person who actually made these payments, we deem it unwise to attempt to modify the judgment conformably to this opinion, believing that upon a retrial the facts can be more fully developed and dissipate the obscurity which the record shows.

The judgment should be reversed and a new trial ordered, with costs to the appellant to abide the event.

McLENNAN, WILLIAMS, HISCOCK and DAVY, JJ., concurred.

Judgment reversed and new trial ordered, with costs to the appellant to abide the event.

HARRY W. TRUE, Respondent, *v.* THE NIAGARA GORGE RAILROAD
COMPANY, Appellant.

*Negligence — injury to a conductor because of car tracks being so close together that
the running board on an open street car overlaps the running board of another
car.*

In an action to recover damages for personal injuries sustained by the plaintiff,
a conductor employed on the defendant's electric railroad, who, while standing
on the running board of his car collecting fares, was swept therefrom by
another car traveling in the opposite direction on the adjacent track, it appeared
that at the point where the accident occurred the tracks were so close together
that if two cars passed each other their running boards would overlap. This
close proximity continued for about one hundred and sixty feet, and was apparently due to an oversight. The plaintiff had been employed upon the road,
which was seven miles in length, for thirty days, and had made from twelve
to fifteen trips daily, but was unaware of the dangerous proximity of the
tracks. It was his custom on each trip to collect fares on the running board
next to the adjoining track, after having first raised the guard rail, which
was let down at the beginning of each trip in order to prevent passengers from
alighting on that side. This was also the custom followed by the conductor
who instructed the plaintiff in the performance of his duties.
It further appeared that it would be impracticable for the plaintiff to stand
between the seats of the car while collecting fares, and that he could not collect fares on the running board on the other side of the car owing to the existence of rocks jutting out from the face of a wall on that side of the track, and
also because the rope attached to the fare register was not accessible from the
running board on that side.
Held, that the questions of the defendant's negligence and of the plaintiff's freedom from contributory negligence were properly submitted to the jury, and
that a judgment entered upon a verdict in favor of the plaintiff should be
affirmed:
That, under the circumstances, the risk incident to the proximity of the tracks
was not one which the plaintiff assumed.
HISCOCK and McLENNAN, JJ., dissented.

APPEAL by the defendant, The Niagara Gorge Railroad Company, from a judgment of the Supreme Court in favor of the plaintiff, entered in the office of the clerk of the county of Niagara on
the 4th day of May, 1901, upon the verdict of a jury for $10,000,
and also from an order entered in said clerk's office on the 17th day
of April, 1901, denying the defendant's motion for a new trial made
upon the minutes.

J. H. Metcalf, for the appellant.

P. F. King, for the respondent.

SPRING, J. :

The plaintiff had been a conductor on the Gorge road, a trolley line operated by the defendant from Niagara Falls to Lewiston, and on September 3, 1899, while acting in that capacity and collecting fares on the running board on one of the defendant's cars, he was struck by another of its cars approaching on a parallel track from the opposite direction, was knocked off and thrown under the car, sustaining injuries resulting in the amputation of both legs below the knees.   He was at the time twenty-nine years of age and had been in the employ of the defendant as a conductor operating its cars on this road, which was only about seven miles in length, for thirty days, going over the road from twelve to fifteen times daily. These cars were open, for summer use by tourists, and consisted of thirteen seats, which extended entirely across the car without any aisle in the car, so that the running board was used by the conductors in the collection of fares.   Each seat was supposed to hold five people when filled, and the car on which the plaintiff was riding at the time he was injured contained fifty-three people.   The seats were somewhat close together, so that when one was occupied there was no space between the passengers and the seat in front and it was inconvenient and even impracticable for the conductor to crowd in front of them between the seats to collect the fares.   The roof of the car was supported by posts which extended out from the body of the car three inches, and they were about thirty-two inches apart and were placed at the ends of the seats.   Iron handle bars were attached to these posts extending out also nearly three inches. Along each side of the car was the running board used by passengers in getting on and off the car and also by the conductor in the performance of his duties.   The outside of the running board extended from the inside of the rail nearest to it twenty-four inches. On each side of the car and just inside the handle bars was a movable guard rail extending along the length of the car for the purpose when down of preventing passengers from alighting or getting on that side of the car.   The road was a double track, and the plaintiff's proof shows that at the point of the injury the distance between the inside rails of these parallel tracks was three feet ten inches, so that two cars could not pass at this point without their running boards overlapping. The witness John Peters, who was an electrician and in charge of the line work for the defendant at the time of the accident, described the situation as follows : " The distance was three feet ten, the inside distance between the two rails. That is the center of the rail, the ball of the rail. I observed cars passing at that point at the time I was measuring the track. Different times I worked right there and I observed the men arguing over it. In testing it a man was working for me and got between the two cars and stood on the running board to let another car pass. I hollered at them to get out of that ; they would get killed. The men had to get up in the car ; they leaned up forward in the car between the two stanchions to let the car pass. I saw the two cars passing and I observed the distance they were apart. Two or three men stood between the cars and they had to get into the car to avoid being struck. I stood there myself ; I stood on the running board and I had to lean up in the car while the car passed."

McGrath, who was a conductor of the defendant and was at the place where the injury occurred within two or three hours thereafter and measured the space between the tracks, testified : " I noticed cars passing each other there ; I noticed the cars could pass together, but the boards would lap ; the edges of the running board would lap over. One would be a little higher than the other, so that it could just lap over the top. This handle bar was about two inches or two inches and a half out from these standards or posts. When the cars pass there a man couldn't stand on the running board ; that is, not with safety. He could stand there and get the same as True got — his legs cut off. It would be impossible for him to stand there without being struck. The next afternoon I went there and measured. I had the point shown to me by the motorman that was on with True at the time, and the two of us took measurements. We measured in two different places there and there was a variation of about two inches in the two measurements ; one place it was three feet ten and the other place three feet eleven."

The usual space between the inside rails of these two tracks was ûve feet three and one-half inches, but the witness referred to and others who measured the space at the point of the accident testified that they were only three feet ten inches apart where the accident occurred. Whatever the actual distance was, the witness who made the experiments and observed others standing on the running board of one of these cars at this place testified that if a man were standing erect on this board he would be hit by a passing car.

It also appears that this narrow space continued only for a short distance, while along the rest of the route, except at the cantilever bridge where the tracks came close together, there was ample space for two cars to pass without injury to one standing erect on either running board, and the conductors did this constantly in the performance of their duties. This close proximity of the tracks continued for about one hundred and sixty feet, varying from three feet ten inches to four feet four inches. The space between the handle bars of contiguous cars was about five or six inches, the witnesses varying somewhat as to the distance. Maps of the tracks were produced upon measurements made subsequently to the accident by engineers in the employ of the defendant which show a space in excess of the standard gauge tracks, but there is evidence adduced tending to show that immediately after the accident to the plaintiff these tracks were relaid and placed farther apart. This road was constructed close to the edge of the Niagara river and the perpendicular wall of rock which extended high above the river was blasted and cut off to make the roadbed. Along where these injuries were inflicted some of the rocks jutted out from the face of the wall so that the conductor could not perform his duties on the running board next to this wall. On the day of the accident the plaintiff had started from Niagara Falls on the track nearest to the granite wall and was on the running board next to the parallel track collecting fares. It was his duty to perform this labor before reaching the Buttery Elevator Station which was the first stop in his northern trip and less than a mile from the starting point. He began at the front of the car collecting from the passengers of each seat, and as he was north of the Steel Arch bridge, perhaps one hundred feet, was hit by a car going in the opposite direction and toward which his back was turned. He testified, and he is corroborated in this, that he stood at the end of the seat and was collecting a fare. One witness, a passenger, testified he was making change for a two-dollar bill which the witness had handed him in payment of two fares. Witnesses on behalf of the defendant testified that plaintiff was swinging around one of the standards when he was struck. The motorman on the approaching car sounded his gong, but the proof tends to show this was a common thing and was not for the purpose of attracting the attention of the conductor of the other car. The roaring noise of the river in a measure drowned the sound of the gong, but the plaintiff if he had heard it would not have apprehended that the gong was ringing to warn him of the danger. It appears that in the month he had been acting as conductor he had always collected fares on the running board, meeting cars on every trip and there was no clashing, nothing to apprise him of any danger. The proof shows also that before he commenced his service as conductor, he was instructed by a brother conductor named Snyder, who had been long in the employ of the defendant. The plaintiff testified, and there is supporting proof of this fact, that Snyder collected fares on the running board and gave him no instructions that they were to be collected elsewhere, and what is more significant, Snyder performed his duties on the north-bound trip on the running board next to the other track instead of on the side nearest to the wall. There was a rope attached to a bell to register the payment of the fares and which it was his duty to pull upon collecting each fare, and this rope was on the river side of the car and not accessible from the running board on the opposite side of the car. The proof shows that the guard rail was down at the time the car started from Niagara Falls to prevent passengers from alighting between the tracks, but this was raised up by the plaintiff to enable him to collect the fares. The evidence also shows that this was usual and had been done by Snyder when tutoring the plaintiff.

A recapitulation of the prominent facts which were established by the verdict of the jury shows that the plaintiff was riding on the running board of the car in the usual manner, engaged in the performance of his duties in accordance with the instructions given him. He was in the proper place to collect his fares and was not aware that while on the running board he was in any danger of being hit by a passing car. The tracks were dangerously close together at this point, not caused by any tapering to unite, for both north and south of the place of the accident the space widened, but the narrow space was probably due to some oversight, for they were removed farther apart after the injuries to the plaintiff and apparently to avoid the recurrence of a like catastrophe. It is not important whether when struck he was standing on the running board or passing around one of the standards as long as he was in the line of his duty, performing it in the ordinary manner and not cognizant of any danger to be apprehended from the passing car. The defendant claims it had a rule requiring the guard rails on the inside of the cars to be kept down, and that this was posted in the usual place for imparting notice to conductors. It is difficult to see any great potency to this question, for the way the proof was presented it was essential for the conductor to collect the fares on the inside running board, and certainly the guard rail if down would be an impediment to this work, and instead of mitigating, would have added to the peril of a person on the running board. But waiving that, it was a question for the jury to determine whether this notice was posted, and their verdict on that proposition settled the fact in plaintiff's favor.

With these facts fixed by the jury, we cannot say the judgment should be disturbed. The proof shows that the defendant had left its tracks at this place in a situation fraught with peril of which no notice had been given to the plaintiff, and the danger could readily have been averted by the exercise of proper care by the defendant. This condition had existed for some time, and Morgan, the manager of the defendant, knew that at this point the space between the tracks was narrower, and yet nothing was done to widen them out or to indicate to the conductors that they must keep off the running board when passing over this space.

It was the duty of the defendant to furnish a reasonably proper place for the plaintiff to carry on his work. The rule is stated in *Kuhn* v. *D., L. & W. R. R. Co.* (92 Hun, 74 [affd. on opinion below, 153 N. Y. 683] at p. 75): "The defendant owed the plaintiff's intestate the duty to exercise reasonable care and prudence to furnish him a safe and proper place in which to prosecute his work, and if it became dangerous, and the danger could be foreseen and guarded against by the exercise of reasonable care, to exercise such care and adopt such precautions as would protect the intestate." *Mohr* v. *Lehigh Valley R. R. Co.* (55 App. Div. 176); *Brown* v.

N. Y. C. & H. R. R. R. Co. (42 id. 548; affd., 166 N. Y. 626);
Mulvaney v. *Brooklyn City R. Co.* (1 Misc. Rep. 425; 49 N. Y.
St. Repr. 637; affd., 142 N. Y. 651); *Herdt* v. *Rochester City &
Brighton R. R. Co.* (48 N. Y. St. Repr. 46; affd., 142 N. Y. 626)
decisively establish that under the circumstances of this case the
defendant's negligence was for the jury.

Nor do we think the plaintiff can be charged with want of care
as matter of law. He was insensible of the danger. It was not
observable to him from the car. He had received no warning of it.
He was in the discharge of his duties in the ordinary way and his
mind was engrossed in their performance. In *Wallace* v. *C. V. R.
R. Co.* (138 N. Y. 302) the plaintiff, a brakeman, was hit by a low
bridge and a verdict was directed in favor of the defendant, which
was affirmed by the General Term of the Supreme Court, but
reversed by the Court of Appeals. The plaintiff knew of the
existence of the bridge, but at the time of the accident had his back
toward it and was engaged in the discharge of his duties and was
oblivious to the proximity of the bridge. The court say (at p. 305):
" We do not think that one thus situated can, as matter of law, be
charged with negligence because he did not take notice of the fact
that he was approaching the bridge, and thus know that he was in
a place of danger. He was in a place where there was danger that
the train might break in two, and he was intent upon the discharge
of his duty. It cannot be said that a brakeman is, as matter of
law, careless because he does not bear constantly in mind the precise
location where the train is and where every bridge is." Of like
effect are *Benthin* v. *N. Y. C. & H. R. R. R. Co.* (24 App. Div.
303); *McGovern* v. *Standard Oil Co.* (11 id. 588); *Fitzgerald* v.
N. Y. C. & H. R. R. R. Co. (88 Hun, 359); *Brown* v. *N. Y. C.
& H. R. R. R. Co.* (42 App. Div. 548, 553, *supra*). The case under
consideration is much stronger for the plaintiff than any of the
cases cited, for in each of those the person injured was conversant
with the defect which was responsible for the injury, while the
plaintiff here had no information of the nearness of the tracks at
this particular point.

The dissenting opinion is upon the assumption that the plaintiff
knew of the location of these tracks or by the exercise of care
ought to have been cognizant of it. None of the conductors or

motormen who testified appeared to be advised of it, and Snyder, when instructing the plaintiff, gave no information on the subject, but occupied the running board between the tracks at this point in collecting fares, indicating that he had not been apprised of the peril incident to carrying on his work in that way. In view of these facts, we cannot say that the jury were in error in acquitting the plaintiff of blame in following the usual practice and in not appreciating the danger.

The pith of the cases cited in the dissenting opinion like *Gibson* v. *Erie R. Co.* (63 N. Y. 449); *De Forest* v. *Jewett* (88 id. 264) and *Kennedy* v. *M. R. Co.* (145 id. 288), is that the person injured in each instance was entirely familiar with the defect which caused the injuries and it was held that the dangers appertained to the employment.

This was not a risk which the plaintiff assumed. It was not an incident to the business, was not manifest, but was due to the oversight of the defendant which proper caution would have prevented. The employer must to a reasonable degree perform the obligation resting upon him to safeguard the interests of his employees before the latter can be charged with assuming the risk with reference to the especial thing which should have been remedied. Assumption of risks must rest upon knowledge upon the part of the servant or the means of acquiring it by the exercise of ordinary diligence. As was said in *Eastland* v. *Clarke* (165 N. Y. 420, at p. 427) : " It is now the settled law of this state that the risks which a servant assumes are either such as are incident to his employment, after the master has discharged his duty of reasonable care to prevent them, or such as are quite as open and obvious to the servant as the master. * * * A servant does not assume risks which are not obvious, and are not known to him, but are or should be within the knowledge of the master."

The judgment and order should be affirmed, with costs and disbursements to the respondent.

Judgment and order affirmed, with costs and disbursements to the respondent.

WILLIAMS and DAVY, JJ., concurred; HISCOCK and McLENNAN, JJ., dissented.

HISCOCK, J. (dissenting):

I am unable to agree with the conclusion reached by a majority of my associates, that the question of plaintiff's conduct, of his assumption of risks incident to the construction of defendant's road, and of his freedom from contributory negligence was for the jury. I think, upon the other hand, that upon the evidence presented he, as matter of law, assumed the risks which resulted in his injury and that it was not permissible for the jury to find otherwise.

Defendant's road was only about seven miles in length. The close proximity of its tracks, which is complained of here and which resulted in the accident, continued for a distance of nearly 200 feet. Plaintiff had been in the employ of defendant as a conductor operating a car on its road for thirty days, going over the road, including the particular portion under criticism, from twelve to fifteen times daily. Most of these trips must have been in daylight. His experience was during the season when there was no snow to cover up or obscure his view of the track. The condition was perfectly patent, and while he might not have known with perfect accuracy to an inch how close together cars would come in passing each other at the point in question, still his acquaintance with conditions was or should have been such as to inform him that they would come very close together and bring into danger one occupying the position which he occupied at the time of his injuries.

Under these circumstances, I think the case can be distinguished from or taken outside of the principles laid down in *Gibson* v. *Erie R. Co.* (63 N. Y. 449); *De Forest* v. *Jewett* (88 id. 264); *Kennedy* v. *M. R. Co.* (145 id. 288); *Appel* v. *B., N. Y. & P. R. Co.* (111 id. 550); *Williams* v. *D., L. & W. R. R. Co.* (116 id. 628).

Upon the other hand, I think it cannot be distinguished upon its facts from those especially relied upon by the respondent.

In *Wallace* v. *C. V. R. R. Co.* (138 N. Y. 302) the plaintiff, who was a brakeman, was injured while on top of a train by coming in contact with an overhead bridge. He had made many less trips under it than plaintiff had made over defendant's road. At the time of his injury he was in a position to which he was called by the discharge of his duty, and inasmuch as this duty related to watching his train and guarding against accidents which were liable

to happen just at that particular point, and inasmuch as he had
no control whatever over the movements of the train, his position
at the time of the accident was largely forced upon him by rules and
circumstances over which he had no power. In the case at bar,
plaintiff might easily have suspended the collection of his fares for
one or two minutes while passing over the portion of the road in
question. Again, as was said by Judge EARL, "It cannot be said
that a brakeman is, as matter of law, careless because he does not
bear constantly in mind the precise location where the train is and
where every bridge is." The weight and common sense of the rule
so laid down is apparent at once. It very well might be a hardship
to hold, as matter of law, that a brakeman should keep in his mind
constantly the precise location of every overhead bridge upon a
long line of road. But that argument hardly applies to such situation as there was upon defendant's road in the short space of seven
miles, and which, so far as the evidence shows, was an exceptional
and not a common condition. But again, what necessarily must have
been of very great weight in the *Wallace* case, was the fact that the
defendant was required to put up "telltales" which should warn
brakemen of the approach to a bridge. The plaintiff in that case
had a right to rely upon the observance of this rule, and such
reliance, under very well-settled principles, exempted him from the
care and caution which he otherwise might have been required to
observe.

In *Benthin* v. *N. Y. C. & H. R. R. R. Co.* (24 App. Div. 303)
the plaintiff's intestate, who was a fireman, was killed while looking
out of the side of the engine by his head coming in contact with a
telegraph pole. It was held that he was not to be charged, as matter of law, with knowledge of the precise location of this pole and
of the danger which followed from its situation near the track.
But the court in laying down this rule, comments upon facts which
distinguish that case very widely from the one at bar and which, as
it seems to me, sustain defendant's rather than plaintiff's contention herein. The court says: "This pole was but one of many,
the location of which could not be borne in mind by any employee.
This pole was not like a bridge or a station house — a structure
— the location of which could not well be forgotten." In addition
to this, the accident happened in the night time, and the ques-

tion was fairly before the jury, as stated by the court, "Whether the night of the accident was so foggy and dark that objects could not be distinctly seen for any considerable distance." It seems to me that the situation and location of the tracks for a distance of nearly 200 feet upon a road only seven miles long, is much more to be governed by the principles applied to the case of "a station house — a structure — " than to a telegraph pole which is one of many thousand upon a long line of railroad.

In *Brown* v. *N. Y. C. & H. R. R. R. Co.* (42 App. Div. 548), where plaintiff's intestate, a fireman, while in the performance of his duty, was killed by being struck by a mail crane located near the road, the court said: " We think it can hardly be said as matter of law, that he ought to have seen and avoided this mail crane, for it was but one of many similar contrivances located along the line of the defendant's road, and, as was said i n the *Benthin Case* (*supra*), it 'was not like a bridge or a station house — a structure — the location of which could not well be forgotten.' "

In this case, as in the *Wallace* case, the intestate at the time of his injury was called upon to perform a duty which was governed by circumstances not at all under his control, and which, therefore, did not give him the opportunity that plaintiff in the case at bar had of selecting a time which should be free from unusual dangers.

In *McGovern* v. *Standard Oil Co.* (11 App. Div. 588) the intestate, a brakeman, while on top of his car was killed by a low crossbeam maintained by an oil .company. As indicated by the opinion in the case, it was a serious question whether, within the authority of the *Williams Case* (*supra*), the plaintiff should be non-suited, or, within the authority of the *Wallace Case* (*supra*), allowed to go to the jury. The court finally reached the conclusion that the latter case governed, referring especially to the rule therein laid down that " A brakeman on top of a moving train, as matter of law, is not chargeable with negligence simply because he does not constantly bear in mind the precise location where his train and where every bridge over the track is."

In *Fitzgerald* v. *N. Y. C. & H. R. R. R. Co.* (88 Hun, 359) plaintiff's intestate, who was a freight brakeman, was killed by coming in contact with a low bridge. It is sufficient, in disposing of this case, to call attention to the fact that at the time of the accident it was not light, and that intestate had only been over the road once before.

The disposition by the Court of Appeals of the recent case of *Young* v. *S., B. & N. Y. R. R. Co.* (166 N. Y. 227) merits con sideration upon this question.

Plaintiffs' intestate in that case was an engineer upon defendant's road. He was killed by having his train, through a misplacement of a switch, run on a siding. While the red light upon the switch indicated that it was open and that, therefore, there was danger, in consequence of the construction of certain obstructions by the side of the track and the location of the switch signals, the intestate could not see the danger signal in time to avoid the collision. Plaintiffs' intestate had been at work upon the road a long time, and upon the trial the plaintiffs were nonsuited upon the ground that the deceased assumed the risks of the dangers resulting in his death, since he had the same knowledge of the location of the switch with reference to the obstructions that the defendant had, and if the place was dangerous he knew or should have known what the situa tion was, and, therefore, assumed the risks. The Appellate Division (45 App. Div. 296) reversed the judgment of nonsuit, saying: " We believe it to be settled * * * by repeated adjudications that a servant is not bound at all times and under all circumstances to be mindful of the dangers which surround him while engaged in the performance of his duty, even though he may be well aware of their existence," and then cited the cases which are now relied upon to sustain plaintiff's contention in this case and to which reference has already been made. The Court of Appeals, while affirming the judgment of the Appellate Division, very distinctly declined to overrule the decision of the trial judge that the deceased assumed the risks of his occupation incident to the situation of the switch light and structures referred to, or to affirm the judgment of the Appellate Division upon this question, placing its decision upon an entirely separate and distinct ground.

It seems to me that unless we are to abrogate the rule once thoroughly established, that an employer was not bound to change the location and situation of his structures like the one in question, and that an employee assumed the risks incident to a perfectly open and patent condition, we must be led to the conclusion in this case that plaintiff is to be charged, as matter of law, with the risks which resulted in his accident.

In addition to this main issue, in my judgment there are exceptions to the rulings of the trial judge which present close and somewhat troublesome questions, but in view of the conclusion reached upon the proposition above discussed it does not seem necessary to go over them at length.

The judgment and order should be reversed and a new trial granted, with costs to appellant to abide event.

McLENNAN, J., concurred.

Judgment and order affirmed, with costs.

FRANCIS X. ZAPF, Respondent, *v.* LULU N. CARTER, Appellant, Impleaded with Others.

3172 NY

Title by adverse possession as against cotenants of real property — effect of an attempt to buy in the title of a cotenant.

One cotenant of real property may acquire title to the interests of the other cotenants by adverse possession, but in order to do so the possession must be open and notorious and coupled with an assertion of exclusive and hostile ownership.

A man died intestate in 1876, seized of certain real estate incumbered by a mortgage, leaving surviving him a widow, a brother and two sisters as his only heirs at law. The widow continued to occupy or lease the premises to tenants until her death, which occurred December 81, 1895. During such occupancy the widow paid a mortgage on the premises and the taxes, repaired a house on the lot, kept up the insurance, received the rents, which considerably exceeded the expense of management, and claimed to strangers that she was the owner of the property and endeavored to sell it. It did not appear that she gave any notice to the heirs at law, who were adults, some of whom lived only a short distance from her, that she was claiming title adversely to them.

By her will she devised the property to her adopted daughter, and the latter continued the same open and exclusive possession until 1899 without hindrance on the part of the heirs at law.

Held, that the adopted daughter had acquired by adverse possession a valid title against the heirs at law;

That the presumption that the widow was occupying as a cotenant was overcome by the character of her possession, and the fact that none of the heirs at law made any claim of ownership even after her death;

That the adopted daughter, by making an unsuccessful attempt to obtain a quitclaim deed of the premises from one of the heirs at law, did not estop herself
from disputing the validity of the title derived by a third person under a deed
from such heir at law.

APPEAL by the defendant, Lulu N. Carter, from an interlocutory
judgment of the Supreme Court in favor of the plaintiff, entered in
the office of the clerk of the county of Jefferson on the 13th day of
March, 1901, upon the report of a referee directing the partition
of the premises described in the complaint.

George C. Carter, for the appellant.

John Conboy, for the respondent.

SPRING, J.:

Chauncey B. Ashley died intestate in the city of Oswego in 1876,
leaving him surviving his widow and no children, but a brother and
two sisters his only heirs at law.   In 1871 he acquired by purchase
the premises described in the complaint, and owned the same undis-
putedly at the time of his death.   After his death his widow continued to occupy or lease the same to tenants, who attorned solely
to her until her death, which occurred December 31, 1895.   At the
time of the death of Chauncey Ashley there was a mortgage covering the premises upon which there was then unpaid the sum of
$450, and this lien was paid off and discharged by the widow in
1877.   During her occupancy the widow paid the taxes, repaired
the house on the lot, kept up the insurance, received the rents and
claimed to strangers she was the owner thereof and endeavored to
sell the same although there is no evidence that she gave any notice
to the heirs at law, who were known to her and lived only a short
distance from her that she was claiming title adversely to them.
During this period the net rents received apparently exceeded considerably all the expenses she incurred in managing and repairing
the property.

In 1863 the defendant, then a young girl of seven years, became
a member of the family of Mr. and Mrs. Ashley, assuming their
name, and continued thereafter to be treated as their daughter, and
that was the ostensible relation at the time of the death of Mr. Ashley.   She was married in 1878, and was then living with her foster

mother, who had remarried a man named Spalisbury, and while she moved west with her husband the filial relations remained unchanged during the lifetime of Mrs. Spalisbury, whose husband died in 1888. Mrs. Spalisbury left a will giving the bulk of her property, real and personal, to the defendant, and the only real estate of which she died seized was that in controversy in this action. After the death of Mrs. Spalisbury the defendant received the rents from the property in question, and the plaintiff, who was the sole executor of the will mentioned, acted as her agent. It soon developed that the defendant had no record title to the premises described in the complaint, and the appeal book discloses considerable correspondence between the parties relative to this situation. In 1898 the defendant obtained a quitclaim deed from the brother of the said intestate for a nominal consideration. The plaintiff on behalf of the defendant endeavored to secure a like conveyance to her from the other heirs at law, but there was some hitch in the matter and no deed was given. In July, 1899, the plaintiff acquired by quitclaim deeds the interests of these two heirs at law for the sum of $75, the entire property being worth from $800 to $1,000, and has commenced this action of partition to effect a division or sale thereof. The defendant sets up title by possession for more than twenty years in hostility to that of the legal owners by her testatrix and in herself after the death of her foster mother.

· If Mrs. Spalisbury and the defendant had been strangers in title to the heirs at law of Mr. Ashley, unquestionably the acts of these occupants, although founded on no muniment of title, were ample to ripen into ownership by open, notorious, adverse possession. (Code Civ. Proc. §§ 371, 372 ; *Barnes* v. *Light*, 116 N. Y. 34 ; *Baker* v. *Oakwood*, 123 id. 16 ; *Lewis* v. *N. Y. & Harlem R. R. Co.*, 162 id. 202.) The rule does not obtain in its severity where the occupancy is by one tenant in common ; yet, if that occupancy is open, notorious, visible and by acts unequivocally conveying to the cotenants the information that the one in possession is holding in defiance of their cotenancy instead of in subordination to it, that possession may be adverse and grow into a title by prescription. (*Jackson* v. *Whitbeck*, 6 Cow. 632 ; *Van Dyck* v. *Van Beuren*, 1 Caines, 84 ; *Abrams* v. *Rhoner*, 44 Hun,

507; *Millard* v. *McMullin,* 68 N. Y. 345, 352; *Florence* v. *Hopkins,* 46 id. 182; Busw. Lim. & Adv. Pos. § 299.) In *Florence* v. *Hopkins* (*supra*) the court say (at p. 186): "But even the possession of one of the tenants in common may become adverse by acts on his part amounting to an exclusion of his co-tenants." Wood, in his work on Limitations, thus gives expression to the doctrine (Vol. 2 [2d ed.], § 266): "*Prima facie,* the possession of one tenant in common is the possession of all. * * * But if one tenant in common enters upon the whole land and takes the entire profits, claiming and holding exclusively for the full statutory period, an actual ouster of his co-tenants may be presumed." And in Angell on Limitations the following appears (6th ed. § 432): "But it is not necessary in order to prove that a tenant in common has claimed the whole exclusively, that it should be proved that he made an express declaration to that effect, for it may be shown clearly by acts as well as words. (*Law* v. *Patterson,* 1 W. & S. [Pa.] 191; *Bracket* v. *Norcross,* 1 Greenl. [Me.] 89.) Where one enters and takes the profits exclusively and continuously for a long period, under circumstances which indicate a denial of a right in any other to receive them, as by not accounting with the acquiescence of the other tenants, an ouster may be presumed in this country." (See, also, *Boll* v. *New York & Harlem R. R. Co.,* 33 Misc. Rep. 42; 102 N. Y. St. Repr. 139.) The authorities relied upon by the appellant do not infringe upon this principle. In *Knolls* v. *Barnhart* (71 N. Y. 474) the widow was in possession as dowress and guardian in socage of the minor heirs, and it was held that her occupancy was presumptively as tenant in common and that her attempt to buy in a title, upon which no sufficient length of possession had existed in her to erect a title by operation of the Statute of Limitations by adverse possession, would inure to the benefit of the *cestuis que trust.* The court decided that her "fiduciary relation to the property and the heirs * * * prevented her from purchasing or foreclosing the mortgage for her individual benefit," and also that "adverse possession was not found or proved." In *Culver* v. *Rhodes* (87 N. Y. 348) the widow and daughter were in possession for more than twenty years, but her possession was that of the life tenant and also as trustee. During the running of the possession a judgment was recovered against her by her cotenants in an action of waste committed by her on the

premises and there was no act of hers impeaching the title of the
co-owners. The court in discussing what is essential to create a title
by adverse possession in favor of one cotenant say that there should
be notice of the adverse holding to the cotenant " or unequivo-
cal acts so open and public that notice may be presumed of the
assault upon his title and the invasion of his rights." We may, therefore, regard the doctrine as settled that one cotenant may acquire
title adversely which will oust that of her cotenant, but in order to
enable that holding to ripen into ownership, the possession must be
open and notorious with an assertion of exclusive and hostile ownership. In the present case Mrs. Spalisbury received the rents and
profits, paid off an outstanding incumbrance, repaired the property,
paid the taxes, and it was continuously assessed to her. She
repeatedly tried to sell it and did by oral agreement dispose of a
strip of the land. After her death the defendant continued the
same open and exclusive ownership without disturbance until about
the time of the commencement of this action. For twenty-three
years, then, occupancy and averment of title continued without ·
interruption. The heirs at law of Ashley were adults. Some of
them lived near this land and must have known of the exclusive
and notorious character of the possession of Mrs. Spalisbury and
later of that of her foster daughter. After the death of the testatrix these heirs were willing to part with their legal interest for a
small sum, which further tends to confirm the position that they
had little faith in their ability to stand out against the title of the
defendant.

The referee finds the facts upon which this maintenance of title
is based but finds that there is no proof to show that it was in hos-
tility to that of the heir at law. We think the presumption that
she was occupying as a cotenant was overcome by the character of
the possession and the fact that none of the heirs at law made any
claim of ownership even after the death of the widow.

What constitutes adverse possession must always depend upon
the facts of each case. The general principles of law governing
such an occupancy have been long settled and are staple and uniform. The possession of a cotenant to become effective against his
co-owners, must be more marked and more open than ·against a
stranger and of that character which is manifestly hostile to the

claim of the cotenants. In this case, every act essential to establish an exclusive ownership was committed by the defendant and her testatrix. Payment and the discharge of the mortgage indebtedness, continuous possession, keeping the property in repair, receiving rents, asserting title, paying insurance and taxes, with the assessments to Mrs. Spalisbury and later to the defendant constituted a series of acts which go to make up this claim of ownership, and are all which any owner would perform. Any one of these acts may have been insufficient to mature into a title by adverse holding, but all combined form a chain which irresistibly establishes it, and it is a significant fact in vindication of this claim that during this long possession the heirs at law were adults and either lived or visited at times a short distance from the land and never sought to disturb the conspicuous acts upon which ownership was being founded.

To give notice to these heirs at law that the possession was with the view of claiming title would have been superfluous, for they must have known it. Nor is there anything in the relationship between these heirs at law and Mrs. Spalisbury which gives color to the suggestion that they were permitting her to ocupy these premises in this exclusive way, intending after her death to assert their title. She was their sister-in-law, and shortly after the death of her first husband, their brother, she remarried. She was not penniless, and the inference seems reasonable that if they had expected to claim title to this property, they would have done so immediately upon the death of their brother. It may be that they knew of the existence of the mortgage lien upon the property and concluded that their interest in excess of this incumbrance was inconsiderable, and did not care ever to be invested with the possession or actual ownership of this property, and it is a noteworthy fact that after the death of Mrs. Spalisbury, when her foster daughter came into possession and assumed proprietorship of this property, and who was of no kin to these heirs at law, there was then no attempt on their part to obtain possession.

The defendant, in seeking to fortify her title and buy peace by obtaining a quitclaim deed from one of the heirs at law of the deceased Ashley, did not estop herself from disputing the title derived from the heirs at law. (*Greene* v. *Couse*, 127 N. Y. 386.)

The course of the plaintiff in procuring the conveyances from the two sisters of Ashley does not require us to scan with too much minuteness the title of the defendant and her devisor. The plaintiff was the executor of the will and learned that Mrs. Spalisbury did not have the legal title and so advised the defendant. He acted as her agent in the collection of the rents and endeavored to purchase the interests of these sisters of the decedent on behalf of the defendant for ten dollars, which was the limit of his authority. After these negotiations had ceased he purchased on his own behalf. To be sure he had ceased collecting rent, had settled with his principal and his account as executor had been judicially settled, but he obtained title because of the knowledge he had acquired while acting for the defendant. The courts have uniformly condemned the acts by which an agent obtains title to property to undermine his principal, and this conduct of the plaintiff is reprehensible in the extreme, although the referee, by evidence which may be said to sustain it, has found he apprised the vendors he was buying the land for himself.

The judgment should be reversed and a new trial granted, with costs to the appellant to abide the event.

ADAMS, P. J., McLENNAN and WILLIAMS, JJ., concurred; HIS-COCK, J., not sitting.

Interlocutory judgment reversed and new trial ordered before another referee, with costs to the appellant to abide the event.

In the Matter of the Judicial Settlement of the Account of MARY S. SACK as Guardian of the Estate of ROSA E. FREELAND.

MARY S. SACK, as Guardian of the Estate of ROSA E. FREELAND, Appellant; ROSA E. FREELAND, Petitioner, Respondent.

Statute of Limitations — when not available to a general guardian called upon to account.

A proceeding commenced by a ward, eighteen years after attaining her majority, to compel her former general guardian to account for moneys received by the guardian for the benefit of the ward is not barred by the Statute of Limitations, where it appears that the guardian never filed any inventory or annual statement or rendered any account, and that, until within six months before the commencement of the proceeding, the ward did not know that the guardian had received any moneys belonging to her, and that, during the period which had elapsed since the ward had attained her majority, the guardian had made no repudiation or disclaimer of the guardianship or denial of the receipt and retention of moneys in that capacity.

APPEAL by Mary S. Sack, as guardian of the estate of Rosa E. Freeland, from an order of the Surrogate's Court of the county of Niagara, entered in said Surrogate's Court on the 18th day of December, 1901, denying her motion to dismiss a petition on the ground that the claim of the petitioner to compel an accounting was barred by the Statute of Limitations, and requiring her to file an account as general guardian of the petitioner.

The petition in this proceeding shows that the appellant was duly appointed the general guardian of the petitioner by the decree of the Surrogate's Court on the 6th day of September, 1866; that as such guardian she received $1,536.40, which consisted of pension moneys paid by the United States government for the benefit of said infant as the minor child of her deceased father; that the petitioner attained her majority April 28, 1883. No inventory or annual statement was ever made by the guardian, and no settlement of her account in that capacity has ever been rendered. The petition further states that the petitioner did not know that her guardian had ever received any money until within six months before the commencement of this proceeding. The petition was presented to the Surrogate's Court in August, 1901, and a citation issued on the twenty-fourth of that month requiring the guardian to show cause why she should not settle her account. The guardian appeared and answered, alleging that she had expended for the benefit of her ward and paid to her all the moneys received, and further averred that the Statute of Limitations was a bar to the maintenance of the proceeding. Subsequently a motion was made to dismiss the petition on the ground that the claim was barred by the Statute of Limitations, which motion was denied and the order appealed from was thereupon entered.

D. E. Brong, for the appellant.

David Millar and *S. E. Graves,* for the respondent.

SPRING, J.:

We must assume upon this appeal that the appellant received over $1,500 belonging to her ward which she still retains, and that the petitioner, until about the time of the commencement of this proceeding, did not know that her guardian had this money in her custody. During the long period elapsing since the petitioner became of age there has been no repudiation or disclaimer of the guardianship by the guardian, or of the receipt and retention of the moneys by her in that capacity. While the duty was upon the guardian to initiate proceedings for the settlement of her account she has disregarded this duty, and if the allegations of the petition are true, has misappropriated the moneys belonging to her *cestui que trust*. To be sure, the respondent could have required an accounting, but the only object of resorting to the proceeding by her was to obtain from the guardian whatever belonged to the petitioner, and if the latter believed there was no money in the custody of the guardian she was not called upon to incur the expense and annoyance which such a proceeding might involve. The bare fact that nothing was done by the guardian, either to settle formally her account in the Surrogate's Court or with the petitioner, indicated to the petitioner that the guardian had no funds in her hands.

While there is considerable conflict in the authorities as to the operation of the Statute of Limitations in favor of a guardian or executor or administrator as against the ward or beneficiaries, we believe the doctrine may be regarded as settled to the extent, at least of holding that where a ward, having reached his majority, believes that his guardian has no money belonging to him, and there has been no act of the guardian known to the ward in repudiation of the guardianship, that the Statute of Limitations is no bar to a proceeding of this kind.

In *Matter of Petition of Camp* (126 N. Y. 377) the infant became of age in 1872, and did not commence the proceeding to compel his guardian to account until 1888 when the latter raised the question of the Statute of Limitations. In that case, as in the present, the petitioner was ignorant of the receipt of the moneys by the guardian until within a year prior to the commencement of the proceeding, and no inventory or account had ever been filed. The court in discussing the proposition as to the running of the Statute of Limitations, uses this language (at p. 389): "Although he may cease to be guardian upon the ward coming of age, yet so long as the property remains in his possession as guardian and unaccounted for, he must remain liable to account. This is no hardship upon the guardian, nor can it be the means of sustaining stale claims against him as such. The moment the ward arrives of age he may cite the guardian to account, and now by the Code of Civil Procedure (§ 2849, following the provisions of the Revised Statutes, vol. 2, p. 152, § 12), the guardian may, in any case where a petition for an accounting may be presented by any other person, present one in his own behalf, and an accounting may then be had. Thus, either party may claim an accounting the moment the ward attains his majority."

In *Matter of Taylor* (30 App. Div. 213) letters of administration were issued in November, 1888, and the order compelling the accounting was entered in January, 1898. A judgment had been recovered against one of the next of kin and the petitioner was appointed the receiver of the property of the judgment debtor. The Statute of Limitations was urged, and the court overruled this defense and required the administrator to account, holding that until the administratrix has legally accounted for the funds that she has received, "or until she has publicly and officially renounced her trust," the statute does not become operative. *Matter of Grandin* (61 Hun, 219); *Matter of Jones* (51 App. Div. 420); *Matter of Beyea* (10 Misc. Rep. 198); *Mount* v. *Mount* (35 id. 62), and *Zebley* v. *Farmers' L. & T. Co.* (139 N. Y. 461) each sustain the principle that there must be a denial or disclaimer of the trust before the Statute of Limitations is set running.

The position is a very reasonable one, for the guardian alone as a rule possesses exact information as to the condition and amount of the funds in his custody. If he has administered the trust properly he has kept the fund invested and is able to present an itemized statement concerning it. A provident and careful guardian will settle his account when his ward arrives at his majority. The guardian's management of the trust estate should then cease. He may voluntarily settle with his ward, and upon filing the proper voucher a decree may be entered discharging him. The proceeding is simple and inexpensive, and if the guardian neglects to have his guardianship properly terminated, he is the delinquent. In the event of his remissness the retention of any funds by him operates to continue his trust management of the property. The relation is not that of debtor and creditor, but the guardian is the custodian of the funds of another which he voluntarily undertook to keep invested in a certain way for a fixed compensation, and all the time the property is his ward's, disconnected from any other, and until its transfer to his *cestui que trust*, the guardian is acting in recognition of his trusteeship.

In this case the guardian, in her answer, does not deny that she received this fund. She alleges, as a defense, that it has been expended for the benefit of the petitioner, to whom, she averred, "large sums" have been paid since she became of age. The petitioner is entitled to know in what way this fund, a portion of which remained unexpended when she attained her majority, has been disbursed by her guardian.

The order should be affirmed, with ten dollars costs and the disbursements of this appeal against the appellant personally.

McLENNAN, WILLIAMS, HISCOCK and DAVY, JJ., concurred.

Order affirmed, with ten dollars costs and disbursements of this appeal against the appellant personally.

CHARLES H. MONNIER, Respondent, *v.* THE NEW YORK CENTRAL AND HUDSON RIVER RAILROAD COMPANY, Appellant.

Railroad — removal from a car of a passenger who has not procured a ticket, because of the absence from the office of the ticket agent, and who refuses to pay an additional five cents — an action lies for assault and battery — the damages are compensatory — a $500 verdict is not excessive.

A railroad company empowered by statute (Laws of 1857, chap. 228) to demand and receive, from a passenger boarding one of its trains without having first purchased a ticket, five cents in addition to the regular fare, provided it keeps its ticket office open for the sale of tickets at least one hour prior to the departure of each passenger train from the station, is not entitled to demand the extra five cents from a passenger who is unable to procure a ticket at a station because of the fact that the ticket agent was not at the ticket office for several minutes immediately prior to the departure of the train.

Where the conductor, after being informed of the facts, attempts to forcibly eject the passenger because of his refusal to pay the additional five cents, the passenger is entitled to resist such attempt to the best of his ability, and if, in the process of ejection, he sustains injury, he may maintain an action against the railroad company for an assault and battery, and his remedy is not limited to an action for the unlawful ejection.

If he elects to bring an action for assault and battery, he can only recover compensatory damages.

Where, on the trial of such an action, it appears that the plaintiff was a business man and that the ejection occurred in the daytime in the presence of a number of his acquaintances, that he was dragged from the car, carried out and put down in the road, a verdict for $500 will not be set aside as excessive.

WILLIAMS, J., dissented.

APPEAL by the defendant, The New York Central and Hudson River Railroad Company, from a judgment of the Supreme Court in favor of the plaintiff, entered in the office of the clerk of the county of Oneida on the 5th day of September, 1901, upon the verdict of a jury for $1,000, which was reduced to $500, and also from an order entered in said clerk's office on the 5th day of September, 1901, denying the defendant's motion for a new trial made upon the minutes.

Thomas D. Watkins, for the appellant.

D. F. Searle, for the respondent.

SPRING, J. :

This action is assault and battery to recover for injuries claimed to have been inflicted upon the plaintiff by reason of his forcible and improper ejection from a passenger train of the defendant by its conductor in charge of the train and upon which the plaintiff was riding as a passenger. On the morning of November 16, 1900, the plaintiff went to the station of the defendant at Oriskany for the purpose of taking the train for Utica and which was scheduled to leave at nine-one. He reached the station from eight to ten minutes before the arrival of the train and applied at the ticket office for a ticket to Utica, but was unable to procure one as the ticket agent was not in his office. That official had left his place of business and did not return until the train was leaving the station, so there was no opportunity for plaintiff to buy a ticket. The fare from Oriskany to Utica is fourteen cents, and when the conductor came to the plaintiff for his ticket he tendered to the officer fifteen cents, explaining to him that the ticket agent was not at the office and for that reason no ticket could be purchased. The conductor insisted that he must pay the extra charge of five cents for the trip to Utica or get off the train. Doctor Aulliame, who had taken the train at Oriskany, also informed the conductor that the agent was not in the office and that plaintiff was not able to purchase a ticket. The conductor still insisted on the extra fare, which plaintiff declined to pay, and as the train was about leaving Whitesboro station the conductor caused it to be stopped and forcibly dragged the plaintiff from the car, the latter resisting to the best of his strength. The conductor after a sharp scuffle carried the plaintiff from the car and set him down in the road, and the plaintiff went from Whitesboro to Utica on the street car line.

By chapter 228 of the Laws of 1857 the defendant was permitted "to demand and receive from" a passenger riding on one of its passenger trains not exceeding five cents in addition to the regular fare, which is two cents a mile, when a ticket office established by it is kept "open for the sale of tickets at least one hour prior to the departure of each passenger train from such station;" and by section 2 of the act the authority to exact this excess of fare exists "if any person shall at any station where a ticket office is established and open" attempt to ride as a passenger "without having first purchased a ticket." The right of the conductor, therefore, to demand the additional sum of five cents from the plaintiff did not exist in the present case, for the defendant had omitted to give him the opportunity to purchase a ticket as required by the statute. He was accordingly rightfully on the defendant's train, and if he tendered the lawful fare of two cents a mile to Utica the defendant was bound to receive it and transport him to his place of destination.

It is, however, contended that the action of assault and battery is not proper against the defendant, reliance chiefly being placed upon *Townsend* v. *N. Y. C. & H. R. R. R. Co.* (56 N. Y. 295) in support of this contention. In that case the plaintiff was improperly and violently ejected from the defendant's passenger train, and an action for assault and battery was commenced by him. Upon

the trial the trial judge instructed the jury that, although the conductor acted in good faith in the line of what he conceived to be
his duty, still the jury might award to the plaintiff punitive damages if they reached the conclusion that he was entitled to recover,
and the judgment was reversed for this manifest error. The judge
in his opinion, however, devotes considerable space to the discussion
of the question whether the plaintiff had the right to use force to
retain his seat in the car and concludes that he had not that right.
This conclusion was not essential to the determination of the case,
and, so far as I have been able to discover, has not been followed
by the courts of this State. In fact, in that case upon the retrial
the plaintiff again recovered a substantial verdict, which was sustained by the General Term. (4 Hun, 217 ; S. C., 6 T. & C. 495.)

In *Muckle* v. *Rochester Railway Co.* (79 Hun, 32) the action
was for assault and battery for personal injuries sustained by the
plaintiff by being forcibly put off the defendant's car by the conductor, and a recovery was sustained. The effect of the *Townsend*
case was discussed and held to be controlling only in that it
restricted the recovery to compensatory damages, and the court
say further : "It is a general rule that a carrier of passengers is
answerable for all the consequences to a passenger of the willful conduct or negligence of the persons employed by it in the execution
of the duty it has assumed towards him. The defendant had, by
its contract with the plaintiff, undertaken for a consideration paid
to carry him to his place of destination and pursuant to it he had
the right of passage, and as between him and the defendant he was at
liberty to refuse to repay his fare and to insist upon having his continuous passage. In violation of that right, the defendant by its
conductor proceeded to forcibly eject him from the car in which he
was rightfully seated as a passenger. Although the conductor personally may have been justified by his instructions to do so, the
defendant was put in the wrong by the act of the other conductor
and was no more justified in the attempted act of ejection than it
would have been if the plaintiff had at the time had and presented
the evidence of his right to remain as a passenger in the car without
further payment."

In *Dwinelle* v. *N. Y. C. & H. R. R. R. Co.* (120 N. Y. 117) the
action was to recover damages for an assault made upon the plain-

tiff by a porter of the sleeping car in which plaintiff had been riding. The train of which it formed a part was detained and the plaintiff with the other passengers was directed to board another train, and as they were walking along by the side of the car the porter made an unprovoked assault upon the plaintiff. The Court of Appeals, after holding that it was incumbent upon the defendant "to protect the passenger against any injury from negligence or willful misconduct of its servants while performing the contract," and after disposing of one or two other questions unimportant here, say: "These and numerous other cases hold that no matter what the motive is which incites the servant of the carrier to commit an unlawful or improper act toward the passenger during the existence of the relation of carrier and passenger, the carrier is liable for the act and its natural and legitimate consequences."

The same principle is upheld in *Stewart* v. *B. & C. R. R. Co.* (90 N. Y. 588); *Weber* v. *Brooklyn, Q. C. & S. R. R. Co.* (47 App. Div. 306); *Franklin* v. *Third Ave. R. R. Co.* (52 id. 512); *Ray* v. *Cortland & Homer Tr. Co.* (19 id. 530); *Geraty* v. *Stern* (30 Hun, 426).

In *Palmeri* v. *Manhattan R. Co.* (133 N. Y. 261) the plaintiff had purchased a ticket of the agent at the station of the elevated railroad in New York and was charged by him with having passed upon him a piece of counterfeit money. He followed up his accusation by detaining the plaintiff at the station and applying vile epithets to her. She sued the railroad company to recover damages for this unlawful restraint with the slanderous charges made publicly against her by the defendant's agent. A recovery was had which was sustained by the Court of Appeals, which (at p. 265) uses this language in discussing the extent of the liability of the defendant for the misconduct of its servant: "For all the acts of a servant or agent, which are done in the prosecution of the business entrusted to him, the carrier becomes civilly liable, if its passengers, or strangers, receive injury therefrom. The good faith and motives of the servant are not a defense if the act was unlawful. Once the relation of carrier and passenger entered upon, the carrier is answerable for all consequences to the passenger of the willful misconduct or negligence of the persons employed by it in the execution of the contract which it has undertaken towards the passenger. This is a reasonable and necessary rule which has been upheld by this court in many cases."

The contention of the appellant's counsel is that if the plaintiff may maintain an action at all it is one for the ejection of the plaintiff. That question is an academic one here, for the jury were instructed that no exemplary damages could be recovered, and hence the rule is restricted to what would have been the proper gauge of the defendant's liability had it been based solely upon the unlawful removal of the plaintiff. All the facts were set out in the complaint and it is the subtlety of refinement to distinguish in a practical way between the two forms of actions, if there is any distinction between them. If the ejection was done by force, it is no more than an assault, and if the form of the action resorted to is the common one for assault and battery, then the damages must be restricted to those which are termed compensatory. If the plaintiff had been removed from the train without personal violence he might have recovered whatever damages were the natural outcome of his expulsion. Had the conductor publicly and in violent language charged him with attempting to steal his ride, that would have been a proper item within the pale of compensatory damages. Had that official slandered the plaintiff, the jury would have been permitted to consider such slander as an element of damages. We can see no difference whether the action is what the counsel terms one for ejection or one for assault and battery. If the facts show that an assault was committed, the gist of the action in any event is that plaintiff, while rightfully on the car, was improperly expelled therefrom, and whatever damages are the legitimate result of that unlawful invasion he can recover.

The common law gives to a person assaulted and beaten an action to recover damages for assault and battery, and it is maintainable against the actual perpetrator of the outrage or the inciter of it. It has been held without variation that a common carrier is responsible for the unlawful acts of its employee while engaged in the general line of his duty (*Rounds* v. *Delaware, Lack. & West. R. R. Co.*, 64 N. Y. 129), and that carries with it the right to resort to any form of action which the facts warrant. If the better remedy is by action for assault and battery, then that form of remedy is available to the person injured. It would be a novel doctrine that, where the defendant is liable for injuries inflicted upon a person in throwing him from a passenger car, he is prevented from recovering because his complaint containing the facts upon which the cause of action rests charges the defendant with having assaulted and beaten the plaintiff. The case in 56 New York referred to makes no such distinction between an action for assault and battery and one for ejection, as is now contended for.

The foundation of the plaintiff's cause of action is that he was rightfully on the car. He, therefore, had a right to defend himself, to resist force by force, and if he was injured by reason of the vigor of his resistance, that would not shield the defendant. (*English* v. *Delaware & Hudson Canal Co.*, 66 N. Y. 454; *Erie Railroad Co.* v. *Winter*, 143 U. S. 60, 73.) The moralist may claim that a person should peaceably surrender his rights rather than fight for their maintenance, but no such superfine doctrine finds support in the law.

The verdict in this case was $1,000. The trial court, in the exercise of its discretion, granted a new trial unless the plaintiff stipulated to reduce the recovery to $500, in which event the motion for a new trial was denied. The stipulation was given, and the appellant's counsel strenuously urges that the recovery is still excessive. The plaintiff was a business man riding in the daytime in a passenger coach with a number of acquaintances. He was in effect publicly charged with lying to the conductor, and trying thereby to evade the payment of the fare to which the defendant claimed to be entitled, and then was dragged by force from the car, carried out and put down in the road. He was not physically injured to any great extent, but the humiliation and indignity of such an open and unprovoked assault constitute the essence of the offense, and were properly permitted to be considered by the jury as compensatory damages. (*Eddy* v. *Syracuse R. T. R. Co.*, 50 App. Div. 109; *Hamilton* v. *Third Ave. R. R. Co.*, 53 N. Y. 25; *Miller* v. *King*, 21 App. Div. 192.) The trial court, in the exercise of its discretion, reduced the recovery to $500, and we see no reason for paring it down any more.

The judgment and order appealed from should be affirmed, with costs and disbursements to the respondent.

MCLENNAN, HISCOCK and DAVY, JJ., concurred; WILLIAMS, J., dissented.

WILLIAMS, J. (dissenting) :

The judgment and order appealed from should be reversed and a new trial granted, with costs to the appellant to abide event.

The verdict of $1,000 was so grossly excessive as to show that the jury were actuated by prejudice against the defendant. They were limited to giving of merely compensatory damages. The plaintiff suffered no substantial physical injuries. The only other element of damages was injuries to his feelings. He offered the conductor fifteen cents, and the conductor required four cents more. The regulations of the company required the conductor to collect the additional four cents or eject the plaintiff from the train. He could not take the plaintiff's word that the ticket office was not open so that a ticket could be purchased.

The plaintiff had a remedy against the company which he could enforce, and he had no occasion to require the conductor to violate his duty by accepting less than the full fare for passage without a ticket. It is inconceivable that a man so small and mean as to create a sensation and render it necessary for the conductor to eject him from the train and to forcibly carry him out and set him down upon the ground, should suffer any appreciable injury to his feelings by the transaction. He practically invited the use of force, and was entitled to no substantial damages therefor. (*Townsend* v. *N. Y. C. & H. R. R. R. Co.*, 56 N. Y. 295.) The jury by rendering a verdict for $1,000 under these circumstances, showed themselves unfit to pass upon the question of damages at all. The court should not have permitted the verdict to stand for any amount. By allowing it to stand for $500, the court was itself passing upon the question of damages without the aid of the jury. If the court assumed to fix the damages at all itself, it should have permitted them to be no larger than $100 in any event. The facts called for no greater verdict.

The judgment and order should, therefore, be reversed and a new trial ordered, with costs to the appellant to abide event, or should at least be so reversed, unless the plaintiff stipulates to reduce the verdict to $100, in which event the judgment and order as so amended should be affirmed, without costs to either party against the other.

Judgment and order affirmed, with costs.

AGRICULTURAL INSURANCE COMPANY, Appellant, *v.* ALEXANDER H. DARROW and H. D. CUMMINGS, Respondents.

Death of an attorney after the submission of the case to a referee — delivery of the referee's report before the expiration of the thirty days' notice to appoint another attorney — waiver.

Where the attorney for one of the parties to a reference dies after the case has been finally submitted to the referee, section 65 of the Code of Civil Procedure, which provides, "If an attorney dies, is removed or suspended, or otherwise becomes disabled to act, at any time before judgment in an action, no further proceeding shall be taken in the action, against the party for whom he appeared, until thirty days after notice to appoint another attorney has been given to that party, either personally or in such other manner as the court directs," does not prohibit the referee from delivering his report before the expiration of the thirty days prescribed by that section, especially where it appears that the thirty days did not expire until after the expiration of the sixty days allowed to the referee within which to deliver his report.

Semble, that where it appears that nothing was done pursuant to the report until after the expiration of the thirty days prescribed by the section, and after other attorneys had been substituted in place of the deceased attorney, it may be said that the actual delivery of the report did not take place until after the lapse of the thirty days.

Assuming that the delivery of the report before the expiration of the thirty days constituted a technical violation of section 65 of the Code of Civil Procedure, it was a mere irregularity, which was waived by the failure of the substituted attorneys to take advantage thereof before the entry of the judgment, it appearing that upon their request such judgment was not entered until ten days after their substitution.

APPEAL by the plaintiff, the Agricultural Insurance Company, from an order of the Supreme Court, made at the Oswego Special Term and entered in the office of the clerk of the county of Jefferson on the 8th day of October, 1901, setting aside the report of a referee and the judgment entered thereon and a stipulation and order of reference.

A. H. Sawyer and *H. W. Steele,* for the appellant.

C. H. Walts, for the respondents.

SPRING, J.:

This action was brought by the plaintiff, a fire insurance corporation, to recover of the defendants, who were its agents in Chicago,

Ill., premiums upon policies of insurance which it is alleged had been withheld. Upon the stipulation of the attorneys for the respective parties an order was entered November 9, 1900, referring the issues to a referee for trial. The action was tried and finally submitted to the referee April 8, 1901. The firm of Porter & Porter represented the defendant Cummings, who alone answered. Judge Porter, the senior member of that firm, died May 21, 1901, and his copartner was at that time in an asylum mentally incompetent, and in the month of June following was adjudged to be of unsound mind.

On the twenty-fifth of May the plaintiff's attorney by notice in writing advised the defendant Cummings of the death of Judge Porter and of the disability of the other member of the law firm and notified the defendant to obtain another attorney to act in his behalf in this action. Walts & Pitcher, by order of the Special Term, entered on the 8th day of July, 1901, were substituted as the attorneys for the defendants at their request. On the 7th day of June the referee delivered his report to the attorneys for the plaintiff directing that judgment be entered in its favor for the sum of $1,106.97. Nothing was done pursuant to this report until after the substitution of the attorneys for the defendants, and judgment was thereupon entered July 18, 1901.

The contention of the respondents is that upon the death of Judge Porter, as his partner was mentally incompetent, all proceedings were stayed by section 65 of the Code of Civil Procedure, and the delivery of the report was in violation of this section. The section reads as follows : "If an attorney dies, is removed or suspended, or otherwise becomes disabled to act, at any time before judgment in an action, no further proceeding shall be taken in the action, against the party for whom he appeared, until thirty days after notice to appoint another attorney, has been given to that party, either personally or in such other manner as the court directs." The referee was required to file with the clerk, or deliver to the attorney for one of the parties, his report within sixty days from the final submission of the case. (Code Civ. Proc. § 1019 ; *Little* v. *Lynch,* 99 N. Y. 112 ; *Russell* v. *Lyth,* 66 App. Div. 290.)

It was important for the referee to comply with this requirement or perhaps lose the fees which he had earned. The object of section 65 is to hold all proceedings in the action "against the party" in abeyance after the death of his attorney for the period of thirty days to enable him to employ another attorney. It is a salutary safeguard for the protection of a party whose attorney has died or become disqualified, but where the referee who tried the case files or delivers his report pursuant to another section of the Code and nothing further is done during the inhibited time we apprehend there is no transgression of the spirit of section 65. No harm can result to the defeated party unless some proceeding is taken in behalf of the successful party. The referee may live at a distance from the litigants or their attorneys, who may not be aware of the death or disability which stays the proceeding, and may innocently cause his report to be filed or delivered, and we apprehend this is not such a step in the action as the statute was intended to prohibit.

In *Commercial Bank* v. *Foltz* (13 App. Div. 603), relied upon by the counsel for the respondents, the decision of the trial judge was followed up by a supplemental decision and judgment of foreclosure and sale entered and the premises were sold, all without any notice to the party defeated, whose attorney had been disbarred and no substitution made. In that case there was a persistent course of proceeding in disregard of the section quoted and to the manifest damage of the defendant. In each of the other cases where it has been held that the statute was violated, there was an explicit affirmative act on the part of the attorney to progress the action.

If we are in error in the foregoing conclusion, we believe it may well be said that the actual delivery of the report was after the lapse of thirty days during which the proceedings were stayed. It was so treated by the attorney for the plaintiff, and the delivery, even after the sixty days given the referee to make and render his report, would be effective against the party who had not sought to terminate the reference.

At best, if there was a technical disregard of section 65 of the Code in delivering the report, it was a mere irregularity, and ten days elapsed after attorneys for the defendants had been substituted upon their request before judgment was entered. These attorneys must have known that sixty days had long expired since the final submission of the case, and they should have proceeded at once, if they expected to end the reference or impeach the delivery of the report. They cannot be permitted to remain quiet until after the entry of the judgment and then claim that all the proceedings were annulled by the action of the referee in delivering the report.

The order should be reversed with ten dollars costs and the disbursements of this appeal, and the motion to set aside the report, judgment, stipulation and order of reference be denied, with ten dollars costs.

McLENNAN, HISCOCK and DAVY, JJ., concurred; WILLIAMS, J., not sitting.

Order reversed, with ten dollars costs and disbursements, and motion to set aside judgment, stipulations, order of reference, report of referee denied, with ten dollars costs.

THE PEOPLE OF THE STATE OF NEW YORK ex rel. JUDSON SACKETT, Appellant, v. EGBERT E. WOODBURY, as Surrogate of Chautauqua County, Respondent.

Execution against an administrator on a surrogate's decree after the expiration of five years — notice to the administrator — peremptory mandamus against the surrogate — review by mandamus.

Sections 1377 and 1378 of the Code of Civil Procedure, which provide that notice of an application to the court for leave to issue execution on a final judgment, after the lapse of five years from its entry, must be served personally upon the adverse party, if he is a resident of the State, are applicable to a decree of the Surrogate's Court judicially settling the accounts of an administrator.

The five years' limitation commences to run from the time of the entry of the decree in the Surrogate's Court, and not from the time that a transcript of the decree is docketed in the county clerk's office.

Where an administrator, pursuant to the terms of a decree of the Surrogate's Court finally settling his accounts, pays into the Surrogate's Court the distributive share of one of the next of kin supposed to be dead, and after the lapse of more than five years after the entry of the decree such next of kin appears and makes application for leave to issue execution upon the decree in order to obtain ¬ayment of his distributive share, the surrogate may, in his discretion, irrespective of any statutory authority, require notice of the application to be served upon the administrator.

A peremptory writ of mandamus, requiring the issuing of an execution by the surrogate, will not be granted unless his refusal to do so is clearly and unmistakably established.

The action of the surrogate in refusing to issue the execution without notice to the administrator cannot be reviewed by mandamus.

APPEAL by the relator, Judson Sackett, from an order of the Supreme Court, made at the Erie Special Term and entered in the office of the clerk of the county of Chautauqua on the 8th day of July, 1901, denying the relator's application for a peremptory writ of mandamus requiring the surrogate of Chautauqua county to issue an execution to enforce the payment of a sum of money in accordance with a decree of the Surrogate's Court of said county.

Thomas H. Larkins, for the appellant.

Frank W. Stevens, for the respondent.

SPRING, J.:

On the 30th day of June, 1894, in proceedings for the judicial settlement of the account of Van Buren Sackett, as administrator of the goods, etc., of Jacyntha Sackett, deceased, a decree was entered in the Surrogate's Court of Chautauqua county finally settling his account, and directing that said administrator pay to the relator Judson Sackett, $498.60, his distributive share as one of the next of kin of said deceased. Said decree further ordered that, in case said payment could not be made to said Judson Sackett, the same be paid into the Surrogate's Court of said county. In 1899 proofs were presented to the said Surrogate's Court sufficient to raise the presumption of the death of said Judson Sackett, and an administratrix of his personal estate was appointed who continued to act in that capacity until May 6, 1901, when the letters of administration were revoked as the alleged decedent was ascertained to be alive and the revocation of the letters was at his instance as well as that of the administratrix. During the incumbency of said administratrix proceedings were commenced on her behalf to enforce the decree of June, 1894, by requiring the respondent to pay over to her the sum adjudged as the distributive portion of the relator. The respondent answered, alleging that he had paid such sum to a former surrogate of said county, but the proceedings were dismissed without determining as to the validity of this payment. On the 16th day of April, 1901, a transcript of said decree was docketed in the clerk's office of said county, and, as a proceeding was to be commenced for the enforcement of the decree directing the payment to the relator, the surrogate wrote to his attorney advising him, among other things, of the propriety of giving notice of the proceedings to the respondent in conformity with sections 1377 and 1378 of the Code of Civil Procedure. A citation was subsequently issued to the administrator requiring him to show cause why an execution should not issue upon the decree entered in the Surrogate's Court. The proceeding was dismissed on the ground that the petition was insufficient, but without prejudice to the renewal of the application. The attorney for the relator thereafter presented the papers used upon this application for the writ of mandamus, and the surrogate questioned their sufficiency and advised the issuing of a citation to the administrator, as that officer desired to test the validity of the payment to the former surrogate, and the fact of such payment was obvious by the records in the surrogate's office. The attorney thereupon asked leave, which was granted, to withdraw his papers, informing the surrogate he would examine the practice regulating applications of this kind. Subsequently, without any further application or request to the surrogate, this proceeding for a peremptory writ requiring the surrogate to issue an execution was commenced.

We think there are several cogent reasons for affirming the order of the Special Term denying the writ:

First. The judicial settlement of the account of the respondent as administrator was clearly within the cognizance of the Surrogate's Court, and its decree was "the final determination of the rights of the parties." (Code Civ. Proc. § 2550.) That decree was conclusive upon their rights and possessed the same force and verity as the judgment of any court of competent jurisdiction. (*Baldwin* v. *Smith*, 91 Hun, 230; *Garlock* v. *Vandevort*, 128 N. Y. 374; *O'Connor* v. *Huggins*, 113 id. 511.)

By section 2553 of the Code of Civil Procedure a transcript of the decree directing the payment "of money into court or to one or more persons therein designated" may be docketed in the clerk's docket book, "kept in his office as prescribed by law for docketing a judgment of the Supreme Court. The docketing of such a decree has the same force and effect * * * as if it was such a judgment." It still remains, however, a decree of the Surrogate's Court (*Townsend* v. *Whitney*, 75 N. Y. 425), and the surrogate or his clerk alone has power to enforce the decree by issuing an execution (Code, § 2554), or in a proper case by punishing the party refusing to obey it for contempt. (Code, § 2555.) In these various proceedings and remedies the surrogate or his court still retains exclusive jurisdiction over the subject-matter of the decree, and the docketing in no way impairs this authority or transmits it to any other court. The object of docketing the decree is to create a lien upon the property of the party charged with the payment of the money, not to change the character of the decree or to divest the surrogate of jurisdiction. In enforcing the decree, section 2554 of the Code, however, after providing that execution can be issued only by the surrogate or the clerk of his court, adds : " In all other respects the provisions of this act, relating to an execution against the property of a judgment debtor, issued upon a judgment of the Supreme Court, and the proceedings to collect it, apply to an execution issued from the Surrogate's Court, and the collection thereof, the decree being, for that purpose, regarded as a judgment."

The mode of procedure, therefore, covering the issuing of an execution on a judgment of the Supreme Court is applicable to one issued to enforce the decree of the Surrogate's Court directing the payment of a sum of money. Section 1377 of the Code permits an execution on a final judgment " after the lapse of five years from the entry * * * where an order is made by the court granting leave to issue the execution." By the following section notice of this application "must be served personally upon the adverse party if he is a resident of the State." The docketing of the decree did not make a new date for the starting of the five years limitation upon the issuing of an execution without leave of the court. The period from which the five years commences to run is the entry of the final judgment, which in this case was the entry of the decree, and there was no merger of the decree into a judgment by its docketing. The decree itself was not even entered in the clerk's office, but a transcript attested by the surrogate or the clerk of his court furnished the data from which it could be docketed.

We are, therefore, satisfied that the surrogate was within the strict line of his official duty in urging upon the attorney for the relator the necessity of complying with the requirements of these sections. There are no reasons which occur to us why these provisions are not applicable to the enforcement of the decree of the Surrogate's Court, and the obvious intention of the Legislature has been to conform the practice of that court as far as possible to that which obtains in other courts of record.

Second. In the present case the surrogate very properly insisted that the administrator should have notice of the application to issue an execution. The records of his court relating to the settlement of this estate showed that the administrator had endeavored to comply with its requirements and had paid the money to the surrogate who signed the decree. It was contended in his behalf that the payment was a satisfaction of the decree so far as it affected the appellant, and whether right or wrong in this contention he ought to be given an opportunity to have its validity determined before any execution was issued. Irrespective of any statutory authority the surrogate was acting within his inherent power, which necessarily vested him with some discretion in insisting that the administrator be given notice that the relator desired to enforce the decree by execution. The requirement that he notify the administrator was not burdensome, could readily be complied with and was in every way reasonable.

Third. But the surrogate did not unqualifiedly require that notice be given to the respondent of the application for leave to issue the execution. He advised this and apparently the attorney for the relator acquiesced in the suggestion of the surrogate. The writ peremptorily requiring the surrogate to issue the execution, and which of itself implies an improper refusal by the surrogate, may not be granted until the declination of the official to act is clear and unmistakable.

Fourth. We apprehend, however, that the remedy by peremptory writ of mandamus is not the proper manner in which to review the conduct of the surrogate, even if tantamount to a refusal to issue the execution without notice to the administrator. Conceding the application for execution was made unequivocally, the surrogate was called upon to act judicially, which he did. While not denying the right of the relator ultimately to have the execution issued, the surrogate in the exercise of his discretion required as a preliminary step that the administrator be called in to be heard.   This judicious course of the surrogate cannot be reviewed by mandamus.   (*People ex rel. Forsyth* v. *Court of Sessions,* 141 N. Y. 288 ; *People ex rel. Lunney* v. *Campbell,* 72 id. 496 ; *People ex rel. Woodward* v. *Rosendale,* 76 Hun, 103.)   The remedy savors too much of an attempt to coerce a public official who was obviously endeavoring to perform his whole duty to both parties interested.   If there had been in fact a refusal to issue the execution without notice, an order denying the application might have been entered and a review had by appeal.

For these reasons, we conclude that the order should be affirmed, with ten dollars costs and the disbursements of this appeal.

McLENNAN, WILLIAMS, HISCOCK and DAVY, JJ., concurred.

Order affirmed, with ten dollars costs and disbursements.

FREDERIKA EGERER, Respondent, *v.* THE NEW YORK CENTRAL AND HUDSON RIVER RAILROAD COMPANY, Appellant.

Railroad grade crossing — the right of an abutting owner to easements of light, air and access in a street is protected by the Constitution — eminent domain.

While the Legislature has the power to provide for the abolition of grade crossings of city streets by steam railroads, still the owners of property abutting upon the streets, although their title extends only to the margin thereof, have incorporeal rights of light, air and access in the nature of easements in the streets themselves, which constitute private property, and of which, under section 6 of article 1 of the Constitution of the State of New York, they cannot be deprived by the Legislature or the city, or both, without compensation.

APPEAL by the defendant, The New York Central and Hudson River Railroad Company, from an order of the Supreme Court, made at the Monroe Trial Term and entered in the office of the clerk of the county of Monroe on the 25th day of September, 1899, denying the defendant's motion for a new trial made upon the minutes, a verdict of the jury having been rendered in favor of the plaintiff for $866.25.

Edward Harris, for the appellant.

Thomas Raines, for the respondent.

WILLIAMS, J.:

The order appealed from should be affirmed, with costs.

The action was brought to recover damages for an obstruction of the street in front of plaintiff's premises, whereby she was deprived of her easements of light, air and access.

There have been three trials of the action. On the first trial there was a verdict directed for defendant. There was an affirmance at General Term (49 Hun, 605), but a reversal in the Court of Appeals (130 N. Y. 108). On the second trial a verdict was again directed for the defendant. There was a reversal by the Appellate Division (39 App. Div. 652). On the third trial a verdict was rendered for the plaintiff, which is here under review.

The obstruction complained of was erected by the defendant, under an agreement with grade crossing commissioners, appointed under chapter 147, Laws of 1880, for the purpose of eliminating grade crossings of railroads in the city of Rochester. No provision was made in that act or in the charter of the city (Laws of 1880, chap. 14) for compensation to property owners for any property interests or rights that might be invaded or taken in carrying out the objects to be secured under the Grade Crossing Act. No compensation has ever been made to the plaintiff, nor steps taken to acquire any rights, or consent of plaintiff, with reference to the obstruction in question.

It is well settled that while the Legislature has the power to provide for the removal of grade crossings of city streets by steam railroads, still the owners of property abutting upon the streets, though their title extends only to the margin thereof, have the incorporeal rights of light, air and access, in the nature of easements, in the streets themselves, which constitute private property, and which they cannot be deprived of by the Legislature or the city or both without compensation, under article 1, section 6, of the Constitution of the State. (*Abendroth* v. *Manhattan R. Co.,* 122 N. Y. 1; *Kane* v. *N. Y. Elevated R. R. Co.,* 125 id. 165; *Reining* v. *N. Y., L. & W. R. Co.,* 128 id. 157; *Egerer* v. *N. Y. C. & H. R. R. R. Co.,* 130 id. 108; *Holloway* v. *Southmayd,* 139 id. 390.)

In the last case GRAY, J., considered and distinguished several cases cited by the appellant herein, viz.: *Jackson* v. *Hathaway* (15 Johns. 447); *Wheeler* v. *Clark* (58 N. Y. 267); *Kings County Fire Insurance Co.* v. *Stevens* (101 id. 411); *King* v. *Mayor* (102 id. 175), and we need not, therefore, discuss them here. It was said by GRAY, J., among other things, that these private easements are independent of the public easement, and are in their nature indestructible by the public authorities.

There can, therefore, be no doubt as to the right of the plaintiff to recover damages for any obstruction of the street in front of her premises by the defendant, whereby she was deprived of her easements of light, air and access.

The defense was based upon the claim, in effect, that the obstruction was not erected in front of her premises. The agreement between the commissioners and the defendant was made, and the obstruction erected, in or about the year 1882. Prior to that time North avenue left North street at the intersection of the latter street by the defendant's railroad. North street ran substantially north and south, and North avenue extended off in a northeasterly direction. Plaintiff's premises faced upon North avenue, and were bounded on the west by the avenue and on the north by the defendant's right of way. The agreement between the commissioners and the defendant provided that North avenue should be changed and diverted into North street, northerly of defendant's right of way, across a triangular piece of land there owned by the defendant and dedicated to the public use for that purpose, and the portion of the avenue required to be inclosed by walls upon its right of way to support the elevated structure and tracks should be abandoned and discontinued. This change in the avenue was made, as agreed upon, and the southerly portion thereof was used for the erection of the walls to support the elevated structure and tracks. The walls were erected within the limits of the avenue, but whether the southerly portion thereof was wholly within the defendant's right of way was a matter in dispute upon the trial. There was a controversy as to the precise location of the southerly line of such right of way, and plaintiff claimed the wall, some part of it, extended southerly beyond such line. In either event, however, the wall was in front of the plaintiff's premises in the part of the avenue abandoned and discontinued by the city. The wall interfered very materially with plaintiff's easements, the right of light, air and access, whether it was in whole, or in part only, within defendant's right of way, and the plaintiff claimed the right to recover damages regardless of the question as to the precise location of the line in controversy.

The plaintiff's right to recover on the trial, however, was limited to a finding by the jury that the obstruction was in part south of the boundary line of defendant's right of way, and this finding was made by the jury upon conflicting evidence. Some difficulty was experienced in satisfactorily establishing the disputed line, and it is claimed by the defendant that the finding of the jury locating the same was against the weight of the evidence and should be set aside for that reason. The parties derived their titles from a common grantor, one Hiram Davis. The defendant's right of way was acquired by the Auburn and Rochester Railroad Company (to whose rights defendant succeeded) in 1839. It was thirty-four feet wide and was on a curve through Davis' lands. At the same time a right of way was acquired through the lands of Benedict and Penny, lying east and west of the Davis lands. This right of way through Davis and Benedict's lands was fenced by the railroad company on its south line, and a portion of this fence was standing at the time the plaintiff's lands were deeded to plaintiff's husband in 1856. The railroad company also constructed a ditch for the purpose of draining its roadbed just north of and near to the fence along the Davis and Benedict property, a foot wide at the bottom and eight to ten feet wide at the top and five feet deep. The fence did not extend, in 1856, all the way to North avenue, then North street, but only fifty or sixty feet westerly from the easterly line of plaintiff's premises. The ditch, however, extended all the way along the plaintiff's premises from her easterly boundary to North avenue and North street, and was covered with planking across the avenue and street. None of the monuments mentioned in the description of the right of way through the Davis, Benedict and Penny lands, as originally acquired, remained at the time of the trial. All had ceased to exist for more than twenty years. The first deed in plaintiff's chain of title was given by Davis to Luckey in 1843 and described lands as bounded on the north by the railroad, on the west by North street (a portion afterwards called North avenue), on the south by Tyler street as laid out on a map filed in the Monroe county clerk's office, but not then opened, and on the east by a line far enough from North street, between Tyler street and the railroad, to include three acres of land. In August, 1854, Luckey first deeded to Washburn a portion of the three acres, other than plaintiff's premises, bounding the property so conveyed as commencing at Tyler street, twenty-five feet west of the corner of Sand's lot, and running thence northerly, in two courses, forty-six feet and one hundred and forty-two feet and ten inches to a stone set in the ground by the railroad fence, the south line of the railroad; thence westerly on the south line of the railroad thirty-five feet six inches; thence southerly in a direct line to Tyler street; thence easterly on Tyler street, in two courses, fifty-nine feet and forty-two feet three inches, to the place of beginning (survey made by Cornell). Luckey next deeded to Frederick Benedict a portion of the three acres, other than the plaintiff's premises, bounding the property so conveyed as beginning at the corner of North street and Tyler street, and running thence northerly along North street to a point within twenty feet and four inches of the railroad fence on the south side of the railroad; thence easterly to a point on the west line of Washburn's lot one hundred and sixteen feet north of Tyler street; thence south on Washburn's line to Tyler street; thence west on Tyler street to the place of beginning.

Then Luckey deeded to Alfred Benedict the plaintiff's premises, describing the same as being on the east side of North street (afterwards North avenue), and on the south side of the railroad, beginning at a point in the west line of the Washburn lot 116 feet north of Tyler street, and running westerly on Frederick Benedict's north line to North street (avenue); thence northeasterly along that street (avenue) to the railroad; thence easterly along the railroad to the Washburn's west line, stated in Cornell's survey to be 112 feet; thence south on Washburn's west line to the place of beginning, marked in the same survey as 66½ feet. Plaintiff's chain of title then continued with this same description, by deed from Benedict to Benedict in 1855, from Benedict to Egerer (plaintiff's husband), in 1856, and from her husband to herself, through one Yeck, in 1859.

Later, and in 1873, the plaintiff deeded through Yeck to her hus-

426 EGERER v. N. Y. CENTRAL & H. R. R. R. CO.

band a triangular piece in the northerly part of this property and described the same as on the east side of North street (avenue), and bordering on the railroad, beginning at a point in the south line of the railroad thirty-seven feet east of its intersection with the east line of North street (avenue); running thence easterly along the railroad about seventy-five feet to the Washburn land; thence along Washburn's northerly line, southerly to the southeast corner of the house on the premises conveyed; thence westerly to the place of beginning.

The precise location of Tyler street as indicated upon the map on file was in dispute on the trial. There were no monuments to locate it, and it was not opened at the time Davis gave his deed to Luckey in 1843.

The Egerers, husband and wife, went into possession of the property in question in 1856, and have continued in possession ever since. There were then no buildings upon the property. The whole tract of land was open between the railroad and Tyler street. There was the fence and ditch constructed by the railroad, and an old fence on Tyler street. No fence along North street or avenue.

The Egerers erected the hotel building in 1856, as it now stands, including the piazza in front of it. In 1859 or 1860 the two-story house was built upon the triangle of land conveyed in 1873 by plaintiff to her husband, and in 1866 or 1867 the shop was built and used originally as a barber shop.

These buildings appear all to be parallel with the south line of the property, the hotel quite close to that line, and the other two buildings over near the railroad line. According to defendant's claim as to the location of its south line, these buildings all extend over such line, while plaintiff claims the line is clearly to the north of all of them.

There was evidence of many other facts and circumstances given at the trial bearing upon the real and true location of this railroad line. We do not think it necessary to recite them in detail here. And then there are extended arguments of counsel in favor of their respective contentions. The plaintiff relies largely upon the fence and ditch constructed by the railroad, the fence being referred to in some of the deeds as the line of the railroad; also the use made by the plaintiff and her husband of the property in the location of buildings, without objection on the part of the railroad, while the defendant relies largely upon the deeds in and connected with the plaintiff's chain of title, the language thereof, the distances stated, and the survey referred to therein.

Very likely it is difficult, with absolute certainty, to locate the disputed line, but we think there was evidence of circumstances sufficient to go to the jury, and that its verdict based thereon should not be set aside by us.

We do not assent to the proposition that a recovery might not be had by the plaintiff, even if the jury were to find the line to be as claimed by the defendant, but that question is not involved on this appeal because of the course the trial took, and the verdict having been rendered based upon a finding that the line was where the plaintiff claimed it to be.

We are of the opinion that the verdict cannot be regarded as excessive, and, therefore, the views hereinbefore expressed lead to the affirmance of the order appealed from, with costs.

McLENNAN, SPRING and HISCOCK, JJ., concurred; DAVY, J., not sitting.

Order affirmed, with costs.

LEHIGH VALLEY RAILWAY COMPANY and LEHIGH VALLEY RAILROAD COMPANY, Respondents, *v.* ROBERT B. ADAM and Others, Constituting the Grade Crossing Commissioners of the City of Buffalo, Appellants.

Buffalo grade crossing commission — power of, to alter the general plan — exercise of the police power in removing grade crossings — impairment of contracts.

Section 6 of the Buffalo Grade Crossing Act (Laws of 1898, chap. 345), as amended by chapter 353 of the Laws of 1892, authorized the commissioners to adopt a general plan of the work, and, from time to time, to alter, amend or modify the same as to any detail, but prohibited them from adopting a general plan extending beyond the one theretofore adopted, under which contracts had already been entered into, and from extending the general plan adopted by them. Pursuant to the amended section, the commissioners adopted and filed a general plan.

Thereafter they proposed to change such general plan by raising a portion of the Lehigh Valley railroad above the grade of the street and carrying it upon an elevated structure. The plan mentioned in the original act and the plan adopted pursuant to the amendment of 1892 treated of the portion of the railroad affected by the proposed change, but neither of such plans provided for raising the tracks above the surface of the street.

Held, that the commissioners had authority, under the amendment of 1892, to make the proposed change in the general plan;

That such change related merely to a detail of the general plan and did not constitute an extension of such plan;

That to extend the general plan meant to enlarge its scope so as to take in streets, crossings or territory not embraced in the original plan;

That the Legislature, in the exercise of the police power, may provide for the abolition of grade crossings, and that the franchises granted to railroads by cities, and contracts entered into between railroads and cities, are subject to the exercise of this power;

That such legislation does not violate the constitutional prohibition against the impairment of the obligation of contracts and the taking of property without due process of law.

APPEAL by the defendants, Robert B. Adam and others, constituting the grade crossing commissioners of the city of Buffalo, from a judgment of the Supreme Court in favor of the plaintiffs, entered in the office of the clerk of the county of Erie on the 16th day of April, 1901, upon the decision of the court rendered after a trial at the Erie Special Term.

Spencer Clinton, for the appellants.

Martin Carey and *James McC. Mitchell,* for the respondents.

WILLIAMS, J. :

The judgment appealed from should be reversed and a new trial ordered, with costs to the appellants to abide event.

The judgment permanently restrained the defendants from adopting any alteration, change or extension of the general plan theretofore adopted under the provisions of the Buffalo Grade Crossing Law that would in any way affect the existing condition of the tracks and property of the plaintiffs between Alabama and Washington streets in the city of Buffalo, and from in any way interfering with the railroad and property of the plaintiffs.

The existing condition of the tracks and railroad was that it traversed the location in question at grade, and the proposed change was to elevate the tracks and roadbed above grade on an elevated structure.

It was claimed by the plaintiffs that the defendants could not make the change because:

First. It would violate the contract rights of the plaintiffs, acquired under a municipal franchise granted by the city of Buffalo, and under an agreement with grade crossing commissions for the city, theretofore made and granted.

Second. No power was given defendants so to do by the Legislature of the State.

Third. If any such power was given by the Legislature, it was unconstitutional and void.

The decision of the trial court was apparently based upon the first two grounds, the constitutional question not being passed upon. The plaintiffs insist upon the constitutional question here, however, in case it shall be deemed essential to an affirmance of the judgment.

The facts in the case, stated as briefly as possible, are as follows:

The plaintiffs' railroad was originally constructed by the rail*road* company, a Pennsylvania corporation, and was leased to the rail*way* company, a domestic corporation, about the year 1890, and has since been operated by the latter company.

The original franchise to run through the city of Buffalo was granted in 1882, and through the locality in question was to be at grade from Alabama street westerly to its terminus at Washington street. This franchise was further ratified and approved in 1885, and the roadbed was constructed prior to 1888, and has been operated since that time. Down to September, 1892, the part of the road in question was operated solely for freight, the passenger business, by a traffic arrangement with the Erie railroad, going over the tracks and into the passenger station of the latter company. Since September, 1892, the part of the road in question has been used for both freight and passenger business.

February 20, 1888, a commission of engineers was held at Buffalo for the purpose of recommending a plan for the relief of the streets of that city, by railroads crossing the same at grade, and a plan was recommended by that commission and was filed in the office of the engineer of the city. That plan, however, provided for no change of grade of that part of the plaintiffs' road in question here.

In May, 1888, the Legislature passed chapter 345 of the laws of that year, which provided, by section 1, that any six of the commissioners therein appointed were authorized to enter into a contract in behalf of the city of Buffalo, with any railroad companies for the relief of the city from obstruction to streets by railroads crossing the same at grade upon the plan recommended by the commission of engineers, then on file in the office of the city engineer of Buffalo, or upon any modification thereof as to detail agreed upon in such contract, subject to the approval of the city engineer, and that such contract should be binding upon the city, and, by section 5, that if within six months from the passage of the act the railroad companies declined or refused to enter into such a contract, then the city might apply to the Supreme Court, upon notice to the railroad companies, for the appointment of a commission of five persons to change and regulate the crossing and occupation by railroads of the streets, avenues and public grounds of the city.

There were then provisions by subsequent sections for the carrying out of the objects of the act.   On the last day of the six months from the passage of the act, and on November 22, 1888, the commissioners named in section 1 entered into a contract with the plaintiffs' railroad company, for certain changes in the grade of the roadbed and tracks of the railroad and of the streets, and for erections, viaducts and cuttings, to be made by the parties, according to the detail plans prepared and placed on file in the city engineer's office, and fixing the proportion of the expenses thereof to be paid by each party respectively, and the contract so made was carried out and complied with by the railroad company.   Under this contract the tracks and roadbed at Michigan street were raised about two feet.

In 1890, by chapter 255 of the laws of that year, the act of 1888 was amended, and again in 1892, by chapter 353 of that year, the acts of 1888 and 1890 were further amended.

By the amendment in 1890 of section 5 of the act of 1888 the commissioners appointed in the original act were substituted for the second commission under the original act, and were directed to proceed to secure the relief to the city from the crossing of streets, alleys and public grounds by railroads at grade.   This section, however, apparently related only to such railroad companies as should have failed to enter into a contract under section 1 of the original act, and the plaintiffs were very likely thereby excluded from the provision of this amendment. By section 6 of the original act, as amended in 1890, the new commission was directed to adopt the general plan mentioned in section 1 of the original act, which was the plan recommended by the commission of engineers in 1888, and they were prohibited from changing this original plan in any material part, and were given power to make new contracts and by agreement with the contracting company to alter, modify or change any contract theretofore made.

By the amendment of 1892 section 1 of the original act was changed so as to provide for the making of " contracts from time to time;" reference to the plan adopted by the commission of engineers was omitted, and in its place were inserted the words, " plans adopted or to be adopted by said commissioners as hereinafter provided;" then by section 6 of the original act, as again amended by this act of 1892, the commission were given power to adopt a general plan and from time to time to alter, amend or modify the same as to any detail, but were prohibited from adopting a general plan extending beyond the one theretofore adopted under which contracts had already been entered into and from extending the general plan adopted by them.

The commissioners, pursuant to this act, on the 19th of November, 1893, adopted and filed a general plan which included no change in the line of plaintiffs' railroad and dealt with the same crossings and in substantially the same manner as the general plan recommended by the commission of engineers in 1888. It was not until December 11, 1899, however, that the commissioners took the action which led to the commencement of this suit. Then in compliance with the provisions of the statute they served upon the plaintiffs' railroad company a notice that they proposed to adopt a modification, amendment or alteration of the general plan theretofore adopted and filed, and that on December 27, 1899, they would hear the city, the plaintiffs' railroad company and all other persons interested, with reference thereto.

The proposed change involved the raising of the tracks of the plaintiffs' railroad from Alabama street to Washington street, about three-fourths of a mile, including the construction of overhead crossings at the intersection of streets, and an elevated railroad through and along Scott street and upon the plaintiffs' own property at least fifteen feet above the surface of the street, the structure across and along the streets to be of steel with stone abutments and steel columns.

The trial court decided that this change was not a *modification, alteration or amendment,* but was an *extension* of the general plan theretofore adopted and filed, and under which the contract was made between the plaintiffs and defendants; that it would be a violation of that contract and of the franchise granted to the plaintiffs by the city to require such change to be made in the tracks and roadbed of the plaintiffs' road, and that the commissioners were never authorized by the Legislature to make such change in the general plan or in the railroad structure, and inasmuch as the franchise had never been abrogated, and the plaintiffs had never consented to such change, the commissioners had no power to make the same.

Upon such decision the judgment appealed from was ordered.

It does not appear that the hearing noticed for December 27, 1899, ever in fact was had. It seems to have been adjourned until February 1, 1900, and on the latter day this action was commenced and a temporary injunction served, which was subsequently continued during the pendency of the action.

We are of the opinion that the commissioners were authorized, under the acts of the Legislature referred to, to make the change in the general plan proposed. By the act of 1892 they were given the power to adopt a general plan (not necessarily the same one already adopted), and from time to time to alter, amend or modify the same as to any detail. They were only prohibited from adopting a general plan *extending beyond* the one theretofore adopted, under which contracts had already been entered into, and from *extending* the same after it had once been adopted. The commission did adopt a general plan in 1893, which did *not* extend beyond the one theretofore adopted. They sought in 1899 to alter, amend or modify the general plan of 1893, and the question is whether the change proposed related merely to a detail of such general plan or whether it constituted an extension of such general plan. No change in the line, no extension thereof, was proposed. The same streets and crossings and territory were treated of. To *extend* the general plan was to enlarge its scope so as to take in other streets, crossings or territory not embraced in the original plan. It would be a forced construction of the statute to hold that it did not permit any change to be made in the grade of the roadbed, rendered necessary by any growth of the city or increase in the use of the streets, or enlargement of the traffic over the railroad, in order to insure the safety of the public in traveling the streets. Until 1892 the passenger trains of the plaintiffs were run over the tracks of the Erie railroad and into its depot. Only the small freight business of the plaintiffs was done over the part of the plaintiffs' road in question. Since then the whole passenger and freight business of the plaintiffs has been done over this part of its road, and fast passenger trains have been run here. This has so changed the condition of things that the safety of the community demands that these dangerous grade crossings shall be eliminated.

Assuming that the Legislature might authorize this·change to be made, we think a fair construction of the act of 1892 gives the commissioners power to make the change in the general plan of 1893, and to compel the plan so changed to be complied with, and the roadbed and tracks to be elevated so as to remove the grade crossings in question.

The Legislature had power to appoint a commission and authorize it to take proceedings to remove grade crossings in the city of Buffalo. These crossings in large cities are *quasi* public nuisances, and their abolition is the subject of the police power of the State, which can by the Legislature provide for their removal, and the franchises granted to railroads by cities, and contracts entered into between railroads and cities, are subject to the exercise of such police power. The constitutional inhibition upon the impairment of contracts and the taking of property without due process of law, are not violated by the exercise of such police power in securing the public safety by the abolition of grade crossings. (*New York & New England R. R. Co.* v. *Bristol*, 151 U. S. 556, 567; *Wabash R. R. Co.* v. *Defiance*, 167 id. 88; *Chicago, etc., R. R. Co.* v. *Nebraska*, 170 id. 57, 74.)

It was held in those cases that it was not only within the power, but was also the duty of the State, through its Legislature, to provide for and secure to the community the safety of railroad crossings of streets in large cities; that it was within the police power of the

State, and that it could not be contracted away by any agreement between the cities and the railroad companies; that any other view involved the proposition that it was competent for the city and the railroad companies, by entering into agreements between themselves, to withdraw the subject from the reach of the police power and to substitute their view of the public necessities for those of the Legislature, and that the acts passed by the Legislature, in the legitimate exercise of the police power in securing public safety at street crossings by railroads in cities, were constitutional and valid. It was also held that this power might be exercised through the medium of a commission such as was constituted in this case.

It seems to us, therefore, that the only question here to be seriously considered is whether the Legislature has clothed the defendants with power to take the action proposed, to make the change in the general plan already adopted and require it to be complied with so that the tracks of the plaintiffs' railroad shall be elevated above the streets intersected and traversed thereby instead of crossing and running along such streets at grade. The language of the acts of the Legislature might have been clearer than it is, but we are of the opinion that by the fair construction thereof such power has been given the grade crossing commissioners.

Whether the result of such change of plaintiffs' tracks and road-bed will injuriously affect the plaintiffs' property or business is not for this court to consider. That is a question which should be addressed to the commission. The question before the court is one of power in the commission to act, to take the proceeding which it has instituted and which the judgment appealed from enjoined.

The views here expressed lead to the conclusion that the judgment appealed from was erroneously ordered and that it should be reversed and a new trial ordered, with costs to appellants to abide event.

McLENNAN, SPRING, HISCOCK and DAVY, JJ., concurred.

Judgment reversed and new trial ordered, with costs to the appellants to abide the event.

70
s 79

JOHN CLEMENS, Appellant, *v.* THE AMERICAN FIRE INSURANCE COMPANY OF PHILADELPHIA, PENNSYLVANIA, Respondent.

Insurance policy — what allegation in an action thereon is insufficient to show that proofs of loss were served — it must be alleged that sixty days have elapsed since such service — a plea of performance must use the word "duly."

Where, by the terms of a policy of fire insurance, the service of proofs of loss is made a condition precedent to the right to maintain an action thereon, a complaint in such an action is demurrable which contains no allegation of the service of any proofs of loss, except that the plaintiff filed a complete inventory of the property destroyed, with the quantity and cost of each article and the amount claimed thereon, which inventory had been and still was in the possession of the defendant, when it does not allege that such inventory (which did not contain all the information required to be set forth in the proofs of loss) was rendered as the proofs of loss and that it was received and retained by the defendant without objection, and that the defendant had required no further or other proofs of loss.

Where the policy in suit specifically provides that the loss should not become payable until sixty days after the proofs of loss are received by the company and that no suit shall be sustainable upon any claim until after full compliance with all requirements of the policy, an allegation that sixty days have elapsed since the proofs of loss were received by the defendant, before the action was commenced, is essential to the sufficiency of the complaint.

A pleader seeking to take advantage of section 533 of the Code of Civil Procedure, providing, "In pleading the performance of a condition precedent in a contract, it is not necessary to state the facts constituting performance: but the party may state generally that he or the person whom he represents, *duly* performed all the conditions on his part," must use the word "duly" in his allegation of performance.

APPEAL by the plaintiff, John Clemens, from an interlocutory judgment of the Supreme Court in favor of the defendant, entered in the office of the clerk of the county of Erie on the 9th day of July, 1901, upon the decision of the court, rendered after a trial at the Erie Special Term, sustaining a demurrer to the complaint.

Philip V. Fennelly, for the appellant.

Seward A. Simons, for the respondent.

WILLIAMS, J.:

The judgment appealed from should be affirmed, with costs.

The action was brought upon a policy of insurance to recover for the loss of household furniture destroyed by fire. The demurrer was upon the ground that the complaint did not state facts sufficient to constitute a cause of action. The particular points made were : *First.* That there was no sufficient allegation of the rendering of proofs of loss to the defendant pursuant to the terms of the policy. *Second.* That there was no allegation that sixty days had elapsed after the proofs of loss were received by the defendant before the action was commenced. These were conditions precedent to a right to recover in the action.

There was no specific allegation as to rendering proofs of loss, except that the plaintiff filed a complete inventory of the property destroyed and injured, with the quantity and cost of each article and the amount claimed thereon, which inventory ever since had been and still was in the possession of the defendant.

The policy, a copy of which was annexed to the complaint, specified in detail what the proofs of loss should contain, and the inventory alleged failed very materially to comply with the provision of the policy. It failed to furnish anything like the amount of information required by the specifications as to the proofs of loss. If it had been alleged that this inventory was rendered *as* the proofs of loss, and that it had been received and retained by the defendant without objection and that the defendant had required no further or other proofs of loss to be furnished, it might have been sufficient ; but the allegation of the complaint fell far short of this. It was manifestly insufficient as a specific allegation of performance of this condition precedent to the right to recover. Nor was this defect cured by the general allegation under section 533, Code of Civil Procedure, which provides : " In pleading the performance of a condition precedent in a contract, it is not necessary to state the facts constituting performance ; but the party may state generally that he or the person whom he represents, *duly* performed all the conditions on his part. If that allegation is controverted, he must, on the trial, establish performance."

The word *duly* was omitted from the complaint, and there was, therefore, a failure to comply with the section quoted, and plaintiff was entitled to no benefit thereunder.

The word *duly* in this, and other like provisions of the Code, has been held to be one of substance and not of form merely. (*Lee*

Successeurs D'Arles v. *Freedman,* 53 N. Y. Super. Ct. 519 ; *Baxter* v. *Lancaster,* 58 App. Div. 380 ; *People ex rel. Batchelor* v. *Bacon,* 37 id. 414; *Tuttle* v. *Robinson,* 91 Hun, 187, 189; *Brownell* v. *Town of Greenwich,* 114 N. Y. 518.)

There was no allegation in the complaint that sixty days had elapsed since the proofs of loss were received by the defendant before the action was commenced. Such an allegation was necessary. (*Porter* v. *Kingsbury,* 5 Hun, 598; 71 N. Y. 588; *Reining* v. *City of Buffalo,* 102 id. 312.)

In the first case it was held that a complaint in an action upon an undertaking upon appeal given pursuant to section 348 of the old Code, which failed to allege service of notice on the adverse party of the entry of the order or judgment affirming the judgment appealed from, ten days before the commencement of the action, was defective ; that the notice was a condition precedent to the commencement of the action, and in the absence of the allegation the complaint did not state a cause of action. The Code prohibited the commencement of the action until ten days after the service of the notice.

In the other case it was held necessary to allege in the complaint, in an action against the city for a tort, the presentation of the claim to the common council and the expiration of forty days thereafter, before the commencement of the action ; that the provision of the charter requiring such presentation of claim and prohibiting the bringing of the action until forty days had elapsed created a condition precedent. The court there said, in referring to *Porter* v. *Kingsbury :* " There the act required to be performed, constituted no part of the cause of action, but was provided, as in this case, to shield the parties liable from cost and trouble, in case of their willingness to pay the claim without suit after notice given. It is immaterial whether a condition be imposed in the statute giving a right of action, or be provided by contract, or exists by force of some principle of common or statute law, the complaint must, by the settled rules of pleading, state every fact essential to the cause of action, as well as those necessary to give the court jurisdiction to entertain the particular proceeding."

In the case we are considering it was specifically provided by the policy that the loss should not become payable until sixty days after proofs of loss were received by the company, and that no suit should be sustainable upon any claim until after full compliance with all requirements in the policy.

The rule laid down in the cases cited is applicable to this case.

The views here expressed lead to the conclusion that the judgment should be affirmed, with costs.

McLennan, Spring, Hiscock and Davy, JJ., concurred.

Interlocutory judgment affirmed, with costs, with leave to the plaintiff to plead over upon payment of costs of the demurrer and of this appeal.

The People of the State of New York, Respondent, *v.* Gilbert Milks, Appellant.

Arson — cross-examination of a witness for the prosecution to show that he entertained ill-feeling toward the defendant — right to have a witness explain his failure to earlier disclose his knowledge — right of the defendant to show that one jointly indicted with him, and called as a witness by him, had been acquitted.

Where, on the trial of an indictment charging the defendant with having induced one Smith to burn a barn owned by the defendant, a witness for the People testifies that after the fire the defendant requested him to go and see Smith and ascertain whether the latter had disclosed any information about the fire, it is error for the court to refuse to allow the defendant to cross-examine the witness as to whether there had not been some trouble between his family and the defendant and whether the witness did not entertain ill-feeling toward the defendant.

Where a witness who testified on behalf of the defense, that upon the night of the fire he saw Smith at such a place that it would have been practically impossible for him to have started the fire, is cross-examined by the district attorney concerning his failure to disclose such knowledge earlier in the litigation, so vigorously as to seriously affect his credibility, the defendant's counsel should, upon the redirect examination of the witness, be permitted to ask him to explain why he had not sooner disclosed his knowledge.

Where Smith, who had been jointly indicted with the defendant and who had been tried and acquitted, was sworn on behalf of the defendant, and it appeared that the jury knew that he and the defendant were jointly indicted, but did not know that he was acquitted, the court considered that the defendant was entitled to present that fact to the jury, in order that it might not appear that Smith had a vital personal interest in establishing the defendant's innocence.

APPEAL by the defendant, Gilbert Milks, from a judgment of the County Court of Cattaraugus county in favor of the plaintiff, entered in the office of the clerk of the county of Cattaraugus on the 14th day of June, 1901, upon the verdict of a jury convicting him of the crime of arson in the third degree, and also from an order entered in said clerk's office on the 14th day of June, 1901, denying the defendant's motion for a new trial made upon the minutes.

M. B. Jewell, for the appellant.

J. M. Congdon and *George W. Cole,* for the respondent.

HISCOCK, J.:

The defendant was jointly indicted with one Mitchell Smith for having upon June 4, 1898, set fire to a certain barn which was the property of said Milks. He was tried separately and apart from Smith. He was convicted upon a previous trial, but such conviction was reversed by this court.

Milks was several miles away from the place of the fire at the time it occurred, and the theory of the prosecution is that he procured Smith to set fire to the barn and other buildings which were burned with it.

Although it does not appear in the record, it did appear without contradiction upon the argument that Smith upon a second trial has been acquitted. We, therefore, start out with the somewhat incongruous and illogical condition that Smith, who was charged with actually having applied the match to the buildings, has been found by the jury not to have done so, and that the defendant, who is charged with having fired said buildings only and solely through the hand of Smith, is found to have committed such act.

Defendant's counsel has urged with great vigor and earnestness that upon the merits the evidence in this case was not sufficient to sustain the verdict of the jury, and that the latter should be set aside as against the weight of evidence. The conclusions we have reached as to the merit and correctness of certain objections and exceptions taken upon the trial in behalf of the defendant, render it unnecessary for us to pass upon such contention. As leading up to and bearing upon the review of the exceptions referred to, however, we

not only may but should bear in mind that the evidence certainly
presented a very close question of fact as to the guilt of the accused.
The decision as to his guilt or innocence upon the testimony offered
called for the most careful deliberation and well-directed consideration by the jury. In addition to the fact, not at all uncommon, that
the evidence against him was purely circumstantial, a large portion
of testimony which, from its nature, must have had great weight
with the jury, related to defendant's alleged attempts to bribe witnesses and suppress evidence. Some of the latter certainly crowded
to the border line of competency.

We refer to these features as indicating the great degree of
protection from the erroneous omission and rejection of evidence to
which the defendant was entitled. Upon a trial where the testimony was so conflicting an error which, in some other case could be
regarded as immaterial, might easily be sufficient to supply the little
additional weight necessary to turn the verdict against him. The
presumption always applicable unless clearly rebutted by the record,
that an error committed against the defendant upon a criminal trial
is material and harmful, especially applies to this case.

In three instances evidence sought by the defendant was, upon
the objection of the People, excluded by the learned county judge,
and in our opinion error thereby was committed.

One Fuller, having been sworn in behalf of the People, testified
to alleged conversations with the defendant after the fire, in which
the latter in substance raised the question whether Smith had
disclosed information about the fire, and procured said Fuller to
go and see the latter upon this subject. Fuller was a connection
by marriage of the defendant. His evidence was quite long, and,
if believed, tended strongly to prove guilty relations by the defendant to the fire. In fact, there was no one witness in our opinion
whose testimony, if believed, was liable to be more potential
against the prisoner. Upon the cross-examination defendant's
counsel sought, first, to show that there had been trouble between
the latter and a brother of the witness who was sworn upon the
former but not upon this trial. Such evidence as was then asked
for was objected to and properly excluded. The defendant's
counsel then asked these questions: " Q. Did you understand that
at one time Gilbert Milks had been instrumental in getting your

brother Wilson D. Fuller indicted for selling hard cider and by reason of that do you entertain some hard feelings against Milks?"

The district attorney "objected to the first part of the question, and the court sustained the objection and the defendant duly excepted."

It was then asked: "Q. Did you know that there had been some trouble between Milks and your family in the past?" This question was objected to and excluded.

We are unable to formulate any sufficient reason for excluding this evidence. The first question fairly called for the attitude of the witness toward the man against whom he was testifying. It not only was not objectionable, but eminently proper to embody in the question calling for his feelings the further query as to the cause upon which they were based. We know of no more elementary rule than that one of the chief purposes of a cross-examination is to disclose the situation and disposition of a witness, whether friendly or unfriendly, towards the respective parties to the litigation in which he is testifying. In this case, with the presumption which would naturally arise in the minds of jurymen, that on account of his relations with defendant he would be favorably predisposed towards him, it was most appropriate that an opportunity should be offered to disclose, if possible, that this was incorrect and that his attitude was really one of unfriendliness.

One Perkins was called in behalf of the defense to testify that upon the night of the fire he saw Smith at such a locality as practically to have rendered it impossible for him to have started the conflagration as claimed by the prosecution. The district attorney most vigorously and pointedly cross-examined this witness as to his failure to disclose this knowledge and information earlier in the litigation. His cross-examination tended to raise a serious doubt as to the probability of this witness having maintained silence so long if he really possessed the knowledge in question. Upon the re-direct examination, the counsel who had called the witness sought to have him explain why he had not so disclosed his information that it might be earlier utilized by the defendants who were on trial. This evidence was objected to and excluded, and thereby we think another simple and elementary rule in regard to the examination of witnesses was violated. The evidence of this witness, if it was true, was of great importance to defendant. The counsel for the People had by his cross-examination apparently seriously affected his credibility, and it was justly due to the defendant that he might call upon the witness to give any explanation which would reinstate him in the good opinion of the jury. The district attorney rather seeks to sustain these rulings upon the theory that it would be impossible for the witness to give any reasonable or decent excuse for his reticence under the circumstances; also that the defendant's counsel in one of his questions indicated the excuse which witness would have given, and that if so given it would have been clearly frivolous. As to the latter, we do not think it can be assumed that the witness would necessarily have given an excuse framed in the words of counsel's question, and as to the former, we think it was his privilege to give his excuse and let the jury pass upon its efficacy.

Defendant called as a witness in his behalf Smith, who was jointly indicted with him for causing this fire, and who gave evidence which, if true, absolutely entitled defendant to an acquittal. The latter's counsel sought to show that Smith had been tried upon the indictment against him and acquitted, and this evidence was objected to and excluded.

We do not believe that this evidence was competent as offering a legal bar to the conviction of this defendant as suggested by counsel. We do, however, think that the evidence was proper for the purpose of disclosing the situation of Smith as a witness. We have no doubt from the record that the jury was fully apprised of the fact that Smith and the defendant were jointly indicted. The fact of the acquittal of the witness does not appear anywhere in the record. Apparently he occupied the stand as a witness who had a vital personal interest in establishing that the defendant was not guilty upon the theory claimed by the prosecution. We think that it was very proper, under all of the circumstances of this case, that it should be made to appear that he had no such personal interest, and that, therefore, his testimony was not subject to the discrediting consideration of bias in that respect.

For these reasons, we conclude that the judgment of conviction and order denying the motion for new trial should be reversed and a new trial granted.

Judgment of conviction and order denying motion for new trial reversed and new trial ordered and proceeding remitted to the clerk of Cattaraugus county, pursuant to section 547, Code of Criminal Procedure.

McLENNAN, SPRING, WILLIAMS and DAVY, JJ., concurred.

Judgment of conviction and order denying motion for new trial reversed and new trial ordered, and proceeding remitted to the clerk of Cattaraugus county, pursuant to section 547 of the Code of Criminal Procedure.

GEORGE T. CHESTER, Individually and as Executor, etc., of MARY P. CHESTER, Deceased, Respondent, v. BUFFALO CAR MANUFACTURING COMPANY and Others, Appellants.

Corporation — issue of stock paid for out of surplus earnings — when it goes to a life tenant and when to remaindermen — when a legatee under the will of the original owner having consented to a division of the stock between himself and the other remaindermen, cannot recover it as such legatee or as executor or as legatee of the life tenant — a surrogate's decree on the final accounting of the executors of his testator is binding on him — what proof of ignorance of the manner of issue of the stock is insufficient.

A corporation having a surplus of accumulated profits may, within the limits of good faith, either distribute it as dividends or retain it and convert it into capital. The substance and intent of the action of the corporation, as evidenced by its treatment of the surplus and its resolutions in issuing new stock against such surplus, will be considered by, if it does not control, the courts in deciding whether or not the new stock is dividend, and hence income belonging to a life tenant.

If the corporation pays money or issues stock as a distribution of profits it will ordinarily go to the life tenant, but if it issues stock as capital and appropriates its surplus as an increase of the capital stock, such issue will be held to inure to the benefit of the remaindermen.

A testator, who left surviving him a widow, a son and three daughters, gave his residuary estate to his wife during her life with the remainder to his four children equally. Included in the residuary estate were sixty shares of the capital stock of a corporation, which had a capital stock of $40,000 and for many years prior to the death of the testator had allowed its earnings to accumulate. At the time of the testator's death the accumulated surplus amounted to $289,341.88, which surplus was then permanently invested in the business of the corporation. After the testator's death, and during the lifetime of the widow, the corporation declared and paid frequent cash dividends upon the stock.   It also issued two thousand one hundred shares of additional stock and divided two thousand of them among its stockholders who paid nothing therefor.   The agreement of the stockholders consenting to the issue of the additional stock and the action of the trustees of the corporation directing its issue denominated the transaction as an "increase of capital stock."   At the time the additional stock was issued, the accumulated surplus of the corporation amounted to $443,030.57.   A few days before the issue of such stock the corporation paid to its stockholders $80,000 in cash, declaring such payment to be a dividend.

Held, that the additional shares were intended to be and were issued to represent an accretion to the permanent working capital of the corporation and did not constitute a dividend of income; that, for this reason, the three hundred additional shares apportioned to the testator's estate belonged to the remaindermen and not to the life tenant.

After the widow's death one of the executors and trustees under the testator's will, wrote to the testator's son, who was also an executor and trustee under the will, stating that the testator's estate owned three hundred and sixty shares of the capital stock of the corporation in question, viz., the sixty original shares and the three hundred additional shares, and that for the purpose of securing an adjustment and settlement of matters as executor and trustee of the testator he would offer the stock for sale at public auction.   The wife of the testator's son, to whom he had previously transferred all his interest in his father's estate, thereupon presented a petition to the Surrogate's Court alleging that as assignee of her husband's interest in his father's estate she was the owner of ninety shares of such stock and that she did not wish to have such ninety shares sold, but desired to keep the same as an investment, and she requested that the executors be compelled to show cause why they should not deliver over to her such ninety shares of stock.   The testator's son joined in the petition, stating that he had read it and that the same was true, and that he desired that the prayer of the petition be granted.   An order was issued restraining the executor from selling the said ninety shares of stock until the further order of the court.   No further proceedings were had in the Surrogate's Court, but by an arrangement between the parties the certificate for three hundred and sixty shares was surrendered to the corporation and four new certificates of ninety shares each were issued to the wife of the testator's son and to the testator's three daughters.   Thereafter the testator's son, his wife and the testator's three daughters signed an acknowledgment that the executors and trustees "have fully and satisfactorily accounted to us as the heirs and next of kin of said deceased for all moneys and property held by them as such Executors and Trustees," and consented to the entry of a decree discharging the executors and trustees from any and all liability or accountability to such heirs.   The decree entered upon such consent adjudged that the executors and trustees thereby were "finally released, exonerated and discharged as the executors and trustees of and from any and all liability and accountability to said interested persons."

Subsequently the testator's son brought an action to establish title to the two hundred and twenty-five shares of additional stock distributed to his three sisters, claiming such stock in a three-fold capacity, namely, as assignee under a reassignment from his wife of his interest in his father's estate, as executor under his mother's will, and as specific legatee under such will of all her interest in the stock of the corporation. He also contended that, at the time of the proceedings in the Surrogate's Court and the distribution of the stock among his wife and his three sisters, he was ignorant of the facts surrounding the issue of the disputed stock and did not know his rights therein.

Held, that he could not maintain the action in the first capacity, as, if the stock belonged to his father's estate, it had concededly been properly distributed;

That, as it did not appear that there were any creditors of his mother's estate or that there were any other persons who claimed to have derived any interest in the stock through her, his qualified title as executor under his mother's will became merged in his beneficial interest as legatee under such will and that, if such stock belonged to his mother's estate, he would be entitled to it as an individual rather than as an executor;

That the plaintiff, having consented to the distribution of the stock among his wife and three sisters, upon the theory that it constituted part of his father's estate, could not subsequently insist that the stock was a part of his mother's estate;

That the decree discharging the executors and trustees was an adjudication that the division of the stock was proper and that such decree was binding upon the plaintiff in favor of the other legatees;

That the contention that, at the time the stock was divided among the plaintiff's wife and his three sisters, he was ignorant of the facts which attended the issue of the additional stock was not supported by the facts found.

WILLIAMS, J., dissented.

APPEAL by the defendants, the Buffalo Car Manufacturing Company and others, from an interlocutory judgment of the Supreme Court in favor of the plaintiff, entered in the office of the clerk of the county of Erie on the 5th day of July, 1901, upon the decision of the court rendered after a trial at the Erie Special Term.

Adelbert Moot, for the appellants.

Frank C. Ferguson, for the respondent.

HISCOCK, J.:

The principal question involved upon this appeal is whether 300 shares of capital stock issued by the defendant car company in January, 1893, against an accumulated surplus, is to be regarded as a dividend and belonging to the life tenant under a will, or whether it is to be regarded as part of the principal of the estate and belonging to the remaindermen.   There are other questions, but they are minor and incidental to this one.

The learned trial justice has found upon the issue above suggested in favor of the life tenant and plaintiff as her legatee and against the remaindermen.   We are unable, however, to agree with the result thus reached by him.   We think the facts found in much detail do not warrant such conclusion, and that under the features of this case it leads to results which are unnatural and inequitable.   We think that the stock was not a dividend and income belonging to the life tenant, also that plaintiff is prevented from asserting such claim by reason of certain settlements and surrogate's decrees to which he was a party.

Thomas Chester, the administration of whose estate presents this controversy, died February 18, 1884, leaving him surviving his widow, Mary P. Chester, and his children, the plaintiff and the individual defendants.   He left a last will and testament which was duly admitted to probate, and which, so far as important here, after certain specific legacies not affecting the stock in issue, contained this clause : "I give, devise and bequeath all and singular the rest, residue and remainder of my property and estate, both real and personal, unto my beloved wife, Mary P. Chester, for her use and benefit during the full term of her natural life but no longer."

Then followed remainder in said property to his said four children, to be divided and distributed to and among them equally, share and share alike, upon the death of his wife.

The will appointed the plaintiff and James F. Chard, husband of the defendant Elizabeth Chard, executors thereof.

The widow, Mary P. Chester, died February 16, 1897.   She left a will which was admitted to probate September 25, 1897, whereby she appointed plaintiff sole executor, and devised and bequeathed to him the greater part of her property and estate, and expressly including all of her interest in the stock of the Buffalo Car Manufacturing Company.

At the time of his death Thomas Chester was the owner of sixty shares of the capital stock of the defendant car company, each share being of the par value of $100, and the total capital stock being $40,000.   Said company had only declared one dividend while testator was alive and the holder of its stock, but, as expressly found by the trial court, "a large surplus of earnings had been allowed to accumulate in the operation of said corporation." Its statement or inventory of January 5, 1884 (just before testator's death), showed an accumulated surplus above the original capital stock of $289,341.88. After the testator's death, and down to the death of his widow, the life tenant, it at frequent intervals declared large cash dividends, at first upon the original 60 shares held by testator and subsequently upon the 360 shares which included the stock issue in dispute. These dividends were all paid or conceded to belong to the widow, although, as matter of fact, she did make provision whereby a large portion of them were ultimately paid to and enjoyed by her four children. These dividends, during the period in question, amounted to $93,450. Notwithstanding their payment, it appears that at the time the stock issue in question was made, the accumulated surplus of the car company was $443,030.57, or $153,688.69 more than at the date of death of the testator. Such amount of increase, however, was subsequently and during the life of Mrs. Chester largely distributed and reduced by cash dividends of which she had the benefit.

Said testator left other valuable property, the income of which his widow was entitled to, and consideration of which we do not regard as of importance here.

Shortly after his death the certificate for the original 60 shares of stock standing in his name was surrendered by the executor Chard and canceled, and a new certificate for said shares issued in form to the estate of Thomas Chester, and when the additional 300 shares were issued it was by a certificate running to the estate of Thomas Chester and delivered to said executor.

Prior to and as authority for the increase in the capital stock of said car company, upon January 7, 1893, the stockholders therein signed an agreement which recited that they "hereby mutually agree one with another to *increase the capital stock* of the said company from forty thousand dollars ($40,000.00), consisting of four hundred shares of one hundred ($100.00) par value each, to two hundred fifty thousand dollars ($250,000.00), consisting of twenty-five hundred shares of one hundred dollars ($100.00) par value each, one hundred shares of which said stock shall be held in the treasury of said company and be sold by the trustees as they may decide to some railroad party, which shall be for the best interests of the company, the balance of the increased stock to be divided *pro rata* among the stockholders of the said company according to their present holdings." This action was followed up by a meeting of the trustees of said car company held January 14, 1893, at which, as specifically found by the trial judge, "the capital stock of the Buffalo Car Manufacturing Company was increased from $40,000.00, consisting of four hundred (400) shares of the par value of $100.00 each, to $250,000.00, consisting of twenty-five hundred (2,500) shares of the par value of $100.00 each. * * * That no new money or property was contributed by any stockholder at the time of said increase of stock." Thereafter the certificate for the 300 shares in question was issued.

There have been various disagreements and controversies between plaintiff and his sisters, the defendants, over the estate of their father. We do not deem it material to go into the details of any of them except the ones which specially relate to the disposition and division of this stock.

While the will of Thomas Chester did not specifically name and appoint his executors also trustees, they were still treated as such. A fair construction of the will and the administration of the property as between the life tenant and the remaindermen properly called upon them to act as such. In addition to this, by the specific request of the widow, the conduct of the other parties and the decrees of the Surrogate's Court they were upon all sides treated and regarded as trustees as well as executors. The plaintiff at some time transferred all of his interest in his father's estate to his wife, Helen R. Chester. In September, 1897, the executor Chard wrote plaintiff a letter commencing "You will remember that the estate of Thomas Chester owns three hundred and sixty shares of the capital stock of the Buffalo Car Manufacturing Company," and then stating that for the purpose of securing an adjustment and settlement of matters as executor and trustee of Thomas Chester he should offer said stock for sale at public auction at a given date.

Thereupon plaintiff's wife, as his assignee, instituted proceedings in the Surrogate's Court of Erie county setting forth various facts in regard to the death of Thomas Chester, the administration of his estate, the provisions of his will, the assignment to her of plaintiff's interest in said estate and that one of the items of property in the hands of the executors was said 360 shares of the capital stock of the Buffalo Car Manufacturing Company. Her petition then further referred to the receipt of the letter just mentioned from the executor Chard alleging " that as the assignee of the interest of the said George T. Chester in the estate of his said father Thomas Chester, deceased, she became and is now the owner of ninety (90) shares of the said three hundred and sixty (360) shares of the Buffalo Car Manufacturing Company's stock. That she does not desire to have her said ninety shares (90) shares sold but wishes to keep same as an investment." Upon her petition she requested that the executors of the will of Thomas Chester be compelled to show cause why they should not deliver over to her " her aforesaid ninety (90) shares of the capital stock of the Buffalo Car Manufacturing Company," and that in the meantime they might be enjoined. George T. Chester, although having assigned his interest in said estate and stock, joined in his wife's petition, saying " that he has read the foregoing petition of his wife Helen Reid Chester, and that the same is true. That he desires that the prayer of the said petitioner be granted." Upon this petition an order to show cause was granted and Chard was restrained from selling, disposing of or incumbering the said ninety shares of stock until the further order of the court. No further proceedings in Surrogate's Court appear to have been had. An arrangement, however, was made by the parties amongst themselves which resulted in the certificates for the three hundred and sixty shares of stock being delivered to the company for cancellation, and upon September 30, 1897, four new certificates of ninety shares each were issued in place thereof to plaintiff's wife and the individual defendants herein respectively.

After such arrangement and division of said stock amongst said four people, and in November, 1898, upon an acknowledgment signed by the three defendant heirs and also by plaintiff and his wife, that James F. Chard and George T. Chester, " as the Executors and Trustees of the Will of Thomas Chester * * * have fully and satisfactorily accounted to us as the heirs and next of kin of said deceased for all moneys and property held by them as such Executors and Trustees ;" and, upon the express consent that said Chard and Chester might have a decree made and entered discharging them of and from any and all liability or accountability to his heirs without further accounting, a decree was duly entered in the Surrogate's Court of Erie county upon the petition of said executors, ordering and decreeing that said Chard and Chester should be and thereby were " finally released, exonerated and discharged as the executors and trustees of and from any and all liability and accountability to said interested persons."

The trial court found that the plaintiff " had no knowledge of the declaration of said stock dividend, nor of the increase of stock, nor of the issuing of said certificate for three hundred (300) shares * * * and did not know of the increase of said stock until after the death of the said Mary P. Chester."

Sometime before the commencement of this action the car company, having disposed of a part of its business and assets, entered upon a course of liquidation.

Upon these and many other facts which it is impossible to recapitulate in detail, the learned trial court found that said 300 shares of the new stock " represented and was a payment and distribution of income upon and from the sixty (60) shares of stock of which the said Thomas Chester died possessed and owning at the time of his death." In accordance with such finding of fact he reached the conclusion of law that plaintiff was entitled to recover from his three sisters the 225 shares of stock delivered to them under the arrangement hereinbefore referred to and was entitled to have them and also the car company account, and be held liable for all dividends paid to such sisters, respectively, on such portion of said 300 shares so delivered to them.

As we indicated in the beginning, we do not come to the decision of this appeal with the feeling that there is any strong and predominating equity inherent in plaintiff's claim and theory. And in saying this, we overlook entirely its incidental surroundings. We disregard the fact that plaintiff comes as the legatee of the life tenant, whose death has terminated any use or need by her for this property viewed as income, seeking through the intervention of her will to procure, as against his sisters, an unequal distribution of his father's estate. Upon the other hand, we hold ourselves subject to the same equitable consideration which should prevail if the life tenant herself were here seeking for a full admeasurement of the provisions made and intended by her husband for her support during her life.   Being so guided, we still think that during her life without the stock in dispute, there was worked out a liberal fulfillment of the bequest to her of the income upon her husband's stock in this company.   Estimated from the dividends declared upon the Chester stock and the other figures found, the company made earnings and profits during the life tenancy of Mrs. Chester amounting to the neighborhood of $700,000.   With her husband's death it apparently entered upon a new policy of distributing in cash dividends amongst its stockholders substantially all of its profits.   We thus find that its surplus between his and her death had only increased $72,000.   All of the remainder of these tremendous earning and profits had been distributed in cash and she had received as her share during the period of twelve years $93,450.   That she did not receive still more was due to the accident of her death between two dividend periods, for soon after her decease the company made another cash dividend of forty per cent.

Using round figures, at the time the new stock was issued the surplus of the company was $443,000, of which $153,000 had accumulated after the death of the testator.   Assuming for the sake of the argument that the new stock is to be deemed issued as against this total surplus, practically two-thirds of it, or 200 shares, would be against that which had accumulated before the death of the testator.   If plaintiff's contention prevails, and in addition to the cash dividends above referred to, the accumulated capital and surplus existing when testator died, is distributed in the proportion of 200 shares to the life tenant as against only 60 shares going to the remaindermen, we believe it must impress the judgment at once as at least an unusual division.

While it is subject to modification and variation, the natural and fundamental idea of life income payable under a will is of that current income which accrues and becomes payable from time to time during the life tenancy upon a principal fixed as of the time when the trust took effect and remaining substantially unchanged.   Sometimes the amount of this principal is fixed by directions for the investment of a definite sum, and at other times by the appropriation of specified securities as bonds or stocks. In the case of the latter, while it may happen that by means of an extraordinary dividend there will be allotted to the life tenant a certain per cent of profits which accrued before his estate commenced, that is the unusual course rather than otherwise. We certainly do not expect or readily accept such a solution between the life tenant and remaindermen through the medium of dividends as will divide a testator's estate as it existed at his death between the former and the latter in the proportion of three or four shares to the former for one to the latter.

It is, however, insisted that unacceptable as such result may be in this case, this court is compelled by controlling decisions to adopt and affirm it. We do not think this is so.

This question, whether additional capital stock issued by a corporation against accumulated earnings and profits shall belong to the life tenant or remainderman, has naturally been a prolific source of dispute and controversy. In trying to deal fairly and equitably with it, the courts have been led by different theories and varying phases under which the issue was presented, into irreconcilably conflicting opinions.

Turning to those decisions which are controlling or at least authoritative, there seem to be, reasonably well defined, two rules which we may utilize in measuring the rights of the parties here.

First. A corporation with a surplus of accumulated profits, within the limits of good faith, has the power either to distribute it as dividends, or to retain it and convert it into capital.

Second. The substance and intent of the action of the company as evidenced by its treatment of the surplus and its resolutions in issuing new stock against it, will be considered by, if not control, the courts in deciding whether such issue is dividend and hence income belonging to the life tenant or not. If the company pays money or issues stock as a distribution of profits, it will ordinarily go to the life tenant. If it issues stock as capital and appropriates its surplus as an increase of the capital stock of the concern, such issue will be held to inure to the benefit of the remainderman. (*Matter of Kernochan,* 104 N. Y. 618, 629, 630; *Gibbons* v. *Mahon,* 136 U. S. 549; *McLouth* v. *Hunt,* 154 N. Y. 179, 194; *Matter of Rogers,* 161 id. 108.)

There is the other general rule always applicable to construction under a will, that we must ascertain, if possible, the meaning and intention of the testator, to be derived from the language employed in the creation of the trust, from the relations of the parties to each other, their condition and all the surrounding facts and circumstances. (*McLouth* v. *Hunt, supra*, 190.)

We shall endeavor to apply these principles and rules to the facts of this case. So far as the last one is concerned, it appears that for years before the testator's death the policy had been pursued by the defendant company of accumulating its profits, only one dividend having been paid to him. The surplus at the time of his death was more than seven times greater than its capital stock. While there is no definite finding upon that subject, we may assume from what incidentally appears that the testator and his wife were elderly people. The wife's demands for income were apparently not extravagant or large. This appears from the fact that most of the income which she did receive or become entitled to receive from this stock during her life was passed over to her children. It is difficult for us to believe that when the testator left the income of this property to his widow he believed or anticipated that the long-continued policy of the corporation would be immediately reversed, and by a stock dividend several shares of the property which it had at his death, would pass to the life tenant, as against one which would then be left for his children. As was said in *Matter of Rogers* (*supra*, 113), in accordance with a well-settled policy then long pursued of retaining accumulated earnings for working capital, it must "have been within the contemplation of the testator that a reasonable amount would be retained by the directors for this purpose."

The first of the other two rules is too well established to require discussion. It must be admitted at once that if, in the exercise of an honest judgment, the defendant corporation saw fit to permanently capitalize its profits, instead of distributing them in dividends, the life tenant could not force a change of policy. She could not compel dividends if the company saw fit to accumulate surplus.

The second rule seems to flow logically from the first. As long as the corporation has power to decide for the purposes of its own management whether it will capitalize or distribute earnings, it is proper that the courts should consider such decision in settling between them the rights of those — remainderman and life tenant — who are interested in its stock.

It perhaps may be granted for the sake of the argument rather than held, the question not being here, that this company in 1893 had the power to distribute amongst its stockholders its surplus and so make it a dividend that this court would have felt constrained to treat such dividend as income payable to the life tenant.

Upon the other hand, we think it undoubtedly had the power to so capitalize its surplus and then issue new stock against it, so clearly and explicitly declaring the latter to represent and be an increase of its actual permanent working capital, that no court could fairly say the new shares were a distribution of profits or income. It will be seen that the question addressed to the court in a given case, whether new shares are dividend and income or increase of capital, must almost necessarily be governed largely by the purpose and attitude and condition of the corporation. This must be so unless every issue of stock against surplus is to be indiscriminately called a dividend and treated as income.

What was the nature of the stock issued in this case? The learned trial court has said, in substance, that it was issued as a stock dividend and was a distribution of income upon the original sixty shares. Such finding, however, is a conclusion dependent upon and governed by many facts.

If, as we think, the detailed facts and circumstances otherwise found do not sustain it, it must yield to them. (*Phelps* v. *Vischer*, 50 N. Y. 69, 72; *Bonnell* v. *Griswold*, 89 id. 122, 127; *Rochester Lantern Co.* v. *S. & P. P. Co.*, 135 id. 209, 212.)

It is perfectly manifest from its statement and otherwise that the profits accumulated by this corporation down to the testator's death and down to the issue of this stock were treated as an accretion to capital and permanently invested in plant and other assets necessary for the conduct of business. Substantially none of them were carried in the form of cash. The real estate and machinery alone upon January 5, 1884, inventoried at $119,832.11, or practically three times the amount of the authorized capital. It is perfectly evident also that this company could not have done its business upon a capital of $40,000, but that it was necessary to accumulate and use a large amount besides. The men who were in charge of its affairs in 1893 and knew its needs realized this and did not divide up a large portion of this surplus by a cash dividend, the equivalent in legal principle of a stock dividend. In fact, a very forcible argument as to what the directors did not intend to do in the way of distributing the surplus in dividends is to be drawn from what they did do in that respect. They appreciated that the stockholders were entitled to liberal dividends from the large earnings, and they declared those in cash. A few days before this new scrip was issued they paid to the stockholders $80,000 in cash. That was a dividend and so intended and declared. Then they issued stock for $210,000 of surplus, and denominated it, not a dividend, but an increase of capital. If they had intended to distribute that amount of surplus, and not keep it for permanent capital, there was no necessity for taking the two different steps.

Read in the light of these facts and considerations, we think the consent of the stockholders and the action of the directors show that they had no intention to make a dividend, but that they intended by an issue of new shares to so add to and increase their paper capital that it would represent and correspond with their actual working capital. We think the predominating purpose was to permanently increase capital rather than to divide up profits. The stockholders' agreement recites that they " mutually agree one with another to *increase* the capital stock of the said company," etc. We do not see how they could well express more plainly the idea of enlarging their capital. It is true, as was said by the court in the *McLouth Case* (*supra*, 195), that no money was paid for this stock and nothing added to the actual property of the company. But that is always so when stock is issued as this was against a surplus. If money or property is paid for new stock upon a subscription it could not possibly be called a dividend. Yet it cannot be doubted that stock may be issued against a surplus as permanent capital instead of a dividend if the corporation so elects. If the words used, "increase the capital stock," are themselves ambiguous, they cease to be so when we again recall that such increase was against an accumulation of assets already in use as working capital and which could not be actually distributed as dividend amongst the stockholders without disrupting its business.

It may be suggested that a stock dividend would not really

divide the assets amongst the stockholders, but would leave them still in the possession of the company. This, however, is not an answer, if we are right that one of the tests by which to determine the question here presented is whether the company intended by this stock issue to make an addition to its permanent principal or capital rather than distribution of income by cash or stock.

We think the construction of the words of the agreement which we have adopted as sustaining the former view is upheld in the *Gibbons Case* (*supra*, pp. 551, 569), and in which respect we do not understand that case to be overruled or questioned by the *McLouth* case. Moreover, the agreement and resolution referred to are significant for what they omit to say in plaintiff's favor.

In the *Kernochan* case, relied upon by him, there was a resolution which expressly provided for a *dividend* at a certain rate per share (p. 627). In the *McLouth* case the parties actually stipulated that the corporation "by a capitalization of accumulated earnings made and retained * * * increased its capital stock * * * and predicated thereon made a *stock dividend* of ten per cent," etc.

Thus in both of these leading cases the corporation having the power to do so, explicitly declared the disputed issue to be a dividend, and that being done the court gave it to the life tenant who was entitled to dividends as income.

In *Lowry* v. *Farmers' Loan & Trust Co.* (56 App. Div. 408) the court manifestly intended to follow the *McLouth* and *Rogers* cases. There again the stock in controversy was issued under a resolution which expressly authorized and directed it as a *stock dividend*.

Further, we think the *McLouth* case fairly outlines the doctrine that in each case the court will look into the surroundings and nature of the transaction which produces the stock issue and adjust the rights of the contending parties according to justice and equity. We do not think that it was intended to hold that every issue of stock against a surplus was income going to the life tenant. There is a manifest difference between a distribution of 10 per cent upon upon the capital and an issue of 500 per cent of stock.

We are thus led to conclude that the 300 shares in question were intended to be and were issued to represent an accretion to the permanent working capital long used and recognized as such, and that they were not a dividend from income or profits belonging to the life tenant.

We believe that a defense to this action is also found in the proceedings had in Surrogate's Court for the settlement of the testator's estate, and in the agreements made and executed between plaintiff and his sisters for the division of the stock in dispute, which were connected with and in whole or part served as a basis for such proceedings in Surrogate's Court.

Plaintiff, in seeking here to enforce his claims, assumes the threefold role of assignee of his wife, who in turn was his own assignee, of any interest in his father's estate; executor of his mother's estate; specific legatee under her will of this stock.

He has no standing in the first character. If this stock belonged to his father's estate it has concededly been distributed in proper proportions. Measuring his demands by their derivation through his mother's estate, we think that, for the purposes of the discussion to follow of the agreements and proceedings above referred to, he must be regarded at the time of their occurrence as having been entitled to this stock as an individual rather than as executor, if entitled to it at all.

He was specific legatee of it. His mother died February 16, 1897, and her will was duly admitted to probate September 25, 1897, before any of the important steps hereinafter recounted occurred. It very clearly appears that no other legatees or distributees had any interest in this stock. It does not appear that any creditors had any such interest. In fact, it is a very permissible inference from all the facts found in regard to Mrs. Chester that there were no creditors to interfere with plaintiff's specific legacy in the stock.

Under such circumstances his qualified title as executor became merged in his beneficial interest as devisee and legatee and as such latter, individually, he became vested with the legal title to the stock if it belonged to his mother's estate. (*Blood* v. *Kane*, 130 N. Y. 514.)

All doubt upon this point is removed by plaintiff's own attitude in this case. He alleges in his complaint that his mother, by her will, devised and bequeathed all her property and estate to him, and that he " thereby became the owner of the said three hundred shares of stock and entitled to receive the same."

Having thus defined the character and capacity through which plaintiff must urge his demands, we come immediately to the question whether he could take part as he did in the various agreements and decrees which treated of, and related to, this stock as part of his father's estate, and then many years afterwards, when these proceedings had long been executed and the stock divided in accordance with them, obtain an entirely new adjustment upon the ground that the stock did not belong to his father's estate at all, but was part of his mother's. We say very frankly we do not believe he can, or ought to. We revert first to the occurrence of September, 1897, when the other executor, Mr. Chard, gave notice in effect that he treated this stock as all belonging to Thomas Chester's estate and proposed to sell it as such, and plaintiff's wife and then assignee took the position in effect that such stock did not belong to the father's estate and that as representative of her husband she was entitled to one-quarter of it, and requested that such proportion and interest be allotted to her, expressing her willingness that the other heirs, defendants here, should have their similar respective shares.

Plaintiff joined in the verification of her petition and requested "that the prayer of the said petitioner be granted." It was granted by the acts of the parties without further proceedings in court. The stock was divided as belonging to the father's estate, under the terms of his will, and plaintiff's wife and assignee, by his request and desire, received, and she or he still holds, ninety shares upon that theory belonging to her. The defendants hold their respective portions which plaintiff now seeks by virtue of the same division which gave hers.

We think it clear, if this arrangement and division by the parties between themselves was otherwise binding and, when executed, irrevocable, that plaintiff, who was a party to, and requested it cannot now be allowed to disrupt and overturn it by a claim through his mother's estate which he then possessed as fully as now, and which he did not then mention or assert.

It is said, however, plaintiff was ignorant of the facts which attended the issue of the 300 shares of stock; also that his sisters parted with no rights upon this division, and that, therefore, there is nothing to now prevent taking the stock away from them by virtue of a different theory of ownership. We shall consider the first proposition later, saying and assuming for the present that it is not sustained.

So far as the second one is concerned, it may be said that such an adjustment as was made may be sustained against a party as well by virtue of gain to him as by loss to those with whom he deals. The executor claimed then as now that all of this stock belonged to the estate of Thomas Chester and was about to sell it. Plaintiff and his wife evidently felt that they might be put to a disadvantage by such sale and, therefore, said, " Give up the sale and let us have our share of this stock and the others can have theirs." This was done, and we think a sufficient consideration is found in the substitution and mutuality of the transaction to uphold it. We may, however, look at it in another light. If we should assume that the three sisters, defendants here, had absolutely no right to this stock, yet if plaintiff and his wife voluntarily consented, as a matter of pure gift and gratuity, that they should have each a quarter thereof, and such consent and gift was executed and the stock delivered, we fail to see how plaintiff, except for some legal reason, as fraud or mistake, could thereafter get the stock back from them.

After this division was made, plaintiff and his coexecutor Chard petitioned to have their accounts as executors and trustees finally settled and themselves discharged. Their petition recited that they had fully accounted for all the property which had come into their possession. An instrument was executed by all the parties interested, including this plaintiff and his wife, which acknowledged distribution to and receipt by the parties of all property " held by them as such executors and trustees," and consented that they be discharged. Upon this a decree was made by Surrogate's Court discharging them, the surrogate " being satisfied that the said executors have duly accounted to all the interested parties for their interest in said estate." The scrip for this 300 shares of stock had been issued to and held and claimed by the estate of Thomas Chester. This had been made patent to the plaintiff at least by the letter and attitude of the executor Chard at the time of its proposed sale. The only way it had ever been distributed was as belonging to his estate and amongst his four children. Therefore, when this decree, founded upon the release and consent of the parties, held that the executors were entitled to be discharged because they had distributed to the persons entitled all the property which had come into their hands, it necessarily adjudicated that the division in question was a proper distribution for which they should receive credit.   If that stock, which indisputably had been issued to this estate and came into the control of its executors at the time of this decree, belonged to plaintiff as legatee of his mother, no proper distribution of it had been made and the decree was improper.   We do not doubt, that the Surrogate's Court had jurisdiction to determine where this personal property belonged, as between the different legatees and their representatives and successors, whether it went to the life tenant or remaindermen.   We also feel equally clear that that was one of the questions necessarily involved in this accounting, and that upon it, unless reversed or annulled in some way, the surrogate's decree was a binding adjudication.

Plaintiff was a party to that accounting and decree.   He was not only a party to it as an executor and petitioner, but he was named and made a party as one of the persons interested in the estate.   He was then vested with just as much right and title as now by virtue of his mother's will to all of this stock.   If his claim is just now it was then, and he was entitled to a very different decree from that which was entered.   We do not deem it necessary to indulge in any extended reasoning to show that the decree if binding in favor of the executors is also a binding adjudication in favor of the different heirs who took the stock from them and were parties to the decree.

It is, however, strenuously urged in behalf of plaintiff for the purpose of relieving him from the conclusions which we have drawn from the proceedings above detailed that he was not cognizant of the facts surrounding the issue of the disputed stock; that he did not know his rights and was laboring under ignorance; that, therefore, he is not bound by what took place.   The trial court in a qualified manner has found for this claim.   We are, however, unable to reconcile such conclusion with the detailed facts found and upon which it would have to rest.

Plaintiff knew that Thomas Chester's estate at his death held only sixty shares of this stock.   He knew by the letter of his coexecutor, if not otherwise, before any of the steps or proceedings now invoked against him were taken, that this holding had increased to three hundred and sixty shares, and that the estate of Thomas Chester held and claimed them. As an executor he must be charged with knowledge that the estate had not expended a large sum of money in buying these additional shares. He knew that a corporation could not at will multiply the number of its capital shares, but that it must have some assets against which they were issued. He knew that when the corporation issued these additional shares without receiving money for them, it must necessarily have issued them against an accumulated surplus of profits over and above the amount of its original capital. The fact that he had taken part in inventorying the original sixty shares at $850 per share instead of par, at least ought to have suggested to a person of average experience that the company was putting its surplus into an increase of its shares. When he knew all these things he was charged with sufficient knowledge to suggest the legal inquiry whether such new stock was income and belonged to him as his mother's legatee. He may not have thought about this question, or if he did he may have thought differently than he does now. But that is not sufficient to relieve him from the consequences of what was done, if he was fairly apprised of the facts. There is no evidence that any effort was made to keep him in ignorance or mislead him. There is nothing in the record of the litigation presented to us which makes us believe that these parties were led astray through too much mutual confidence or that plaintiff was slow to see or assert his rights in this estate. In April, 1898, and thus many months before the surrogate's decree, plaintiff's wife called upon the defendant corporation under the statute for a detailed, verified statement of its affairs, which was furnished to her. We have no idea that plaintiff was a stranger to this step or that with his attorneys to guide him he felt unable to secure more information upon this subject if he desired it.

We are impressed upon all of the facts as they are unfolded in the findings, that the difference between plaintiff's attitude in 1898 and now is not due to his having been then disabled by ignorance of the essential facts. It is more probably due to the conclusion which has come to him since, that upon those facts known then as now, it might have been possible for him to have obtained more stock.

The conclusions reached upon the main proposition carry with them a decision of the other minor and incidental questions involved in the case.

The judgment appealed from should be reversed, with costs to the appellant to abide event.

ADAMS, P., J., McLENNAN and SPRING, JJ., concurred; WILLIAMS, J., dissented.

WILLIAMS, J. (dissenting):

The interlocutory judgment appealed from should be modified as hereinafter stated, and as modified affirmed, with costs to respondent against appellants other than corporation, and with costs to corporation appellants against respondent.

The action was brought to determine the ownership of 225 shares of the capital stock of the defendant corporation and for equitable relief incidental to such ownership. The questions involved may be stated generally to be :

First, whether the stock was at any time owned by the plaintiff, or the widow, his mother ; and, *second*, whether anything has occurred since to deprive them of such ownership or to prevent plaintiff's recovery thereof.

The facts are somewhat complicated and should be clearly understood. There was no case or case and exceptions made or inserted in the record, and I must, therefore, be controlled by the decision of the trial court as to the facts upon which the conclusions of law were based.

One Thomas Chester died February 18, 1884. At the time of his death, and for some time prior thereto, he was the owner of 60 shares of the capital stock of the defendant corporation. The capital stock was then $40,000, divided into 400 shares of $100 each. He left him surviving his widow, Mary P. Chester, and four children, the plaintiff George T. Chester, and Elizabeth Chard, Kate C. Miller and Cora C. Tripp. He left a will, whereby he gave to each of his three daughters $20,000 and to his son a bond and mortgage for $40,000, made by the son and held by the father, and then gave his widow all the residue of his estate, real and personal, for her use and benefit during life, and after her death, in fee to his four children, to be divided equally between them, and made his son and son-in-law, James F. Chard, executors. The will was admitted to probate April 18, 1884, and letters testamentary were issued to the executors named, who qualified and entered upon the discharge of their duties. On the 29th day of December, 1884, the certificate for the 60 shares of capital stock of the defendant corporation was surrendered by the executor Chard to the corporation and canceled, and a new certificate for said 60 shares was, by the procurement of said executor Chard, issued to the estate of Thomas Chester. On the 14th day of January, 1893, the capital stock of the defendant corporation was increased from $40,000 to $250,000; from 400 to 2,500 shares. Of the 2,100 shares newly issued, 100 shares were set aside as treasury stock and 2,000 shares were divided *pro rata* among the holders of the old stock, that is, 5 shares of new for each share of old stock. On the 28th day of February, 1893, the corporation issued a certificate for 300 shares of the newly issued stock to the estate of Thomas Chester, based upon its holding of 60 shares of the old stock. The widow, Mary P. Chester, died February 16, 1897, leaving a will whereby she gave all her interest in the capital stock of the defendant corporation to the plaintiff, George T. Chester, and made him executor. The will was admitted to probate September 25, 1897, and letters testamentary were issued to the executor named, who qualified and entered upon the discharge of his duties.

Before proceeding further with the statement of facts, let us understand the claims made by the parties as to the first question involved herein, the original ownership of the stock, old and new. There is no dispute but that the 60 shares held by the father at the time of his death was a part of the *corpus* of his estate, and at the death of the widow belonged to all the children, one-fourth to each. The controversy arises over the 300 shares of newly issued stock. The plaintiff claims these shares never belonged to the *corpus* of the estate, but were income from the estate, and as such belonged to the widow absolutely and passed under her will to the plaintiff absolutely. Of the 360 shares of stock, the plaintiff was concededly the owner of 15 shares of the old stock, and 75 shares of the new stock. The question is whether he was the owner of the remaining 225 shares of the new stock, and this involves the question whether the 300 shares of new stock when issued, belonged wholly to the widow as income, or to the *corpus* of the estate, to the income from which alone she was entitled during her life. The further facts bearing upon the determination of this question are as follows :

The only dividend received by Thomas Chester upon the 60 shares of stock during his lifetime was February 7, 1882, $1,500. A large surplus of earnings was allowed to accumulate, which at the time of his death amounted to $289,341.88. The value of the stock at the time of his death was $850 per share, in all $51,000, as appraised in the inventory of the estate, based upon the last yearly statement made by the defendant corporation.

The dividends received by the widow, Mary P. Chester, upon the 60 shares of stock from the time of her husband's death, until the increase of the capital stock in January, 1893, were: April 15, 1884, $1,500; October 9, 1884, $3,000; October 3, 1885, $3,000; November 1, 1886, $6,000; December 5, 1887, $1,500; August 20, 1888, $6,000; August 22, 1888, $6,000; August 31, 1888, $6,000; December 30, 1888, $7,050; September 16, 1889, $1,500; January 27, 1891, $1,500; January 30, 1892, $6,000; January 11, 1893, $12,000; making in all for the nine years $61,050, and at the time of the increase of the capital stock the surplus of earnings allowed to accumulate were $443,030.51, an increase during the nine years since the death of Thomas Chester of $153,688.69. After deducting the amount of the stock dividend made in increasing the capital stock $210,000, the surplus earnings still on hand were $233,030.57, which was $56,311.31 less than at the time of Thomas Chester's death.

The dividends received by the widow, Mary P. Chester, from the time of the increase of the capital stock, in 1893, until her death in 1897, upon the 360 shares of stock, were, December 28, 1893, $7,200; January 10, 1895, $7,200; September 25, 1896, $18,000, making in all $32,400, and at the time of her death the surplus of earnings allowed to accumulate were $362,006.29, an increase during the four years of $128,975.63. These figures show that during the lifetime of the widow and after her husband's death she received in all of cash dividends on the stock, the 60 shares of old and 300 shares of new, $93,450. There was also the stock dividend of 300 shares, or $30,000 at $100 per share, and there was during the time a total increase of the surplus earnings from $289,341.88 to $362,006.29, that is, $72,664.41.

After the death of the widow, Mary P. Chester, and February 4, 1898, there was a dividend of forty per cent paid upon the stock of the defendant corporation, which upon the 360 shares belonging to the parties to this action amounted to $14,200. And then in the month of February, 1899, the corporation sold out all its property, except bills and accounts receivable and cash, for $553,861.71, and went into liquidation. It has paid certain liquidation dividends to its stockholders. The dividends upon the 360 shares have, however, been deposited in the Fidelity Trust Company of Buffalo, N. Y., to the amount of $79,200, to await the result of this action. There will be added to this amount of deposited dividends about $3,366, less some expenses of liquidation.

The plaintiff, George T. Chester, knew nothing of the increase of the stock and the issue of the 300 new shares, until after the death of the widow, his mother, Mary P. Chester. Whether she knew of it does not appear. In August, 1886, the widow and the plaintiff and Mrs. Chard and Mrs. Miller, by a writing executed by them, directed the executors of the estate to divide all moneys received by them from the defendant corporation from the date of such writing to January 1, 1889, belonging to the estate, equally between the four heirs, Mrs. Chard, Mrs. Miller, Mrs. Tripp and George T. Chester, the plaintiff. All the dividends received from the defendant corporation upon the 60 shares of stock, from the time of the death of Thomas Chester until the increase of the capital stock, were, with one exception, divided among the four children by the direction of the widow, and all the dividends received upon the 360 shares of stock, after the increase and up to the time of the widow's death, were also divided among the four children by direction of the widow. Whether the writing above referred to was relied upon as such direction, or whether there was other direction, does not appear. It does appear that by a writing made by the widow, February 27, 1888, she stated that she had always regarded the executors named in the will as trustees of her husband's estate, for her benefit, and that she had always dealt with them as such, she being thus relieved personally of the charge and management of the estate, and asked that their accounts be settled before the surrogate, the same as if the will had expressly made them such trustees for her benefit during her life, and that the executors thereafter act as such trustees. And thereupon the settlement was made and decree entered April 17, 1888, upon a petition filed February 29, 1888 ;

and in such petition and settlement the writing of August, 1886, was recognized as signed by all the four heirs, though the name of Mrs. Tripp does not appear signed to the writing in the record of the findings by the trial court. The executor James F. Chard was, prior to the death of Thomas Chester, a trustee of the defendant corporation and secretary thereof, and continued to be such trustee and secretary until the death of the widow, while the plaintiff, George T. Chester, was at no time a trustee or officer of the corporation. After the settlement of the estate above referred to, the executors continued to hold the stock of the defendant corporation with the consent of the widow and all the next of kin, the four children. When the certificate for the 300 shares of newly issued stock was made out, it was to the estate of Thomas Chester, and was delivered to the executor James F. Chard. Under these circumstances we can hardly assume, in the absence of an express finding to that effect, that the widow had actual knowledge *of* the issue of the 300 shares of new stock, and that it was issued in the name of the estate and not in her name. The findings are that she received all the dividends from the old and the new stock, but this is rather a conclusion than otherwise. The real fact apparently was that the executor Chard, who acted for her and who had sole charge of this part of the business as trustee or otherwise (because the plaintiff had no knowledge of the increase of the stock), received all the dividends and divided them, and there was no more reason why the widow should inquire and know that the dividends were on 360 rather than on 60 shares of the stock than that the plaintiff should. She had no personal charge or management of the business. She had imposed such care and management upon the executors as trustees or otherwise. There was more reason why the plaintiff should know about the increase of stock and form of the new certificate than the widow.

Finally, as bearing upon this branch of the case, the court has found as a fact that the 300 shares of new stock represented and was a payment and distribution of income upon and from the 60 shares of stock owned and possessed by Thomas Chester at his death, but it is not found whether such income was earned before or after the death of Thomas Chester.

These seem to me to be all the facts bearing upon the first question involved here, the original ownership of the 300 shares of newly issued stock.

I think it is now well settled in this State as a general rule that as between a tenant for life and remaindermen, stock dividends belong to the life tenant if made during the life tenancy, though from earnings accumulated wholly or in part before such tenancy commenced.

In *Riggs* v. *Cragg* (89 N. Y. 487) it was said that this question had not then been considered by the court of last resort in this State, and it was not passed upon in that case. The question seems first to have been considered by the Court of Appeals in the case of *Matter of Kernochan* (104 N. Y. 618).

The will there gave to the executors portions of the estate in trust, to receive the rents, interest and income, and apply the same to the use of the widow during life, remainder to the beneficiaries named. The trust fund included certain shares of stock upon which a dividend was declared after the death of the testator, in part from earnings accumulated before his death. It was held that the widow was entitled to the whole of the dividend; that whether the earnings were accumulated before or after the death of the testator, they were not profits accruing to, or owned by, the stockholders unless set apart by the corporation for their use, and they belonged to the widow because ascertained and declared after her husband's death.

The court below had apportioned to the beneficiaries that portion of the dividend earned before the death of the testator, and to the widow that portion earned after such death, thus applying a rule said to be founded on general equity, viz., "that when a fund is given for life to one beneficiary, and remainder over, the first shall have its earnings after his life tenancy begins, and the remainderman the balance." JUDGE DANFORTH, however, said : "I find nothing in the will which indicates that the testator intended any such investigation or division, or that any other than the ordinary rule which gives cash dividends, declared from accumulated earnings or profits, to the life tenant, should be applied. The direction to his executors is to receive the rents, interest and income of his estate, and apply the net amount of such rents or other income * * * to the use of his wife. From the shares in question no income could accrue, no profits arise, to the holder until ascertained and declared by the company and allotted to the stockholder, and that act should be deemed to have been in the mind of the testator, and not the earnings or profits, as ascertained by a third person, or a court upon an investigation of the business and affairs of the company either upon an inspection of their books or otherwise."

In *McLouth* v. *Hunt* (154 N. Y. 179) the residuary estate was by a will given to his executors in trust, to "take, receive, hold, care for, preserve, maintain, invest and reinvest, convert, sell, lease and collect the same," and pay over a portion of such income to the use and benefit of his grandsons respectively during their minority, and after arriving at the age of twenty-one years, to pay over to them the full income, and upon their arriving at the age of thirty-five years, the full amount of principal with any accumulations thereon remaining, and in case of death before arriving at the age of thirty-five years, the fund was given to other persons in fee. The testator died September 18, 1888. There was included in the trust estate 254 shares of Western Union Telegraph Company stock, upon which a stock dividend of ten per cent was declared November 10, 1892, upon the surplus earnings of the telegraph company accumulated during the ten years prior thereto. The court, among other things, was asked to determine whether this stock dividend belonged to the life tenants (so called) or to the remaindermen, whether it was income or part of the *corpus* of the estate. The trial court held that the dividends belonged to the life tenants and they were entitled to the same as earnings or income, and the Court of Appeals affirmed that decision. Judge O'BRIEN, writing for the court, considered all the cases in this State and elsewhere and arrived at the conclusion that the decision made by the court below was equitable and just and was supported by reason and authority. It is apparent the surplus earnings from which the dividend was declared were accumulated, a part before and a part after the death of the testator. The opinion was certainly based upon such an understanding of the facts, because Judge O'BRIEN states therein that "the resolution recites that the earnings of the corporation had been withheld from the shareholders for almost ten years; that they had accumulated, and that it was the intention of the directors in taking such action, and the shareholders in consenting to it, to distribute such accumulated earnings to the shareholders in the form of stock certificates instead of money."

In *Matter of Rogers* (22 App. Div. 428; 161 N. Y. 108) the

will created trusts for the benefit of testator's children during their lives with remainders to their issue. In the trust fund were shares of stock in a corporation. The testator died August 25, 1888. The corporation continued in business until 1893, paying yearly dividends, at first of ten per cent and later of twenty per cent. Then it sold its plant, with raw material and that in process of manufacture, for $2,750,000, to be paid for in the stock of a new corporation. The stock of the new company was divided among the stockholders of the old company in the proportion of ten shares of the new stock for one of the old. The old corporation had still other property, of the value of $3,000,000, and the corporation sold this property and distributed the proceeds among its stockholders. The question was as to the rights of the life tenants and remaindermen in the new stock and proceeds of the other property sold. The referee before whom the case was first heard held that the whole fund was to be treated as capital or part of the *corpus* of the trust estate, and that the life tenants were entitled to no share in it. The surrogate modified the report of the referee, holding that 100 per cent of the cash dividend, and the dividends of the new stock, were capital, and that the remainder were profits or income, to which the life tenants were entitled. The decision of the surrogate was affirmed in the Appellate Division and in the Court of Appeals. The case was decided in the Appellate Division November, 30, 1897, the week after the decision of the Court of Appeals in *McLouth* v. *Hunt* (*supra*), which was decided November 23, 1897. No reference was made by the Appellate Division to the *McLouth-Hunt* case, and we assume, therefore, the latter case was not brought to the attention of the Appellate Division in the *Rogers* case. Justice CULLEN did, however, say in the *Rogers* case, "While the corporation continues to do business or as is sometimes said, is a going concern, the law is settled in this State that a cash dividend is income and goes to the life tenants, no matter at what time the profits from which the dividend was declared may have accrued or have been accumulated." (Citing the *Kernochan Case*, 104 N. Y. 618, above.)

In view of the *McLouth-Hunt* case we must add that the same is true of a stock dividend as of a cash dividend. The Appellate Division, however, held that the rule stated had no application to the *Rogers* case, where there was no dividend by a going corporation, but a division made of the assets of a liquidating corporation among its stockholders. Later in his opinion Justice CULLEN says: "Had the company before transferring its plant to the new corporation, distributed this whole surplus or reserve fund among its stockholders, it would have gone to the life tenant, and no well-founded complaint could have been made that such a distribution was either illegal or inequitable." It further appears from the opinion of the Appellate Division that the life tenants took no exceptions, and made no objection to the decision of the surrogate, so far as it held that a portion of the fund was capital and belonged to the remaindermen. The case cannot, therefore, be regarded as an authority so far as the Appellate Division or Court of Appeals is concerned for the proposition that any part of the fund was capital and belonged to the remaindermen. No authorities were cited by the Court of Appeals in its opinion, the only reference thereto being the statement that the cases to which their attention had been called furnished but little aid in the determination of the question presented under the peculiar facts of the case. The appeal to the Court of Appeals was by the remaindermen alone. The life tenants did not appeal. This case, therefore, cannot be said in any way to have modified or overruled the former decision of the court in the *McLouth-Hunt* case.

It may be further noted that the Appellate Division in the first department, in December, 1900, followed the law as laid down in the *McLouth-Hunt* case in *Lowry* v. *Farmers' Loan & Trust Co.* (56 App. Div. 408), and held that a stock dividend, declared out of undivided profits or surplus (a portion of which was earned before the testator's death), upon stock of a corporation set apart by a trustee of a trust fund created by a will, belonged to the life beneficiary of the trust, and not to the remaindermen.

In the case we are considering it does not appear when the surplus earnings were accumulated from which the stock dividend was made, whether before or after, or both before and after the death of the testator. There was a surplus at the death of $289,341.88, and at the time this dividend was made this surplus had increased to $443,030.57. The dividend was $210,000. The whole of it may have been made from the surplus accumulated before the death. The whole of it could not have been made from the surplus accumulated after the death, because the surplus so accumulated was only $153,688.69. It was made from the whole surplus accumulated up to the time it was made, without any limitation to that accumulated during any particular time. In any event, under the authorities we have referred to, the 300 shares of new stock issued upon the 60 shares of old stock owned by the estate belonged to the widow, and the children had no interest therein.

I have very carefully considered the suggestions of counsel for the appellant and I find no justification for any different result growing out of the language of the will in question or the facts found by the trial court. It is suggested that in the *McLouth-Hunt* case the language of the will was peculiar in that it provided that the executors should pay the life tenants *the full income*, but this language was used because it had already been provided that prior to the life tenants coming of age, only portions of the income were to be paid to them, and then followed the provision that from the age of twenty-one to thirty-five the *full income* should be so paid.

This language could have no bearing upon the testator's intention with reference to the disposition of any dividends upon the sixty shares of stock, made after his death. The remarks of Judge DANFORTH in the *Kernochan* case, above quoted, are quite applicable here. I find nothing in the will or in the condition of the property or of the widow and next of kin, indicating any intention on the part of the testator to take this stock dividend out of the ordinary rule which gives the whole of it to the life tenant to the exclusion of the remaindermen. There is no basis for any claim that the widow assented or admitted that the new stock belonged to the estate, by permitting the certificate to be taken to, and the stock to stand during her whole lifetime, in the name of the estate. It does not appear that she had any knowledge or information as to the form of the certificate or that the stock stood in the name of the estate.

My conclusion is that the 300 shares of new stock belonged to the widow from the time they were issued until her death, and the children had no interest therein. At her death the stock under her will passed to her son, the plaintiff George T. Chester. The remaining question is whether anything has occurred since the death of the widow which deprives the plaintiff of the present ownership of the stock, or prevents his recovery of the same.

As already stated, the widow died February 16, 1897, but her will was not admitted to probate until September 25, 1897. At some time prior to September 30, 1897 (just when does not appear), the plaintiff assigned and transferred to his wife, Helen R. Chester, all his interest in his father's estate, and this assignment covered and included whatever interest he had in the 360 shares of stock as residuary legatee under that will. It did not cover or include whatever interest he acquired in the 300 shares of stock by his mother's will. September 6, 1897, James F. Chard, plaintiff's coexecutor under the father's will, wrote the plaintiff that the estate owned 360 shares of stock in the defendant corporation, and that as all parties desired the estate matters settled and adjusted, he, as executor and trustee, would offer all the interest of the estate in such stock for sale to the highest bidder on the 4th day of October, 1897. Thereafter, and September 14, 1897, Helen R. Chester presented to the surrogate a petition wherein she stated the facts necessary to enable her to secure the relief asked for, which already appear, and need not be again repeated here, and stated, among other things, that the executors held the 360 shares of stock, and that she, as her husband's assignee, was entitled to 90 shares thereof, and she asked that the stock belonging to her might be delivered to her and not sold. As a result of this application, with the assent of all the parties, the certificate for the 300 shares and the certificate for the 60 shares of stock were surrendered up to the corporation and canceled, and September 30, 1897, four new certificates of 90 shares each were issued, one to Helen R. Chester and one to each of the three daughters of Thomas Chester, and the proceeding before the surrogate was discontinued. The plaintiff assented to this division of the stock. It was while Helen R. Chester held this stock that the forty per cent dividend was paid. February 4, 1898, she received on the 90 shares $3,600. On the 20th day of January, 1899, she assigned and transferred to her husband, the plaintiff, all her right, title and interest in the property and stock of the defendant corporation. This action was commenced January 31, 1899.

It does not appear when the plaintiff first claimed the whole 300 shares of stock under his mother's will, except that it was prior to the commencement of this action.

It is apparent that neither the plaintiff nor his wife supposed, when the stock was divided between the four parties, that such a division was other than in accordance with the real rights of the parties. Just how much information they had as to the facts connected with the issue of the 300 shares of stock it is impossible to say. They evidently were not informed as to the law, if they were as to the facts. No question was made as to the division being in accordance with the strict legal rights of the parties until just before the commencement of this action. There was no disagreement, no controversy as to the real rights of the parties in the stock at the time the division was made. That being so, I am unable to see how there was any compromise or settlement of any controversy or any consideration for the assent or agreement by plaintiff or his wife to divide the stock, giving each party 90 shares, or any estoppel preventing the plaintiff from recovering his stock and the dividends paid and unpaid thereon since the death of his mother. It would seem that all the parties supposed that the 300 shares of stock belonged to the estate of Thomas Chester, and acted upon that theory. Even if the facts were fully known, the law applicable to the facts was not understood, as the court has since held it to be.

In the absence of any consideration for the division, even a consideration growing out of a compromise or settlement of a disputed controversy, I am unable to see how the fact of the division of the stock has operated to deprive the plaintiff of the interest he would otherwise have therein.

Much litigation was had between the parties to this action other than the defendant corporation as to matters growing out of their interests in the residuary estate of Thomas Chester and the business of the old firm of Thornton & Chester, of which Thomas Chester was a member at the time of his death, and which was continued during the lifetime of the widow, and there was also a contest of the will of the widow and mother, Mary P. Chester. None of these litigations, however, in any way related to or involved the interests of the parties in the stock in question, unless it was the contest over the will of Mary P. Chester, and the parties did not evidently regard that contest as in any way affecting their rights in the stock. Finally, November 14, 1898, there were papers and writings executed between the parties settling their differences and litigations, except one action that was particularly specified, and then it was provided that it was expressly understood and agreed that none of the papers, nor all of them together, should be construed to release any claim between the parties except those expressly enumerated.

No claim had then been made or suggested as to this stock in question, and no such claim was enumerated in the writings and agreements constituting the settlement thus made between the parties. The controversy in this action was not, therefore, settled by any express agreement made at that time. It was not in the minds or within the contemplation of the parties. Under these circumstances, I am unable to see how any estoppel as to this claim by plaintiff, of an interest in this stock, could arise. The consent to the discharge of the executors of the estate of Thomas Chester in no way affected this claim. No relief is sought against them. No remedy against them in behalf of the defendants, the three daughters, as to this stock was lost by this discharge. The 300 shares of stock never belonged to the estate, but to the widow. The executors never dealt with this stock so as to render them liable to the daughters of the testator in any way. The plaintiff now makes no claim and asks no relief against his coexecutor. Such coexecutor is not a party to the action. More than this, these shares of stock were surrendered by the coexecutor of plaintiff and canceled, and the new certificates for 90 shares each were issued by consent of all the parties. No further claim could, therefore, be made against him on account of such stock by any of the parties.

The claim here sought to be enforced is not one against the estate or its executors, but against the three daughters of the testator, who have received a portion of the 300 shares of stock, which never belonged to the estate nor to them at all, but which has been received by such daughters without legal right and without their paying any consideration therefor.

I am unable to perceive any reason why such claim should not be enforced, and the judgment, so far as it affords relief against them, should not be affirmed.

The corporation whose capital stock is in litigation is also a party to the action. It was a necessary party for various reasons.

The court, however, erroneously directed judgment in favor of the plaintiff and against the corporation itself for $9,000, the dividends upon the stock of plaintiff paid to the three daughters after the certificates of stock had been issued to them, and before the corporation had gone into liquidation or had any notice of plaintiff's claims to the stock, and also for the costs of the action. This relief was granted upon the theory that the dividends were wrongfully paid to the daughters. It is said that the corporation knowing all the facts was bound to know the law, and, therefore, knew that these 300 shares of stock belonged to the plaintiff, and that the daughters had no interest therein. The stock, however, stood upon the corporation's books in the name of the three daughters, and they held their certificates with the assent, and it may be said by the procurement, of the plaintiff and his wife. She commenced the proceeding to procure the division of the stock, and the plaintiff added his affidavit to his wife's petition, swearing to the truth thereof and stating his desire that the petition be granted. Thereupon the daughters and plaintiff's coexecutor acceded to the desire of plaintiff and his wife, the proceeding was dismissed, and the division was made upon consent of all the parties. How could the corporation do otherwise than pay the dividends as it did? It was not a wrongful payment. No matter who were the legal owners of the stock, all the parties directed its division as it was divided, and assented to the payment of the dividends in accordance with such division, and such payment relieved the corporation from all liability to respond again for such dividends. The payment of the dividends to the daughters was not wrongful, and the judgment, so far as it provided for a recovery of the dividends from the corporation, and for costs, was erroneous and should be modified and corrected.

My conclusion is, therefore, that the judgment appealed from should be modified by striking therefrom all provisions to the effect that the defendant corporation wrongfully issued certificates of stock to the other defendants, and wrongfully paid dividends thereon to such other defendants, and that plaintiff have personal judgment and execution against such defendant corporation therefor, with interest and costs, or for any other amount, and as so modified affirmed, with costs to the respondent against the appellants other than the corporation, and with costs to such corporation appellant against the respondent.

Judgment reversed and new trial ordered, with costs to the appellants to abide the event.

EMILIE R. SEIDENSPINNER, Respondent, *v.* METROPOLITAN LIFE
INSURANCE COMPANY, Appellant.

*Insurance — application therefor — whether a question as to other insurance covered
insurance in an incorporated benevolent association — when a question of fact.*

An application for a policy of life insurance contained the following questions
and answers:

"A. Have you ever applied to any company, order or association for insurance on your life without receiving exact kind and amount of insurance applied
for? (If yes, give particulars.) No.

"B. State name of company, order or association which has declined to issue
a policy on your life or postponed you. None.

"C. State whether any company had refused to restore a lapsed policy on
your life. (If yes, give particulars.) None.

"D. Is any application or negotiation for other insurance on your life now
pending or contemplated? (If yes, give particulars.) No.

"E. State amount of insurance you now carry on your life, with name of
company or association by whom granted and the year of issue. (Enumerate
each.) None.

"F. If insured in this company, in ordinary, industrial or intermediate, give
policy numbers. None.

"Is there any other insurance in force on your life? None."

At the time of the insured's death he was a member of an incorporated benevolent association whose certificate of incorporation provided that the "object of
its creation is to accumulate by initiation fees, quarterly dues, fines and interest, a fund out of which to assist each other (the members) in time of sickness
and death as prescribed by the Constitution and By-laws of the same." The
constitution provided: "At the death of a member in good standing for six
months the widow or legal heirs of the deceased shall receive the sum of $150;
at the death of the wife of a member in good standing for six months he shall
receive from the treasury $50." The association issued no certificates of membership and the constitution designated the person to whom the sum, payable
upon the death of a member or his wife, should be paid and did not confer any
power upon the member to name any other beneficiary.

Held, that an examination of question E, contained in the application, in connection with the questions which preceded it, indicated an insurance in a
company or association which issued some form of certificate;

That men's minds might reasonably differ as to whether or not the last
question, taken in connection with the others, did not mean some form of
other insurance evidenced by a policy or certificate, and also upon the issue
whether such question fairly called upon the insured to state his connection
with the benefit association above alluded to;

That as to these matters a question of fact was presented.

Semble, that membership in an association, whose constitution and by-laws provided simply for the payment of certain funeral expenses, did not constitute an insurance within the meaning of the questions contained in the application.

APPEAL by the defendant, the Metropolitan Life Insurance Company, from a judgment of the Supreme Court in favor of the plaintiff, entered in the office of the clerk of the county of Erie on the 6th day of June, 1901, upon the verdict of a jury rendered by direction of the court, and also from an order entered in said clerk's office on the 12th day of June, 1901, denying the defendant's motion for a new trial made upon the minutes.

Seward A. Simons, for the appellant.

Moses Shire, for the respondent.

HISCOCK, J. :

Plaintiff is seeking to recover the sum of $1,000 and interest upon a policy of life insurance issued by the defendant April 30, 1900, upon the life of Gottlieb Seidenspinner, and wherein plaintiff was designated as beneficiary. The insured died October 28, 1900.

The only questions litigated upon the trial or presented here, were and are whether the insured in procuring said policy was guilty of a breach of warranty which avoided it through misstatements as to other policies of insurance in force upon his life, and as to sicknesses which he had suffered.

At the close of the trial, which was before a jury, each side asked to have a verdict directed in its favor. Among the questions and answers contained in the application of the insured for the policy in question were the following:

" A. Have you ever applied to any company, order or association for insurance on your life without receiving exact kind and amount of insurance applied for ? (If yes, give particulars.) No.

" B. State name of company, order or association which has declined to issue a policy on your life or postponed you. None.

" C. State whether any company had refused to restore a lapsed policy on your life. (If yes, give particulars.) None.

" D. Is any application or negotiation for other insurance on your life now pending or contemplated ? (If yes, give particulars.) No.

" E. State amount of insurance you now carry on your life, with name of company or association by whom granted and the year of issue. (Enumerate each.) None.

" F. If insured in this company, in ordinary, industrial or intermediate, give policy numbers. None.

" Is there any other insurance in force on your life ? None."

At and for some time prior to the date when said questions were
asked and answered as aforesaid, plaintiff was a member of four
associations, namely, Wuertemburger Suavia Benevolent Association
No. 1 of Buffalo, N. Y., East Buffalo Wuertemburger Schwaben
Verein No. 2, Freiheit Court No. 144 of the Foresters of America,
and of one of the lodges of Odd Fellows. -

Under the constitution and by-laws of two of those associations,
provision was made simply for the payment of certain funeral
expenses, and it is hardly claimed that these provisions constituted
an " insurance " within the meaning of the questions in the application. Stronger facts in behalf of the appellant are presented in
connection with the Wuertemburger Suavia Benevolent Association,
the constitution and certificate of incorporation of which were put
in evidence. It appears from them that such association was incorporated under the acts, chapter 368 of the Laws of 1865, as
amended by chapter 668 of the laws of the same year. By its certificate of incorporation it is provided that " the particular business
or object of its creation is to accumulate by initiation fees, quarterly
dues, fines and interest, a fund out of which to assist each other
(the members) in time of sickness and death, as prescribed by the
Constitution and By-laws of the same." The constitution provides
that the object of the association shall be " To support one another
in word and deed, in days of need and sickness; to bury the dead
with honors, as well as to help the widows and orphans of deceased
members according to means, and to cultivate moral education." It
further provided certain qualifications of membership, amongst
which was the examination of every proposed candidate by a
physician. Small quarterly dues were provided for and then the
further provision was made that at the death of each member " each
brother is to pay one dollar until the treasury shows the amount of
$3,000." Under the heading " In Regard to Benefits," it was pro-
vided that " At the death of a member in good standing for six
months the widow or legal heirs of the deceased shall receive the
sum of $150; at the death of the wife of a member in good stand-
ing for six months he shall receive from the treasury $50."

The question is whether membership by the insured in this association made his answers false and avoided the policy.

While such associations are brought within some of the statutory provisions with reference to the supervision of the general subject of life insurance and while they are sometimes spoken of as being engaged in the business of life insurance, it is apparent that that feature in the organization and existence of the association in question was, to say the least, very primitive. No separate fund was provided out of which death losses should be payable. There probably was no practical way in which the association could enforce the payment by members of dues and assessments from which to pay the benefit sums which became payable upon the death of a member or his wife. No certificate of membership was issued such as in the case of many benefit and aid associations takes the place of a regular insurance policy. The constitution designated the person to whom the sum payable upon the death of a member or his wife should go, and there was no power given to the member to name any other beneficiary. While the sum paid at death necessarily partook somewhat of the character of the moneys payable under a regular life insurance policy upon death, still evidently the predominating idea was that of aiding and helping members rather than engaging in what might be regarded as a regular insurance business.

Having these considerations in mind, we come to the more particular consideration of the questions and answers. It is claimed by appellant that the insured especially was untruthful in answering " none " to the following two questions : " State amount of insurance you now carry on your life, with name of company or association by whom granted and the year of issue," and " Is there any other insurance in force on your life ? "

We think that an examination of the first question in connection with the other questions which preceded it, fairly warrants the conclusion that it indicated an insurance in some company or association which had issued some form of policy or certificate. We think further, that men's minds might reasonably differ as to whether or not the last question, taken in connection with the others, did not mean some form of formal insurance evidenced by policy or certificate, and might differ upon the issue whether this question fairly called upon the insured to state his connection with the benefit associations to which we have referred. It was very easy for the defendant, if it desired to, to ask such questions as would plainly and fairly call upon the applicant to disclose any membership in benefit or aid associations. The language of the questions which were asked and prepared by itself are to be construed most strongly against it. The insured should not be convicted of having given fraudulent and untruthful answers unless such inference is fairly warranted by the evidence.

If, as we think, different inferences might be drawn as to whether the questions stated called for different answers and information than was given, then an issue of fact was presented for a jury to pass upon. Each party, however, asked the trial justice to direct a verdict. Neither side requested to go to the jury upon the question indicated. Under those circumstances, a verdict having been directed, it is to be presumed that the trial justice found upon any question of fact involved in such manner as to authorize and sustain the verdict. (*Kirtz* v. *Peck*, 113 N. Y. 222; *Provost* v. *McEncroe*, 102 id. 650.)

Upon the trial the learned counsel for the defendant sought to have admitted certain evidence in regard to the payment to the insured of sick benefits by the associations already named as indicating that he was sick at different and other times than admitted in his application. We think, however, if it should be assumed that such evidence was competent, that by his questions and offer he did not make it sufficiently clear that such evidence, if admitted, would have indicated sicknesses at other dates than those admitted in the application to present error. Further than that, while excepting to the rulings of the court, the counsel admitted that the evidence sought for was not the best evidence which could be given of illness. We think an examination of all that took place at this point of the trial discloses that no such material error was committed as to call for reversal.

In accordance with these conclusions we think the judgment and order appealed from should be affirmed, with costs.

MCLENNAN, SPRING, WILLIAMS and DAVY, JJ., concurred.

Judgment and order affirmed, with costs.

CAROLINE B. WOODRUFF and Others, as Executors and Trustees under the Will of NELSON BEARDSLEY, Deceased, Plaintiffs, v. THE OSWEGO STARCH FACTORY, Defendant.

Tax on rent reserved under a perpetual lease — what covenant by the tenant to pay all taxes, etc., does not require him to pay the tax on the rent — when the lessor is estopped to claim that the statute imposing the tax is unconstitutional.

Taxes upon rents reserved in a perpetual lease assessed against the lessor pursuant to section 8 of the Tax Law (Laws of 1896, chap. 908) re-enacting chapter 327 of the Laws of 1846, are not payable by the lessee under a covenant binding him to pay "all taxes, charges and assessments, ordinary and extraordinary, which shall be taxed, charged, imposed or assessed on the hereby demised premises and privileges, or any part thereof, or on the said parties of the first part (the lessors), their heirs and assigns, in respect thereof."

The fact that the lease was executed about a year after the enactment of chapter 327 of the Laws of 1846, does not establish that the lessor had these taxes in mind when he executed the lease and intended to relieve himself from the payment of such taxes by the covenant contained therein.

Assuming, without deciding, that the taxation of such rents is unconstitutional, that fact will not prevent the lessee from setting off against the rents reserved under the lease, moneys involuntarily paid by it for taxes assessed upon the rents, which the lessor had refused to pay, where it appears that the lessor did not assert his claim that the assessments were invalid until after the payments had been made.

SUBMISSION of a controversy upon an agreed statement of facts pursuant to section 1279 of the Code of Civil Procedure.

Frederic E. Storke, for the plaintiffs.

H. L. Howe, for the defendant.

HISCOCK, J.:

This action involves the construction of a covenant with reference to the payment of taxes contained in certain leases executed in perpetuity of premises situated in Oswego. The plaintiffs have become owners and landlords, and the defendant the tenant under said leases.

Between June 2, 1847, and the year 1867, Charles Carrington and Myron Pardee, being the owners of certain lands and water power on the Oswego river, executed to various persons seven leases in fee, reserving in each case to the lessors a perpetual rent. Prior to 1898 the plaintiffs' testator, one Nelson Beardsley, had acquired an undivided half interest in said seven leases and the rents reserved thereunder, and the defendant had acquired under said leases the fee of the land therein described.

May 13, 1846, and, therefore, a little more than a year before the first lease was drawn, there had been passed the act* imposing a tax upon rents reserved in leases such as those under consideration. By chapter 908, Laws of 1896, known as the Tax Law, the provisions of this original act for this species of taxation were in the main re-enacted. Section 8 provided that " Rents reserved in any lease in fee * * * and chargeable upon real property within the state shall be taxable to the person entitled to receive the same as personal property in the tax district where such real property is situated." Subdivision 5 of section 21 provided for setting down in the fifth column of the assessment roll the value of such taxable rents estimated upon a certain prescribed basis.· Section 75 provided that if said taxes could not be collected out of the persons against whom they were assessed, the same might be collected of the tenant or lessee in possession of the premises on which the rent was reserved, and in that case such tenant or lessee should be entitled to have the amount paid or collected of him, with interest, deducted from the amount of rent reserved upon such premises then or thereafter to become due.

The rents reserved upon the leases in question were never actually assessed until the year 1898. Since then they have been, and the plaintiffs having failed to pay the taxes, they have been collected by appropriate proceedings from the defendant, which now seeks to deduct the amount so collected, amounting to several hundred dollars, from the rents reserved under its leases to the plaintiffs. Plaintiffs deny its right so to do, claiming that the obligation rests upon defendant to pay said taxes, and these opposing contentions of the respective parties as to the liability to pay said taxes lead to and involve a construction of the tax covenant written in substantially similar language in each of said leases. This covenant binds the lessee to pay "all taxes, charges and assessments, ordinary and extraordinary, which shall be taxed, charged, imposed or assessed on the hereby demised premises and privileges, or any part

*Laws of 1846, chapter 327.— [REP.

thereof, or on the said parties of the first part (the lessors), their heirs and assigns, in respect thereof."

The learned counsel for the plaintiffs has approached the immediate interpretation of the clause with a most extended and careful review and analysis of early English statutes and decisions bearing upon the subject of taxation as related to and involved in leases after which the ones in question are largely patterned and formulated. The review thus made, however, while extremely interesting for the historical light which it throws upon the general subject of leases and taxes, fails to disclose any authority which to our minds is decisive of the precise question here presented. In the solution of that, and the construction of the covenant in dispute, we must mainly be governed by the reasonable and natural meaning of the words used in the clause itself, considered in the light of the entire contract of which the latter is a part. Some aid can be derived from general considerations which may be supposed to have affected the minds and intentions of the parties when the leases were made, and at least one authority has been cited from the reports of this State adjudicating the meaning of a somewhat analogous provision.

Passing, then, to a consideration of the language employed in the covenant, we think it very apparent that plaintiffs' contention of defendant's liability finds a broader support in the last than in the first clause. We easily conclude that taxes, etc., " taxed, charged, imposed or assessed on the hereby demised premises and privileges" do not include a tax assessed upon the rents springing therefrom. The word " premises" is used throughout the leases as meaning and referring to the lands and rights which are the subject of the leases. When we join with it the other words used, with the resultant term "hereby demised premises," we think it becomes clear beyond doubt that there is meant and indicated exclusively the land and property which is leased to and put in the possession of the tenant, and that it would be a violent construction to hold the latter liable under this clause to pay a tax upon rents which the landlord received as the consideration and consequence of so demising such premises.

It is to be observed that the law providing for this taxation expressly treats and defines it as a tax upon personal property.

Plaintiff's counsel, in support of his theory that rents are so an incident or a part of the premises that a tax upon them may be regarded as one upon the latter within the terms used, has especially urged upon our attention the opinions delivered in the recent Income Tax cases in the Supreme Court of the United States (*Pollock* v. *Farmers' Loan & Trust Co.*, 157 U. S. 429; 158 id. 601), in which it was held or said by various of the judges, in substance, that the term "lands" included the rents issuing therefrom. The issues in those cases naturally and equitably seem to have permitted of such a conclusion. The question arose as to the legality of a law which taxed the income, including the rents, of real estate. Concededly a constitutional prohibition existed which forbade direct taxation upon real estate after the manner pursued in the statute, and the question was presented whether Congress might evade such prohibition against said tax upon lands by levying the same upon the income thereof. The opinion was expressed by various members of the court that it might not be allowed to avoid the prohibition which covered the subject, simply by proceeding against what was clearly an incident and a part thereof. The principles there evoked and declared, however, do not seem to us to apply to this case. Here is no attempt to escape a broad constitutional provision which protects a certain class of property, by attacking some incident thereof. The question simply is of the apportionment of what may be assumed to be proper and legal burdens, between two parties to a contract as governed by the terms of that contract. The construction to be sought is one which will simply, legally and properly determine the rights of the two parties to a contract.

We, therefore, are remitted to the final query, whether this tax can be said to be one imposed on the "parties of the first part (lessors of the premises and privileges), their heirs and assigns *in respect thereof*." Technically and gramatically the words "in respect thereof," relate and have reference to the preceding words "demised premises and privileges," so that the words describe a tax imposed upon the lessors "in respect of" or in relation to the leased premises. If this wording covers this tax it must be because such tax upon rents may be said to be one in respect of or in relation to the demised premises.

While perhaps it might be said that a tax upon the rents reserved under a lease had some very general relation to the demised premises which produced them, we do not think that it would be a natural or reasonable construction to hold that the relation was such as to satisfy the requirements of this covenant. The tax here indicated is one which is directed specifically against the property which is demised or against the lessors in respect of, or on account of, such property. We call to mind at once the class and character of such taxes which should be so charged against said premises. In form, when the owners were non-residents of the county where the premises were situated, as in this case, the ordinary taxes would be assessed in the name of the defendant as occupant. But the Legislature might at any time provide that the plaintiffs should be assessed for them, and then immediately a case would be presented for the application with its natural meaning of this last provision. Plaintiffs would be assessed in respect of the demised premises, and it would become the duty of the defendant to protect them and the premises against such assessment by paying the tax thereon. But when we pass beyond this class of assessments and assume one made against the lessor upon his income or rents received under a lease, and otherwise in no manner based upon, or measured by the lands leased, their value, character or condition, it seems to us that it would be a strained construction to say that such tax was on account of, related to, or "in respect" of, the demised premises, within the meaning of the covenant.

Sufficient reason is found in the general scope of the contract between the parties for imposing upon the tenant the obligation to pay all taxes which naturally and legitimately could be said to be assessed upon the leased lands and privileges, in whosoever's name the assessment might be. Under the lease it became practically the owner of the premises. They were its to occupy, improve and enjoy with all of the profits to be derived therefrom. The burden would naturally follow of discharging all taxes which might be assessed against them and which theoretically, in large part, would represent benefits and improvements making the lands more valuable. There would, however, be no such appropriateness in making the tenant pay taxes upon the rents. Those were the property of the landlord, which it was his right to utilize and enjoy as best he could, and a similar process of logic would naturally call upon him, rather than the tenant, to discharge any burden of taxation which the government might see fit to impose upon them.

If it should be urged that this argument of what would be the reasonable division of burdens between the parties is subject to the defect that the imposition of some unexpected tax upon the rents might so diminish the landlord's net revenue from the premises as to make the contract inequitable towards him, it may readily be answered that the same unforeseen contingency might deprive the tenant of all his profits, and that in this case no such consideration is presented because this species of taxation was framed before the leases were made.

Coming to some of the general arguments outside of the words themselves of the covenant in question, it is forcibly and ably argued by plaintiffs' counsel that this taxation of rents under leases such as these was the result of a strenuous and widespead public agitation which had culminated in the passage of the original act for this manner of assessments only a year or two before the first of these leases was made; that, therefore, it must be assumed that the landlords in making them had this taxation in mind and intended to guard against it and that this intention of the parties should be taken into account in construing the covenant. We are unable, however, in this argument to find much support for plaintiffs' contention. It is fair to assume that these contracts were the product and evolution of much experience and care upon the part of the landlord class, and that if there is any ambiguity upon this particular subject it is to be charged against the lessors rather than otherwise. If, then, counsel is correct that they had in mind the imposition of this tax at the time the leases were made and it was the intention and the agreement of the parties that the same should be paid by the tenant, it is difficult for us to understand why the latter obligation was, to say the least, left in so much doubt, when the use of three or four words would have placed it beyond any uncertainty whatever. It would perhaps be more reasonable to infer that the lessors, taking into account the possibility of this taxation, fixed the consideration for, and the rents reserved under the leases at such a figure as would indemnify them against the same when the hour of payment came.

But one case has been called to our attention passing upon a clause in a lease somewhat similar at least to the one in question. (*Van Rensselaer* v. *Dennison*, 8 Barb. 23.)

Plaintiffs' counsel in a careful analysis of this case seeks to so distinguish it that it will not be an authority for defendant in its contention herein. While the clause there construed was not absolutely identical with the one here, it still did contain, amongst other phrases, substantially the language under review by us, and we think the reasoning employed by the court in that case does support very strongly the theory of defendant adopted by us that the tax upon rents was for the landlord and lessor to pay.

Upon the assumption that this court might hold as above indicated, it was next urged by plaintiffs' counsel that the law under which the assessments in question were made was unconstitutional and the latter void; that, therefore, the tenant had no right to pay the taxes upon such assessments and charge the same up against the rents reserved under the leases. We do not find it necessary to consider the first proposition, because, even if we should adopt plaintiffs' views in relation thereto, we should still hold that under the facts of this case defendant would be entitled to the offset claimed.

In substantially the same form as now, the provisions for this manner of taxation have been embodied in the statutes of this State for over half a century. During that time we must assume that they have been enforced in a multitude of instances and that they have imposed a burden which was exceedingly irksome to and unpopular with those who were its objects. Notwithstanding this, no one, so far as we are aware or are advised by plaintiffs' counsel as the result of his great research, has secured from any court a decision that the law was unconstitutional. We refer to this history not, of course, as deciding the question of law presented, but as bearing upon the conduct and good faith of the defendant in paying the taxes imposed under it. It did not hurry forward to pay them. Its payment was not voluntary, but enforced by levy and sale of its property. Plaintiffs are not only presumed to have had knowledge of the law providing for these assessments, but as a matter of fact did have such knowledge, and were aware that after a long period of non-enforcement of the law the same was to be invoked against these rents. The prepared statement of facts recites that plaintiffs " prior to the completion of the assessment roll of 1898, notified the defendant of the proposed assessment and of plaintiffs' claim that defendant was bound to pay all taxes levied thereon." Such notice assumed the validity of the assessment rather than otherwise. The assessment in form was against the plaintiffs. If we are right in the conclusions which we have reached, the liability rested upon them rather than upon defendant to make payment thereof.

Under all of these circumstances,·we think that if they desired to resist this species of taxation upon the ground that it was unconstitutional and illegal, they themselves either should have done so or should have fairly advised defendant of their claim and position before the payments were made; that under the circumstances the obligation did not rest upon defendant upon its own motion without demand or offer of indemnity by plaintiffs to resist the payment of the taxes further than it did. We think that it is entitled, in accordance with the provisions of the statute, to set off the latter which have been collected from it against the rents reserved under the leases.

In accordance with these conclusions, plaintiffs are entitled to the sum of $552 heretofore tendered to them by defendant, and defendant is entitled to recover of plaintiffs the balance in amount of taxes upon rents collected from it during the year 1899 over and above rents accrued and unpaid or accruing during said year, and judgment should be had accordingly.

Judgment ordered for defendant for $101.19, with interest from November 1, 1900, with costs.

ADAMS, P. J., McLENNAN, SPRING and WILLIAMS, JJ., concurred.

Judgment ordered for the defendant for $101.19, with interest from the 1st day of November, 1900, with costs.

70
81

FRANK WHITAKER, Respondent, *v.* JOHN F. EILENBERG, Appellant.

Contract to buy grapes — remittance of check for less than the contract price, with a statement that the grapes were below the contract standard — the vendor, if he accepts the checks, cannot thereafter recover the balance of the contract price.

A commission merchant made a contract with a grape grower to purchase the latter's crop of grapes then upon the vine at eighteen dollars per ton. The merchant found no fault with the first few shipments of grapes and paid the full contract price therefor. Upon receiving each of the next three or four lots, he notified the grower that the grapes were below the contract standard and inclosed a check for the price of the grapes, figured upon the basis of sixteen dollars instead of eighteen dollars per ton. The grower received the communications and checks and retained and used the latter. He expressly accepted the reduction in the first instance and made no complaint or protest in the other instances, until several months later.

Thereafter there was a frost in the territory including the grower's vineyard and the commission merchant telegraphed him, "grapes since the freeze will be sold to your account," and also wrote him the following letter: "We find, this being our first car since the freeze, that the grapes show the cold very badly and will be compelled to sell them to your account. We wired you to-day thinking perhaps you would prefer to consign to some one else. We will do the very best we can for you under the circumstances," etc. The grower made no reply to such communications and subsequently shipped to the commission merchant three lots of grapes. The latter disposed of each lot for the grower's account and sent him a full statement of the transaction, inclosing checks with such statements for the full balance due, in accordance therewith. The grower retained and used the checks without making any protest or objection of any kind until some months later.

In an action brought by the grower against the commission merchant to recover the balance due for the grapes in accordance with the terms of the original contract, it was

Held, that the plaintiff could not recover;

That the acceptance by the plaintiff of the commission merchant's checks constituted, as matter of law, an accord and satisfaction, even though such checks did not themseves explicitly state that they were in full payment, it appearing that the plaintiff fully understood that they were so intended;

That it was error for the court to submit the case to the jury upon the theory that it was for them to say whether the parties had made a new contract which took the place of the original contract and made the defendant's payments sufficient.

APPEAL by the defendant, John F. Eilenberg, from a judgment of the County Court of Yates county in favor of the plaintiff, entered in the office of the clerk of the county of Yates on the

22d day of June, 1901, upon the verdict of a jury, and also from an order entered in said clerk's office on the 15th day of June, 1901, denying the defendant's motion for a new trial made upon the minutes.

The action was originally commenced in a Justice's Court where a judgment was recovered by the plaintiff. The defendant appealed to the County Court and demanded a new trial.

Thomas Carmody, for the appellant.

Calvin J. Huson, for the respondent.

HISCOCK, J.:

This controversy springs out of the sale and delivery of a crop of grapes by plaintiff to defendant. Part of them have concededly been paid for in full. Upon the remainder plaintiff seeks to recover an alleged unpaid balance of about $150 computed upon the basis of prices fixed in the original contract. Although having accounted for quite a portion of the crop only at a sum below such prices, defendant nevertheless urges that he has been discharged from all further obligations because plaintiff has accepted and retained his checks therefor knowing that they were intended to be in full payment on account of the inferior quality of the grapes.

Plaintiff was a grower of grapes in Yates county. Defendant was a commission merchant in Philadelphia. They had had dealings before those in question. September 19, 1896, apparently in answer to a letter from him, plaintiff wrote defendant, "I have a good crop of grapes * * * and they are very fine * * * would sell at a fair price. * * * The crop is much better than last year; but very little rot." A short time thereafter defendant went to plaintiff's vineyard and, after a limited examination, made a contract to purchase his grapes, then upon the vines, at eighteen dollars per ton. There is some conflict about some of the terms of the contract which was not reduced to writing. Defendant claims that he kept calling attention to rotten berries in the bunches and asked plaintiff what was to be done with them, to which the latter replied, "they would be taken out as much as possible." "He said he would put the grapes up in a saleable condition." Plaintiff differs with him some as to what was said upon this subject.

The shipments were commenced about October first. No fault was found with the first lots, and the full contract price was promptly remitted for them. Between October sixteenth and twentieth three or four lots were shipped which defendant claimed then, and testifies now, were below his contract standard. Upon receipt of each lot he plainly and fairly made this complaint to plaintiff, figured up the price at sixteen dollars instead of eighteen dollars per ton, and remitted the full sum and balance due upon that claim and basis. Plaintiff received his communications and checks and retained and used the latter. He expressly accepted the reduction in the first instance and made no complaint or protest in the others except that in January following he sent a bill for a balance due upon all the grapes shipped computed upon the basis of contract prices.

About October eighteenth there was a frost in the territory including plaintiff's vineyard. Apparently the grapes subsequently shipped by him were still upon the vines. October twentieth defendant telegraphed him, " Grapes since the freeze will be sold to your account," and the same day wrote him, "We find, this being our first car since the freeze, that the grapes show the cold very badly and will be compelled to sell them to your account. We wired you to-day thinking perhaps you would prefer to consign to some one else. We will do the very best we can for you under the circumstances," etc. Plaintiff duly received these communications, but made no reply thereto, shipping thereafter to defendant three lots of grapes. Defendant probably had not, as matter of fact, received from plaintiff any grapes after the frost when he wrote his letter referring to his " first car since the freeze," but may have received such grapes from others. At any rate, he testifies that these last three lots, received on and after October twenty-seventh, were full of dry and frozen berries, and there is no satisfactory contradiction of this. In accordance with his telegram and letter, he disposed of these grapes for plaintiff's account, as he claims, at the full market price and without any charge for commissions. He wrote plaintiff and sent him a full statement showing what he had done; that he had sold the grapes for his account; the amount realized upon the sales and the charges against the same for freight, cartage, etc. He inclosed checks with such statements for the full balances due in accordance therewith. The plaintiff received the letters and statements and checks. He retained and used the latter, making no protest or objection of any kind except the bill hereinbefore referred to.

Defendant claimed upon the trial, as he does upon this appeal, that the checks sent to plaintiff, when accepted and used by him under the circumstances referred to, constituted a full payment and satisfaction of all claims on account of the grapes involved in controversy. He presented this proposition in various forms upon the trial. The county judge ruled against him and attempted to cover the subject by allowing the jury to say whether the parties by their acts above referred to made a new contract which took the place of the original one and made defendant's payments sufficient. We believe he committed error therein.

In the first place, we do not think that there was any issue of fact at this point to be submitted to the jury.

The material acts of the parties by which are to be established their respective rights with reference to the shipments of grapes and remittances therefor, are not the subject of conflicting testimony, and do not permit different and contradictory inferences. Upon the other hand, in our opinion, they are undisputed and simple, and lead plainly and decisively to but one line of conclusions.

In the next place, we do not think that the learned county judge was entirely fortunate and accurate in defining the questions between the parties as one whether a new contract had been made between them. While it may be said that in a very general way this issue was involved, the more exact and specific question was whether the acceptance by plaintiff of defendant's checks, under all of the circumstances, constituted a payment and satisfaction of all claims, and this even though no new contract had been made covering the disputed shipments, and even though defendant was not justified in his original contention that the grapes were below the grade he was entitled to, and that he had a right, therefore, to treat them upon a basis different from that provided in the original contract. We conclude that this question must be answered, as matter of law, in the defendant's favor.

Upon receipt of the two shipments in dispute here which reached him, respectively, October nineteenth and twentieth, defendant clearly and plainly took the position with plaintiff that they were inferior in quality, and that he was only willing to allow eighty cents per hundred instead of ninety cents, and he remitted the full balance due upon that theory. Upon October twentieth he as clearly and plainly notified plaintiff that on account of the frost he would sell the grapes thereafter received on his account, instead of accepting them under the contract. Plaintiff had the right upon receipt of that notice either to treat and proceed against defendant as having repudiated his contract or to ship grapes under the new arrangement proposed by him. He chose the latter. But independent of this, when defendant received the three shipments sent after such notice, he fairly and explicitly took the position that the grapes had been injured by the frost, were inferior in quality, and that in accordance with the notice theretofore served he had disposed of them for plaintiff's account, and he again remitted the full balance due upon such disposition.

In each case plaintiff, with full knowledge of defendant's position and claim and clearly understanding that it was intended to be in full payment of the shipment in question, accepted, retained and collected the money upon defendant's check. He did not even make any protest or objection until several months afterwards. He fully understood the conditions upon which the checks were sent, and, when he accepted and used the latter, we think it must be held that he accepted and assented to the conditions which accompanied them.

It is true that there must be some sufficient reason and consideration to render a payment of less than the amount originally and primarily due a full satisfaction thereof. If plaintiff's claim were liquidated and undisputed, defendant would not be able to satisfy the same by paying part thereof. But in this case there is a sufficient consideration for treating the payments made as a full satisfaction. Independent of the question whether defendant by his notices of October twentieth established a new relation which should govern the future shipments, there is nothing which impugns the apparent good faith of his claim that the shipments received by him on and after October nineteenth were inferior and below the grade called for by his contract. Plaintiff has scarcely questioned the fact that the grapes were more or less damaged and defective. He does, it is true, dispute somewhat defendant's claim as to what the terms and meaning of the original contract were. But this does not at all deprive defendant of the force of his position, duly taken, that the goods which he received were not what he was entitled to, thereby furnishing a reason and consideration for a less price than originally fixed ; that he has paid this and plaintiff accepted it, thus making a complete settlement and satisfaction of their dealings.

We do not regard it as of any significance in this case that the checks sent did not upon themselves explicitly state that they were in full payment. The letter or account or both sent with each one clearly showed that it was intended to be in full settlement of the balance for the given shipment in question. Plaintiff understood this clearly enough.

We think, therefore, that these checks operated as a payment and satisfaction and that plaintiff was not entitled to recover the balance due in accordance with the terms of the original contract, and that error was committed in the trial and submission of the case within the views expressed in *Wisner* v. *Schopp* (34 App. Div. 199); *Fuller* v. *Kemp* (138 N. Y. 231) ; *Nassoiy* v. *Tomlinson* (148 id. 326).

There is some controversy between the parties about some covering put upon the grape boxes and about the alleged failure of defendant to return to plaintiff certain boxes. These items only involve a small amount, and inasmuch as a new trial must be had, they do not seem to require consideration.

The judgment and order appealed from should be reversed and a new trial granted.

McLENNAN, SPRING, WILLIAMS and DAVY, JJ., concurred.

Judgment and order reversed upon questions of law only, the facts having been examined and no error found therein, and new trial ordered, with costs to the appellant to abide the event.

JEANNETTE E. DEVOE, as Administratrix, etc., of WILLIAM H. DEVOE, Deceased, Respondent, *v.* THE NEW YORK CENTRAL AND HUDSON RIVER RAILROAD COMPANY, Appellant.

70
|r174 N
70
r174 N

Negligence — injury to a car inspector who, outside of his duty as such, assists in uncoupling cars and is crushed between them — effect of his disregard of a rule requiring him to station a man by the side of cars while he is between them — act of a fellow-servant.

A car inspector in the employ of a railroad company who, while voluntarily engaged in assisting the conductor of a shifting engine and not in the course of his duties as car inspector, goes between two cars for the purpose of uncoupling them, assumes the risk incident thereto, and if he is killed in consequence of the shifting engine backing other cars against those which he is endeavoring to uncouple, the railroad company is not liable for the damages resulting from his death, especially where it appears that when he went between the cars he did not station a man by the side thereof as required by a rule promulgated by the railroad company for the protection of car inspectors and which had been communicated to the deceased.

If the engineer of the shifting engine was negligent in pushing cars against those which the deceased was endeavoring to uncouple, it was the negligent act of a fellow servant of the deceased and not of the master.

APPEAL by the defendant, The New York Central and Hudson River Railroad Company, from a judgment of the Supreme Court in favor of the plaintiff, entered in the office of the clerk of the county of Onondaga on the 13th day of April, 1901, upon the verdict of a jury for $7,000, and also from an order entered in said clerk's office on the 16th day of April, 1901, denying the defendant's motion for a new trial made upon the minutes.

Leroy B. Williams, for the appellant.

William S. Jenney, for the respondent.

DAVY, J.:

This action was brought to recover under the statute (Code Civ. Proc. § 1902), damages for the death of plaintiff's intestate, alleged to have occurred through the negligence of the defendant.

The intestate had been in defendant's service as car inspector at its passenger station in Syracuse for seven years prior to the accident, which occurred shortly after noon on July 19, 1899. While he was between two empty passenger cars, either in uncoupling or inspecting them, they were suddenly pushed together and his head was caught and crushed between the cars, from which injury he died the following day.

The negligence of the defendant, it is alleged, was its failure to enjoin upon its car inspectors the use of blue lights and blue flags, for the purpose of protecting its employees while at work in and about trains at passenger stations, instead of pursuing the system adopted and followed by the company at the station in Syracuse, which required a car inspector to protect himself, when making repairs to cars standing in the train-shed, by stationing a man opposite the car which he was under.

It appears that in 1895 the defendant printed rules, one of which required a blue flag by day and a blue light by night, to be placed on the end of a car, engine or train while men were at work under or about them. This rule was not enforced by the car inspectors. Mr. Beatty, the foreman of the car department, testified that in 1893 the company adopted and promulgated verbal rules, to the effect that inspectors should not, in the ordinary inspection, go between cars or under them ; and in case it became necessary to go between or under cars, they should station a man at or near the car to stand on guard for their protection. These rules were communicated by Beatty to the section master, the engineers, firemen, conductors, the entire train crew and the men working around the trains, who were instructed that they must not, under any circumstances, go under or between the cars, whether there was an engine attached or not, without protecting themselves by having a man stand on guard. He repeated these orders frequently to the deceased and other employees of the defendant. This system of inspecting cars had been adopted and pursued at the Syracuse station for a number of years, and had been universally followed by the inspectors. Mr. Beatty said he had occasionally used the blue flag and blue light, but he found them comparatively useless, as they did not afford sufficient protection to the employees; that, under his plan, the inspectors were as safe as it is possible to make them, and more safe than they could be under the blue light and blue flag system. The reasons he gave for placing a man on guard were, that inspectors under cars are out of sight of a blue light or flag, and would not know how long the signal would remain on the car after they began work; a new trainman or an outsider might take the signal down; the light might blow out or the flag be removed; a car being run in on the track might go too far owing to a failure of the brakes to respond promptly; an engine backing up to connect with the train might fail to stop in time; a train entering a station might be going too fast to stop; a misplaced switch might throw a train or car into the cars that were being inspected or repaired. Under these circumstances, a man on guard, while he might not be able to prevent a collision of the cars, could warn the repairmen and have them out from under the cars in time to avoid any accident, and he could also give signals to the approaching engine or train to stop. It is evident that Mr. Beatty's long experience in conducting inspection and repairs entitles his testimony to great weight, especially when it appears that, during his long term of office at the Syracuse station, he never knew of a train being moved when workmen were under it, when the instructions as to protecting workmen were complied with, and that the accident to the deceased was the first accident received by any of his inspectors during the ten years that he had been in charge of this station, where from fifty to sixty passenger trains are inspected daily.

It appears that shortly before the accident, train No. 10 came in from the north on the Rome, Watertown and Ogdensburg track which joins the northerly tracks known as Nos. 7 and 6 in the New York Central station by a "Y" and a switch. The time of the arrival was about twelve o'clock noon. The engine on No. 10 went west on track 6 to the engine house, leaving six or seven cars composing train No. 10 standing on track 6. When train No. 4 came in, it stopped on track 6 just west of the switch, and its engine also went west on track 6 to the engine house.

The deceased was between the two easterly cars of train No. 4, when the shifting engine backed train No. 10 against it, and the deceased was caught between the two cars. No one saw just how the accident occurred. Hugh Crocker, a car cleaner at the New York Central station in Syracuse, was working inside of a car at the time, and was the last man to converse with the deceased before he went between the cars. He says that he first saw the deceased at the end of the smoker, which was the first passenger car east of the baggage car on train 4, and at that time Crocker was on the platform and the deceased was on the ground. Crocker asked him to come into the coach, and he said no, he would go down and uncouple the cars and help Sweeney, who was the conductor of the shifting engine, and who was handling these cars at the time of the accident. Crocker says that the deceased laid his hammer on the platform when he went between the cars.

A witness by the name of Peck, who was a trainman on the Auburn road, and who was standing beside his train on the south track opposite the scene of the accident, saw the deceased come down from the platform of one of the cars just before the accident and go between the cars. Immediately after the acccident, it was discovered that the safety chains were uncoupled and the air cock was turned off, and there is no evidence that this was done by any of the other employees.

The inference to be drawn from all the testimony and the surrounding circumstances is, that the deceased went between the cars for the purpose of uncoupling them. This fact seems to be so clearly established that no construction of the facts as drawn from the evidence would warrant a different conclusion.

There was no excuse for the conduct of the deceased in exposing himself to danger. The notice to him not to go between or under the cars under any circumstances, unless a man was stationed by the side of the car, and the continuance of the deceased in the service of the company, with the knowledge of such a rule, made its terms a part of the contract of employment, so that it was a breach of duty on his part to go between the cars, either to inspect or to uncouple them.

There were no defects in the brakes or about the cars, and there was no occasion for him, as inspector, to go between them. The rule is well settled that where an employce, at the time of receiving an injury, is in the performance of duties outside of his regular employment, he will be held to have assumed the risk incident to those duties and cannot recover. (*LaCroy* v. *N. Y., L. E. & W. R. R. Co.*, 132 N. Y. 570; *Sutherland* v. *Troy & Boston Railroad Co.*, 125 id. 737.)

It is an elementary principle of law that, between master and servant, the servant who undertakes the performance of hazardous duties assumes the ordinary risks incident to the business.

It is undoubtedly the duty of the employer to provide the employees with a safe working place and with safe machinery and appliances. The employer is not bound, however, to exercise the highest degree of skill and care in discharging this duty, but is only required to exercise ordinary care and skill. This duty is one which the law imposes upon the master, and it is one which cannot be delegated so as to relieve him from responsibility. The agent to whom it is intrusted, whatever his rank may be, acts as the master in discharging it. There are likewise duties resting upon the employee as well as upon the employer. The law imposes obligations upon one as well as upon the other. One of the obligations imposed upon the employee is that he shall assume the risks and dangers which are known to him, incident to the employment, or which, by the exercise of reasonable care, he might have known. No employee is obliged to remain in the service of a railroad company when he knows that the service is dangerous, but if he does remain, he assumes all the risks arising from the known danger.

There is another familiar rule, and that is that when an employee enters into or remains in the service of a railroad company, having knowledge of its rules and regulations, he must be held as undertaking to acquiesce therein, and if he is afterwards injured by reason of his violation of such rules and regulations he cannot claim damages, because they were unreasonable. (*LaCroy* v. *N. Y., L. E. & W. R. R. Co.* *supra*; *Byrnes* v. *N. Y., L. E. & W. R. R. Co.*, 113 N. Y. 251.)

The deceased, when he entered the employment of the defendant, was informed of the rules which he and other car inspectors were to follow. At the time of the accident he had been in the employ of the company as car inspector and had worked under these rules for a number of years; he had witnessed the mode of switching and coupling cars at the station almost daily, and knew the risks incident to that kind of business. He knew that it was dangerous to go between the cars for any purpose, either to inspect or to couple them, for the reason that cars were being moved continuously from one track to another, and pushed against each other; the danger was as apparent to him as it was to the defendant, and to every ordinary workman about the station. The danger was not of such a character as to require a skilled mechanic or an expert to detect it.

If the engineer was negligent in pushing the engine against the cars that the deceased was between, it was the negligent act of a fellow-servant of the deceased, and not of the master. (*Berrigan* v. *N. Y., L. E. & W. R. R. Co.*, 131 N. Y. 582.)

It was held in *Haskin* v. *N. Y. Central & H. R. R. R. Co.* (65 Barb. 134) that where one enters into the employ of a railroad company, with full knowledge that no provision has been made for protecting its servants against injury from moving trains or engines, he has no claim to recover damages if he sustains an injury.

Railroad companies must be permitted, in order to protect passengers and employees, to make such reasonable rules as they think best. In this case the defendant had made and promulgated rules for the protection of the car inspectors at the Syracuse station, and these rules at the time of the accident were actually in force which rendered any other rules unnecessary. (*Corcoran* v. *Del., Lack. & W. R. R. Co.*, 126 N. Y. 673; *Kudik* v. *Lehigh Valley R. R. Co.*, 78 Hun, 492; *Davis* v. *S. I. R. T. R. Co.*, 1 App. Div. 178.)

The evidence shows that the cars and couplings where the deceased was injured were not out of repair, and that there was no occasion for his going between them. He well knew that his duty to the defendant and a proper regard for his own safety required him to obey the rules. Had he obeyed them, or exercised that reasonable care and caution which the situation demanded, he would have avoided the accident. Had he exercised the same degree of care that is demanded of a traveler upon the highway in approaching a railroad crossing he would not have been injured. If he had looked he would have seen Sweeney, the conductor, who was only fifteen feet from him, and he would also have seen the train backing down. (*Albert* v. *N. Y. Central & H. R. R. R. Co.*, 80 Hun, 152.)

It seems to us that the evidence fails to establish negligence on the part of the defendant, but the contributory negligence of the deceased was clearly established as a matter of law, and the judgment and order appealed from should be reversed and a new trial granted, with costs to the appellant to abide the event.

Judgment and order reversed and a new trial ordered, with costs to the appellant to abide event.

McLennan, Spring, Williams and Hiscock, JJ., concurred.

Judgment and order reversed upon questions of law only, the facts having been examined and no error found therein, and new trial ordered, with costs to the appellant to abide the event.

Antonio Di Pietro, as Administrator, etc., of Domenico Di Pietro, Deceased, Respondent, *v.* The Empire Portland Cement Company, Appellant.

Negligence — injury to an employee who, outside of his duty, volunteers to assist other employees and goes upon a scaffold near a cogwheel in plain sight and is crushed thereby.

In an action brought to recover damages resulting from the death of the plaintiff's intestate, it appeared that, while two workmen in the defendant's cement mill were engaged in removing belts from a broken shaft, the intestate, who was employed in another department of the mill where his duties were not at all dangerous, volunteered to assist them. Thirteen feet above the floor of the mill was a scaffolding, consisting of two planks, one ten inches wide and the other twelve inches wide, the twelve-inch plank being placed on top. These planks extended close to some shafting and some unguarded cogwheels. This scaffold was not designed for employees to stand upon while removing the belts for which purpose the defendant had provided ladders. During the progress of the work the intestate got upon the scaffold and remained there notwithstanding the fact that the room was light enough to enable him to see the proximity of the shafting and cogwheels and that he was notified by his companions that the scaffolding was a dangerous place. After the work of removing the belts was completed it was discovered that the intestate had been crushed to death beneath the cogwheels. No one saw just how the accident occurred or what was the cause thereof.

Held, that the danger of working upon the scaffold while the machinery was in motion was obvious to the intestate and that he assumed the risk incident thereto, and that a judgment entered upon a verdict in favor of the plaintiff should be reversed.

Appeal by the defendant, The Empire Portland Cement Company, from a judgment of the Supreme Court in favor of the plaintiff, entered in the office of the clerk of the county of Onondaga on the 26th day of April, 1901, upon the verdict of a jury for $1,500, and also from an order entered in said clerk's office on the 24th day of April, 1901, denying the defendant's motion for a new trial made upon the minutes.

James Devine, for the appellant.

B. J. Shove and *Lamont Stilwell,* for the respondent.

DAVY, J.:

Plaintiff's intestate, a married man, about thirty years of age, was killed at defendant's mill in the village of Warners, Onondaga county, N. Y., about three o'clock in the afternoon of December 23, 1899, by falling upon unguarded cogwheels, into which he was drawn and killed. The question was whether the accident was the result of negligence on the part of the defendant. The jury found that it was, and the inquiry here is, whether the proofs in the case sustain the finding.

The plaintiff's contention is that the accident was the result of negligence on the part of the defendant in not erecting and maintaining a proper scaffolding for the deceased to work upon. The scaffolding, which was thirteen and a half feet above the floor, consisted of two planks, the one ten and the other twelve inches wide. The wider plank rested on top of the other. These planks extended along next to the machinery and rested on cleats made of inch boards about twelve inches wide, and were not nailed or fastened to the cleats. It was claimed by some of the plaintiff's witnesses that they were loose and wobbled.

During the afternoon of December twenty-third a shaft broke in the mill, and the assistant superintendent, who had charge of the men and machinery, instructed Flynn and James Sandy, who were employees of the defendant, to run off the belts in what was called the Ball mills room and to hang them up. Sandy took a stick, and while in the act of throwing them off, the deceased, who had been in the employ of the defendant for two years as a common laborer and who was at that time operating the hopper in the kiln room on the floor above, came down and tendered his services, but Sandy informed him that he could throw them off alone and requested him to get a piece of rope to tie them up. When the deceased returned with the rope Sandy told him that he did not need it; that he had found some lacings and would use them in tieing up the belts. At this time, the deceased went upon the plank or scaffolding next to belt No. 2 and was passing by the flywheel, when Sandy, who stood upon the ladder, called to him to get off the plank, that it was a dangerous place, but he shrugged his shoulders and said, " I don't believe." He was also told by his companion, Antonio Di Pietro, not to go upon the scaffolding, as it was dangerous, but he remained there, notwithstanding this warning. When the belts were adjusted Sandy and Di Pietro started to go down stairs, and after they had gone a short distance Di Pietro looked back and saw the deceased was between the cogwheels. It appears that this scaffolding was constructed at a time when some repairs were made to the machinery and a shaft was put in the mill, and it had remained there ever since. It was intended to be used only in repairing the machinery. The defendant had furnished three ladders for the employees to use in oiling the machinery and removing the belts from the pulleys and tieing them up, so there was no occasion for using the scaffolding for doing the work referred to.

The case was tried upon the theory that if the scaffolding had been properly built this accident would not have happened. It must be remembered that the scaffolding was not constructed for the employees to stand upon in removing the belts from the pulleys, or to use for any purpose while the machinery was in motion.

The accident occurred in the daytime, the room was also lighted by electricity, and while there was some dust, it was not enough to prevent the deceased from seeing the movements of the machinery. The shafting and cogwheels were so close to the platform upon which the deceased stood that he could plainly see it was a dangerous place. He had been assigned by the master to another department where his duties were not in any sense dangerous, and had he remained there he would not have been killed. It was only when he volunteered to do work more hazardous and not assigned to him that the accident occurred. When he went upon this platform, the danger of the situation was as obvious to him as it was to the other employees, and after he was notified of the danger he was either negligent or indifferent as to the consequences.

In Shearman & Redfield on Negligence (5th ed.), section 207, the authors say: "The servant cannot recover for an injury, which he would not have suffered if he had not voluntarily left his post of duty to take a position of greater danger, even though his act may be well-meant and his object to continue serving his master."

In *McGovern* v. *C. V. R. R. Co.* (123 N. Y. 287) the court says: "If the servant puts himself in the way of dangerous machinery, with knowledge of its character, or places himself in the way of bodies moving in their accustomed orbit with irresistible force, and is thereby injured, it will generally be regarded as the result of his own carelessness."

In *Maltbie* v. *Belden* (167 N. Y. 312) the court held that "A servant assumes not only the risks incident to his employment, but all dangers which are obvious and apparent, and so, if he voluntarily enters into, or continues in the service, having knowledge, or the means of knowing, the dangers involved, he is deemed to assume the risks and to waive any claim for damages against the master in case of personal injury." (*Crown* v. *Orr*, 140 N. Y. 452.)

It is also claimed that the defendant was negligent in not placing guards around the machinery. The deceased knew from observation that there were no guards; he also knew the dangers to be apprehended from the movements of the machinery, and, having knowledge of these facts, he assumed the risks. (*Knisley* v. *Pratt*, 148 N. Y. 372.)

The immediate cause of the death of the intestate was his being crushed between the cogwheels. No one saw just how the accident occurred. Whether the platform wobbled or he stubbed his toe, or slipped, or became dizzy and fell, or whether his clothes were caught in the machinery, no one knows. That is purely a matter of speculation.

It is a well-settled rule of law that in an action for damages based on negligence of the defendant, the absence of negligence contribut-ing to the injury must be clearly shown by the plaintiff, either by direct proof or by circumstantial evidence.

We are of the opinion that the application of well-settled princi-ples of law to the facts and circumstances in this case requires a reversal of the judgment.

Judgment and order reversed and a new trial granted, with costs to the appellant to abide the event.

McLENNAN, SPRING, WILLIAMS and HISCOCK, JJ., concurred.

Judgment and order reversed upon questions of law only, the facts having been examined and no error found therein, and new trial ordered, with costs to the appellant to abide the event.

MAY A. FLANAGAN, as Administratrix, etc., of PETER FLANAGAN, Deceased, Respondent, v. THE NEW YORK CENTRAL AND HUDSON RIVER RAILROAD COMPANY, as Lessee of the ROME, WATERTOWN AND OGDENSBURG RAILROAD COMPANY, Appellant.

Negligence — injury from a collision at a grade crossing — negligence of a driver, when not imputed to his companion — $5,000 verdict, when not excessive — the credibility of witnesses is for the jury — proof of the speed of a train.

In an action brought to recover damages resulting from the death of the plaintiff's intestate who, while riding in a buggy at the invitation of one Horan, was killed in a collision with one of the defendant's north-bound trains at a grade crossing in the village of Fulton, at about eight o'clock on a dark August evening, while the electric street lights were not burning, it appeared that, as they approached the crossing, the occupants of the buggy could not see a train approaching from the south until they reached a point about thirty feet westerly from the crossing, at which point they could see the engine for a distance of one hundred and fifty-nine feet; that at twenty-five feet from the crossing the engine of an approaching train could be seen for a distance of twelve hundred and seventy-five feet. It appeared that the intestate and his companion looked both ways when they were about twenty-five or thirty feet from the crossing, and that when they again looked south the train was upon them.

There was evidence tending to show that the train was traveling at a speed of twenty-five miles an hour, and it was conceded that the locomotive whistle was not blown and that the automatic signal at the crossing was out of order. The evidence was conflicting as to whether the bell on the engine was rung or not. It further appeared that a large crowd of people had assembled at the crossing and that there was a great deal of noise and commotion there.

Held, that a judgment entered upon a verdict in favor of the plaintiff should be affirmed;

That the questions, whether the defendant was negligent and whether the intestate exercised that degree of care and caution that a prudent man would have exercised under similar circumstances, were properly submitted to the jury;

That the negligence of the intestate's companion, who was driving, could not be imputed to him, but that the mere fact that the intestate had no control over the horse did not relieve him from the duty of looking and listening for himself and doing all that a prudent man should do under similar circumstances;

That, as it appeared that the deceased was forty eight years of age at the time of his death; that he had accumulated $5,000, and was earning from $1,000 to $4,000 a year, and that his family consisted of a wife who had since died and an unmarried daughter, twenty-one years of age, a verdict of $5,000 should not be set aside as excessive;

That the credibility of the plaintiff's witnesses presented a question for the jury and not for the court;

That it was competent to prove the speed of the train by the the testimony of persons of ordinary experience.

McLENNAN and WILLIAMS, JJ., dissented.

APPEAL by the defendant, The New York Central and Hudson River Railroad Company, as lessee of the Rome, Watertown and Ogdensburg Railroad Company, from a judgment of the Supreme Court in favor of the plaintiff, entered in the office of the clerk of the county of Oswego on the 11th day of May, 1901, upon the verdict of a jury for $5,000, and also from an order entered in said clerk's office on the 25th day of April, 1901, denying the defendant's motion for a new trial made upon the minutes.

Henry Purcell, for the appellant.

Thomas Hogan, for the respondent.

DAVY, J.:

This action was brought to recover damages for the alleged negligence of the defendant in causing the death of plaintiff's intestate, who was killed at a grade crossing in the village of Fulton, Oswego County, New York, about eight o'clock in the evening of August 19, 1900.

The original plaintiff was Bridget Flanagan, as administratrix, etc., who was the widow of the deceased, but she having died since the entry of judgment, the present plaintiff, a daughter of the deceased, has been substituted in her place.

The railroad tracks run north and south through Seneca street in said village, and the highway crossing, upon which the deceased was killed, runs east and west.

It appears from the testimony that upon the afternoon of the day that the intestate was killed, which was Sunday, he left his home with one James Horan, with a horse and top buggy, driven by the latter.   They reached Fulton about six o'clock, stopped at a hotel, and remained there until a quarter after eight o'clock that evening.   The road that they took in returning was through Cayuga street, which crosses the tracks of the New York, Ontario and Western railroad at right angles.   As they approached the crossing the view of the deceased and his companion was obstructed by a block of buildings on the southerly side of Cayuga street, so that an approaching train could not be seen until they reached a point about thirty feet westerly from the center of the crossing, where the engine could be seen at about one hundred and fifty-nine feet from the same center, and when at twenty-five feet from the crossing, it could be seen, if they looked, at a distance of twelve hundred and seventy-five feet.

It appears that at the time of the accident the night was dark and the electric lights were not burning on the street; that there was a great deal of commotion at the crossing, and a large crowd of people had assembled at the depot and crossing; that there was noise from the pavements made by horses and wagons, and the Salvation Army band was nearby, playing and singing.   The automatic gong or signal, which rung when trains approached this crossing, was not in working order and did not sound an alarm upon the occasion when this accident occurred.

It also appears from the testimony that the schedule time for making the distance between the two stations was but three minutes, which included starts and stops, and that the train went some four hundred feet after the air brakes were applied.   The engineer testified that a train going five miles an hour could be stopped within one hundred feet.   The baggageman testified that the train stopped so suddenly that it tipped him over.   All of this testimony indicates that the train was running at a high rate of speed.

It is urged on behalf of the defendant that plaintiff should have been nonsuited on account of the intestate's own carelessness, for the reason that the place where he looked both ways was about twenty-five or thirty feet from the tracks, and at that point his view of the approaching train was obstructed by the buildings on the southwest corner of Cayuga street, and that if he had looked again to the south before reaching the tracks, he would have seen the train.

It appears that the intestate and his companion did look both ways as they approached the tracks. They looked first to the south and then to the north, and when they again looked south, the train was upon them.

It cannot be held as a matter of law that it was the duty of the deceased to have been more vigilant in looking to the south. The noise at the crossing may have attracted his attention for a few seconds. The silence of the automatic signal was an implied invitation to the deceased and his companion to cross the tracks. They had a right to consider it as safe to cross as if a gate had been opened or a flagman had signaled them to cross over. It may not have been the defendant's duty to repair the signal, but when defendant discovered that it was not in repair and that it did not warn, those who had occasion to cross the tracks, that a train was approaching, it became defendant's duty to exercise greater care and caution in running its trains over the crossing.

When the surroundings render a crossing dangerous to travelers on the highway on account of obstructions to the view, or the failure of an automatic signal to work, or the removal of a flagman or gatetender, it is the duty of the railroad company to take precautions commensurate to the danger, and it is for the jury to determine whether or not the absence of any particular precaution is negligence. (*Glushing* v. *Sharp*, 96 N. Y. 676.)

The plaintiff contends that this train was run at an unusual and dangerous rate of speed. There is no evidence that the municipal authorities had fixed the speed at which trains might run through the village so that it was a question of fact whether, under the circumstances, the actual rate of speed that the train was running was excessive or dangerous, and that would to some extent depend upon whether there was anything to obstruct the view of those about to cross the tracks, and whether proper safeguards had been adopted by the railroad company to prevent accidents. The employees of the defendant and other witnesses testified that the speed of the train did not exceed eight miles an hour. On the other hand, a number of the plaintiff's witnesses, who were standing at the crossing and at the depot, testified that when the train reached the crossing it was running at twenty or twenty-five miles an hour. There was such a conflict of testimony upon that point that it would have been error for the trial judge to have taken that question from the jury, even if that were the only act of negligence charged against the defendant.

It was conceded upon the trial that when the train approached the crossing neither the steam whistle was blown nor the automatic signal sounded. Signals of some kind are usually necessary when trains are run at a high rate of speed over crossings, especially through cities and villages.

The rights of the public and the railroad company as to the use of street crossings at the point of intersection are mutual and reciprocal, and both the company and those using the highway must exercise reasonable care and caution to avoid a collision. While a railroad train from its force and momentum has the preference in crossing first, yet those in charge of it are required to give reasonable and timely warning so that a person about to cross with a horse and buggy may stop and allow the train to pass.

A number of plaintiff's witnesses, who were standing near the station and the crossing, testified that they observed the train as it approached the crossing, and that the bell on the engine did not ring. Others testified that they did not hear it ring. Some of the defendant's employees swore that the bell was rung and two or three other witnesses who stood near the crossing swore that it was rung; so that upon this point there was a conflict of testimony.

It was held in *Henavie* v. *N. Y. C. & H. R. R. R. Co.* (166 N. Y. 284) that where a witness is shown to have been in a position to hear, and testifies that he observed the engine, but did not hear the bell ring, it furnishes some evidence that the bell was not ringing, and if he is positive that the bell was not rung, it furnishes strong evidence that the bell was not ringing. The court said : " A railroad company which runs a locomotive, rapidly, in the night time, upon a public street in a populous city, crossing other streets at grade, with no gate or flagman to protect the public and without taking any precaution to warn travelers by bell, whistle or otherwise, except by means of its headlight, may properly be found guilty of neglecting its duty to operate its cars with the care and caution required by the circumstances."

The conflict of evidence upon the question of ringing the bell and upon the other disputed questions of fact in the case made them proper questions for the consideration of the jury, in determining whether or not the defendant was negligent, and whether the deceased exercised that degree of care and caution that a prudent man would have exercised under similar circumstances.

The court could not have held as a matter of law that the testimony of plaintiff's witnesses was false; it was for the jury and not the court to determine that question. (*Williams* v. *Del., Lack. & West. R. R. Co.*, 155 N. Y. 158.)

The negligence, if any, of the driver, who was the owner of the horse and carriage, could not be imputed to the deceased, who was not responsible for the acts of the driver, over whom he had no control. The deceased accepted an invitation to ride in the buggy with him, but the mere fact that he had no control over the horse did not relieve him from the duty of looking and listening for himself, and doing all that a careful and prudent man should do under similar circumstances.

The plaintiff's intestate was forty-eight years old at the time of his death. His family consisted of his wife, who was forty-eight years of age, and has since died, and his daughter, twenty-one years of age and unmarried.

We think the damages awarded were not excessive. The plaintiff's intestate had accumulated some $5,000 and he was earning from $1,000 to $4,000 a year. These facts constitute such a reasonable expectation of a greater pecuniary benefit to the next of kin, if the deceased had lived, than the amount recovered that we do not feel justified in reducing the amount of the judgment.

No valid exceptions were taken upon the trial. It was competent to prove the rate of speed at which the train was running by the testimony of persons of ordinary experience. This question was not one that could be answered only by experts. (*Salter* v. *Utica & Black River Railroad Company*, 59 N. Y. 632.)

The judgment and order appealed from should be affirmed, with costs to the respondent.

Judgment and order affirmed, with costs.

SPRING and HISCOCK, JJ., concur; McLENNAN and WILLIAMS, JJ. dissented.

Judgment and order affirmed, with costs.

70
a174 N

· The City Trust, Safe Deposit and Surety Company of Philadelphia, Plaintiff, *v.* The American Brewing Company,
Defendant.

Undisclosed principal — when liable to a surety company against which a judg-
ment has been recovered on a bond accompanying a liquor tax certificate — parol
evidence to show that the principal named in the bond was an agent of the undis-
closed principal — subrogation.

A surety upon a bond accompanying a liquor tax certificate, who becomes such
without knowledge that the principal named in the bond is acting as the agent
of a third person, and who, because of the maintenance of a gambling device
upon the licensed premises, in violation of the conditions of the bond, is
obliged to pay a judgment recovered by the State Commissioner of Excise
against him and the nominal principal for the penalty of the bond, may maintain an action against the undisclosed principal to recover the amount so paid.

In such a case the admission of parol evidence of the existence of the undisclosed principal does not violate the rules of law relative to the admission of
such evidence in actions upon written contracts.

Semble, that if neither the nominal principal nor the surety had paid the judgment recovered by the State Commissioner of Excise, the latter could maintain
an action against the undisclosed principal to recover the amount of the judgment, and that the surety, upon payment of the judgment, would become subrogated to this right.

McLennan and Hiscock, JJ., dissented.

Motion by the plaintiff, The City Trust, Safe Deposit and Surety
Company of Philadelphia, for a new trial upon a case containing
exceptions, ordered to be heard at the Appellate Division in the first
instance, upon the dismissal of the complaint by direction of the
court at the Monroe Trial Term.

Charles Van Voorhis, for the plaintiff

George F. Yeoman, for the defendant.

Davy, J. :

At the Monroe Trial Term on the 27th day of November, 1901,
and before any evidence was given, the defendant moved to dismiss
the complaint on the ground that it did not state facts sufficient to
constitute a cause of action. The motion was granted and the plaintiff excepted. The exception so taken was ordered to be heard by

the Appellate Division in the first instance and that judgment be suspended in the meantime.

The only question to be considered upon this motion is, does the complaint state a cause of action.

The complaint alleges, in substance, that on or about the 11th day of November, 1897, a liquor tax certificate was duly issued to one John M. Kurtz, authorizing him to engage in the traffic of liquor at No. 153 Main street, East, in the city of Rochester, N. Y.; that in order to obtain said license a bond was given to the People of the State of New York in the penal sum of $1,000, which was signed by John M. Kurtz, as principal, and the City Trust, Safe Deposit and Surety Company of Philadelphia, the plaintiff herein, as surety; that the conditions of this bond were, that the said Kurtz would not suffer or permit any gambling upon the said licensed premises; that he would not permit or suffer said premises to become disorderly, and that he would not violate any of the provisions of the Liquor Tax Law (Laws of 1896, chap. 112, as amd.). It further alleges that on or about the 12th day of July, 1898, the Commissioner of Excise of the State of New York commenced an action against said Kurtz and this plaintiff to recover the penal sum mentioned in said bond, on the ground that there had been a breach of its conditions by said Kurtz in maintaining and suffering to be maintained upon said licensed premises a nickle-in-the-slot machine, which was a gambling device upon which people did play for money by chance; that a judgment was obtained in that action against said Kurtz as principal and the plaintiff as surety, and an appeal was taken from that judgment to the Appellate Division and to the Court of Appeals, and the judgment was affirmed in both courts, which judgment was subsequently paid by said plaintiff as surety upon the bond.

The complaint also alleges that the defendant was the undisclosed principal on said bond, and was the owner of the liquor tax certificate; that the business in said saloon was conducted for the benefit of the defendant, and that defendant owned the lease of the store furnished the stock of goods therein, including fixtures; that it paid all expenses of running said place; that said Kurtz was employed by the defendant as manager and paid twelve dollars a week for his services, and that he had no interest whatever in the said business.

The learned justice before whom the case was moved for trial held that the decision of the court in *Farrar* v. *Lee* (10 App. Div. 130) is decisive and controlling in the case at bar. It appears that that action was brought upon a bond against an undisclosed principal, and the court held that as the contract was in writing and under seal, and was not executed in the name of the undisclosed principal, and as it did not appear on the face of the instrument that the same was made in his behalf, that no recovery could be had against him in an action founded upon the bond.

This action is brought, not upon the bond, but against the defendant, an undisclosed principal, to recover the money which the plaintiff, as surety, was compelled to pay for the defendant's benefit. Although the principal was concealed, the contract, however, was made by its agent, upon its authority and for its benefit and advantage. It is a rule of law that an undisclosed principal, when subsequently discovered, may, at the election of the other party, if exercised within a reasonable time, be held liable upon all contracts made in his behalf by his duly authorized agent, although the credit was originally given to the agent under a misapprehension as to his true character.

In this action the complaint alleges that when the plaintiff executed the bond at the request of Kurtz, it was not aware of the fact that Kurtz was acting as agent for the defendant. The fact that Kurtz executed the bond as principal does not preclude the plaintiff from maintaining this action, upon parol proof that the contract, in fact, was the contract of the defendant; that the act of Kurtz was the act of the defendant, and that, therefore, the defendant was liable for the breach of the contract.

In *Briggs* v. *Partridge* (64 N. Y. 362), in discussing the question under consideration, Judge ANDREWS said: "The doctrine that must now be deemed to be the settled law of this court, and which is supported by high authority elsewhere, that a principal may be charged upon a written parol executory contract, entered into by an agent in his own name, within his authority, although the name of the principal does not appear in the instrument, and was not disclosed, and the party dealing with the agent supposed that he was acting for himself, and this doctrine obtains as well in respect to contracts which are required to be in writing as to those where a writing is not essential to their validity." (*Brady* v. *Nally*, 151 N. Y. 262; *Coleman* v. *First National Bank of Elmira*, 53 id. 393; *Meeker* v. *Claghorn*, 44 id. 349; *Jessup* v. *Steurer*, 75 id. 613; *Nicoll* v. *Burke*, 78 id. 580; Story Agency [9th ed.], § 270.)

In *Coleman* v. *First National Bank of Elmira* (*supra*) it was held that the rule does not preclude a party who has entered into a written contract with an agent from maintaining an action against the principal, upon parol proof that the contract was made, in fact, for the principal, although the agency was not disclosed by the contract and was not known to such party at the time of making it. (*Briggs* v. *Partridge, supra; Pierson* v. *Atlantic National Bank*, 77 N. Y. 310.)

The rule of evidence which makes a written contract conclusive proof of what the parties have agreed to, and which rejects parol proof to vary or contradict the writing or its legal import, applies only in controversies between the parties to the instrument. (*Folinsbee* v. *Sawyer*, 157 N. Y. 196.)

There is another well-settled principle of law applicable to this case, and that is that where a surety pays the debt of his principal, the surety has a right to be put in the place of the creditor, and to avail himself of every means the creditor had to enforce payment against the principal debtor. This principle of law comes under the rule of subrogation, which is not founded upon contract, but upon principles of equity and justice, and may be enforced where no contract or privity of any kind exists between the parties.

In *Arnold* v. *Green* (116 N. Y. 571) Judge VANN says: "The remedy of subrogation is no longer limited to sureties and *quasi* sureties, but includes so wide a range of subjects that it has been called the 'mode which equity adopts to compel the ultimate payment of a debt by one who in justice, equity and good conscience ought to pay it.'" (*Cole* v. *Malcolm*, 66 N. Y. 363; *Townsend* v. *Whitney*, 75 id. 425; *Jessup* v. *Steurer, supra; Pease* v. *Egan*, 131 N. Y. 262.)

In *Lewis* v. *Palmer* (28 N. Y. 271) the court held that a surety who pays a debt for his principal is entitled to be put in the place of the creditor, and to all the means which the creditor possessed to enforce payment against the principal debtor.

Assuming that in the action upon the bond the execution had

been returned unsatisfied against both the plaintiff and Kurtz, can there be any question but that the excise commissioner, acting for the People, could have maintained an action in equity against the defendant, who was the undisclosed principal, to recover the amount of the judgment? I think not. The defendant had authorized Kurtz, its agent, to make the contract, and it was done for defendant's benefit and with its consent and approval. The defendant received the emoluments of the business, which it could not have carried on without giving the bond.

If the State Excise Commissioner could maintain such an action, then the plaintiff can maintain this action, for the reason that, when plaintiff paid the judgment, it became subrogated to all the rights of the State, and could avail itself of every means that the State had to enforce payment of the judgment.

In the case of *Kane* v. *State ex rel. Woods* (78 Ind. 103), where a party applied to the board of excise commissioners for a license to sell intoxicating liquors, and in order to obtain his license was required to give a bond to the State with sureties in the penal sum of $2,000, conditioned, among other things, that he would pay all judgments that might be recovered against him for any violation of the provisions of the act regulating the sale of liquors, the principal was four times convicted for violating the provisions of said act; judgments were obtained against him, and, having failed to pay them, they were paid by the surety; and it was held that the surety was entitled to be subrogated to all the rights of the State, the judgment creditor. (*Boltz's Estate*, 133 Penn. St. 77; *Matter of Churchill*, 39 Ch. Div. 174; *Richeson* v. *Crawford*, 94 Ill. 165; *Dias* v. *Bouchaud*, 10 Paige, 461.) It will be seen from these cases that no distinction is made between an official bond given to the State and an ordinary bond given to an individual; the surety in either case, upon paying the debt of the principal, has a right to be subrogated to all the rights of the creditor, and may invoke every remedy for its enforcement.

Benham v. *Emery* (46 Hun, 160) was a contract under seal made by the husband in his own name for a building on his wife's land. It appeared that the contractor was ignorant that the husband was acting as the agent of his wife, the undisclosed principal. The court said: "The plaintiff may pass by the written agreement and recover upon an implied promise for the work and labor done and material furnished, as the same was done for the benefit of the defendant, and with her consent and approbation; it is fair that she should pay the plaintiff for his work and labor and the material which he furnished to improve her own property, as the same was done with her consent and she now enjoys the benefit and the advantages derived therefrom." The court, in further discussing this question, said: " As a test that the defendant is liable for the work and labor and materials furnished, suppose the defendant had authorized her husband, as her agent, to borrow in her name and on her account, a sum of money, not authorizing him to execute any written promise in her name for the repayment of the loan, and in pursuance of such authority he had borrowed a sum of money of a third party, who was ignorant that he was acting as agent and executed in his own name a promise under seal to repay the loan himself, and had delivered the money received over to his wife, his principal, can there be any doubt but that she would be liable in an action for the money had and received? The authorities are abundant that the lender could pass by the special agreement made by the agent and sue for the money loaned and advanced, upon an implied promise to repay the money which she had received from the loaner by the hand of her agent." (*Donegan* v. *Moran*, 53 Hun, 21 ; *Higgins* v. *Dellinger*, 22 Mo. 397.)

It would be against public policy to permit the defendant to give a bond in the name of an irresponsible servant, to enable it to carry on the liquor business and to violate the conditions of the bond through its servant in order that it might derive a pecuniary benefit therefrom and then be screened from any liability, on the ground that it did not sign the bond. Fair and honest dealings should be upheld, but courts of justice should not help parties to consummate fraud and deception.

Upon the facts, as alleged in the complaint, we think the action can be maintained, and that the court erred in dismissing the complaint. Plaintiff's exceptions, therefore, should be sustained and the motion for a new trial granted, with costs to the plaintiff to abide the event.

SPRING and WILLIAMS, JJ., concurred; MCLENNAN and HISCOCK, JJ., dissented.

McLENNAN, J. (dissenting):

It seems to me that the law of principal and agent has no application to this case. The conditions of the bond related solely to the personal acts and conduct of Kurtz. By its terms he was not liable for the acts of any one else, unless permitted or authorized by him upon the premises covered by the liquor tax certificate. Neither was any one else liable for his acts. It was purely a personal obligation on the part of Kurtz. Whether the bond should be violated or not, and thus the surety become liable, was wholly with Kurtz and for him to determine. The act of the brewing company, or of any one else, could not create an obligation under the bond. It seems to me that it might as well be said that if an agent gave a bond to keep the peace, and violated it while acting as agent, the principal would be liable on such peace bond, or for the amount the surety had to pay.

It seems to me clear that upon principle as well as upon authority the case was rightly disposed of by the court below. I, therefore, think the motion for a new trial should be denied, and judgment ordered for the defendant.

HISCOCK, J., concurred.

Plaintiff's exceptions sustained and motion for new trial granted, with costs to the plaintiff to abide the event.

RUDOLF DOLGE, Plaintiff, v. ALFRED DOLGE, Defendant.

In the Matter of the Claims of ADRIAN M. HEKKING and Others, Appellants, v. ALBERT M. MILLS, as Receiver, etc., of ALFRED DOLGE & SON, Respondent.

Wages of employees — what plan for pension, insurance and endowment does not create claims enforcible against a receiver of a partnership — what is necessary to establish a preference of wages under the Labor Law — "winding up of the business" defined.

A firm, desiring to share a portion of the profits of the business with its employees, adopted a plan known as the "Earnings Division Accounts," which embraced pension, insurance and endowment features. The rules and regulations governing the respective features were embodied in laws called respectively the Pension Law, Insurance Law and Law of Endowment. Each of these laws contained the following provision: "It is distinctly understood that all and every of the provisions of this law are voluntary on behalf of said house of Alfred Dolge, and that this law does not, nor does any of the provisions herein contained, confer any legal right or create any legal right in favor of any employee of said house mentioned herein, or of any person or persons whomsoever, nor any legal liability on behalf of said house of Alfred Dolge, or of said Alfred Dolge, either in law or in equity." The preamble to the laws stated that it was entirely discretionary with the firm to say how much of the net earnings of the business should be set aside for distribution among the employees.

Upon entering the service each employee received a pass book containing a copy of the preamble and the various laws. Each year the pass book was called in and the amount to which the employee was entitled entered therein.

After the plan had been in existence for some time the firm was dissolved and a permanent receiver was appointed. No fund had been set apart out of the assets of the business for the payment of the amounts entered in the pass books.

Held, that the employees did not have a valid claim against the receiver for the amounts credited to them in the pass books;

That the crediting of such amounts in the pass books did not create a valid gift thereof, and that the facts did not sustain the contention that they represented wages;

That, assuming that such amounts did represent wages which the employees had contributed to the business, the claims of the employees for such amounts would not be entitled to a preference under section 8 of the Labor Law (Laws of 1897, chap. 415), providing that, upon the appointment of a receiver of a partnership, the wages of the employees of the partnership shall be preferred to every other debt or claim, as the wages so contributed lost their character as such by the contribution and became mere claims for money loaned;

That the words "winding up of the business," used in the Insurance and Endowment Laws, referred to a voluntary winding up of the business.

APPEAL by the claimants, Adrian M. Hekking and others, from an order of the Supreme Court, made at the Onondaga Special Term and entered in the office of the clerk of the county of Herkimer on the 2d day of May, 1901, sustaining the exceptions filed by the receiver to the report of a referee, and disallowing the claims of the appellants.

John F. Wilson, for the appellants.

William P. Quin, for the respondent.

DAVY, J.:

This action was commenced to dissolve the copartnership between plaintiff and defendant, who were engaged in the manufacture of felt, under the firm name of Alfred Dolge & Son.

A judgment was entered on the 2d day of May, 1898, dissolving the copartnership and appointing a permanent receiver, with the usual powers and duties as such. By the provisions of said judgment a referee was appointed to receive claims against the funds of the copartnership, to take proofs concerning the same, to ascertain as to the validity and amounts of such claims and to report thereon with his proceedings to the court.

There were a number of claims presented by the employees of the firm, some of whom had worked for Alfred Dolge prior to the formation of said firm. A preference was sought upon the ground that the claims represented wages for labor performed. The receiver disputed all of these claims and the claimants' right to a preference.

It was agreed between the attorneys for the claimants and the receiver that the claims of the appellants should be reported upon by the referee, and the decision of the court obtained thereon, so that the rules applicable to similar claims might be ascertained and determined. The referee reported that the appellants were unpreferred creditors under the so-called "Laws of the House of Dolge" for the following amounts : Adrian M. Hekking, insurance, $244.96 ; endowment, $102.77 ; T. Jefferson Abrams, endowment, $106.20 ; Adelbert House, endowment, $518.01. The total claims presented by the appellants and other employees amounted to the following sums : Pension, $10,000 ; insurance, $3,600 ; endowment, $5,500.

The Special Term refused to confirm the report of the referee as to there being any indebtedness, and decided that the claimants were not creditors of the firm upon the ground that they did not have enforcible claims against Alfred Dolge or the said copartnership firm. From that decision and the order of the court entered thereon the claimants appealed to this court.

The principal questions presented upon this appeal arise under the title printed on the first page of the employees' pass book as follows : "System of Distribution of Earnings for the Employees of Alfred Dolge."

In the year 1874, Alfred Dolge, then being engaged in the manufacture of felt, established a scheme known as the "Earnings Division Accounts," and as a part of this scheme he made certain rules and regulations as to what employees should be entitled to receive and share in the benefits of the said earnings division account. In 1886 he introduced and made a part of the earnings division account, a feature known as "Life Insurance and Deposit Benefits." In 1890 the feature of "Endowment Benefits" was introduced and made a part of the earnings division account. Each pass book contained a "Preamble," which was followed by the "Pension Law," "Insurance Law" and "Law of Endowment."

Upon placing the name of the employee upon the roll of the earnings division account he was given a pass book, in which was recorded the first payment and the year he entered the service; this book contained the printed rules and regulations for the distribution of earnings, and the provisions were classified under headings called the "Pension Law," "Insurance Law" and "Law of Endowment;" there was also entered on this book the amount that was placed to his credit on the several accounts, and each year the pass book was called in and the separate amounts were added. After the amounts were entered the pass book was returned to the employee.

A provision contained in each one of the so-called pension, insurance and endowment laws reads as follows: "It is distinctly understood that all and every of the provisions of this law are voluntary on behalf of said house of Alfred Dolge, and that this law does not, nor does any of the provisions herein contained confer any legal right or create any legal right in favor of any employee of said house mentioned herein, or of any person or persons whomsoever, nor any legal liability on behalf of said house of Alfred Dolge, or of said Alfred Dolge, either in law or in equity."

The appellants contend that while the offers were voluntary on the part of Dolge, and in and of themselves have no binding force, yet when accepted, acted upon and complied with by the employees, they become binding upon Dolge, and when the promised credits were actually given upon the pass books the employees had a vested right in the sum or sums so created, which should be enforced in these proceedings.

We are of the opinion that the contention of the appellants is not well founded. This plan, as adopted by Dolge, did not constitute a binding agreement between him and his employees. It was simply a benevolent plan proposed by him, and it was solely within his power and discretion to carry it out or not. It was expressly agreed between him and his employees that the agreement did not confer any legal right in favor of any employee or of any person or persons whomsoever, or any legal liability on the part of said house of Dolge, either in law or in equity.

These transactions could not be upheld as a gift to the employees. Merely giving credit upon their pass books for certain amounts did not constitute a valid gift. To sustain a gift of this character there must have been on the part of Dolge an intent to give and an actual payment and complete delivery of the money to or for the employees, wholly divesting Dolge of the control of it.

At the time of the assignment, if a fund had been set apart and the amounts entered in the pass books, so that the claimants could have drawn the sums placed to their credit, then the claims of the appellants might be upheld, but as there was no fund set apart, they can have no legal claim to any of the assets of the firm in the hands of the receiver.

In *McNevin* v. *Solvay Process Company* (32 App. Div. 610; affd. in the Court of Appeals, 167 N. Y. 530) it was held that an employee could not demand payment of the sum credited on his account, under a somewhat similar plan ; that it was for the trustees to determine when payments would be made and their decision was final. It was also held that the amount credited was an incomplete gift which was unexecuted and could not be enforced.

It is urged by the learned counsel for the appellants that the sums credited to the employees on the pass books were wages, but the facts do not sustain this contention. The preamble to the so-called laws states that the object of the plan was to have the male employees receive a share of the net earnings of the business over and above their wages, and to secure a just distribution of such net earnings among its employees, and that it was entirely discretionary with the house of Dolge to decide how much of the net earnings of the business should be set aside for the distribution account. It will be seen from the substance and the language of the preamble that the scheme of crediting the employees on the pass books was entirely distinct from wages, which were paid weekly to the employees.

The question here is, whether these claims were entitled to a preference under the provisions of the statute. The statute under which the employees of the firm might claim preference is section 8, chapter 415, Laws of 1897, known as the Labor Law, which reads as follows: " Upon the appointment of a receiver of a partnership, or of a corporation organized under the laws of this state, and doing business therein, other than a moneyed corporation, the wages of the employes of such partnership or corporation shall be preferred to every other debt or claim." This is purely a statutory preference, which neither Dolge nor the firm could enlarge by any agreement. Even if the agreement could be so construed that the employees contributed to the business the sums actually due them for wages, by so doing they would waive their statutory right to the preference. The amounts contributed would then lose their character as wages and would become mere claims for money loaned.

In *Matter of Stryker* (158 N. Y. 528) Judge O'BRIEN, in discussing the provisions of this statute, says: " The most important word in the statute is the word ' wages.' It was wages that the legislature intended to prefer in the distribution of the assets of the insolvent corporation, not salaries, nor earnings, nor compensation." He also says (p. 529): " In order to give the preference provided by the statute, the claim must be for wages in the ordinary sense of that term."

It is also urged by the appellants that the winding up of the business by the receiver and assignee is within the meaning of the words "winding up of the business," as used in section 6 of the insurance law and section 10 of the endowment law. These provisions evidently referred to liquidation by Dolge or the firm, in case they were solvent and were winding up the business, but even so it was entirely discretionary with them whether or not they should pay any of the claims.

It follows, therefore, that the appellants and those having similar claims have no legal right to any of the copartnership funds that passed into the hands of the receiver.

The order appealed from should be affirmed, with ten dollars costs and disbursements to the respondent.

McLENNAN, SPRING, WILLIAMS and HISCOCK, JJ., concurred.

Order affirmed, with ten dollars costs and disbursements.

In the Matter of the Probate of the Last Will and Testament of HERMAN S. BARNES, Deceased.

KITTIE M. LARZELERE, Appellant; J. FRANKLIN BARNES and Others, Respondents.

Will — when revoked by proof of the subsequent execution of another will — the attorney superintending the execution of the subsequent will may testify as to what was done — presumption of destruction animo revocandi — proof required to overcome it.

On an application for the admission of a will to probate, it appeared that, subsequent to the execution of the will offered for probate, the testator executed another will, with all the statutory formalities, expressly revoking all former wills made by him; that the testator took possession of such subsequent will immediately after its execution, and that it could not be found after his death, although a careful search was made therefor. It did not appear what became of the subsequent will after it was delivered to the testator, or that the latter ever made any attempt to revive the former will. No proof was given as to the contents of the subsequent will, except that it in terms revoked all former wills.

Held, that the former will was not entitled to probate.

An attorney who superintended the execution of the subsequent will, and who, with the assent and approval of the testator at that time, read aloud the revocation and attestation clauses of the will, is not incompetent, under section 885 of the Code of Civil Procedure, to testify as to what was said and done at the time the will was executed.

In such a case the failure to find the subsequent will after the testator's death raises a strong presumption that it was destroyed by the testator *animo revocandi*, and in a proceeding for the probate of such will, as a lost or destroyed will, the burden of overcoming such presumption rests upon the petitioner. It is not sufficient for the petitioner to show that some one whose interest was adverse to the will had an opportunity to destroy it, but he must go further and show by facts and circumstances that the will was actually lost or destroyed.

APPEAL by the proponent, Kittie M. Larzelere, from a decree of the Surrogate's Court of the county of Yates, entered in said Surrogate's Court on the 28th day of July, 1901, refusing to admit to probate an instrument purporting to be the last will and testament of Herman S. Barnes, deceased.

Calvin J. Huson, for the appellant.

Thomas Carmody, for the respondents.

DAVY, J.:

On the 2d day of January, 1901, the appellant presented her petition to the Surrogate's Court of Yates county, praying that the last will and testament of Herman S. Barnes, deceased, bearing date June 17, 1897, be admitted to probate, and a citation was duly issued thereon to all parties interested in said estate. On the return of said citation, J. Franklin Barnes, a son of the deceased, filed an answer, denying that the paper so presented for probate was the last will and testament of said deceased, and alleging that subsequent to the execution thereof, and on or about the 30th day of November, 1900, the deceased made another will, revoking the former will, and that the last will had been lost or destroyed since the death of the testator. Subsequently said J. Franklin Barnes presented a petition for the probate of the will alleged to have been executed by deceased on the said 30th day of November, 1900, as a lost will, to which the appellant interposed an answer, putting in issue all the material allegations of the petition. After hearing the proofs offered by the respective parties, the acting surrogate found, as conclusions of law based upon the findings of fact, that upon the execution of the will dated November 30, 1900, the deceased thereby revoked the former will of June 17, 1897, and that said last-mentioned will had no legal existence. He also found that the will dated November 30, 1900, was lost or destroyed ; that by the terms of said will the testator expressly revoked all former wills by him made ; that the contents of said will were not established by sufficient evidence, and, therefore, it could not be admitted to probate ; and that the said decedent, since the loss or destruction of said will of November 30, 1900, did not execute, re-establish or republish said will of June 17, 1897; therefore, neither of said wills was entitled to probate.

Under the statute a lost or destroyed will can be admitted to probate in the Surrogate's Court only in a case where a judgment establishing the will could be rendered by the Supreme Court. (Code Civ. Proc. § 2621.) The statutory enactment which provides for the proof of a lost or destroyed will in the Supreme Court states that " The plaintiff is not entitled to a judgment establishing a lost or destroyed will, as prescribed in this article, unless the will was in existence at the time of the testator's death, or was fraudulently destroyed in his lifetime; and its provisions are clearly and distinctly proved by at least two credible witnesses, a correct copy or draft being equivalent to one witness." (Code Civ. Proc. § 1865.) It will be seen from this provision of the statute that the petitioner was obliged to prove either that the will was in existence at the time of the testator's death, or that it had been fraudulently destroyed in his lifetime. It appears from the testimony that the testator took possession of the last will immediately after its execution, and it does not appear what he afterwards did with it, and no evidence was given that it was in existence at the time of the testator's death or that it was fraudulently destroyed during his lifetime. It appears that a careful and thorough search was made among the private papers and effects of the deceased, and the will could not be found.

It was held in *Collyer* v. *Collyer* (110 N. Y. 486) that where a will previously executed cannot be found after the death of the testator, there is a strong presumption that it was destroyed by the testator *animo revocandi*. (*Matter of Kennedy*, 167 N. Y. 163.)

The burden of overcoming this presumption rested with the petitioner. It was not sufficient to show that some one of the relatives had an opportunity to destroy it. The petitioner should have gone further and shown by facts and circumstances that the will was actually lost or destroyed. The fact that the testator's daughter, who was with him during his last illness, and whose interest was adverse to the will, refused to allow her brother to examine the papers in the testator's bureau drawer a short time before his death is a suspicious circumstance; it is not sufficient evidence, however, of the existence of the will at the time of testator's death, or of a fraudulent destruction of it during his lifetime.

The learned counsel for the appellant contends that the acting surrogate erred in holding that the last will was properly executed. It appears from the evidence that the testator read the will before it was executed, and that the attorney who drew it read over to the testator and the subscribing witnesses, all of whom were present in the attorney's office at the time of its execution, from the place in the will where the name of the executor is mentioned down to and including the clauses, "revoking any and all former wills by me at any time made," and the attestation clause; that after he had finished reading these clauses the deceased signed the will, and then the attorney said to him, " do you say this is your last will and testament, and do you request these gentlemen to sign it as witnesses," and he said "yes," and they sat down to the table one by one and signed it. These facts are corroborated by the attesting witnesses.

It is urged by the appellant that this is not a compliance with the statute that prescribes the formalities to be observed in the revoca_ tion of wills. The statute provides: "No will in writing except in the cases herein after mentioned, nor any part thereof, shall be revoked, or altered, otherwise than by some other will in writing, or some other writing of the testator, declaring such revocation or alteration, and executed with the same formalities with which the will itself was required by law to be executed; or unless such will be burnt, torn, cancelled, obliterated or destroyed, with the intent and for the purpose of revoking the same, by the testator himself, or by another person in his presence, by his direction and consent; and when so done by another person, the direction and consent of the testator, and the fact of such injury or destruction, shall be proved by at least two witnesses." (3 Birdseye R. S. [3d ed.] 4020, § 10.)

Section 21 of the statute referred to provides that " If, after the making of any will, the testator shall duly make and execute a second will, the destruction, cancelling or revocation of such second will shall not revive the first will, unless it appear by the terms of such revocation that it was his intention to revive and give effect to his first will, or unless after such destruction, cancelling or revocation, he shall duly republish his first will." (Id. 4022.)

In *Matter of Stickney* (161 N. Y. 42) the court held that a will that has been revoked by a subsequent one, which is destroyed by the testator, is not revived by his declaration that he desires his first will to stand, made to others than the subscribing witnesses.

There is no evidence in this case that the testator either intended or attempted to revive the former will, so we have the uncontradicted proof of the execution of a will by the testator upon the 17th day of June, 1897, also the proof of the making and execution of a subsequent will upon the 30th day of November, 1900, which subsequent will was executed with the prescribed formalities required by law, declaring in express terms in the instrument itself that all former wills made by the testator were revoked. It is urged that even if the subsequent will were executed with all the formalities required by statute, it did not revoke the former will, for the reason that the subsequent will had not been admitted to probate. The fact that the proofs did not authorize the surrogate to admit the subsequent will to probate does not afford any valid reason why the former will should be revived. The first will, when revoked by the subsequent will, had no longer any legal existence.

It was said in *Wallis* v. *Wallis* (114 Mass. 512), that " When a testamentary instrument is lost or destroyed it cannot be admitted to probate without clear and satisfactory proof of its whole contents. * * * If it can be proved that a later will was duly executed, attested and subscribed, and that it contained a clause expressly revoking all former wills, but evidence of the rest of its contents cannot be obtained, it is, nevertheless, a good revocation, and it can be made available only by allowing it to be set up in opposition to the probate of the earlier will." (*Nelson* v. *McGiffert*, 3 Barb. Ch. 158, 164; *Day* v. *Day*, 3 N. J. Eq. 549; *Matter of Forbes' Will*, 24 N. Y. Supp. 841.)

In Page on Wills (§ 270) it is stated that " If the lost will is shown to have contained a clause of express revocation, the first will is not in force, even where it is impossible to prove the contents of the lost will further than such revocation clause."

Underhill on the Law of Wills (Vol. 1, § 266) lays down the rule that where a will, proved to have been executed, is shown to have been lost or to have been destroyed by the testator or some other person, all the contents of the lost will need not be proved, if enough is proved to show that it revoked the former one. If the court is satisfied that the subsequent will was properly executed, the revocation clause may be proved in opposition to an application to probate an earlier will, even though the revocatory writing, which was lost, has never been admitted to probate.

It is urged by the learned counsel for the appellant that the evidence given by the attorney Evarts, pertaining to the execution of the will of November 30, 1900, was incompetent under section 835 of the Code of Civil Procedure, which prohibits the disclosure by an attorney of a communication made by his client to him, or his advice given in the course of his professional employment. His testimony was undoubtedly very material and important in its bearing upon the question as to whether the will was properly executed, and if erroneously admitted, would lead to a reversal of the judgment appealed from. When Evarts read the attestation and revocation clauses of the will in the hearing and presence of the testator and the subscribing witnesses, with the testator's assent and approval, it was an express waiver of secrecy within the meaning of the statute; it would seem that the testator had no intention that the lips of the attorney should be sealed as to what took place at the time the will was executed, or that he should be prevented from testifying in support of the will. (*Hurlburt* v. *Hurlburt*, 128 N. Y. 424; *Rosseau* v. *Bleau*, 131 id. 183.)

In *Matter of Chase* (41 Hun, 204) Justice FOLLETT said : " The draughtsman of a will, though he is an attorney, is not incompetent under section 835, Code Civil Procedure, to testify in support of the will to the instructions received from the testator in respect to the provisions to be incorporated in the will." (*Sheridan* v. *Houghton*, 16 Hun, 628; affd., 84 N. Y. 643; *Hebbard* v. *Haughian*, 70 id. 55.)

The act of the attorney in asking the testator if he acknowledged the instrument to be his last will and testament, and if he desired the parties present to sign it as witnesses, is not an unusual one. It frequently occurs in executing wills that words of request or acknowledgment come from the party who is assisting the testator in the preparation and execution of his will.

It was held in *Matter of Nelson* (141 N. Y. 157) that a request to sign as a witness, made by the person superintending the execution of a will in the hearing of the testator and with his silent permission and approval, is a sufficient compliance with the requirements of the statute. (*Gilbert* v. *Knox*, 52 N. Y. 128; *Peck* v. *Cary*, 27 id. 9.)

The fact that the instrument in question was the will of the testator, was made known to the witnesses by the declaration of Evarts, who acted and spoke for the testator, not only in preparing the will, but seeing that it was properly executed. We are of the opinion that the testimony of Evarts as to what was said and done at the time the will was executed was competent.

It is not necessary to discuss the other exceptions, for the reason that the will was not admitted to probate and, therefore, the appellant was not prejudiced by the rulings of the court.

The decree of the Surrogate's Court should be affirmed, with costs to the respondent, to be paid by the appellant personally.

Decree affirmed.

MCLENNAN, SPRING, WILLIAMS and HISCOCK, JJ., concurred.

Decree of Surrogate's Court affirmed, with costs of this appeal to the respondent, payable by the appellant personally.

CARL MEYER and CASPER TEIPER, Respondents, *v.* WILLIAM R. HAVEN, Appellant, Impleaded with THE NEW YORK CENTRAL AND HUDSON RIVER RAILROAD COMPANY.

Delay by a sub-contractor in placing iron trusses on a wall — damages resulting from the blowing down of the wall by reason thereof — items of damage, interest on delayed payments to the principal contractor, increased cost of working in winter and the longer employment of men and the personal service of the principal contractor — they are not too remote.

In an action to foreclose a mechanic's lien, it appeared that the defendant Haven entered into a contract to construct a number of shops for the New York Central Railroad Company, and that Haven sublet the structural iron work for two of the shops to the plaintiffs. During the progress of the work, a portion of the brick walls of one of the shops erected by Haven was blown down, owing, as found by the court, to the negligent failure of the plaintiffs to place iron trusses on such walls. The amount of damages did not clearly appear upon the trial, and the court, by an interlocutory judgment, directed a reference to take proof of, and ascertain and determine the amount of damages sustained by Haven, through the failure of said plaintiffs to erect said trusses. Upon the reference, the referee ruled that the defendant was entitled to recover a sum stated representing the necessary expenses of repairing and rebuilding the walls that were blown down, the value of the property destroyed, the amount expended in removing the debris of the fallen walls, in cleaning the brick and the cost of the work required to lay the new walls.

It also appeared that by reason of the walls being blown down, the defendant lost the use of a sum of money which the railroad company retained for several months under a clause in the contract, because the work was not completed within the contract period; that he was obliged to perform a large portion of the work during the winter season, at an increased expense; that he was obliged to retain the services of a number of employees, and that he was compelled to devote his own time and personal services to the completion of the work.

The referee found that, under the terms of the interlocutory judgment, he had no legal authority to pass upon the question of the allowance to the defendant of the last-mentioned items of damage and also that such items were uncertain, remote and contingent and could not be allowed.

Held, that the language of the interlocutory judgment was broad enough to cover all damages sustained by the defendant on account of the blowing down of the walls;

That the parties might fairly be supposed, had they considered at the time the contract was entered into the effect of a failure to perform it, that the items of damage disallowed by the referee would have resulted therefrom;

That the items of damage in question were not remote, speculative and uncertain and that the referee erred in refusing to consider them.

APPEAL by the defendant, William R. Haven, from a judgment of the Supreme Court in favor of the plaintiffs, entered in the office of the clerk of the county of Erie on the 15th day of January, 1900, upon the report of a referee, and also from so much of an order of the Supreme Court, made at the Erie Special Term and entered in in the office of the clerk of the county of Erie on the 7th day of February, 1901, as denies the said defendant's motion to set aside and vacate the said judgment.

C. M. Bushnell and *Warren F. Miller*, for the appellant.

Merton S. Gibbs, for the respondents.

DAVY, J.:

The defendant Haven, on the 12th of May, 1892, entered into a contract in writing with the New York Central and Hudson River Railroad Company to construct and complete certain shops at Depew, N. Y. Haven sublet the structural iron work for erecting shops " A " and " B," so called, to the plaintiffs. The brick work on the walls of shop " B " was erected by the defendant to the height of twenty-six feet. The work was then suspended, for the reason that the plaintiffs were not in readiness to erect the iron trusses. This condition of things continued with respect to shop " B " until the fifth or sixth day of the following September, when plaintiffs requested the defendant to complete the walls of shop " B " to the required height of thirty-four feet, as they were ready to place upon the walls of said building the iron trusses. In compliance with this request, Haven commenced and prosecuted the work, so that on Friday, the 9th of September, 1892, he had the walls of shop "B" completed to the height of thirty-four feet. On that day he gave notice to the plaintiffs in writing that the walls of shop "B," had been erected and were ready for the trusses, and that he should hold them responsible for any damages which he might sustain by reason of their failure to furnish the trusses and iron work as agreed upon, and that the walls were in such a condition that they were liable to be blown down or injured by the elements, unless the iron trusses were at once placed thereon.

On the night of the 13th of September, 1892, the walls of shop "B," between the point where the trusses had been placed upon them, and the point where the walls had been raised to the height of thirty-four feet, were blown down.

The defendant Haven procured an order of the Supreme Court discharging the plaintiffs' lien, upon executing a bond in the sum of $17,500, conditioned for the payment of any judgment which might be rendered against the property. The action was brought to foreclose a mechanic's lien for $13,789.10, and interest thereon. An answer was interposed, alleging that, by reason of the failure of the plaintiffs to perform their agreement with the defendant, in omitting to place upon the walls of said buildings the iron trusses in time to prevent the destruction of the walls by wind, the defendant was damaged in a large amount, which is set up as a counterclaim to the plaintiffs' demand. The issues were tried at the Erie County Special Term, and the court found as conclusions of law:

. I. That the plaintiffs are liable to the defendant Haven for the damages suffered by him, because of the failure of plaintiffs to erect the trusses on the walls of shop "B" as soon as the walls were in readiness for said trusses, owing to which failure said walls were left in an exposed and unprotected condition and were blown down by the wind.

II. That the amount of said damages not clearly appearing on the trial, the defendant Haven is entitled to a reference to some referee, to be appointed by the court, to take proof of, ascertain and determine the amount of damages sustained by him through the failure of said plaintiffs to erect said trusses.

III. That the amount of said damages being so ascertained and determined, the same shall be applied upon the said sum of $13,019.04, remaining unpaid from defendant Haven to plaintiffs in reduction thereof.

IV. That plaintiffs are entitled to recover any balance which may appear to be owing and unpaid from said defendant Haven to the plaintiffs herein, after applying said damages as aforesaid.

The interlocutory judgment was entered thereon. An appeal was taken therefrom to this court, which was affirmed. (37 App. Div. 202.) A referee was then appointed, and after taking the testimony, he found that the defendant Haven was entitled to recover from the plaintiffs the sum of $8,660.82, and that the damages, estimated as directed by the interlocutory judgment and the order of reference, were the necessary expenses of repairing and rebuilding the walls that were blown down, the value of the property destroyed, the amount expended in removing the debris of the fallen walls, in cleaning the brick and the cost of the work required to lay the new walls, amounting in the aggregate to the said sum of $8,660.82. He also found as a conclusion of law that, under the interlocutory judgment and the order of reference, he was limited to the question of damage growing directly out of the failure of the plaintiffs to put the trusses upon said walls, and the falling of the same in consequence thereof.

The referee, in his supplemental report, found that the failure of the plaintiffs to perform their contract prevented the defendant from performing his contract with the railroad company until June 25, 1893; that under the ten per cent clause in the contract with said company the defendant Haven lost the use of $27,800 from December 12, 1892, until June 25, 1893, which amounted to the sum of $834; that Haven was compelled to perform and complete a large portion of the work during the winter season, at an increased expense, amounting to at least $2,435; that he was required to retain the services of the engineers, foreman, bookkeepers and time-keepers employed on the work, at a salary and wages amounting to the sum of $4,166; that defendant was also compelled to devote his time and personal services to the performance and completion of the work, which were reasonably worth the sum of $2,000. The referee, in his supplemental report, found as conclusions of law that, under the decision of the trial judge, the interlocutory judgment entered thereon and the orders of reference entered therein, he had no legal authority or right to pass upon the question of the allowance to the defendant of the foregoing items of damages. He also found that said items of damages were not such as were contemplated by the plaintiffs and defendant when they entered into the contract, and that the same were uncertain, remote and contingent, and could not be allowed to the defendant.

The principal question involved upon this appeal is, whether the defendant Haven is entitled to all or any portion of the damages referred to in the referee's supplemental report.

The referee, in his opinion which accompanied his report, states that "By reference to the opinion of Judge LAMBERT (the learned justice who tried the case), we find this expression : ' The principal question arising for a determination upon the issues litigated is, whether the plaintiffs should pay the reasonable costs made necessary in re-erecting the walls blown down, and the damage done to property as a consequence.' * * * That upon no other theory than that indicated in the opinion of Judge LAMBERT could the learned judge who wrote for the Appellate Division in this case have said : ' There is no question about the measure of damages, providing the plaintiffs' responsibility is established. Those damages would be the necessary expense of repairing and rebuilding the walls that were blown down.' (*Meyer* v. *Haven*, 37 App. Div. 201.)"

The referee construed this language as binding upon him and as limiting his authority to determine the cost of reconstructing the walls and the value of the property destroyed. This rule of esti-mating damages would not fully compensate the defendant for all the injuries sustained by him from the falling of the walls. Had the findings and interlocutory judgment limited defendant's recov-ery to these particular items, the referee might then have properly held that no recovery could be had for any of the items of loss mentioned in the supplemental report. The defendant's right to recover for losses is governed by the interlocutory judgment based upon the findings. The opinion did not modify or change the judg-ment. The language of the judgment is plain and unambiguous and broad enough to cover all damages sustained by the defendant on account of the blowing down of the walls. What the learned justice intimated in his opinion as to plaintiffs' paying the reasonable costs made necessary by re-erecting the walls was merely *obiter* and not essential to the disposition of the case and could not affect the legal rights of the parties fixed by the interlocutory judgment.

The rule of law is well settled that after entry of a judgment in an equity action based on findings of fact and conclusions of law, the Special Term which tried the action has no power to make amendments therein, altering the decision on the merits. (*Heath* v. *New York Building Loan Banking Company*, 146 N. Y. 260.) Section 723 of the Code of Civil Procedure was designed to confer upon courts the amplest power to correct mistakes in process, pleadings, and in all other respects, so long as the substantial rights of the parties are not affected.

If the findings and interlocutory judgment were changed so as to allow the defendant only the cost of rebuilding the walls instead of all the damages sustained, it would materially diminish the amount of his recovery and thereby affect his substantial rights. The interlocutory judgment, therefore, is conclusive and binding upon the parties until set aside or reversed by an appellate court.

In *McLean* v. *Stewart* (14 Hun, 472) the court held that after a decision had been made and filed in a case a subsequent Special Term had no power, upon motion, to alter the judgment entered on such decision as to matters relating to the merits, and that such a change could only be made after a rehearing before the trial judge upon the case being sent back to him or after a review by an appellate court.

The courts have found it difficult to apply a rule of damages that would meet all cases; the decisions upon the subject are not harmonious, but the general rule is clearly stated by Chief Judge PARKER in *Witherbee* v. *Meyer* (155 N. Y. 449). He says: "The general rule is, * * * that the party injured is entitled to recover all of his damages, including gains prevented as well as losses sustained, but this rule is subject always to two conditions:

"*First*, that the damages shall be such as must have been fairly within the contemplation of the parties to the contract at the time it was made; and,

"*Second*, they must be certain, not only in their nature, but as respects the cause from which they proceed, for the law wisely adopts that mode of estimating damages which is most definite and certain."

In *Leonard* v. *New York, etc., Tel. Co.* (41 N. Y. 566) Judge EARL says: " It is not required that the parties *must* have contemplated the actual damages which are to be allowed. But the damages must be such as the parties may fairly be *supposed* to have contemplated when they made the contract. Parties entering into contracts usually contemplate that they will be performed and not that they will be violated. They very rarely actually contemplate any damages which would flow from any breach, and very frequently have not sufficient information to know what such damages would be. As both parties are usually equally bound to know and be informed of the facts pertaining to the execution or breach of a contract which they have entered into, I think a more precise statement of this rule is, that a party is liable for all the direct damages which both parties to the contract would have contemplated as flowing from its breach, if, at the time they entered into it, they had bestowed proper attention upon the subject and had been fully informed of the facts."

It is presumed that a party violating his contract contemplates the damages which directly ensue from the breach ; for instance, where two parties have made a contract, which one of them has broken, the damages which the other ought to receive in respect to such breach would be such as may fairly and reasonably be considered either as arising naturally, that is, according to the usual course of things, from such breach of the contract itself, or such as may reasonably be supposed to have been in the contemplation of both parties at the time they made the contract. Now in this case, if the circumstances under which defendant's contract with the railroad company was made were communicated to the plaintiffs and known to both parties at the time the sub-contract was made, the damages resulting from the breach of such contract, and what the parties reasonably contemplated, would be the extent of the injury which would ordinarily and naturally flow from the breach of the contract.

It is a rule of interpretation that the intention of the parties is to be ascertained from the whole contract considered in connection with the surrounding circumstances known to them both.

The plaintiffs, when they entered into the contract with this,

FOURTH DEPARTMENT, MARCH TERM, 1902.   [Vol. 70.

defendant, must have known that the trusses and iron work would have to be completed in time to enable the defendant to fulfill his contract with the railroad company, and that the walls could not be erected to their full height until the trusses were in readiness for the building, for the reason that the wind might blow them down.

The next question is, whether the damages referred to in the referee's supplemental report are so remote, speculative and uncertain that the referee was justified in not taking them into consideration in estimating the defendant's damages.

It appears that the plaintiffs did not perform their contract or work in time to enable defendant to carry out his agreement with the railroad company at the time fixed by the contract, which was December 12, 1892; that by reason thereof the railroad company, under the ten per cent clause in its contract with Haven, retained the sum of $27,800 from December 12, 1892, until June 25, 1893, on account of which defendant lost during that period the use of the money. It also appears that if the plaintiffs had fulfilled their contract, and put the trusses on the walls when they were completed, the walls would not have blown down, which would have enabled the defendant to have completed his contract with the railroad company in time to have received this sum of money, and have had the use of it during the period referred to. So that this item of loss can be traced directly to the plaintiffs' breach of the contract. The defendant, in rebuilding the shop, claims that he was compelled to perform a large portion of the work during the winter season at an increased expense of at least double the cost of doing the same work in the summer or fall; that he could not abandon his contract or wait until the weather was warmer or the days longer and more favorable for doing that kind of work, because his contract with the railroad company called for the completion of the work on or before the 12th day of December, 1892, and in case of a failure he was to pay to the railroad company the sum of $50 a day for each and every day, Sundays and holidays excepted, during the period that the building or any part thereof remained incomplete or unfinished. It is not claimed but that the defendant prosecuted the work vigilantly and in good faith in rebuilding the shop and putting it in the same condition it was in at the time the walls were blown down, and that he incurred an increased expense over the sum the work would have cost if it had been done during the summer or fall. The defendant claims that he was compelled to retain the services of certain workmen from December 12, 1892, to June 25, 1893, at stated wages paid to them; that he was also compelled to devote his time and personal service to the performance and completion of the work from February 12, 1893, to June 25, 1893, and that this labor was necessary in order to complete the building, and was a part of the extra labor and expense incurred by the defendant.

The general rule is, that when it is certain that damages have been caused by a breach of contract, a recovery is not prevented by the mere fact that the amount of damages is uncertain or its ascertainment is difficult. One who violates his contract with another is liable for all the direct and proximate damages which result from the violation, including gains prevented as well as losses sustained. The damages, however, must not be speculative or imaginary, but they must be reasonably certain. (*Wakeman* v. *Wheeler & Wilson Mfg. Co.*, 101 N. Y. 209; *Griffin* v. *Colver*, 16 id. 489.) This rule is subject to the qualification that the person injured by the breach of the contract is bound to do whatever lies in his power to render the damages as light as possible. (*Allen* v. *McConihe*, 124 N. Y. 347.)

In the case of *Murdock* v. *Jones* (3 App. Div. 221) it was held that where a sub-contractor agrees to furnish materials of special design to be used in the construction of a particular house, although he may be ignorant of the time within which the contractor is required by his contract to complete it, he will be liable to the contractor for any unnecessary delay in furnishing the materials, and be bound to indemnify him against any damage he may suffer under his contract because of such delay. (*Louisville & Nashville Railroad Company* v. *Hollerbach*, 105 Ind. 137.)

We are of the opinion that the learned referee erred in refusing to consider and pass upon the several items of damages referred to, for which error the judgment and order appealed from should be reversed.

Judgment and order reversed, with costs to the appellant to abide the event, and the case remanded to the Special Term for further hearing upon the items of damages mentioned in the referee's supplemental report.

McLENNAN, SPRING and HISCOCK, JJ., concurred; WILLIAMS, J., dissented.

Judgment and order reversed, with costs to the appellant to abide event, and case remanded to the Special Term for further hearing upon the items of damages mentioned in the referee's supplemental report.

538|
515|

THE OSWEGO CITY SAVINGS BANK, Respondent, *v.* THE BOARD OF EDUCATION OF UNION FREE SCHOOL DISTRICT No. 2, TOWNS OF MANHEIM AND OPPENHEIM, COUNTIES OF HERKIMER AND FULTON, STATE OF NEW YORK, Appellant.

Typewritten bonds issued by a school board—printed bonds subsequently substituted therefor are enforcible by a bona fide *holder for value — want of authority in the holder of the bonds to sell them is not a defense — interest payable after default.*

Brokers, to whom typewritten bonds regularly issued by the board of education of a school district were offered for sale by the holder thereof, having refused to purchase them unless they were printed, bonds were printed in the precise form of the typewritten bonds and were executed by the same officers of the school district under the same seal. The printed bonds were then delivered to the brokers, and at the same time the typewritten bonds were canceled by mutilating them with a knife and were delivered to and retained by the president of the school district. No claim was ever made against the board of education on account of the typewritten bonds.

In an action on the printed bonds by a *bona fide* purchaser thereof for value,

Held, that the board of education was liable on the printed bonds, assuming that it would have been liable on the typewritten bonds if the printed bonds had not been substituted therefor;

That the objection that the person who sold the bonds to the brokers did so without authority from the owner thereof was not available to the board of education as against a *bona fide* holder of the printed bonds;

That the board of education, having refused to comply with a demand made after the maturity of one of the bonds for payment of the principal of such bond, was liable for interest on such principal from the time of such demand and refusal, computed at the statutory rate, and not at the rate fixed by the bond.

APPEAL by the defendant, The Board of Education of Union Free School District No. 2, Towns of Manheim and Oppenheim, Counties of Herkimer and Fulton, State of New York, from a judgment of the Supreme Court in favor of the plaintiff, entered in the office of the clerk of the county of Herkimer on the 26th day of September, 1901, upon the decision of the court rendered after a trial at the Herkimer Trial Term, a jury having been waived.

George W. Ward and *A. M. Mills,* for the appellant.

Elisha B. Powell, for the respondent.

WILLIAMS, J. :

The judgment should be affirmed, with costs.

The action was brought to recover the amount of a bond for $1,000, and coupon upon such bond, and coupons upon fourteen other bonds of $1,000 each, the whole fifteen bonds being of one and the same issue. There is little or no dispute as to the facts. The questions involved are mostly questions of law. In 1895 the defendant and the Dolgeville School Society were two domestic corporations, located at Dolgeville, N. Y. The school society owned a school site and property at Dolgeville and the defendant desired to purchase the same.

The transfer was agreed upon at $18,000. Proper legal proceedings were had on the part of both corporations to carry out their agreement. The school society was authorized to sell and convey the property, and the defendant to purchase the same and take title thereto, and to issue and negotiate bonds to raise the $18,000 to pay the purchase price. Alfred Dolge was president and Nathan A. Snell was treasurer of the defendant, and continued such until the year 1897. On the 5th day of August, 1895, eighteen bonds of $1,000 each were duly issued by defendant, having been signed by Dolge, its president, and Snell, its treasurer, and sealed under the direction of the defendant. These bonds were sold at public auction, August 6, 1895, as required by law, and were bid in at par by one Armstrong, representing the school society. August 7, 1895, Armstrong borrowed money from the bank and paid the defendant in cash for the bonds, and the defendant thereupon paid the school society the $18,000 for the site and property and took a conveyance thereof. The school society gave the $18,000 in cash to the bank, in payment of the money borrowed, to pay for the bonds. Defendant at once took possession of the property and has ever since retained the same. The bonds were placed in the custody of the said Armstrong, to be kept for the school society, and were so kept by him until June 25, 1896, when Dolge, who was still president of the defendant and was also a member of the executive committee of the school society, went to bond brokers in New York city and offered for sale seventeen of the bonds, numbered 2 to 18, both inclusive, representing himself to be the owner thereof. All the bonds were typewritten, and Dolge had with him at the time bond No. 18. A certified copy of the proceedings by the defendant, authorizing the issue of the bonds, was delivered to the brokers. They expressed a willingness to purchase the seventeen bonds, but told Dolge that they could not use typewritten ones and it would be necessary to have them printed or lithographed as was usual for such bonds. Dolge agreed to have them put in print, and left the bond No. 18 with the brokers, who procured the printing to be done.

The next day, June 26, 1896, Dolge sent to the brokers the remaining sixteen typewritten bonds. The next day, June 27, 1896, the brokers sent to Dolge the printed forms of the seventeen bonds of precisely the same language as the typewritten ones. The printed bonds were executed by Dolge as president, and Snell as treasurer, the same as the typewritten ones had been executed, the same seal being used. On June 30, 1896, Dolge took the printed bonds so executed to New York and delivered them to the brokers, and the typewritten bonds were at the same time canceled by cutting and mutilating the same with a knife and delivered to Dolge who carried the same away and thereafter retained them, he being the president of the defendant. The brokers at the same time paid Dolge for the bonds. No claim against the defendant upon the seventeen typewritten bonds has ever since been made by any one. They have never been transferred to any one. Some time afterwards, but before the maturity of any of the seventeen printed bonds, the same were in the regular course of business sold and delivered to the plaintiff. The certified copy of the proceedings authorizing the issue of the bonds was at the same time delivered to plaintiff. The plaintiff relied thereon and was a *bona fide* purchaser for value of the bonds.

Bond No. 2 and the first coupon upon each of the other sixteen bonds became due and payable October 1, 1897, and were presented to and paid by the defendant and were canceled and delivered to the defendant. Bond No. 3 and the second coupon on each of the remaining fifteen bonds became due and payable October 1, 1898, and were presented to and paid by the defendant and were canceled and delivered to the defendant.

Bond No. 4 and the third coupon upon each of the remaining fourteen bonds became due and payable October 1, 1899, and were presented to defendant and payment thereof demanded and refused. This was the first time any question was raised as to the validity of the printed bonds.

This action was commenced January 10, 1900, to recover the amount of this bond and the coupons, payment of which was refused October 1, 1899. The complaint alleged the execution of the bonds at the date thereof and the transfer thereof to the brokers and to the plaintiff, and no allegation was made as to the surrender or cancellation of the typewritten bonds and the issue and substitution of the printed bonds for the typewritten ones, and the transfer of the printed bonds to the brokers and to the plaintiff. The answer was a general denial, except as to the incorporation of the defendant. The transaction between Dolge and the New York brokers in changing the seventeen bonds amounted to a mere substitution of the printed form for the typewritten form of the bonds. There was no new issue of bonds and the liability of the defendant was in no manner changed or increased. The typewritten bonds were not in shape to be used on the market. The printed ones were. No one was injured or affected in any way by the change. The defendant certainly was not, nor was the school society. The printed bonds were just as good and valuable as the typewritten bonds and were more marketable. The typewritten bonds were canceled and delivered up to the president of the defendant, who never parted with them until this litigation arose, and then the whole transaction as to the substitution of the printed bonds therefor was known, and the typewritten bonds were of no validity and could not be enforced againts the defendant while the printed bonds were outstanding.

The question as to any misappropriation of the bonds by Dolge was

just the same as to the printed as it was to the typewritten bonds.
If, as claimed, Dolge had no authority from the school society to dispose of the bonds and misappropriated the same, then the injury to
the school society arose out of the disposition of the bonds to the
New York brokers and not out of the substitution of the printed
for the typewritten ones.   Such misappropriation could not be
insisted upon as a defense against the plaintiff, however, because it
was a *bona fide* holder thereof for value.   (*Dutchess County Mut.
Ins. Co.* v. *Hachfield*, 73 N. Y. 226.)

The question of the substitution of bonds was passed upon in two
cases : *Town of Solon* v. *Williamsburgh Savings Bank* (114 N. Y.
122); *Williamsburgh Savings Bank* v. *Town of Solon* (136 id.
465).   The transaction there involved was a surrender and cancellation of the bonds originally issued, and the delivery in place
thereof of other bonds of different denomination and payable at a
different place.

The court, however, held that the substituted bonds in no manner
increased the liability of the town, and refused to invalidate them.
The town was held liable thereon.   The questions there passed upon
are applicable to this case, and are authority for holding the defendant liable upon the bonds here in litigation.   The first action as to
the town of Solon bonds was in equity to declare the substituted
bonds invalid.   The court refused the relief asked for.   The second
action was at law to recover the amount of the bonds, and the court
held a recovery could be had.

Here there has been no action in equity.   The first action brought
is one at law to recover upon the written bonds.   It can hardly be
said that two actions were necessary when the parties are before the
court and the relief can as well be afforded in one action as in two
actions between the same parties.   All the facts are before the court,
and the question of liability can be determined in this action, whatever its technical form may be.   No equitable relief is called for.
We need only determine that upon the conceded facts the defendant
is liable upon the bonds and the plaintiff is entitled to recover the
amount thereof.   It is not suggested that the defendant was in any
way prejudiced by allowing all the facts to be proved under the
pleadings as they were.   It is not claimed that any other facts would
have been shown if the plaintiff had alleged the same more fully in

its complaint as originally served, or if it had amended its complaint upon the trial so as to present the whole facts as they appeared.

Our conclusion, therefore, is that the trial court properly decided that the plaintiff could recover upon the printed bonds if, in the absence of such substitution, it could have recovered upon the type-written ones. The court properly allowed interest upon the $1,000 of principal upon the bond from the time payment thereof was demanded and refused. (*O'Brien* v. *Young*, 95 N. Y. 429.) The rate of interest before the time fixed for the payment of the principal was governed by the contract itself, but after demand and refusal, interest was allowed as damages for breach of the contract, and the rate was not controlled by the contract, but was that fixed by the statute.

The views herein expressed lead to an affirmance of the judgment appealed from, with costs.

McLENNAN, SPRING and DAVY, JJ., concurred; HISCOCK, J., not sitting.

Judgment affirmed, with costs.

———

THE PEOPLE OF THE STATE OF NEW YORK ex rel. NIAGARA FALLS HYDRAULIC POWER AND MANUFACTURING COMPANY, Appellant, *v.* THOMAS J. SMITH and Others, as Assessors of the City of Niagara Falls, New York, Respondents.

Use of the water of a river for manufacturing purposes by a riparian owner — it does not constitute a franchise, although defined by statute — its value enters properly into an assessment for taxation.

The right of the Niagara Falls Hydraulic Power and Manufacturing Company to draw water from Niagara river for the purposes of its business, which right is confirmed and defined by chapter 968 of the Laws of 1896, is not a franchise but an incorporeal hereditament appurtenant to its land, and the value of such right should be considered in assessing its land for the purposes of taxation.

APPEAL by the relator, the Niagara Falls Hydraulic Power and Manufacturing Company, from an order of the Supreme Court, made at the Erie Special Term and entered in the office of the clerk of the county of Niagara on the 6th day of May, 1901, quashing a writ of certiorari theretofore issued to review the assessment of relator's property and denying the prayer of the relator's petition.

Eugene Cary, for the appellant.

Franklin J. MacKenna, for the respondents.

Order affirmed, with ten dollars costs and disbursements, upon opinion of CHILDS, J., delivered at Special Term.

McLENNAN, SPRING, WILLIAMS, HISCOCK and DAVY, JJ., concurred.

The following is the opinion of CHILDS, J., delivered at Special Term:

CHILDS, J.:

The relator is a private corporation, organized under the Business Corporations Law of 1875. (Laws of 1875, chap. 611.) It is the owner in fee of the property embraced in the assessment here sought to be reviewed, which is situate wholly within the tax district of the city of Niagara Falls, and consists of a canal and power plant, extending from a point on the Niagara river above the falls to a point on the Niagara river below the falls, such premises being used as an entirety; they embrace, *first,* lands under the waters of the Niagara river, near the mouth or intake of the relator's canal; *second,* the canal proper, being a strip of land 100 feet wide and about one mile long through the heart of the city of Niagara Falls; *third,* the canal basin near the edge of the high bank of the Niagara river below the falls; *fourth,* a strip of land from the canal basin to the edge of the high bank containing sluiceways; *fifth,* land below the high bank of the Niagara river about 4,000 feet long and 160 feet wide; *sixth,* the power house, with machinery and appurtenances, on land below the high bank.

The canal was constructed for power development, and was first used in or about the year 1857, and was acquired by Mr. Jacob F. Schoellkopf and his associates as individuals in or about the year 1878. The entire property embraced in the assessment was subsequently deeded to the relator, which has since continued to own and hold it. All of the land on the American shore of the Niagara river, between the intake of relator's canal at Port Day (so called)

PEOPLE ex rel. NIAGARA FALLS P. CO. v. SMITH. 545

App. Div.]   Fourth Department, March Term, 1902.

to the brink of the Falls of Niagara, was acquired by the State of
New York for a State park in the year 1883, in pursuance of chapter 336 of the laws of that year. The relator has received and
accepted the grants of land under the waters of Niagara river at
Port Day, extending into and under said waters of said river for a
distance of more than 200 feet from the bulkheads at the head of
its canal, over which lands all waters taken into said canal are
drawn.

In the year 1896 the Legislature of the State passed an act (Laws
of 1896, chap. 968) entitled, "An Act confirming and defining
certain Riparian Rights of The Niagara Falls Hydraulic Power
and Manufacturing company," of which the following is a copy:

"Section 1. The right of The Niagara Falls Hydraulic Power
and Manufacturing company to take, draw, use and lease and sell
to others to use the waters of Niagara river for domestic, municipal, manufacturing, fire and sanitary purposes, and to develop power
therefrom for its own use and to lease and sell to others to use for
manufacturing, heating, lighting, and other business purposes, is
hereby recognized, declared and confirmed, and the exercise thereof
by said company, its successors and assigns, to take and to draw
water from Niagara river for use and disposal to others to use for
the purposes above specified, and for the development of power for
use, and for disposal to others to use, for purposes above mentioned is hereby limited and restricted to such quantity of water as
may be drawn by means of the hydraulic canal of said company
when enlarged throughout its entire length to a width of one hundred feet, and to a depth and slope sufficient to carry at all times a
maximum uniform depth of fourteen feet of water, provided that
exercise by said company of the rights hereby declared and confirmed shall not impair the practical navigation of Niagara river.

"§ 2. This act shall take effect immediately."

The position of the relator is that its right to draw water from the
Niagara river is a franchise and as such not assessable; that the
assessment of its property as a whole, including such water rights,
is illegal; that its property, for all purposes of assessment, must be
treated as though no water right or privilege was attached to and
used in connection therewith; that the true basis for assessment is

546 PEOPLE ex rel. NIAGARA FALLS P. CO. *v.* SMITH.

FOURTH DEPARTMENT, MARCH TERM, 1902. [Vol. 70.

the cost of reproducing the relator's property, exclusive of any water right.

The relator, as a riparian owner and as owner of the lands under the waters of the Niagara river adjacent to its uplands from which the water is immediately taken, has the right to the use of the waters of the river for manufacturing purposes, and to divert the same for that purpose, returning them to the river, as it does, after passing over its own lands (Gould Waters [3d ed.], § 213; *People v. Tibbetts,* 19 N. Y. 523; *People* v. *Canal Appraisers,* 33 id. 461; *Chenango Bridge Company* v. *Paige,* 83 id. 178; *Smith* v. *City of Rochester,* 92 id. 480; *Groat* v. *Moak,* 94 id. 115; *Sweet* v. *City of Syracuse,* 129 id. 336), subject only to the paramount right of the State to utilize these waters for a public use, without compensation to such riparian owners; all riparian rights remaining unimpaired until the exercise of such paramount right by the State. This being so, it appears that the relator, as riparian owner, had the right to take waters from the Niagara river for manufacturing purposes, not interfering thereby with the navigability of the stream, such right being in no sense in the nature of a franchise but a corporeal hereditament, not depending either upon grant or prescription. This subject is fully discussed in chapter 6 of Gould on Waters (3d ed.) at page 393, to which reference is made. And this view of the relator's rights is confirmed by the act of 1896, above quoted, which in terms confirms and defines the *riparian rights* of the relator and is wholly inconsistent with the claim of the relator as to the nature thereof. The fact that the State might destroy relator's riparian rights does not convert such right into a mere franchise. Interference with the relator's rights by the State is a contingency too remote to require serious consideration.

We learn from the map in evidence that Niagara river, at all the points affected by the exercise of the relator's rights, is an unnavigable stream and will so remain, and when it is considered that not even the State is at liberty to interfere with the riparian rights of the relator arbitrarily, but that such interference, if attempted, must be in the interest of some substantial right of the State affected by the exercise of the right of the relator to use the waters of the river, the claim of the relator appears to be wholly unfounded. (*People* v. *Mould,* 37 App. Div. 35.)

Having reached the conclusion that the relator, in the use of the waters of the river, is in the enjoyment of its riparian rights, acquired before 1896, and confirmed by the act of the Legislature of that year, it becomes unnecessary to examine the other questions argued by both the relator and the defendants. In reaching this conclusion, the cases cited by the relator have been carefully examined, and the arguments in support of its contention fully considered, and no benefit could result from considering the same further in this opinion.

The stipulation of the parties submitted on this argument, to the effect that "if it is decided as matter of law that relator's water rights and right to take water from the Niagara river are elements which the assessors may have properly considered in fixing the valuation upon relator's said property, the assessment made by them of relator's said property for the year 1900 shall not be reduced," renders it unnecessary to examine the basis upon which the assessors have fixed the value of the relator's property and included the same in the roll.

The relator's writ should be quashed and set aside, with costs to the defendants.

Let an order be entered accordingly.

Cases

FIRST DEPARTMENT

IN THE

APPELLATE DIVISION,

April, 1902.

CANDACE P. HEDGES, Respondent, v. METROPOLITAN STREET RAIL-
WAY COMPANY, Appellant.

*Evidence — testimony of a physician that asthma "could have been occasioned" by
an accident — when, similar testimony having been admitted without objection, it
affords no ground for a reversal.*

Upon the trial of an action to recover damages for personal injuries, sustained
by the plaintiff in a collision with one of the defendant's street cars, the court
permitted one of the physicians to be asked whether the asthmatic condition
which he observed in the plaintiff and the attack of asthma which he found
to have occurred after the accident "could have been occasioned" by reason
of the plaintiff's receiving an injury by coming in contact with some large
body with sufficient violence to cause the injury he observed. The physician
replied, "This asthmatic condition, in my opinion, could have been the result
of some violence; * * * that is, as far as I know."

Held, that, upon a consideration of the other similar evidence in the case upon
the same subject, not objected to, and of the record, the error, if any, was not
prejudicial or such as would require the reversal of a judgment in favor of the
plaintiff.

APPEAL by the defendant, the Metropolitan Street Railway Company, from a judgment of the Supreme Court in favor of the
plaintiff, entered in the office of the clerk of the county of New
York on the 16th day of November, 1901, upon the verdict of a
jury for $1,500, and also from an order entered in said clerk's office
on the 22d day of November, 1901, denying the defendant's motion
for a new trial made upon the minutes.

Theodore H. Lord, for the appellant.

Otto H. Droege, for the respondent.

PER CURIAM:

The plaintiff was injured by a collision with one of the defendant's cars at the "Circle" at Fifty-ninth street while she was riding her bicycle; and the negligence averred is that the motorman, after motioning to her to cross the track, ran into her. The single question urged upon this appeal from the judgment entered on the verdict of the jury in favor of the plaintiff for $1,500 is whether error was committed by the court in permitting one of the physicians to be asked whether the asthmatic condition which he observed in the plaintiff and the attack of asthma which he found to have occurred a few days after the accident "could have been occasioned" by reason of the plaintiff's receiving an injury by coming in contact with some large body with sufficient violence to cause the injury he observed. The question was objected to as incompetent and improper, but was allowed under exception, and the answer was: "This asthmatic condition in my opinion could have been the result of some violence; * * * that is, as far as I know." The question was not asked whether, in his opinion, the plaintiff's asthma was so caused. Previously, however, the physician had testified that a few weeks prior to the accident he had noticed no difficulty with her breathing, and that on the evening of the accident he found her suffering great pain and difficulty in breathing, and he examined her chest and found she was suffering from an attack of asthma and coughing. And he explained that asthma has its typical sign, which is difficulty in getting breath through the bronchial tubes, pain under the chest bone and on the side, increased by any exertion, which gives rise to the peculiar breathing, and "that is all there is to the attack of asthma." He also said, "An attack of asthma always presupposes that there must be an asthmatic condition of the patient at the time," and it sometimes comes from nervous shock, or fright would bring it on. No exception was taken to this, which is similar testimony to that excepted to. The physician also testified that he set the plaintiff's ribs. The plaintiff testified that the doctor was sent for to relieve her difficulty in breathing; that she had never had trouble in breathing before the accident, but now had severe attacks of asthmatic trouble. Another physician testified that he had seen the plaintiff two days before the accident, as she had a severe headache, and she then had no symptoms of asthma — none whatever, and that asthma was one of his specialties. He was then asked if with reasonable certainty he could give an opinion whether that attack of asthma could have been produced by reason of the plaintiff's coming in violent contact with a heavy body, and after some colloquy with the court, he answered that in his opinion physical injuries may be the cause of asthmatic conditions, but he had no knowledge of this case.

It will be seen that substantially the same question was asked of the two physicians, except that in the latter case the words "reasonable certainty" were used, and both answered affirmatively that physical injuries might produce asthmatic conditions. The first question, therefore, although it did not include the words "reasonable certainty," was not really prejudicial; and, moreover, the question whether the injury here resulted in asthma was not asked. Apart from this, however, we have the positive testimony that the plaintiff was never before troubled with her breathing or with asthma, and when seen by physicians before the accident showed no such symptoms, but when seen after it, and as she herself testifies, she had an attack of asthma. When it is further remembered that the plaintiff broke a rib, which had to be set, and that she suffered pain and had difficulty with her breathing as the result of the accident, and that asthma is such difficulty in breathing, and that the complaint avers that the accident and shock brought on an attack of asthma, there was sufficient evidence properly presented upon which the jury could return a verdict.

There was no exception to the charge, nor any request to charge. No mention was made in it of asthma, but the jury was left to determine on the whole evidence what with reasonable certainty were the direct and natural results of the defendant's negligence.

We think, therefore, that the error, if any, was not prejudicial or such as would require a reversal. The judgment and order should, accordingly, be affirmed, with costs.

Present — VAN BRUNT, P. J., O'BRIEN, MCLAUGHLIN, HATCH and LAUGHLIN, JJ.

Judgment and order affirmed, with costs.

James J. Phillips and Others, Partners, Trading under the Name and Style of Phillips. & Sons, Respondents, v. Joel G. Curtis and Alfred D. Curtis, Partners, Trading as J. G. Curtis & Sons, and Others, Appellants.

Discovery asked of an agreement under which the defendants transacted business — denied, where it was made to ascertain whether the plaintiffs had a cause of action — allegations on information and belief, not stating the source thereof.

The complaint in an action, brought to recover damages because of the alleged wrongful and malicious conduct of the defendants in injuring the plaintiffs' business, which was that of selling calves, alleged that the defendants were carrying on business in the city of New York under a written agreement, pursuant to which they willfully and maliciously conspired to secure to themselves a monopoly of the business of selling calves in certain stock yards in that city, and that they had destroyed the business of the plaintiffs in such yards. One of the defendants answered, admitting the existence of an agreement under which they did business, but denying that it was made for the purposes alleged in the complaint. Such answer also denied all allegations in the complaint of malicious and improper acts.

The plaintiffs then made application for a discovery of the agreement under which the defendants did business, alleging in their petition their ignorance of the contents of the agreement and their inability to obtain knowledge thereof, and that it was necessary that they should make an examination of the agreement prior to the trial, in order to be fully advised of the character of such agreement and in order that they might properly prepare for trial.

Held, that it was apparent that the application was made for the purpose of ascertaining whether or not the plaintiffs had a cause of action, and that an order granting the application should be reversed, especially as all the material allegations of the petition were made upon information and belief without any statement as to the sources of the information and the ground of the belief.

Appeal by the defendants, Joel G. Curtis and Alfred D. Curtis, partners, trading as J. G. Curtis & Sons, and others, from an order of the Supreme Court, made at the New York Special Term and entered in the office of the clerk of the county of New York on the 26th day of December, 1901, directing the defendant Joel G. Curtis to deliver to the plaintiffs' attorneys a sworn copy of a certain writing or agreement between the defendants.

Philip J. Britt, for the appellants.

J. S. Wise, for the respondents.

VAN BRUNT, P. J. :

This action is brought to recover damages because of the wrongful and malicious conduct of the defendants, whereby the business of the plaintiffs was injured. It is alleged in the complaint that the defendants were carrying on business in the city of New York under an agreement in writing, and that a combination existed between the defendants, pursuant to which the defendants willfully and maliciously conspired together to secure to themselves a monopoly of the business of selling calves (which was the plaintiffs' business) in certain stock yards in the city of New York, and which injured, harassed and destroyed the business of the plaintiffs in said yards, and that they succeeded in destroying the business of the plaintiffs and in driving them out of the same.

The defendant Curtis answered the complaint, admitted the existence of an agreement between the defendants under which they did business, but denied that the agreement was for the purpose set out and alleged in the plaintiffs' complaint. All the allegations in the complaint of malicious and improper acts were denied.

Upon a petition the plaintiffs applied for a discovery of the agreement (the existence of which was admitted) under which the defendants did business. The defendants resisted such application, and it being granted by the court below this appeal was taken.

The authority of the court to grant the relief in question was challenged by the defendants upon the ground, amongst others, of defects in the allegations contained in the petition. An inspection of the petition shows that after setting out the formal matters in regard to the residence of the plaintiffs and defendants, the appearances in the action, the fact of the service of an amended summons and complaint and the joining of issues by the service of answers, and that the action was brought to recover a certain sum for damage sustained by the plaintiffs by reason of the wrongful acts of the defendants, it proceeds to state what the allegations of the complaint are, and then avers : " That, as will appear from the foregoing and from the pleadings herein, the defendants are now and at the times referred to in the complaint herein were, co-operating under an agreement in writing, which said agreement the defendants admit to be in existence at the present time ; that plaintiffs have no way of knowing the contents thereof, and have no copy thereof ;

that plaintiffs, through their attorneys aforesaid, have requested defendants through their attorney aforesaid, to permit them to inspect said agreement, which said request has been denied." It then swears to advice of counsel, and further states that they are advised by the pleadings that the aforesaid writing or agreement between defendants herein is now in the possession or under the control of the defendant Curtis, as the plaintiffs are advised by their counsel and believe. Then follows an allegation that owing to the nature of the charges of an illegal combination and conspiracy on the part of the defendants, it is necessary that the plaintiffs should make an examination of the aforesaid writing or agreement prior to the trial of said action in order to be fully advised of the character of the written agreement under which the defendants are, and were, at the time of the committing of the offenses herein stated operating, and in order that they may properly prepare for the trial of said action, and that without an examination and inspection of the aforesaid document, writing or agreement, plaintiffs cannot safely proceed to the trial of this case; and further that, owing to the fact that they have not been able to secure a copy of said agreement, or to inspect the same, they are unable to more particularly describe the said writing, but that the writing which they refer to and which they desire by this petition to secure an inspection of is the writing or agreement referred to on page 4 of the amended complaint herein in paragraph 6 of said complaint, and which is admitted on page 3, paragraph 7, of the answer of defendant Curtis herein.

These allegations show beyond question that this application is a mere expedient for the purpose of seeing whether they may or may not have a cause of action by reason of the provisions of the agreement under which these defendants were co-operating or acting. There is no statement whatever tending to show that if any wrong acts were done by any of these defendants they were in anywise authorized by this agreement, and that it could in any way affect the questions which were to be presented upon the trial of this action. The rules in relation to discovery provide that the party applying shall show to the satisfaction of the court the materiality and necessity of the discovery or inspection sought, the particular information which he requires, and in the case of books and papers that there are entries therein as to the matter of which he seeks a discovery or inspection. There is no allegation whatever in this petition that this agreement contains the particular information which the plaintiffs require, or that there is any entry or writing therein which is in any way material to the questions which are to be presented upon the trial of this action. They desire to make amongst the private papers of these defendants an experimental voyage of discovery in the hope that, perhaps, they may be able to fish out something they may turn to their advantage. It does not seem to us that such a mere fishing expedition should be countenanced by the court, and it never has been heretofore.

If a discovery of this kind can be allowed then the private papers of every competitor in trade may be compelled to be produced for inspection in the hope that something may be found in them which will subject them to criticism. It does not seem to us that the rule of discovery has ever been carried to any such length.

It is to be observed that all the material allegations in the petition in reference to these questions are made upon information and belief only, without the slightest statement as to the sources of information and the grounds of belief. It has become a reasonably familiar maxim that allegations of this kind contained in an affidavit are of no value. Allegations upon information and belief in a complaint answer the purpose of a pleading, but furnish no proof when contained in a petition or affidavit which is supposed to represent evidence.

We think, therefore, that the motion was improvidently granted and that the order should be reversed, with ten dollars costs and disbursements, and the motion denied, with ten dollars costs, with leave upon payment of such costs to renew the application upon additional papers.

PATTERSON, O'BRIEN and LAUGHLIN, JJ., concurred.

Order reversed, with ten dollars costs and disbursements, and motion denied, with ten dollars costs, with leave upon payment of such costs to renew the application upon additional papers.

JOHN BURNS, Respondent, *v.* REUBEN E. BOLAND, Appellant.

Appeal — what was decided below is not established by the opinion— deductions of an
· *affiant presumed to be from a paper not produced, and not from oral statements of*
a party.

Upon an appeal from an order the Appellate Division cannot advert to the opinion of the court below in order to ascertain what has been decided.

Deductions made by an affiant from papers which he fails to produce have no probative force.

Where an affidavit used upon a motion alleged "that deponent thereafter had several interviews with the defendant, Reuben E. Boland, at one of which the said Boland exhibited a written statement of the account of said sales to Skidmore and collections on account thereof, purporting to be taken from the books of the said Boland, that from the said statement the said Boland admitted to deponent that he had received from the said Skidmore the sum of sixty-eight and 78 / 100 dollars, $68.78, in excess of the amount which he had remitted to the plaintiff after deducting all items of commissions and discounts," the court considered that the admission mentioned in the affidavit was a deduction drawn by the deponent from the statement of account and not from anything that Boland orally stated at the time of the exhibition of the account.

LAUGHLIN, J., dissented.

APPEAL by the defendant, Reuben E. Boland, from an order of the Supreme Court, made at the New York Special Term and entered in the office of the clerk of the county of New York on the 26th day of December, 1901, denying the defendant's motion to vacate an order of arrest theretofore granted in the action.

W. Benton Crisp, for the appellant.

Charles K. Carpenter, for the respondent.

VAN BRUNT, P. J.:

It appears from the opinion of the court below, which was handed down at the time of the denial of the motion to discharge the defendant from arrest, that such motion would have been granted had it not been for the fact that the court was of the opinion that Mr. Carpenter in his affidavit swore to an oral admission upon the part of the defendant that he had received sixty-eight dollars and seventy-eight cents in excess of the amount which he had remitted to the plaintiff, after deducting all items of commissions and disbursements.   Under these circumstances, we need consider only the question as to this alleged admission. While it is true that we cannot advert to the opinion of the court in order to ascertain what has been decided, it seems hardly necessary to reconsider questions in the solution of which we concur; and, therefore, we need only examine the affidavits upon the point as to whether Mr. Carpenter's affidavit bears the construction put upon it by the learned judge below. It seems to us, upon a reading of that affidavit, that the true interpretation of the language used is that Mr. Carpenter is averring facts which he learned from the statement of account submitted to him by the defendant, rather than giving any oral statement which the defendant made to him in connection with such statement of accounts. Of course, the rule is well settled that deductions made by an affiant from papers which he fails to produce have no probative force, because such deductions are the mere conclusions of the affiant, and it is a question for the court to determine from the papers as to whether such conclusions are properly drawn, which it cannot do in their absence.

Mr. Carpenter states as follows: "That deponent thereafter had several interviews with the defendant Reuben E. Boland at one of which the said Boland exhibited a written statement of the account of said sales to Skidmore and collections on account thereof, purporting to be taken from the books of the said Boland. That from the said statement, the said Boland admitted to deponent that he had received from the said Skidmore the sum of sixty-eight and 78/100 dollars ($68.78), in excess of the amount which he had remitted to the plaintiff after deducting all items of commissions and discounts." It seems to be reasonably apparent that the admission is taken from the statement of account, and not from anything that the defendant orally stated. The language used is: "That from the said statement, the said Boland admitted." If the affiant was testifying to an oral admission, certainly this language would not have been used. As already stated, the admission sworn to is only "from the said statement," and not from anything that Boland orally stated at the time of the exhibition of the account. This being, in our judgment, the necessary construction of the affidavit, it is clearly nothing but the conclusion of the affiant from papers which were presented to him, and of the contents of which the court is entirely ignorant. It is impossible, therefore, for the court to determine whether the conclusion of Carpenter was borne out by the statement submitted by Boland or not.

We think that the order of arrest should have been wholly vacated upon the ground that there was no legal evidence tending to establish a right to arrest. The order should be reversed with ten dollars costs and disbursements, and the order of arrest vacated, with ten dollars costs.

O'BRIEN, J., concurred; PATTERSON, J., concurred in result; LAUGHLIN, J., dissented.

Order reversed, with ten dollars costs and disbursements, and motion to vacate order of arrest granted, with ten dollars costs.

EDMUND L. BAYLIES, as Trustee under the Last Will and Testament of HERMAN C. LE ROY, Deceased, Respondent, v. THE AUTOMATIC FIRE ALARM COMPANY, Appellant.

Contract to install automatic sprinklers — obligation created by a provision in the specifications as to the annual cost of connecting them with a central station — construction of a unilateral contract.

A fire alarm company entered into a contract with the owner of a building to equip it with a system of automatic sprinklers and to connect the alarm system in said building with the central station of the fire alarm company for one year. Added to the specifications for the work, which were signed by the fire alarm company alone, was the following clause: "It is further understood that if you desire us to maintain the Alarm System connection to our Central Station longer than one year, we will do so at an annual expense to you of thirty-five dollars per year."

Connection with the central office was no part of the sprinkler system, but was a separate and distinct device.

Held, that the clause quoted did not bind the fire alarm company to furnish the connection with its central office at the rate of thirty-five dollars a year as long as the owner of the building desired, but was a mere statement of the practice and intention of the fire alarm company in reference to furnishing the service and did not prevent it from thereafter modifying or withdrawing the privilege.

In order that a contract shall be interpreted to be perpetually obligatory upon one side, when there is no obligation whatever upon the other side, the language must be clear and convincing.

APPEAL by the defendant, the Automatic Fire Alarm Company, from a judgment of the Supreme Court in favor of the plaintiff, entered in the office of the clerk of the county of New York on the 28th day of June, 1901, upon the decision of the court, rendered after a trial at the New York Special Term, decreeing that the defendant maintain the electric alarm connection between the defendant's central office and the building No. 26 Beekman street, both in the city of New York, as long as the plaintiff pays to the defendant the sum of thirty-five dollars a year therefor.

Elijah S. Cowles, for the appellant.

Edward Harding, for the respondent.

VAN BRUNT, P. J.:

This action was commenced to compel the specific performance of an alleged contract between the plaintiff's predecessor and the defendant, decreeing that the defendant maintain an electrical alarm connection, as then maintained, between the defendant's central office and the building No. 26 Beekman street, both in the city of New York, as long as the plaintiff pays to the defendant thirty-five dollars a year for the maintenance of such connection. The facts as they appeared upon the trial were substantially as follows: On the 25th of January, 1889, a contract was made by one Elizabeth A. Le Roy, the plaintiff's predecessor, as trustee under the last will and testament of Herman C. Le Roy, deceased, and the defendant corporation, by which, for a consideration of $2,000, the defendant agreed to equip the building No. 26 Beekman street, then owned by said Le Roy as such trustee, with a system of Grinnell Sensitive Automatic Sprinklers, and to connect the alarm system from said building with the central station of the defendant for one year. This contract was signed by the defendant and by said Le Roy as trustee. Attached to said contract were specifications of work, signed only by the defendant, to which specifications was added the following clause : " It is further understood that if you desire us to maintain the Alarm System connection to our Central Station longer than one year, we will do so at an annual expense to you of thirty-five dollars per year."

The sprinkler in question was installed and the connection with the central station was maintained by the defendant until the 1st of May, 1900, at the request of the plaintiff, who paid after the first year thirty-five dollars a year therefor. It further appears from the evidence that connection with the central office was no part of the sprinkler system, but was a separate and distinct device. The defendant refused to continue the service of connection with the central station after the 1st of May, 1900, at the rate of thirty-five dollars a year, claiming that in consequence of the law requiring the removal of all overhead wires the company was unable, by reason of the additional expense, to furnish this service at the price named. The plaintiff claims, however, that the paragraph in question constituted a contract between the defendant and the plaintiff by which the defendant was bound to furnish this connection at the rate of thirty-five dollars a year during the plaintiff's pleasure.

It is to be observed that there was no obligation whatever upon the part of the plaintiff to maintain this connection and to pay thirty-five dollars a year for a single moment after the expiration of the first contract, and that he can discontinue it at any time when he sees fit. In other words, so far as the maintenance of this service is concerned, the contract between the parties is entirely unilateral — obligation upon the one part and none upon the other. We do not think that any construction can be put upon this paragraph which would forever compel the defendant to the maintenance of this connection. The sprinkler system was entirely complete without the connection with the central station. That was a mere additional precaution for which, after the first year, the plaintiff had agreed to pay the additional price so long as he was furnished by the defendant at his request with the service. The paragraph in question was a mere statement of what the defendant's price was for the service. It formed no part of the contract of installation. It was a mere inducing statement as to what the defendant's practice was in reference to the maintenance of this additional connection. It clearly was not an agreement upon the part of the defendant that it would be bound forever to furnish this connection, no matter at what cost it might be put to maintain it; and it is difficult to see how the plaintiff could have understood that the defendant was under an obligation to him while he was under no obligation to it.

It seems to us that in order that a contract shall be interpreted to be perpetually obligatory upon one side, where there is no obligation whatever upon the other, the language must be clear and convincing. It may undoubtedly have been the expectation of both parties that this service would continue. But it is perfectly apparent that the paragraph under consideration was a mere statement of what the intentions of the defendant were in regard to the cost of keeping up this central connection in the future. It was in no way of such a character that the defendant had not the right to alter its terms or to withdraw the privilege; and it cannot be otherwise construed than as a mere statement of the terms upon which it expected in the future to be able to furnish this service. Such being the conditions, they were far from binding the defendant to a perpetual contract in respect to which the plaintiff was under no obligation whatever.

We think, therefore, that the judgment of the court below was erroneous and should be reversed and a new trial ordered, with costs to the appellant to abide the event.

PATTERSON, O'BRIEN and LAUGHLIN, JJ., concurred.

Judgment reversed, new trial ordered, costs to appellant to abide event.

RUDOLPH LOUIS BLUMENTHAL and Others, Doing Business under the Firm Name and Style of MANHATTAN MILLS, Respondents, *v.* AMOS L. PRESCOTT and C. OSCAR LITTLEFIELD, Appellants.

Landlord and tenant — injury to goods from a roof being insufficiently protected while being repaired after a fire — right of a sub-lessee to recover from his lessor, although the repairs are made by the owner of the building — agency — measure of damages.

The Le Conte estate demised certain premises to the firm of Prescott & Co. by a lease, which contained the following clause:

"Said parties of the second part further covenant that they will not assign this lease nor make any alteration in said premises without the written consent of the said parties of the first part under the penalty of forfeiture and damages."

"And it is further agreed between the parties to these presents that in case the building or buildings erected on the premises hereby leased shall be partially damaged by fire, the same shall be repaired as speedily as possible at the expense of the said parties of the first part."

"And it is further understood and agreed that all repairs that may become necessary to or about said building, steam engine and elevators, during the term hereby granted (except repairs to the roof), shall be made and paid for by the said parties of the second part."

Prescott & Co. subsequently sub-let the premises to a firm known as the Manhattan Mills, the sub-lease also containing the provisions above quoted. The course of dealing between the Manhattan Mills and Prescott & Co. was such that when occasion arose for repairs, which the landlord was bound to make, the Manhattan Mills were referred to E. H. Ludlow & Co., who were the agents of the Le Conte estate, and the repairs were then made through the agency of Ludlow & Co. The communications between the Manhattan Mills and Prescott & Co. were through an employee of the latter firm, named Miller.

During the term of the sub-lease a fire occurred upon the premises, which burned a large hole in the roof. Neither of the members of the firm of Prescott & Co. was within the State of New York at the time the fire occurred, and the Manhattan Mills, as claimed by them, gave personal notice of the fire to Miller, who represented Prescott & Co. in their absence. They also gave notice of the fire to Ludlow & Co., and the latter undertook to make the necessary repairs, employing a contractor for that purpose. The contractor began his work on Friday, and on Saturday left the roof in an unfinished condition, and without taking proper precautions to cover the hole therein. Rain storms occurred on the following Sunday and Monday, and goods belonging to the Manhattan Mills were damaged in consequence thereof.

In an action brought by the Manhattan Mills against Prescott & Co. to recover for the damage thus done to the goods, it was

Held, that, as it appeared that the defendants had constituted Ludlow & Co. their representative for the purpose of carrying out the obligations of their lease to the plaintiffs, and Ludlow & Co. had undertaken to make the repairs through the medium of a contractor, it was immaterial whether, upon a strict interpretation of the covenants of the lease, it was the duty of the plaintiffs to repair at the defendants' expense, or whether it was the duty of the defendants to make the repairs in the first instance;

That the defendants had created a privity between themselves and the person who made the repairs, when they referred the plaintiffs to Ludlow & Co. as agents of the Le Conte estate;

That the defendants were liable for any negligence on the part of the contractor employed by the Le Conte estate;

That, the injury to the building being susceptible of quick and easy reparation, and the contractor having been negligent, the plaintiffs were entitled to recover the damages for the injury done to their goods, and not simply the difference between the rental value of the premises as they were and their rental value as they would have been if repaired in accordance with the landlord's covenant.

APPEAL by the defendants, Amos L. Prescott and another, from a judgment of the Supreme Court in favor of the plaintiffs, entered in the office of the clerk of the county of New York on the 21st day of October, 1901, upon the report of a referee.

Herbert J. Hindes, for the appellants.

John Bogart, for the respondents.

VAN BRUNT, P. J.:

This action was brought to recover from the defendants damages for injuries to goods, the property of the plaintiffs, claimed to have been caused by the negligence of the defendants, who were their landlords. In June, 1896, Harriett G. Le Conte, as trustee, etc., and Robert G. Le Conte, parties of the first part, executed a lease of the premises No. 11 Jay street, in the city of New York, to the defendants, composing the firm of J. L. Prescott & Co., parties of the second part. The said lease, amongst other things, contained the following clauses :

"Said parties of the second part further covenant that they will not assign this lease nor make any alteration in said premises without the written consent of the said parties of the first part under the penalty of forfeiture and damages."

" And it is further agreed between the parties to these presents that in case the building or buildings erected on the premises hereby leased shall be partially damaged by fire, the same shall be repaired as speedily as possible at the expense of the said parties of the first part."

" And it is further understood and agreed that all repairs that may become necessary to or about said building, steam engine and elevators during the term hereby granted (except repairs to the roof), shall be made and paid for by the said parties of the second part."

On the 9th day of December, 1898, the defendants leased said premises to the plaintiffs for the period of five years and four months, commencing January 1, 1899, the said lease also containing the provisions above quoted. On the 3d day of August, 1900, a fire took place on the premises, which was limited to the rear of the building, burning a large hole in the roof. From about August third up to Friday, August tenth, the fire department had charge of that portion of the demised premises which was injured by the fire and kept the roof covered. Upon the last-mentioned day one

Scherer, a contractor, and his men undertook to make repairs to the roof. Before such repairs were completed, and while the premises remained open, rainstorms occurred on Sunday and Monday, August twelfth and thirteenth, causing damage to the plaintiffs' goods. The claim is that Scherer and his workmen left the roof on Saturday, August eleventh, in an unfinished condition, and without taking any proper precaution to protect it from rain, and it is to recover for the alleged damage to the goods of the plaintiffs that this action is brought.

It is claimed upon the part of the defendants that no liability attached to them for the damage sustained by the plaintiffs, because :

First. The defendants were not absolutely bound to repair.

Second. The plaintiffs failed to give notice to the defendants of the damage to the roof and to repair.

Third. It was the duty of the plaintiffs to repair at the defendants' expense or move out of the premises if the defendants failed to repair agreeably to their covenant.

Fourth. There was no privity between the defendants and the person who made the repairs.

Fifth. The repairs were not negligently done.

And, *sixth*, the plaintiffs were guilty of contributory negligence.

The referee has found, and we think that there was evidence sufficient to justify the finding, that the course of dealing between the defendants and the plaintiffs had been that, when occasion arose for repairs which the landlords were liable to make, the plaintiffs had been referred to E. H. Ludlow & Co., who were the agents of the Le Conte estate, and that such repairs were then made through the agency of Ludlow & Co., and that the communications had by the plaintiffs with the defendants were principally through an employee of the defendants of the name of Miller, who, the referee found, represented the defendants in their absence.

It further appears that at the time of the occurrences in question neither of the defendants was in the city of New York, or the State of New York, one of them being in the Yellowstone Park and the other in the State of Maine. Under these circumstances, it was, of course, impossible for the plaintiffs to give notice of the occurrence of the fire to the defendants personally. There is evidence that personal notice was given to Miller of the fire. It is

FIRST DEPARTMENT, APRIL TERM, 1902.   [Vol. 70.

true that he denies it; but that he was aware of the happening of the fire is apparent from the fact of his having received a letter addressed to J. L. Prescott & Co. from E. H. Ludlow & Co., which he had opened and read, and then forwarded to the plaintiffs.

It further appeared that Ludlow & Co., in pursuance of the practice which had been suggested by the defendants, were notified of the fire, and, in accordance with the obligations of the lease, they undertook to make the repairs.

It seems to us, therefore, that the first objection is clearly not well taken, because the plaintiffs did everything which it was incumbent upon them to do in order to give the defendants notice of the fire, so that the proper repairs might be made. Miller, who was the representative of the defendants, certainly in their absence, had notice of the fire; and Ludlow & Co., the parties to whom the plaintiffs were referred whenever there was a question of repairs to be done under the lease by the landlords, also had notice. And further, Ludlow & Co. undertook to perform the duty of making these repairs, admitting themselves obligated so to do by the terms of the lease to the defendants. Under these circumstances, it is apparent that the defendants had constituted Ludlow & Co. their representatives for the purpose of carrying out the obligations of their lease to the plaintiffs; and they having undertaken to do these repairs in this manner, it is entirely immaterial, so far as this case is concerned, whether upon a strict interpretation of the covenants in the lease it was the duty of the plaintiffs to repair at the defendants' expense, or whether it was the duty of the defendants to make the repairs in the first instance. This also makes immaterial the objection that there was no privity between the defendants and the person who made the repairs. The defendants had created such privity when they referred the plaintiffs to Ludlow & Co., as agents of the Le Conte estate in reference to the subject of repairs to be made under the clause. It is, of course, readily to be understood why this reference was made. While the defendants were bound to make certain repairs for the plaintiffs, the Le Conte estate was bound to make the repairs for the defendants; and thus, in order to avoid the necessity of their communicating with Ludlow & Co., the defendants instructed the plaintiffs to do so directly; and, the plaintiffs having acted upon this instruction, it is too late now for the defendants to claim that there was no privity between themselves and the contractor employed by the Le Conte estate to make the repairs. They handed over this business to the Le Conte estate, and the estate consented, and in so doing, so far as the plaintiffs were concerned, Ludlow & Co. were acting as the agents of the defendants, and the defendants were liable for whatever the estate did in the carrying out of the defendants' contract with the plaintiffs. Of course, this whole position depends upon the fact that this reference was made, and that the defendants had held out Miller as being authorized to act for them in respect to this matter. We do not see how the referee could come to any other conclusion than that Miller was the representative of the defendants, as we have already said, certainly during their absence from the State. This being the case, the question of an independent contractor in no way enters into the discussion. The defendants, if not bound in the first instance, assumed, by their representative the Le Conte estate, to make repairs. If they did so, they were bound to make them with diligence and care. They could choose their own method of doing the work. They could do it themselves, or they could make a contract with others to do it. But whichever method they adopted, the doing of the work was their act. They were simply fulfilling their contractual obligations to the plaintiffs, who had no interest in the manner of its being done, or by whom. The case is absolutely different from one in which a claim is made by a stranger for damage caused by negligence in the performance of work.

It is also claimed that the plaintiffs were guilty of contributory negligence, in that, knowing that their merchandise was exposed to damage or injury from storms, they left it to this hazard, and, therefore, they cannot recover from any one, not even the owner of the property, who made the repairs; and our attention is called to various cases where the landlord was under a covenant to repair, and it was held that where, the landlord having failed to comply with his covenant to repair, the tenant leaves his goods subject to the action of the weather, he cannot recover for the damages sustained in consequence of a storm. But those cases have no application to the one at bar. Here the landlords, representing the defend-

FIRST DEPARTMENT, APRIL TERM, 1902.   [Vol. 70.

ants, were in the act of performing their covenants, and were making the repairs, and it was in consequence of the negligent manner in which the work was conducted that the injury occurred. It is true that the proof shows that the plaintiffs knew that this roof was not secured as it should have been when the contractor quitted work on the Saturday preceding the Sunday and Monday when it rained; but the plaintiffs had no reason to suppose that when the storm came up the contractor would not take means to protect the roof which he knew he had left open. It is entirely different from a case where the tenant knew that his landlord was not going to perform his covenant and he deliberately allowed his goods to be destroyed   The whole difficulty in the case was that the carpenters did not get their work done. The evidence shows that the man who was to put on the tar roof and make the roof watertight was there ready to do the work and would have completed it on Saturday had the carpenters had their part of the work in condition.

It is further claimed on the part of the defendants that the repairs were not negligently done. The point needs no discussion; the circumstances attending the making of the repairs speak loudly enough to answer this proposition.

The claim made by the defendants, that the rule of damages adopted by the referee was an improper one, and that he should have allowed only the difference between the rental value of the premises as they were and their rental value as they would have been if repaired in accordance with the landlords' covenant, is clearly untenable. The plaintiffs were not bound to abandon the lease because of the damage to the building which occurred. It was susceptible of quick and easy reparation. It was the duty of the defendants to make the repairs in a manner which would protect the plaintiffs from loss; and if that work was so negligently carried out that the plaintiffs' goods were damaged by water, there is no reason why they should not be allowed to recover the damages they have sustained.

The judgment must be affirmed, with costs.

PATTERSON, O'BRIEN and LAUGHLIN, JJ., concurred.

Judgment affirmed, with costs.

In the Matter of the Petition of Herman H. Kipp, Respondent, | 70
for an Order Directing the Payment of Funeral Expenses by   e 78
Henry B. Wesselman, Temporary Administrator, etc., of
Charlotte Miller, Deceased, Appellant.

*Reference of a claim for funeral expenses — subdivision 3 of section 2729 of the Code
of Civil Procedure applies to claims previously accruing — an objection to the constitutionality of an act is not first available upon appeal.*

Subdivision 3 of section 2729 of the Code of Civil Procedure, added by chapter
293 of the Laws of 1901, relating to the collection of a claim for the funeral
expenses of a decedent, is a mere regulation of a form of procedure and applies
to a claim which accrued before the subdivision became operative.

The objection that such subdivision violates the constitutional provision that
trial by jury in all cases in which it has heretofore been used shall remain
inviolate forever, is not available for the first time upon an appeal from an
order of reference made pursuant to such subdivision.

Appeal by Henry B. Wesselman, temporary administrator, etc.,
of Charlotte Miller, deceased, from an order of the Surrogate's
Court of the county of New York, entered in said Surrogate's
Court on the 26th day of December, 1901, referring the matter to a
referee to take proof as to the claim of the petitioner and to report
the same to the court with his opinion thereon.

Bertram L. Kraus, for the appellant.

Peter Cook, for the respondent.

Van Brunt, P. J.:

The services were performed and the materials furnished for
which this claim is made on or about the 19th of March, 1901, and
the claim was presented to the temporary administrator on the 17th
of June, 1901 ; and, pursuant to the authority conferred by section
2729 of the Code of Civil Procedure, as amended by chapter 293
of the Laws of 1901, which went into effect September 1, 1901, the
Surrogate's Court on the 26th of December, 1901, made the order
in question.

It is objected by the appellant that the holder of a claim for funeral
expenses is not a creditor, nor a person interested in the estate,

within the meaning of those terms as used in section 2727 of the Code; and that as the amendment to section 2729, constituting subdivision 3 thereof, went into effect on September 1, 1901, it is not applicable to the matter at bar, as the claim accrued before the amendment became operative. It seems to be sufficient to say upon this point that the amendment of section 2729 was a mere regulation of procedure; and it is a well-settled rule that no matter when a claim may mature, the form of procedure provided for by the law for its collection at the time the proceeding for collection is commenced must be the one adopted, and consequently the claimant was required, at the time at which he presented his application, to proceed in the manner then provided by the law for enforcing its collection.

It is further urged that chapter 293 of the Laws of 1901, constituting subdivision 3 of section 2729 of the Code, is in violation of the constitutional provision that trial by jury in all cases in which it has been heretofore used shall remain inviolate forever. (Art. 1, § 2.) It is not necessary to discuss this question upon this application, for the reason that it does not appear that any such objection was taken in the court below. If the party desired to avail himself of an objection of this kind, he was bound to do so before the court entered upon the disposition of the case as provided for by subdivision 3 of section 2729. It is too late to raise that question for the first time upon appeal from the order which was made pursuant to the provisions of that section.

The order should be affirmed, with ten dollars costs and disbursements.

PATTERSON, O'BRIEN and LAUGHLIN, JJ., concurred.

Order affirmed, with ten dollars costs and disbursements.

HENRY A. WOLFF, Appellant, *v.* HENRY B. LOCKWOOD and Others, as Copartners Doing Business under the Firm Name of LOCK-WOOD, HURD & Co., Respondents.

Unauthorized sale by a broker of a customer's stock — measure of damages.

Where stock, carried by a firm of stock brokers for a client upon margins, has been sold by the brokers without the consent of the client, at a time when the brokers held sufficient margins to protect the stock from arbitrary sale, the client's measure of damages is the difference between the price at which the stock was sold and the highest market price brought by such stock within a reasonable time after the sale.

APPEAL by the plaintiff, Henry A. Wolff, from a judgment of the Supreme Court in favor of the defendants, entered in the office of the clerk of the county of New York on the 26th day of July, 1901, upon the report of a referee.

Lewis H. Freedman, for the appellant.

Edwin C. Ward, for the respondents.

PATTERSON, J.:

The judgment from which this appeal is taken was entered upon the report of a referee in favor of the defendant dismissing the complaint and allowing a recovery upon a counterclaim. The transactions between the plaintiff and the defendants out of which their respective demands arose consisted of dealings in stocks. The plaintiff's claim is based upon allegations that the defendants, as brokers, were employed by him to buy and sell shares on his account; that there were two accounts with the defendants standing in his name, known, respectively, as accounts No. 1 and No. 2; that on account No. 1 no transactions were had after February 7, 1898, and he claims further that on account No. 2 a balance apparently due from him to the defendants was paid by the check of a third party. The claim of the defendants is, in substance, that the transactions of the plaintiff with them extended beyond February 7, 1898, and included items of stock, the purchase of which on the plaintiff's account is now repudiated by him. The determination of the issues arising upon the transactions contained in account No. 1 depends upon the authority of the defendants to charge the plaintiff with certain alleged purchases made by them on his behalf. All the stocks bought or held by the defendants for the plaintiff were carried on margins. The referee found that on the 14th day of February, 1898, the defendants were carrying on the plaintiff's account 1,600 shares of stock on which the margins had become exhausted; that the defendants made due and reasonable efforts to advise the plaintiff of the condition of his account and to secure further margin from him; that they failed to receive further margin and sold out the account on the fifteenth day of February, at a loss. The plaintiff's contention is that on the 7th of February, 1898, the defendants were carrying for him only 1,000 shares of stock; that he ceased dealing with them on his account No. 1 at that time, and that he never gave any orders to buy stock on his account after that date, and that the sale of his stocks on the fifteenth of February was unauthorized. If the defendants, by authority of the plaintiff, bought shares on margin for him after the seventh of February, and in excess of the 1,000 shares carried for him on that date, or if the plaintiff ratified purchases of shares made by the defendants on his account after the seventh of February, and without excuse failed to respond to calls for margin after being duly advised, then the plaintiff was not entitled to recover.

All the transactions had by the plaintiff with the defendants were by orders given through one Ranger. The referee has found that Ranger was an employee of the defendants whose business it was to solicit accounts for the firm and that he received a salary for so doing; that while in such employment Ranger secured the account of the plaintiff for the defendants, and plaintiff authorized a number of transactions on said account, giving his orders through Ranger, who, in addition to those authorized, sent other orders to buy and sell stocks on account of the plaintiff of which the plaintiff was ignorant; but the referee also found that those transactions were executed in good faith by the defendants, who did not know, and had no reason to know, that they were unauthorized.

The evidence fully sustains the contention that through all those transactions Ranger was the agent of the defendants and not of the plaintiff. The dealings of the plaintiff with Ranger as the representative of the defendants must stand respecting account No. 1 upon the same footing as to their liability as if the plaintiff had dealt directly with the defendants. The shares with which he is sought to be charged by the defendants over and above the 1,000 which they were carrying can be no other than the 600, the purchase of which on his account the plaintiff disclaims. The referee has found that the plaintiff must bear the loss arising from the purchase and sale of these 600 shares, because of his neglect in the transactions and because the defendants themselves were free from negligence, and this conclusion requires an examination of the evidence to ascertain what was the situation and what were the acts of the parties concerning the account No. 1.

Eliminating from that account those 600 shares, we find that on the 15th of February, 1898, the day upon which the stock was sold, there was a margin upon 1,000 shares of $1,770 and the referee very properly states in his opinion that if the plaintiff's contention is correct, his account was sufficiently margined to protect it from an arbitrary sale, while if the defendants' contention is correct, they were unquestionably justified in selling out the account, provided they had performed their obligation in giving notice. We are unable to gather from all the evidence a satisfactory reason why, as an original proposition, the plaintiff should be charged with the fraud of Ranger upon his principals, or with the consequences of the imposition he practiced upon them. It is conceded that he had no direct transactions with the defendants. Ranger was employed by them to solicit and take orders from customers. The defendants put Ranger in the position which enabled him to deceive them, and as his agency was solely for them it is apparent that if no other element is introduced in the case those who were invited by the defendants to deal with him on their account should not be made to suffer for his transgressions. Good faith or honesty of purpose on the part of the defendants in buying these stocks and charging them to the plaintiff does not affect the question. The defendants may have believed that the plaintiff had ordered the purchase of the additional shares, but that would give them no right, unless the plaintiff did something to confirm that belief or acted in such a way as to justify it and to subject them to some loss in consequence of such acts of confirmation. The defendants contend that such was the case. They claim that accounts were furnished from day to day to the plaintiff of the transactions he

FIRST DEPARTMENT, APRIL TERM, 1902.   [Vol. 70.

now repudiates; that the ordinary notifications were sent to him
at the address given by him; that he paid no attention to those
notices, and that, therefore, they were justified in believing that
the orders for the purchase emanated from him, and that they
were thus prevented from taking such steps as would have been
appropriate to save themselves from loss had they been notified
that Ranger had no authority to give the orders for these repudiated purchases. The course of dealings established between the
parties was the following: The account, referring now to account
No. 1, was originally opened at the solicitation of Ranger and by
a transfer to the defendants of an account which the plaintiff had had with another firm of brokers. The defendants
conducted their business at their office at 44 and 46 Broadway in the city of New York. Ranger, their agent, transacted
his business at the Waldorf-Astoria Hotel in the city of New
York; orders were given to him by the plaintiff and were then
transmitted by telephone to the defendants' principal office on
Broadway, and the orders were then executed in the customary
way. On the day on which each order was executed, a memorandum showing the transaction was sent in the usual way to
the customer. The plaintiff had stated that his address was the
Reform Club in the city of New York. There is no reason to
doubt that on each occasion on which an order was given by Ranger
for the account of the plaintiff, whether such order were genuine or
spurious, the usual notification was sent to the Reform Club. The
plaintiff swears that he received no such notices. The evidence
upon this subject is in such a condition that we are unable to hold
that the plaintiff was bound to these unauthorized purchases by
reason of inattention to those notices. But the contention of the
defendants is further to the effect that on the fourteenth day of
February, the day before they closed the plaintiff's account, they
sent to him notices, the delivery of which at the Reform Club is
proven, that the margins upon his account were exhausted, and in
that notice it was specifically mentioned that they were carrying
for him 1,600 shares of stock. That notice is in the following
words: "At the closing prices your account is short and during the
day we have endeavored to communicate without success. Will
you kindly send us $1,000 at least by the opening to-morrow to

protect your stocks, and another $1,000 as additional margin if you wish to carry them.   You are long 800 shares Penna., 300 Northern Pac. Pf., Union Pacific Pfd. and 200 B. & O. S. W. Pfd." The reference is undoubtedly to 300 shares each of Northern Pacific and Union Pacific stock.   The plaintiff swears that he never received this notice, but at all events, on the fifteenth of February, the defendants sold out the plaintiff's account, and they again sent by special messenger a notification to the plaintiff, who again swears he never received it, although this notice as well as the one the day before was proved to have been delivered by a special messenger at the Reform Club.

All this might have been satisfactory evidence to bind the plaintiff to an account by which he was charged with the 1,600 shares, and which would have been sufficient as a notification to him that his margins were exhausted and his stock would be sold unless the margin was kept up, if the inference could fairly be drawn that the plaintiff actually received these notices and there were nothing further in the case to show that he was not concluded by them and their contents.   On the fifteenth day of February, the day on which the account was closed, the plaintiff had a conversation over the telephone with a Mr. Kelly, one of the defendants, and he asked for Ranger.   That communication was opened by the plaintiff in consequence of a letter he received that day from Ranger asking him to call him up personally at the office of the defendants in Broadway.   Ranger was not there, but Kelly informed the plaintiff that his stocks had been sold.   The plaintiff swears that he understood that as referring to certain stocks which the defendants were carrying for him and which he had authorized or directed to be sold at a fixed price, and that he did not regard that communication as referring to the whole account.   On the evening of that day the plaintiff saw Ranger, who requested him to call next day.   On the sixteenth the plaintiff had a conversation with Ranger at the Waldorf-Astoria Hotel, and there they figured up the margin which was in the defendants' hands on the plaintiff's account, and it was found to be about $1,600.   Ranger then assured the plaintiff that his stocks were secure, but asked for additional margin and received it in the shape of a draft or check drawn upon London for £200. On the same day the plaintiff left the city of New York for Boston, where he remained for some days and, on returning, found that his whole account had been closed and his stock sold on the fifteenth.

We are of the opinion, upon all these facts, which are in the main uncontradicted, that the plaintiff might safely rest upon the conviction that in dealing with Ranger he was entitled to regard him, if not as one of the defendants, then (as he was in fact) the representative and agent of the defendants in all the transactions concerning account No. 1, and that all that Ranger did with the plaintiff was binding upon the defendants. We think that the defendants closed the account and sold the plaintiff's stock without right on the fifteenth of February; that the plaintiff is not precluded by the notices claimed to have been sent to him, and that on the sixteenth although the day after the sale), when the communication was made by Ranger, that the plaintiff had sufficient margin for the time being, and additional margin was put up, the plaintiff was entitled to believe that his stocks were secure and his account protected. On the sixteenth the defendants, through their agent, were dealing with the plaintiff with reference to a then existing account, and the plaintiff is not estopped from insisting that the sale on the fifteenth was unauthorized, and he is not bound to an admission that the defendants were carrying for him the 600 additional shares which they claimed to have bought on his account. On all the evidence as to this account No. 1, our conclusions are, *first*, that the defendants were not authorized to buy the 600 shares with which they seek to charge the plaintiff; *second*, that the plaintiff's account on the fifteenth of February consisted of the 1,000 shares upon which on that day there was sufficient margin; *third*, that although the defendants may honestly have believed that they were carrying 1,600 shares for him on that day, and sent a notice containing a statement that they held that number of shares and that the margin was exhausted, nevertheless the plaintiff was not bound by such notice, he having on the same day made the effort to see the defendants' agent concerning the matter, and on the next day, having seen their agent (with whom the transactions were had), and agreed with him that the margin was sufficient to carry his stock, and he having given to such agent a check for an additional sum as margin. We think, therefore, on this account No. 1 that the plaintiff is entitled to recover from the defendants whatever loss he sustained by reason of their closing it out, the measure of damages being the difference between the price at which they sold his 1,000 shares and the highest price which shares of a similar character brought in the market within a reasonable time after the fifteenth of February.

Concerning account No. 2, the finding of the referee is correct. That was a speculative account carried in the name of the plaintiff, but in which he, Ranger and one Bowles were jointly interested. Whatever may have been the relations existing between these three parties was a matter of no consequence to the defendants in the absence of knowledge on their part of the fact that this was other than just such an account as it purported to be, namely, one for which the plaintiff is individually responsible. The defendants may look to him for liability on that account, and no fair contest can be made as to the fact that the defendants were entitled to close that account as they did. A balance was due on it to them. For a portion of that balance Bowles gave a check through Ranger, but did not satisfy the whole indebtedness nor was it received by the defendants in extinguishment of that whole indebtedness. Bowles and Ranger were interested with the plaintiff in this account No. 2, and the plaintiff was properly held liable for all of the balance of that account except the amount that had been paid by the check of Bowles given to Ranger. It cannot be said that Ranger was the agent of the defendants with respect to this account No. 2, for, by the arrangement between the plaintiff and Bowles and Ranger, those three were engaged in transactions in the very nature of which Ranger could not have been the agent of the defendants, but was, in effect, a partner with the plaintiff, and the defendants are entitled to avail themselves of the real nature of the transactions. The plaintiff is, therefore, liable for the balance, and the amount of it is a proper offset to any recovery to which the plaintiff might be entitled on account No. 1.

The foregoing considerations lead to a reversal of the judgment, and a direction that a new trial be had before another referee, with costs to appellant to abide the event.

Van Brunt, P. J., O'Brien and Laughlin, JJ., concurred.

Judgment reversed, new trial ordered before another referee, with costs to appellant to abide event.

Minnie G. Glean, by George Dodson, her Guardian ad Litem, Appellant, v. Robert G. Glean, Respondent.

Concealment, by a husband from his wife, of his prior unlawful cohabitation with another woman — it is not such "fraud" as authorizes the annulment of the marriage.

The concealment by a husband from his wife of the fact that prior to his marriage he had unlawfully cohabited with another woman and had had children by her, is not a ground for the annulment of the marriage. The fraud which will authorize the annulment of a marriage, under subdivision 4 of section 1748 of the Code of Civil Procedure, is a fraud relating to the essentials of the
* contract.

Appeal by the plaintiff, Minnie G. Glean, by George Dodson, her guardian ad litem, from an order of the Supreme Court, made at the New York Special Term and entered in the office of the clerk of the county of New York on the 29th day of January, 1902, denying the plaintiff's motion for leave to serve an amended complaint.

Maurice Meyer, for the appellant.

Charles G. Stevenson, for the respondent.

Patterson, J.:

The plaintiff and the defendant were married at the city of New York on the 20th of November, 1899. In May, 1900, she brought, through her guardian *ad litem,* this action to annul the marriage upon allegations that at the time of such marriage the defendant had a former wife then living to whom he had been married several years before, and that such last-mentioned marriage was in full force and effect at the time of the marriage of herself and the defendant. The defendant answered, denying the allegations of the complaint, and the cause being at issue it appeared upon the calendar of the Special Term of the court in June, 1901, when upon the application of the plaintiff the trial was postponed in order to enable her to take testimony, upon a commission, of witnesses to prove the alleged prior marriage of the defendant. Subsequently, and in January, 1902, when the case was about to appear again upon the calendar for trial, the plaintiff suggesting that grave obstacles existed to her procuring proof of the alleged prior marriage of the defendant, moved to amend her complaint by setting up a second cause of action, and she obtained an order to show cause why she should not be allowed to serve an amended complaint containing such second and independent cause of action. A proposed amended complaint was served with the order to show cause, and its averments are in substance that for the purpose of inducing the plaintiff to consent to marriage, the defendant falsely and fraudulently represented to her that he was a respectable and honorable unmarried man of good social position, and of good moral character; that he concealed his real position and character from plaintiff; that he was not a respectable or an honorable man, or a man of good moral character, but on the contrary at the time such representations were made, and at the time of his marriage to plaintiff, he *either* had been married to *or* had unlawfully cohabited for many years with a woman in the island of Cuba, by whom he had at least two children, such woman and children being alive to defendant's knowledge at the time said representations were made and his marriage with the plaintiff *consummated*, and that defendant without the knowledge of the plaintiff recognized and treated the woman in Cuba as his wife and his children by her as his own, but that he now denies his marriage with that woman; that the plaintiff was induced to consent to her marriage with defendant by his said representations, which she believed at the time of her marriage to be true, and by her ignorance of the facts he concealed; and that if the said representations had not been made to her and said concealment had not been practiced, she would never have consented to the said marriage. The court at Special Term denied the motion to amend the complaint by allowing a second cause of action to be set forth, and from that order the plaintiff now appeals.

The general rule is, that marriage covers with oblivion antenuptial incontinence and lapses from virtue. (*Graves* v. *Graves*, 3 Curt. 238; *Brooks* v. *Brooks*, 145 Mass. 574; *Van Epps* v. *Van Epps*, 6 Barb. 320; *Weatherley* v. *Weatherley*, 1 Spinks Ecc. & Ad. 193.) In the case last cited, the learned Dr. Lushington says, "the doctrine universally maintained is, that marriage operates as an oblivion of all that has passed, *and as oblivion of all that can possibly have occurred.*" Notwithstanding this general rule, the law authorizes the annulment of a marriage when one of the parties to it has been induced to consent, or enter into the contract, by fraud. In the State of New York, that authority is contained in the 4th subdivision of section 1743 of the Code of Civil Procedure, by which it is enacted that an action may be maintained to procure a judgment declaring a marriage contract void, and annulling the marriage where it appears " that the consent of one of the parties was obtained by force, duress or fraud." What amounts to such a fraud as would authorize a judicial decree annulling a marriage has not been and cannot be defined in general terms, but it has been regarded as a fraud relating to the essentials of a contract of marriage, namely, that the parties are competent to contract and to fulfill the obligations of that contract. There are cases in the books in which the views of individual judges respecting the facts of particular cases as furnishing proof sufficient to annul a contract on the ground of fraud are set forth, but our attention has not been called to any adjudication in which it has been held that the mere concealment of antenuptial incontinence and the consequences thereof, so long as they do not affect the essentials of the contract of marriage, have been sufficient to require a judicial annulment of that contract. In *Fisk* v. *Fisk* (6 App. Div. 432) this court said that the rule is well settled that no fraud will avoid a marriage which does not go to the very essence of the contract, and which is not in its nature such a thing as either would prevent the party from entering into the marriage relation, or, having entered into it, would preclude performance of the duties which the law and custom imposes upon the husband or wife as a party to that contract (1 Bish. Marr. & Div. [6th ed.] §§ 183, 184 ; Schouler Husb. & Wife, § 27 ; *Reynolds* v. *Reynolds*, 3 Allen, 605), and it is further said that, within that rule, no misconception of one party as to the *character* or fortune or temper of the other, however brought about, will support an allegation of fraud on which a dissolution of the marriage contract, when once executed, can be obtained in a court of justice. (1 Bish. Marr. & Div. *supra; Wier* v. *Still*, 31 Iowa, 107.) The gist of the proposed additional cause of action in this case is the concealment of illicit relations of the defendant with a woman prior to his marriage with the plaintiff, for the alternative allegation that he was married to that other woman adds nothing to this second cause of action as that is made the substantive ground of relief in the complaint as it now stands.

It is not necessary to expand the discussion of the subject beyond what is said in *Fisk* v. *Fisk* (*supra*) and in the well-considered opinion of Mr. Justice PRYOR in *Shrady* v. *Logan* (17 Misc. Rep. 330), in which latter case it was held that concealment by the wife from her husband that before her marriage she had given birth to an illegitimate child did not in itself constitute such fraud as would authorize annulment of the marriage.

The order appealed from should be affirmed, with costs.

VAN BRUNT, P. J., O'BRIEN and LAUGHLIN, JJ., concurred.

Order affirmed, with ten dollars costs and disbursements.

———— — — ——— ——

THE PEOPLE OF THE STATE OF NEW YORK v. THE AMERICAN LOAN AND TRUST COMPANY.

In the Matter of the Proofs of Claim upon the Final Accounting of J. EDWARD SIMMONS, as Receiver of THE AMERICAN LOAN AND TRUST COMPANY.

EUPHEMIA A. HAWES, as Executrix, etc., of GRANVILLE P. HAWES, Deceased, and Others, Appellants; LOUIS BAUER and Others, Appellants and Respondents; J. EDWARD SIMMONS, Receiver of THE AMERICAN LOAN AND TRUST COMPANY, Respondent.

Receivership of a trust company — claims of an attorney for services to the trust company, not increasing the fund, are not preferred — interest, when not allowed on preferred claims — excepting creditors, only, entitled to share in the benefits of a reversal.

A claim by the attorney of a trust company, which has been dissolved, for services rendered by him in connection with securities held by the trust company as collateral to a loan, is not entitled to a preferential payment out of the assets in the hands of the receiver of the trust company, appointed in the action to dissolve it, where it does not appear that there were any judicial proceedings in connection with the collateral securities which would support a common-law or a statutory lien, or that the attorney did anything which created or preserved any of the securities or resulted in any advantage to the receiver or to the trust company; nor is a claim for services, rendered by the attorney, at the request of the trust company, in opposing the appointment of the receiver of the company, entitled to such a preference, where it appears that the attorney's efforts did not augment or preserve the funds of the trust company.

Where the charter of the trust company provides, "In case of the dissolution of the said company by the Legislature, the Supreme Court or otherwise, the *debts due* from the company as trustee, guardian, receiver or depositary of moneys in court or of savings bank funds, shall have a preference," the amount of such preferred debts should be determined as of the date of the appointment of the receiver. If there are sufficient assets to pay all the creditors, interest accruing after the appointment of the receiver on the preferred debts will be allowed, but if there are not sufficient assets to pay all the creditors, interest will not be allowed on the preferred debts.

Where only a portion of the unpreferred creditors file exceptions to the report of a referee, erroneously allowing interest accruing after the appointment of the receiver on debts preferred by the charter, the excepting creditors are alone entitled to share in the benefits resulting from a reversal of the referee's ruling upon that point.

APPEALS by Euphemia A. Hawes, as executrix, etc., of Granville P. Hawes, deceased, and others, from portions of an order of the Supreme Court, made at the New York Special Term and entered in the office of the clerk of the county of New York on the 11th day of December, 1901, upon a motion to confirm the second report of the referee appointed in the matter of the final accounting of the receiver of the American Loan and Trust Company.

Barclay E. V. McCarty, for the appellant Hawes.

Vincent P. Donihee, for the appellant Wickes.

C. L. Stone, for the appellant Onondaga County Savings Bank.

Christian N. Bovee, Jr., for the appellant Union Dime Savings Institution.

James Dunne, for the appellants respondents Bauer and others.

William S. Opdyke, for the respondent.

PATTERSON, J. :

The several matters requiring consideration in this case are brought up by appeal from an order made at the Special Term sustaining some and overruling other conclusions of a referee. The duty imposed upon the referee by the order of his appointment was to make a proper distribution among creditors of a balance of moneys remaining in the hands of the receiver of the American Loan and Trust Company. That corporation had been dissolved by an order of the Supreme Court made on the 1st day of May, 1891, and in and by such order J. Edward Simmons was appointed its receiver. He entered upon the discharge of his duties, collected the assets of the corporation and from time to time, in pursuance of orders of the court, made payments to preferred creditors of the corporation, but none to unpreferred creditors.

Among the preferred creditors are the Onondaga County Savings Bank, the Monroe County Savings Bank, the Union Dime Savings Institution and the Farmers and Mechanics' Savings Bank. These several institutions with other preferred creditors have been paid by the receiver the full amount of the principal of their respective claims upon the dissolved corporation. Those claims were for moneys on deposit with that corporation and under agreements by which interest at varying rates was to be paid upon such deposits. On the 21st day of July, 1891, a dividend of thirty-five per cent was paid to the preferred creditors on the principal of their claims; on July 13, 1892, another payment of thirty-five per cent was made to them in the same way; on June 21, 1893, another dividend of twenty per cent was paid them, and on the 2d of July, 1894, a fourth dividend of ten per cent was paid. Each of these several dividends was receipted for as a dividend on the principal amount of the claims of these preferred creditors. The receipt for the fourth and final dividend recited that it was on and completed the payment of the principal of the claim of the creditor receiving it as a preferred creditor of the trust company. The referee in his report allowed these savings institutions and their preferred creditors interest upon their claims. They had insisted before him that they were entitled to legal interest down to the time of the payment of the first dividend, and that such payments should be treated as being first on account of interest and then the balance applied to the payment of the principal and so on with the three other dividends. The referee did not adopt that contention, but reported that the preferred creditors were entitled to interest upon the prin-

cipal of their claims down to the time of the payment of the first
dividend, then to interest upon the balance as upon a new principal
until the payment of the second dividend, and so on through the
whole series of payments.   The allowance of interest upon the preferred claims, including those of the savings institutions, would
exhaust the whole of the balance in the hands of the receiver, leaving nothing for the unpreferred creditors.   Certain of those unpreferred creditors, namely, Louis Bauer, William L. Koester and
Louise B. O'Connor, individually and as administratrix of James
Owen O'Connor, deceased, excepted to the report of the referee.
The claims of those parties amount to about $153,000.   The aggre-
gate of unpreferred claims allowed by the referee was $455,000, but
none of the unpreferred creditors other than those above named
excepted to the report of the referee.   Euphemia A. Hawes, the
executrix of the last will and testament of Granville P. Hawes,
deceased, presented claims aggregating $14,786.46, and of that
amount she claimed to be entitled to a preference for $8,365
on one ground and to $5,000 with interest on another ground.
The referee refused to allow the preference, but recognized the
whole amount of these claims as unpreferred debts.   They had
their origin in legal services rendered by Mr. Hawes to the American
Loan and Trust Company, some of which services apparently were
continued after the appointment of the receiver.   Thomas P.
Wickes, as receiver of the firm of Stanton & Co., was included
by the referee in the schedule of preferred creditors and was
allowed interest upon the claims of that firm.   By the order
appealed from, the learned judge at Special Term, adopting the
conclusion of the referee, adjudged that the claim of Mrs. Hawes,
as executrix, was not entitled to a preference.   Contrary to the conclusion of the referee, he held that the savings banks and the preferred creditors appearing before him were not entitled to interest.
He further held that all the unpreferred creditors were entitled to
share in the distributable balance in the hands of the receiver, and
not those only who had filed exceptions to the referee's report.
The several specific matters we are to consider on this appeal may,
therefore, be stated as follows: *First.* Is the executrix of the last
will and testament of Granville P. Hawes, deceased, entitled to a
preference of either or both of the items of $8,000 and $5,000, which

the referee ranked as unpreferred claims? *Second.* Are the savings banks and Thomas P. Wickes, receiver, entitled to interest on their respective preferred claims? *Third.* If those preferred creditors are not entitled to such interest, is the distribution of the balance of the moneys in the hands of the receiver to be made among those unpreferred creditors who excepted to the report of the referee, or is that balance to be distributed among such unpreferred creditors generally?

First. An examination of the evidence respecting the services rendered by Mr. Hawes shows that the summary of the facts in relation thereto, made by the referee in his report, is an accurate statement of all that Mr. Hawes did under his employment. From those facts no other conclusion was permissible than that reached by the referee. The claim to a preference for these services must stand upon the right to a statutory lien, or the right to a common-law lien as distinguished from a statutory lien, or upon equitable considerations indicating that a fund from which payment is preferentially demanded was either created in whole or in part, or preserved by the services of the attorney who makes a specific claim upon that fund. The $8,000 item is for services rendered by Mr. Hawes as the regular attorney and counsel of the American Loan and Trust Company. That corporation was a trustee under a mortgage made to secure bonds of the Decatur, Chespeake and New Orleans Railway Company. The American Loan and Trust Company held in its own right some $400,000 at par value of those bonds and about the same amount of its stock. These securities were held as collateral to a loan made by the trust company to the railway company of about $310,000. The mortgage upon default of the bonds was foreclosed and Mr. Hawes was paid for his services in that foreclosure. He also rendered services in connection with the collateral securities held by the trust company, and it would seem that the claim is made to a lien upon the funds in the hands of the receiver, or a right to a preferential payment thereof on the ground that Mr. Hawes had some specific right or lien upon the bonds and stocks so held by the trust company as collateral. All that was ever received by the trust company out of these collaterals appears to have been the sum of $5,950. There does not appear to have been any judicial proceedings in connection with this collateral security; and, hence, there was no statutory lien, nor was there any judgment concerning them to which a common-law lien could attach, nor was there anything done by him that created or preserved any of these securities, or increased in any way a fund, or resulted in any advantage to the receivership or the trust company; and, therefore, we think, with reference to this item, the decision of the referee was right. As to the $5,000 claim, the services for which that amount is charged were rendered at the request of the American Loan and Trust Company, and apparently not otherwise than in endeavors to prevent the appointment of a receiver of that company. Those services are clearly not entitled to preference in payment out of the moneys belonging to the creditors of the receivership. Nothing came through the opposition to the appointment of a receiver which in any way augmented or preserved the funds of the trust company. Conceding that they are valid claims against the receivership, they are entitled to rank only as unpreferred claims. The disposition made of both these items by the court below we, therefore, consider to have been correct.

Second. Interest upon the preferred claims was not allowed by the Special Term for the reason stated in the opinion of the court that such preferred creditors having given receipts for and accepted the principal of their claims, they are debarred from now recovering interest. The learned judge held that the interest claimed by the preferred creditors is not contractual interest, but interest as damages for non-payment of the debts, and the rule is that where interest is recoverable merely as damages for non-payment of a debt, the creditor cannot maintain an action for its recovery after accepting the principal, citing cases in support of that proposition. It is very doubtful whether the view of the relations of these preferred creditors to this fund are such as they were deemed to be by the Special Term, but it is unnecessary to consider that question for the reason that, as we regard the rights of these preferred creditors, they were not entitled to interest at all in the situation of this fund until all the other creditors were fully satisfied. Upon this broad ground we think the decision of the Special Term may be upheld. The right of these preferred creditors, namely, the savings banks and Wickes, receiver, arises out of the provisions of the charter of the American Loan and Trust Company, and not out of those of the

Banking Law. The charter provision is in the following words: " In case of the dissolution of the said company by the Legislature, the Supreme Court or otherwise, the *debts due* from the company as trustee, guardian, receiver or depositary of moneys in court or of savings bank funds, shall have a preference." This provision is in derogation of the well-known rule that, in the distribution of the assets of debtors, equality is equity. The widest scope has been given to the application of that equitable principle, and the provision of the charter of this corporation should not be expanded to cover anything more than such a preference as may reasonably be regarded as having been within the intention of the Legislature when that provision was inserted in that charter. The real question is, what is the extent of the preference, and that depends upon the time at which the debt preferred is to be deemed due. The provision is " in case of the dissolution of the said company," the creditors mentioned shall have a preference for debts due, and we conceive that that provision was made with the intention that the preference should take effect at the time at which all claims against the corporation would be presentable, and that it was not the intention of the Legislature to allow either contractual interest or interest as damages to run on indefinitely through all the protracted proceedings that might continue (as they did in this case) for many years after the court took possession of the assets for the purpose of making distribution of them. By the appointment of the receiver the law took possession of this corporation, stopped its business and at once entered upon the collection and distribution of its assets. In *People* v. *Commercial Alliance Life Ins. Co.* (154 N. Y. 95) the court says : " It is the day on which the court practically takes possession of the assets of the company for the purpose of distribution among its creditors and consequently (that) is the day on which the rights of creditors should be ascertained and the value of their claims determined." In that case the court cites the *Matter of Equitable Reserve Fund Life Association* (131 N. Y. 354), and quotes from the opinion of PECKHAM, J., as follows: " In this case, the proceeding had for its end the dissolution of the company. We hold that after the commencement of the proceedings no assessments need be levied or paid and if the proceedings terminate in dissolution the status of the claimants at the commencement of the

proceedings is the proper one upon which to base the distribution."
These were cases of life insurance companies involving the rights
and relations of policy holders, but they illustrate the rule we think
applicable here in construing the words "debts due." We are of
opinion that the point of time at which the status of the preferred
debts, that is, the amount preferred, is to be fixed, is the date of
the appointment of the receiver, when the court took into its hands
the distribution of the fund or it may relate back to the institution
of the proceeding. The claim is against assets. As against the
corporation itself, interest may be continued, and if there is enough
to pay all creditors, would be allowed. There is nothing in the
provision quoted of the charter of this corporation which in terms
allows interest as part of the preference. "Debts due" from the
company in case of dissolution have the preference and the inference to be drawn from these words is rather that when the company
is dissolved, the debts *then* due (which includes both owing and payable) to the specified creditors shall have a preference as they exist
when that event takes place. The enlargement of this provision
into a right to interest on the debts after the dissolution and until
protracted judicial proceedings are terminated, is only done by
another and contrary and inequitable inference. The case of *Upton
v. N. Y. & Erie Bank* (13 Hun, 271) is cited in opposition to
our view, but that case is distinguishable. There the court held,
under the provisions of section 48, chapter 371, Laws of 1875, that
savings bank deposits were entitled to a preference with interest to
the date of payment. The provision of the law is that all the property of any bank or trust company which shall become insolvent
shall be applied by the receiver thereof in the *first place* to the *payment in full* of any sum or sums of money deposited therewith by
any savings bank. In the *Upton* case no reason is given by the
court for allowing interest, but it was taken for granted that under
the provision of the law then under consideration the savings bank
was entitled to interest until it was paid in full. There is a difference between the provision of law in that case and the charter of
this corporation. Here the provision merely is that in case of a
dissolution the savings banks shall have a preference. We think
the rule should be applied that each creditor gets his or its status in
proving claims against the assets of the corporation as of the date

of dissolution, and that where preference is given it takes effect for the amount established as of that. date. We have seen that such was the rule in the cases above cited, applied on the dissolution of insurance companies. It is an equitable rule, which, in the absence of statutory declaration that another must prevail, ought to be applied here. We think, consequently, that these savings banks are not entitled to interest, either as damages or as arising out of contract, after the appointment of the receiver.

Third. Only the unpreferred creditors who filed exceptions to the report of the referee are before this court. It certainly seems inequitable that the exceptants alone should receive the distributable funds in the hands of the receiver, but the other unpreferred creditors have not pressed their claims nor put themselves in an attitude to receive the benefit of the ruling now made, or to review that of the referee. They acquiesced in his findings and are concluded thereby.

The order appealed from should be modified by restricting the right of the unpreferred creditors to distribution of the fund created under the exceptions to those who filed exceptions to the report of the referee and were represented on this appeal.

VAN BRUNT, P. J., McLAUGHLIN and HATCH, JJ., concurred.

INGRAHAM, J. (concurring):

I concur with Mr. Justice PATTERSON, except as to the disallowance of interest upon the deposits by the savings banks, as I think under the contract between the corporation and the savings banks the latter were entitled to contractual interest up to the time of payment, as the contract with the savings banks provided for the payment of such interest.

Order modified as directed in opinion, with costs of appeal to the respondent as against the savings banks, appellants.

THE SHOE LASTING MACHINE COMPANY OF NEW YORK, Appellant, *v.* THE WESTERN NATIONAL BANK OF THE CITY OF NEW YORK, Respondent.

Banking — checks on a deposit made by a corporation which has left signature cards with the bank — how the checks should be signed.

The secretary and treasurer of a corporation, acting on behalf thereof, opened two accounts with a bank, one known as the general account and the other known as the dividend account. At the time he opened the accounts he left with the bank two signature cards designed to guide the bank in the payment of checks upon the two accounts. One of such cards read:

"AUTHORIZED SIGNATURES OF

"*Dec* 10*th* 1897.

"*THE SHOE LASTING MACHINE CO.*

" *T. Mayo Blackwell*

" *Treas*

" *General Account.*

" *Walter Shaw, Prest.*"

The other read:

"AUTHORIZED SIGNATURES OF

" ....189......

" *THE SHOE LASTING MACHINE CO.*

" *Dividend Account.*

" *T. Mayo Blackwell*

" *Secty & Treas* "

Held, that the bank had authority to pay checks drawn on the dividend account and signed by Blackwell as secretary and treasurer, but that it had no authority to pay checks drawn on the general account and signed by Blackwell as treasurer and not by Shaw as president.

APPEAL by the plaintiff, the Shoe Lasting Machine Company of New York, from a judgment of the Supreme Court in favor of the defendant, entered in the office of the clerk of the county of New York on the 7th day of February, 1901, upon the verdict of a jury, and also from an order entered in said clerk's office on the 8th day of March, 1901, denying the plaintiff's motion for a new trial made upon the minutes.

Justus P. Sheffield, for the appellant.

John Quinn, for the respondent.

PATTERSON, J. :

This appeal is from a judgment, entered upon a verdict in favor of the defendant, and from an order denying a motion for a new trial. The action was brought to recover balances of money which the plaintiff claimed to be due it upon two deposit accounts it had with the defendant — one called the general account and the other the dividend account. The plaintiff was a corporation of the State of Massachusetts, but it had its main office or agency in the city of New York in charge of one Blackwell, who was the secretary and treasurer of the corporation, and is also referred to in the evidence as being practically a local manager. Blackwell opened the bank accounts for the plaintiff with the defendant, and it fully appears that the officers of the corporation in Massachusetts were cognizant of the opening of such accounts, and if original authority was not conferred upon Blackwell to open them, his acts in so doing were fully ratified by continuous dealings through those accounts with the defendant which were known to and acquiesced in by the plaintiff. In answer to the causes of action stated in the complaint, the defendant set up, in substance, the defense of payment. On the trial, the affirmative of the issue being with the defendant, it sought to establish its contention by evidence of the disbursement of moneys upon checks, which it claims were properly signed to authorize it to charge against the accounts of the plaintiff all the moneys withdrawn from the bank on such checks. It is admitted by the plaintiff that on the general account, all moneys were withdrawn on proper and sufficient checks, except the sum of $500.85. Those checks, which the plaintiff recognizes and admits to have been properly drawn on the general account, bore the name of the plaintiff corporation and the signatures of " T. Mayo Blackwell, Treas.," and " Walter Shaw, Prest." The checks drawn upon the general account and repudiated by the plaintiff, were subscribed in its name but bore only the signature of " T. Mayo Blackwell, Treas." The checks disclaimed by the plaintiff and paid by the defendant out of the dividend account, were subscribed in the name of the plaintiff, but bore only the signature of " T. Mayo Blackwell, Secty. and Treas."

When Blackwell opened the accounts with the defendant he left with it two signature cards. It is admitted that those cards were intended to guide the bank in its payment of checks drawn upon the plaintiff's two accounts, but the plaintiff contends that checks drawn upon those accounts should have borne the signatures of two officers while the defendant insists that the signature of either of the two officers would suffice upon checks drawn on the general account and of Blackwell alone on the dividend account. When the two accounts were opened by Blackwell, if he had original authority to open them, that authority embraced the right to do everything that was necessary to the constitution of an active bank account, and included furnishing the bank with examples of the signatures upon which checks upon those accounts should be honored. If he did not have original authority to open the accounts, but his acts in so doing were ratified by the plaintiff, then that ratification also extended to such acts as he performed and were necessary to the constitution of a current bank account or accounts. Of the two signature cards that applicable to the general account reads as follows:

"AUTHORIZED SIGNATURES OF

"*Dec.* 10*th* 1897.

"*THE SHOE LASTING MACHINE CO.*

"*T. Mayo Blackwell*

"*Treas.*

"*General Account.*

"*Walter Shaw, Prest.*"

"Address 123 *Liberty St. N. Y.*

"Business *Shoe Machinery*

"Introduced by *U. S. Nat. Bank*

"For THE WESTERN NATIONAL BANK, New York."

There is some conflict of testimony as to this card in its completed shape having been left by Blackwell with the Western National Bank at the time the account was opened. Mr. Shaw, the president of the company, says that it was sent to him signed by Blackwell and that then he added his signature and forwarded the card by mail to the defendant; but it is immaterial how it reached the bank. The signature card for the dividend account is in the following words:

"AUTHORIZED SIGNATURES OF

"........ ... .189....

" *THE SHOE LASTING MACHINE CO.*

" *Dividend Account.*

" *T. Mayo Blackwell*

" *Secty. & Treas.*"

" Address 123 *Liberty S. N. Y.*

" Business *Shoe Machinery*

"Introduced by *U. S. Nat. Bank*

" For The WESTERN NATIONAL BANK, New York."

The object for which these signature cards were left with the bank being as above stated, the interpretation to be given to them as indicating the duty of the bank in the payment of checks is a subject for determination by the court, and it seems to be obvious that on the general account one set of signatures was required while on the dividend account another and distinct signature was necessary. Checks on both accounts were to be drawn in the name of the plaintiff, but on the general account two signatures were required, namely, that of the president and that of Blackwell as treasurer. That the differences in signatures were material is emphasized by the fact that on the dividend account Blackwell's signature was to be in an entirely different form and was to be made in a different capacity from that in which checks were to be drawn on the general account. On checks drawn on the general account he was to sign as treasurer alone ; on checks drawn on the dividend account he was to sign both as treasurer and secretary.

Obviously, checks drawn on the general account were to be signed by two officers ; checks on the dividend account by one. We can find nothing on the signature card relating to the general account which can be construed as authorizing the bank to pay checks on one of two signatures, and, on the other hand, nothing on the signature card relating to the dividend account which can be construed as authorizing the plaintiff to insist that two signatures were required to checks drawn upon that account. Consequently, we are of the opinion that the bank had no authority to pay moneys out of the general account upon the signature of Blackwell, Treas., alone, and that the defendant is not protected in making payment of the $500.85 upon insufficiently signed checks, and that the plaintiff was entitled to recover that amount, and, further, that the bank was authorized to make payment on checks on the dividend account signed by Blackwell, Sect. & Treas., alone. No such course of dealing was established between the parties as would have compelled the defendant to reject checks on that dividend account signed in the manner last indicated. The question as to the general account is sufficiently raised by the exception to the refusal of the court to charge the 8th request of the plaintiff.

It follows that the judgment and order appealed from should be reversed and a new trial ordered, with costs to the appellant to abide the event.

VAN BRUNT, P. J., INGRAHAM, McLAUGHLIN and HATCH, JJ., concurred.

Judgment and order reversed, new trial ordered, costs to appellant to abide event.

THE PEOPLE OF THE STATE OF NEW YORK, Respondent, *v.* ARTHUR MILLER, Appellant.

Abduction — what evidence does not corroborate the testimony of the girl abducted.

Where, upon the trial of an indictment framed under section 282 of the Penal Code, which provides that "a person who * * * takes, receives, employs, harbors or uses or causes, or procures to be taken, received, employed or harbored or used, a female under the age of eighteen years for the purpose of prostitution * * * is guilty of abduction," the female alleged to have been abducted testifies that, at her own request, the defendant made arrangements with the keeper of a disorderly house to have her received therein and that he took her to the house and left her there with knowledge of her purpose, evidence given by a person employed in the alleged disorderly house to the effect that she saw the defendant standing in the hallway of the house with other men and the female is not sufficiently corroborative of the testimony of the female to sustain a conviction of the defendant.

APPEAL by the defendant, Arthur Miller, from a judgment of the Court of General Sessions of the Peace in and for the city and county of New York in favor of the plaintiff, entered on the 19th day of July, 1901, upon the verdict of a jury convicting the defendant of the crime of abduction.

Charles Haldane, for the appellant.

Edward Sandford, for the respondent.

PATTERSON, J. :

The defendant was brought to trial in the Court of General Sessions of the Peace in and for the city and county of New York upon an indictment for the crime of abduction, which indictment contained two counts, the first charging that the defendant at the city of New York on a day named did feloniously take, receive, harbor, employ and use one Gussie Eslofsky, who was then under the age of eighteen years, to wit, of the age of fifteen years, for the purpose of sexual intercourse, he, the said defendant, not being then and there the husband of the said Gussie Eslofsky; and the second count charging that the defendant, at the time aforesaid, did feloniously take, receive, harbor and employ the said Gussie Eslofsky, she being then and there a female under the age of eighteen years, for the purpose of prostitution, against the form of the statute.

Upon the trial of the indictment the first count was virtually abandoned, the district attorney saying that he was willing to have the court instruct the jury that there was no corroboration sufficient to establish that count. Upon the second count the charge was substantially reduced to an accusation of the defendant taking the girl to a house of prostitution in order that she might become an inmate of that house for the purpose of prostitution. The testimony to establish the charge was given by the girl herself, who swore that she was a servant in the employment of the defendant. She was a wayward girl, addicted to vice, of which fact she says the defendant was aware. She states that she requested the defendant to put her in a place of prostitution, and that he told her that he had arranged with the keeper of a house of ill-fame in Stuyvesant place to have her received there, and that he took her there and left her with a knowledge of her purpose, and that she there pursued her career of a common prostitute. The prosecution relied for a conviction upon the fact of the defendant taking the girl to this place in order that she might there pursue her vicious life, and the court remarked on the trial, what was undoubtedly the condition of the case, that there was but one material fact to be established, namely, that the defendant brought the girl to that house for the purpose of prostitution. That statement of the court presented the only aspect in which the defendant could have been found guilty under the second count.

The provision of the statute referring to the crime of abduction, under which this indictment was framed, is contained in section 282 of the Penal Code, which, so far as it relates to this case, is as follows : " A person who * * * takes, receives, employs, harbors or uses or causes, or procures to be taken, received, employed, or harbored or used, a female under the age of eighteen years for the purpose of prostitution * * * is guilty of abduction." It was not claimed here under the second count of the indictment that the defendant received, employed, harbored or used a female under the age of eighteen years for the purpose of prostitution or caused or procured to be received (except so far as the girl testified to an arrangement having been made by the defendant with the keeper of the house of prostitution), employed, harbored or used such female for such purpose ; but the ground that the prosecution relied upon for conviction was that the defendant took the plaintiff to the house of ill-fame in Stuyvesant place. That explicit proof was made by the testimony of the girl herself cannot be doubted ; but, in order to a conviction being had, it was required that her statements should be corroborated, not necessarily by the oaths of witnesses who could confirm what she testified to upon the material facts, but by circumstances, if such existed.

We have searched this record in vain to find corroboration that the defendant took this girl to this house of prostitution or made any antecedent arrangement with the keeper of that house that she should be received and harbored there for an unlawful purpose. The only evidence, other than that of the girl herself, tending to connect this defendant with her is that of a witness who was employed in the house in Stuyvesant place, who testified that she saw the defendant standing in the hallway of that house with other men and the girl. There is not a word of corroboration of the statement of the girl that she ever was employed by or lived in the household of the defendant or ever knew him before the date charged in the indictment. There is not a word of testimony nor a circumstance shown to corroborate her statement that the defendant ever had any communication with the keeper or proprietor of the house of prostitution. There is no evidence to show, other than the statement of the girl, that the defendant advised her to go there or took her there or went with her there or had any agency whatever in inducing her to go there. The witness employed in this alleged disorderly house swore that she saw the Eslofsky girl at the house on the eighteenth of May. "I saw the girl with that young fellow over there (meaning the defendant); * * * I said that when this girl came to the place, I saw her with this defendant; I did see them in the hall; * * * I don't know whether she came with him or not." Her testimony simply amounts to a statement that she saw this girl and the defendant in the hall together, and that she recognized them. That is not sufficient corroboration of the fact that he took her there. The whole story of this girl may have been fabricated. What the law requires is confirmation of her story on the material facts, or on so much of the material facts as would lead to the conclusion beyond a reasonable doubt that the defendant was guilty of the crime with which he was charged.

The judgment must be reversed and a new trial ordered.

VAN BRUNT, P. J., O'BRIEN and LAUGHLIN, JJ., concurred.

Judgment reversed and new trial ordered.

MORRIS ORLICK, Appellant, *v.* BERTHA ORLICK, Respondent.

Party — action by a husband to establish a trust, in property conveyed absolutely by him to his wife, for the support of herself and her children and as a residence for himself — the children are not proper parties.

Where a husband has conveyed land to his wife by a deed, absolute upon its face, in reliance upon his wife's promise that she would hold the property in trust for the term of her natural life, would apply the rents, profits and income thereof to the repair of the buildings on the land and to the support and maintenance of the husband, after deducting a reasonable sum for the support of herself and her children, and would use the premises as the joint residence of herself and her husband, and would forthwith make her will, devising the property to her husband for the term of his natural life, the children of the husband and wife are neither necessary nor proper parties to an action brought by the husband against the wife to establish the existence of the trust.

APPEAL by the plaintiff, Morris Orlick, from an interlocutory judgment of the Supreme Court in favor of the defendant, entered in the office of the clerk of the county of New York on the 4th day of January, 1902, upon the decision of the court rendered after a trial at the New York Special Term, overruling the plaintiffs' demurrer to the "third and further defense" contained in the answer.

Saul S. Myers, for the appellant.

George M. S. Schulz, for the respondent.

PATTERSON, J. :

The defendant, who is the wife of the plaintiff, holds the legal title to certain real estate in the city of New York which was conveyed to her by the plaintiff by a deed absolute on its face. This action is brought to engraft a trust upon this title, the allegations of the complaint in that behalf being that the defendant induced the plaintiff to make the conveyance to her upon the representation, promise and agreement that if the plaintiff would make such conveyance she would hold the property in trust for the term of her natural life, would apply the rents, profits and income thereof to the repair of the buildings on the land, and to the support and maintenance of plaintiff, after deducting a reasonable sum for the support of herself and her children and would use the premises as the joint place of residence and abode of the plaintiff and defendant and would forthwith make her will devising to plaintiff the property for the term of his natural life. In answer to the complaint the defendant denies making any agreement whereby the property was to be charged with a trust, and claims that that property was bought with her own money, the title by mistake being placed in the name of her husband, the plaintiff, and that the conveyance to her was for the purpose of correcting that mistake. She asserts that she is the absolute owner of the premises. She then proceeds to set up as a third and separate defense that at the times mentioned in the complaint when the contract or agreement therein set forth was alleged to have been made, the plaintiff's and defendant's family consisted of five children, and that under the allegations of the complaint the said five children have an interest in the subject-matter of the action and are necessary parties and should be made parties to the action, and that they have not been joined with the defendant in the action and that, therefore, there is a defect of parties defendant. To this third defense the plaintiff demurred; the demurrer was overruled and from the interlocutory judgment thereupon entered, this appeal is taken.

Under the allegations of the complaint, the children have no such interest in the subject-matter of the action as requires that they be made parties. If there were any agreement of the character mentioned in the complaint, specific performance of that agreement, if it could be awarded at all, could be decreed without the presence in the action of those children. It was an agreement exclusively between a grantor and grantee of real estate, expressing the condition upon which a conveyance of that real estate was made. It was a condition for the benefit of the plaintiff, one upon which he parted with the property. The children took no interest in the land by virtue of the conveyance, and whatever contribution to their support would come from the rents, issues and profits of the land, if the trust were declared, would come entirely through the mother, who is to take in the first instance from the rents, issues and profits enough thereof for her and their support. They are not brought in privity with this agreement in any way. The right of the mother under the trust, as stated, would be personally to retain from the rents, issues and profits enough to support herself and those children who receive that support through her and not independently. They cannot claim, unless it be as against her, and then only during her natural life. The purpose of this action is the establishment of the trust as against the defendant. The issue is confined to an agreement with her. If no such agreement were made, the action fails, and if it were made, all rights are established when the adjudication against her is made.

We think, therefore, these children were neither necessary nor proper parties, and that the demurrer should have been sustained, with costs.

The interlocutory judgment should be reversed, with costs, and judgment ordered sustaining the demurrer to the third defense, with costs.

O'BRIEN and LAUGHLIN, JJ., concurred; VAN BRUNT, P. J., concurred in result.

Judgment reversed, with costs, and judgment ordered sustaining demurrer to the third defense, with costs.

HERMANN H. CAMMANN and Others, Surviving Executors of and
Trustees under the Last Will and Testament of NATHANIEL
PLATT BAILEY, Deceased, Respondents, *v.* SIDNEY SMITH WHIT-
TLESEY and Others, Appellants, Impleaded with ALLETTA R.
BAILEY and Others, Defendants, and ALLETTA NATHALIE BAILEY,
Respondent.

*Will — a gift of two mortgages, one held by the testator at his death and the other
directed by him to be purchased by the executors — both treated as specific legacies
in order to carry out the testator's intention.*

The will of a testator provided in the 12th clause thereof: "As the largest part
of my property consists of lands at Fordham Heights * * * and said lands
at the time of my death may yet be unsold and, therefore, unproductive of
income, and my wife may desire to occupy the property or some part thereof
during the term of my son's and granddaughter's lives — upon whose lives I
have limited her enjoyment of mine estate, or any other good reasons may then
exist why the same should not all be forthwith sold, and as my other property
will be sufficient to pay the taxes on said Fordham lands and most, if not all,
the other charges and legacies hereinbefore provided in the first to the eleventh
inclusive sections of this my will, and as the following legacies cannot be paid
unless said Fordham lands or some portions thereof are sold and a part of the
avails thereof used for that purpose, I hereby direct my executors to pay the
following legacies out of the body of my estate as soon as it can be done without embarrassment to my wife's comfort and an undue sacrifice of said lands,
but at any time within the lives of my son and granddaughter or the survivor
of them should my wife, if she then be living, consent in writing thereto; but
should any two of the three beneficiaries who are to receive the income of the
trust estate created under the succeeding sections of my will die, then I direct
such sale to be forthwith made, whether my said wife be living or not, and after
the provisions of the foregoing and succeeding sections of this my will have
been duly complied with, then I hereby give and bequeath the following sums
to the following persons hereby charging the estate of my said son and granddaughter and the residuary estate or estates hereby created with the payment
of the following legacies. Subject, therefore, to the above restrictions, I
hereby give and bequeath unto the following persons the following sums, viz.:
* * * To my niece Catherine Whittlesey, Twenty thousand dollars ($20,000),
payable as follows: Ten thousand 00/100 dollars ($10,000) thereof by transfer
to herself personally in her own right of a mortgage for that amount made by
her and her husband in favor of my wife and in case said mortgage shall not
belong to me at my decease then my executors are hereby directed to purchase
the same in order to comply with this bequest or otherwise to pay said legatee
that amount in money; six thousand dollars ($6,000) thereof to be paid by
transfer to her in her own right by executors of a mortgage made by her and

her husband in my favor for that amount and the balance of said legacy, the sum of four thousand dollars ($4,000) in money."

At the time of the testator's death, which occurred October 12, 1891, he owned the $6,000 mortgage alluded to and his wife owned the $10,000 mortgage. Letters testamentary were issued upon the testator's estate, January 8, 1892. December 1, 1899, the testator's executors purchased the $10,000 mortgage from the testator's wife and on that day, the Fordham Heights property still remaining unsold, assigned both mortgages to the next of kin of Catherine Whittlesey, who had died intestate.

Held, that the next of kin of Catherine Whittlesey should be charged with interest on both the mortgages for a year following the granting of the letters testamentary on the testator's estate, and not for any period thereafter;

That, although it appeared that the bequest of the $10,000 mortgage was not a specific legacy (the testator not having owned it at the time of his death), and that the bequest of the $6,000 mortgage was a specific legacy, the artificial rules relating to the allowance of interest upon specific, demonstrative and general legacies did not apply, as the testator did not intend to make any distinction between the benefits the legatee was to receive from the transfers of the two mortgages.

VAN BRUNT, P. J., dissented.

APPEAL by the defendants, Sidney Smith Whittlesey and others, from the following portions of a judgment of the Supreme Court in favor of the plaintiffs and the defendant Alletta Nathalie Bailey, entered in the office of the clerk of the county of New York on the 17th day of December, 1900, upon the report of a referee:

First. From the summary statement of said judgment.

Second. From so much and such part of said judgment as decides that none of the legacies under the 12th clause of the will of the testator, excepting in regard to the partial payment of the legacy to Catherine Whittlesey by transfer of the $6,000 mortgage were payable until the sale of the Fordham Heights property, and the receipt from such sale of funds applicable to the payment of such legacies; and from so much and such part of said judgment as decides that the said legacies only became payable at the date of the death of Eliza Meier Bailey and only began to draw interest from that date.

Third. From so much and such part of said judgment as decides that the provisions regarding the $10,000 mortgage mentioned in the legacy to Catherine Whittlesey in the 12th clause of the will of testator did not establish a specific or demonstrative legacy of the same, and from so much and such part of said judgment as decides that the purchase of said mortgage could only be made with funds raised in the same manner and at the same time as those from which payment of the other legacies in said clause was to be made, and that the provision in that regard was subject to all the limitations attached to such other legacies, and from so much and such part as decides that the amount of the legacy paid by transfer of said mortgage was not payable until the death of Eliza Meier Bailey.

Fourth. From so much and such part of said judgment as decides that the provisions in regard to the $6,000 mortgage contained in said legacy to Catherine Whittlesey did not establish a specific gift of the same, but simply indicated and set apart the mortgage as a fund from which $6,000 of said legacy was primarily to be paid by transfer to the legatee, and from so much and such part as decides that the time for this transfer was at the expiration of one year after the issuance of letters testamentary, and from so much and such part as decides that the appellants are only entitled to receive the income earned and paid to the executors upon said mortgage after that date.

Fifth. From so much and such part of said judgment as decides and states the account of the amount due to these appellants upon said legacy, which account is stated as follows :

" Amount of legacy................	$20,000 00	
" Amount of interest due on $6,000 mortgage....	2,184 00	
		$22,184 00
" Amount paid by transfer of $10,000 mortgage......................	$13,450 00	
" Amount paid by transfer of $6,000 mortgage..	6,000 00	
		$19,450 00
" Balance remaining due.................		$2,734 00 "

Sixth. From so much and such part of said judgment as decides that only the sum of $2,734, with interest from May 23, 1900, is due these appellants upon said legacy.

Seventh. From so much and such part of said judgment as decides that by the transfer of the said $10,000 mortgage the sum of $13,450 was paid to appellants on account of said legacy.

The action was brought by executors and trustees of the will of Nathaniel P. Bailey, who died October 12, 1891, for the construction thereof, and a determination of the rights and interests of the beneficiaries.

The testator left surviving him as heirs at law and next of kin his widow, Eliza M. Bailey, who subsequently died May 23, 1900, and a son, James M. Bailey, who died February 27, 1897, leaving a widow and a daughter. By his will, which was dated January 24, 1891, and was admitted to probate December 31, 1891, letters testamentary being issued January 8, 1892, the testator disposed of his estate, which amounted to over $800,000, both by specific bequests and by the creation of trusts. The sum of $325,669.77 was thus given in the first eleven paragraphs. The more important of these legacies were those named in the 3d paragraph, directing the executors to set aside $100,000 for the widow, and in the 5th, creating a trust of $150,000 for the benefit of his son with remainder over for the benefit of the son's wife and daughter.

The 12th clause, wherein legacies amounting to $221,000 were given, among which was one of $20,000 to the testator's niece, Catherine Whittlesey, the mother of the appellants, provided: " As the largest part of my property consists of lands at Fordham Heights * * * and said lands at the time of my death may yet be unsold and, therefore, unproductive of income, and my wife may desire to occupy the property or some part thereof during the term of my son's and granddaughter's lives — upon whose lives I have limited her enjoyment of mine estate, or any other good reasons may then exist why the same should not all be forthwith sold, and as my other property will be sufficient to pay the taxes on said Fordham lands and most, if not all, the other charges and legacies hereinbefore provided in the first to the eleventh inclusive sections of this my will, and as the following legacies cannot be paid unless said Fordham lands or some portions thereof are sold and a part of the avails thereof used for that purpose, I hereby direct my executors to pay the following legacies out of the body of my estate as soon as it can be done without embarrassment to my wife's comfort and an undue sacrifice of said lands, but at any time within the lives of

FIRST DEPARTMENT, APRIL TERM, 1902.   [Vol. 70.

my son and granddaughter or the survivor of them should my wife, if she then be living, consent in writing thereto; but should any two of the three beneficiaries who are to receive the income of the trust estate created under the succeeding sections of my will die, then I direct such sale to be forthwith made whether my said wife be living or not and after the provisions of the foregoing and suc- ceeding sections of this my will have been duly complied with, then I hereby give and bequeath the following sums to the follow- ing persons hereby charging the estate of my said son and grand- daughter and the residuary estate or estates hereby created with the payment of the following legacies. Subject, therefore, to the above restrictions, I hereby give and bequeath unto the following persons the following sums, viz.: * * * To my niece Catherine Whit- tlesey, Twenty thousand dollars ($20,000) payable as follows: Ten thousand 00/100 dollars ($10,000) thereof by transfer to herself personally in her own right of a mortgage for that amount made by her and her husband in favor of my wife and in case said mort- gage shall not belong to me at my decease then my executors are hereby directed to purchase the same in order to comply with this bequest or otherwise to pay said legatee that amount in money; six thousand dollars ($6,000) thereof to be paid by transfer to her in her own right by executors of a mortgage made by her and her husband in my favor for that amount and the balance of said legacy, the sum of four thousand dollars ($4, 000) in money."

The trust estate referred to as "created under the succeeding sections" for the benefit of three beneficiaries, is stated in the 14th clause which disposes of all the rest and remainder of the testator's real and personal property.

The Fordham Heights property was occupied and held by the widow down to the time of her death, May 23, 1900. Meanwhile, on February 12, 1895, Catherine Whittlesey died intestate leaving as her heirs at law the appellants herein. The $10,000 mortgage was not owned by testator at his death, but belonged to his wife, and interest was paid on it by Mrs. Whittlesey up to March 1, 1894. It was purchased by the executors from Mrs. Bailey for $10,000 on December 1, 1899, the unpaid interest at that time amounting to $3,450. Mrs. Whittlesey paid as interest on the $6,000 mortgage after the death of the testator $2,631, of which $447 was for interest for the year after letters testamentary were granted. Both mortgages were assigned to these appellants on December 1, 1899.

The referee in his report determined with regard to the sum which the appellants were entitled to receive from the executors in payment of what remained due under the legacy, that the legatees were to be charged with $3,450 interest due and unpaid on the $10,000 mortgage when it was purchased from the widow and that they were not to receive back the interest which had been paid thereon from the time of the testator's death to March 1, 1894; that they were to be charged with interest on the $6,000 for the year following the death of the testator but were to be credited with $2,184 earned and collected on that mortgage after January 8, 1893. From the judgment entered on the report the legatees referred to appeal, claiming that the referee erred (1) in charging them with interest of $3,450 unpaid when the $10,000 was assigned; (2) in not crediting them with $1,500 paid thereon prior to March 1, 1894, and (3) in charging them with $447 interest on the $6,000 mortgage for the year following the granting of letters testamentary.

Thomas F. Conway, for the appellants.

Fordham Morris, for the executors, respondents.

Stephen H. Olin, for the respondent Bailey.

O'Brien, J.:

We concur with the referee in his conclusion and for the reasons stated by him, that interest should be charged on the $6,000 mortgage for the year following the granting of letters testamentary. It seems anomalous, however, that he should have reached the further conclusion that the legatee was chargeable with interest that accrued on the $10,000 mortgage beyond that time.

Undoubtedly there is a distinction between the two mortgages growing out of the fact that the testator held one at his death, while the other, the $10,000 mortgage, was at that time the property of his wife; and, owing entirely to this consideration, the referee held that while the $6,000 mortgage was a demonstrative legacy, the one for $10,000 was neither a specific nor a demonstrative legacy, and that as its purchase could only be made with funds raised through the sale of the Fordham property, it was payable in the same way as the remaining legacies in the 12th clause, namely, after such sale, and that interest-ran only after the date so fixed. The results of the decision of the referee are, the legatee receives the $6,000 mortgage as of a date one year after the granting of letters testamentary, but the transfer to her of the $10,000 mortgage is made as of such time as it was purchased by the executors, which purchase could be deferred until the Fordham property was to be sold.

The referee has correctly stated the general rule upon the subject of when interest runs upon legacies and the distinction made in the cases between specific, demonstrative and general legacies; but we think he has overlooked what is, after all, the controlling principle in all cases involving the construction of wills, and that is the intention of the testator. Notwithstanding the difference in his relation as to the ownership of the two mortgages, it is reasonably certain that the testator intended to make no distinction as to the benefits which the legatee was to receive from the transfer to her of both mortgages, because he distinctly states that if he did not own the $10,000 mortgage at his decease, then his executors were to purchase it in order to comply with his wishes, which were that in part payment of her legacy of $20,000 his niece should receive the two mortgages and the remaining $4,000 in money. Although, therefore, this was not, strictly speaking, a specific legacy, it was in the nature of such; and the testator, having in mind the fact that there rested upon the legatee the obligation of paying not only the principal, but also the interest, of the two mortgages, intended, as is fairly inferable from the context, that these obligations should not be extended, as in the case of the other legacies in the 12th clause, until the time arrived for the sale of the Fordham property. He thought, no doubt, that at sometime between the making of his will and his death this mortgage of $10,000 would come into his possession, or else that after his death his executors might arrange the matter with his wife; but, either failing, he gave the express direction to his executors that if he did not at his death own the mortgage, they were to purchase it. Had he owned it at his death, clearly the rights of the legatee therein would have been the same as to the $6,000 mortgage.

In view, therefore, of the evident intent of the testator, as shown by the exact provision he made as to the manner of payment of this legacy, we think the referee gave undue weight to legal definitions and artificial rules which, in doubtful cases, are necessarily resorted to for the purpose of construing and administering wills, but which must give way and can play no part where the intent is clear. Our reading of this 12th clause of the will before us, providing that the Whittlesey legacy of $20,000 is payable in a specified and different manner from all the other legacies embraced in that clause, is, that the testator intended that his niece should receive the benefit of these mortgages and that in this connection he did not intend to make any distinction between the $6,000 and the $10,000 mortgage.

Our conclusion, therefore, is that the referee erroneously charged the legatee with the interest which had accumulated on the $10,000 mortgage during the period beyond the year after the letters testamentary were issued and that the judgment appealed from should be modified in that respect and as so modified affirmed, with costs to the appellant payable out of the estate.

McLAUGHLIN, HATCH and LAUGHLIN, JJ., concurred; VAN BRUNT, P. J., dissented.

VAN BRUNT, P. J. (dissenting):

I agree that it is anomalous that the referee did not charge interest on the $6,000 mortgage as well as on the $10,000 mortgage; and I am of the opinion that he should have charged interest upon both. The mortgagor was bound to pay the interest upon these mortgages until the legacy of $20,000 became payable, which it is conceded would not occur until the Fordham Heights property was sold. It is entirely immaterial as to who held these mortgages. The bonds accompanying the mortgages were debts of the mortgagor, and they naturally drew interest until the time came for their being turned over to the mortgagor in part payment of the $20,000 legacy when such legacy became due. It might just as well be claimed that the mortgagor was entitled to recover interest upon the sum of $4,000 which was to be paid in cash, as that she was not to pay interest upon her debts until, under the terms of the will, it became proper for the executors to discharge the same.

Judgment modified as directed in opinion, and as modified affirmed, with costs to the appellant payable out of the estate.

WILLIAM CSATLOS, an Infant, by JOHN CSATLOS, his Guardian ad Litem, Respondent, *v.* METROPOLITAN STREET RAILWAY COMPANY, Appellant.

Negligence — injury to a child stepping upon street railroad tracks directly in front of a car — charge that the railroad company might be held liable notwithstanding the plaintiff's contributory negligence.

In an action to recover damages for personal injuries sustained by the plaintiff, a boy four and a half years of age, in consequence of being run over by one of the defendant's street cars while crossing a street in the city of New York, it appeared that the plaintiff was accompanied by his mother and another woman; that the entire party stepped upon the defendant's track when the horses attached to the car were but a few feet distant; that the driver shouted and that both of the women stepped back in time to avoid the accident, but that the plaintiff, who was walking between the two women, was knocked down and run over. The evidence tended to show that the driver applied the brake, pulled in his horses and did his utmost to avert the accident.

The defendant's negligence was predicated upon the theory that the brake with which the car was fitted was defective.

The court charged, over the objection of the defendant, that, if the car, properly equipped, could have been stopped, after the driver saw the child in time to have prevented the accident, the jury might find that there was negligence on the part of the defendant, even if the person with the child was negligent; that it was a rule of law that, notwithstanding negligence on the part of the injured person he could recover, if the defendant, by care, could have avoided the accident; that if the driver might have stopped the car and avoided the accident, the fact that the plaintiff's negligence or that of the person in whose care he was, contributed to the injury, would not be a bar to a recovery.

Held, that, while the propositions charged may have been correct in the abstract, they were not applicable to the case at bar;

That they tended not only to confuse, but to mislead the jury, and that they constituted prejudicial error.

APPEAL by the defendant, the Metropolitan Street Railway Company, from a judgment of the Supreme Court in favor of the plaintiff, entered in the office of the clerk of the county of New York on the 22d day of January, 1901, upon the verdict of a jury for $10,000, and also from an order entered in said clerk's office on the 22d day of January, 1901, denying the defendant's motion for a new trial made upon the minutes.

The action was brought to recover for personal injuries sustained by the plaintiff, a boy four and a half years of age, who was run over on the afternoon of August 11, 1898, by defendant's westbound Twenty-third street horse car at Second avenue, and as a result of the accident lost his leg.

The plaintiff, accompanied by his mother, who was carrying a younger child, and by another woman, Miss Mick, alighted from the south side of an east-bound Twenty-third street car at the west side of Second avenue in order to transfer north, and started diagonally to the northeast corner. As they were stepping on the westbound Twenty-third street track they heard a shout and saw a horse car approaching. The women stepped back, but the plaintiff was struck by the horses, and before the car had stopped at the westerly crosswalk was run over by the front wheel on the north side of the car. It was testified by a truckman, Harrison, who was standing on the northwest corner looking across, that when he saw the boy in the middle of the track, crossing diagonally, the horses' heads were about three feet from him and the driver was trying to stop the car. Miss Mick testified that they were walking across and went to step on the track when she heard shouting, saw the car coming and drew back, and the boy was then standing on the track, screaming, and the horses' heads were about five or six feet away. The mother testified that the boy was walking between her and Miss Mick, and when she heard the shout and jumped back the horses' heads were about five yards away, and then when she saw the child on the track they were four yards away; that the horses were not going fast and not going slow. The driver of the car, called by the plaintiff, testified that he did not see the women till he was on top of them, his horses' heads being about five feet from them, and he did not see the boy until they had stepped back and the horses then were right on him. Further, he testified that although he had put on the brake and pulled hard the car would not stop, and the brake was worn and full of holes and of no use to a car at all, and before the accident its bad condition had been reported; that the car, after he applied the brake, went fifteen feet; but if there had been no defect he could have stopped within five feet. An affidavit of the driver, made just after the accident, gives substantially the same account, but makes no mention of a defective brake.

In behalf of the defendant there was testimony that the brake was in good order when inspected a few days prior to the accident, and that no report of defect had been made, and that ordinarily the car might be stopped in twelve or fifteen feet.   It was further testified by one witness that he heard a shout and turning around saw the women step back and the child run forward and get struck and he was dragged two feet.   Another witness testified that the car first stopped on the east side of the avenue when the people started across.

In charging the jury the court said : " The railway company * * * was bound to act under the rules of ordinary prudence. This driver says that it did not ; that the brake was defective, and while the truckman Harrison says that he was doing all that he could to stop the car, and that it happened so suddenly, and the driver himself says that he put on the brake, the driver says that because the company had furnished him with a car with a bad brake he could not stop.   Now you will consider all the circumstances * * * so as to make up your minds whether he told the truth."   No exception was taken to the charge, but the plaintiff made several requests, among which the following were charged, the defendant excepting :

" *Tenth*. If the car of the defendant, properly equipped, could have been stopped in time to have prevented the accident after the driver saw the child approaching or on the track, you are authorized to find that it was negligence on the part of the defendant to have permitted the accident even if you find that the person in whose care the child was, was negligent in permitting the child to get into a position of danger.   * * *

" *Eleventh*. It is a rule of law that notwithstanding negligence upon the part of the person injured, he may recover if the railway company after such negligence occurred could by the exercise of ordinary care have discovered it in time to have avoided inflicting the injury.   * * *

" *Twelfth*. If the driver might by the exercise of ordinary care have stopped the car and so have avoided the injury to the boy, neither the fact of plaintiff's own negligence or that of his parent or the person in whose care he was (in being on the track) contributed to the accident, constitutes a bar to plaintiff's recovery."

The jury's verdict was for $10,000, and from the judgment

entered thereupon and from order denying motion for a new trial, the defendants appeal.

Charles F. Brown, for the appellant.

William H. Leonard Edwards, for the respondent.

O'BRIEN, J. :

There is no evidence in this record to support a finding that the driver failed to do his utmost after knowledge that those crossing in front of him were in danger to avert the accident. His shouting enabled the women to step back in time to avoid being struck by the horses, and his testimony, supported by that of the witness Harrison, is that he at once applied the brake and pulled in the horses. The witnesses state that the boy went upon the track but a few feet in front of the horses, and the circumstances and manner in which the accident occurred show that only a brief interval of time and space separated the existence of danger and the collision. Although the car had stopped on the other side, when the people started to the northeast corner there is nothing to show that the driver was not, as were those crossing, suddenly made aware of the danger. And, although it appears that the child was dragged two feet, it is not shown that this was the fault of the driver. The negligence in fact was predicated upon the failure of the defendant to furnish the car with a suitable brake, and it was upon this theory that the court submitted the issue to the jury.

Not satisfied, however, with the charge to which neither side took exception, the plaintiff's counsel urged upon the court numerous requests to charge and introduced propositions of law which, however good in the abstract, were not applicable to the case at bar, and as will be seen would necessarily tend not only to confuse, but to actually mislead the jury. Thus the court charged at plaintiff's request, the defendant duly excepting, that if the car properly equipped could have been stopped after the driver saw the child, there was negligence on the part of the defendant even if the person with the child was negligent. The next request went a step further and charged that " It is a rule of law " that notwithstanding negligence on the part of the injured person, he may recover if the company might still by care have avoided the accident. And the following request was that if the driver might have stopped the car and avoided the accident, the fact of plaintiff's negligence contributing to the injury was not a bar to recovery.

A request similar to this last was charged in *Goodman* v. *Met. St. Ry. Co.* (63 App. Div. 84), and resulted in a reversal of judgment for the plaintiff. What the counsel had in mind undoubtedly in submitting these various requests were cases like *Weitzman* v. *Nassau Elec. R. R. Co.* (33 App. Div. 585); *Green* v. *Met. St. Ry. Co.* (42 id. 160), and *Totarella* v. *N. Y. & Queens County R. Co.* (53 id. 413). In the *Weitzman Case* (*supra*), which is a good illustration, a child five years of age, upon being struck by an electric street car, fell upon the fender and was carried along for a distance of from 32 to 150 feet when he rolled from the fender in front of the advancing car and was run over and killed, and it was held that, assuming the child to have been *sui juris* and that his falling upon the fender resulted from his contributory negligence, it was the duty of the railroad company when the child had reached a position upon the fender, to have prevented the injury and death of the child if it had time and could have done so by the exercise of reasonable care. As was therein said : " Whatever the degree of negligence on the part of the individual in the original contact, that negligence culminated in the accident which landed him in the net of the fender. From that moment a new relation existed between the parties and any act or omission on the part of the defendant, amounting to a lack of the care demanded by the situation and resulting in the death of plaintiff's intestate, is sufficient to charge the company with negligence."

In the case at bar, however, there were presented the ordinary questions of negligence and contributory negligence, and there was no suggestion, either in the pleadings or in the testimony, of any new situation being created after the plaintiff had come into a position of danger. Neither the cases referred to, therefore, nor the rule of law invoked by the plaintiff and embodied in the requests, had any application. It had been shown that the driver, with his utmost vigilance and endeavor, could not stop the car, and the testimony would support the inference that the child, when the accident occurred, was walking between his mother and another woman, and was well taken care of. The tendency of the two first requests and the effect of the last was to instruct the jury that, regardless of contributory negligence, there might be a recovery. Of course, if the jury had found that the parent was negligent in attempting to cross in the manner testified, such negligence, assuming the child to be *non sui juris,* would bar recovery, yet the jury were instructed that a recovery could be had upon proof merely that there was negligence on the part of the defendant. The last request, particularly, was, in view of the facts, erroneous and most prejudicial.

The judgment and order, accordingly, must be reversed and a new trial ordered, with costs to the appellant to abide the event.

VAN BRUNT, P. J., PATTERSON and LAUGHLIN, JJ., concurred.

Judgment and order reversed, new trial ordered, costs to appellant to abide event.

NOTE.— The rest of the cases of this term will be found in the next volume, 71 App. Div.— REP.

DECISIONS

IN

CASES NOT REPORTED IN FULL.

FIRST DEPARTMENT, MARCH TERM, 1902.

Thomas W. Bracher, Plaintiff. v. Jessie C. McBride, Defendant.— Submission dismissed, with costs to the plaintiff.— Submission of a controversy upon an agreed statement of facts pursuant to section 1279 of the Code of Civil Procedure.—

PER CURIAM: It appearing by concession of counsel in open court that there is now no controversy between the parties to this submission, the defendant having taken title, the submission should be dismissed, with costs to the plaintiff. Present — Van Brunt, P. J., O'Brien, Ingraham, Hatch and Laughlin, JJ.

Lyman G. Bloomingdale, Suing on Behalf of Himself and of all Other Creditors of the Harlem Casino Company, Appellant, v. August Luchow and Others, Respondents.— Order modified as directed in opinion and as modified affirmed, without costs.— Appeal from an order permitting plaintiff to discontinue the action upon certain conditions.—

PER CURIAM: This order should be modified by confining the award of costs to the only defendants opposing the motion, namely, August Luchow, Richard Stein and Charles H. Lellman. It is true that the latter died; but his attorney was served with notice and appeared and opposed the motion. As so modified, the order should be affirmed, without costs of this appeal. Present — Van Brunt, P. J., O'Brien, McLaughlin, Hatch and Laughlin, JJ.

Johanna Kalish and Others, as Executors, etc., of Joseph Kalish, Deceased, Respondents, v. Luke Higgins and Elizabeth Higgins, Appellants. (Action No 2.) — Judgment reversed, new trial ordered, costs to appellant to abide event.— Appeal from a judgment entered upon the decision of the court at Special Term.—

INGRAHAM, J.: The action is brought to set aside a conveyance of property made by the defendant Luke Higgins to the defendant Elizabeth Higgins, his wife. The case was tried with, and depends upon the same facts, as the case of Kalish v. Higgins (No. 1) (ante, p. 192), and for the reasons stated in the opinion in that case the judgment appealed from should be reversed and a new trial ordered, with costs to the appellant to abide the event. Van Brunt, P. J., McLaughlin, Hatch and Laughlin, JJ., concurred.

Charles F. Frothingham, Respondent, v. Frank Le Roy Satterlee, Appellant. — Judgment affirmed, with costs.— Appeal from a judgment entered upon the report of a referee.—

INGRAHAM, J.: The action is brought to recover the balance of an account due from the defendant to the plaintiff, who was a broker engaged in the business of buying and selling stocks and bonds and other securities in the city of New York, and the complaint alleges that the plaintiff and the firm of which he is surviving partner purchased and sold various stocks and bonds for the defendant; that on or about the 3d day of April, 1894, there was an account stated between the plaintiff's firm and the defendant by which it was agreed that the balance due to the plaintiff was on that day $8,199.91, which sum the defendant agreed to pay to the plaintiff; that thereafter, from the 31st day of March, 1894, to the 1st day of January, 1899, the said firm continued to act as brokers for the defendant under said employment, and at his request made certain purchases and sales of stock for him, and that on the 1st day of January, 1899, there was a balance due the plaintiff from the defendant of $5,142.53, for which sum the plaintiff asks to recover judgment. The answer admits the statements of this account, but alleges that the same was agreed to relying upon the assurances of one James R. Nichols, then the plaintiff's partner, that the same were just and correct statements of the account; and upon information and belief that "the aforesaid statements wrongfully contained entries of stocks, etc., bought or sold without the order or knowledge of defendant, and charges of commission thereon, and likewise included charges of interest at usurious and unlawful rates, and also of interest claimed to have been paid on account of stocks embraced in said statements, but which amounts of interest had not, in fact, been paid thereon," and the defendant asks that the complaint be dismissed; that an accounting between the plaintiff and the defendant be directed, and that the defendant recover judgment against the plaintiff for the amount found due. The reply denied the allegations constituting a counterclaim, and the case was referred to a referee to hear and determine. Upon the trial the plaintiff proved the statement of the account by a letter dated April 3, 1894, addressed to the plaintiff and signed by the defendant, as follows:

"DEAR SIRS.— Your statement of my account to March 31, 1894, is received and found correct.

"Very truly yours,
"F. LE ROY SATTERLEE.'

The plaintiff also proved the subsequent transactions alleged in the complaint and the rendering of the final account to the defendant to December 31, 1897, which showed a balance against the defendant of $4,847.80; and testified to several interviews with the defendant after the rendition of this account at which the defendant admitted that he was indebted to the plaintiff in this amount and promised to pay the same when able to do so. Upon this evidence the referee held that there was an account stated which was binding upon the defendant, unless such account was impeached for fraud, mistake or manifest error. This ruling was correct. (Spell-

629

man v. *Muehlfeld*, 166 N. Y. 245.) The plaintiff thus having established his cause of action, the burden was on the defendant to impeach the account. To sustain this defense the defendant was examined as to certain conversations between himself and Mr. Nichols, who was the plaintiff's partner, but who died before the commencement of the action. He testified that he signed the statement approving the account upon the statement of Mr. Nichols that it was only a matter of form and it was understood to be a simple receipt of the account and not an approval of it; that Mr. Frothingham, his partner, insisted upon having the statements receipted and that he had to satisfy Mr. Frothingham; but this testimony of the defendant was uncorroborated. Mr. Nichols had died before the commencement of the action, and, if admissible as against the plaintiff, it presented a question of fact for the referee, and his finding in favor of the plaintiff was supported by the evidence. The only other question presented is as to the right of the defendant to offset as against this amount due the damages sustained by the defendant by reason of the failure of the plaintiff to sell certain bonds of the defendant held as collateral security for the amount due the plaintiff upon this account. There was evidence that the plaintiff tried to sell the bonds; that they had no market value in New York, and were not listed upon the Stock Exchange; and that finally, being unable to sell the bonds in the regular way, the defendant requested the plaintiff not to sacrifice them at auction, which request the plaintiff complied with. The counterclaim that was alleged in the answer would not justify a recovery by the defendant for a failure to sell these bonds. Assuming, however, that such a counterclaim had been pleaded, it was a question of fact for the referee as to whether the plaintiff obeyed the instructions of the defendant in respect to the sale of the bonds, and the finding of the referee on this subject was sustained by the evidence. There are various rulings upon the admission and rejection of evidence to which the defendant excepted. They relate principally to the refusal of the referee to allow upon the cross-examination of the plaintiff and his bookkeeper, proof of purchases and sales of stock prior to the statement of the account between the plaintiff and the defendant. The referee sustained these objections to questions upon cross-examination, upon the ground that the evidence was only admissible as a part of the defendant's case and that there first had to be some evidence tending to show that the account as assented to by the defendant was incorrect. After the plaintiff had rested, the defendant recalled the plaintiff, and no evidence was excluded that could have helped defendant. So far as appears, all the testimony that was offered by the defendant to prove his case which was admissible was admitted, and nothing was excluded that could bear upon the question at issue. The main defense of the defendant was as to his understanding with Nichols, who was a member of the plaintiff's firm, as to these various purchases and sales and the conditions upon which he approved the account. These were all questions of fact for the referee, and were found against the defendant. The evidence excluded could not have aided him in his defense. Upon the whole case we think that none of the rulings would justify a reversal of the judgment, and it should be affirmed, with costs. Van Brunt, P. J., McLaughlin, Hatch and Laughlin, JJ., concurred.

Henry S. Moore, as Executor, etc., of Theron R. Butler, Deceased, Respondent, v. Tillie E. Smith and Others, Defendants, and Lena Vogel, Appellant. Wilmore Anway, Receiver, Respondent. (Action No. 1.) — Order modified as directed in opinion, and as so modified, affirmed, without costs. — Appeal by the defendant Lena Vogel from an order of the Special Term adjudging her guilty of a contempt of court in disobeying an order directing her to pay certain moneys to the receiver in the action. —

HATCH, J.: It was sought by this action to foreclose a mortgage upon the premises No. 57 East One Hundred and Seventeenth street, in the city of New York, consisting of a double flat apartment house, five stories in height. After the action was commenced, the plaintiff applied for the appointment of a receiver of the rents of the premises, and by an order duly entered such application was granted and the receiver appointed. The latter immediately notified all of the tenants in the building who paid their rents monthly in advance to make such payments to him. This the tenants refused to do, and the receiver instituted a proceeding in the Municipal Court to dispossess one of said tenants. When the proceeding came on for hearing, it appeared for the first time that Lena Vogel, who had not then been made a party to the action, was possessed of a lease of the whole premises executed by the defendant owner, dated April 8, 1901, and expiring May 1, 1902, and proof was given tending to show that she had paid rent in advance under the terms of the lease in the sum of $1,750. This lease was not recorded or acknowledged. After the lease had been produced and proven, the receiver discontinued the summary proceeding, and the plaintiff procured an order making the said Vogel a party defendant in the action, and leave was given to serve an amended supplemental summons and complaint upon her. This order was complied with, and the defendant Vogel was duly made a party to the action. Subsequently, she was brought into court upon an order to show cause why the receivership should not be extended so as to embrace the rents collected by her accruing since July 1, 1901. Upon the return day of this order, Lena Vogel made default. She subsequently applied to have the order set aside for the reason that she had never been served with a copy of the papers or notice to appear in such proceeding. This motion was denied, and she was given leave to make a motion to vacate the order upon the merits, and upon that motion being heard, the same was denied. From the orders entered upon these respective motions, the defendant did not appeal, and the same now stand in full force and effect. Thereafter the receiver duly demanded of the said Vogel payment to him of all rents which she had collected, accruing in July, 1901. Compliance with this demand was refused, and thereupon a motion was made to punish her for contempt, under a claim of disobedience of the order extending the receivership to the rents collected by her. This motion coming on to be heard, she was adjudged guilty of contempt of the order and fined the sum of $332.50, being the amount of rents collected by her, and an additional sum of $35, together with $10 costs of the motion. From that order this appeal is taken. The order which extended the receivership so as to embrace the rents collected by Lena Vogel made provision therefor in these words: "It is further ordered that said Lena Vogel pay to said receiver any rents of said premises which she may have collected from the monthly tenants for rent accruing since July 1, 1901." It is undisputed that of the rents collected by Lena Vogel, $232.50 were of rents which accrued on the 1st day of July, 1901, and that no rents which accrued thereafter were collected by her, except the sum of $50, and this sum she claimed was expended in renovating the rooms in the building. It is clear, therefore, that to the extent of $232.50 the order extending the receivership did not embrace such moneys. Its express language was for rents accruing since July 1, 1901. There could be, therefore, no violation of the order so far as these rents were concerned, as they were not covered by its terms, and she could not be adjudged guilty of contempt for refusing to pay over these moneys, for, so far as the terms of the order were concerned, they belonged to her. As to the $50, however, she was clearly in contempt. She was not authorized to collect that sum, as it was of rent which accrued subsequent to July 1, 1901. She was neither justified in receiving it nor was she justified in paying it out for any purpose. It belonged to the receiver, and the order commanded that she pay it to him. It is quite probable that there was a lack of good faith upon her part in connection with the lease and these premises; but such fact, assuming it to exist, does not justify the imposition of a punishment for the violation of an order which she did not violate. It follows, therefore, that the order should be modified by deducting therefrom $232.50 of the sum imposed by way of fine, and as so modified the order should be affirmed, without costs to either party in this court. Van Brunt, P. J., O'Brien, Ingraham and McLaughlin, JJ., concurred.

Gertrude S. Kramer, Respondent, v. Edwin G. Kramer, Appellant. — Order reversed, with ten dollars costs and disbursements, and motion denied, with ten dollars costs.— Appeal from an order vacating an order for the examination of plaintiff before trial.— HATCH, J.: This action was brought upon the following promissory note, alleged to have been duly made and delivered to the plaintiff herein by the defendant:

"$12,000. BOSTON, MASS., April 1st, 1901.
"—— after date I or my estate promise to pay to the order of Gertrude Short Kramer, Twelve thousand Dollars at 6% interest from date, at 474 Commonwealth Ave., Boston, Mass.
"Value received $12,000
"No. 1 Due EDWIN G. KRAMER."

Defendant, in his answer, admits the making of such a note, and as an affirmative defense avers that it was delivered to Alfred E. Kramer, the husband of the plaintiff, without any consideration and upon the express condition and promise that the said note was not to be delivered, or negotiated under any circumstances, nor the possession thereof parted with. Defendant further alleges, upon information and belief, that the said note was never delivered, but that plaintiff obtained the same wrongfully and fraudulently, without the consent of Alfred E. Kramer and without any consideration. The defendant obtained an order for the examination of the plaintiff before trial, which was subsequently vacated, and it is from such order vacating the examination that this appeal is taken. We think it fairly appears that the answer in this case is interposed in good faith, and that the defendant intends in good faith to use the testimony to be taken upon the examination on the trial of the action. It is evident that the testimony of the plaintiff, in view of the

peculiar circumstances surrounding the execution and delivery of the note, is material and necessary to the defense in this action, and under such circumstances, where the application is made in good faith and is for the purpose of procuring testimony to be used upon the trial, a case is made entitling the party to an examination. (Leary v. Rice, 15 App. Div. 897.) The facts as to how the plaintiff became possessed of the note and the consideration, if any, that she paid therefor are peculiarly within the knowledge of the plaintiff, and upon such subject the defendant must be presumed to be absolutely ignorant. It devolves upon him to show that the plaintiff is not a bona fide holder of the note, and it is quite likely that he can only show such fact by an examination of the plaintiff. There is no presumption that she will be present at the trial, and it is clear that if she is she will be a hostile witness; and there is no certainty that the defendant, unless he be permitted to have this examination, will be enabled to obtain her testimony at all. The facts appearing upon the motion show a clear case, not only in the averment of the answer and in the affidavit, but also in the circumstances surrounding the whole transaction for an examination of plaintiff before trial, and the order, therefore, was properly granted. It follows that the order vacating the order for examination should be reversed, with ten dollars costs and disbursements, and the motion to vacate denied, with ten dollars costs. Van Brunt, P. J., Ingraham, McLaughlin and Laughlin, JJ., concurred.

Demie W. Hildreth and Henry Segelken, Respondents, v. Joseph M. McCaul, Appellant. — Order affirmed, with ten dollars costs and disbursements.— Appeal by defendant from an order of the Special Term of the Supreme Court, entered in the clerk's office of the county of New York on the 9th day of August, 1901, adjudging him guilty of contempt in having violated an injunction order granted herein and imposing a fine of $250.— LAUGHLIN, J.: The injunction order, for the violation of which appellant has been adjudged guilty of contempt, is the one considered on the appeal decided herewith. After that order was granted and served, appellant issued and mailed a circular to retail dealers in honey, beeswax, maple sugar and maple syrup, announcing the death of Henry P. Hildreth, which occurred several weeks before, and stating that he, as survivor, was the sole owner of the business carried on at Nos. 120 and 122 West Broadway. It appears by an affidavit, which is, however, controverted by the defendant, that in one instance, at least, this circular was inclosed in an envelope, upon which was originally printed "After 5 days return to Hildreth, McCaul Co., Jos. M. McCaul, Prop.. 190 & 122 West Broadway, New York," and upon which the name "Hildreth" was left plainly legible, although some blue ink had been spread over it. The court was justified in finding that this circular thus issued was calculated and intended to continue the deception which it was the design of the injunction order to prevent, and the defendant was properly adjudged guilty of contempt. (Devlin v. Devlin, 69 N. Y. 212.) The order should, therefore, be affirmed, with ten dollars costs and disbursements. Van Brunt, P. J., O'Brien, McLaughlin and Hatch, JJ., concurred.

Clark W. Dunlop, Appellant, v. Frederic T. James and Marietta Wilsey, Respondents.— Judgment affirmed, with costs.— Appeal by the plaintiff from so much of a judgment of the Supreme Court, entered in the clerk's office of the county of New York on the 8d day of July, 1901, as adjudges that he is not entitled to recover any sum from the defendant James or a deficiency judgment against said defendant.—

LAUGHLIN, J.: This action is brought to foreclose a mortgage on a leasehold interest in premises No. 20 Warren street, New York city, and to have the defendant James adjudged liable for any deficiency to the extent of $850. The court had granted a decree in foreclosure but has decided that the defendant James is not personally liable. The material facts are not controverted. On the 3d day of April, 1899, the defendant James owned, by assignment, a lease of the premises in question made by the Trinity church corporation on the 15th day of April, 1890, for twenty-one years from May 1, 1890, and on that day he executed an assignment thereof in writing to the defendant Wilsey, the consideration recited being $25,000. On the same day the defendant Wilsey executed a bond to the plaintiff in the penal sum of $28,000, conditioned for the payment of $14,000 in five semi-annual payments of $500 commencing November 1, 1899, and the balance on May 1, 1902, with six per cent interest semi-annually and conditioned that the whole amount should, at the option of the mortgagee, grow due on default for thirty days in the payment of interest, or for ninety days in the payment of any tax or assessment upon the premises. The mortgage accompanying the bond covers the lease and describes the property, recites the assignment by defendant James to defendant Wilsey and that the latter was justly indebted to the plaintiff in the sum of $14,000, secured by a bond of even date therewith and recites the conditions of the bond as to default in payment of interest but not as to default in payment of taxes and assessments, but makes reference to the bond as more fully showing the default as to interest and the effect thereof. It also recites that the mortgage is intended "for the better securing" the sum of money mentioned in the bond, together with interest thereon. The mortgage further provides that it is made subject to the rents, covenants, conditions and provisions of said lease and that if the mortgagor shall pay the sum mentioned in the condition of the bond and interest as therein provided, that in that event the mortgage should be void. The mortgagor covenanted to pay the money as conditioned in the bond. It was further therein provided that if default should be made in the payment of the sum specified on the bond or interest, then it should be lawful for the mortgagee to sell the lease, and the remainder of the term at public auction "according to the act in such case made and provided," and out of the moneys arising from the sale to retain the principal and interest then due, together with costs and charges of the sale and advertising, and pay the surplus, if any, to the mortgagor. The mortgage also contained an agreement that the mortgagor should keep the buildings insured and assign the policy to the mortgagee, and in default thereof that the mortgagee might effect such insurance, and the cost thereof should be a lien on the mortgaged premises and forthwith become due; that the mortgagor should pay all taxes and assessments, and in default thereof for ninety days the mortgagee might pay the same, and the amount so paid should forthwith become due and payable, and be deemed secured by the mortgage and collectible in the manner provided for the collection of interest on the principal, and in default of such payment

the whole principal should, at the option of the mortgagee, immediately become due and payable; that the mortgagor would pay the ground rent reserved in the lease when the same became due as therein provided, and in default on her part of any covenant or condition of the lease, the mortgagee might at his election consider the entire principal due and payable forthwith, and he might pay the ground rent if the mortgagor should default in paying the same, and the amount so paid should be a lien on the premises payable on demand; that if ground rents should remain unpaid for ten days after becoming due, the mortgagee might forthwith, without notice to any person or application to any court, enter upon and take possession of the premises, and for that purpose the mortgagor therein assigned the rents and profits to him with power to let the premises, receive the rents, issues and profits thereof, and apply the same, after paying necessary expenses and charges on account of the ground rent, taxes and amount secured by the mortgage. At the time of the execution of this bond and mortgage the defendant Wilsey signed, sealed, acknowledged and delivered to the plaintiff a written instrument as follows:

"WHEREAS, Marietta Wilsey has executed a bond of even date herewith, conditioned for the payment to Clark W. Dunlop of the sum of Fourteen thousand Dollars and interest and secured by a mortgage, of even date herewith, covering leasehold premises No. 20 Warren Street, in the Borough of Manhattan, City of New York, and

"WHEREAS, it is intended that an amount sufficient to meet the amounts that shall grow due for the ground rent, interest and installment on said mortgage, taxes, water rates and insurance shall be accumulated from the rents of said premises.

"Now this indenture witnesseth, that Four hundred and twenty-five ($495.00) on each and every month, during the continuance of said mortgage, from the rents of said premises, shall be deposited with Wells, Waldo & Snedeker, attorneys and counsellors-at-law, No. 84 Nassau Street, New York City, who agree to retain said amounts and deposit them in a trust company for the purposes aforesaid and to allow the trust company's rate of interest, to wit, two per cent while they remain on deposit as aforesaid, and said Marietta Wilsey hereby agrees to pay, each and every month, until the aforesaid mortgage is paid in full, to said Wells, Waldo & Snedeker, from said rents said amount of Four hundred and twenty-five Dollars." It will be observed that this declaration does not recite any consideration, does not purport to be an agreement with anybody and that it is not referred to in the bond or mortgage. At the time of the execution of the bond the defendant James indorsed a guaranty thereon of the first two installments falling due thereunder and of the interest falling due at the same time. These have been paid. After the execution of these papers and on the same day the defendant Wilsey re-assigned the lease to the defendant James. The assignment recites a consideration of $25,000, being the same as that stated in the assignment from him to her. The assignment was expressly made subject to "a mortgage of even date herewith given to secure the payment of fourteen thousand dollars and interest." The defendant James did not assume the payment of the mortgage or the obligations of the defendant Wilsey under the declaration herein quoted, although he was present at the time of its execution and knew the contents thereof. These facts were fully known to all of the parties. There is no claim of fraud or deception on the part of the defendant James. The papers were all executed, as has been seen, the same day, and they were all drawn by the plaintiff's attorneys, who were aware of the fact that the defendant James did not wish to become personally liable on the bond or mortgage to a greater extent than the two installments which he guaranteed. The appellant concedes that there was no personal obligation assumed or intended to be assumed by the defendant James for the payment of any part of the principal or interest represented by the bond other than the first two installments which are not in question. It is claimed, however, that, inasmuch as James knew of this declaration with reference to depositing the rents made by his assignor, he received the rents impressed with a trust to apply the same according to that declaration. Not only did James not assume the liability of his assignor under that declaration, but it does not even appear that he received the money that was loaned on the faith of the bond and mortgage, nor, in fact, is it shown that any money whatever was loaned thereon. It is not alleged nor was any proof offered tending to show any mistake, mutual or otherwise, with reference to the contents of any of the documents enumerated. It has neither been alleged, proved or claimed that the defendant James agreed to turn over the rents in accordance with the declaration made by his assignor or that any such agreement was omitted from the writings through fraud or mistake. While it appears that the lease was reassigned to James the same day he assigned it to the defendant Wilsey, yet it was not shown that at the time of the execution of the bond and mortgage and declaration by her that the agreement to reassign had been made or that it was then understood by the parties that it was to be reassigned to James. We are of opinion that, on the facts proved, the defendant James is not personally liable for rents received which were not paid over to the plaintiff's attorneys in accordance with the defendant Wilsey's declaration. If there was default in the payment of the principal, interest, taxes, assessments or ground rents, the appellant was at liberty to pursue his rights and remedies under the bond and mortgage. One right and remedy was to obtain possession of the premises and collect the rents himself; but, inasmuch as the defendant was under no legal obligation to the plaintiff, the latter could not suffer the former to collect them and then hold him personally liable therefor. It follows that the judgment appealed from should be affirmed, with costs. Van Brunt, P. J., O'Brien, Ingraham and Hatch, JJ., concurred.

Joseph Freeman, Respondent, v. The Manhattan Railway Company and The Metropolitan Elevated Railway Company, Appellants.— Judgment modified by reducing the amount awarded for fee damage to the sum of $1,200; and by reducing the judgment for rental damage, interest, costs and allowances as entered to the sum of $1,542.72, and as so modified affirmed, without costs to either party. No opinion.

James W. Murphy and Michael McCormack, Appellants, v. John E. Parsons and Others, Respondents.— Judgment and order affirmed, with costs. No opinion.

Daniel Tyrrel, Appellant, v. Seamen's Bank for Savings, Respondent.— Judgment and order affirmed, with costs. No opinion.

Charles F. Rivoir, Respondent, v. Metropolitan Street Railway Company, Appellant.— Upon

the respondent's stipulating to reduce judgment to $5,407.44, the same including costs and allowance, the judgment, as so reduced, and the order will be affirmed, without costs. If such stipulation be not given, judgment and order reversed and new trial ordered, with costs to appellant to abide event. No opinion.

In the Matter of Henry C. Valentine, Appellant, v. Collector of Assessments, etc., of New York, Respondent.— Order affirmed, with fifty dollars costs and disbursements. No opinion.

Albert Luther, Respondent, v. Julius Meyer Hanser, Appellant.— Order affirmed, with ten dollars costs and disbursements. No opinion.

William H. Rolston and Others, Appellants, v. Evert Van Slyke, as Administrator, etc., of Sarah D. Van Slyke, Deceased, Respondent. — Order affirmed, with ten dollars costs and disbursements. No opinion.

Ellen B. Cudlip, Respondent, v. The New York Evening Journal Publishing Company, Appellant.— Judgment and order affirmed, with costs. No opinion.

Eric Hope (Earl of Yarmouth), Respondent, v. The Daily Telegraph Company, Appellant.— Judgment and order affirmed, with costs. No opinion.

Estella A. Thurber, Respondent, v. The Preferred Accident Insurance Company of New York, Appellant.— Judgment and order affirmed, with costs. No opinion. (Ingraham, J., dissented.)

The People of the State of New York, Respondent, v. Gus Hart, Appellant.— Judgment affirmed. No opinion.

Lyman G. Bloomingdale, Suing on Behalf of Himself and of all Other Creditors of the Harlem Casino Company, Respondent, v. August Luchow and Others, Appellants.— Order affirmed, with costs to each of the respondents appearing on this appeal. No opinion.

Jessie Schwab, Appellant, v. The City of New York, Respondent.— Judgment and order affirmed, with costs. No opinion.

Christina Just, Respondent, v. The Manhattan Railway Company and the New York Elevated Railroad Company, Appellants. — Judgment modified by reducing the amount awarded for fee damages to $2,000, and by reducing the judgment for rental damage, interest, costs and allowance as entered, to the sum of $2,908.06, and as so modified, affirmed, without costs to either party. No opinion.

Charles A. Stevenson, Respondent, v. The Daily Telegraph Company, Appellant.— Order affirmed, with ten dollars costs and disbursements. No opinion.

John F. Douglas and Another v. Emma L. Jones.— Motion denied, with ten dollars costs. Memorandum per curiam.

John G. Gray v. Metropolitan Street Railway Company.— Motion denied, with ten dollars costs.

Augustus V. Stuyvesant v. Mary A. Early.— Motion denied, with ten dollars costs.

Otto H. Droege, as Receiver, v. Edwin W. Baxter and Another.— Motion granted; question certified as stated in memorandum per curiam.

In the Matter of Seward Park.— Motion for reference granted.

Boyle & Evarts Company v. John D. Fox and Others.— Motion denied upon payment of ten dollars costs, and upon payment of an additional ten dollars, leave given to apply to the court below to open default.

The People of the State of New York ex rel. William A. Hart v. Bernard J. York and Others, Commissioners. — Motion denied, with ten dollars costs.

70
Case
s171 NY
r174 NY

Allan L. Smidt v. May E. Wood — Motion denied upon payment of ten dollars costs, and upon payment of an additional ten dollars, leave given to apply to the court below to open default.

William Jones v. Robert E. Moss. — Motion granted, with ten dollars costs.

In the Matter of The John Spry Lumber Company. — Motion denied, with ten dollars costs.

Leopold Adler v. Sigmar Cohn. — Motion denied upon payment of ten dollars costs, and upon payment of ten dollars additional, leave given to apply to the court below to open default.

The People of the State of New York v. John Bremer. — Motion denied, with ten dollars costs.

Thomas J. Backes v. James P. Curran and Others. — Motion denied, with ten dollars costs.

Lawrence V. Mulry v. Daily Telegraph Company. — Motion denied upon payment of ten dollars costs, and upon payment of an additional ten dollars, leave given to apply to the court below to open default.

Charles Philips v. Burr W. McIntosh. — Motion denied, with ten dollars costs.

Country Club Land Association v. Frederick Lohbauer and Others. — Motion granted, unless defendant stipulates to consent to the withdrawal of the plaintiff's appeal to the Court of Appeals, and pays ten dollars costs and also the costs of appeal which had accrued to the plaintiff, and any disbursements which it had made at the time of the entry of the order amending the order of reversal. Memorandum per curiam.

James Ford v. The Mayor, etc. — Motion granted so far as to dismiss appeal, with ten dollars costs.

Ellen B. Cudlip v. The New York Evening Journal Publishing Company. — Motion for leave to go to the Court of Appeals denied.

Ellen B. Cudlip v. The New York Evening Journal Publishing Company. — Motion for reargument denied, with ten dollars costs. Memorandum per curiam.

William Shipman, as Trustee, etc., Plaintiff, v. Nathaniel Niles, Defendant. — Case sent back for decision. Memorandum per curiam.

In the Matter of the Judicial Settlement of the Accounts of John H. Hayward, Surviving Trustee under the Will of John R. Hayward, Deceased, Appellant; Amanda M. Halsted, Petitioner, and Others, Respondents. Decree affirmed, with costs. No opinion.

In the Matter of Fulton Avenue. — Motion granted, with ten dollars costs.

In the Matter of the Will of Joseph F. Weber, Deceased. — Motion denied, upon payment of ten dollars costs; appellants allowed to serve a proper undertaking upon payment of an additional ten dollars; and appellants allowed to serve notice of appeal upon Herman C. Weber and Emeline A. Weber upon payment of an additional ten dollars. Memorandum per curiam.

Fanny Rayne McComb, Appellant, v. Title Guarantee and Trust Company of New York and Others, as Executors of and Trustees under the Last Will and Testament of James Jennings McComb, Deceased, Respondents; Jennings Scott McComb, Appellant, Impleaded with Others, Defendants. — Judgment affirmed, with costs, on opinion of court below. (Reported in 36 Misc. Rep. 370.)

THIRD DEPARTMENT, MARCH TERM, 1902.

Herbert L. Handy and Others, Respondents, v. Joseph A. Powers and Others, Appellants, Impleaded with Others. — Order affirmed, with ten dollars costs and disbursements. — Appeal by the defendant The J. B. Orcutt Company and the defendants Joseph A. Powers, Albert E. Powers and Nathaniel B. Powers from an order entered in the clerk's office of Saratoga county upon the 23d day of December, 1901. —

PER CURIAM: The appellants' complaint is that the bill of particulars ordered was not sufficiently comprehensive. The plaintiffs were ordered in substance to serve a bill of particulars of "the class and kind and amount, in general terms, of the property thus claimed by the plaintiffs to have been converted by said defendants, but without particularly specifying the number of feet of lumber, or panes of glass, or any further amounts than they are able to ascertain from the examination of the inventory made by the assignee of Barnes and La Dow and by the trustee in bankruptcy of said Barnes & La Dow respectively." The inventories referred to in the order are not before the court. It is impossible, therefore, for us to tell how comprehensive or satisfactory the bill of particulars ordered may be. The order, therefore, should be affirmed, leaving to the defendants their motion to make more specific the bill of particulars if one inadequate be furnished. In the complaint it is alleged that the plaintiffs have been denied access to this lumber a part of which they are claiming. The defendants thus denying access to the property cannot with good grace ask that the

plaintiffs be required to specify particularly what parts of the property are claimed. The order, we think, properly confined the obligation of the plaintiffs to specify such amounts as they were able to ascertain from the inventories which had been made, their only apparent means of knowledge of the property in the hands of the defendants which was the subject of their mortgage. All concurred.

The People of the State of New York ex rel. Dayton T. Eastman, Respondent, v. Michael Scott and William Veyhl, as Commissioners of Highways of the Town of Callicoon, Sullivan County, N. Y., Appellants. — Order reversed, with ten dollars costs and disbursements. Motion for mandamus denied, with costs as in an action. — Appeal from an order of the Supreme Court, entered in the office of the clerk of Sullivan county on the 8th day of August, 1901. In August, 1896, an order made by the commissioners of highways of the town of Callicoon was filed in the clerk's office of the town, laying out a highway over certain lands therein specified. No proceedings were taken to open such road until in June, 1899, the owner of some of such lands applied to the highway commissioners of such town to open and work the same. The commissioners refused, on the ground that no release of such lands, as is required by section 80 of the Highway Law (Laws of 1890, chap. 568), had been filed and recorded in such office, and that, therefore, such order was inoperative. Such owner, the relator herein, then applied for a mandamus requiring the commissioners to open the road. An alternative writ was granted, and a trial thereon subsequently had at a Special Term of this court, and upon such trial the court found as a fact that the written consent of all the property owners through whose lands the road was to run, releasing all claims for damages and dedicating the necessary lands for such road, was delivered by the commissioner to the town clerk for filing and recording; that such order was regular and still operative, and thereupon made an order that a mandamus be issued directing the commissioners to proceed and open the road as therein laid out. From that order this appeal is taken.—

PARKER, P. J.: Section 80 of the Highway Law requires that a road shall not be laid out over lands dedicated to the town, unless there be "filed and recorded in the town clerk's office " at or before the time of filing the order laying it out a " release of the land " over which the road is to pass. Such is not the language, but it is the plain provision of the section in question. If, therefore, no such release, as is by that section required, had been filed with the order in question, the order was illegal and without force, and the commissioners were without authority to proceed under it. I am of the opinion that the proof before the Special Term utterly failed to sustain the conclusion that such a release had ever been filed. That none had ever been recorded is conceded. Without discussing or deciding whether a filing without recording would be sufficient, let us examine the evidence upon which it is claimed that one had been filed. It appears that when the order was signed by the commissioners, a paper purporting to be a release was given to one of them. The evidence is very unsatisfactory as to whether it was signed by all the several owners of lands over which the road is laid; but, conceding that it had been, what did that commissioner do with it? He has since died and gives no evidence on that subject. Two witnesses testify that some two years afterwards they saw that paper in the town clerk's office. Neither says he saw it on file there, or that it was there as one of the records of the office, or in the custody of the clerk. Merely that he saw it there. The relator further swears that the clerk told him that he did not file the paper because the town board directed him not to. The clerk, however, denies that he ever told him so, and, moreover, testified that no such paper was ever left at the office for filing. None can now be found on file in the office, nor is there any entry in the office referring to any filing or recording of one. The clerk testified distinctly that none was ever filed or recorded. On this evidence it seems clear that the paper was never actually filed. Neither does the court find that it was. It merely found that it was left for filing. Also the clear weight of evidence is against the claim that the paper was ever left there to be filed. The alleged *declaration* of the clerk that it was is not evidence of that fact against the commissioners or the town. The evidence of the witnesses that they had seen it there is also too indefinite as to the situation and condition in which it was seen there to overcome the positive testimony of the officer in charge that it never was left there for filing. But suppose the paper referred to as being left with the one commissioner had been left at the clerk's office to be filed, concededly it cannot now be found there. It is a lost instrument, and no evidence of its contents has been intelligently given by any witness. Those who

claim to have seen it call it a release. But that is merely giving the paper a name, not giving a statement of its contents. It is, in effect, their opinion merely. What have we before us to show that it was a "release of the land" such as the statute requires? Was it witnessed or acknowledged? Was it under seal or not? Was it anything more than a consent that the road might be laid out? Did it release anything more than damages for laying it out? What was its language and what its legal effect? We have no information whatever on either of these subjects. We know only that the witness called it a release. Now, the clear purpose of the statute is to secure to the town some sure and permanent evidence of its title to a right of way over the lands claimed to be dedicated for the purpose of a road, and to protect the town against the expense and liabilities incident to the opening and working of the road unless it has acquired a clear right to do so. Surely, if the town in the case before us has no better evidence of title to the lands through which this road is to be opened than was shown to the Special Term, these commissioners have slight protection against an action for trespass should they proceed to take possession of and construct a highway across them. Such evidence would hardly be put forward as establishing a release against any *owner* of the lands in question, and I am of the opinion that the commissioners should not be compelled to enter upon and appropriate lands to which the town can establish scarcely the shadow of a title. Their right is much too doubtful to be enforced by a writ of mandamus, and the order appealed from should be reversed. All concurred; Fursman, J., in result.

Charles O. Landers, Respondent, v. William H. Forbes, as Executor, etc., of Nancy Landers, Deceased, Appellant.— Judgment reversed on the law and facts, referee discharged and new trial granted, with costs to appellant to abide event.— Appeal from a judgment entered upon the report of a referee allowing $1,174.77, besides disbursements, on a claim for $2,901.54 presented to the defendant, as executor, and disputed by him.—

KELLOGG, J.: The plaintiff presented an itemized bill to the executor of the estate of Nancy Landers aggregating $2,901.54, which was rejected. The deceased left personal estate worth $3,000 or $3,400. She was the widow of one Garrett V. Landers, who died in 1888, leaving a farm of fifty acres to his widow for life, then to the plaintiff in fee. So far as the record discloses, the plaintiff was the adopted son of Garrett and Nancy Landers. He always lived with them, called them father and mother, always lived on this farm of fifty acres, and this farm was always the home of Garrett and Nancy Landers. The plaintiff lived on the farm for forty-four years and was never married. In the lifetime of Garrett Landers he worked the farm on shares from the time he was twenty-one until Mr. Landers' death, some ten or twelve years, and lived with the others at the common house, which was the dwelling house on the farm. It does not appear that his father and mother by adoption paid him for board or that he paid them for board. After the death of Garrett Landers he, by an arrangement with his adopted mother, continued to work the farm on shares. The lease seems to have been in writing. By the terms of the lease, as stated by witness Forbes, who drew it up, the parties were to share equally in the farm produce and each was to pay one-half the taxes, and the mother, Nancy

Landers, was to have her home on the old place as she always had. Nothing was said about board of either. They continued to live together as they had always done. From all the testimony it seems to be beyond question that what was raised upon the farm without division supplied the table. Plaintiff took eggs and butter and such produce to the village store and brought back such articles for table use as were needed, and Nancy Landers did the same. There is no evidence that the table was supplied from plaintiff's share. The mother owned all the furniture and table equipment in the house. She, without a servant, was housekeeper, and did for the most part the household work and prepared the food for herself and plaintiff and for the farm hands when any were employed; and the witnesses Hiram Harris and Elmira Harris, the nearest neighbors and persons in position to know what Nancy Landers did, say that her services were worth more than her board, and on this point no other witness definitely speaks, though all the witnesses who give any of their observations say that Nancy Landers did the house work when she was not ill, and she is shown to have been ill during the twelve years from 1888 to the time of her decease only some fifteen weeks; only for that length of time was she so far ill as to require the attention of a nurse. She was eighty-three years old when she died, but seems to have been gifted with such an unusual temper and bodily health as to successfully resist the ordinary effects of old age. It appears that the claimant, without objection and without regard to the provisions of section 829 of the Code of Civil Procedure, was permitted to testify to every personal transaction had with the deceased, and yet it is impossible to read the testimony and not be entirely convinced that there was never any expectation on the part of the claimant to be paid for board of his mother by adoption, nor was there ever any intention on her part to pay for board otherwise than by services as housekeeper such as she was able to render and did render during these twelve years. There is no testimony in the case which remotely suggests that a claim for board was contemplated by either mother or son in the lifetime of the mother, except the testimony of the witness Catherine Hutchins, a servant, who worked in the household a few weeks some six years before her testimony was given. The witness undertakes to give her recollection of a conversation which did not in any way interest her. Taking into account the lapse of time, the manner in which the witness testifies, the fact that her memory fails to recall anything but such fragments of the conversation as might benefit plaintiff, the surroundings, the occasion which it appears prompted the petulant expressions of the mother, what is claimed to have been said seems so improbable that very little weight should be given to the recollection of this witness. On the other hand, we have the testimony of Frances Wetherbee, giving a conversation with plaintiff soon after the mother's decease in which he disclaims all intention of making claim for board, and when plaintiff was asked as witness if he had not made this statement he did not deny having done so. We have the further fact in the case that both plaintiff and the mother were very particular to make prompt settlement and payment in all matters of business between them; that plaintiff made frequent payments of money to his mother; that the mother was in no need of money and plaintiff had none to spare; the further fact that after six years all claim for

board became stale and uncollectible; the further fact that the table was supplied for the most part if not wholly from the undivided product of the farm or the proceeds of such product. Plaintiff's witness, Catherine Hutchins, says that plaintiff would take eggs and butter and bring back tea, sugar and ordinary groceries. Witness Burr, the storekeeper, says "during the past ten or twelve years she came to the store about once in two weeks and brought butter and eggs which she exchanged for groceries sometimes and she would take due bills for the balance some other times: I thought she traded at our store more than Charles Landers did;" the further fact that she was the owner of the cooking utensils, the table appointments and all the furniture in the house but one bed; the further fact that she was mistress in the house and sole housekeeper and doing, without help, all the household work the same as she always had done, with no servant to do this work for her. This, altogether, makes the suggestion that she was a boarder in her own home and liable to be charged as such by her adopted son much too absurd for belief. The item thereupon allowed by the referee for six years' board at $3 per week, amounting to $936, was error. There is no evidence to support this finding. The item for fire insurance allowed for premiums paid during the six years next prior to the decease of the testatrix at $29.58 is too large. The referee evidently overlooked the testimony of the plaintiff that the insurance was joint and at most Nancy Landers was liable for only one-half that sum. The item for taxes paid, which was allowed by the referee, for the said six years, of ninety dollars, at fifteen dollars a year, is also too large. This is the total tax for these years. The lease called for payment of only one-half the taxes by the deceased. By the evidence of the collector of taxes she paid the whole tax in the years 1896 and 1898. If plaintiff paid for two years there would be only two other years to be divided and the item at most would not exceed fifteen dollars chargeable to her estate. The item for board of nurses, allowed at fifty-four dollars and eighty-six cents, seems to be too large, The proof discloses not to exceed twenty weeks' board at three dollars per week. This board was furnished from the food jointly owned and was prepared by these so-called nurses; the item could not exceed thirty dollars, from this evidence. The allowance of twelve dollars for twelve "trips" has no evidence to support the charge. This, among civilized people, is of the nature of service without pay. The item allowed at thirty-eight dollars, for extra work performed by claimant when his mother was sick, has no proof to support it. The judgment should be reversed, the referee discharged, and a new trial granted, with costs of this appeal to appellant to abide the event. All concurred.

Annie Bell, Respondent, v. New Jersey Steamboat Company, Appellant.— Judgment and order unanimously affirmed, with costs. Fursman, J., not sitting.

James Fulton, Respondent, v. John F. Simpson, Appellant.— Judgment unanimously affirmed, with costs. No opinion.

Lena Garrett, Appellant, v. Bradford R. Wood, Individually and as Executor, etc., of Bradford R. Wood, Deceased, and as Committee, etc., of Thomas G. Wood, and Others, Respondents.— Judgment unanimously affirmed, with costs. No opinion.

Lyman H. Hills, as Trustee of the Estate of Chester M. Hapgood, a Bankrupt, Appellant,

70
Case
a174 NY

v. Chester M. Hapgood and Others, Respondents.—Judgment unanimously affirmed, with costs. No opinion.

Willis T. Honsinger and Albert F. Jerry, Respondents, v. The Union Carriage and Gear Company, Appellant.—Judgment unanimously affirmed, with costs. No opinion.

Smith Lane, Respondent, v. Rosa Frey, as Administratrix, etc., of Christian F. Frey, Deceased, Appellant.—Interlocutory judgment affirmed, with costs, with usual leave to the defendant to answer on payment of costs. No opinion. All concurred.

In the Matter of the Judicial Settlement of the Accounts of J. W. Allen, as Trustee under the Last Will and Testament of Elizabeth Gibbard, Deceased, Appellant; Minerva Cleveland and Irving H. Cleveland, as Administrators, etc., of Ezekiel Cleveland, Deceased, Respondents.— Decree of surrogate unanimously affirmed, with costs. No opinion. Smith, J., not sitting.

Bridget O'Reilly, as Sole Administratrix, etc., of Michael O'Reilly, Deceased, Appellant, v. The Lawrence Cement Company, Respondent.—Judgment affirmed, with costs. No opinion. All concurred, except Smith, J., dissenting; Chase, J., not sitting.

Arthur S. Pierson, Appellant, v. Caleb B. Hill, Respondent.—Judgment unanimously affirmed, with costs. No opinion.

George B. Smith, Respondent, v. The City of Johnstown, Appellant.—Judgment and order unanimously affirmed, with costs. No opinion.

Peter Favo, Respondent, v. The Remington Arms Company, Appellant.—Motion denied.

Joseph Greenwald and Others, Respondents, v. Augustus G. Wales, as Sheriff of Broome County, Appellant.—Motion denied.

Oliver C. Latimer, Respondent, v. Frank H. McKinnon and Others, as Trustees in Bankruptcy of Frank H. McKinnon and Walter R. Burrows, Bankrupts, Appellants. — Motion granted. Order settled to conform to Exhibit A in moving papers.

In the Matter of the Probate of the Last Will and Testament of Sarah Gallagher, Deceased.—Appeal dismissed, with ten dollars costs.

In the Matter of the Application of the Schenectady Railway Company for the Appointment of Three Commissioners to Determine whether an Extension or Branch of its Railroad ought to be Constructed and Operated, etc., in the Town of Glenville, Schenectady County.— Application granted. Hon. Samuel Edwards, Jeremiah Day, of Catskill, N. Y.,

and Peter Walker, of Dunsville, N. Y., appointed commissioners.

In the Matter of the Examination of Edgar C. McKallor and Martha Bell Scott, Judgment Debtors, in Proceedings Supplementary to Execution upon a Judgment, etc.— Motion granted on default, with ten dollars costs.

J. Samuel Lemon, as Administrator, etc., of Hope A. Lemon, Deceased, Appellant, v. Maxwell Smith, as Administrator, etc., of Adon Smith, Jr., Deceased, and Others, Respondents; Ina S. Cowell and Others, Infants, Appellants, Impleaded with Others.— Judgment affirmed, with costs. Opinion by Parker, P. J. (withheld from publication by direction of Parker, P. J.) All concurred, except Smith, J., dissenting. Order to be entered as of January 8, 1902.

Annie Bell, Respondent, v. New Jersey Steamboat Company, Appellant.—Motion denied.

Winthrop N. Finkle, Respondent, v. Oscar G. Finkle and Jerusha Finkle, Appellants.— Judgment affirmed, with costs. No opinion. All concurred.

The First National Bank of Plattsburgh, N. Y., Respondent, v. David B. Sickels and Marie Blanche Sickels, Appellants, Impleaded with Charles R. Sickels.— Order affirmed, with ten dollars costs and disbursements. No opinion. All concurred.

Willis Sharpe Kilmer, Appellant, v. Evening Herald Company, Respondent. — Order modified by striking out provision requiring plaintiff to stipulate not to bring another action against the defendant for the same cause, and as so modified affirmed, with ten dollars costs and disbursements on appeal on grounds stated in opinion in *Kilmer* v. *Evening Herald Co.* (ante, p. 291). No opinion. All concurred.

Jacob Slingerland, Respondent, v. Emma Buchholtz, Appellant.—Judgment unanimously affirmed, with costs. No opinion.

Esther J. Smith, as Administratrix, etc., of Richard O. Smith, Deceased, Appellant, v. Maxwell Smith, as Administrator, etc., of Adon Smith, Jr., Deceased, and Others, Respondents; Ina S. Cowell and Others, Appellants, Impleaded with Others.—Judgment affirmed, with costs, on grounds stated in opinion in *Lemon* v. *Smith* (ante, p. 621). All concurred, except Smith, J., dissenting. Order to be entered as of January 8, 1902. No opinion.

Watertown Carriage Company, Respondent, v. Edwin L. Hall, Appellant.—Motion for reargument granted.

70   621
3d Dept
Case 13
p 70   621

FOURTH DEPARTMENT, MARCH TERM, 1902.

John Buehler, Appellant, v. Robert D. Pierce, Respondent.—Judgment affirmed, with costs, upon mem. of Merwin, J., delivered at Special Term.—All concurred, except Williams and Hiscock, JJ., dissenting.—The following is the memorandum of Merwin, J., delivered at Special Term:

MERWIN, J.; According to the doctrine laid down in *Littauer* v. *Goldman* (72 N. Y. 506), I see no way to escape the conclusion that, upon the transfer by defendant to plaintiff of the note and mortgage in question, there was no implied warranty of validity as regards any usury of which the defendant had no notice. The *Littauer* case has been criticised (*Meyer* v. *Richards*, 163 U. S. 411) but it is the law of the State. There was here, as in that case, the transfer of a promissory note, and if as to the note there was no implied warranty, there was none as to the collateral mortgage. (See 1 Jones Mort. [5th ed.] § 824,

p. 783.) The same principle would be applicable to both. In the assignment from defendant to plaintiff there was a covenant by defendant that there is due on said bond (note) and mortgage the sum of $188.72, with interest included therein to date, January 20, 1899. The face of the note and mortgage was $330, payments had been made thereon, and the amount specified in the covenant evidently represents the amount unpaid after deducting the payments. The plaintiff claims that this covenant is in effect an express warranty of the validity of the instruments. The defendant, by the covenant, says that of the debt secured by the note and mortgage there remains a certain sum unpaid. He does not say that the security is enforcible for that amount. That idea could be carried into the covenant only by implication, and that would not be allowable under the *Littauer* case. The covenant does not go to the origin of the debt, but to the condition at the time of the assignment. It assumes the validity of the security, but does not warrant it any more than it would be warranted by a verbal sale and delivery for its face value. In the latter case there would be no warranty as held in the *Littauer* case. So that practically the *Littauer* case is fatal to plaintiff's claim in either aspect, and judgment must, I think, go for defendant.

Hannah Wickham, Respondent, v. John Bennett, Appellant.—Judgment and orders affirmed, with costs. All concurred, except McLennan and Davy, JJ., dissenting on the ground that the verdict is against the weight of the evidence.

Sidney B. Breese, as Administrator, etc., of Catharine H. Graves, Deceased, Appellant, v. Maurice A. Graves and Charles E. Stevens, as Executors, etc., of Nathan F. Graves, Deceased, Respondents. — Order affirmed, with ten dollars costs and disbursements. All concurred.

Sidney B. Breese and Others, Appellants, v. Maurice A. Graves and Charles E. Stevens, as Executors of and Trustees under the Will of Nathan F. Graves, Deceased, and Others, Respondents.—Order affirmed, with ten dollars costs and disbursements. All concurred.

Adeline S. Thomson, Respondent, v. LaMott Thomson and Others, Appellants, Impleaded with Others.—Judgment and order affirmed, with costs. All concurred.

William H. Rees, as Trustee in Bankruptcy of Angeline J. Drake, Appellant, v. Anson A. Leonard and Others, Respondents.—Judgment affirmed, with costs. *Held*, that the admission of the assessment rolls in evidence, even if error, was not sufficiently prejudicial to require a reversal. All concurred.

Walter L. Wilhelm, by Josephine P. Wilhelm, his Guardian ad Litem, Appellant, v. Byron J. Tillman, Respondent.—Judgment modified by striking out that part which directs a reference, and as so modified affirmed, without costs of this appeal to either party. *Held*, that no accounting is demanded in the answer and it can relate only to a few unimportant items, while a general adjustment between the parties seems to be inevitable. All concurred.

Ball & Wood Company, Respondent, v. Louis K. Comstock and Others, Appellants — Order affirmed, with ten dollars costs and disbursements. All concurred.

Ball & Wood Company, Respondent, v. Louis K. Comstock and Others, etc., Appellants.—Judgment affirmed, with costs. All concurred.

William P. Clark and Charles E. Clark, Appellants, Respondents, v. Erie Railroad Company, Respondent, Appellant. — Judgment and order affirmed, without costs of this appeal to either party. All concurred.

Rochester Savings Bank, Plaintiff v. Caroline F. Bailey, Individually and as Executrix, etc., of Franklin Bailey, Deceased, Respondent, Impleaded with John R. Bailey, Appellant, and Others.—Order affirmed, with ten dollars costs and disbursements. All concurred.

The National Gramophone Corporation, Respondent, v. Norman McMillan, Appellant.—Judgment affirmed, with costs. All concurred.

Carrie E. Drake, as Administratrix, etc., of Delbert M. Drake, Deceased, Respondent, v. Auburn City Railway Company, Appellant. — Judgment and order affirmed, with costs. All concurred, except McLennan, J., dissenting.

Frederick Miller, an Infant, Respondent, v. M. Stuart Benedict and Another, Appellants.—

Motion for reargument denied, with ten dollars costs. Motion for leave to appeal to the Court of Appeals denied.

G. Frank Lapham, Appellant, v. Clayton D, Leonard and Another, Respondents.—Motion to dismiss appeal granted, with ten dollars costs, unless the appellant, within thirty days, procures a case and exceptions to be settled and filed and the papers printed, filed and served, and pays the ten dollars costs of motion.

Asa E. Dye, Respondent, v. Ashton M. Parks, Appellant.—Motion to dismiss appeal denied, without costs, but without prejudice to the right to renew the motion at the opening of the next term of this court in case of failure to exercise due diligence in procuring the case and exceptions herein to be settled and filed and the papers printed, filed and served.

Meyer Lichtenstein, Appellant, v. Harry Rabonlinski, Respondent.—Motion to dismiss appeal denied, without costs, but without prejudice to the right to renew the motion at the opening of the next term of this court, in case of failure to exercise due diligence in procuring the case and exceptions herein to be settled and filed and the printed papers filed and served.

The City of Buffalo v. The Delaware, Lackawanna and Western Railroad Company.—Motion for reargument denied, with ten dollars costs.

Alice H. Butler, Respondent, v. William H. Hawley and Sarah Hawley, Appellants.—Order affirmed, with ten dollars costs and disbursements. All concurred.

Isaac C. Clark, Appellant, v. John W. Smith, 2d, Respondent.—Order affirmed, with ten dollars costs and disbursements. All concurred; Davy, J., not sitting.

William Whipple, as Administrator, etc., Appellant, v. The New York Central and Hudson River Railroad Company, Respondent.—Order affirmed, with ten dollars costs and disbursements. All concurred.

Curtis B. Ellison, Respondent, v. Elmira Industrial Association of Elmira, N. Y., Appellant. —Interlocutory judgment affirmed, with costs, with leave to the appellant to withdraw its demurrer and answer within twenty days, upon payment of the costs of the demurrer and of this appeal, upon authority of *Whiting* v. *Elmira Industrial Association* (45 App. Div. 349). All concurred.

Jasper P. Easterbrook, Respondent, v. Elmira Industrial Association of Elmira, N. Y., Appellant.—Interlocutory judgment affirmed, with costs, with leave to the appellant to withdraw its demurrer and answer within twenty days, upon payment of the costs of the demurrer and of this appeal, upon authority of *Whiting* v. *Elmira Industrial Association* (45 App. Div. 349). All concurred.

John Scanlon, Appellant, v. The Village of Weedsport, Respondent.—Order reversed, with ten dollars costs and disbursements, and motion to set aside the verdict denied, with ten dollars costs. *Held*, that the defendant, because of its proceedings taken by it subsequent to the rendition of said verdict and of its delay in making said motion, waived and lost its right, if it had any, to have said verdict set aside. All concurred; Davy, J., not sitting.

The Second National Bank of Utica, N. Y., Respondent, v. Solomon A. Campbell, Appellant.— Order affirmed, with ten dollars costs and disbursements. All concurred.

Charles Coolman, Appellant, v. The Whitestown Water Works Company and Others, Respondents. — Order affirmed, with ten dollars costs and disbursements. All concurred.

Ida E. Van Etten, Respondent, v. Charles H. Van Etten, Appellant.— Order reversed, with ten dollars costs and disbursements, and motion granted, without costs. All concurred.

Merwin Tripp, Respondent, v. The New York Central and Hudson River Railroad Company, Appellant.— Order reversed, with ten dollars costs and disbursements, and motion granted, with ten dollars costs to abide event, upon condition that, within ten days after service of a copy of this order, the defendant make and file with the clerk of Onondaga county the stipulation to pay transportation of plaintiff's witnesses in accordance with the tender recited in the order appealed from. Held, that, under the circumstances of this case, the trial should be had in the county wherein the cause of action arose. All concurred.

George Rudd v. John King and Others, as Receivers of Union Steamboat Company.— Ordered that the motion for new trial upon exceptions ordered to be heard in the Appellate Division in the first instance be, and and the same is hereby denied, for want of prosecution, with costs, and that the judgment be entered upon the verdict.

In the Matter of the Application of Howland P. Wells for the Appointment of a Committee of the Person and Property of Eugene P. Clark, an Alleged Incompetent Person.— Motion to dismiss appeal denied, without costs.

In the Matter of the Application of Howland P. Wells, for the Appointment of a Committee of the Person and Property of Eugene P. Clark, an Alleged Incompetent Person.— Motion to strike from notice of appeal the words "and all intermediate orders herein" granted upon consent of counsel, without costs.

The People of the State of New York ex rel. Charles E Hequembourg, Respondent, v. John G. Doherty and Others, Assessors of the Town and City of Dunkirk, Chautauqua County, New York, Appellants.— So much of the order as is appealed from affirmed, with ten dollars costs and disbursements. All concurred.

623 | In the Matter of the Judicial Settlement of
le 7 | the Estate of Philip Chase, Deceased.— De-
Y 615 | cree of Surrogate's Court affirmed, with costs against the appellant personally. All concurred.

George Dennison, as, etc., Appellant, v. Joseph H. Wilcox and Another, Respondents.— Judgment affirmed with costs. All concurred.

In the Matter of the Estate of Lucinda A. Watson, Deceased; The Comptroller of the State of New York, Appellant; Young Men's Christian Association of the City of Rome, New York, and the Missionary Society of the Methodist Episcopal Church, Respondents.— Order affirmed, with ten dollars costs and disbursements to each of the respondents, upon the opinion of Calder, Surrogate (reported in 36 Misc. Rep. 504). All concurred.

Henry W. Lynch, Appellant, v. Syracuse, Lakeside and Baldwinsville Railway, Respondent. — Argument herein stayed and record returned to Onondaga County Court in accordance with the opinion of this court this day filed with the clerk.

The Spinroller Company, Respondent, v. The Homer P. Snyder Manufacturing Company, Appellant.— Order affirmed, with ten dollars costs and disbursements. All concurred.

In the Matter of the Estate of Louise T. Doolittle, Deceased.— Order affirmed, with ten dollars costs and disbursements to each of the respondents, upon the opinion of Calder,

Surrogate, in Matter of Watson (reported in 36 Misc. Rep. 504). All concurred.

Joseph Schwartz, Appellant, v. The Buffalo Railway Company, Respondent.— Judgment affirmed, with costs. All concurred.

Judson W. Loomis and Others, Respondents, v. George H. McChesney, Appellant.— Judgment reversed and new trial ordered, with costs to the appellant to abide the event. Held, that without passing upon the other questions involved, the damages allowed by the referee were in excess of those suffered by the plaintiff. All concurred.

William H. Golden, Appellant, v. Ezra Hilts and Walter Hilts, Respondents.— Judgment and order affirmed, with costs. All concurred.

The City of Rochest r, Respondent, v. Rochester Bill Posting Company, Appellant.— Judgment affirmed, with costs. All concurred.

Mary E. Tomney, Respondent, v. George Rankert, Appellant.— Judgment affirmed, with costs. All concurred.

Minnie Morrison v. The City of Syracuse.— Motion to amend order and judgment herein entered July 30, 1900, granted by adding thereto, "upon questions of law only, the court having examined the facts and found no error therein," without prejudice to any right which the defendant may have to move the Court of Appeals to dismiss the plaintiff's appeal for not having been duly and properly taken.

Sarah J. Aikens, Respondent, v. The City of Rome, Appellant.— Judgment and order reversed and new trial ordered, with costs to the appellant to abide the event, unless the respondent stipulates within twenty days to reduce the verdict to $1,000, as of the date of the rendition thereof, in which event the judgment is modified accordingly, and as thus modified the judgment and order are affirmed, without costs of this appeal to either party. All concurred.

The People of the State of New York ex rel. Joseph Seal, Appellant, v. The New York, Chicago and St. Louis Railroad Company, Respondent.— Judgment and order affirmed, with costs. All concurred.

Margaret M. Rich, as Administratrix, etc., Appellant, v. The New York Central and Hudson River Railroad Company, Respondent.— Judgment and order affirmed, with costs. All concurred, except Davy, J., dissenting upon the ground that the evidence warranted the submission to the jury of the questions of the defendant's negligence and the freedom from contributory negligence of the plaintiff's intestate.

David H. Morgan and Charles R. Morgan, Respondents, v. The Merchants' Co-operative Fire Insurance Association of Central New York, Appellant.— Judgment and order affirmed, with costs. All concurred.

Mary Shelderberg, Appellant, v. The Village of Tonawanda, Respondent.— Judgment and order affirmed, with costs. All concurred, except Hiscock and Davy, JJ., dissenting upon the ground that the evidence warranted the submission to the jury of the questions of defendant's negligence and plaintiff's freedom from contributory negligence.

Schwartzchild & Sulzberger Beef Company, Respondent, v. Hiram R. Winney, Appellant.— Judgment and order affirmed, with costs. All concurred.

Lena Kelly, as Administratrix, etc., of Thomas Kelly, Deceased, Respondent. v. Steel Storage and Elevator Construction Company, Appellant, Impleaded with Another.— Judgment and order affirmed, with costs. All concurred.

Industrial Savings and Loan Company, Respondent, v. The Realty Investment and Improvement Company, Impleaded with Wesley H. Beck and Others, Appellants.— Order affirmed, with ten dollars costs and disbursements. All concurred.

Industrial Savings and Loan Company, Respondent, v. The Realty Investment and Improvement Company, Impleaded with Frank D Kenyon and Others, Appellants.— Order affirmed, with ten dollars costs and disbursements. All concurred.

James M. Thomas, Respondent. v. George H. White and Bert E. Flagg, Appellants.— Order affirmed, with ten dollars costs and disbursements. All concurred.

Spencer Kellogg and Spencer Kellogg, Jr., Respondents, v. George F. Sowerby, as President of the Western Elevating Association, and Others, Appellants.— Order affirmed, with ten dollars costs and disbursements. All concurred.

The People of the State of New York, Respondent, v. Gates Thalheimer, Impleaded with Louis Windholtz, Appellant.— Order reversed, with ten dollars costs and disbursements, and motion granted, with ten dollars costs. *Held,* that the plaintiff's complaint purports to state two or more causes of action, and that appellant is entitled to have the same separately stated and numbered. All concurred.

Byron D. Nellis, Respondent, v. The Village of Weedsport, Appellant.— Interlocutory judgment affirmed, with costs, with leave to the defendant to withdraw its demurrer and serve an answer within twenty days, upon payment of the costs of the demurrer and of this appeal. All concurred.

Edward Wunch v. David Shankland, as President of Typographical Union Number Nine. -- Motion denied, with ten dollars costs.

Alice M. Colvin v. Sophia Shaw and Others.— Motion granted, without costs to either party.

In the Matter of the Judicial Settlement of the Accounts of Mary S. Sack, as Guardian of the Estate of Rosa E. Freeland.— Motion for leave to appeal to the Court of Appeals denied, with ten dollars costs.

William Hennesey, Respondent, v. John R. Collins, as Executor, etc., Appellant.— Judgment affirmed, with costs. All concurred.

George J. Keyes, Appellant, v. C. Walter Smith, Respondent.— Order affirmed, with ten dollars costs and disbursements. All concurred.

Charles Cohen, Respondent, v. Thomson-Houston International Electric Company, Appellant.— Judgment and order affirmed, with costs. All concurred; Hiscock, J., not sitting.

Central Bank of Rochester, Appellant, v. Laura M. Kimball and Harold C. Kimball, as Executors, etc., of William S. Kimball, Deceased, Respondents.— Order affirmed, with ten dollars costs and disbursements. All concurred.

Goachimo Porcella, as Administratrix, etc., of James Porcella, Deceased, Appellant, v. The New York, Chicago and St. Louis Railroad Company, Respondent.— Judgment and order affirmed, with costs. All concurred.

Martin V. Benson, Respondent, v. Charles F. Burley and Jane L. Burley, Appellants.— Judgment affirmed, with costs. All concurred; McLennan, J., not sitting.

Charles B. Clark, Appellant, v. The Standard Oil Company of New York, Respondent.— Judgment affirmed, with costs. All concurred; Hiscock, J., not sitting.

The People of the State of New York, Respondent, v. Fred Gabel, Appellant.— Judgment and order affirmed, with costs. All concurred, except Adams, P. J., not voting.

INDEX.

ADVERSE POSSESSION — *Title by adverse possession as against cotenants of real property — effect of an attempt to buy in the title of a cotenant.*] One cotenant of real property may acquire title to the interests of the other cotenants by adverse possession, but in order to do so the possession must be open and notorious and coupled with an assertion of exclusive and hostile ownership.

A man died intestate in 1876, seized of certain real estate incumbered by a mortgage, leaving surviving him a widow, a brother and two sisters as his only heirs at law. The widow continued to occupy or lease the premises to tenants until her death, which occurred December 81, 1895. During such occupancy the widow paid a mortgage on the premises and the taxes, repaired a house on the lot, kept up the insurance, received the rents, which considerably exceeded the expense of management, and claimed to strangers

ADVERSE POSSESSION — *Continued.* PAGE.

that she was the owner of the property and endeavored to sell it. It did not appear that she gave any notice to the heirs at law, who were adults, some of whom lived only a short distance from her, that she was claiming title adversely to them.

By her will she devised the property to her adopted daughter, and the latter continued the same open and exclusive possession until 1899 without hindrance on the part of the heirs at law.

Held, that the adopted daughter had acquired by adverse possession a valid title against the heirs at law;

That the presumption that the widow was occupying as a cotenant was overcome by the character of her possession, and the fact that none of the heirs at law made any claim of ownership even after her death;

That the adopted daughter, by making an unsuccessful attempt to obtain a quitclaim deed of the premises from one of the heirs at law, did not estop herself from disputing the validity of the title derived by a third person under a deed from such heir at law. ZAPF *v.* CARTER. 895

—— *Effect of, on rights of action.*
   See LIMITATION OF ACTION.

AFFIDAVIT:
   See DEPOSITION.

AGENCY — *Generally.*
   See PRINCIPAL AND AGENT.

ALBANY — *Designation of official city newspapers — the president of the common council in a city of the second class can vote only in case of a tie vote.*
   See PEOPLE EX REL. ARGUS CO. *v.* BRESLER 294

ALIEN — *Title acquired by virtue of an escheat act — release "subject to any right," etc.— the Statute of Limitations does not run.*] 1. Where the widow of a deceased owner of real property acquires title thereto under an escheat act of the Legislature, by the terms of which the release by the State is "subject to any right, claim or interest of any purchaser, heir at law or devisee, or of any creditor by mortgage, judgment or otherwise, in the said real estate," the Statute of Limitations does not run in her favor.
   FOWLER *v.* MANHEIMER.......... 56

2. —— *Devise to a non-resident alien.*] A non-resident alien devisee takes a good title to land under chapter 38 of the Laws of 1875 until escheat is declared. SMITH *v.* SMITH...... ·.. 386

ALLOWANCE:
   See COSTS.

AMENDMENT — *Of the constitution and by-laws of a mutual benefit association — when not applicable to an existing member who has become insane.*
   See INSURANCE.

ANNULMENT — *Of a marriage for fraudulent concealment.*
   See HUSBAND AND WIFE.

APPEAL — *From a justice's judgment — the return, not the preliminary statement in the "case," prevails as to the time of the entry of the judgment.*
   See ERDMAN *v.* UPHAM...................................... 815

—— *Upon an appeal from an order the Appellate Division cannot advert to the opinion of the court below in order to ascertain what has been decided.*
   See BURNS *v.* BOLAND........ ....·............. 555

—— *Excepting creditors, only, entitled to share in the benefits of a reversal.*
   See PEOPLE *v.* AMERICAN LOAN & TRUST CO.................. 579

ARSON — *Cross-examination of a witness for the prosecution to show that he entertained ill-feeling toward the defendant — right to have a witness explain his failure to earlier disclose his knowledge — right of the defendant to show that one jointly indicted with him, and called as a witness by him, had been acquitted.*
   See PEOPLE *v.* MILKS.............................. 483

ATTORNEY AND CLIENT — *Continued.*

tho expenses of the litigation did not necessitate such a demand, and upon his refusal to comply therewith notified him that the contract was terminated. Thereafter Warren withdrew from the firm and refused to take any further part in the conduct of the litigation. Hatch subsequently procured the action to be tried (but not by Warren), and it resulted in a judgment that the client had no cause of action.

In an action brought by Nelson against Hatch & Warren to recover damages for a breach of the contract,

Held, that Nelson's failure to pay the $1,000 demanded by Hatch & Warren did not justify them in electing to terminate the contract, as he was not obliged to pay the second $5,000 upon the arbitrary demand of Hatch & Warren, but only when the proper conduct of the litigation required it;

That the refusal of Hatch to apply the money advanced by Nelson to the diligent prosecution of the action, and the attempted cancellation of the contract because of Nelson's failure to pay the $1,000, and the refusal of Warren to perform his contract with the client, constituted a breach of the contract with Nelson, and absolved the latter from the necessity of continuing to perform it;

That it could not be successfully contended that the measure of the plaintiff's damages was the benefit to him of having the contract performed, and that as the action to which the contract related had resulted in a judgment of no cause of action the plaintiff's damages were purely nominal;

That, as the contract had been rendered impossible of performnce by the action of the defendants, this rule of damages did not apply, and that, under the circumstances, the plaintiff should be permitted to recover the moneys which he had advanced under the contract and the expense which he incurred in connection therewith.

A claim by the attorney of a trust company, which has been dissolved, for services rendered by him in connection with securities held by the trust company as collateral to a loan, is not entitled to a preferential payment out of the assets in the hands of the receiver of the trust company, appointed in the action to dissolve it, where it does not appear that there were any judicial proceedings in connection with the collateral securities which would support a common-law or a statutory lien, or that the attorney did anything which created or preserved any of the securities or resulted in any advantage to the receiver or to the trust company; nor is a claim for services, rendered by the attorney, at the request of the trust company, in opposing the appointment of the receiver of the company, entitled to such a preference, where it appears that the attorney's efforts did not augment or preserve the funds of the trust company.

Where the attorney for one of the parties to a reference dies after the case has been finally submitted to the referee, section 65 of the Code of Civil Procedure, which provides, "If an attorney dies, is removed or suspended, or otherwise becomes disabled to act, at any time before judgment in an action, no further proceeding shall be taken in the action, against the party for whom he appeared, until thirty days after notice to appoint another attorney has been given to that party, either personally or in such other manner as the court directs," does not prohibit the referee from delivering his report before the expiration of the thirty days prescribed by that section, especially where it appears that the thirty days did not expire until after the expiration of the sixty days allowed to the referee within which to deliver his report.

Semble, that where it appears that nothing was done pursuant to the report until after the expiration of the thirty days prescribed by the section, and after other attorneys had been substituted in place of the deceased attorney, it may be said that the actual delivery of the report did not take place until after the lapse of the thirty days.

ATTORNEY AND CLIENT — *Continued.* PAGE.

4. —— *Waiver.*] Assuming that the delivery of the report before the expiration of the thirty days constituted a technical violation of section 65 of the Code of Civil Procedure, it was a mere irregularity, which was waived by the failure of the substituted attorneys to take advantage thereof before the entry of the judgment, it appearing that upon their request such judgment was not entered until ten days after their substitution. *Id.*

—— *Competency as a witness of an attorney superintending the execution of a will.*
 See EVIDENCE.

AUCTION — *Agreement not to bid at, is against public policy.*
 See CONTRACT.

AUDITOR — *In a town.*
 See TOWN.

AUTOMATIC SPRINKLERS — *Contract to install.*
 See CONTRACT.

BANKING — *Deposit, in a bank account in the name of a firm of brokers, of moneys of an insurance company and of a navigation company — under what circumstances they are respectively impressed with a trust — effect of the moneys being from time to time wrongfully withdrawn and thereafter being replaced.*]
1. The firm of Weatherby & Wilbur, who were engaged in the insurance and brokerage business, kept a bank account in the name of "Weatherby & Wilbur." In August and September, 1898, Weatherby, who was the agent for the Travelers' Insurance Company, deposited in the account premiums collected by him for that company amounting to $318.64. In September, 1898, he deposited in the account $360.08, which represented the avails of drafts sold by the firm for the International Navigation Company. Weatherby died October 5, 1898, at which time the account contained $724.87. Several times during the month of September Weatherby, by means of withdrawals, made without the knowledge of the insurance company or the navigation company, reduced the account below the sums needed to discharge the two claims, but, as many times, made good such deficiency from some undisclosed source. It did not appear that Weatherby deposited in the account any money except trust money, or that he had deposited therein moneys held in trust for any one but the insurance and navigation companies.

Held, that the several withdrawals and restorations made by Weatherby in his lifetime did not operate to extinguish the identity of the moneys originally deposited belonging to the insurance and navigation companies;

That, in the absence of any other claimants of the $724.87 than the creditors of Weatherby or his administratrix, such moneys constituted a trust fund, applicable to the discharge of the claims of the insurance and navigation companies. UNITED NATIONAL BANK *v.* WEATHERBY......... 279

2. —— *Checks on a deposit made by a corporation which has left signature cards with the bank — how the checks should be signed.*] The secretary and treasurer of a corporation, acting on behalf thereof, opened two accounts with a bank, one known as the general account and the other known as the dividend account. At the time he opened the accounts he left with the bank two signature cards designed to guide the bank in the payment of checks upon the two accounts. One of such cards read:

"AUTHORIZED SIGNATURES OF
 "*Dec* 10*th* 1897.
"*THE SHOE LASTING MACHINE CO.*
 "*T. Mayo Blackwell*
 "*Treas*
"*General Account.*
 "*Walter Shaw, Prest.*"

The other read:

"AUTHORIZED SIGNATURES OF
 "........... ....189......
"*THE SHOE LASTING MACHINE CO.*
"*Dividend Account.*
 "*T. Mayo Blackwell*
 "*Secty & Treas*"

BILLS AND NOTES — *Continued.*

"AUTHORIZED SIGNATURES OF
"*Dec* 10*th* 1897.
"*THE SHOE LASTING MACHINE CO.*
"*T. Mayo Blackwell*
"*Treas*

"*General Account.*
"*Walter Shaw, Prest.*"

The other read:

"AUTHORIZED SIGNATURES OF
"......................... 189.. ...
"*THE SHOE LASTING MACHINE CO.*
"*Dividend Account.*
"*T. Mayo Blackwell*
"*Secty & Treas*"

PAGE.

Held, that the bank had authority to pay checks drawn on the dividend account and signed by Blackwell as secretary and treasurer, but that it had no authority to pay checks drawn on the general account and signed by Blackwell as treasurer and not by Shaw as president.

SHOE LASTING CO. *v.* WESTERN NAT. BANK............ 588

2. —— *Usury — recovery of, where paper is discounted by a national bank.*] Where a national bank discounts a note for a customer, retaining as the discount an excessive rate of interest, and on the maturity of the note the customer pays the excessive discount in cash and executes a renewal note for the same amount, and this process is repeated several times, each actual payment constitutes a usurious transaction within the meaning of section 5198 of the United States Revised Statutes, which provides that a person who pays an excessive rate of interest to a national bank may maintain an action to recover, "twice the amount of the interest thus paid, from the association taking or receiving the same, provided such action is commenced within two years from the time the usurious transaction occurred."

SMITH *v.* FIRST NATIONAL BANK................................ 876

8. —— *When the Statute of Limitations begins to run.*] The two years' Statute of Limitations commences to run from the date of each cash payment of an excessive discount. *Id.*

BOARD — *Of town officers.*
See TOWN.

BOARD OF CLAIMS — *Statute of Limitations — what does not suspend its operation — claim against the Buffalo Asylum for work and materials — it might have been presented to the State Board of Audit — what statute conferring jurisdiction on the Board of Claims gives a reasonable time for the presentation of a claim.*
See BISSELL *v.* STATE OF NEW YORK... 288

BOND — *Undertaking on opening a default in the City Court of New York — the liability thereunder extends to a judgment entered on a remittitur from the Court of Appeals — variance between the undertaking and the provisions of the order.*] 1. Judgments having been taken by default against the defendants in two actions brought in the City Court of New York, the court opened the default upon condition that the defendants should give an undertaking in each of said actions, "to secure any judgment that may be recovered in said two actions which undertakings are to be approved upon notice to plaintiff's attorney and justification of the sureties by one of the justices of this court, and each to be given in the penalty of twice the amount of the claims of the plaintiff in each of the above-entitled actions." Pursuant to this order the defendants gave an undertaking conditioned to pay "the just and full amount of any judgment which may be finally recovered against them * * * in a certain action now pending in the City Court of New York." One of the actions was then brought to trial in the City Court and the defendants recovered a verdict upon which judgment was entered. This judgment was affirmed by the General Term of the City Court of New York and also by the Appellate Term of the Supreme Court, but was

BOND— *Continued.*   PAGE.

reversed by the Appellate Division which ordered a new trial. The plaintiff then appealed to the Court of Appeals, stipulating for judgment absolute. The Court of Appeals affirmed the Appellate Division and directed judgment absolute against the defendants pursuant to the stipulation. Thereafter, on the remittitur from the Court of Appeals, the judgment of the Court of Appeals was made the order and judgment of the City Court. In an action brought upon the undertaking, after an execution issued upon the judgment entered upon the remittitur had been returned unsatisfied, it was

Held, that the order opening the default and the undertaking contemplated that the liability on the undertaking should not be limited to a judgment recovered in the first instance in the City Court, but should be construed to embrace a judgment entered as the result of a stipulation for judgment absolute in the Court of Appeals;

That, as the undertaking was not a statutory one, the variance between the language thereof and of the order opening the default did not affect the validity of the undertaking;

That, whether the liability on the undertaking was to be determined by the phraseology of the order opening the default or by that of the undertaking, the plaintiff was entitled to recover. CAPONIGRI *v.* COOPER........ **124**

2. —— *Typewritten bonds issued by a school board—printed bonds subsequently substituted therefor are enforcible by a bona fide holder for value—want of authority in the holder of the bonds to sell them is not a defense—interest payable after default.*] Brokers, to whom typewritten bonds regularly issued by the board of education of a school district were offered for sale by the holder thereof, having refused to purchase them unless they were printed, bonds were printed in the precise form of the typewritten bonds and were executed by the same officers of the school district under the same seal. The printed bonds were then delivered to the brokers, and at the same time the typewritten bonds were canceled by mutilating them with a knife and were delivered to and retained by the president of the school district. No claim was ever made against the board of education on account of the typewritten bonds.

In an action on the printed bonds by a *bona fide* purchaser thereof for value,

Held, that the board of education was liable on the printed bonds, assuming that it would have been liable on the typewritten bonds if the printed bonds had not been substituted therefor;

That the objection that the person who sold the bonds to the brokers did so without authority from the owner thereof was not available to the board of education as against a *bona fide* holder of the printed bonds;

That the board of education, having refused to comply with a demand made after the maturity of one of the bonds for payment of the principal of such bond, was liable for interest on such principal from the time of such demand and refusal, computed at the statutory rate, and not at the rate fixed by the bond. OSWEGO CITY SAV. BANK *v.* BD. EDUCATION...... **588**

3. —— *Surety on the bond of an insurance agent—what modification of the contract between the company and its agent discharges the surety.*] A contract between an insurance company and one of its agents provided that the agent should pay all the expenses and claims of his district and, in addition thereto, pay to the company ten per cent of the gross premiums collected in the district. Pursuant to the terms of the contract, the agent furnished a bond conditioned that he should well and truly perform the terms of the contract, which bond was executed by a surety who had knowledge of the terms of such contract. After the delivery of the bond to the insurance company, the insurance company and the agent, without the knowledge or consent of the surety, made an agreement whereby the agent was to deduct ten dollars weekly from the receipts as a living fund and the insurance company was to pay from the home office sick claims, doctors' bills and rent and the agent was to remit to the insurance company all collections, less commissions due to sub-agents and the ten dollars weekly for living purposes.

Held, that the alteration of the arrangement between the insurance company and the agent operated to release the surety from any liability upon the bond. AMERICAN CASUALTY INS. CO. *v.* GREEN **267**

CONTRACT — *Continued.*

CONTRACT — *Continued.*

& Warren's share of the proceeds, agreed to advance $10,000 to the attorneys for the purposes of the litigation, the first $5,000 to be advanced by a specified time, and the second $5,000 to be advanced in such sums as might be desired by Hatch & Warren.

After Nelson had advanced $7,000 under his contract, Hatch & Warren refused to advance moneys necessary to the diligent prosecution of the action, although they had in their hands funds applicable to that purpose. They also demanded of Nelson an additional payment of $1,000 under the contract when the expenses of the litigation did not necessitate such a demand, and upon his refusal to comply therewith notified him that the contract was terminated. Thereafter Warren withdrew from the firm and refused to take any further part in the conduct of the litigation. Hatch subsequently procured the action to be tried (but not by Warren), and it resulted in a judgment that the client had no cause of action.

In an action brought by Nelson against Hatch & Warren to recover damages for a breach of the contract,

Held, that Nelson's failure to pay the $1,000 demanded by Hatch & Warren did not justify them in electing to terminate the contract, as he was not obliged to pay the second $5,000 upon the arbitrary demand of Hatch & Warren, but only when the proper conduct of the litigation required it;

That the refusal of Hatch to apply the money advanced by Nelson to the diligent prosecution of the action, and the attempted cancellation of the contract because of Nelson's failure to pay the $1,000, and the refusal of Warren to perform his contract with the client, constituted a breach of the contract with Nelson, and absolved the latter from the necessity of continuing to perform it;

That it could not be successfully contended that the measure of the plaintiff's damages was the benefit to him of having the contract performed, and that as the action to which the contract related had resulted in a judgment of no cause of action the plaintiff's damages were purely nominal;

That, as the contract had been rendered impossible of performance by the action of the defendants, this rule of damages did not apply, and that, under the circumstances, the plaintiff should be permitted to recover the moneys which he had advanced under the contract and the expense which he incurred in connection therewith. NELSON *v.* HATCH.................. 206

8. —— *Delay by a sub-contractor in placing iron trusses on a wall — damages resulting from the blowing down of the wall by reason thereof — items of damage, interest on delayed payments to the principal contractor, increased cost of working in winter and the longer employment of men and the personal service of the principal contractor — they are not too remote.*] In an action to foreclose a mechanic's lien, it appeared that the defendant Haven entered into a contract to construct a number of shops for the New York Central Railroad Company, and that Haven sublet the structural iron work for two of the shops to the plaintiffs. During the progress of the work, a portion of the brick walls of one of the shops erected by Haven was blown down, owing, as found by the court, to the negligent failure of the plaintiffs to place iron trusses on such walls. The amount of damages did not clearly appear upon the trial, and the court, by an interlocutory judgment, directed a reference to take proof of, and ascertain and determine the amount of damages sustained by Haven, through the failure of said plaintiffs to erect said trusses. Upon the reference, the referee ruled that the defendant was entitled to recover a sum stated representing the necessary expenses of repairing and rebuilding the walls that were blown down, the value of the property destroyed, the amount expended in removing the debris of the fallen walls, in cleaning the brick and the cost of the work required to lay the new walls.

It also appeared that by reason of the walls being blown down, the defendant lost the use of a sum of money which the railroad company retained for several months under a clause in the contract, because the work was not completed within the contract period; that he was obliged to perform a large portion of the work during the winter season, at an increased expense; that he was obliged to retain the services of a number of employees, and that he was compelled to devote his own time and personal services to the completion of the work.

CONTRACT — *Continued.*

that between August 1, 1899, and May 1. 1900, the plaintiff maintained and
supported Philip with the knowledge and consent of the defendant, and that
such support and maintenance was worth the sum of $180. The answer
admitted the execution of the deed referred to in the complaint and denied
each and every other allegation thereof.

Upon the trial the plaintiff offered in evidence a "deed of property from
Philip Erdman to George Upham" (the defendant), but made no statement
as to the character of its contents. The court excluded the deed upon the
objection of the defendant, and no other evidence being offered by the plaintiff the justice entered a nonsuit against him.

Held, that, in the absence of any information as to the contents of the deed
offered in evidence, it could not be said that the justice erred in excluding it;

That, if the contract set forth in the complaint had actually been made,
the plaintiff being neither a party nor a privy thereto could not maintain an
action upon it;

That, in the absence of any proof or offer to prove that the plaintiff had
furnished support to Philip Erdman upon the consent of the defendant, the
justice properly granted the nonsuit. ERDMAN *v.* UPHAM.................. 815

6. —— *Breach of a contract to give the plaintiffs the exclusive sale of a hat
manufactured by the defendants — measure of damages — the plaintiffs are not
entitled to recover for unsold hats at the price at which they contracted to sell
them.*] In an action for the breach of a contract made between the plaintiffs, who were the proprietors of a retail hat store in Binghamton, N. Y., and
the defendants, who were the manufacturers of the "Hawes Guarantee Hat,"
it appeared that the plaintiffs agreed to handle, advertise and push the sale
of such hat in the city of Binghamton and the county of Broome and to make
it their "leader" in preference to all other makes of hats, in consideration
of which the defendants agreed to sell such hats to the plaintiffs at the price
of twenty-four dollars per dozen, the plaintiffs agreeing to sell the hats for
three dollars each and the defendants agreeing not to sell such hats to any
other person in that locality — the contract to continue in force as long as
the plaintiffs performed on their part. The breach consisted of the action
of the defendants in refusing to sell the hats to the plaintiffs and in selling
the hats to another dealer in the city of Binghamton. It appeared that at
the time such breach occurred, the plaintiffs had on hand 197 hats. Nothing in the contract prevented the plaintiffs from thereafter selling the hats
and it was not shown that the breach had in any way depreciated their
value.

Held, that the measure of the plaintiffs' damages was the value of the
contract;

That they were not, however, entitled to recover the value of the 197 hats
still on hand and unsold at the time of the breach, at the rate of three
dollars for each hat. VOSBURY *v.* MALLORY......... 247

7. —— *Agreement to pay to a materialman a specified sum out of an installment to fall due to the contractor at a certain stage of the work — the payment
before it becomes due, of the balance of such installment to the contractor, who
then abandons the work, entitles the materialman to his money.*] Under an
arrangement between the owner of certain premises and a mortgagee thereof,
the owner was to erect a number of buildings thereon and the mortgagee
was to advance to him certain sums at various stages in the erection of the
buildings. During the progress of the work the mortgagee, in order to
induce a firm which had furnished a portion of the stone used in the construction of the buildings, and for which it had not been paid, to furnish the rest
of the stone, made an agreement with the firm by which he undertook to
withhold, from the payment to which the owner would be entitled when the
buildings were inclosed, $800 and pay the same to the firm. After the firm
had furnished the stone, but before the building had been entirely inclosed
and before it was due under the terms of the contract, the mortgagee paid
to the owner $4,950, which represented the amount of the inclosure payment
less the $800 which he had contracted to withhold. After receiving such
payment, the owner abandoned his contract and never entirely inclosed the
buildings.

CONTRACT — *Continued.*   PAGE.

with a third person to sell it and pay over the proceeds, creates an agency or a loan with collateral, not a trust. In the event of the death of the third person, the devisee becomes a creditor of his estate. MATTER OF WALKER.....263

CORPORATION — *Issue of stock paid for out of surplus earnings — when it goes to a life tenant and when to remaindermen under the will of the original owner.*] 1. A corporation having a surplus of accumulated profits may, within the limits of good faith, either distribute it as dividends or retain it and convert it into capital. The substance and intent of the action of the corporation, as evidenced by its treatment of the surplus and its resolutions in issuing new stock against such surplus, will be considered by, if it does not control, the courts in deciding whether or not the new stock is dividend, and hence income belonging to a life tenant.

If the corporation pays money or issues stock as a distribution of profits it will ordinarily go to the life tenant, but if it issues stock as capital and

CORPORATION — *Continued.*   PAGE.

appropriates its surplus as an increase of the capital stock, such issue will be
held to inure to the benefit of the remaindermen.

A testator, who left surviving him a widow, a son and three daughters,
gave his residuary estate to his wife during her life with the remainder to
his four children equally. Included in the residuary estate were sixty shares
of the capital stock of a corporation, which had a capital stock of $40,000 and
for many years prior to the death of the testator had allowed its earnings to
accumulate. At the time of the testator's death the accumulated surplus
amounted to $289,341.88, which surplus was then permanently invested in
the business of the corporation. After the testator's death, and during the
lifetime of the widow, the corporation declared and paid frequent cash
dividends upon the stock. It also issued two thousand one hundred shares
of additional stock and divided two thousand of them among its stockholders who paid nothing therefor. The agreement of the stockholders consenting to the issue of the additional stock and the action of the trustees of
the corporation directing its issue denominated the transaction as an "increase
of capital stock." At the time the additional stock was issued, the accumulated surplus of the corporation amounted to $443,030.57. A few days before
the issue of such stock the corporation paid to its stockholders $80,000 in
cash, declaring such payment to be a dividend.

Held, that the additional shares were intended to be and were issued to
represent an accretion to the permanent working capital of the corporation
and did not constitute a dividend of income; that, for this reason, the three
hundred additional shares apportioned to the testator's estate belonged to the
remaindermen and not to the life tenant.

2. —— *Subscription to the stock of a corporation to be organized — what
departure in its organization from the prospectus discharges the subscribers.*]
Where subscriptions to the stock of a corporation about to be formed are
obtained in connection with a prospectus stating that the object of the corporation is "to acquire all patents and rights for all countries, except the
United States and Canada, to metal turning machines, known as the 'Hoffmann machine,' and of which F. G. Hoffmann is the inventor and patentee,
as well as all improvements, additions, etc.," the organization of a corporation, "to make, contract for the manufacture, or purchase of, buy, use, sell,
lease, rent or mortgage all mechanical or other apparatus, machinery and
implements for metal turning machines, or any other article or articles connected therewith or incident thereto, or any or all of them, and *in general to
do a manufacturing business*," constitutes such a material departure from the
agreement entered into by the subscribers as will render the subscriptions
unenforcible as to non-assenting subscribers. STERN *v.* McKEE............

3. —— *Proof that money of a corporation was paid upon its void notes to a
director thereof.*] What evidence given in an action brought by the receiver
of a co-operative insurance corporation against a former director thereof, to
recover moneys of the association paid to the director in extinguishment of
void notes executed by the association to the director, is sufficient to warrant
a jury in finding that the defendant took such money with knowledge
that it belonged to the corporation, considered. McCLURE *v.* WILSON.....

4. —— *Knowledge imputable to a director.*] In such a case the defendant
is chargeable with such knowledge as he gained in the capacity of director,
or which he might have acquired by the exercise of reasonable care. *Id.*

5. —— *Parties to an action to dissolve a corporation and sequestrate property
fraudulently transferred by it.*] In an action brought by a judgment creditor
of a corporation to procure a dissolution thereof and a sequestration of property fraudulently transferred by it, the persons or corporations who hold such
property in their possession may be joined as parties defendant.

6. —— *Examination, before suit brought, of an officer of such corporation
— that it will tend to incriminate him is not a defense to the application.*] On
an application, under section 870 of the Code of Civil Procedure, to take the
testimony of a person whom the applicant intends to make a party to an
action to be thereafter commenced by him, the question whether the informa-

CRIME — *Continued.*

been practically impossible for him to have started the fire, is cross-examined by the district attorney concerning his failure to disclose such knowledge earlier in the litigation, so vigorously as to seriously affect his credibility, the defendant's counsel should, upon the redirect examination of the witness, be permitted to ask him to explain why he had not sooner disclosed his knowledge. *Id.*

5. —— *Right of the defendant to show that one jointly indicted with him, and called as a witness by him, had been acquitted.*] Where Smith, who had been jointly indicted with the defendant and who had been tried and acquitted, was sworn on behalf of the defendant, and it appeared that the jury knew that he and the defendant were jointly indicted, but did not know that he was acquitted, the court considered that the defendant was entitled to present that fact to the jury, in order that it might not appear that Smith had a vital personal interest in establishing the defendant's innocence. *Id.*

6. —— *Circumstantial evidence of the crime of arson — to justify a conviction it must be inconsistent with innocence.*] To justify a conviction upon circumstantial evidence the circumstances must not only point to guilt, but must also be absolutely inconsistent with innocence, that is, the inference of guilt must be the only one that can reasonably be drawn from the facts.

What circumstances, adduced on the trial of an indictment charging the defendant with burning her dwelling house for the purpose of obtaining the insurance thereon, are insufficient to sustain a conviction, considered.

DAMAGES — *Delay by a sub-contractor in placing iron trusses on a wall — damages resulting from the blowing down of the wall by reason thereof — items of damage, interest on delayed payments to the principal contractor, increased cost of working in winter and the longer employment of men and the personal service of the principal contractor — they are not too remote.*

—— *Action for breach of a contract only partially performed by the plaintiff — the expense of the full performance of the contract may be shown by the defendant.*

—— *For the breach of an agreement by one since deceased to make another his sole heir — the claimant is entitled to recover on* quantum meruit *for his services and disbursements.*

—— *Measure of damages for an injury to goods of a sub-tenant occasioned by a roof being insufficiently protected while being repaired after a fire by the landlord.*

—— *Attorney and client — contingent fee — agreement by a third person with the attorney to pay the disbursements of the action and share in the recovery — failure of the attorney to perform the latter agreement — measure of damages where the complaint in the action to which the contract related was dismissed.*

—— *Breach of a contract to give the plaintiffs the exclusive sale of a hat manufactured by the defendants — measure of damages — the plaintiffs are not entitled to recover for unsold hats at the price at which they contracted to sell them.*

—— *Unauthorized sale by a broker of a customer's stock — measure of damages.*

DEATH — *Of an attorney after the submission of a case to a referee.*
See ATTORNEY AND CLIENT.

DEED — *To parties "trustees of the separate estate of Margaretta Persse"
— the words quoted are descriptive — a deed signed by the grantees as individuals
conveys a good title.*] 1. At the beginning of a conveyance of certain premises following the names of the grantees were the words "*trustees of the separate estate of Margaretta Persse, wife of Dudley Persse.*" Nothing else in the
deed indicated the existence of a trust or an intention to limit the estate conveyed to the grantees, and there was no extrinsic evidence of the existence
of such a trust. Thereafter the trustees mentioned in said deed and Margaretta Persse conveyed the premises to one O'Gorman for a nominal consideration of one dollar. No other consideration appeared. The trustees
signed this deed as individuals and were not described therein as trustees.
Held, that the words "*trustees of the separate estate of Margaretta Persse,
wife of Dudley Persse,*" contained in the first-mentioned deed, were to be
regarded as descriptive merely, and that the persons so described acquired
thereunder an estate in fee as individuals:
That, consequently, the deed executed by them for a nominal consideration operated to convey a marketable title which a subsequent purchaser of the premises would be required to accept.
 KANENBLEY *v.* VOLKENBERG... 97

EVIDENCE — *Continued.*   **PAGE.**

FRAUDULENT CONVEYANCE — *Where an absolute deed is held to be a mortgage, a judgment creditor should be adjudged to have a lien upon the premises subject to the mortgage.*] 1. In an action brought by the plaintiff, a judgment creditor of the defendant Mrs. Rosenberg, to set aside as fraudulent

INSURANCE — *Continued.* PAGE.

insurance by which it "contracted to insure and did insure this plaintiff, upon certain terms and conditions in said contract of insurance specified, * * * against legal liability for damages" to the extent of $5,000 to any one person "respecting fatal or non-fatal injuries from accidents occurring to any person or persons at the place or places mentioned and specified in the application for the said contract of insurance and in the policy of insurance issued on said application * * * against the hazards enumerated and set forth under a certain premium schedule to said contract of insurance annexed;" that while said contract of insurance was in force, one Brown, a workman in the employ of the plaintiff, sustained injuries by reason of an accident occurring at the place specified in the policy, and that Brown and the work in which he was employed were included in the class of persons and hazards covered by the contract of insurance and against "liability to whom and because of which, due to injuries from accidents, this defendant insured plaintiff;" that subsequently Brown brought an action against the plaintiff to recover for the injuries sustained by him, and recovered $8.856.57 damages, interest and costs, which the defendant refused to pay; "that plaintiff duly complied with and observed all the provisions of the said contract of insurance by him to be complied with and observed as conditions precedent to defendant's liability to him thereunder, except in so far as such compliance and observance were waived or rendered unnecessary by the position and action of this defendant." Judgment was demanded for the sum of $5,000 and interest.

The policy on which the defendant's liability was predicated was not made a part of the complaint

Held, that the complaint was demurrable, as it alleged simply that the defendant insured the plaintiff upon certain terms and conditions, which were not specified, against certain hazards which were not set forth, and that the plaintiff had performed in so far as performance had not been waived — setting forth no facts from which a waiver could be presumed.

8. —— *By-law of a mutual benefit association — when an amendment thereof need not be complied with by a member.*] The constitution and by-laws of a mutual benefit association provided that, on the death of a member, the endowment should be paid to his widow, children, father and mother, in the order named, and if he left surviving him none of such relatives, to such beneficiaries as he might direct; that if he left neither wife, child nor parents, and failed to designate other persons as his beneficiaries the endowment should fail. Thereafter, pursuant to a provision thereof authorizing it, the constitution and by-laws were amended so as to provide that the endowment should be paid to the member's widow and children, in the order named, and that a member having neither wife nor child must designate in writing in a book provided for that purpose the person to whom the benefit should be paid, and that, in the event of the member's failure to make such designation, the endowment should not be paid.

Held, that the amendment was not applicable to a member who, prior to its enactment, became insane and after its enactment died without recovering his sanity and without having designated his beneficiaries, leaving surviving him a mother, but neither wife nor children;

That, as the deceased member's disability was created by an act of God, and as the act required to be performed could not be performed for him by any other person, his failure to make the designation which the by-laws required did not work a forfeiture.

Semble, that an amendment to a by-law must furnish the person upon whom it is to operate with an opportunity to comply therewith, and if, by the intervention of the *vis major*, or other equivalent condition, such opportunity is not given, the party will usually be held excused and no forfeiture will result.

9. —— *For the benefit of the wife of the assured — how affected by chapter 272 of the Laws of 1896.*] Section 22 of chapter 272 of the Laws of 1896, relating to policies of insurance procured by married women upon the lives of their husbands, and which provides that a married woman shall be "entitled to receive the insurance money payable by the terms of the policy as her separate property, and free from any claim of a creditor or representative of

LANDLORD AND TENANT — *Continued.*

The defendant admitted the plaintiffs' right to such fixtures, as, in his opinion, could be removed without serious injury to the freehold, and accordingly permitted the plaintiffs to remove the bar which was attached to the wall by screws, and purchased some of the gas fixtures from the plaintiffs, but declined to permit the removal of the chattels in suit.

Upon the trial of the action, the defendant based his title solely upon his deed.

Held, that a judgment in favor of the plaintiffs should be affirmed.

Semble, that, as it appeared that the sale of the chattels, their annexation to the freehold and the execution of the chattel mortgage constituted one transaction, the law presumed that the parties intended that the chattels should remain personal property, and that when the defendant acquired title he took subject to the plaintiffs' rights therein.

Semble, that, even if the lease to Lee & Block was terminated by the foreclosure, the rights of the plaintiffs survived for a reasonable time, to enable them to remove their property.

Semble, that, as the defendant did not claim title on account of the failure of the plaintiffs to remove the fixtures within a reasonable time, the plaintiffs were not obliged to prove facts excusing their failure in this respect.

Semble, that the defendant was estopped from asserting that the right to remove the fixtures had been lost by the failure to reserve such right in the lease executed to Mrs. Mahoney, inasmuch as he did not assert such claim at the time the plaintiffs attempted to remove the chattels in suit, nor set it up in his answer.

Semble, that, even if he were in a position to assert this claim, his contention could not be sustained, as it appeared that the property in question consisted of ordinary trade fixtures as distinguished from fixtures which were distinctively realty, and that they could be removed without injury to themselves and without any material, substantial or serious injury to the freehold.

Semble, that, if fixtures are distinctively realty, the acceptance of a new lease without reserving the right to remove them constitutes an abandonment of such right, but that this rule does not apply to trade fixtures not distinctively realty and which are designed to retain their character as personal property, and are capable of removal without material injury to the freehold. BERNHEIMER *v.* ADAMS...... 114

2. —— *Injury to goods from a roof being insufficiently protected while being repaired after a fire — right of a sub-lessee to recover from his lessor, although the repairs are made by the owner of the building — agency — measure of damages.*] The Le Conte estate demised certain premises to the firm of Prescott & Co. by a lease, which contained the following clause:

"Said parties of the second part further covenant that they will not assign this lease nor make any alteration in said premises without the written consent of the said parties of the first part under the penalty of forfeiture and damages."

"And it is further agreed between the parties to these presents that in case the building or buildings erected on the premises hereby leased shall be partially damaged by fire, the same shall be repaired as speedily as possible at the expense of the said parties of the first part."

"And it is further understood and agreed that all repairs that may become necessary to or about said building, steam engine and elevators, during the term hereby granted (except repairs to the roof), shall be made and paid for by the said parties of the second part."

Prescott & Co. subsequently sub-let the premises to a firm known as the Manhattan Mills, the sub-lease also containing the provisions above quoted. The course of dealing between the Manhattan Mills and Prescott & Co. was such that when occasion arose for repairs which the landlord was bound to make, the Manhattan Mills were referred to E. H. Ludlow & Co., who were the agents of the Le Conte estate, and the repairs were then made through the agency of Ludlow & Co. The communications between the Manhattan Mills and Prescott & Co. were through an employee of the latter firm, named Miller.

During the term of the sub-lease a fire occurred upon the premises, which burned a large hole in the roof. Neither of the members of the firm of Pres-

LIFE ESTATE — *Continued.*   PAGE.

and for many years prior to the death of the testator had allowed its earnings to accumulate. At the time of the testator's death the accumulated surplus amounted to $289,341.88, which surplus was then permanently invested in the business of the corporation. After the testator's death, and during the lifetime of the widow, the corporation declared and paid frequent cash dividends upon the stock. It also issued two thousand one hundred shares of additional stock and divided two thousand of them among its stockholders, who paid nothing therefor. The agreement of the stockholders consenting to the issue of the additional stock and the action of the trustees of the corporation directing its issue denominated the transaction as an "increase of capital stock." At the time the additional stock was issued, the accumulated surplus of the corporation amounted to $443,080.57. A few days before the issue of such stock the corporation paid to its stockholders $80,000 in cash, declaring such payment to be a dividend.

Held, that the additional shares were intended to be and were issued to represent an accretion to the permanent working capital of the corporation and did not constitute a dividend of income; that, for this reason, the three hundred additional shares apportioned to the testator's estate belonged to the remaindermen and not to the life tenant.

   CHESTER *v.* BUFFALO CAR MFG. CO............................ **443**

  2. —— *Trust estate — assessments made during a life estate charged against the principal.*] An assessment for sewers and pavements made during the continuance of a life estate is properly charged against the principal of a trust fund. PELTZ *v.* LEARNED.. **812**

LIFE INSURANCE:
  See INSURANCE.

LIMITATION OF ACTION — *What does not suspend its operation — claim against the Buffalo Asylum for work and materials — it might have been presented to the State Board of Audit.*] 1. The operation of the Statute of Limitations upon a claim against the State of New York, for work performed and material furnished under written contracts with the managers of the Buffalo Asylum, between 1871 and 1877, was not suspended by the commencement, in 1878, of a proceeding by mandamus against the managers of the Buffalo Asylum to compel them to measure stone furnished under the contracts, as that proceeding was not a proceeding or suit against the State of New York or a necessary step preliminary to bringing the matter before the State Board of Audit of the State of New York, the body which then had jurisdiction of such claims.

The fact that the claim was payable out of the appropriations for the construction of the asylum and that this fund was placed practically in charge of the managers, did not operate to deprive the claimant of the right to have his claim adjudicated by the State Board of Audit. The running of the statute against the claim was not suspended by an action brought by the State against the original claimants or by an action brought by the original claimants against the State, which actions apparently related to the contracts upon which the claim was based, but in neither of which the claim was litigated or directly involved. BISSELL *v.* STATE OF NEW YORK...... **288**

  2. —— *What statute conferring jurisdiction on the Board of Claims gives a reasonable time for the presentation of a claim.*] Chapter 60 of the Laws of 1884, which took effect March 25, 1884, and remedied the omission of chapter 205 of the Laws of 1883 (abolishing the Board of Audit and creating the Board of Claims) to give the Board of Claims jurisdiction to determine certain claims which had accrued prior to the passage of that act, by authorizing the court to adjudicate such claims, provided they should be filed on or before July 1, 1884, allows a reasonable time for the presentation of a claim which had accrued five years, nine months and twenty-five days prior to the passage of the act of 1883.

Semble, that if there had been no provision in the act of 1884 limiting the time in which the claim should be filed, the Statute of Limitations would run against the claim in two months and five days after the act of 1884 went into effect.

LIMITATION OF ACTION — *Continued*.

does not appear that the claimant was related to the decedent, and no facts and circumstances are shown from which it can be presumed that the services were rendered or the disbursements made gratuitously, the law will imply a promise on the part of the decedent, not only to reimburse the claimant for the moneys expended, but to pay the reasonable value of his services. *Id.*

9. —— *In the case of an agreement to make the claimant the heir of the decedent the statute does not begin to run before the latter's death.*] Where it appears that the decedent agreed to compensate the claimant for his services and disbursements by making him his sole heir, and that he never repudiated such agreement, but failed to perform it owing to the fact that his death was both sudden and unexpected, the claimant is entitled to recover on *quantum meruit* compensation from the estate for his services and disbursements, and as there was no breach of the agreement until the decedent died without having performed it, the Statute of Limitations is not a bar to his right to recover for services rendered and disbursements made more than six years prior to the decedent's death. *Id.*

10. —— *Title acquired by virtue of an escheat act — release "subject to any right,"* etc.] Where the widow of a deceased owner of real property acquires title thereto under an escheat act of the Legislature, by the terms of which the release by the State is "subject to any right, claim or interest of any purchaser, heir at law or devisee, or of any creditor by mortgage, judgment or otherwise in the said real estate," the Statute of Limitations does not run in her favor. FOWLER *v.* MANHEIMER 56

11. —— *Tax — chapter 908 of 1896 is a short Statute of Limitations.*] The provision of the Tax Law relative to the effect of a deed executed by the Comptroller, pursuant to a tax sale, is a Statute of Limitations.
WALLACE *v.* INTERNATIONAL PAPER CO 298

LIQUOR SELLING — *Regulation of.*
See INTOXICATING LIQUOR.

LIQUOR TAX CERTIFICATE:
See INTOXICATING LIQUOR.

LOAN — *With collateral.*
See CONTRACT.

LUNATIC:
See INSANE.

MANDAMUS — *Execution against an administrator on a surrogate's decree — notice to the administrator.*] 1. Where an administrator, pursuant to the terms of a decree of the Surrogate's Court finally settling his accounts, pays into the Surrogate's Court the distributive share of one of the next of kin supposed to be dead, and after the lapse of more than five years after the entry of the decree such next of kin appears and makes application for leave to issue execution upon the decree in order to obtain payment of his distributive share, the surrogate may, in his discretion, irrespective of any statutory authority, require notice of the application to be served upon the administrator. PEOPLE EX REL. SACKETT *v.* WOODBURY 416

2. —— *Peremptory mandamus against the surrogate.*] A peremptory writ of mandamus, requiring the issuing of an execution by the surrogate, will not be granted unless his refusal to do so is clearly and unmistakably established. *Id.*

8. —— *Review by mandamus.*] The action of the surrogate in refusing to issue the execution without notice to the administrator cannot be reviewed by mandamus. *Id.*

4. —— *When a property owner is entitled to a mandamus to compel the opening of a street.*] The remedy of a property owner who has been assessed for the opening of a street which has not been actually opened is to proceed by mandamus against the city authorities.
COLEMAN *v.* CITY OF NEW YORK 218

MARGIN — *Purchase of stock on margin.*
See PRINCIPAL AND AGENT.

MARKETABLE TITLE:
    See SPECIFIC PERFORMANCE.

MASTER AND SERVANT — *Wages of employees — what plan for pension, insurance and endowment does not create claims enforcible against a receiver of a partnership — what is necessary to establish a preference of wages under the Labor Law — "winding up of the business" defined.*] A firm, desiring to share a portion of the profits of the business with its employees, adopted a plan known as the "Earnings Division Accounts," which embraced pension, insurance and endowment features. The rules and regulations governing the respective features were embodied in laws called respectively the Pension Law, Insurance Law and Law of Endowment. Each of these laws contained the following provision: "It is distinctly understood that all and every of the provisions of this law are voluntary on behalf of said house of Alfred Dolge, and that this law does not, nor does any of the provisions herein contained, confer any legal right or create any legal right in favor of any employee of said house mentioned herein, or of any person or persons whomsoever, nor any legal liability on behalf of said house of Alfred Dolge, or of said Alfred Dolge, either in law or in equity." The preamble to the laws stated that it was entirely discretionary with the firm to say how much of the net earnings of the business should be set aside for distribution among the employees.

Upon entering the service each employee received a pass book containing a copy of the preamble and the various laws. Each year the pass book was called in and the amount to which the employee was entitled entered therein.

After the plan had been in existence for some time the firm was dissolved and a permanent receiver was appointed. No fund had been set apart out of the assets of the business for the payment of the amounts entered in the pass books.

Held, that the employees did not have a valid claim against the receiver for the amounts credited to them in the pass books;

That the crediting of such amounts in the pass books did not create a valid gift thereof, and that the facts did not sustain the contention that they represented wages;

That, assuming that such amounts did represent wages which the employees had contributed to the business, the claims of the employees for such amounts would not be entitled to a preference under section 8 of the Labor Law (Laws of 1897, chap. 415), providing that, upon the appointment of a receiver of a partnership, the wages of the employees of the partnership shall be preferred to every other debt or claim, as the wages so contributed lost their character as such by the contribution and became mere claims for money loaned;

That the words "winding up of the business," used in the Insurance and Endowment Laws, referred to a voluntary winding up of the business.

—— *Injury to a servant through negligence.*
    See NEGLIGENCE.

MEASURE OF DAMAGES:
    See DAMAGES.

MILK — *License to sell — penalty for holding oneself out as having a license.*
    See LICENSE.

MILL — *Law relating to.*
    See RIPARIAN RIGHTS.

MORTGAGE — *Arrangement between a third mortgagee and the holders of the first and second mortgages for a certain disposition of the rents — a receiver appointed thereafter at the instance of the third mortgagee without notice will be compelled to dispose of them in the same way — how far the act of the attorney binds the client.*] 1. An action having been brought to foreclose a third mortgage upon certain property, the first and second mortgagees, who were not parties to the action, entered into negotiations with the third mortgagee's attorney respecting the appointment of a receiver of the rents and profits of the property. The negotiations resulted in an agreement that the

MORTGAGE — *Continued.*   <small>PAGE.</small>

mortgagor should execute an assignment of the rents to the third mortgagee and that the rents should be applied in the manner set forth in the assignment. After the assignment of the rents had been executed by the mortgagor and while the first and second mortgagees supposed that the rents were being collected under the assignment, the third mortgagee, without notice to the first and second mortgagees, obtained an order appointing a receiver of the rents and pro ts of the mortgaged premises.

Held, that the first and second mortgagees were entitled to intervene in the action brought by the third mortgagee and to obtain an order directing the receiver of the rents and profits to apply the money collected by him in the manner stipulated in the assignment of the rents;

That, assuming that the attorney for the third mortgagee had no authority to make a binding arrangement as to the application of the rents collected, he had actual knowledge that the first and second mortgagees were taking steps to secure their rights in connection with the rents, and that such knowledge was imputable to the third mortgagee;

That, under such circumstances, the third mortgagee could not defeat the superior rights of the first and second mortgagees in the rents, by procuring the pointment of a receiver, without notice to them.

2. —— *Landlord and tenant — right of a mortgagee of a leasehold to pay the rent which the tenant's assignee has assumed and to sue the assignee therefor.*] Where a lease for a term of twenty-one years contains a covenant obligating the lessee and its assignee to pay a stipulated rent and the taxes assessed upon the premises during the term of the lease, and authorizes the lessor to re-enter in case of a breach of said covenant, a mortgagee of the leasehold interest, in the event of the failure of an assignee of the lease, who took the same subject to the "rents, covenants, conditions and provisions therein," and also subject to the mortgage, to pay the rent and taxes in compliance with the covenant, may pay such rent and taxes and then maintain an action against the assignee to recover the amount so paid.

3. —— *Basis of such right.*] Such right is not based upon any contract relation between the mortgagee and the assignee of the lease, but rests upon the mortgagee's right to protect his interest in the estate. *Id.*

4. —— *Specific legacy of.*] A gift of two mortgages, one held by the testator at his death and the other directed by him to be purchased by the executors, will both be treated as specific legacies in order to carry out the testator's intention.

5. —— *Absolute deed held to be a mortgage — judgment creditor's lien*] Where an absolute deed is held to be a mortgage, a judgment creditor of the grantor should be adjudged to have a lien upon the premises subject to the mortgage.

MOTION AND ORDER — *Deductions made by an affiant from papers which he fails to produce have no probative force — such deductions presumed to be from a paper not produced and not from the oral statements of a party.*

MUNICIPAL CORPORATION — *Contract to erect a city building — obligation of a sub-contractor as to work covered by the plans but not by the specifications of the principal contract — provision that anything mentioned in one should be deemed to be included in the other — provision for a reference of disputes to the architects — a provision of the principal contract as to extra work, not applicable to the sub-contract — a provision as to following the direction of the commissioner of public works as to changes — rejection of proof that the sub-contractor had the city plans and specifications — when a reformation of the contract should be asked for.*] 1. The firm of Dawson & Archer obtained a contract for the erection of the new criminal court building in the city of New York. The plans and specifications, which were made a part of the contract, provided for a cellar, a basement and four stories above the basement. The basement rested on the solid earth on one side of the building, but on the other sides of the building it was supported by pillars and beams.

MUNICIPAL CORPORATION — *Continued.*   PAGE.

The plans indicated that terra cotta arch blocks were to be set between the iron beams of the basement, but the specifications, as well as the principal contract for the erection of the building, expressly excepted the "ground floors" from that work. The specifications clearly indicated that the term "ground floors" meant the basement.

Dawson & Archer sublet the fire proof work to one Isaacs by a contract by which the sub-contractor agreed, among other things, to "Furnish and set between the iron beams on all floors (except ground floors), also in top story ceilings and roof, best approved terra cotta arch blocks 8 inches deep." The sub-contract contained an agreement to do the work in conformity with the specifications and drawings made by the architects, but it did not definitely appear whether the reference to the specifications referred to the city specifications or to those contained in the sub-contract. Isaacs refused to set terra cotta arch blocks between the iron beams of the basement floor, but subsequently did the work under the express direction of Dawson & Archer.

In an action brought by Isaacs against Dawson & Archer to recover the value of such work, it was

Held, that, assuming that the reference to the specifications contained in the plaintiff's contract referred to the city specifications, such contract did not require him to furnish or set terra cotta arch blocks between the iron beams of the basement floor;

That a clause in the sub-contract providing, "Should any dispute arise respecting the true construction or meaning of the said drawings or specifications, the same shall be decided by said architects and their decision shall be final and conclusive." had no application to the case, as the dispute related to the construction of the contract and not to the construction of the drawings or specifications;

That a provision in the city specifications to the effect that the specifications, plans and drawings were intended to mutually explain each other, and that anything mentioned or referred to in one and not shown on the other, and *vice versa,* were to be deemed included in both, was inapplicable, as the plaintiff only contracted to execute that portion of the plans and specifications which was expressly embraced in the sub-contract;

That the provisions of the city specifications with reference to the formalities to be observed with respect to claims for extra work, were designed to protect the city against the principal contractors, and were not binding upon the sub-contractor;

That a provision of the sub-contract requiring the plaintiff to deviate therefrom by omitting work or doing extra work when directed by the commissioner of public works or the architects, and in such a case providing for a deduction from the contract price or extra pay as the case might be, did not preclude the defendants from doing the extra work;

That the refusal of the court to allow the defendants to show that the plaintiff had the city plans and specifications when he contracted with them did not constitute a reversible error.

Semble, that if it was the intention of the parties to include the basement floor, the defendants should have pleaded the facts and asked for a reformation of the contract. ISAACS *v.* DAWSON........................ 282

2. —— *New York city street — right of the city while it remains unopened to maintain a dumping board thereon.*] Chapter 697 of the Laws of 1887, as amended by chapter 272 of the Laws of 1888 and chapter 257 of the Laws of 1889, which vested in the board of the department of docks in the city of New York authority to establish the boundary lines of Exterior street along a portion of the East river and authorized the board of street opening and improvement to institute proceedings to acquire the necessary lands, provided that the street should be laid out as provided by the plan adopted by the dock department, "and the same shall be the sole plan according to which any wharf, pier, bulk-head, basin, dock or slip or any wharf, structure or superstructure shall thereafter be laid out or constructed in that part of the water front included in and specified upon said plan, and from the time of the adoption thereof, no wharf, pier, bulk-head, basin, dock or slip, nor any wharf structure or superstructure shall be laid out, built or rebuilt in that part of the water front aforesaid, unless in accordance with such plan. Excepting, nevertheless, that the board of the department of docks may

MUNICIPAL CORPORATION—*Continued.* PAGE.

build or rebuild, or license the building or rebuilding of temporary wharf structures or superstructures to continue and remain for a time not longer than until the construction of said Exterior street shall be begun, all such licenses to be then determined without any right to damages or compensation in favor of the licenses*." A plan of the street was adopted by the dock department and the lands necessary for the street were acquired by eminent domain. Nothing has been done by the city to open or grade the street and it has never been opened for public use and exists only upon paper, except so far as the city has made use of a part of the land so acquired for its own purposes. Prior to the condemnation of the land the board of dock commissioners passed a resolution authorizing the street cleaning department to erect and maintain a dumping board on the land taken for the purposes of the street and this dumping board has since been maintained.

Held, that as long as the street remained unopened, the department of docks had the right, under the exception contained in the act of 1887, to permit the maintenance of a dumping board upon the land taken for the purposes of the street. COLEMAN *v.* CITY OF NEW YORK.. 218

3. —— *When a property owner is entitled to a mandamus to compel the opening of the street.*] *Semble*, that the remedy of a property owner, who had been assessed for the opening of the street, was by mandamus proceedings to compel the city authorities to lay out the street. *Id.*

4. —— *Right to maintain the dumping board after the street is opened.*] *Quære*, whether the city would have a right to maintain the dumping board on the dock after the street had been actually opened. *Id.*

5. —— *Assessment on real property in the city of New York for a street opening—when it becomes a lien—breach of a covenant against incumbrances.*] February 25, 1898, the Supreme Court, upon the presentation of the report of commissioners of estimate and assessment appointed in a proceeding to open a street in the city of New York, made an order confirming the report in respect to the awards of damages and sent it back to the commissioners with directions to assess two specified lots separately, and also not to exceed one-half the tax valuation of 1896 in determining the assessment for benefits. The city of New York alone appealed from the order, and its appeal was only from the provision thereof relating to the tax valuation of 1896.

December 8, 1899, the Appellate Division reversed the portion of the order appealed from and ordered that in all other respects the report of the commissioners be confirmed. A property owner took an appeal from this order to the Court of Appeals, which court, May 1, 1900, affirmed the order of the Appellate Division. May 14, 1900, the order of the Court of Appeals was made the order of the Supreme Court. July 18, 1900, the commissioners of estimate and assessment filed an "amended and supplemental report," stating that they had assessed the two specified lots separately. This report was confirmed August 15, 1900, and on October 4, 1900, the lists of assessments were, for the first time, entered with the collector of assessments in arrears, in pursuance of the statute.

December 3, 1900, an assessment levied upon property affected by the proceeding (but not one of the two lots as to which the report had been sent back to the commissioners) was paid by a person to whom such property had been conveyed on January 23, 1900, by a deed containing a covenant against incumbrances.

Held, as under sections 159, 986 and 1017 of the Greater New York charter (Laws of 1897, chap. 378) the report was not *wholly* confirmed until August 15, 1900, that the assessment was not a lien upon the property in question at the time the conveyance was made;

That consequently there had been no breach of the covenant against incumbrances, and that the grantee was not entitled to recover the amount of the assessment from the grantor. REAL ESTATE CORPORATION *v.* HARPER. 64

6. —— *Buffalo grade crossing commission—power of, to alter the general plan—exercise of the police power in removing grade crossings—impairment*

---

* *Sic.*

MUNICIPAL CORPORATION — *Continued.*

of contracts.] Section 6 of the Buffalo Grade Crossing Act (Laws of 1888, chap. 345), as amended by chapter 353 of the Laws of 1892, authorized the commissioners to adopt a general plan of the work, and, from time to time, to alter, amend or modify the same as to any detail, but prohibited them from adopting a general plan extending beyond the one theretofore adopted, under which contracts had already been entered into, and from extending the general plan adopted by them. Pursuant to the amended section, the commissioners adopted and filed a general plan.

Thereafter they proposed to change such general plan by raising a portion of the Lehigh Valley railroad above the grade of the street and carrying it upon an elevated structure. The plan mentioned in the original act and the plan adopted pursuant to the amendment of 1892 treated of the portion of the railroad affected by the proposed change, but neither of such plans provided for raising the tracks above the surface of the street.

Held, that the commissioners had authority, under the amendment of 1892, to make the proposed change in the general plan;

That such change related merely to a detail of the general plan and did not constitute an extension of such plan;

That to extend the general plan meant to enlarge its scope so as to take in streets, crossings or territory not embraced in the original plan;

That the Legislature, in the exercise of the police power, may provide for the abolition of gra e crossings, and that the franchises granted to railroads by cities, and contracts entered into between railroads and cities, are subject to the exercise of this power;

That such legislation does not violate the constitutional prohibition against the impairment of the obligation of contracts and the taking of property without due process of law. LEHIGH VALLEY R. Co. *v.* ADAM 427

7. —— *License to sell milk — penalty for holding oneself out as having a license without having it or after it has expired — when not incurred.*] The board of health of the city of Gloversville adopted, pursuant to law, the following regulation: "All venders of milk shall register their names with the clerk of the board, who shall issue to them a certificate of authority to sell milk, under his hand and seal. Every person so authorized to sell shall place in a conspicuous place on both sides of his milk wagon or sleigh the number of the license. Mi k tickets shall be used but once. The certificates issued as above shall continue in force one year from the date of issue. Every person who holds himself out as possessing such certificate without having taken out the same, or after the same has been revoked, or has expired, shall be liable to a penalty of ten dollars." A person engaged in vending milk in the city obtained a certificate of authority from the city board of health and placed the number of the certificate in metal figures on the front end of the dashboard of his milk wagon. When the certificate of authority expired the milk vender refused to register his name with the clerk of the board of health and procure a new certificate of authority, contending that such a certificate was not necessary. He also had his wagon repainted, the metal figures being painted over with the rest of the wagon.

H ld, that the milk vender was not l'able for the penalty imposed by the regulation, as such penalty was directed only against a person who held himself out as possessing a certificate, without having taken out the same or after the same had been revoked or had expired.

CITY OF GLOVERSVILLE *v.* ENOS........ 326

8. —— *Trust estate — assessments for sewers and pavements made during a life estate charged against the principal of the trust fund.*] A testator devised certain city real estate to a trustee in trust to receive the income thereof and pay the same over to his daughter during her life, the will providing that at the death of the daughter, the trustee should convey the property to such persons as the daughter might appoint by her last will and testament, and that in the event of her failure to exercise the power of appointment the property should pass to her issue then living. During the continuance of the trust the city constructed sewers and vitrified brick pavements along the streets upon which the various parcels of real estate were situated and levied assessments to defray the expense thereof upon such real estate. The testator's daughter was then forty-four years old and unmarried.

1. In an action brought to recover damages resulting from the death of the plaintiff's intestate who, while riding in a buggy at the invitation of one Horan, was killed in a collision with one of the defendant's north-bound trains at a grade crossing in the village of Fulton, at about eight o'clock on a dark August evening, while the electric street lights were not burning, it appeared that, as they approached the crossing, the occupants of the buggy could not see a train approaching from the south until they reached a point about thirty feet westerly from the crossing, at which point they could see the engine for a distance of one hundred and fifty-nine feet; that at twenty-five feet from the crossing the engine of an approaching train could be seen for a distance of twelve hundred and seventy-five feet. It appeared that the intestate and his companion looked both ways when they were about twenty-five or thirty feet from the crossing, and that when they again looked south the train was upon them.

There was evidence tending to show that the train was traveling at a speed of twenty-five miles an hour, and it was conceded that the locomotive whistle was not blown and that the automatic signal at the crossing was out of order. The evidence was conflicting as to whether the bell on the engine was rung or not. It further appeared that a large crowd of people had assembled at the crossing and that there was a great deal of noise and commotion there.

Held, that a judgment entered upon a verdict in favor of the plaintiff should be affirmed;

That the questions, whether the defendant was negligent and whether the intestate exercised that degree of care and caution that a prudent man would have exercised under similar circumstances, were properly submitted to the jury;

That the negligence of the intestate's companion, who was driving, could not be imputed to him, but that the mere fact that the intestate had no control over the horse did not relieve him from the duty of looking and listening for himself and doing all that a prudent man should do under similar circumstances;

That, as it appeared that the deceased was forty-eight years of age at the time of his death; that he had accumulated $5,000, and was earning from $1,000 to $4,000 a year, and that his family consisted of a wife who had since died and an unmarried daughter, twenty-one years of age, a verdict of $5,000 should not be set aside as excessive;

That the credibility of the plaintiff's witnesses presented a question for the jury and not for the court;

That it was competent to prove the speed of the train by the testimony of persons of ordinary experience.

2. —— *A pedestrian injured by a street car in full view, which, without slowing up, strikes him just as he has crossed the tracks — a nonsuit is improper.*] In an action brought to recover damages resulting from the death of the plaintiff's intestate, who, while crossing from the east to the west side of Third avenue, in the city of New York, at a point seventy feet south of Seventy-second street, about nine o'clock on a summer evening, was struck by one of the defendant's south-bound electric street cars and killed, the evidence tended to show that when the intestate started from the sidewalk, which was thirty-three feet from the south-bound track, the car was at the south crosswalk of Seventy-second street; that the intestate pro-

NEGLIGENCE — *Continued.*

ceeded at an ordinary walk and that when he had reached the easterly rail of the south-bound track the car was fifteen or twenty feet away; that when he reached the westerly rail of the south-bound track the car was only five feet awa , and that, before he could step off the westerly rail, he was struck by the car.

The evidence also tended to show that the car was traveling about twenty miles an hour and that the motorman made no effort to stop it until after the collision, and did not succeed in doing so until it had traveled about ninety feet.

The plaintiff offered to show that the motorman did not sound his gong, or give any other warning to the intestate; but this evidence was excluded by the court. Both the car and the avenue were brilliantly lighted, and if either the motorman or the intestate had looked he could have ascertained the position of the other.

Held, that it was error for the court to dismiss the complaint;

That the jury might infer that the motorman's failure to slacken the speed of the car or to give any warning of its approach was due to an error of judgment, in assuming that the intestate would be able to cross in safety, which error of judgment would not necessarily constitute negligence, or else that his failure to slacken the speed of the car or to give any warning of its approach was a failure to observe that degree of care which he should have observed with respect to a person in the position in which the intestate then was;

That, by the same process of reasoning, the jury might have found that the intestate was guilty of a mere error of judgment, and not of contributory negligence, in attempting to cross the street in front of the car without accelerating his steps.

Upon an appeal from a judgment, entered upon a nonsuit, the plaintiff is entitled to the most favorable inference which can be drawn from the evidence admitted or which should have been admitted.

3. —— *Injury to a conductor because of car tracks being so close together that the running board on an open street car overlaps the running board of another car.*] In an action to recover damages for personal injuries sustained by the plaintiff, a conductor employed on the defendant's electric railroad, who, while standing on the running board of his car collecting fares, was swept therefrom by another car traveling in the opposite direction on the adjacent track, it appeared that at the point where the accident occurred the tracks were so close together that if two cars passed each other their running boards would overlap. This close proximity continued for about one hundred and sixty feet, and was apparently due to an oversight. The plaintiff had been employed upon the road, which was seven miles in length, for thirty days, and had made from twelve to fifteen trips daily, but was unaware of the dangerous proximity of the tracks. It was his custom on each trip to collect fares on the running board next to the adjoining track, after having first raised the guard rail, which was let down at the beginning of each trip in order to prevent passengers from alighting on that side. This was also the custom followed by the conductor who instructed the plaintiff in the performance of his duties.

It further appeared that it would be impracticable for the plaintiff to stand between the seats of the car while collecting fares, and that he could not collect fares on the running board on the other side of the car owing to the existence of rocks jutting out from the face of a wall on that side of the track, and also because the rope attached to the fare register was not accessible from the running board on that side.

Held, that the questions of the defendant's negligence and of the plaintiff's freedom from contributory negligence were properly submitted to the jury, and that a judgment entered upon a verdict in favor of the plaintiff should be affirmed;

That, under the circumstances, the risk incident to the proximity of the tracks was not one which the plaintiff assumed.

4. —— *Injury to a passenger stepping from a street railroad car into a hole in an asphalt pavement within two feet of the tracks, which a paving company*

PARTNERSHIP — *Continued.*

the same, provided he acts in good faith and does not deceive the public or mislead those with whom he seeks to do business, as to the identity of his business or his firm, to the injury or prejudice of others competing in the same line of business.

What affidavits, submitted on a motion made in an action, brought by Demie W. Hildreth and Henry Segelken, partners, doing business under the firm name of Hildreth & Segelken, against one Joseph M. McCaul, who claimed to have entered into a copartnership with one Henry Phelps Hildreth, and who had leased premises formerly occupied by the firm of Hildreth & Segelken, and erected a sign bearing the words "Hildreth, McCaul Co.," in large letters and the words "Jos. M. McCaul, Prop.," in small letters underneath, establish that McCaul was not using the name "Hildreth" in good faith and justify the granting of a temporary injunction restraining the defendant from using, in his business, the name "Hildreth" separately or conjunctively with any other name, designation or description until the further order of the court, considered. HILDRETH *v.* McCAUL. 162

2. —— *Accounting — when the partners are, and when they are not, entitled to interest on money advanced to the firm.*] Where the shares of the several members of a copartnership in the partnership profits depend upon the amount of capital furnished by them, respectively, interest should not, upon an accounting between the partners, be allowed on money furnished by the several partners as part of the original capital or as an addition thereto, but when the amount to be furnished by each partner is fixed and certain and the share of each of the respective partners in the partnership profits is a fixed proportion thereof, advances by one of the partners, in excess of his prescribed proportion, although credited to the special account of such partner and called capital of the firm, are, as between the partners, loans and advancements for the benefit of the partnership and interest should be allowed thereon. GRANT *v.* SMITH 801

PARTY — *To an action to dissolve a corporation and sequestrate property fraudulently transferred by it.*] 1. In an action brought by a judgment creditor of a corporation to procure a dissolution thereof and a sequestration of property fraudulently transferred by it, the persons or corporations who hold such property in their possession may be joined as parties defendant.
 MATTER OF SAYRE.... 329

2. —— *Action by one as legatee rather than as executor.*] When an executor of an estate is also a legatee under the will and, as such, is entitled to certain stock which belonged to the testator, an action in respect thereto, where there are no creditors of the estate, should be brought by him in his individual capacity, rather than by him as executor.
 CHESTER *v.* BUFFALO CAR MFG. CO...................... 443

3. —— *Action by a husband to establish a trust, in property conveyed absolutely by him to his wife, for herself and her children — the children are not proper parties.*] In an action by a husband to establish a trust, in property conveyed absolutely by him to his wife, for the support of herself and her children and as a residence for himself, the children are not proper parties.
 ORLICK *v.* ORLICK.... 595

4. —— *Excessive insurance on a husband's life for the wife's benefit — who may sue therefor.*] An action for insurance money in excess of the statutory amount in which a husband may insure his life for the benefit of his wife lies by the legal representatives and not by a creditor of the deceased husband.
 KITTEL *v.* DOMEYER. 134

5. —— *An administrator, withholding a sum to pay a tax.*] An administrator, withholding on a settlement of the estate a sum to pay a tax, cannot, after he has been released as administrator by the next of kin and a decree entered settling the estate, be sued therefor in his individual capacity.
 THOMPSON *v.* THOMPSON.... 242

6. —— *Action for the maintenance of a third person — by whom it can be enforced.*] A contract for the maintenance of a third person with whom the

PRINCIPAL AND AGENT — *Real estate broker — proof insufficient to establish his right to commissions.*] 1. In an action brought by a real estate broker to recover commissions upon the sale of a parcel of real estate owned by the defendant, it appeared that the plaintiff suggested to one Smith the advisability of purchasing the piece of property in question, and upon being informed by Smith that he would be interested in the property if it was in the market, went to the defendant's house and was informed that one Potterton was the defendant's agent; that the plaintiff called upon Potterton, who said that he represented the defendant but that the property could not be sold until the defendant returned from Europe; that subsequently the plaintiff and Smith called upon Potterton, who informed the plaintiff that, if he would make a written offer for the property, it would be delivered to the defendant upon his return from Europe; that Smith then made a written offer of $325,000 for the property and delivered it to Potterton: that at a subsequent interview Potterton told the plaintiff that the defendant wanted $375,000 for the property; that the plaintiff made an appointment to see the defendant, and at the hour appointed the plaintiff

PRINCIPAL AND AGENT — *Continued.*　　　　　　　　**PAGE.**

and Smith called upon the defendant and were introduced to him by Potterton, who then left the room; that the defendant then offered to sell the
property for $375,000, which proposition Smith accepted.

The contract between Smith and the defendant contained a provision that
"George A. Potterton is the only broker who brought about this transaction, and, so far as the vendee knows, no other broker is concerned herein."
It did not appear that Potterton employed or had authority to employ the
plaintiff to act on behalf of the defendant, or that the defendant had any
knowledge that the plaintiff was a broker or claimed any commissions on
the sale or that he had assumed to represent the defendant.

Held, that there was no evidence of any employment of the plaintiff by
the defendant;

That the defendant was not chargeable with the knowledge possessed by
Potterton of the plaintiff's relation to the transaction, which he did not communicate to the defendant. BENEDICT *v.* PELL.......... ... ... **40**

2. —— *Deposit, in a bank account in the name of a firm of brokers, of moneys
of an insurance company and of a navigation company — under what circumstances they are respectively impressed with a trust — effect of the moneys being
from time to time wrongfully withdrawn and thereafter being replaced.*] The
firm of Weatherby & Wilbur, who were engaged in the insurance and brokerage business, kept a bank account in the name of "Weatherby & Wilbur."
In August and September, 1898, Weatherby, who was the agent for the
Travelers' Insurance Company, deposited in the account premiums collected
by him for that company amounting to $313.64. In September, 1898, he
deposited in the account $360.08, which represented the avails of drafts sold
by the firm for the International Navigation Company. Weatherby died
October 5, 1898, at which time the account contained $724.87. Several times
during the month of September Weatherby, by means of withdrawals, made
without the knowledge of the insurance company or the navigation company, reduced the account below the sums needed to discharge the two
claims, but, as many times, made good such deficiency from some undisclosed
source. It did not appear that Weatherby deposited in the account any
money except trust money, or that he had deposited therein moneys held in
trust for any one but the insurance and navigation companies.

Held, that the several withdrawals and restorations made by Weatherby
in his lifetime did not operate to extinguish the identity of the moneys originally deposited belonging to the insurance and navigation companies;

That, in the absence of any other claimants of the $724.87 than the credit-
ors of Weatherby or his administratrix, such moneys constituted a trust
fund, applicable to the discharge of the claims of the insurance and navigation companies. UNITED NATIONAL BANK *v.* WEATHERBY. **279**

3. —— *Unauthorized sale by a broker of a customer's stock — measure of damages.*] Where stock, carried by a firm of stock brokers for a client upon
margins, has been sold by the brokers without the consent of the client, at a
time when the brokers held sufficient margins to protect the stock from arbitrary sale, the client's measure of damages is the difference between the
price at which the stock was sold and the highest market price brought by
such stock within a reasonable time after the sale. WOLFF *v.* LOCKWOOD... **569**

4. —— *Agreement of sale by a devisee, having a life estate and a right to use
the proceeds of property — the devisee becomes a creditor.*] An agreement by a
devisee, having a life estate and a right to use the proceeds of property, with
a third person to sell it and pay over the proceeds, creates an agency or a
loan with collateral, not a trust. In the event of the death of the third
person, the devisee becomes a creditor of his estate. MATTER OF WALKER. **263**

5. —— *Undisclosed principal — when liable to a surety company on a bond
accompanying a liquor tax certificate — parol evidence.*] An undisclosed principal is liable to a surety company against which a judgment has been recovered on a bond accompanying a liquor tax certificate issued to the agent, and
parol evidence is competent to show that the principal named in the bond
was an agent of the undisclosed principal.

CITY TRUST CO. *v.* AMERICAN BREWING CO....................... **511**

See MASTER AND SERVANT.

PRINCIPAL AND INTEREST — *Receivership of a trust company — interest, when not allowed on preferred claims.*] 1. Where the charter of a trust company which has been dissolved provides, "In case of the dissolution of the said company by the Legislature, the Supreme Court or otherwise, the *debts due* from the company as trustee, guardian, receiver or depositary of moneys in court or of savings bank funds, shall have a preference," the amount of such preferred debts should be determined as of the date of the appointment of the receiver. If there are sufficient assets to pay all the creditors, interest accruing after the appointment of the receiver on the preferred debts will be allowed, but if there are not sufficient assets to pay all the creditors, interest will not be allowed on the preferred debts.

2. —— *Bonds issued by a school board — interest payable after default.*] Where a board of education refuses to comply with the demand made upon it for the payment of the principal of a bond issued by it, it is liable for interest on such principal from the time of such demand at the statutory rate and not at the rate fixed by the bond.

PRINCIPAL AND SURETY — *Surety on the bond of an insurance agent — what modification of the contract between the company and its agent discharges the surety.*] 1. A contract between an insurance company and one of its agents provided that the agent should pay all the expenses and claims of his district and, in addition thereto, pay to the company ten per cent of the gross premiums collected in the district. Pursuant to the terms of the contract, the agent furnished a bond conditioned that he should well and truly perform the terms of the contract, which bond was executed by a surety who had knowledge of the terms of such contract. After the delivery of the bond to the insurance company, the insurance company and the agent, without the knowledge or consent of the surety, made an agreement whereby the agent was to deduct ten dollars weekly from the receipts as a living fund and the insurance company was to pay from the home office sick claims. doctors' bills and rent and the agent was to remit to the insurance company all collections, less commissions due to sub-agents and the ten dollars weekly for living expenses.

Held, that the alteration of the arrangement between the insurance company and the agent operated to release the surety from any liability upon the bond.

2. —— *Undisclosed principal — when liable to a surety company on a bond accompanying a liquor tax certificate — parol evidence.*] An undisclosed principal is liable to a surety company against which a judgment has been recovered on a bond accompanying a liquor tax certificate issued to the agent, and parol evidence is competent to show that the principal named in the bond was an agent of the undisclosed principal.

PRIVILEGED COMMUNICATION — *To physician.*
See PHYSICIAN.

PROMISSORY NOTE:
See BILLS AND NOTES.

PROOF OF LOSS — *Under insurance policies.*
See INSURANCE.

PROPERTY — *Real.*
See REAL PROPERTY.

PUBLIC POLICY — *What contract is contrary to.*
See CONTRACT.

PUBLIC STREET:
See MUNICIPAL CORPORATION.

PURCHASE — *Of personal property.*
See SALE.

RECEIVER — *Of a trust company — claims of an attorney for services to the trust company, not increasing the fund, are not preferred.*] 1. A claim by the attorney of a trust company, which has been dissolved, for services rendered by him in connection with securities held by the trust company as collateral to a loan, is not entitled to a preferential payment out of the assets in the hands of the receiver of the trust company, appointed in the action to dissolve it, where it does not appear that there were any judicial proceedings in connection with the collateral securities which would support a common-law or a statutory lien, or that the attorney did anything which created or preserved any of the securities or resulted in any advantage to the receiver or to the trust company; nor is a claim for services, rendered by the attorney, at the request of the trust company, in opposing the appointment of the receiver of the company, entitled to such a preference, where it appears that the attorney's efforts did not augment or preserve the funds of the trust company. PEOPLE *v.* AMERICAN LOAN & TRUST CO......................... 579

2. —— *Interest, when not allowed on preferred claims.*] Where the charter of the trust company provides, "In case of the dissolution of the said company by the Legislature, the Supreme Court or otherwise, the *debts due* from the company as trustee, guardian, receiver or depositary of moneys in court or of savings bank funds, shall have a preference," the amount of such preferred debts should be determined as of the date of the appointment of the receiver. If there are sufficient assets to pay all the creditors, interest accruing after the appointment of the receiver on the preferred debts will be allowed, but if there are not sufficient assets to pay all the creditors, interest will not be allowed on the preferred debts. *Id.*

3. —— *Excepting creditors, only, entitled to share in the benefits of a reversal.*] Where only a portion of the unpreferred creditors file exceptions to the report of a referee, erroneously allowing interest accruing after the appoint-

SALE — *Continued.*

hats for three dollars each and the defendants agreeing not to sell such hats to any other person in that locality — the contract to continue in force as long as the plaintiffs performed on their part. The breach consisted of the action of the defendants in refusing to sell the hats to the plaintiffs and in selling the hats to another dealer in the city of Binghamton. It appeared that at the time such breach occurred, the plaintiffs had on hand 197 hats. Nothing in the contract prevented the plaintiffs from thereafter selling the hats and it was not shown that the breach had in any way depreciated their value.

Held, that the measure of the plaintiffs' damages was the value of the contract.

That they were not, however, entitled to recover the value of the 197 hats still on hand and unsold at the time of the breach, at the rate of three dollars for each hat. VOSBURY *v.* MALLORY 247

3. —— *Complaint for goods sold at "prices mutually agreed upon" — proof of market value is not sufficient.*] Where the complaint in an action alleged that the plaintiffs sold and delivered to the defendant merchandise "at and for prices mutually agreed upon, which were worth and amounted at the prices so agreed upon as aforesaid, to the sum of $16,702.30, which said price and value the defendant promised to pay to the plaintiffs for said goods, wares and merchandise," and the answer admits that the goods were sold and delivered at prices mutually agreed upon, but denies that the total prices amounted to the sum stated in the complaint, the plaintiffs are not entitled to recover under proof of the market value of the goods.
    VEDDER *v.* LEAMON......... 252

4. —— *An allegation that the goods were worth "the prices so agreed upon" is surplusage.*] The allegation of the complaint that the goods were worth "the prices so agreed upon" should be regarded as surplusage. *Id.*

5. —— *How far such proof is competent.*] *Semble,* that, under such an issue, evidence of the value of the goods would be competent for the limited purpose of determining what were the actual prices agreed upon. *Id.*

6 —— *Unauthorized sale by a broker of a customer's stock — measure of damages.*] Where stock, carried by a firm of stock brokers for a client upon margins, has been sold by the brokers without the consent of the client, at a time when the brokers held sufficient margins to protect the stock from arbitrary sale, the client's measure of damages is the difference between the price at which the stock was sold and the highest market price brought by such stock within a reasonable time after the sale. WOLFF *v.* LOCKWOOD... 569

7. —— *Contract to buy grapes — remittance of check for less than the contract price, with acceptance of the checks.*] Where a contract is made to purchase a crop of grapes then upon the vine at a certain price per ton, and, after receiving the grapes, the purchaser remits his check for less than the contract price, with a statement that the grapes were below the contract standard, the vendor, if he accepts the check, cannot thereafter recover the balance of the contract price. WHITAKER *v.* EILENBERG.................. 489

8. —— *Authority to cut wood.*] The liability of a purchaser from the vendees in a contract for the sale of a wood lot, of timber growing thereon, for a refusal to stop cutting such timber in obedience to a notice given by the vendor after the vendees had surrendered the contract to him, considered. SMITH *v.* MORSE......... 818

—— *Of a decedent's real estate for the payment of debts.*
    See EXECUTOR AND ADMINISTRATOR.

—— *Power of, by executors.*
    See EXECUTOR AND ADMINISTRATOR.

—— *For taxes.*
    See TAX.

SATISFACTION — *Of a debt.*
    See PAYMENT.

SCAFFOLD — *Injury on.*
    See NEGLIGENCE.

SOCIETY — *To effect insurance.*
See INSURANCE.

SPECIFIC LEGACY:
See WILL.

SPECIFIC PERFORMANCE — *Marketable title — what is — title acquired by a widow of the deceased owner by virtue of an escheat act of the Legislature — when the release by the State is "subject to any right," etc., the Statute of Limitations does not run in her favor.*] 1. In 1860, John Furgeson died seized of real property, located in the city of New York, having been naturalized

SPECIFIC PERFORMANCE — *Continued.*   PAGE.

5. ——*Marketable title — the projection of a stoop beyond the building line in a street.*] The fact that the stoop of a house projects beyond the building line into the street, does not constitute a defect in the title to the premises upon which the house stands, where it appears that the stoop has occupied such position for upwards of thirty years without objection on the part of the municipality or of adjoining property owners or any other person.

In such a case, the contingency that the removal of the stoop will ever be compelled by the municipality or by any person having authority in the premises, is so remote as not to be within reasonable contemplation.

LEVY *v.* HILL... 95

6. —— *Venue — of an action by a vendor to compel a vendee to specifically perform a contract to buy land.*] An action brought to compel the vendee in a land contract to accept the title tendered by the vendor and to pay the contract price therefor, is an action brought "to procure a judgment establishing, determining, defining, forfeiting, annulling, or otherwise affecting an estate, right, title, lien or other interest in real property," within the meaning of section 982 of the Code of Civil Procedure, which provides that such an action shall be brought in the county where the land is situated.

TURNER *v.* WALKER... 306

SPIRITUOUS LIQUOR:
  See INTOXICATING LIQUOR.

STATE BOARD OF AUDIT — *Statute of Limitations — what does not suspend its operation — claim against the Buffalo Asylum for work and materials — it might have been presented to the State Board of Audit — what statute conferring jurisdiction on the Board of Claims gives a reasonable time for the presentation of a claim.*
  See BISSE.... *v.* STATE OF NEW YORK................................. 238

STATEMENT — *Of facts required to be stated at the beginning of a case on appeal.*
  See APPEAL.

STATUTE — *Where a title, acquired by a widow of the deceased owner by virtue of an escheat act of the Legislature, by the terms of the release by the State is "subject to any right," etc., the Statute of Limitations does not run in her favor.*
  See FOWLER *v.* MANHEIMER... 56

—— *Constitutionality of.*
  See CONSTITUTIONAL LAW.

—— *Of limitation.*
  See LIMITATION OF ACTION.

  See SESSION LAWS.
  See UNITED STATES REVISED STATUTES.

STIPULATION — *Discontinuance of action for libel — a stipulation by the plaintiff not to bring another action, not required as a condition thereof.*] Where, on a motion to discontinue an action of libel on the calendar at a Trial Term, it appears that no rights of the defendant will be injuriously affected by such discontinuance, the court has no power to require the plaintiff, as a condition of the discontinuance, to file a stipulation not to bring another action for the same cause. KILMER *v.* EVENING HERALD CO....... 291

STOCK — *In corporations.*
  See CORPORATION.

—— *Sale by a broker of a customer's stock.*
  See PRINCIPAL AND AGENT.

STOOP — *Projection of a stoop beyond the building line of a street — how far an objection to the title.*
  See SPECIFIC PERFORMANCE.

STREET — *In a city.*
  See MUNICIPAL CORPORATION.

SUBROGATION — *Of a mortgagee of a leasehold who pays the rent which the tenant's assignee has assumed as against such assignee.*
 See LANDLORD AND TENANT.

 —— *Of sureties.*
 See PRINCIPAL AND SURETY.

SUBSCRIPTION — *To stock of a corporation.*
 See CORPORATION.

SURETY — *On bonds.*
 See BOND.

 See PRINCIPAL AND SURETY.

TRUST — *Deposit, in a bank account in the name of a firm of brokers, of
moneys of an insurance company and of a navigation company — under what
circumstances they are respectively impressed with a trust — effect of the moneys
being from time to time wrongfully withdrawn and thereafter being replaced.*]
1. The firm of Weatherby & Wilbur, who were engaged in the insurance and
brokerage business, kept a bank account in the name of "Weatherby & Wilbur." In August and September, 1898, Weatherby, who was the agent for
the Travelers' Insurance Company, deposited in the account premiums collected by him for that company amounting to $313.64. In September, 1898,
he deposited in the account $860.08, which represented the avails of drafts
sold by the firm for the International Navigation Company. Weatherby
died October 5, 1898, at which time the account contained $724.87. Several
times during the month of September Weatherby, by means of withdrawals,
made without the knowledge of the insurance company or the navigation
company, reduced the account below the sums needed to discharge the two
claims, but as, many times, made good such deficiency from some undisclosed source. It did not appear that Weatherby deposited in the account
any money except trust money, or that he had deposited therein moneys held
in trust for any one but the insurance and navigation companies.
    Held, that the several withdrawals and restorations made by Weatherby in
his lifetime did not operate to extinguish the identity of the moneys originally
deposited belonging to the insurance and navigation companies;
    That, in the absence of any other claimants of the $724.87 than the creditors
of Weatherby or his administratrix, such moneys constituted a trust fund,
applicable to the discharge of the claims of the insurance and navigation
companies. UNITED NATIONAL BANK *v.* WEATHERBY........ 279

2. —— *Assessments for sewers and pavements made during a life estate,
charged against the principal of the trust fund.*] A testator devised certain
city real estate to a trustee in trust to receive the income thereof and pay
the same over to his daughter during her life, the will providing that at the
death of the daughter the trustee should convey the property to such persons as the daughter might appoint by her last will and testament, and that
in the event of her failure to exercise the power of appointment the property
should pass to her issue then living. During the continuance of the trust
the city constructed sewers and vitrified brick pavements along the streets
upon which the various parcels of real estate were situated and levied assessments to defray the expense thereof upon such real estate. The testator's
daughter was then forty-four years old and unmarried.
    Held, that the sewers and pavements were permanent improvements, and
that, in view of the peculiar provisions of the will and of the fact that there
was no remainderman in existence, the entire amount of the assessments
should be charged against the principal of the trust estate.
    PELTZ *v.* LEARNED........... 312

3. —— *Action to have real estate purchased by a committee adjudged to have
been purchased with the money of the lunatic — proof required to sustain it.*]
In an action brought by the heirs at law of a lunatic against the heirs at law
of the committee of the lunatic, to establish a resulting trust in property
purchased by the committee in her individual name, with money alleged to

ULTRA VIRES — *A mutual benefit insurance certificate.*
See INSURANCE.

UNDERTAKING — *Other than on appeal.*
See BOND.

UNILATERAL CONTRACT:
See CONTRACT.

PAGE.

UNITED STATES REVISED STATUTES — § 5198 -- *Usury* — *recovery
of, where paper is discounted by a national bank* — *when the Statute of Limitations begins to run.*
See SMITH *v.* FIRST NATIONAL BANK........................ 876

[See table of United States Revised Statutes cited, *ante*, in this volume.]

USURY — *Recovery of, where paper is discounted by a national bank.*] 1.
Where a national bank discounts a note for a customer, retaining as the discount an excessive rate of interest, and on the maturity of the note the customer pays the excessive discount in cash and executes a renewal note for the same amount, and this process is repeated several times, each actual payment constitutes a usurious transaction within the meaning of section 5198 of the United States Revised Statutes, which provides that a person who pays an excessive rate of interest to a national bank may maintain an action to recover, "twice the amount of the interest thus paid, from the association taking or receiving the same, provided such action is commenced within two years from the time the usurious transaction occurred."
SMITH *v.* FIRST NATIONAL BANK....................... 876

2. —— *When the Statute of Limitations begins to run.*] The two years' Statute of Limitations commences to run from the date of each cash payment of an excessive discount. *Id.*

VENDOR AND PURCHASER — *Contract sale of a wood lot accompanied with authority to cut the wood* — *surrender of the contract to the vendor while a licensee of the vendees is cutting the wood* — *liability of such licensee for wood cut before and after notice to stop cutting.*] 1. The vendor in a contract for the sale of a wood lot authorized the vendees to cut and sell the timber growing upon the lot. Thereafter the vendees sold to one Smith the timber growing upon a portion of the lot to be thereafter cut by him. Subsequently the vendees surrendered their contract to the vendor, and the latter, who knew that Smith was cutting timber upon the lot and had made no previous objection thereto, notified him to stop cutting. Smith continued cutting for a few days thereafter, and the vendor thereupon brought an action of trespass against him for the cutting done by him both before and after the vendor had notified him to stop.
The jury awarded a verdict of $200 to the plaintiff, and judgment was entered thereon for treble that amount.
Held, that, assuming that the license given by the vendor to the vendees was personal to the latter, the vendees might while it remained unrevoked employ the defendant to do the acts which they were authorized to do, and that consequently the defendant was not a trespasser up to the time when he received notice to quit;
That it was error for the court to allow the plaintiff to prove the value of the timber cut by the defendant before being notified to stop, and at the same time to refuse to allow the defendant to show that he acted in good faith under a claim of right and with the knowledge and consent of the plaintiff;
That, as it was impossible to tell whether the verdict was based upon the cutting done before or that done after the defendant received notice to stop, the judgment entered upon the verdict for three times its amount should be reversed. SMITH *v.* MORSE.. 818

2. —— *Marketable title* — *the projection of a stoop beyond the building line in a street.*] The fact that the stoop of a house projects beyond the building line into the street, does not constitute a defect in the title to the premises upon which the house stands, where it appears that the stoop has occupied

After the widow's death one of the executors and trustees under the testator's
will, wrote to the testator's son, who was also an executor and trustee under
the will, stating that the testator's estate owned three hundred and sixty shares
of the capital stock of the corporation in question, viz., the sixty original
shares and the three hundred additional shares, and that for the purpose of
securing an adjustment and settlement of matters as executor and trustee of
the testator he would offer the stock for sale at public auction. The wife of
the testator's son, to whom he had previously transferred all his interest in
his father's estate, thereupon presented a petition to the Surrogate's Court
alleging that as assignee of her husband's interest in his father's estate she
was the owner of ninety shares of such stock and that she did not wish to
have such ninety shares sold, but desired to keep the same as an investment,
and she requested that the executors be compelled to show cause why they
should not deliver over to her such ninety shares of stock. The testator's
son joined in the petition, stating that he had read it and that the same was
true, and that he desired that the prayer of the petition be granted. An
order was issued restraining the executor from selling the said ninety shares
of stock until the further order of the court. No further proceedings were
had in the Surrogate's Court, but by an arrangement between the parties the
certificate for three hundred and sixty shares was surrendered to the corporation and four new certificates of ninety shares each were issued to the wife
of the testator's son and to the testator's three daughters. Thereafter the
testator's son, his wife and the testator's three daughters signed an acknowledgment that the executors and trustees "have fully and satisfactorily
accounted to us as the heirs and next of kin of said deceased for all moneys
and property held by them as such Executors and Trustees," and consented
to the entry of a decree discharging the executors and trustees from any and
all liability or accountability to such heirs. The decree entered upon such
consent adjudged that the executors and trustees thereby were "finally
released, exonerated and discharged as the executors and trustees of and
from any and all liability and accountability to said interested persons."

Subsequently the testator's son brought an action to establish title to the
two hundred and twenty-five shares of additional stock distributed to his
three sisters, claiming such stock in a three-fold capacity, namely, as assignee
under a reassignment from his wife of his interest in his father's estate, as
executor under his mother's will, and as specific legatee under such will of
all her interest in the stock of the corporation. He also contended that, at
the time of the proceedings in the Surrogate's Court and the distribution of
the stock among his wife and his three sisters, he was ignorant of the facts
surrounding the issue of the disputed stock and did not know his rights
therein.

Held, that he could not maintain the action in the first capacity, as, if the
stock belonged to his father's estate, it had concededly been properly
distributed;

That, as it did not appear that there were any creditors of his mother's
estate or that there were any other persons who claimed to have derived any

interest in the stock through her, his qualified title as executor under his mother's will became merged in his beneficial interest as legatee under such will and that, if such stock belonged to his mother's estate, he would be entitled to it as an individual rather than as an executor;

That the plaintiff, having consented to the distribution of the stock among his wife and three sisters, upon the theory that it constituted part of his father's estate, could not subsequently insist that the stock was a part of his mother's estate;

That the decree discharging the executors and trustees was an adjudication that the division of the stock was proper and that such decree was binding upon the plaintiff in favor of the other legatees;

That the contention that, at the time the stock was divided among the plaintiff's wife and his three sisters. he was ignorant of the facts which attended the issue of the additional stock was not supported by the facts found. *Id.*

4. —— *When revoked by proof of the subsequent execution of another will.*] On an application for the admission of a will to probate, it appeared that, subsequent to the execution of the will offered for probate, the testator executed another will, with all the statutory formalities, expressly revoking all former wills made by him; that the testator took possession of such subsequent will immediately after its execution, and that it could not be found after his death, although a careful search was made therefor. It did not appear what became of the subsequent will after it was delivered to the testator, or that the latter ever made any attempt to revive the former will. No proof was given as to the contents of the subsequent will, except that it in terms revoked all former wills.

Held, that the former will was not entitled to probate.

5. —— *The attorney superintending the execution of the subsequent will may testify as to what was done.*] An attorney who superintended the execution of the subsequent will, and who, with the assent and approval of the testator at that time, read aloud the revocation and attestation clauses of the will, is not incompetent, under section 835 of the Code of Civil Procedure, to testify as to what was said and done at the time the will was executed. *Id.*

6. —— *Presumption of destruction* animo revocandi — *proof required to overcome it.*] In such a case the failure to find the subsequent will after the testator's death raises a strong presumption that it was destroyed by the testator *animo revocandi,* and in a proceeding for the probate of such will, as a lost or destroyed will, the burden of overcoming such presumption rests upon the petitioner. It is not sufficient for the petitioner to show that some one whose interest was adverse to the will had an opportunity to destroy it, but he must go further and show by facts and circumstances that the will was actually lost or destroyed. *Id.*

7. —— *When an estate in fee simple absolute is conveyed thereby.*] A testator by his will. after devising certain specified real property in fee to each of his children with the exception of his daughter Charlotte, devised certain specified real property to Charlotte "to have the income and rents thereof during her natural life, at her death to be divided amongst all my remaining children, share and share alike " The residuary clause provided as follows: " All my other real estate and personal property to be divided share and share alike between all my children." After the residuary clause was the following: " I hereby appoint my son Henry Duchardt to act as trustee for my daughter Charlotte D. Duchardt, her houses to be rented and kept in repair, the money her share to be put in bank or bond and mortgage for her benefit while living." " The real and personal estate of which my daughter Charlotte D. Duchardt is possessed during her lifetime, at her death is to be divided equally between my heirs."

Held, that the testator's children acquired an estate in fee simple absolute in all the property which passed under the residuary clause, and that the clauses following the residuary clause related solely to the property in which Charlotte had a life estate.